AULUS GELLIUS

AULUS GELLIUS

Leofranc Holford-Strevens

The University of North Carolina Press
Chapel Hill

First published in Great Britain 1988 by
Gerald Duckworth & Co. Ltd.
The Old Piano Factory
43 Gloucester Crescent
London NW1

First published in the United States 1989
by The University of North Carolina Press

Library of Congress Cataloging-in-Publication Data
Holford-Strevens, Leofranc.
  Aulus Gellius.

  Bibliography: p.
  Includes index.
    1. Gellius, Aulus—Criticism and interpretation.
I. Title.
PA6391.H65 1989   878'.01   88–14340
ISBN 0–8078–1818–6

Typeset at Oxford University Computing Service
by S. & A. Cope.
Printed in Great Britain.

Contents

D. M.
AVLI GELLI

Si tibi post cineres uitalia saecula curae,
    Aule, nec omnino mens requiescit iners,
haec faueas, oro, munuscula parua ferenti,
    noscere qui studui scriptaque teque simul.
iam facies Vrbis, mores, res publica, lingua
    non tua, iam didicit spernere Roma deos;
sed cum perpetuis Caesar quoque cesserit umbris,
    nondum nox Noctes obruit illa tuas.
quod legeris gratum est; quod amaris num tibi mirum,
    quo nil commodius candidiusque nihil?
crede mihi, tua te pietas, doctrina, lepores,
    ipsaque, mi Gelli, Musa perire uetat.

... Gellius a suis commentariis, quibus nihil fieri potest neque tersius, neque eruditius ...

(Erasmus, Adagia, chil. 1, cent. 4, adag. 37.)

... (Gellius) uir bonus fuit ac doctus ...

(J. C. Scaliger, Oratio [sc. I] pro M. Tullio Cicerone contra Des.
Erasmum Rotterodamum (Paris, 1531), sig. E2^r)

<blockquote>
Attica nox haec est nulli cessura diei,
   Quod dedit egregiae Gellius artis opus.
Sermonis Veneres hic sunt, omnesque latinae
   Deliciae, uulgo non patet ista penus.
</blockquote>

(N. Borbonius, 'In Fronte Gelliani codicis, Ex tempore', Nugae
(Paris, 1533), sig. e1^r; cf. rev. edn. (Lyon, 1538) 1. 196, p. 70.)

<blockquote>
These Attic Nights, that to no day shall yield,
Gellius hath written with uncommon skill.
All sweets of speech, all Latin pleasures fill
His page; that store is to few eyes reveal'd.
</blockquote>

Preface

HAVING been admired since the Renaissance, with few dissenting voices, as a scholar who united elegance with erudition, in the nineteenth century Aulus Gellius was commonly despised as a bookish blockhead whose only virtue lay in citing fragments otherwise unknown. The mighty Niebuhr pronounced him the compeer of Wagner, *Famulus* to Faust; the mild Hertz compared him to the dogs that eat of the crumbs which fall from their masters' table and the sergeant who can clear his throat and spit like Wallenstein but from whom his mind is hidden. More such judgements, condemning not only Gellius but his torpid and trivial times, were delivered in the standard handbooks; concurrently, the source-critics in whom the age abounded portrayed him as a mere copying compiler, with nothing to contribute of his own.

Especially since 1945, the twentieth century has been zealous to reverse, on merit or on principle, the verdicts of its predecessor; Gellius, though no longer read by the *dilettanti* for whom he wrote, has regained respect from scholars. Much service has been rendered him by René Marache, Heinz Berthold, Iancu Fischer, and other writers; one complete edition has appeared, two are in progress, and two more are promised. Nevertheless, much remains to be done, both in the asking of new questions and the answering of old ones; in particular, source-criticism has not advanced since the beginning of the century, the notions then current being either swallowed whole or indiscriminately rejected.

The reader of these pages will observe that I have learnt, not only from modern scholars and those of the nineteenth century, but from the humanists and antiquarians, who were less far removed from Gellius in spirit and who in their own works often made use of his language and his procedures. The proportion of truth to error in Gruter's *Lampas* is possibly no lower than in the same wordage of a modern periodical, nor is the present always right against the past.

There was a time when all grammatical notices not nailed down to other authors were freely assigned to Probus; now even explicit reports of his opinions are debated and denied. On the other hand, having written that single combat in the fourth century BC is not inconceivable, I am accused in a recent study, not of over-ready belief, but of excessive doubt. *Periculosum est credere et non credere.* I have done my best to steer a middle course between credulity and hyperscepticism, guided by no general principle but my view of probabilities. 'Du sollst den Namen Methode nicht unnütz im Munde führen'; having seen how the nineteenth-century critics were led astray through love of system, I offer no short cut to certainty. I have tried to state no case more strongly than the evidence will permit; but the reader is warned that 'Gellius has not read' and 'Gellius does not know' are compressions of 'Gellius shows no sign of having read' and 'Gellius does not appear to know'. He himself avows in his preface that his discussions are introductory and not exhaustive; perhaps another will undertake to distinguish those things that he consciously omitted from those not present to his mind, and those not present to his mind from those that he had never learnt. 'The writer shall often in vain trace his memory at the moment of need,' as the wise Johnson writes, 'for that which yesterday he knew with intuitive readiness, and which will come uncalled into his thoughts tomorrow.'

No doubt the same is true of me; but the reader should not assume that what is not cited is not known. To be sure, the volume of modern periodical literature, which distracts us from that study of texts in which our ancestors excelled, is scarcely within the grasp of any mortal; nevertheless, I have read more, both there and in older writings, than I choose to mention, and pass over much that I might have pilloried, all the while aware that work from which I should have benefited may have escaped my notice. So many topics does Gellius cover that some deficiencies seem inevitable; nevertheless, I have attempted to illustrate his subject-matter when his commentators, and Hosius' parallels, seem inadequate.

I admit further that my work is by no means comprehensive: Gellius' narrative skills, his use and neglect of Cicero, his knowledge and ignorance of Greek, the clues in his language to works read, his evidence for Roman scholarship and Antonine social life, all demand additional research. Nor have I treated, except in occasional observations, of his literary afterlife: not because I hold such studies in disrespect, but because an adequate account of Gellius' presence in the works of later ages would require not a single chapter but another book or more. Hertz, indeed, in the preface to his great edition and in articles on Nonius and Ammianus, largely covered late antiquity and the Middle Ages, though additions to our knowledge have accrued since he wrote, and we have been made aware that many quotations come from florilegia; but far less has been published in this field on the Renaissance and more modern times, despite valuable observations especially by Berthold. Gellius not only contributed literary modes to scholars from Politian and Crinitus down to Falster, but supplied ideas and information to Castiglione, Guevara, Mejía, Rabelais, Montaigne, Kirchhof, Burton, Browne, and Holberg; he also provided themes for the moral emblems beloved of the sixteenth and seventeenth centuries. It would be no easy task to collect even the admitted borrowings, to segregate the false citations, to recognize unacknowledged and often distorted echoes, to distinguish direct from indirect citations; but the archives of the book-trade would need to be perused, and studies made of schoolmasters' purchases and gentlemen's libraries. I claim no competence in such matters: that art let each man practise which he knows.

My interest in Gellius, kindled by reading him over twenty years ago, led me to write my doctoral thesis on his second book, successively supervised by Sir Roger Mynors and Robin Nisbet, whom I gladly thank for their criticism and encouragement. At Christ Church I drew benefit from the friendship of many learned men; I am especially grateful for the support my studies have received from Hugh Lloyd-Jones, Peter Parsons, and the Revd Henry Chadwick. I am beholden to Heinz Berthold for an offprint of a recent article, to Raymond J. Starr for a copy of one not yet published, to John Waś for my discscript, and to many others, too numerous to name, for particular discussions and responses.

The scholar in Oxford is fortunate in his libraries; my gratitude is due both to their staff, who have rendered me their usual friendly service, and to the great collectors, such men as Francis Douce and Ingram Bywater, by whom their stocks have been augmented. It is no light thing to work with volumes of Turnebus' *Aduersaria* that bear the arms of Thuanus and the signature of Boissonade. Often, too, in the Ashmolean Library, I would find that the volume I was reading had belonged to Eduard Fraenkel, who had represented to me as to many others the true exemplar of a scholar. Books not available in Oxford or in the British Library were supplied at my request, and through the diligence of the Bodleian staff, by librarians from Berkeley to Budapest. At Trinity College, Cambridge, I inspected Bentley's manuscript (which had been William III's) of the Valerio-Gellian florilegium. I spent an agreeable week in Copenhagen, where Erik Petersen gave me access to the resources of Det kongelige Bibliotek, in particular Christian Falster's 'Noctes Ripenses' and for light relief Triller's 'Emendationum et obseruationum libellus'; subsequently, Torben Nielsen, chief librarian of Første afdeling, Universitetsbiblioteket, sent me photocopies of Falster's manuscript additions to his *Vigiliae primae Noctium Ripensium*, and made available the annotated copy of the Gronoviana mentioned in Madvig's *Aduersaria critica*, presented to Falster by the enlightened nobleman Peter Fogh of Ryomgård. T. I. Kondakova of the Gosudarstvennaja biblioteka SSSR imeni V. I. Lenina answered my enquiries about early Russian translations reported in Schweiger's bibliography.

Despite these debts, only I am responsible for what I write; and all would have been in vain had not Colin Haycraft, *uir de studiosis humanitatis optime meritus*, been willing to publish a work on one whom the elder Scaliger called a good and learned man, than whose writings Erasmus knew nothing more polished or more erudite, and who has imparted to later ages far more than they are aware of owing him.

Oxford,   LEOFRANC HOLFORD-STREVENS
31 March 1987

Abbreviations and Modes of Reference

Most authors will be easily recognized. 'Ar.' = Aristophanes, 'Arist.' = Aristotle, 'D.S.' = Deutero-Servius, 'Luc.' = Lucian. Abbreviations for epigraphic and papyrological collections follow convention; they will be found in LSJ and *OCD*. Periodicals are generally abbreviated as in *L'Année philologique*.

ALL	*Archiv für lateinische Lexikographie und Grammatik*, ed. E. Wölfflin (Leipzig, 1884–1909)
ANRW	*Aufstieg und Niedergang der römischen Welt*, ed. H. Temporini (Berlin (West), 1972–)
Bonner HAC	*Bonner Historia-Augusta-Colloquium*
C.	Codex Iustinianus
CA	*Collectanea Alexandrina*, ed. J. U. Powell (Oxford, 1925, repr. 1970)
CCSL	Corpus Christianorum, series Latina
CGL	*Corpus glossariorum Latinorum*, ed. G. Götz (Leipzig, 1888–1923)
Coll.	Mosaicarum et Romanarum legum collatio (*FIRA* ii. 541–89)
CSEL	Corpus scriptorum ecclesiasticorum Latinorum
C.Th.	Codex Theodosianus
D.	Digesta
DEI	*Dizionario etimologico italiano*, ed. C. Ballisti and G. Alessio (Florence, 1950–7)
DK	H. Diels, rev. W. Kranz, *Die Fragmente der Vorsokratiker*[6] (Berlin, 1951)
EFHE	*Ennius*, Fondation Hardt, Entretiens sur l'antiquité classique, 17 (Vandœuvres–Geneva, 1972)
FGrH	*Die Fragmente der griechischen Historiker*, ed. F. Jacoby (Berlin and Leiden, 1923–57)
FIRA	*Fontes Iuris Romani Anteiustiniani*[2], ed. S. Riccobono *et al.* (Florence, 1968–72)
FV	Fragmenta Vaticana (*FIRA* ii. 461–540)
G.	Gaius, *Institutiones*
GDK	*Die griechischen Dichterfragmente der römischen Kaiserzeit*, ed. E. Heitsch, Abh. der Gött. Ges. d. Wiss., phil.-hist. Kl.[3] 49 (Göttingen 1963), 58 (Göttingen, 1964)
GLK	*Grammatici Latini*, ed. H. Keil (vols. ii–iii M. J. Hertz, Supp. H. Hagen) (Leipzig 1855–80)

GRR	*Grammaticae Romanae fragmenta*, ed. H. (i.e. G.) Funaioli (Leipzig, 1907)
GW	*Geflügelte Worte*[33], ed. G. Büchmann, rev. W. Hofmann (Frankfurt am Main, 1981)
HRR	*Historicorum Romanorum fragmenta*, ed. H. Peter (Leipzig, 1914)
I. Mem.	*Les Inscriptions grecques et latines du Colosse de Memnon*, ed. A. and É. Bernand (Paris, 1960)
J.	Justinian, *Institutiones*
JbClPh	*Jahrbücher für classische Philologie*
KlP	*Der Kleine Pauly*[2], ed. K. Ziegler and W. Sontheimer (Munich, 1979)
L&S	C. T. Lewis and C. Short, *A Latin Dictionary* (Oxford, 1879)
LCL	Loeb Classical Library
LdÄ	*Lexikon der Ägyptologie*, ed. W. Helck, E. Otto, and W. Westendorf (Wiesbaden, 1975–86)
LSJ	H. G. Liddell and R. Scott, rev. H. S. Jones, *A Greek–English Lexicon*[9] (with Supp., Oxford, 1968)
OCD	*Oxford Classical Dictionary*, ed. N. G. L. Hammond and H. H. Scullard (Oxford, 1970)
ODEP	*Oxford Dictionary of English Proverbs*[3], ed. W. G. Smith, rev. F. P. Wilson (Oxford, 1970)
OLD	*Oxford Latin Dictionary*, ed. P. W. Glare (Oxford, 1982)
PG	Patrologia Graeca
PIR	*Prosopographia Imperii Romani*
PL	Patrologia Latina
PLM	*Poetae Latini Minores*, ed. E. Bährens (Leipzig, 1879–86)
PMG	*Poetae Melici Graeci*, ed. D. L. Page (Oxford, 1962)
PS	Sententiae receptae Paulo tributae (*FIRA* ii. 317–417)
RAC	*Reallexikon für Antike und Christentum*, ed. Th. Klauser *et al.* (Stuttgart, 1950–)
RE	*Real-Encyclopädie der classischen Altertumswissenschaft*, ed. A. Fr. von Pauly, rev. G. Wissowa *et al.* (Stuttgart, 1894–1980)
RLM	*Rhetores Latini Minores*, ed. K. Halm (Leipzig, 1863)
RS	Rolls Series
SH	*Supplementum Hellenisticum*, ed. P. H. J. Lloyd-Jones and P. J. Parsons (Berlin (West), 1983)
SVF	*Stoicorum ueterum fragmenta*, ed. H. von Arnim (Leipzig, 1903–24); cited by vol. and fr.
Tijdschr.	*Tijdschrift voor Rechtsgeschiedenis*
TLL	*Thesaurus linguae Latinae* (Leipzig, 1900–)

Fragments of ancient authors are cited by standard numerations; for Ennius I use O. Skutsch in the *Annales*, Jocelyn in the plays, otherwise Vahlen. Nonius appears with Lindsay's page and printed line-number. Favorinus is cited by

Mensching where available and Barigazzi, Fronto by van den Hout, save where Portalupi corrects him.

References to Gellius are in modern form, even if older editions are being cited. Editions and translations are discussed in the appendix; the more significant are:

Editions

Giov. And. Bussi (Rome, 1469, *ed. pr.*; reset 1472)

Phil. Beroaldus (Bologna, 1503), rev. Nic. Ferrettus (Feretrius) (Venice, 1509), Jo. Connellus (Paris, 1511)

Car. Aldobrandus (Florence, 1514; Juntine)
  [Dated Jan. 1513 (sc. Florentine style = 25 Mar. 1513–24 Mar. 1514), in the papacy of Leo (sc. X, el. 11 Mar. 1513)]

Joh. Bapt. Egnatius (Venice, 1515; Aldine)

Jod. Badius Ascensius (Paris, 1517 with a few nn., [2]1519 with more nn., [3]1524 with further nn., [4]1531 [15 Mar. 1530 curial style] with Mosellanus' comm. and remarks thereon, [5]1532 with revisions; posth. by M. Vascosanus, 1536)
  [I cite the 1532 edn. The nn. added in 1519 are avowed to be mostly the work of Aegidius Maserius, to whom many of those appended in 1524 are specifically attributed; only the latter are assigned to him below.]

L. Carrio (Paris, 1585; for H. Stephanus)

J. F. Gronovius (Amsterdam, 1651; 1665; Leiden, 1687 with nn.)

A. Thysius and J. Oiselius (Leiden, 1666)

J. Proust (Paris, 1681; Delphin)

Jac. Gronovius (Leiden, 1706); rev. J. L. Conradi (Leipzig, 1762)

P. D. Longolius (Hof, 1741)

A. Lion (Göttingen, 1824)

M. J. Hertz ([1]Leipzig, 1853; [2]Berlin, 1883–5; [3]Leipzig, 1886)
  ['Hertz' alone denotes the *ed. mai.* of 1883–5.]

C. Hosius (Leipzig, 1903)

P. K. Marshall (Oxford, 1968)

Bilingual editions

J. C. Rolfe (New York and London, 1927; rev. Cambridge, Mass., and London, 1946)

M. Mignon (Paris, 1934)

R. Marache (Paris, 1967–)

F. Cavazza (Bologna, 1985–)

Translations

J.-F.-I. (Donzé-)Verteuil (Paris and Brussels, 1776–7)
A. H. Freiherr von Walterstern (Lemgo, 1785)
Afanasij Ivanov (Moscow, 1787)
W. Beloe (London, 1785)
F. Weiss (Leipzig, 1875–6)
D. Popescu (Bucharest, 1965; introduction and notes by I. Fischer)

The above works are not included in the bibliography; the commentaries by
Mosellanus, Carolus, and others are. Carrio's *Castigationes et notae*, appended
to his edition, are cited as 'Carrio, comm.' Books, articles in multi-author
works (other than reference-books listed above), and all periodical-articles
quoted more than once are cited by author and (where necessary) short title
only, full title and place-date being reserved for the bibliography.

In quoting modern Latin, I have not in general felt obliged to respect the
use of *I i*/*J j*, *U u*/*V v*, ligatures, or accents; but it is worth noting that Falster,
like other Danes of his day, wrote not *qu* but *qv*.

I have not compelled classicizing scholars to resume their vernacular
names: having been taught that Milton defended the English people against
Salmasius, I do not know why Gellius must be emended by Claude Saumaise.
The Polish editor of Cicero is known to his countrymen as Andrzej Patrycy
Nidecki; but we still say that a fragment of *De republica*, cited by Gellius from
the second book, was assigned to the third by Andreas Patricius. Perhaps no
one will let Geert Geertszoon be abused by Giulio Bordon, rather than
Erasmus by Julius Caesar Scaliger; but those who insist on calling Stephanus
Henri Estienne (for which they may plead his vernacular writings) must
decide the nationality of his editor, 'Ludovicus Carrio patre Hispano, matre
Belga natus', as Barthius tells us, in order to style him Luis Carrión or
Lodewijk Carrion, since we may no longer Anglicize to Henry Stephens and
Lewis Carrio. Such folk, moreover, must be warned against receiving for
original Latin names with vernacular veneer, so that Piero Del Riccio Baldi
becomes Crinito, and Adrien de Tournebu Turnèbe.[1] Even Johannes
Fredericus Gronovius, so called in the vernacular of his adopted
Netherlands,[2] has appeared as Gronov, a form best confined to his homeland
(where Sir Thomas More is Morus); his Low German ancestors will have
answered to Gronouwe, that is Gronau, still a frequent name in his native
Hamburg. Worst of all, certain editors have ascribed to the non-existent
Italian Ciacconi a conjecture in Sallust's description of Sertorius by the

---

1. Politianus, *il Poliziano*, is not the family name of Agnolo degli Ambrogini but an ethnic
adjective, 'the man from Montepulciano'.
2. Antonius Thysius and his homonymous father thus appear in the *Biographisch Woordenboek
der Nederlanden*, though the grandfather is 'Christophel Thys'; his colleague Oiselius, descended
from the Huguenot family of Loisel, is registered as Oesel with the variants Oezel, Ousel, and
Ouzel.

Spaniard Pedro Chacón of Toledo, the Varro of his age, styled in Latin Petrus Ciacconius.

However, I prefer Giovanni Andrea Bussi to the purely notarial Joannes Andreas de Buxis, and retain the vernacular style for Louis d'Orléans and Jacques Proust, whom the younger Gronovius and Falster Latinize as Aurelius and Prousteus, but whose title-pages, though themselves in Latin, give their surnames in the mother-tongue. Some will say that Filelfo should have been Philelphus or Huetius Huet; but few would call Pricaeus Price. Perfect consistency is no more to be attained than in other matters.

Introduction

FEW modern writers will concede to Gibbon that the condition of the human race was most happy and prosperous between the death of Domitian and the accession of Commodus,[1] that fatal moment (his melancholy monarchs reflected) 'when some licentious youth, or some jealous tyrant, would abuse, to the destruction, that absolute power which they had exerted for the benefit of the people', described by one then living as the transition from an age of gold to one of rusty iron.[2] Zealous to burnish iron and tarnish gold, we rehabilitate Severus, if hardly Commodus, and observe not only tensions between Hadrian and the senate, war and plague under Marcus, but increasing misery among the poor, rebellion, desertion, and banditry, the social rise of Christianity, financial pressure on decurions, and ever more harshness in the criminal law towards *humiliores*.[3] Nevertheless, the rich élite, free of the terror that especially senators had known under Domitian, basked in the afternoon sun of ancient culture; if enjoyment predominated over achievement, and synthesis over discovery, yet intellectuals received public honour, the private law grew more humane, and the future was not suspected. Some persons, as at other times, sought the comfort of religion or the consolation of philosophy; but although Marcus, far from bestriding the world like a Colossus, groaned underneath it like an Atlas,[4] the second century was anything but the age of anxiety the twentieth, judging by itself, has seen in it.

The war waged on the free intellect by successive emperors was over, but it had been won: the liberty restored, as by a master's grace,[5] under Nerva and Trajan was employed—not least by Martial, the shameless flatterer of Domitian living—to denigrate Domitian dead and praise the new rulers. To have a message had been dangerous; now there were no more messages, save from two men of strong mind, Juvenal and Tacitus, who, having endured the evil times, portrayed the blindness of mankind and the darkness of despotism

---

1. Gibbon i. 85–6; cf. Bacon, *The Advancement of Learning* 1. 7. 4–8 Wright. It is still a happy time one would have liked to live in for Cavazza, edn. i.10.

2. Cass. Dio 71. 36. 4 (contrast Ael. Arist. 26. 106 Keil); from other standpoints the modern historian may reckon the decline from 161, or prolong the Antonine age till 235, but it was in 180 that Rome ceased to be governed by virtuous emperors who respected the Senate.

3. For Antonine social evils see e.g. MacMullen, *Enemies* 193–4, Garnsey 153–72, de Ste. Croix 467–9, 476; and note the growth of legislation about *fugitiui* (D. 11. 4). Christianity attracts the polemic of a Celsus even as its faithful are being killed in Lyon and Vienne.

4. *Onus est honos, qui sustinet rem publicam.* Yet Marcus did his duty, albeit without a Trajan's joy.

5. 'Iubes esse liberos: erimus' (Plin. *Pan.* 66. 4).

with a force and insight that give their works a relevance even to those who read them in translation.[6]

But not, it seems, to the Romans. Other minds could not bear so much reality; neither the survivors nor the successors of an era when thinking as one wished brought peril had any wish to think about such miseries; far pleasanter was picturesque description, the pretty poetry of wine and love, the indulgence of sentiments that sterner ages had restrained. Juvenal and Tacitus sank almost without trace.[7] No kinder fate befell the modernists of Julio-Claudian days and the neo-classicists of the Flavian reaction: rendered odious by the rulers under whom they wrote, they also cloyed the palate of the second as of the nineteenth century. Conceits and compression, the excellencies of Silver writing, palled: a jaded public turned instead to the rude vigour of a Cato or an Ennius.

Furthermore, the recent writers, who amid much artificiality of language had not eschewed usages of educated speech unsanctioned by the classics, afforded no solid bulwark against linguistic change that threatened to sever living Romans from their greatest authors. Even in the first century a scholar could find *uexare*, which to Vergil as to Cicero had meant 'ravage', too feeble in sense for Scylla's depredations; in Juvenal it means 'bother'.[8] Early literature both filled the gap left by the rejection of Imperial writers, and served to correct corruption of language as of eloquence—which some extremists detected even in the classics.

Among both Greeks and Romans, the second century saw a reversion to the past. The show-orators—'sophists'—of the east increasingly affect the language of free Athens; that city revives her epichoric alphabet, others erect inscriptions in artificial dialect. Trajan, who acted the bluff soldier, received dedication of Aelianus' treatise on the Macedonian phalanx; his successor, the investigator of all curiosities,[9] who surrounded himself with intellectuals in order to upstage them, not content with reviving the beard of the ancient Romans, or with exalting Cato and Ennius above Cicero and Vergil like any other snob, preferred to Sallust, greatest of archaists, the even more archaic Coelius Antipater.[10] This judgement, indeed, reflected the same exhibition-ism that made him rank Homer below the learned and long-forgotten Antimachus of Colophon, while taking care to disparage the latter's most

6. Yet even they knew the limits: Juvenal (whose intention was perhaps less than his achievement) belabours the dead, Tacitus says little about events after Domitian's murder.

7. Fronto, *Princ. hist.* 2. 18, a commonplace, need not come from Juv. 10. 80 (where see Courtney). For Tacitus see ch. 13 n. 2.

8. See ch. 11 n. 41. Cf. Aristotle's misunderstanding of οὐδεὶς ἑκὼν πονηρός at *EN* 1113ᵇ14–16. Dionysius of Halicarnassus, though no doubt (like Malherbe) polemically exaggerating his incomprehension, appears to find Thucydides more difficult than we do.

9. Tert. *Apol.* 5. 7.

10. *HA Hadr.* 16. 6. Lebek, who minimizes the annalists' use of archaisms as opposed to expressions still current but refused by Cicero and Caesar, confesses Coelius' taste for Ennian diction (*Verba prisca* 222–3, 264–5, cf. Fronto, *Ep. M. Caes.* 4. 3. 2). For Cicero, Coelius was the best of a bad bunch (*Leg.* 1. 6, but see *Brut.* 102, *Orat.* 230).

famous admirer Plato in favour of we know not whom;[11] yet even Fronto, who having praised Hadrian without love pursues his memory with sneers and slanders, allows that his style afforded a hint of ancient eloquence;[12] the remnants show only a capable speaker who permitted himself the occasional markedly classical or even pre-classical expression, but the occasional Silver or Brazen usage too.[13] This foreshadows the practice of Fronto, Gellius, and Apuleius as his dispute with Terentius Scaurus on the Latinity of *obiter* foreshadows Gellius' puristic chapters.[14]

Yet though a monarch may set fashions of grooming and architecture,[15] if Hadrian's example had sufficed to propagate linguistic pretiosity and learned small-talk, the same effect would have followed from the same tastes in Tiberius.[16] But Tiberius, the Republican *nobilis* compelled to administer Augustus' empire, was a misfit in his world; Hadrian's affectations coincided at once with the predilection for the past through which Rome was preening herself on the recovery of ancient virtue,[17] and the desire of a rising élite, not least in the provinces, to display its new-found cultivation.[18]

The survival, throughout the early Empire, of a taste for early writers has caused the archaizing of the second century to be seen as a triumph of the long-mocked *antiquarii* over modernists who reeked of Nero and neo-classicists tainted by Domitian, over wit that had lost its novelty and pastiche that fell

11. Cass. Dio 69. 4. 6 (cf. *AP* 7. 674), *HA Hadr.* 16. 2, 6, cf. Casaubon, comm. 69. The preferred philosopher was perhaps Aeschines of Sphettos, who as the least original of the Socratics passed for the most faithful portraitist, whom Plato reputedly disliked (D.L. 2. 60, 3. 36), and in whom the 2nd c. took no little interest, to judge by quotations and papyri; or else Xenophon, idolized by the emperor's friend Arrian. On Plato's alleged admiration for Antimachus see Lefkowitz 172–3.

12. *Ver.* 2. 1. 17 (§ 12 *m²* d v.d.H.), correctly translated by Portalupi, wrongly by Haines (L. A. Holford-Strevens, *CR²* 28 (1978) 54 n. 14); cf. *Eloq.* 4. 7, 11; Gell. 10. 3. 15; 12. 4. 3; D.H. *Dem.* 5 (*Opusc.* i. 137. 1–2 Usener–Radermacher) ὅ τε πίνος . . . ὁ τῆς ἀρχαιότητος. See too *Ep. M. Caes.* 2. 1. 1; Champlin, *Fronto* 94–6.

13. *Vti* for *ut*, besides *uiduuium* first found in the elder Pliny (*CIL* xiv. 3579); classical *saluistis* for current *saliistis*, together with *conuertuit* paralleled only in the Itala (*ILS* 2487 + 9134). Did Hadrian, like Augustine, use a vulgar form when addressing the uneducated—or did he take it from an *Atellania* or a mime to be gleefully quoted at any officer who questioned it over dinner? (Cf. D. M. Lewis, *JHS* 104 (1984) 180 *fin.* for epigraphic reflection of Hadrian's views on language.)

14. Charis. 271. 10–20 Barwick: he dismissed Augustus (his proclaimed model in politics) as 'non pereruditus homo'.

15. Cass. Dio 69. 4. 1–4; his 'gourds' will have been domes, as on the Pantheon.

16. Suet. *Tib.* 70. 1–3, cf. Aug. 86. 2; Syme, *RP* iii. 937–52 (noting the archaisms at Tac. *A.* 4. 38. 1, 3); A. F. Stewart, *JRS* 67 (1977) 76–90. The works written to exploit his tastes in Greek poetry proved ephemeral; the fashion for learned conversation neither arose nor fell with him.

17. Not, as has been thought (cf. ch. 2 n. 75), demanding such a return in the face of perceived decline: these contented writers display less anxiety than their predecessors. In a society that laid great stress on the ruler's moral qualities, antique virtue could want no better guarantors than Pius and Marcus. (Fronto does not laud the ancient ways; but he did not create the spirit of the age.)

18. See e.g. Wallace-Hadrill 26–49; on Hadrian, id. 78–80.

short of its original.[19] Indeed, as opponents of Ciceronian bombast had invoked Lysias,[20] those of modernism Cicero with his coevals,[21] so neo-classicism promoted by repulsion the cause of Early Latin;[22] yet the antiquarians had posed as champions of four-square artlessness against the false glitter, or the bland smoothness, of the fashionable *delatores*, exalting a straightforwardness that in their mimicries was merely raw.[23] Nothing could be less like Fronto, let alone Apuleius.

To arrest the attention of impatient courts and blasé audiences, the modernists had favoured brief and pithy *sententiae* that could be taken out and quoted,[24] but left the orator no way of expanding his declamation into a full-length speech except to clothe the same thought in a different epigram;[25] even Pliny, who professes Ciceronian fullness, in fact constructs his periods out of brief modernistic phrases. The next step was not back to the classical subordination of part to whole, but onwards to concentration on an even smaller unit than the *sententia*, the individual word. This was to be not merely the *mot juste*, but the startling word, the *insperatum atque inopinatum uerbum*.[26] Tacitus' Aper had complained that Cicero offered no extractable *sententiae* until his later years; Fronto complains that he does not exhibit words the reader could not have guessed for himself. By contrast, the heir to the purple, M. Caesar, is bidden to discriminate amongst kindred terms[27] and search for striking words, which since coinage is in theory frowned on[28] must be looked for in the early writers. Even Cicero and Quintilian had in principle allowed that an archaic word might lend distinction to one's style;[29] now the principle became practice, the early authors being read and even classified for their vocabulary.[30] The result is not presented as a new style, or that

19. For early imperial archaism see e.g. Knapp 134–8, Brock 27–31; for the distinction between it and mannerism see Marache, *Critique* 13–78 (but note Cousin's review). Whereas in the 1st c. BC the old poets had been classics, their prose contemporaries mere primitives (Lebek 81), in the Silver Age they stood or fell together.

20. Indeed, Cicero can afford to blame Lysias' admirers for neglecting Cato (*Brut.* 68, cf. p. 144); Atticus thinks he is joking (§§ 293–4). Cf. the patriotic Quintilian (12. 10. 39, cf. 1. 8. 8); implicitly, and without praise, Plin. *Ep.* 1. 20. 4; Greek incredulity at Plut. *Cat. mai.* 7. 2–3.

21. So Tacitus' Messalla. But there were archaizers in Seneca's day (*Ep.* 114. 13), and Sallust, himself in vogue for a time (ibid. §§ 17–20), had set off a brief Catonian fashion (Lebek 160–70, 336–9).

22. Probus' scholarship played a part (Suet. *Gram.* 24. 2).

23. Quint. 2. 5. 21; 8. 5. 33–4; but there was also affectation (8. 2. 12).

24. Tac. *Dial.* 20. 2–3, 22. 3; cf. Plin. *Ep.* 6. 2. 5–9 for judicial dispatch.

25. Cf. Fronto, *Orat.* 5–7, 9 (on Lucan as well as Seneca).

26. Fronto, *Ep. M. Caes.* 4. 3. 3 (mispr. 4 v.d.H.); contrast Quint. 8. pr. 31. But unexpected thoughts require disguise: Fronto, *Eloq.* 4. 10. ('Tacitus' Aper had commended careful choice of words, *Dial.* 18. 2, 21. 2, 22. 2, but mainly in avoiding archaisms, 21. 4, 22. 5.)

27. Fronto, *Ep. M. Caes.* 4. 3. 4–6.

28. Fronto, *Eloq.* 2. 4 *m²* d, *Orat.* 18; see in general L. Calboli Montefusco, edn. of Fortunatianus, pp. 428–30.

29. Cic. *De Or.* 3. 153; Quint. 1. 6. 39; 8. 3. 24; 9. 3. 14; a successful exponent was Pompeius Saturninus (Plin. *Ep.* 1. 16. 2–3). See too Steinmetz 28–33.

30. Fronto, *Ep. M. Caes.* 4. 3. 2; see in general ch. 7 nn. 14–15.

appropriate to the age;[31] for Fronto it is simply the proper way to write, and the old writers afford the true model for oratory as Roscius (whom Aper had thought unbearably old-fashioned) does for acting.[32]

Nevertheless, the mannerists—for so they should be called, not archaists —did not attempt to write in Early Latin as an Aristeides or a Lucian attempts to write in Attic.[33] Admittedly, Roman rhetoric in this age, and the contemporary Greek phenomenon that Philostratus terms the Second Sophistic, are marked by the same love of show, the same supremacy of form over content and technique over thought, the same retelling of old tales, the same taste for the picturesque and the paradoxical, the same sentimentality, the same trick of finding a word and fitting a sentence round it, the same excessive zeal for the speech of bygone days. But Greek culture, less inert than Roman, carried its escapism to further extremes; thus was expressed the contradiction between the reviving fortunes of the Greek élite and its constant awareness of subjection.

The Greek world, prostrated by Roman conquest and ravaged by the civil wars, had begun to recover, no little encouraged by Nero;[34] the upper class, secured in local power by Roman policy, did not want for wealth, and much of Asia returned to prosperity. Greeks penetrated the Roman Senate, even obtaining consulates; Greek rhetoric, astronomy, architecture, medicine, and philosophy all flourished. These pursuits combined prestige with safety;[35] although the Greek world was not so closely controlled as the capital, the Greeks (however fulsomely they praised the universal empire of prosperity and peace) knew full well they were not masters in their own house.[36] Yet their classical literature came from the age of free cities, whose monuments the tourists flocked to see, above all from Athens, the Hellas of Hellas, to whose language another route was already taking them. The same 'Atticism' that found fault with Cicero caused the 'Asianism' of the Greek orators he

31. For 'elocutione nouella' (*Eloq.* 5. 1) see pp. 163–4. Neither Quintilian nor Fronto possessed Tacitus' insight into the connection between society and style.

32. Tac. *Dial.* 20. 3, Fronto, *Eloq.* 2. 16.

33. When writing in Greek, Fronto uses the Atticistic dialect, not as the counterpart to his Latin style, but as that *de rigueur* among educated Greeks; even the Christians pour their new wine into the old bottle. Naturally Latin developments were encouraged by the Greek example; and the archaistic element in mannerism played off the Romans' glorious past against the Greeks' (Cameron 161, cf. Cavazza, edn. i. 25 n. 17). But mannerism and Atticism each had their own causes; indeed, the Greek counterpart of mannerism would seem to be the jargon affected by Pompeianus of Philadelphia (Athen. 97 F–98 C) and the sophists 'a little before our time' (Luc. *Lexiph.* 23), a minor aberration.

34. The significance attached by Plut. *Mor.* 567 F–568 A to the liberation of Hellas is confirmed by the appearance of false Neros in the east.

35. Stoicism and Cynicism (Peregrinus perhaps apart) had ceased to express or affect political opposition; in any case the major philosophical developments took place in other schools. Architecture did not prove safe for Apollodorus of Damascus; but tactlessness undoes anyone.

36. Plut. *Mor.* 813 E. For the sophists, Greek history ended with the death of Alexander. The Greek élite had no desire to rebel against the βασιλεύς; the idealization of free Athens sublimated, rather than expressed, residual regrets. See in general Bowie.

knew to be challenged by a soberer, more classical manner; Atticism of style led in due course to Atticism of language, which during the course of the second century was interpreted with increasing, if not always successful, strictness.[37]

By attempting to speak in classical Attic, one could imagine oneself a citizen of the city that had defeated the Great King, for whose fleet Macedon felled her timbers, and in which the name of Rome had not been heard.[38] A Roman, by contrast, however greatly he admired the men of old, did not dream of enduring the harshness of their lives in a brick-built city with a smaller empire; Cato's style and sentiments might be applauded, but no one wished to walk in fear of his censorial note. Nor was early Latin, for all its wild beauties, either as rich or as elegant as the classical language, let alone as Attic; and sophisticates prefer the primitive in small, tame doses. To the extent that archaism asserted the upholding of ancient ways, it was a qualified assertion of a qualified truth.

The intellectual contrast in this age between Greek and Latin culture induced Romans of such unlike stature as Marcus and Aelian to write in Greek. Fronto, the champion of Latin, might disapprove;[39] but though he illustrated a style that long outlived him,[40] he had nothing to say. In the very mansion on the Esquiline where Maecenas had heard the poetry of Horace and of Vergil, Fronto discoursed on niceties of grammar.[41]

Yet this social erudition, by now habitual with the Roman élite, enabled the rising rich to display the general education of the gentleman and the orator. Instead of reviling it out of Seneca and Epictetus, as if the ancients should have paid more attention to their moralists than we do to ours, one might more reasonably rejoice that men of wealth did not confine their discourse to houses and horses. In this satisfied age, the collection of existing knowledge engaged more zeal than the pursuit of new; but the demand for its diffusion that accompanied the greater comfort of the upper class encouraged the writing of handbooks to help their readers shine at cultured tables. One of these was Gellius' *Attic Nights*.

37. For the difference between Atticism of style—not yet triumphant in the elder Seneca's day (Winterbottom, 'Declamation')—and Atticism of language, contrast Man. 5. 475 'doctior urbe sua linguae sub flore Menander' with Phrynichus' constant charges of carelessness and defilement; see especially his outburst at p. 418 Lobeck.

38. Similarly the brutal Spartan ἀγωγή commended itself to parents and tourists alike, who as they watched boys flogged to death could daydream of Thermopylae and Plataea. Severity may be no less sentimental than softness: cf. ch. 2 n. 77.

39. See ch. 7 n. 40.

40. In the sense that such writers as Arnobius, Ammianus, and Sidonius seek out unusual words (so too, *si dis placet*, the hisperical barbarians); but Fronto's virtues do not survive.

41. The point is made by Hertz, *R. und R.* 5–8; it concerns not individuals (Maecenas' prose was far more extravagant than Fronto's) but literary cultures.

PART I

THE MAN AND HIS WORK

Chapter 1

Life and Date

THE subject of our study bore the name of Aulus Gellius.[1] His *nomen* is generally derived from a Samnite *praenomen* attested from the Roman wars of the late fourth century BC—not that he shows partiality towards Samnites.[2] He mentions, in no proprietary spirit, Cn. Gellius, the annalist of the second century BC, and L. Gellius L. f., consul in 72 BC and censor two years later;[3] but modern scholars sometimes forget that Romans with the same *nomen*, unlike Highlanders with the same surname, did not conceive of themselves as kinsmen,[4] for a gentile name might come from the manumission of a slave or the enfranchisement of a provincial. However, the style 'Aulus Gellius', at a time when most male Roman citizens bore the *tria nomina* and were normally called by *nomen* and *cognomen* to the neglect of the *praenomen*, indicates that Gellius' family had, by a defiant conservatism, maintained the older practice of using only *praenomen* and *nomen*, being demarcated thus from superiors and inferiors alike; if, as seems probable, he was of colonial stock, the lack of a *cognomen* proclaimed Italian ancestry in contradistinction to three-named natives.[5]

The earliest of the incidents, real and fictitious, that Gellius recounts from his past life is his first encounter with the grammarian Sulpicius Apollinaris, when he had already taken the *toga uirilis* and was seeking, in person, more advanced teachers: 18. 4. 1 'magistrosque tunc nobis nosmet ipsi exploratiores

---

1. So Serv. on *Aen.* 5. 738, D.S. *Georg.* 1. 260; cf. the covert allusion at *HA Prob.* 1. 1 (Hertz ii, p. vi); the corruption *Agellius* (cf. *CIL* vi. 1056*b* (2). 33, Schulze, *ZGLE* 440, and the Novatianist bishop Ἀγέλιος), normal in the Middle Ages and intermittently defended in the Renaissance till Lambecius' *Dissertatio*, is attested at Prisc. *GL* ii. 246. 6, 259. 23, 355. 20 (cf. 134. 14), supported by the position of *quoque* at Greg. Tur. *Vita patrum* pr. (MGH Scr. Mer. i¹/2. 662. 20), presented in the 7th-c. *codex unicus* of Lact. *Epit.* 24. 5, and implied by the constantly repeated 'A.' in our texts of Aug. *CD* 9. 4, *Q. Hept.* 1. 30. MSS of the *Nights* offer both *a. gellii* and *agellii*; a single chapter shows *m. accii* for *Macci* and *laelius* for *L. Aelius* (3. 3. 9, 12). But Gellius is by far the commoner *nomen*, MS incipits and explicits usually offer at least two names (or name and epithet), and 'Gellius' intended to publish matter by Fronto (pp. 98–9).

2. Cf. ch. 16 n. 26.

3. The annalist, cit. 8. 14; 13. 23. 13; 18. 12. 6, may be the shady Cn. Gellius of Cato fr. 186 SbC = 206 M (*NA* 14. 2. 26), cf. Peter, *HRR*, p. ccvi, and the uncle of the *uir censorius*, who proposes a civic crown for Cicero at 5. 6. 15: R. J. Evans, *LCM* 5 (1980) 201–3, cf. id., *LCM* 8 (1983) 124–6.

4. Some scholars have an obsession with finding gentle kin for ancient authors, as if to make them worthier a snob's attention: observe the constant attempts to derive the poet T. Lucretius Carus—surely the social as well as poetical peer of Memmius' other client Catullus—from the long-defunct Lucretii Tricipitini.

5. For lack of *cognomen* in imperial times see G. W. Houston, *ZPE* 16 (1975) 33–5; Courtney on Juv. 5. 127; add *CIL* iii. 6611 and Martial's friend Q. Ovidius.

quaereremus'. The emphatic pronouns indicate that his was the power of decision: his father either respected his maturity of judgement or was already dead. Gellius, in fact, says nothing of either ascendants or collaterals.

At all events, Gellius' education was not inhibited by lack of funds: he spent several years in study at Rome and Athens, after which he could pursue the literary life without the need to earn a living; at Rome, this apparently required the equestrian census of 400,000 sesterces.[6] He had a residence at Praeneste (11. 3. 1), for use as a summer retreat; and when he and other pupils of the rhetor Antonius Julianus saw a tenement-building ablaze on the Mons Cispius, there is no thought (as there is in Juvenal) of the tenants who have lost their all, but only of the risk that made urban property less attractive to the landlord than rural despite the higher returns.[7] He became a friend of the fashionable sophist Favorinus, and had the entrée to the consular orator Cornelius Fronto; in Athens he was frequently the guest of the rich and powerful Herodes Atticus.[8]

On the other hand, in no anecdote is Gellius himself the host, and the prominent acquaintances who appear in his pages were, so far as we can tell, encountered in the course of his studies, not in an independent social life. It is not Gellius himself who, on beholding the fire, declares that if only the buildings could be fireproofed he would sell all his farms, and invest in urban properties; and one house out of town would have seemed abject poverty to Cicero or Pliny. In particular, he does not seem to have owned any property in the Bay of Naples: he is there only in the company of Julianus. At Tibur, too, he is the guest of a friend, a 'rich man' (19. 5. 1); no doubt this means one considerably wealthier than himself. Although he is an accepted member of good society, he is one of its lesser members; not for nothing does he take to heart Ennius' verses on the ideal confidant for a man of higher station (12. 4).

Although, by the time he meets Apollinaris, Gellius is resident in Rome, his place of origin (not necessarily of birth) appears to have been a *colonia*. At 16. 13. 2 he asks: 'How many of us (*quotus enim fere nostrum*), though coming from a *colonia*, do not wrongly use the word *municeps* of themselves and their fellow townsmen?' In English, this might not be taken to include the speaker; but in Latin the use of *nostrum* in such expressions always seems to do so.[9]

6. P. White, *JRS* 68 (1978) 88–9. The relevance of Gellius' judicial appointment (14. 2. 1) is unclear: Plin. *NH* 33. 33 would suggest that by Caligula's time there were more than enough *equites* to fill all five decuries without recourse to the poorer men of Suet. *Aug.* 32. 3, but *quadringenarii* were still distinguished under Pius (*CIL* x. 7507).

7. *NA* 15. 1 (presumably a normal fire, not the disaster of *HA Pius* 9. 1), contrast Juv. 3. 203–11. Cf. the unruffled jest of Cic. *Att.* 14. 9. 1.

8. No doubt on Favorinus' recommendation (cf. Philost. *VS* 491); perhaps on Fronto's too, if *Epp. M. Caes.* 1. 7–8 belong to the mid-140s (so tentatively Champlin, 'Chronology' 141).

9. At 16. 9. 2 'ita plerique nostrum, quae remotiora uerba inuenimus, dicere ea properamus, non discere', Gellius is admitting, in the Horatian manner, to a human weakness (even if in hopes to be disbelieved); cf. 16. 5. 1. But if Gellius did not himself come from a *colonia*, he had no need to associate himself with *coloni* and their errors. (When Gellius classes himself among 'Roman' students in Athens, 2. 21. 1; 18. 2. 2, he means 'Latin-speaking', cf. ch. 5 n. 15; they cannot all have been *Stadtrömer*. So too 'apud nos' in the African Apuleius, *Apol.* 9. 8.)

The theory that the mannerism of Fronto, Apuleius, and Tertullian was the fruit of their African birth, and 'therefore' that Gellius, also a mannerist, was also an African, has long since been discredited;[10] nor, given the prominence of Africans in the cultural life of Antonine Rome, is African origin proved by their appearance in the *Attic Nights*. His teacher Apollinaris, probably a Carthaginian (cf. pp. 61–2), also taught P. Helvius Pertinax from Alba Pompeia in Liguria. In Fronto's circle Gellius encountered M. Postumius Festus from near Cirta and became friendly with Julius Celsinus the Numidian (pp. 110–11); this was only to be expected, for Fronto took a keen interest in his fellow Africans,[11] but Gellius was introduced to him by Favorinus the Gaul. He knows a grammarian called Fidus Optatus, probably from Africa (pp. 107–8); this too proves nothing. In the classical age of Roman jurisprudence, the one contemporary jurist named is Sex. Caecilius Africanus of Thuburbo Minus, but Gellius met him through Favorinus.[12]

Tantalizing, however, is the lemma to the lost chapter 8. 13: 'Cupsones quod homines Afri dicunt non esse uerbum Poenicum sed Graecum', the African provincialism *cupsones* is not a Punic word but Greek. The term is elsewhere attested only in the African Augustine, and in an African context: 'In Numidia ... in cupsonibus habitant.'[13] Proposing the gloss 'in crags and caves' (*in rupibus et speluncis*), the Maurist editors (v. 246 n. e) noted that elsewhere in Augustine the Donatist Africans at Rome are called *Montenses* or *Cutzupitae/-tani*;[14] if *cupsones* and *Cutzupitae* are related, the parent tongue will have allowed metathesis.

Gellius' interest in foreign etymologies is often on display.[15] Sometimes the source is Varro, who shows knowledge of Phoenician or Punic;[16] but Varro had no reason to expound an African word. In Gellius' day, Africans may have brought a few local terms with them to Rome; but since polite society demanded full assimilation,[17] and the mannerists drew their startling

10. See W. Kroll, *RhM*[2] 52 (1897) 569–90; Brock 161–261.

11. Pflaum 545–7.

12. Kunkel, *Herkunft* 172–3. But no trace of the apparently Carthaginian Scaevola (Syme, *RP* iii. 1407); perhaps too exalted, like the Cirtensian consular Pactumeius Clemens (Fronto, *Amic.* 2. 11. 2, cf. Kunkel, op. cit. 155 n. 229).

13. *Serm.* 46. 39 (CCSL 41. 567), attacking an African heresy; see P. K. Marshall, *Mnem.*[4] 15 (1962) 273.

14. Aug. *Ep.* 53. 2 (CSEL 34. 154), *Ep. Cath.* 6 (CSEL 52. 237).

15. *NA* 1. 18; 4. 3. 3; 11. 1. 5; 13. 23. 7; 15. 30; 16. 12.   16. *LL* 5. 113, 8. 64.

17. Cf. Stat. *Silv.* 4. 5. 45–8. His addressee's namesake allegedly retained his African accent (*HA Sev.* 19. 9), but this may be no more than a guess (Birley, *Sept.* 63, 73–4; for the story of his sister's poor Latin see ibid. 204). Provincialism was undesirable (Quint. 8. 1. 2–3; 11. 3. 30; but accents might remain unlevelled, *NA* 19. 9. 2, cf. § 7). Porcius Latro could not unlearn his Spanish rough-and-readiness (Sen. *Contr.* 1. pr. 16); the Annaei were more successful. We cannot hope to detect Hispanisms in Silver writing (contemporaries were doubtless more sensitive): Quintilian's and Martial's use of *fabulari* (ch. 3 n. 6)—taken up by Tacitus—will reflect educated Roman usage; not even Martial ventures on such terms as *disex* (?) and *paramus* (> Sp. *páramo* 'high plain'), exhibited to a local public at *Carm. epigr.* 1526 A 6 (where *pace* Bücheler 'ut cursu certare, ut disice ferri' should exhibit parallel infinitives), C 3. Africanisms would be no less elusive even if we possessed a vernacular through which to detect them.

words from books not speech, who but an African would have cared about *cupsones*? Nor does the distancing expression 'quod homines Afri dicunt' show that Gellius was not himself an African: M. Fabius Quintilianus of Calagurris, whom the proud Spaniard Martial does not venture to claim as a compatriot, affects only to have heard that a popular term for blockheads is of Spanish derivation.[18] If we have not pressed this lemma and 16. 13. 2 too far, Gellius' *origo* will have been a *colonia* in the province of Africa.[19]

Even if Gellius' anecdotes be fictitious, it does not follow that they flout chronology; in order to extract consistent dates from the *Attic Nights*,[20] nothing need be disregarded except the temporal expressions like 'recently',[21] 'last night', 'today', which either belonged to the original annotations, not adjusted in the final redaction,[22] or imitate similar language in Plato and Cicero.[23]

Gellius was born between 125 and 128; having taken the *toga uirilis* (18. 4. 1), he became a pupil of the grammarian C. Sulpicius Apollinaris, who was twice consulted by Sex. Erucius Clarus, prefect of the City in the early years of Pius,[24] to his death early in 146, the year of his second consulate. From *NA* 7. 6. 12 'Erucio Claro praefecto urbi [*V*, urbis *C*]', we naturally conclude that he was already prefect, but not yet consul; 13. 18. 2 'qui praefectus urbi et bis consul fuit' is an identification, not a date.[25] Within a few years Gellius had passed from grammar to rhetoric and from rhetoric to philosophy. In 20. 1 his friend and teacher Favorinus is pitted against the jurist Africanus when Rome is nearly nine hundred years old; the anniversary was celebrated in 148. By then Gellius had probably gone to Greece, attending the Pythian Games of 147;[26] he speaks of the Attic summer (2. 21. 2), autumn (1. 2. 2),

18. Quint. 1. 5. 57.

19. Gellii without *cognomen* are found in Africa, but not in such numbers or concentration to advance the argument any further. For African origin cf. Schettino 81–7.

20. See Holford-Strevens, 'Chronology', as amended in the present discussion; Marshall, 'Date' was the first treatment to take account of Erucius' death in 146.

21. *Nuper*, in any case, is vague enough to span 60 years (Tac. *Hist.* 4. 17. 4), 34 (Cic. *In Caec.* 67, *Verr.* 2. 118), and 31 ('Q. Cic.' *Comm. pet.* 11).

22. Cf. the present tenses of 11. 3. 1 and the reminders for future research (p. 24).

23. Holford-Strevens, 'Chronology' 107 n. 70.

24. Apparently succeeding Bruttius Praesens (*cos. II* 139), Syme, *RP* ii. 491, *Arctos* Supp. 2 (1985) 286–7; L. Vidman, edn.² of *Fasti Ostienses*, p. 123.

25. At 17. 15. 6 Livius Drusus, 'qui tribunus plebi fuit', travels to Anticyra, not, as Gellius knew (3. 2. 11; 13. 12. 9), during his year of office. Cf. 11. 8. 2 ∼ Peter, *HRR*, p. cxxv.

26. Holford-Strevens, 'Chronology' 96, 98–9 (the argument at pp. 97–8 from Polydeucion's death falls, ch. 7 n. 67). W. Ameling, *Hermes* 112 (1984) 484–90 makes Gellius spend 165–7 in Athens, when rising or past forty; he would have been no good Roman *paterfamilias* to abandon his *negotia* and sit at the feet of Greek rhetors and philosophers, the laughing-stock of his fellow students, an opsimath worthy of his own scorn (11. 7. 3; 15. 30. 1). Nor had Peregrinus, when Gellius first encountered him (12. 11. 1), yet taken the name Proteus he would discard before his death in 165 (Luc. *Per.* 27). The argument from Gellius' use of *adulescens* and *iuuenis* (Friedländer–Wissowa iv. 286 n. 2) is refuted by Marshall, 'Date' 147–8; and a long interval between schooldays and visit would make 'priusquam Athenas concederem' (19. 8. 1) pointless.

and winter (pr. 4), but not of spring, though 'soliti simus' (18. 2. lemma) and the imperfects of 18. 2. 1–6; 18. 13. 1–6 should refer to keeping Saturnalia more than once rather than to the seven days of a single celebration. Unlike Apuleius he was concluding, not commencing, his higher education. After his return, he retreated into literature and rhetoric, till at the age of twenty-five or not much more he was appointed a judge.[27] Both Favorinus and Sulpicius Apollinaris were still alive; we do not know the dates of their deaths, but Apollinaris died soon enough for the future emperor Pertinax to take over his school, fail to make a living, seek a centurion's vine-staff through Lollianus Avitus (proconsul of Africa 157/8), become prefect of a cohort in Syria, and be disciplined—still under Pius (d. 7 March 161)—for using official transport without a pass.[28]

At 11. 3. 1 Gellius states, in the present tense, that when he has time to spare from his judicial business and walks or rides for exercise, he sometimes ponders linguistic questions; thus it was that recently, 'nuper', on an evening walk in Praeneste, he considered the various senses of the preposition *pro*. The adverb is no more to be taken strictly than at 18. 2. 7, where it refers to Gellius' days at Athens, but if it speaks from the time, not of publication but of original writing, so may the present tenses: at pr. 23, where Gellius undertakes to continue his scholarly collections so long as the gods allow him life and he has leisure from looking after his estate and seeing to his children's education, there is no mention of judicial distractions, from which he had presumably obtained discharge by threefold paternity. In the first preserved sentence of his preface, he states that he had also ('quoque') written for his children's amusement in their free time, 'quando animus eorum interstitione aliqua negotiorum data laxari indulgerique potuisset'. Unfortunately it is not clear from the mangled context whether any child was yet of an age to have *negotia*, but since the theme is the published text, there was probably one (at least) who would already appreciate the handy book for the purpose stated; if so, and if Gellius married about the age of twenty-five, publication could hardly have been much earlier than 170. It appears, however, to have been later: in 19. 12. 1 Gellius reports that he heard Herodes Atticus discoursing at Athens 'in the Greek language',[29] in which he excelled all others in Gellius' lifetime for the merits of his style. The aorist 'praestitit' implies that Herodes, who

---

27. The loose language of 13. 13. 1; 14. 2. 1 does not show that Gellius became a judge before studying philosophy, but rather that it was no longer his main concern (Holford-Strevens, 'Chronology' 99–100).

28. *HA Pertinax* 1. 4–6.

29. This, not 'in a Greek speech', is the sense of 'Graeca oratione'; so rightly Rolfe. See Holford-Strevens, 'Chronology' 101 n. 33; to praise a particular speech in Greek Gellius writes 'Graece disserentem egregia atque inlustri oratione' (14. 1. 1).

continued successfully declaiming till the very end, is dead, and therefore that the notice was written in or after 177.[30]

The same tense is used in 20. 1. 1 of Africanus' standing as a jurist: 'Sextus Caecilius in disciplina iuris ... scientia, usu auctoritateque inlustris fuit.' If the imperfect in two of Paul's three citations indicates attendance at Africanus' lectures, he will hardly have died before 170,[31] and may have survived for some years longer; his master and presumably senior Julian was still alive in 169.[32]

In 16. 4 Gellius quotes three extracts from the probably Triumviral antiquary L. Cincius: the fetial formula for declaring war; the oath administered to recruits in 190 BC; and a note on the names of military units, including the obsolete maniple. The third passage has no more contemporary relevance than the list of weapons and ships in 10. 25;[33] interest in the levy of 190 BC, in which one consular army was reinforced and another, of two legions, raised from scratch (Liv. 37. 2. 2–4), might be stimulated by the creation in AD 165–6 of Legiones II Pia and III Concors (later called II and III Italicae), startling reversion as it was to the practice of the venerated elders. But before departing, on 3 August 178, to the continuing northern war, the emperor Marcus hurled the *hasta sanguinea* in fulfilment of the fetial rite.[34] Among the hostile peoples were the Hermunduri (or their more southerly portion), till then Rome's faithful friends.[35] The *fetialis'* words, as recorded by Gellius, specify as enemy the 'populus Hermundulus'; the name is not known save as a dissimilated form ('Hermundolus', Jord. *Get.* 114) of *Hermundurus*. Even if Cincius lived to see Ahenobarbus' assignation of territory *c.*2 BC (Cass. Dio 55. 10a. 2) and Tiberius' expedition to the Elbe in AD 5 (Vell. 2. 106. 2), he had no reason to make this tribe the typical foe;[36] but Gellius could have interpolated the name to make the quotation topical,

30. Castorina 121–33 (= *GIF* 3 (1950) 137–45); on Ameling's chronology (ii. 2) the *terminus a quo* will be 179. Marache, 'Fronton et A. Gellius' 229 takes 'praestitit' to mean 'achieved pre-eminence'; but whereas 'superauit' and 'uicit' at Cic. *Brut.* 154, of the living Ser. Sulpicius, narrate an intellectual development, Gellius is summing up a lifetime's merit. Had he meant 'while I knew him', the obvious form was *praestabat*.

31. Holford-Strevens, 'Chronology' 101–2, modifying Honoré, 'Julian's Circle' 4, 12; for the imperfect see id., *Gaius*, pp. xvi, 6 (but cf. R. Reitzenstein, *Hermes* 35 (1900) 611 n. 1, D. Nörr, *ANRW* II. xv. 511 n. 66). Since Paul, deduced from D. 27. 1. 13. 2 to be Ulpian's senior, was still responding under Severus Alexander (D. 31. 87. 3–4, cf. 49. 1. 25), birth *c.*155 seems probable.

32. E. Bund, *ANRW* II. xv. 412–13 (on the possibility that he was *cos. II* in 175 see ibid. 429–30, cf. D. Nörr in Watson (ed.) 237–42). For Africanus' relation to Julian see Honoré, 'Julian's Circle' 9–10, A. Wacke, *ANRW* II. xv. 461–3.

33. On military matters in Gellius (only to be expected in a Roman) see Berthold 160, 168; add 17. 2. 9 (*copior* a term of the camps).

34. Cass. Dio 71. 33. 5, indicating above all by his reference to eye-witnesses that this was no routine event, *pace* Birley, *Marcus Aurelius* 206–7; were only the emperor's participation noteworthy (though even that might have attracted Gellius' attention), we should have expected Dio to add αὐτός. For *sanguinea* see J. Bayet, *MEAH* 52 (1935) 29–76, cf. Turnebus, *Aduersaria* 8. 23, 11. 17. Date of departure: *HA Commodus* 12. 6.

35. Tac. *Germ.* 41. 1, *HA Marcus* 22. 1, 27. 10.

36. Even if, as L. Schmidt, *Germania* 23 (1939) 264 suggests, there were 'patriotic' Hermunduri among the Germans facing Tiberius across the Elbe, no fighting ensued.

choosing it as less obviously non-Italic (cf. *Aequiculus*, *Apulus*) than *Marcoman-nus* or *Quadus*.[37] If he did so after Marcus had revived the ritual, the *terminus post quem* of summer 178 suits well with our other evidence. Gellius would be in his fifties, an appropriate age for referring to the remnant of his life in the diminutive ('cum ipsius uitae quantuli quomque fuerint progressibus', pr. 24), or for excusing a young man's ardour ('atque ego his eius uerbis ut tum ferebat aetas inritatior', 15. 9. 7). Indeed, it is not inconceivable that Gellius published after Marcus' death, though before the fire late in 192 that destroyed the temple and library of Peace;[38] the précis of *NA* 2. 22. 13–29 at 'Apul.' *De mundo* 13–14 is of no assistance, since this work may well belong to the third century.[39]

To have collected, over more than thirty years, only enough material for twenty books may seem rank idleness by the elder Pliny's standards; but not all authors are equally productive. The failure to mention in 3. 16 that Pius admitted birth on the 182nd day of pregnancy (D. 38. 16. 3. 12) and in 5. 19 that he permitted adrogation of *pupilli* (G. 1. 102), no more proves publication before 161 than the failure in 10. 2 to mention the famous quintuplets shown to Hadrian (D. 5. 4. 3; 34. 5. 7. pr.) proves publication before 138.[40] In particular, 5. 19 comes from a favourite but long outdated lawyer, Masurius Sabinus: in general, Gellius does not feel obliged to cram his *commentarii* with everything that might be said upon a topic (cf. pr. 17).[41]

The obscure and fragmentary letter of Fronto to Claudius Julianus apparently concerning Gellius (*Amic.* 1. 19) is of no help here, since both date and subject are obscure (pp. 98–9). Champlin has made it probable that Fronto died in the great plague of 166–7,[42] but his achievements were too well known at Rome to require a necrology like those for the Greek Herodes,

37. The identification was made by Louis d'Orléans in his edn. of Tacitus (Paris, 1622), p. 289 on *A.* 2. 63. 5; Gellian interpolation was deduced by Friedrich Lachmann (half-brother to Karl) 30. To suppose an unknown Italic tribe (J. F. Gronovius *ap. filium*) or a random procedure of Cincius' (Hertz, *De L. Cinciis* 78–9) seems desperate. Liv. 1. 32. 11 interpolates 'Prisci Latini' in the formula. Casaubon reports -*l*- from MS R at *HA Marcus* 22. 1 (comm. 163); MS Z of Jordanes has -*r*-.

38. See Grosso 361–4; add Gal. *Scr. min.* ii. 117. 22–3 Müller. The library is treated as extant at 5. 21. 9, though not necessarily at 16. 8. 2. For a possible echo of Gellius in Tertullian's *Apolegeticum* of 197 see L. A. Holford-Strevens, *RAC* ix. 1051.

39. *De Platone* and *De mundo* exhibit the *cursus mixtus*, on which see S. M. Oberhelman and R. G. Hall, *CPh* 79 (1984) 114–30, 80 (1985) 214–26, *CQ*² 35 (1985) 201–14. The undisputed Apuleius, Gellius, Fronto, and Tertullian ignore the accent in their clausulae; the first writer to regard it is Minucius Felix. Composition by Apuleius (or anyone else) *c.*150 seems impossible; a Commodian date, though compatible with use of Gellius, would require the Platonist to have forgotten a good deal about Plato. The self-reference in Π. ἑρμ. 4 poses no problem (cf. Victorinus, *RLM* 188. 4–7); but clausulae suggest a third author.

40. Holford-Strevens, 'Chronology' 105–6. For the 182nd day of 'Hipp.' *Octim.* 4. 8 (88. 17–18 Grensemann). The quintuplets are misdated to the next reign by *HA Pius* 9. 3, to that preceding by Phlegon, *Mir.* 29 ('Ἀδριανοῦ Meursius; the reverse corruption at Ael. Tact. pr. 1 in MS B), who makes the woman bear triplets a year later.

41. Sabinus: p. 221. In 10. 1 COS. TERTIVM is not cited from Hadrian's inscription on the Pantheon pronaos (too well known?).

42. *Fronto* 139–42; cf. Whitehorne. *Aliter scripsimus alibi: sed falsi sumus.*

or the specialists Africanus and Apollinaris; it seemed better to praise his private conversation, which not all Gellius' readers had enjoyed the privilege of hearing (19. 8. 1). We need therefore not suppose that Fronto was still alive when Gellius wrote.

In 12. 11 there is no mention of Peregrinus Proteus' spectacular suicide at the Olympic Games of 165; perhaps there was in 8. 3 for Ammianus Marcellinus, an avid exploiter of Gellius,[43] to draw on at 29. 1. 38–9, but Gellius was under no obligation to say a word about it. His silence thus does not imply an early date; nor do the persons of his acquaintance who had known the grammarian M. Valerius Probus, since no reliance should be placed on the latter's *floruit* of 56 in Jerome.[44]

The twelfth-century chronicler Ralph of Diss ('Diceto'),[45] in the preliminary table to his *Abbreuiationes chronicorum*, 'de uiris illustribus quo tempore scripserint', absurdly states 'Agellius scribit anno centesimo nono-decimo'; the chronicle proper assigns 'Agellius' to both 118 and 119.[46] This last entry explicitly sets him in Hadrian's time; that is no more than an inference by one who observed Hadrian to be the last emperor named in the *Nights*,[47] and who, having seen 'beatae memoriae' used of a living pope,[48] was not put on his guard by *diuus*. Yet although 'centesimo nonodecimo' in the table not only accords with the chronicle, but appears in a manuscript owned by Diceto himself and another of like age from the same scriptorium, the corruption 'CLXIX', induced by the preceding entry for 162, was discovered in the nineteenth century and adopted, as possibly resting on a good tradition, by classical scholars ignorant of their own ignorance.[49]

There remains Marache's theory that Gellius had already published before Apuleius drew on *NA* 19. 9 in his *Apologia* of 158/9.[50] That chapter portrays the birthday-party at which the scornful remarks of Greek guests on the inadequacy of Latin love-poets provoked Antonius Julianus to recite two epigrams by Valerius Aedituus and one each by Porcius Licinus and Q. Catulus—all three early poets[51]—than which (as Gellius believes) nothing more neat, delightful, polished, or refined can be found in Greek or Latin. Apuleius, charged with sorcery before Claudius Maximus, proconsul of

---

43. Hertz, *Opusc. Gell.* 146–201, cf. Pricaeus, comm. on Apul. *Met.*, pp. 44, 487, 530, 721.

44. *NA* 1. 15. 18; 3. 1. 5–6; 6. 7. 3; 9. 9. 12; 13. 21. 1; Helm 79.

45. Dean of St Paul's 1180/1–*c*.1200. The interpretation of *de Diceto* as 'of Diss', rejected by Stubbs (i, pp. xi–xvii RS), is defended by Diana Greenway in her re-edn. of J. Le Neve, *Fasti Ecclesiae Anglicanae, 1066–1300* (i. 5 n. 11; I owe this reference to Professor Christopher Brooke); Dr Greenway would maintain it now with greater emphasis (pers. comm.).

46. Diceto i. 20, 64 Stubbs; other quotations at Marshall *et al.* 374 n. 32. (MS B does not exhibit the entry for 118; that relating to Hadrian is assigned to 120. *Ipse contuli*.)

47. G. Gundermann, *Ber. über d. Verh. d. Sächs. Akad. d. Wiss.*, ph.-hist. Kl. 78/2 (1926) 29.

48. I am informed of this sporadic usage by Dr Martin Brett.

49. Holford-Strevens, 'More Notes' 151.

50. *Critique* 331–2; 'Fronton et A. Gellius' 228–31; edn. i, pp. x–xii.

51. Dates discussed by Holford-Strevens, 'Chronology' 103 nn. 42–4.

Africa, repels the prosecutor's attempt to brand his writing of love-poetry as a suspicious circumstance by declaring, at *Apol.* 9. 6–8, that he had good precedents: among the Greeks Anacreon, Alcman, Simonides, and Sappho —all identified by city and not by name, to mock provincial ignorance with allusive erudition—'apud nos uero Aedituus et Porcius et Catulus', the same three poets in the same order, and again as counterparts of Greeks—yet not at all those one would have expected.[52]

Usener supposed an anthology on which not only Gellius and Apuleius drew, but also M. Caesar, who addresses to Fronto (*Ep.* 1. 2. 1) a thought very much like that in Catulus' epigram: the writer's soul has left him for the beloved.[53] But the migration of the lover's soul is a commonplace;[54] Marcus need not have even known the epigram.

No one would have doubted that Apuleius' source was Gellius had chronology not seemed an obstacle; Marache indeed draws the consequence that the *Nights* appeared in the mid-150s, assuming that Apuleius derived his information from the published book. But his period of study in Athens overlapped with Gellius' own;[55] they could have met as Taurus' pupils or as Herodes' house-guests. They could have met again in Rome, perhaps as guests of Apuleius' leading compatriot Fronto.[56] They must have met if the 'friend of mine, a highly cultured youth' who rendered into Latin an epigram ascribed to Plato (19. 11. 3) is rightly identified with Apuleius, whose favourite turns of phrase recur in the translation and who claimed Plato as his authority for writing erotic verse.[57] Apuleius, having returned to Africa, would remain in Gellius' mind as the 'adulescens' he had known.

If Apuleius saw the poems later quoted in *NA* 19. 9, the hemistich 'dum potiar patiar' (*Apol.* 9. 12) may show the influence of Aedituus' 'dum pudeo pereo'.[58] Marache does not support his theory with other resemblances between Gellius and Apuleius;[59] these are not few, but prove little in an age

52. If the Augustans were out of favour, yet Laevius, Calvus, and Catullus all appear in the *Apologia* (Calvus admittedly as an orator); Apuleius preferred to be obscure.
53. Usener ii. 65.
54. Even old Cato knew (and complained) that the lover's soul inhabited another's body (Plut. *Cat. mai.* 9. 8, cf. *Mor.* 759 C). And Marcus read Callimachus (*Ep.* 1. 4. 6), Catulus' model.
55. See *Flor.* 18. 15; 20. 4; cf. H. E. Butler in his and A. S. Owen's edn. of *Apol.*, p. ix n. 5.
56. For Apuleius' time in Rome see *Flor.* 17. 4.
57. H. Dahlmann, *AAWM* 1979, no. 8. Despite Fischer, p. xxv n. 7 and ad loc., G. Bernardi Perini, *AAP* 82 (1969–70) 15–34, Steinmetz 336 n. 107, it is hard to credit Gellius with a poem; but if he had written these charming lines, he would have confessed the fact with a show of shame (cf. ch. 2 n. 4).
58. Emended by Usener ii. 60.
59. Echoes in *Met.* which may well be Commodian, would not help him. Such resemblances as *risum subicere* 1. 21. 8 ∼ *NA* 17. 3. 4 (cf. Lucil. 648 M), *latebra* 'trick' 2. 22. 4 ∼ *NA* 17. 9. 4, *caedes* metaph. 3. 16. 3 ∼ NA 19. 12. 7 (from the Greek sources, cf. Philost. *Ep.* 16?), *perdius* + *pernox* 5. 6. 2; 9. 5. 5 ∼ *NA* 2. 1. 2, *fallaciosus* 8. 10. 4; 9. 6. 4 ∼ *NA* 6. 3. 34; 14. 1. 34, *uenenum praesentarium* 10. 4. 6; 10. 9. 1 (cf. 2. 25. 4) ∼ *NA* 7. 4. 1, *gestuosus* 10. 29. 4; 11. 11. 2 ∼ *NA* 1. 5. 2, mostly noted by Pricaeus, are inconclusive; in 'poculis crebris grandibusque ... ingurgitat' 7. 11. 3 ∼ 'crebris et ingentibus poculis ... ingurgitabat' *NA* 15. 2. 3 the direction of influence, if any, cannot be determined. Gellian priority would be established if 'qui robore ceteros antistabat'

whose literature is largely lost. Who can say what may have been derived
from Lollianus Avitus, so extravagantly praised in *Apol.* 95? from Fronto, or
Postumius Festus, or Licinius Montanus? Such shared neologisms as *cohibilis*,
fetutinae, and *pensiculare*, found in *Apol.* and the *Nights*, may have been
vogue-words of the age; the literal use of *fetutinae* at *Apol.* 8. 3. can hardly
come from the figurative at *NA* 13. 21. 1. Nor is coincidence to be excluded: the well-read and inventive Madaurensian could independently
find 'mea delicia' (9. 12 ~ *NA* 19. 8. 6) in Plautus, and hit on 'agrestis ... et
barbarus' (10. 6 ~ *NA* 19. 9. 7), 'asseuerate' (25. 1 ~ *NA* 6. 5. 3), 'molli
condicione' (92. 5 ~ *NA* 4. 18. 3). At *NA* 7. 6. 5 Gellius makes Annianus
cite, as an example of stressed intensive *ad-*, the adverb *adfabre*, which
Apuleius uses at *Apol.* 61. 6; but anyone could find it at Cic. 1 *Verr.* 14. *Apol.*
15. 10 'rhetori iurganti an philosopho obiurganti' displays both a figure and a
predication affected by Gellius,[60] but an orator of half Apuleius' talent could
have devised them for himself. The antithesis between reminding and
informing (*Apol.* 48. 13 ~ *NA* 16. 8. 3) was a commonplace, as were the oath
'Iouem lapidem' (*Socr.* 5 ~ *NA* 1. 21. 4) and Protagoras' instruction by
Democritus (*Flor.* 18. 19 ~ *NA* 5. 3);[61] his suit against Euathlus (*Flor.* 18.
19–29 ~ *NA* 5. 10) was a favourite of the rhetoricians'.[62] Both authors
discuss vision, mirrors, and the silence of Pythagorean neophytes (*Apol.* 15.
12–15; 16. 2–6; *Flor.* 15. 23–5 ~ *NA* 5. 16; 16. 18. 3; 1. 9. 3–4), but their
treatments differ widely. Both cite Neoptolemus' dislike in Ennius for lengthy
philosophizing (Apol. 13. 1 ~ *NA* 5. 15. 9; 5. 16. 5), but so did Cicero;[63] if
Apuleius shares the adjective *Ennianus* with Gellius, he shares 'necesse' with
Tusc. 2. 1, and the formation was quite normal.[64] The injustice of Philemon's
victories over Menander (*Flor.* 16. 6 ~ *NA* 17. 4. 1–2) was established

---

4. 8. 6, cf. 4. 14. 8 (but also 8. 2. 1; 11. 28. 1; Mela 3. 54) came from Quadr. at *NA* 9. 13. 7 (cf. 6.
5. 1); the moderate beauty of Psyche's sisters (4. 32. 3; contrast 4. 28. 1) not from the Greek
source but *NA* 5. 11. 10–13; or 'non mordacem nec calcitronem' 8. 25. 1 from Cael. Sab. at *NA*
4. 2. 5 (but cf. Varro, *Sat.* 479 Bücheler; presumably technical, and cf. X. *Mem.* 2. 2. 7, Pollux 1.
198). In the disputed works, *Mund.* 13–14 apart (p. 15), 'dentium uallum' (*Plat.* 1. 14) sides with
NA 1. 15. 3 against the undoubted Apuleius' *murus* at *Apol.* 7. 4, *Flor.* 15. 23. No use is made of
NA 16. 8 in *Π. ἑρμ.*

60. For 'iurganti ... obiurganti' see ch. 2 n. 5 and Owen's n.; for objurgating philosophers
Pricaeus, comm. 37. 9–28; 219. 4–8. For 'rhetori' = *causidico* (also Gellian: ch. 3 n. 50) see
Cic. *Tusc.* 3. 63 (~ [Plut.] *Mor.* 119 C).

61. *Admonere*/*docere* Quint. 4. 1. 36, cf. X. *Hell.* 2. 4. 13, Hygin. *Astr.* pr. 1 Le Bœuffle, Justin,
pr. 4 (?from Trogus, Seel 44–7), Men. Rhet. 337. 10–12; at *NA* pr. 17 the sense is 'moins pour
exposer que pour avertir' (Marache). Oath: Hosius ad loc. Gell. Protagoras' education: DK 80 A
1–3.

62. The story (sometimes told of Corax and Teisias) was, as Gellius remarks (§ 3)
'peruolgatum' (see Hosius ad loc.; Mullach, *FPG* ii, pp. lxxx f.; Rabe at *Rh.* xiv, pp. vi f.; DK ii.
266. 10 n.). Both Gellius (§ 7) and Apuleius (§ 22) use, at different points in the story, the adverb
'diutule'; but cf. *NA* 11. 16. 6, *Flor.* 2. 1; 16. 21; 21. 7. Only Gellius makes Euathlus pay half the
fee in advance; the rhetorical terminology is different.

63. *De or.* 2. 156, *Rep.* 1. 30, *Tusc.* 2. 1; see Enn. *Sc.* 95 J.

64. *NA* 5. 15. 9 'Ennianum Neoptolemum' (cf. 5. 16. 5); *Apol.* 13. 1 'Neoptolemi Enniani';
such phrases abound in Cicero. *Ennianus* is also found in Seneca and M. Caesar; Apuleius'
Vergilianus (e.g. *Apol.* 10. 6) does not happen to occur in Gellius.

doctrine (Quint. 10. 1. 72); if Apuleius' 'fortasse impar', 'uicit saepenumero', 'pudet dicere' resemble Gellius' more vivid 'nequaquam pari scriptore', 'saepenumero uincebatur',[65] 'non erubescis?', we do not know what stood in their sources.

Nevertheless, although individual resemblances may be explained away, and the loss of contemporary literature distorts comparison, the cumulation is not unimpressive; but it does not prove that at the outset of his career Apuleius possessed a complete copy of the *Nights* in twenty books, from which he continually borrowed words and themes while ignoring its author's linguistic purism. Having struck up acquaintance in Rome, the two men may well have corresponded for some years after Apuleius' return to Africa, Gellius happily communicating his latest *trouvaille* and Apuleius his latest speech; the one could still think of the other as young, especially if their correspondence, as these things do, slackened with the years and died. Publication of the *Nights* before 158/9, and heavy dependence on them in Apuleius, pose greater problems.[66]

65. For the imperfect in preference to the aorist see *NA* 10. 3. 12 (though descriptive not iterative). Apuleius uses *saepenumero* at four other places; here it is preferred to *saepe*, as weightier, in the emphatic post-verbal position.

66. Astarita 431–2 has Gellius die before Herodes comes to Rome *c*.160 for Favorinus' bequests—or rather to defend himself against the charge of murder (Ameling i. 103–9)—because no mention is made of the visit; but nothing is said of his presence in 143 as *consul ordinarius*, and he will not have troubled to renew his acquaintance with a person of so little consequence.

Chapter 2

Composition and Purpose

IN HIS preface (§ 4) Gellius declares that, since the project of the commonplace-book he is now publishing first occurred to him during the long winter's nights in Attica, he has imposed on it the name of *Attic Nights*, 'inscripsimus Noctium esse Atticarum', again at § 10, 'Atticas Noctes inscripsimus'.[1] The name implies midnight oil, traditional both in titles (*Λύχνοι*, quoted at § 7; Furius Bibaculus' *Lucubrationes*) and in prefaces.[2] He affects to find it unimaginative as compared with names of similar works by other authors, of which he recites a long list in Greek and Latin (§§ 8–9);[3] their increasing dullness indicates his modesty to be as much for show as the accompanying disclaimer of good style,[4] belied by its very form: 'tantum ceteris omnibus in ipsius quoque inscriptionis laude cedentes, quantum cessimus in cura et elegantia scriptionis' (§ 10). The word-play 'inscriptionis ... scriptionis' exemplifies a favourite device.[5]

But Gellius was not the first miscellanist to compare his workmanlike title with others' fantasies: the elder Pliny (*NH* pr. 24–6) had remarked 'inscriptionis apud Graecos mira felicitas', listed a few examples, complained that these wonderful titles were not matched by the contents, added some Latin specimens, returned to the Greeks with the comment that Diodorus Siculus ceased trifling, and averred 'me non paenitet nullum festiuiorem excogitasse titulum', words recalled by Gellius' 'nihil imitati festiuitates inscriptionum, quas plerique alii utriusque linguae scriptores in id genus libris fecerunt' (§ 4). Although the list of titles at Clem. Alex. *Strom.* 6. 2. 1 suggest that such a review was standard, when we find among these more

1. For 'commentationes hasce', cf. 18. 4. 11 'ut commentariis harum Noctium inferrem ... commentationibus istis' and 9. 4. 5; 13. 7. 6 'his commentariis'; Clem. Alex. describes his *Στρωματεῖς* in their title as *ὑπομνήματα*, cf. Pamphila's *Ἱστορικὰ ὑπομνήματα* ∼ *NA* 15. 17. 3 'in conmentario Pamphilae nono et uicesimo'. For the gen. pl. see §§ 6–9 (where it varies with the acc.); 11. 5. 5. See too pr. 19 'a Noctibus his' (cf. 1. 25. 18), 14. 6. 1 'Noctes tuas' (cf. § 6). The variation of word-order between §§ 4 and 10 is of no significance, ancient titles being more fluid than our own; G. Bernardi Perini's notion, *AAP* 80 (1967–8) 357–68, that the adjective should precede, against the entire direct and indirect tradition, is devoid of merit.

2. Janson 97–8, 147–8.

3. For identifications see Hertz's comm. of 1877 and Faider.

4. Cf. Janson 125, 136. Studied elegance in such disclaimers is as old as Antiphon, *Or.* 5. 1–5; for the topos cf. Barrett on E. *Hipp.* 986–7. Gellius' modesty, here and at 12. 1. 24; 14. 1. 32; 17. 20. 8, need not be taken too seriously (10. 22. 3 is more sincere); for the convention see Curtius 83–5, *GW* 289–90. Cf. Tac. *Agr.* 3. 3 'uel incondita uel rudi uoce'.

5. For this *adnominatio* with prefixes see 1. 3. 29; 1. 4. 7; 2. 9. 5; 2. 23. 22; 6. 3. 24; 17. 5. 13; 19. 11. 2; 10. 1. 20. 'Inscriptionis' (so also C) was restored by Connellus, whose printer Ascensius retained the transmitted *scriptionis* in his own edns.

elegant titles 'Natural History' (§ 8), far less inspired than 'Attic Nights', we cease to take Gellius' humility at face value.[6] 'Pliny was a dry old stick,' he is saying, 'but I can improve on even the fancy titles, let alone his.' He was right.[7]

From *NA* pr. 5–9 it is sufficiently clear how many works there were that offered 'uariam et miscellam et quasi confusaneam doctrinam'; nor was Gellius' to be the last.[8] The volume of Greek and Latin writing had swollen far beyond the capacity of any normal person to read (let alone remember),[9] even if copies were available, which they were often not. Since in polite society a man was expected to have some acquaintance with books and things to be found in them, he would be all the more grateful for summaries and selections from which to acquire the veneer of culture that is all most people can aspire to. When even 'an individual scholar could only hope to see a few of the books that he had heard of',[10] the cultivated *homme du monde* had every reason to rely on Gellius and those like him.[11]

The works that Gellius lists include comprehensive 'encyclopaedic' compilations such as Pliny's; but the *Nights* are of a different kind, making no pretensions to completeness but offering isolated facts and self-contained discussions that should retain the reader's interest by brevity and variety. That this corresponded with the taste of the times is shown by the miscellanies of Plutarch, Aelian, and Athenaeus; so popular was the genre that the Christian Clement of Alexandria adopted it for a work imparting not a general culture but a specific message.[12] Lost specimens include works by Pamphila (twice cited in the *Nights*),[13] Sotion (cf. *NA* 1. 8), Favorinus (p.

6. For Gellius' attitude to Pliny, cf. pp. 121–2.

7. The more imaginative titles (still prosaic by Oriental standards) at once displayed refinement and invited purchase (H. Zilliacus, *Eranos* 36 (1938) 23–4). Since the Renaissance, 'Noctes Atticae' has been adapted for works ranging from H. Stephanus' *N. Parisinae* on Gellius in Carrio's edn. (1585) and the 18th-c. *N. Corythanae* of the Accademia Etrusca at Cortona, to F. Betera, *N. Brixianae* (1601) on a pestilence at Brescia, and R. Johnson's *N. Nottinghamicae* (1718), in English, on over-simplifications in Lily's grammar. There is an ecclesiastical mutation in J. Gussetius, *Vesperae Groninganae* (1688, ²1711), of theological content. Imitation of Gellius' title remains distinct from that of his form: Chr. Falster, who designated his Gellian studies 'N. Ripenses' (i.e. of Ribe, where he was rector of the cathedral school), called his learned miscellany *Amoenitates philologicae*. For the contribution of the title to the work's success cf. M. Dolç in *Roma en el siglo II* 49.

8. See H. Fuchs, *RAC* v. 504–15.

9. Cf. Quint. 1. 8. 18–21, Sen. *Ep.* 88. 37, Demet. Troez. *SH* 376, though Bibaculus fr. 3 M–B is otherwise interpreted by Suet. *Gram.* 9. 5.

10. Russell, *Plutarch* 42.

11. Fischer, *passim* ('om de lume'). Such a reader would find in Gellius' injunction that the uncultured and unlearned should let his work alone (pr. 19–21), and in particular the extracts from the parabasis of Aristophanes' *Frogs*, the compliment of being thought worthy to dance with the mystae as a man of taste and learning.

12. His Στρωματεῖς; for the title see Hertz, 'Praefatio' and Faider on *NA* pr. 7; [Plut.] fr. 179, cf. 'Lamprias', no. 62.

13. *NA* 15. 17, 15. 23; cf. Phot. *Bibl.* 175 (119ᵇ16–120ᵃ4), *Suda* s.v. Παμφίλη (Π 139). She is credited with epitomes of historical and other authors, including Ctesias; a work Περὶ ἀμφισβητήσεων; and a treatise on sex that a lady with her *sprechender Name* could have imputed to her without the trouble of writing it.

81), Granius Licinianus, Apuleius,[14] and Herodes Atticus ('which gathered into a small compass the flowers of former ages' wide learning': Philost. *VS* 565).[15]

The *Noctes Atticae*, as they left Gellius' pen, comprised a preface, a list of contents ('capita rerum', pr. 25), and twenty books (pr. 22), divided into chapters (11. 10. 1 'in capite superiore'; at pr. 25 and 17. 21. 2 the word is *commentarius*, at 1. 3. 29 *tractatus*), for each of which there was an item in the summary;[16] lost in transmission are book 8 (a few fragments apart), the beginning of the preface, the end of book 20,[17] and some of the *capita* or lemmata, which, though still in their place in the fourth century when the original text of the palimpsest Vat. Pal. 24 (MS A) was written, were subsequently distributed to precede the corresponding books. Surviving texts from the ninth to fourteenth centuries offer either books 1–7 or books 9–20; in the fifteenth nearly a hundred manuscripts combine both parts, many also containing the lemmata of book 8.[18] Altogether we know of 398 chapters (including the fifteen recorded for book 8); if the original total was 400, squaring the number of books, two are lost—perhaps after 20. 11, but one fragment of book 8, 'Historia ex libris Heraclidae Pontici iucunda memoratu et miranda', though just conceivably relating to the tale of Socrates and

14. Granius' *Cena*; Apuleius' *Quaestiones conuiuales*.

15. Ἐγχειρίδια and καίρια (but see Broccia 22–3 with n. 39, 35). For the floral image cf. Cass. *Var.* 9. 25. 5 with Seel 23–6; below, n. 51.

16. For *caput* 'chapter' in a work of information see Cels. [5. 8]; 6. 12; 8. 9. 2; cf. κεφάλαια, Clem. Al. *Strom.* 2. 147. 5 (the reference to length shows they are not topics but discussions). In MSS P and V the chapters are distinguished with Greek alphabetic numerals.

17. We also lack the beginning of 5. 1 and the end of 5. 5 (cf. n. 40). The opening 40 words of bk. 7 survive only at Lact. *Epit.* 24. 5–9, not discovered till the 18th c.; they are first included in Beloe's tr. and Lion's edn. From 8. 1; 8. 15 come Macr. *Sat.* 1. 4. 17–19; 2. 7. 1–5; other frr. of bk. 8 are preserved in Nonius and Priscian, but stray mediaeval citations from 'Agellius' are best ignored (Holford-Strevens, 'More Notes' 151; at Petrus Cantor, *Verb. abb.* 53 (PL 205. 164 C) 'Agellius' is either a mistake for 'Anacharsis' or due to use of the Valerio-Gellian florilegium, which includes Val. Max. 7. 2. ext. 14). William of Malmesbury, *Polyhistor* 62. 17–20 Ouellette makes him tell of Arthur's sword (cf., without attribution, MS B of Diceto, i. 96 n. 2 St s.a. 516); Diceto i. 42 St attributes Peregrinus' sermon (12. 11) to Varro. For [Agellius], *De bellis Armenie*, see Smalley 232–3, 349–50.

18. See Marshall, 'Gellius'; editors' prefaces; Gamberale, 'Note'; L. A. Holford-Strevens, *CQ²* 29 (1979) 226–7, showing that B is not dated 1173; Munk Olsen i. 395–402; Marshall *et al.* on the important new Cambridge MS (C) and knowledge of Gellius in mediaeval France and England. In bks. 1–7 aPR (where a is the putative ancestor of V and its highly emended nephew C) represent a single tradition; in bks. 9–20 Marshall posits three branches of tradition Fγδ, but Marache assigns F to γ and Gamberale, 'Note' 51–5 holds it a contamination of early γ with early δ. The two moieties of the Nights were present (in part and out of order) in the lost Codex Buslidianus (β), allegedly 12th-c. (Carrio, comm. 9), which preserves portions of the text otherwise unknown or found only in A and contains readings of variable quality (Hertz ii, pp. lxxxv–lxxxvii, xcviii–civ); both apparently stood in a MS owned by Richard de Fournival (Marshall *et al.* 379–80), and were known to anthologists and certain authors (eid. 357–8, 374 n. 32; Sabbadini, *Scoperte* 13; cf. W. Suerbaum in *EFHE* 332 n. 2 on Petrarch). MSS of *totus Agellius* were created by combining discrete copies (e.g. Cod. Vat. Lat. 3452, from V and 'V *pars alt.*'; cf. Marshall *et al.* 378, 380 with n. 60).

Xanthippe in chapter 11, looks more like a lemma.[19] In any case, Gellius may not have intended the round number, or may have miscounted if he did.[20] The books are unequal in number of chapters (eight in book 14, thirty-one each in books 13 and 15) as in length (books 1, 2, 7, and 11 occupy respectively 51, 53, 24, and 25 pages in Hosius' edition, 47, 47, 21, and 21 in Marshall's); individual chapters range from seventeen words in 16. 15 to some 2,100 in 6. 3.

Valerius Soranus' *Epoptides* included a summary of contents; citing this precedent,[21] Pliny lists in the first book of his *Natural History* the subjects and sources of the other thirty-six. However, whereas Pliny's summaries are brief and matter-of-fact, Gellius' are longer and written in his characteristic style.[22] Their authenticity, sometimes doubted before the finding of the palimpsest,[23] is not disproved by inaccuracies in their formulations:[24] the final redaction of the *Nights* was distinctly careless.

Gellius states (pr. 2–3) that he made brief notes of things read or heard, in no order, 'ad subsidium memoriae'. The *aide-mémoire* recurs as a cure for forgetfulness in Clement;[25] the convenient habit of excerpting is shared with the elder Pliny, Fronto, and Marcus;[26] Gellius' admissions that he has not the book by him, or cannot recall the details,[27] suggest notes that prove

19. e.g. 6. 5. lemma: 'Historia de Polo histrione memoratu digna'; all told, 18 lemmata exhibit 'historia' thus used. Socratic anecdotes seem not in Heracleides' line; but the other chs. are even less promising.

20. Book-numbers, often wrong in MSS (Hertz ii, pp. lxxxiv f.) and absent from Bussi's *ed. pr.*, run from one to nineteen in Nic. Jenson's edn. (Venice, 1472); the lemmata to bk. 8 first appear in Chr. 'de Quaietis'–Mart. 'de Lazaronibus' (Venice, 1493). All edns. before Hertz[1], following the *recentiores* (so too C), transpose bks. 6–7 of VPR and present 13. 14–16 as either one chapter or two. J. F. Gronovius restored the preface from the tail (as in the *recentiores*) to the head as in P (cf. Salmasius i, sig. [b6]ʳ; so CR; *om.* V). Other errors in capitulation were corrected at the latest in Carrio's edn.; section-nos. were introduced by Longolius.

21. Plin. *NH* pr. 33; cf. Scrib. Larg. ep. 15; Ael. Tact. pr. 7 (noted by Falster in his interleaved copy of *Vig. pr.*, opp. sig.):(4ʳ). A concluding *table des matières* originally stood after Col. 11. 3. 65. For Valerius' title ('Initiated Books') see Henriksson 176–7.

22. These lemmata often remodel phrases appearing in the text: 1. 10. lemma 'casce nimis et prisce loquentem' improves on 'uoces nimis priscas et ignotas' (§ 1); to the three synonyms 'conferas', 'componas', 'committas' of 2. 23. 3 and the two of § 22 'comparo et contendo' are added 'consultatio diiudicatioque' in the lemma; 'interpretatio' 15. 26. 2 becomes 'interpretamentum' (as at 5. 18. 7; 7. 2. 2).

23. Stephanus' objections, *Noct. Par.* IV–V, were met by Falster, *Vig. Pr.*, sig.):(4ʳ–[10]ʳ. A. Mai, *ed. pr.* of Cic. *Rep.*, p. 249 n. *b* adduced the palimpsest.

24. At 1. 18. lemma 'humanarum' is put for 'diuinarum' by confusion of polar terms; at 12. 1. lemma Favorinus' advice is bestowed on the baby's mother (the subject) instead of its grandmother; 18. 7. lemma shows untimely reminiscence of 8. 4, and in 18. 10. lemma misuse of the *word* 'vein' for 'artery' becomes misconception about the *thing*. But all these mistakes could be made in rereading matter written long before and half-forgotten. *NA* 15. 7. lemma 'Gaium filium', § 3 'Gaium nepotem suum', both correctly designate the same person; cf. Gascou 501.

25. *Strom.* 1. 11. 1 (cf. Stählin ad loc.); 1. 14. 2–3; 6. 2. 2.

26. Plin. *Ep.* 3. 5. 10; M. Caes. *Ep.* 2. 5. 2; 3. 19. 2; (M. Ant.) *Med.* 3. 14. Cf. Marache, edn. i, pp. xv–xvi.

27. e.g. *NA* 1. 23. 1; 2. 24. 14; to be distinguished from the affectation of 'if I remember aright', 'so far as I recall', when copying from the book (Kroll 290), e.g. 1. 3. 10, 6. 16. 4. But despite Mercklin 688 Gellius surely had certain noble texts by heart.

defective on subsequent expansion. Lapses of memory indeed occur, especially with names (p. 227); at 12. 11. 7, where a poet whose name Gellius does
not recollect makes Truth Time's daughter,[28] one may suspect a blend of
Plut. *QR* 12, Saturn/Κρόνος (= Χρόνος) the father of Truth, and Pi. *Ol.* 2.
17, Time the father of all things.[29] Nor are all references checked: even
Ennius, at 17. 21. 43, is quoted out of Varro.[30] Sometimes additional
information is promised when available: at 13. 7. 6, Homer and Herodotus
having disagreed on the lioness's litter, Gellius undertakes to cite Aristotle,[31]
but does not; at 18. 12. 10 he declares that other unusual deponents will be
recorded as encountered. Although at pr. 23–4 he intends to compile more
such 'memoriarum delectatiunculas', he has not reserved his unsolved
problems for them. At 2. 19. 3 he is still trying to understand a peculiar use of
re-;[32] at 12. 14. 7, dissatisfied with the available etymologies of *saltem*, he
decides that further research is needed; at 2. 22. 31, where Nigidius uses a
strange phrase, 'we must therefore consider what is meant by *secundo
sole*'[33]—a note to himself that has slipped through his redaction.[34]

Not only was the final editing somewhat slipshod,[35] but some chapters
were largely written up long before publication, apart perhaps from the
closing notes of further information or alternative accounts. We cannot
suppose, even disbelieving all Gellius' anecdotes, that he did not discover the
value of note-taking till he went to Greece,[36] or that his masters did not
instruct him to make excerpts; all that could have come to him in Athens was
the idea of putting his notes into literary form. Nothing else is meant by the
statement (pr. 4) that the title *Noctes Atticae* reflects the circumstances in
which Gellius had begun 'commentationes hasce ludere ac facere'. These
commentationes are the same *commentarii* in which, he has just confessed, the
same disunity of subject-matter obtains as 'in illis annotationibus pristinis', in

28. 'Veritas Temporis filia' (Mary Tudor's motto) was a favourite maxim in the Renaissance
(Baron 197 n. 2, cf. Bacon, *Nou. Org.* 1. 84, *ODEP* 844, Berthold, 'Interpretationsprobleme' 15
and nn. 9, 18).

29. See pp. 104, 246, ch. 12 n. 51, ch. 14 n. 97; A. Otto 343; cf. Eur. fr. 222 Nauck (Justice
Time's child). For another possible error see ch. 13 n. 23.

30. Cf. ch. 4 n. 40.

31. *HA* 579[a]31–[b]14; Kurth cites a modern authority. Some loose ends may be left deliberately
(cf. n. 72 below), but hardly all. Note the promise at 17. 6. 9 'alio in loco dicetur': in a
subsequent chapter? in the projected sequel?

32. In *resci(sce)re*, to learn a secret, or bad news (p. 135).

33. Nig. fr. 104 Sw., etesians and λευκόνοτοι blow 'secundo sole', with the sun (loosely)
behind them (Salmasius ii. 1261[a]A–[b]C; cf. Rutgersius 296, L. A. Holford-Strevens, *CR*[2] 36
(1986) 135–6); so fr. 113 Sw. 'secunda squama', with scales following the water. (Swoboda's
'cum sol iis oportunus est' seems too facile.) It certainly does not, as in several trs., mean
'following the sun'.

34. So Augustine admonishes himself or his amanuensis to check Gellius, *Q. Hept.* 1. 30.

35. Gellius admits to losing track at 18. 4. 11: 'intulisse iam me aliquo in loco
commentationibus istis existimo' (if so it was in 8. 14: 'a P. Nigidio origines uocabulorum
exploratae', lemma).

36. At 20. 6. 15 he takes a note of Apollinaris' discourse while still his pupil (§ 1), as any
teacher would expect.

the original notes. Marache correctly renders 'j'ai commencé de m'amuser à rédiger ces essais', with a note distinguishing the *commentationes* or *commentarii* from the *annotationes* and relating 'ludere' to the nature of the work; this word, commonly used of light verse,[37] is applied by Cicero to his *Paradoxa Stoicorum*.[38]

Sporadically Gellius repeats such matter as praises of the eminent,[39] vocalic quantity in *con-* (2. 17; 4. 17. 6), and the term *spadix* 'bay (horse)' (2. 26. 9–10; 3. 9. 9). The information that Varro called his satires *Menippeae*, but others said *Cynicae* (2. 18. 7), recurs in a less exact form ('partim ... alii') at 13. 31. 1; the model is Varro's phrase at 3. 10. 2 'stellas quas alii erraticas, P. Nigidius errones appellat', which Gellius appropriates at 14. 1. 11 when translating Favorinus' πλάνητες. The sophism known as the κερατίνης (what you have not lost you have; you have not lost horns; therefore you have horns) is alluded to at 16. 2. 10, and said at 18. 2. 9 to have been discussed by the Roman students keeping Saturnalia at Athens; their festivities return in 18. 13, with another of the sophisms already ascribed to them. Some doublets may be due to carelessness, but others show the same matter being put to different uses: the quotation from Cato's *Pro Rodiensibus* discussed for its content at 6. 3. 14 appears at 13. 25. 14 for its congeries of synonyms.[40] Gellius, having noted a passage down for one purpose, saw that it would also serve another, and that repetitions would bind his text together.[41]

According to Photius, *Bibl.* 175 (119^{b}27–32), Pamphila deliberately abstained from imposing an order on her historical, apophthegmatical, rhetorical, philosophical, and poetical matter, easy though it would have been, but wrote the items up at random as they came to her, holding that assortment and variety were more pleasing and charming than uniformity. Clement of Alexandria declares (*Strom.* 6. 2. 1, cf. 7. 111. 1–3) that as in a meadow the flowers bloom in various colours, and in an orchard the fruit-trees are not segregated by their kind (whence the use of such names as 'Meadows' for learned miscellanies), so his work is variegated like a meadow with matters that chanced to come to mind, subjected neither to discrimination in their order nor refinement in their language, but scattered on purpose higgledy-piggledy. Gellius too in his preface claims to have followed the chance order of his notes: 'usi autem sumus ordine rerum fortuito, quem antea in excerpendo feceramus' (§ 2), retaining their 'rerum disparilitas' (§ 3), although he does not, at least in the preserved text, say explicitly that this

37. See Fordyce on Cat. 50. 2.
38. Cic. *Par.* 3.
39. e.g. of the learned Paulus, 1. 22. 9; 5. 4. 1; 16. 10. 9; 19. 7. 1. Vogel, 'De compositione' 11–12, records inconsistencies and duplications, which he explains by Gellius' sudden death; his denial of protracted composition seems ill grounded.
40. Hertz, *Opusc. Gell.* 102 n. 10 suggests (cf. Thysius ad loc.) that Cato fr. 84 P, cited at 10. 1. 10 for adverbial *sextum*, had illustrated *duouicesimus* in 5. 4, cf. Non. 142. 9–14.
41. Cf. Berthold 10–11 ('unausgesprochene Selbstverweise').

was for the reader's delectation. The younger Pliny, who well knew the pleasure afforded by variety (*Ep.* 2. 5. 7–8; 4. 14. 3; 8. 21. 4), asserts that his letters stand in the published collection 'as each came to hand' (*Ep.* 1. 1. 1), which Sherwin-White in his commentary roundly and rightly denies; it is a mere commonplace. Solinus (pr. 4) states openly that he has employed variety to sustain the reader's interest.

Sure enough, there are ample signs in the *Nights* of deliberate disruption. Four explicit quotations from Cicero's *Orator*, standing in the original at §§ 158, 159, and (two extracts) 168, appear respectively at 15. 3. 2–3; 2. 17. 2; 13. 21. 24; 18. 7. 8. At 5. 12. 10 Gellius professes to have mentioned ('admonuimus') some words prefixed with *ue-* in a fuller discussion elsewhere, yet we must wait till 16. 5. 5–7. In 10. 16, from Hyginus' commentary on Vergil, three passages from *Aen.* 6 are considered in the order vv. 365–6, 122–3, 617–19; the commentary is also used at 1. 21. 2; 5. 8; 7. 6; 16. 6. 14–15. Not even the twenty passages of linguistic interest recorded in 17. 2 from the first book of Quadrigarius' *Annales* appear in sequence: indeed, the first extract cited (§ 3, fr. 22 Peter) belongs some eighty years after the last (§ 26, fr. 5). Nor are Gellius' narratives arranged in chronological sequence: if we read the *Nights* straight through, there are twenty changes of locale between Greece and Italy.[42] Two different stories about the landfall at Brundisium (9. 4; 16. 6) precede the stormy voyage from Cassiope (19. 1), which is followed by an incident 'before I went to Athens' (19. 8); the holiday with Julianus in Naples and Puteoli is divided between 9. 15 and 18. 5. Contrariwise, at 17. 21. 1 Gellius claims to have gathered together his disparate notes on Graeco-Roman synchronisms, but has compiled the chapter out of pre-existing lists (p. 179). What Gellius says is no guide to what he does.

To be sure, chapters linked by source or content may stand together (e.g. 2. 8–9 from the second book of Plutarch's *Homeric Studies*, on alleged illogicalities in Epicurus; 4. 1–4 on legal matters)[43] or in close proximity (9. 11, 9. 13 on *cognomina* won in single combat against Gauls; 15. 17, 15. 23 from Pamphila). But whereas excerpts from the same source may have been made at the same time, those of like content but unlike source may not. On the one hand Gellius has not always separated what was clustered in his notes, on the other he has sometimes brought together items there found far apart.

Some attempt at deliberate arrangement is detectable in the care taken that the initial chapter of each book shall afford a seat of honour for a favoured person or be of especial interest in its content:[44] Gellius' adored teacher Favorinus inaugurates books 2, 3, 4, 12, 14, 18, and 20; the genial Antonius Julianus, expounding Gellius' favourite historian Claudius Quadrigarius, has pride of place in books 9 and 15, the much-admired moralist

42. Mercklin 706, cf. 664–71.
43. Other exx. at Vogel, 'De compositione' 4, Berthold 17 n. 1.
44. Cf. Mercklin 707–8.

Musonius Rufus in 5 and 16; the nature of fate is the first topic of 7 and 13; a vivid storm at sea provides the overture to 19, and a solemn detestation of Cicero's critics introduces 17. Book 8 began with striking quotations from Ennius and the Twelve Tables; 10. 1 shows Pompey, in a question of grammar, letting discretion be the better part of valour; the etymology of *Italia* in 11. 1, opening the second half of the work,[45] and 6. 1 on the elder Scipio, exert a patriotic appeal; and the first chapter of all, on Pythagoras' calculation of Heracles' height, whets our curiosity by propounding a puzzle we shall not solve for ourselves.[46]

Gellius proclaims (pr. 11–12) that whereas his predecessors, especially the Greeks, had pursued mere bulk without discrimination, exhausting the bored reader long before he has found the odd snippet pleasant to read, educative to have read, or useful to remember ('quod sit aut uoluptati legere aut cultui legisse aut usui meminisse'), he himself, taking to heart Heracleitus' dictum that much learning does not impart intelligence,[47] has, out of his wide reading, selected only those few things that should either afford lively minds a short cut to a desire for honourable learning ('honestae eruditionis') and the study of the useful arts,[48] or at least redeem men engaged on other business from a shameful and boorish ignorance of words and things. In § 13 he states that in such specialist disciplines as grammar, logic, geometry, and sacral law he has given only such elementary information of which ignorance in an educated member of polite society ('uirum ciuiliter eruditum') is, if not harmful, then at any rate improper ('si non inutile, at quidem certe indecorum est'); we shall find in the course of the work that our gentleman not only ought to know a little law (20. 10. 6) and a little anatomy (18. 10. 8), and not make gross mistakes in chronology (17. 21. 1), but must show some acquaintance with silly fables about strange tribes with single eyes or canine heads in order to play his part in conversation (9. 4. 5). The test for

45. Conradi, Lion, and (in all three edns.) Hertz begin their second vols. with bk. 10 because of a late-imperial owner's epigram (*Anth. Lat.* 904 Riese) after bk. 9 in our MSS; but even if in his copy the break between codices fell here, it is as irrelevant to Gellius' conception as that between bks. 8 and 9 reflected in our tradition.

46. Berthold finds implied 'even so does my miscellany surpass its rivals [but in quality, not in quantity]' ('Aulus Gellius' 49 n. 6; cf. 'Interpretationsprobleme' 12, adducing Castiglione, *Cortegiano* 3. 1); Cavazza deduces from the lightweight subject that the work was meant to be dipped into rather than read straight through (edn. i. 21 n. 11). I see an engaging chapter to entice the reader into reading on.

47. Cf. p. 195: contrast Arist. fr. 62 Rose ('polymathy affords many points of departure'). Read 'Heracliti [*CR recc.*, *om. P*] Ephesii, uiri summe nobilis' (Marshall *et al.* 368; the paradosis, being explicit, is more Gellian). After 'ita est' the *recentiores* and the incunabula have a lacuna, which Beroaldus (edn.) filled with 'introite: nam et hic dii sunt' (cf. DK 22 A 9); this, with the ascription 'apud Gellium', is Lessing's epigraph to *Nathan der Weise*. Carrio replaced 'dii sunt' with asterisks; Stephanus, *Noct. Par.* 204 devised a fantastic explanation. The true text, reported by Salmasius i, sig. [b6]ᵛ, cf. Lambecius 109–14, was printed by J. F. Gronovius.

48. Cf. the 'fermentum cognitionis' of Solin. pr. 2, the spark and the graft of Clem. Alex. *Strom.* 1. 10. 4. For inexhaustiveness as a spur to study see below; Clement's reticence has a different motive (*Strom.* 1. 13. 3–1. 15. 1; 1. 18. 1). See too Janson 127.

Gellius' pieces of information (§ 16) is whether they are not too jejune to feed the love of study, or too frigid to warm and delight the spirit,[49] but make the mind livelier, or the memory better furnished, or the style more painstaking, or the diction purer, or the pleasure of free time and amusement more refined. This pedagogic programme is further expressed in the exhortations to take obscure or incomplete expositions as stimuli to study (§ 17), and when Gellius' statements conflict with those found elsewhere, to weigh both reasons and authorities (§ 18): not only does he teach ill that teaches all, but Gellius would gladly inspire his more serious readers to scholarly researches that they would not otherwise have thought of pursuing. However, he also knows that his less serious readers would have been bored by excessive detail.

The criteria of § 16 would cover most reasons, other than the stylistic elegance it was conventional to disclaim, why anything Gellius chose to include in his book should appeal to an educated readership: rather as a good political manifesto professes enough ideals to justify whatever its presenter does in office. But the principle of utility, stressed here and elsewhere in the *Nights*, will have been a commonplace among miscellanists: Clement of Alexandria expects his compilation to make the reader concerned with true knowledge labour hard in search of the advantageous and useful (*Strom.* 6. 2. 2)—given a Christian twist and identified with eternal salvation (§ 3). Brevity and selectivity are also standard themes:[50] Justin, the epitomator of Pompeius Trogus,[51] claims to have left out those things that were neither pleasing to learn nor necessary for their example (pr. 4).[52] Example having long since become the purpose of studying history, this means that Justin will provide only the pleasant and the useful. That is Gellius' promise.

However, his assertions that his prime aim is utility are not confined to the preface. In 14. 6 a literary friend offers him a large book of miscellaneous learning.[53] It treated of various problems, many of them Homeric: as who was the first grammarian, how many notable men were called Pythagoras and Hippocrates, the nature of the λαύρη in Odysseus' house, why Telemachus woke Peisistratus with a kick, in which verse each word is a syllable longer than its predecessor.[54] We are not told the answers; but when Gellius adds that it recorded the original names of lands and cities, he passes

49. Or as we should say 'dull', 'trivial', 'pretentiously null'; *frigidus* is frequently so used in Gellius.

50. Janson 96, 154; but excessive brevity is 'damnosa' (Solin. pr. 2).

51. The epitomator is one with the anthologist in spirit (Justin, pr. 4: 'breue ueluti florum corpusculum', cf. Seel 35; above, n. 15) or even person (e.g. Pamphila, Apuleius, Granius Licinianus).

52. Cf. Festus 242. 30–5 L, and in turn Paul. Diac. 1. 10–13 L.

53. Not Favorinus' Παντοδαπὴ ἱστορία; see pp. 82–3.

54. *Il.* 3. 182, if Ἀτρείδη is pronounced as a trisyllable; cf. Sacerdos, *GLK* vi. 505. 27–506. 6, Serv. *GLK* iv. 467. 15–17, 'Oratio consulis Ausonii' (pp. 84–5 Prete). Such verses are called 'rhopalic', or club-shaped. This ζήτημα, with some others, was solved by Muretus, *Var. lect.* 14. 13 (Gruter ii. 1123–5).

on the information: Boeotia used to be called Aonia, Egypt Aeria,[55] etc. Gellius, however, returns the book, congratulating his friend on his polymathy (as damned by Heracleitus), but declaring that the *Nights* are mainly concerned with one Homeric verse, reportedly Socrates' favourite:

ὅττι τοι ἐν μεγάροισι κακόν τ' ἀγαθόν τε τέτυκται

What ill and good have happened in thy halls. (*Od.* 4. 392.)

Socrates' fondness for this verse, symbolizing his ethical preoccupation, is asserted by the Peripatetic Demetrius of Byzantium (D.L. 2. 21) and the Stoic Musonius Rufus (fr. 3, p. 10 Hense);[56] the latter stands in high authority with Gellius. The attack on useless knowledge recalls Sen. *Ep.* 88,[57] *Breu. uit.* 13; both authors allude to the problem 'Whether Odysseus wandered in the Mediterranean or the Atlantic' (Sen. *Ep.* 88. 7, Gell. 14. 6. 3). Gellius speaks of isopsephic verses (§ 4);[58] Seneca quotes Apion's argument (*Ep.* 88. 40) that the proem to the *Iliad* was written after both epics' completion, because the first two letters of the opening word (μῆνιν 'wrath') indicated the number of books (μη′ = 48). Scorn for such trifles came even more readily to Cynics (D.L. 6. 27, Ath. 610 B–C); Gellius, I suggest, followed a Stoic or Cynic assault on these discussions, which abounded in Homeric commentaries and elsewhere (e.g. Plut. *Mor.* 739 A, B–D),[59] himself adding the early place-names from another source. Had he considered them equally useless, he could have written simply 'quibus urbibus regionibusque uocabula iam mutata sint', without the ten examples that follow; by the time he composed the lemma, he certainly deemed the information to be worth while, in contrast to what has gone before.[60] Certainly it passed for fact, not speculation; but although this knowledge is useful in reading poetry, and there was a current fashion for the old names' revival,[61] they do not illuminate the Socratic question, 'How should one live?' Perhaps the moralist had asked 'What boots it to know the position of Homer's Ephyre, yet not to discover (ἐφευρίσκειν) the disposition of your

55. For Ἀερία = Egypt see A. *Supp.* 75.

56. Ascribed to Diogenes at D.L. 6. 103.

57. Cit. Carolus 536, Oiselius; Weiss suspects a connection.

58. Consecutive verses whose constituent letters' numerical values yield the same sum. Thus (*Anecd. Gr.* ii. 461 Boissonade) *Il.* 7. 264–5 each add up to 3498 (3508 with iota adscript), 19. 306–7 each to 2848; but only with defective writing of elisions.

59. But Gellius may have added problems he found in Homeric scholarship (cf. ch. 9 n. 1); echoes remain in the scholia and Eustathius ad locc.

60. 'Cuimodi sint quae speciem doctrinarum habeant, sed neque delectent neque utilia sint; atque inibi de uocabulis singularum urbium regionumque inmutatis.' Ascensius observes the utility of the toponymic information; its inclusion is not of itself decisive, cf. the Varronian parenthesis at Sen. *Breu. uit.* 13. 4 ~ Varro fr. 212 Fun. (= *Vit. p. R* fr. 99 Riposati), but the lemma is.

61. Bowie 198 n. 89.

soul?', and Gellius, far from searching his soul, had been put in mind of poetic place-names; it would be in character (p. 49).

The trivial questions about acrostics,[62] and why Homer knows rose-oil but not the rose,[63] are easy to despise; but what is absurd about the question 'cuiusmodi fuisse Homerus dicat in Vlixis domo λαύρην'? Gellius' readers (to whom λαύρα meant 'town street', and perhaps 'lavatory') would, in a society that expressed wealth and status in its houses,[64] desire full details of Odysseus' home; a Roman was likelier to care about the λαύρη in a palace than the σπάρτα in a ship, yet Gellius happily discusses the latter in 17. 3, even considering whether the traditional accentuation is correct. This does not pave the path to virtue;[65] 14. 6. 5 is not the guiding principle of the *Nights*.

When Gellius represents his inclusion of Philip's letter to Aristotle on the birth of his intended pupil Alexander as an inspiration to parents (9. 3. 4), he need not be insincere; but since similar letters between Alexander and Aristotle are quoted at 20. 5. 10–12 for their elegance in brevity, and one from Olympias to Alexander at 13. 4. 2 for its wit,[66] primary interest may be rather the private life of Macedonian royalty, and all the rest mere dressing. If at 13. 26. 5, after an exposition of Nigidius' orthographical distinctions between *ei* and *i*, his statement that they have been included for those who seek knowledge 'even of these matters' is meant to distance Gellius from such folk, it does not distance him very far, though *ei* is not apparently among the archaic spellings he himself indulges in.[67]

In any case, Gellius can find reasons for repeating total rubbish, though he usually feels obliged to give them. At 9. 4. 5 his tall stories serve the social convenience of the reader, yet at § 12 he declares that he is too bored to continue copying such useless and unprofitable stuff: 'tenuit nos non idoneae scripturae taedium, nihil ad ornandum iuuandumque usum uitae pertinentis'. At 10. 12. 4 he affects to be in two minds whether he should record an unlikely story about the chameleon, and to do so only that he may state his view of the danger in such tales of marvels to the lively and enquiring mind; if we take this seriously and not as sheer hypocrisy, the curious student must be an undiscriminating magpie who will snap up a ludicrous story

---

62. If two-letter words be excluded, *Il.* 1. 2–4, 29–32, 40–3 offer ὀπή, Τήια, ἥττω. See Eustath. 1335. 29–53 on *Il.* 24. 1–5 (yielding λεύκη), who reports word-games with Homer (cf. Ath. 458); the Authorized Version has served for like sport.

63. But what of rosy-fingered Dawn?

64. A whole poem or letter may describe a single building: Stat. *Silu.* 1. 3, 2. 2, Plin. *Ep.* 2. 17, 5. 6.

65. Sen. *Ep.* 88. 3; *Breu. uit.* 13. 8 scorns the topic of *NA* 13. 14.

66. For these figments cf. ch. 13 n. 56.

67. Spellings such as *scribtum* and *uolgo* are found in his MSS, but *ei* for *ī* only at 13. 14. 1 (from Messalla, *cos.* 53 BC?) and in the unetymological QVEINTA of A at 1. 7. 1; however, scribes may remove or add archaic forms. On Nigidius see Bernardi Perini, 'Sistema'. Fronto's correspondence frequently exhibits *ei* even in the gen. sg.; note 'ingeniei' *Ep. M. Ant.* 1. 5. 3 (Early Latin *ingeni*).

without perceiving what it is. That is a hit at Pliny, often deserved but not here; yet in both chapters Gellius continues to transcribe his *miracula*. A modern reader, noting Gellius' repeated warnings against too deep a study of physics and logic, might suspect that he recognized in himself an unhealthy interest in silly tales and useless knowledge; but Romans should not be lightly credited with self-awareness.

In other matters the concern for utility is more genuine: in showing how well he could transform a Greek μελέτη into a Latin *declamatio*, Gellius also thought Favorinus' plea for mothers to suckle their own babies worth reporting for the common good (12. 1. 24);[68] the same seems true of his speech against astrology in 14. 1, despite Gellius' initial doubt whether Favorinus meant it (§ 2). The man of property, writing for men of property, knows that a method of fire-prevention will be of interest (15. 1). Nor, for Gellius, was there any doubt over the usefulness of stylistic studies, such as Fronto's of *mortales* put for *homines*, quoted to confer awareness of such subtleties (13. 29. 6); and the very name of χρεία given by the Greeks to pithy quotations from great men, such as he abounds in, testifies to their utility.

Gellius is a good Roman suspicious of Greek cleverness for its own sake, and speculations remote from life;[69] but he pursues intellectual hobbies that the unsympathetic have found no less pointless. In an age when educated men made learned conversation, there was little that could not be described as in some way useful to the reader; and it was naturally advisable so to describe what one had to offer. Certainly, Gellius is not interested in purely theoretical questions: speculative philosophy floats about his head, and even as a grammarian he derides a discussion of the correct vocative singular masculine for adjectives in *-ius* (14. 5), which in his day was generally avoided. But the overriding concern for morality proclaimed in 14. 6. 5 is true only of his philosophical chapters; that it is less important to him than literary taste is proved by his treatment of Seneca at 12. 2 (p. 204).

Granted, Gellius quotes moral saws and discusses moral problems in the light of philosophy (obedience to one's father, 2. 7) or Roman custom (character as determining credibility in court, 14. 2); Roman history may be

68. By this time 'women ... were rebelling against biologically determined roles' (Pomeroy 166); the moralizing cult of ancient ways would exalt the chaste, homekeeping matron of old against the freedom of upper-class women in the late Republic and early Empire (at § 8 Favorinus condemns abortion, to be prohibited in wives by Severus). There will thus be a reactionary (if fashionable: ch. 6 n. 38) point to Gellius' chapter; he does not disapprove of the harsh laws against drink and infidelity in women (for the connection see D.H. *Ant.* 2. 25. 6) reported in 10. 23 (§ 1 perhaps inspired Augustine's example of *temetum* for a hard and obsolete word, *Trin.* 10. 1. 2; the topic had domestic interest, *Conf.* 9. 8. 18). Pius and Marcus showed leniency to husbands who murdered unfaithful wives (D. 48. 5. 39. 8). In *ILS* 7213. 12 a woman of Gellius' own day abides by the ancient rule (Pomeroy 243 n. 9); his contemporary Granius Licinianus discussed the matter in his *Cena* (Serv. on *Aen.* 1. 737). On the permitted and prohibited beverages see André, *Alim.* 162–3, 170, 172.

69. See ch. 14, and especially pp. 192–3.

invoked even in philosophical questions (orders in apparent conflict with the superior's interest, 1. 13), but easily slides into antiquarianism (the hierarchy of duties in the *mos maiorum*, 5. 13, on which his authorities disagree). But we miss firm guidance on ethical choices likely to confront the reader: in 1. 3, where Gellius' sources fail to determine the limits within which one may stretch morality to help a friend, he himself does not supply an answer; at 2. 7. 20 the proposition that one must not obey one's father if his command be shameful is presented as self-evident ('non scilicet parendum', cf. §§ 10–11), not as Gellius' own ruling in a case of conscience.

If we take Gellius' protestations literally, we shall be dismayed by the yawning gulf between them and his practice; Marache, who erects them into an 'humanisme gellien', admits sadly that it applies the noblest notions of man and morality to justify 'un enseignement de manuel'.[70] The contradiction should give us pause: did Gellius really entertain such exalted notions, or were his professions of utility conventional clichés that took away the need to devise a guiding principle, and whose mechanical repetition dulled the perception of conflict or neglect? Fischer, who is not deceived, is also not disappointed, but calmly registers the coincidence between a *jeu de société* reported at 18. 2. 6 and the contents of the *Nights*:[71] the Roman students in Athens discussed a passage from an old poet that was pleasantly, not bafflingly, obscure ('lepide obscura', as Fischer observes, is a profession of faith), a problem in ancient history, the correct meaning of a philosophical doctrine commonly misunderstood (Plato on community of women and kisses for war-heroes; cf. 15. 2 on the value of drunkenness), the solution of a sophistic catch (see p. 25), or the investigation of a rare and unexpected word (cf. 15. 13. lemma), or a strange tense-form (as whether the perfect subjunctive belongs to the future, § 14; in 17. 7 Gellius considers whether the future perfect has a past force). The *Nights* thus afford a means to 'delectatio in otio atque in ludo liberalior' (pr. 16), not devoid of intellectual stimuli;[72] Gellius' claims of purpose do not seem absurd when his miscellany is

---

70. *Critique* 264; but then for Gellius *humanitas* consisted in polite learning (13. 17).

71. Fischer, p. lxix n. 2; cf. *NA* 13. 11. 4. *Anxius/-e* (frequent in Gellius) implies the taking of pains, with positive, neutral, or negative connotations; see Timpanaro, *Contributi* 385 n. 25. The dinners were financed out of forfeits for unsolved sophisms at bathtime (18. 13. 1–6); the prizes (garlands apart) were ancient Greek and Latin texts (18. 2. 3). For the Collegium Gellianum set up at Leipzig in 1641 under the inspiration of *NA* 18. 2 see Gebauer, pp. x, xvi–liii, cf. Berthold, 'Interpretationsprobleme' 13.

72. According to Gellius, the guests solved all the problems in 18. 2 but one, to which alone he gives the answer—a plain matter of fact (but see Skutsch on Enn. *Ann.* 374). The others include the Liar Paradox, which killed Philitas and exercises philosophers even now. In 19. 14 (but not 17. 7) Nigidius' observations are offered without explanation 'ad exercendam legentium intentionem'; they are as straightforward as the riddle of 12. 6, for whose solution we are referred to Varro. It was found by Politian, *Misc. I*, ch. 36, sig. g2ʳ; cf. Wind 164, id. *JWS* 1 (1937) 66–9.

compared with Aelian's. Only those should complain who require their scholarship to be solemn and their amusement vacuous.

The hypothesis underlying much of Heinz Berthold's work on Gellius is that passages cited for grammatical purposes had originally been excerpted for their content.[73] Sometimes there can be no doubt, as when Cic. *Or.* 168, on the effect of well-turned speech, at 18. 7. 8 attests a sense of *contio*; Gellius' extracts from *Orator* are all concerned with euphony, a subject that certainly engaged him (pp. 120, 137–8). Sometimes attention to content is explicit: at 12. 9. 6 Gellius professes to have cited a passage from Numidicus not merely because it displays a semantic rarity but also because it conveys a Socratic precept. But sometimes Gellius found his example preselected by his source; and style has at least an equal claim. When the fourth-declension dative in -*u* is illustrated from Caesar's *Anticato*, 'unius arrogantiae, superbiae dominatuque' (4. 16. 8: 'to one man's arrogance, pride, and overmightiness'), Berthold suggests that Gellius had noted down the core of Caesar's argument; but perhaps it was more the vigour of the phrase that attracted him than its historical significance. The causes of the Civil War, like many other topics that had *ex hypothesi* made the excerpts worth excerpting, are not discussed in their own right: we should have to suppose, either that Gellius' view had contracted with age, or that he left his readers free to take what hints they would. Certainly some quotations show thematic links with Gellius' own material: thus Enn. *Ann.* 371–3 Sk, cited in 6. 2 for Caesellius' misinterpretation, portrays the strained relationship between Hannibal and Antiochus the Great already exhibited in 5. 5, though each chapter was included on its own merits. In any case, succeeding ages have reflected with advantage on Gellius' quotations as on his own statements, whether or not in ways he intended or could envisage.[74]

In recent years Gellius has frequently been thought a moralist;[75] Fischer, however (p. lxx), noting his concern to equip his readers for social pastimes,

73. Berthold 7–9; cf. id., 'Aulus Gellius' 47 (citing 4. 16. 8), 'Interpretationsprobleme' (on later, especially Renaissance, use of Gellian matter).

74. Bussi (to Pope Paul II, fo. [5]ʳ: Botfield 88–9) bids the reader perpend Gellius' themes in their entirety, not merely his own comments. That advice is in the spirit of pr. 12–17; Berthold does much to help us. For creative reading of Gellius see J. Martin, *Viator* 10 (1979) 57–76, on John of Salisbury; cf. ead., *JWI* 40 (1977) 1–20.

75. Marache's theory of 'le primat de la morale' was anticipated by R. Ju. Vipper, *VDI* 1948/2, 58–64, for whom Gellius is 'the best exponent of the optimistic, non-religious Antonine morality' (p. 58) and more humane than Seneca towards slaves. K. I. Novickaja, *VDI* 73 (1960) 145–54 easily refutes him (esp. pp. 153–4, cf. ch. 14 n. 96), yet accepts the primacy of ethics in the *Nights*: like Apuleius' writings, they bear witness that Roman society had entered upon a period of ideological crisis and vainly desired to find a way out of it, which Gellius sought in a return to the past (p. 150; cf. Romano 115–18, Cousin 442). But F.-F. Lühr, *AU* 19/1 (1976) 5–19, comparing *NA* 5. 14 with Petr. 61. 6–62. 14 and Plin. *Ep.* 9. 33, observes that entertainment in Gellius is 'völlig trivialisiert' (p. 17). D. Nörr, *ANRW* II. xv. 557 finds in Gellius virtually no trace of emotional withdrawal to a better past; a-historical antiquarianism is an end in itself (cf. id., 'Rechtskritik' 144 n. 5), reference to its utility a cliché of self-justification

sees in the moral maxims an ancient counterpart to our dictionaries of quotations or the *pages roses* of the Petit Larousse. Gellius deals in such matter no less than other Romans; but his maxims and *exempla* are intended for the reader's delectation (which includes the restatement of accepted beliefs) and for assistance in conversation or in public speaking; reformation of manners was no more his main end than Valerius Maximus'. Medieval writers would derive from Demosthenes' retort to Lais (1. 8) an exhortation to chastity;[76] for Gellius it is a good joke, and even better in Greek. His fascination with punishment, especially by censors, whatever its psychological significance, directs no serious protest at current laxity;[77] even Castricius' rebuke to his casually shod pupils in 13. 22 becomes a peg for grammatical discussion, and is probably a fiction based on Cic. *Phil.* 2. 76.[78] At 3. 3. 8 Gellius states that he copied down verses from an early comedy to investigate the Arretine oracle there mentioned, but cites them as stylistic proof of Plautine authorship.[79] His researches, presumably fruitless,[80] were undertaken not from interest in oracles, or Arretium, but to elucidate a text; in Theodor Vogel's phrase, he was a visitor to other disciplines, but a citizen of Grammar.[81]

('eine apologetische Phrase'). Yet the acquisition of knowledge is itself useful; for Gellius' pedagogic aim cf. Berthold, 'Interpretationsprobleme' 13–14. Insofar as Gellius has a social purpose (so too Gassner 210–23), it is undoubtedly conservative (cf. n. 68) but subsidiary to the provision of erudite amusement. No lesson or moral is drawn from Androclus' experience (contrast Ael. *N. An.* 7. 48, *Aesopica* 563 Perry, Romulus 51 Thiele, *Gesta Romanorum* 104, 278 Österley). For trivialized history see pp. 179–80.

76. J. Salis. *Polic.* 6. 25 (ii. 64–5 Webb); Walter Map, *Nug. Cur.* 4. 3 (p. 304 James–Brooke–Mynors); Gir. Cambr. *Gemma eccles.* 2. 1, 5, *Princ. Instr.* 1. 4. (ii. 172–3, 185, viii. 13–14 RS); contrast Wm. Malmes. *Polyh.* 66. 15–24 Ou., Diceto i. 46 St. The moral was not unthinkable in the 2nd c.: cf. Apul. *Met.* 11. 15. 1.

77. 11. 18. 18, a general truth even in the good old days, and 20. 1. 53, impractical grumbling. Punishment: justified 7. 14; of thieves 8. 1, 11. 18; Appia fined for verbal *incivisme* 10. 6; soldiers compelled to open veins 10. 8 (but worse at Cato fr. 131 P); fines 11. 1; cutting-up of judgement-debtors 20. 1; cf. Berthold 175–7. Censors: e.g. 4. 8; 4. 12; 4. 20; 6. 18. 10; 6. 22—evocations of the distant past, not appeals for Marcus to emulate Domitian. Note too the avenging of Regulus (7. 4. 4) and the portrait of inflexible Justice (14. 4), as whose priest (§ 3, cf. Nörr, 'Iurisperitus sacerdos' 561) Gellius no doubt dreamt of pronouncing grander sentences than civil suits allowed. A sheltered life may breed sternness no less than indulgence (cf. p. 91).

78. The contrast between proper and improper dress, and the new word *gallica*, are both in Cicero; Castricius was an appropriate mouthpiece (pp. 64–5).

79. Was Gellius induced by Cinna fr. 10 M–B (9. 12. 12) to seek out information on the Psylli (16. 11. 3)?

80. The text is corrupt; the conjecture 'responsum Arreti' (see Hertz ad loc.) eliminates Arretium and its oracle—since in Early Latin the locative of *Arretium* was *Arretiei*, cf. Enn. *Var.* 37 V, Ter. *Eun.* 519—to give the no less problematic 'Arretius'/Arrhetos' answer'. Gellius, unaware of the locative as a separate case (G. Funaioli, *ALL* xiii. 301–3), was hunting for a mare's nest.

81. Vogel, 'Iudicium' 14; sc. γραμματική in its broad ancient sense (ch. 9 n. 2). Such isolated interests as embassies (ch. 16 n. 34) and perhaps athletics (pp. 203–4) merely remind us that nothing in human affairs is absolute. At 11. 1. 6–7 Gellius quotes and justifies an abnormal expression in Cato that he uses himself at 6. 14. 8; the fr. (82 P) concerns punishment for unauthorized attack, the theme of 9. 13. 20; 17. 21. 17 (cf. 1. 13. 7), but even if recorded for its content it is cited for a phrase. Which interested Gellius more?

Chapter 3

Language and Style

GELLIUS' language has been frequently studied,[1] mostly for its archaisms, sometimes for its novelties; but as Hazel Hornsby observes (p. xxxiv), 'With the exception of some remarkable chapters ... the text of the "Noctes Atticae" shows surprisingly few strange words or constructions on any given page, though the aggregate for the whole twenty books is considerable', and those strange words or constructions may as well be post- as pre-classical. Although some formations not attested before Gellius would not be out of place in an early author, the distinction between Antonine Latin and Republican is plain enough even in such 'remarkable chapters' as 2. 29 (an apologue retold after Ennius), 3. 7 (a paraphrase of Cato immediately followed by a direct quotation), and 9. 11 (renarration of a story probably taken from Valerius Antias).[2]

The Valencian humanist Vives likened Gellius' style to rainwater collected drop by drop: it had no natural source of its own, but was scraped together as by a beggar out of recent and ancient writers, poets and orators, commonplace words and rarities.[3] This account is true of the parts and false of the whole: Gellius is not a beggar but an artist. The unusual words are not thrown haphazardly together; they embellish a distinctive style that was much to the taste of later readers.[4]

---

1. See biblio. s. nn. Ebert; Gorges; Hache; Knapp (also *AJPh* 14 (1893) 216–25, 16 (1895) 52–65, *TAPhA* 28 (1897), pp. v–vii); Marache, *Mots*; Müller; Neubauer; Portalupi, *Ricerca*; Ronconi; Vogel, 'De sermone' (also *JbClPh* 127 (1883) 185–92); Yoder; see too J. C. Rolfe, *CPh* 15 (1922) 144–6. There is a useful résumé in Hornsby's edn., pp. xxxii–lxv. These studies, however, are not free from human frailty: Ebert, who severely censures Gorges, takes 'inspirantis [acc. pl.] primae litterae [dat. sg.]' (2. 3. 2) for gen. sg. and the ablatives of 2. 6. 11 for datives (p. 579); Neubauer's causal conjunctions do not include *cum* (for instances with the indicative, all following the main clause, see Hornsby, p. lvii); Müller 17–18, through not consulting Proust's word-index, fails to find *forsitan* at 2. 26. 20, *immo* at 15. 9. 4, and *usquequaque* at 3. 2. lemma; 9. 16. 2; 11. 3. 3; 14. 1. 9; Foster, who continues and corrects Knapp's work, implausibly opposes 'survival' archaisms in Apuleius to 'revival' archaisms in Gellius, and in unsuccessfully defending *Africitas* against Brock displays a remarkable discourtesy (pp. 5–11), as if English maiden ladies had no rightful place in these studies.

2. See ch. 11 n. 74, pp. 183, 179.

3. *De ratione dicendi* 2. 2 (*Opera* ii. 141); but Vives was a *Gelliomastix* (p. 237). Good observations in Stephanus' letter to Henri III's man of confidence Jean de Vulcob 12–16. Ruhnken, in Oudendorp's edn. of Apul. *Met.*, p. ii, found Gellius, despite his taste for words from comedy, less extravagant than Apuleius.

4. Augustine calls him 'uir elegantissimi eloquii' (*CD* 9. 4); Ammianus plunders him (ch. 1 n. 43).

Pre-classical diction in the *Nights* comprises such words as *amasius* (6. 8. 1; 19. 9. 9), *castus* subst. (10. 15. 1), *cuius* adj.,[5] *derepente* (10. 12. 3), *fabulor* 'I speak',[6] *ingeniatus* (12. 1. 17), *miscellus* (pr. 5), *prolubium* (5. 10. 12; 16. 19. 13), *publicitus* (7. 14. 4), *rupex* (13. 9. 5), *uaciuus*;[7] such formantia as *-arius* adj. *-ter*, and *-tudo*;[8] such inflexions as *cornum* (1. 8. 2; 14. 6. 2; 18. 6. lemma), *feruit* (2. 29. 10; 17. 8. 8), *ferundum*,[9] *insilibat*,[10] *quitast*,[11] *uidierier* (3. 7. 8; 15. 2. 1); and such constructions as appositive *id genus*;[12] *clam* + accusative (2. 23. 16), *quam* for *potius quam*,[13] causal *prae* in positive context,[14] *nemo quisquam*,[15] and *plerique omnes*.[16] Prepositions are constantly repeated and frequently superfluous;[17] prepositional phrases are presented in concatenation;[18] anaphoric *is* abounds, in sequence or anacoluthon;[19] we find abnormalities in voice or transitivity,[20] and a general taste for redundance, as in *terra Italia*

5. *NA* 1. 13. 7; 1. 22. 6; 2. 29. 15; 9. 16. 5 (unless in Pliny); all imitating early legal language. Whereas Sp. *cuyo*, Ptg. *cujo*, are normally relative and attributive, in Early Latin *cuius* adj. is the regular predicate, whether relative or interrogative, but outside set formulae already archaic as an attribute (Holford-Strevens, 'Select Commentary' on 2. 29. 15).

6. Frequent in Early Latin (56× in Plautus); abandoned in late Republican literature though retained by the Iberian colloquial (Sp. *hablar*, Ptg. *falar*); occasionally used by early imperial writers for lies (Liv. 45. 39. 15) and myth (Plin. *NH* 29. 3; cf. μυθολογεῖν); applied in the late 1st c. AD to undignified oratory (Quint. 11. 3. 131, Tac. *Dial.* 23. 3, 39. 1) and conversation (Mart. 3. 64. 6; 4. 61. 4); given the general sense of 'speak' by Suetonius and the mannerists. (But of fable Apul. *Socr.* pr. 4.)

7. *NA* 1. 22. 10, Sp. *vacío*, Ptg. *vazio*. Gellius does not use the spelling *uo-*, commoner in the extant comedies, and the sense 'superfluous' is recent (so *uacuus* Petr. 102. 7, Gell. *NA* 11. 15. 6).

8. Vogel, 'De sermone' 16–17 (cf. Knapp 155); 30–1; 4 (cf. Knapp 147–8).

9. Gorges 5–7, Knapp 143.

10. *NA* 9. 11. 7, cf. *gestibat* 15. 2. 1. So Fronto, *Fer. Als.* 3. 9 (Portalupi silently trivializes); 5 × in Apul. *Met.* But Gellius does not use the future in *-ibo* (quoted at 6. 17. 13); contrast Apul. *Met.* 6. 28. 5. For his selectivity in archaism cf. Ronconi 140.

11. *NA* 20. 1. 52, cf. Apul. *Apol.* 2. 6; for Quint. 1. 6. 26 it was impossibly harsh.

12. To the exx. at Gorges 28–9, add 14. 7. 11; in general see E. Wölfflin, *ALL* v. 389–98.

13. *NA* 2. 7. 13; see Timpanaro, *Contributi* 39–81.

14. 'Prae studio laudis et honoris' 2. 27. 5. In Early Latin the context may be positive, but the cause must (as here) be psychological (Plaut. *Men.* 181 is comparative, not causal); in classical usage the context must be negative (or quasi-negative: 'oblitae' Liv. 4. 40. 3 = *immemores*), but the cause may be physical. (Holford-Strevens, comm. ad loc., E. D. Francis, *YCS* 23 (1973) 10–12.) Suet. *Aug.* 34. 1 shows the classical, *Claud.* 32 the early use; no archaist (Wallace-Hadrill 203–4), he also has *derepente*, *fabulari* = *loqui*, *lauare* = *lauari*, *miscellus*, *nemo quisquam*.

15. *NA* 2. 6. 9; 9. 10. 4; 12. 7. 4; so *nihil quidquam*, Gorges 63.

16. *NA* 1. 7. 4 etc.; cf. 8. 12; Gorges 62, Ebert 583, Hache 6–7.

17. See Knapp, 'Prepositions' 6–9, 12.

18. *NA* 2. 10. 3 etc.; Hache 28–9.

19. The referent of sequential *is* may vary (e.g. 1. 8. 1–3 'is [sc. Sotion] ... ea uox ... in eo libro') or remain constant (e.g. 2. 18. 2–5 'eius ... is Phaedon ... eum ... is ... eius'; less naïve Macr. *Sat.* 1. 11. 41); cf. Hache 38–9. Anacoluthon: e.g. 2. 3. 1 'H litteram ... inserebant eam ueteres'; Hertz, 'Vind. Gell. alt.' 69–70, Hache 43–4. Other anacolutha too can be found, e.g. 14. 2. 11 'et ipsum illud ... et cetera ... earum rerum'.

20. Discussed by Gellius at 15. 13, 18. 12: note e.g. 'mutare' intr. (2. 23. 7), 'comperior' dep. (3. 3. 1), 'percontantur' pass. (16. 6. 11), 'eiaculauerat' act. (16. 19. 21). Gerundives are used actively at *NA* 3. 10. 7 'ad homines ... nascendos', § 10 'adolescendi humani corporis' (cf. Varro, the source of this ch., *LL* 6. 11 'senescendorum hominum'); for newly transitive verbs see n. 30. Note too such reflexives of rapid motion as 'se ... festinantes' (14. 2. 9); Kühner–Stegmann i. 96.

and *tum postea*.[21] Even the pot in which lentils are served in 17. 8 is a Plautine *aula*, not a Catullan *olla*. Excerpts from early authors and expressions discussed in grammatical chapters or exhibited in quotations appear in Gellius' text.[22] Republican usages like *septentriones* and *superuacaneus*, rare after Cicero, return to oust their long-victorious rivals;[23] letter-names are neuter,[24] *plenus* always takes the genitive,[25] the *rerum gerendi* construction is revived.[26] There is also the false archaism *absque* 'without', 'apart from';[27] and since *dies*, in Imperial Latin, is often feminine where Republican usage would have made it masculine, Gellius writes 'ut in diem certum non pugnetur' (1. 25. 15) and 'diem dictum esse' (3. 4. 1) for the Republic's *certam*, *dictam*.[28]

Yet we also find such imperial innovations in syntax, semantics, and vocabulary as *compendium* 'short cut' (pr. 12), *emaculare* (7. 5. 9), *Graeciensis* (19. 10. 1), *iactantia* (18. 6. 1), *improprie* (7. 6. 2 etc.), *inquies* subst. (19. 9. 5), *inuidere* with accusative (but not ablative) and dative (15. 31. 3), *occiduus* (2.

21. Gorges 61–5, Ebert 581–3, Hache 10–25; on otiose possessives, Yoder 11–14.

22. Thus *in medium relinquo, pugnare in, ne ... quoque*, cited from Quadrigarius in 17. 2, all reappear (7. 14. 9; 17. 21. 17; 1. 2. 5, etc.), as does Laevius' *intolerans = intolerandum* (19. 7. 10, cf. 13. 8. 5); cf. e.g. *defendo = depello* 9. 1. 8–9 ~ 5. 8. lemma, 15. 1. 4, *priui = singuli* 10. 20. 4 ~ 11. 6. 1, apodotic *atque* 10. 29 ~ 17. 20. 4; see Hache 5–10, cf. Hertz, 'Vind. Gell. alt.' 12. For usages shared with quotations see esp. Hache 10–51: e.g. 'parsisset' 5. 14. 15 ~ 'parsissem' Plaut. *Pseud.* 5 at 20. 6. 9 (cf. Nov. 78 R at 17. 2. 8). Quotations may also be echoed at short range (e.g. 'quo in tempore' 2. 13. 4 ~ 'in eo tempore' Asell. fr. 7 P at § 5), even for ordinary words (e.g. 'etiam' 12. 2. 6 ~ Seneca ibid.); cf. Skutsch on Enn. *Ann.* 549). But practice conflicts with precept on *harenae* (ch. 7 n. 33), *maturare* (ch. 10 n. 18), *soloecismus* (ch. 10 n. 38). 'Aeditui' 2. 10. 4 against 12. 10 (cf. 6. 1. 6) may be a MS trivialization, but the restriction of *humanitas* to learning in 13. 17 is not observed at 15. 21 (cf. 20. 1. 11, 24, 26; Falster, 'Noct. Rip.' 445), the distinction between *necessitas* and *necessitudo* scorned in 13. 3 is followed in practice (cf. 16. 13. 6, 8). Cf. Maselli 52, 97 nn. 72, 89.

23. *NA* 2. 21. 4 etc.; 1. 22. 9. Imperial Latin uses *septentrio* (so 'Apul.' *Mund.*), *superuacuus*; Varro fr. 216 Fun. (= *Vit. p. R.* fr. 129 Riposati) disapproves of the latter. Gellius also confines *quantus* and *tantus* to magnitude, *equidem* to the sense ἔγωγε, and *solstitium*, *-alis* to the summer solstice; but the Republican subjunctive *edint* (20. 8. 7) is countered by the post-classical *edit* pres. ind. (11. 7. 3), *ederent* (19. 2. 7 beside classical *esse*).

24. 2. 14. 2; 4. 17. 7; 5. 21. 8; 9. 14. 3; 14. 5. 2; cf. Tiro fr. 7 Fun. at 10. 1. 7. Cicero and Varro use the neut., Quintilian the fem.

25. *NA* pr. 19; 1. 15. lemma; 1. 24. 2; 3. 5. 2; 6. 3. 29 (Gellius, not Tiro, who would not have written 'ea fini'); 7. 16. 8; 9. 3. 3; 14. 2. 6, 10; 17. 5. 1; 18. 12. 4; 19. 8. 1; 20. 1. 13 (Gellius, not Labeo); contrast Quint. 9. 3. 1, and see Krebs ii. 309, E. B. Lease, *AJP* 21 (1900) 450, cf. 30 (1909) 304. Fronto has the abl. at *Amic.* 2. 4; 2. 7. 13, Verus the gen. at *Ver.* 2. 10. 1. Apuleius (both certain and disputed) shows a slight preference for the gen.; neither appears in *Met.* (gen. by conjecture 7. 16. 1; 7. 20. 2).

26. *NA* (3. 16. 1 conj.); 4. 15. 1; 5. 10. 5; 16. 8. 3 (Gorges 53); at 7. 14. 4 Hertz, but not Marshall, reports 'imponendi poenae' in V. Cf. Fronto, *Amic.* 1. 26, *Princ. hist.* 2. 2 m² f, Apul. *Flor.* 17. 9.

27. In Early Latin only in the formula *absque te esset/foret* 'but for you (etc.)'; the correct sense, but not construction, at *NA* 2. 26. 13, Fronto, cf. *Ep. M. Caes.* 5. 48. 1. But the frequency of *absque* in Late Latin, including the subliterary Bible, indicates some spoken currency (cf. Lombard *asca* 'except', Meyer-Lübke no. 47).

28. Hypercorrect masc. throughout 1. 25. 15–16; fem. used correctly at 5. 10. 15; 12. 13. 6; 19. 5. 3 and never wrongly. On the distinction see Fraenkel, *Kl. Beit.* i. 27–72; on hypercorrect masculines ibid. 37 n. 1, 47 n. 1, 70 n. 2; on incorrect feminines in Fronto and Apuleius 57 n. 2, 58 n. 1. See too Tac. *A.* 6. 12. 2; 15. 46. 2.

22. 12), and *tamquam*-clauses of questionable assertion (3. 9. 2; 13. 31. 1). The 'most of others' construction, familiar like many other illogicalities in Greek but rare in Latin (Tac. *Agr.* 34. 1, cf. Plin. *NH* 25. 5), appears at *NA* 1. 3. 12 'hunc autem locum ... omnium rerum aliarum difficillimum'.[29] There further appear such post-classical usages as *adniti* transitive,[30] *arbitrarius* (10. 4. 3 etc., borrowed from the lawyers), *cohibilis* (16. 19. 1), *crastino* 'tomorrow' (2. 29. 9), *demirari* fully conjugated,[31] *dicere ad*,[32] *diutule*,[33] *fauisor* (14. 3. 9), *petitu* 'at the request (of)' (18. 3. 6), and the frequent use of *quod* (with indicative or subjunctive) introducing reported speech,[34] sometimes to avoid one infinitive-clause dependent on another. The *quod*-construction, previously substandard, is not in Gellius a vulgarism; the writer who derives his colloquial diction from Plautus ('Verbero, inquit ridens Taurus, nonne is curriculo atque oleum petis?' 17. 8. 8, complete with trochaic rhythm) does not draw directly on the *sermo plebeius*,[35] but admits certain features that had gained acceptance in the educated *consuetudo*. Like most inveighers against linguistic change, he concentrates his fire on isolated targets while other infiltrators remain unscathed. Moreover, Gellius, far more than Fronto, abounds in words not previously recorded, such as *aequiperatio* (5. 5. 7; 14. 3. 8), *confusaneus* (pr. 5), *deiurium* 'solemn oath' (6. 18. 8), *diluculare* (2. 29. 7; 6. 1. 6), *infacundia* (11. 16. 9), *inludiare* (1. 7. 3), *insubidus/-e* 'stupid', 'tasteless' (1. 2. 4 etc.), *noscitabundus*,[36] *obsequibilis* (2. 29. 12), *positiuus* (10. 4. lemma), *praedaticius* (4. 18. 12; 13. 25. 28), *retaliare* (20. 1. 16), *simulamentum* (15. 22. lemma), *subsecundarius* (pr. 23). First attestation does not prove first use: much early (and other) Latin is lost; some derivations could be made at will; semantic change implies that *insubidus* (from *in-* and *subidus* 'on heat') already

---

29. Cf. Macr. *Sat.* 7. 8. 9. (Contrastive *alius* at *NA* 10. 25. 1, cf. e.g. Lucr. 1. 116).

30. *NA* 2. 12. 5 (gdve., but cf. Fronto, *Ver.* 2. 1. 4; with neut. pron. from Livy). Other new transitives are *suscensere* (7. 2. 5 gdve., 16. 11. 6; with neut. pron. Ter., Cic.); *inolescere* (12. 1. 20 gdve., 12. 5. 7); in gerundive only, *obsequi* 1. 13. 9 (but cf. D. 24. 1. 5. 15), *consistere* 5. 10. 9 (but cf. Iren. 2. 28. 8). *Congredi* (1. 11. 2 gdve.) is transitive at Plaut. *Epid.* 545, *decertare* (10. 18. 6 gdve.) at Stat. *Theb.* 1. 2. At 6. 18. 9 'iureiurando satisfacto' we dare not hope that 'iureiurando' is the old dative and 'satisfacto' impersonal. Cf. Draeger ii. 856–7.

31. *NA* 1. 17. 2 etc. (10×); previously (Plaut., Ter., Cic., Plin. *NH*), and not seldom, only the single form 'demiror'. Free conjugation in Jul. Val. and later. (The restriction is noted in L&S, but not *TLL* or *OLD*.)

32. Knapp, 'Prepositions' 7.

33. See ch. 1 n. 62.

34. Gorges 51–2, Ebert 581, Neubauer 13–14. *Variatio* at 15. 7. lemma, 18. 15. 2; dependent acc. + inf. in turn at 2. 10. 2. But not used at 18. 9. 4 to save ambiguity (ch. 9 nn. 55–6).

35. Which he disdains (p. 128); but no word can be vulgar that was used by good authors (19. 10. 10, cf. ch. 10 n. 14, Lebek 15 n. 12). Some originally substandard uses, like *iste = hic* (pr. 14 etc.), had become entrenched in Silver times (note too weak *ipse*, Yoder 91); others, colloquial in the early writers, are for Gellius simply ancient (e.g. *rupex* 13. 9. 5, from Lucil. 1121 M); cf. Cameron 156.

36. *NA* 5. 14. 11; on -*bundus* adjectives see 11. 15, Marache, *Mots* 185–8; Pianezzola 214–21. Never with dir. obj. (despite 11. 15. 7) as frequently in Apuleius—who (unlike Fronto) relishes this formation (Pianezzola 222–9).

existed;[37] terms of philosophy or rhetoric, modelled on the Greek, may have been picked up in the schools.[38] Nevertheless, when at 1. 20. 9 Gellius ventures a translation of ἀπλατές, 'quod exprimere uno Latine uerbo non queas, nisi audeas dicere inlatabile', using a word not found before or since, the inference is plain that he has coined it himself;[39] he has likewise produced his own equivalents for ἄπηκτος ('incongelabile' 17. 8. 16) and ἀναμάρτητος ('inpeccabilis' 17. 19. 6).[40] The man who approves of coinages by Furius Antias, Cn. Matius, and Sallust is ready to forge his own; he knows that there are limits, and that not every Greek word can be rendered by a single Latin one, but a new term, if not too awkward, is perfectly acceptable.[41] Nevertheless, Greek words, naturalized or not, are freely used, sometimes wantonly (ῥαθυμότερον 6. 2. 11, *aelurus* 20, 8. 6 instead of *negligentius, feles*),[42] and may be glosed (pp. 167–8).

A neologism or a Graecism may be the unexpected word of mannerist theory; so may an archaism, or a word used in an unfamiliar way: *discerniculum*, elsewhere a kind of hairpin,[43] receives at 17. 15. 4 its etymological sense 'distinguishing feature', *genuinus*, properly 'inborn', acquires the meaning 'authentic, genuine' (3. 3. 7, cf. 9. 9. 15). The striking word may also be diminutive, a comparative, a diminutive comparative, a superlative,[44] or a frequentative (often without frequentative import, e.g. 11. 8. 2 'Albinus ... res Romanas oratione Graeca scriptitauit', of a single work).[45]

37. Sexlessness betrays a want of sophistication (cf. Plut. *Mor.* 57 D). M. Leumann, *Glotta* 20 (1931–2) 284–5 finds the original sense at 19. 9. 9 'tamquam profecto uastos quosdam et insubidos ἀναφροδισίας condemnetis' of persons insensitive to love-poetry (*subidus* appears uniquely in Val. Aed. fr. 1. 3–4 M–B at § 11), but the pairing with 'uastos' (cf. Cic. *De or.* 1. 115, 117, *Tusc.* 5. 77) implies the usual Gellian sense of ἀναισθήτους, *stolidos*. He will have found the word in some old text (Marache, *Mots* 123; a current term should have appeared in Fronto or Apuleius).

38. We cannot identify the 'quidam e nostris' who called ἀντιστρέφοντα *reciproca* (5. 10. 2; perhaps Gellius heard the term from Julianus or Castricius) or the 'quidam' who render ἀσώματος *incorporeus* (5. 15. 1–3).

39. See Gamberale 71–4; contrast 'ἄπορον ... Latine autem id non nimis incommode inexplicabile dici potest' (9. 15. 6), where *inexplicabilis* is Ciceronian (and cf. 20. 1. 15).

40. Note too *inopinabilis*, proposed for ἄδοξος at 17. 12. 1 (and used for παράδοξος 11. 18. 14; 17. 9. 18); see too p. 168.

41. See 11. 16. 4–5; 16. 8. 5; 18. 14. 2 (but cf. ch. 12 n. 26); 19. 2. 2 (literal translation of ἀκόλαστος would be 'nimis ... insolens'; Gamberale 124 n. 126 points out the existence of *incastigatus* and *impunitus*, but neither is used in the sense required).

42. For Greek comparatives (not infrequent in Cicero's letters; note too Lucil. 86 M) cf. 1. 22. 12; 13. 27. 3; 13. 29. 4; 14. 1. 5 (from Favorinus); 17. 19. 4. *Aelurus* had been used at Juv. 15. 7, where as in Gellius (see App. n. 3) it was restored by conjecture before being found in a MS.

43. Non. 51. 29–31, citing Lucil. 991 M; cf. Varro, *LL* 5. 129.

44. Vogel, 'De sermone' 11–12, 21, 22–3; Knapp 156–7; Portalupi, *Ricerca* 110–12, 123–4.

45. Hence 2. 25. 4 'ille ἀναλογίαν, hic ἀνωμαλίαν defensitauit' does not imply a prolonged campaign of book and counter-book; in general see Knapp 161–3. In some places, where the notion of frequency is otherwise expressed, we have redundance (Hornsby, pp. xlviii f.), e.g. 12. 11. 1 'cum ad eum frequenter uentitaremus'; cf. 6. 1. 6 'solitauisse ... uentitare', where the notion is expressed thrice over.

It may dominate its sentence, composed as a mere foil;[46] sometimes, however, Gellius exhibits, not a single brilliant, but a whole string. At 10. 22. 24

> Haec Plato sub persona quidem sicuti dixi non proba, set cum sensus tamen intellegentiaeque communis fide et cum quadam indissimulabili ueritate disseruit

the sole word *indissimulabili*, of a truth that cannot be ignored,[47] thrusts the rest of the clause into the shade; but at 15. 30. 1

> Qui ab alio genere uitae detriti iam et retorridi ad litterarum disciplinas serius adeunt, si forte idem sunt garruli natura et subargutuli, oppido quam fiunt in litterarum ostentatione inepti et friuoli

we mock the opsimaths' display far less than we wonder at Gellius', so completely has the word taken over from the sentence and the sense.[48] Alternatively the jewels may be grouped round a centrepiece: at 5. 1. 6

> 'Idcirco' inquit 'poetarum sapientissimus auditores illos Vlixi labores suos inlustrissime narrantis, ubi loquendi finis factus, non exsultare nec strepere nec uociferari facit, sed consiluisse uniuersos dicit quasi attonitos et obstupidos delenimentis aurium ad origines usque uocis permanantibus'

Portalupi rightly sees *consiluisse* as the most important word in the sentence,[49] but it does not obscure *inlustrissime*, or the many other emphatic expressions surrounding it.

As a variation on the unexpected word, Gellius offers at 2. 7. 20 the unexpected example: one should disobey a paternal command to defend a Catiline or Tubulus or Clodius in court.[50] Keeping company with the two Ciceronian malefactors, Catiline and Clodius, is not the obvious Verres but the praetor of 142 BC, L. Hostilius Tubulus, who fled Rome rather than face

---

46. Portalupi, *Ricerca* 132–8; Quint. 8. 3. 30; Luc. *Lex.* 24. Cf. Fronto, *Orat.* 11 'quod ubi uerbum inuenisti, cauere pulchre sciuisti'.

47. Often misunderstood as 'a frankness that cannot dissemble'.

48. Cf. Schibel's judgement on 9. 11 (see below, pp. 179–80).

49. *Ricerca* 134–5.

50. The problem whether one should speak in an undeserving cause was considered by Plato (*Gorg.* 480 B 7–D 6), Aristotle (*Rhet.* 1355ª31), Cicero (*Off.* 2. 51, following Panaetius; cf. *Cluent.* 57, *Sulla* 81 for the forensic topos), Quintilian (12. 1. 33–45; 12. 7. 4–7), and Plutarch ('Lamprias', no. 156); more robustly by Dr Johnson (Boswell, *Life* ii. 47–8, v. 26 Hill-Powell; canonical in England). By Gellius' day the court appointed advocates for those with none (D. 3. 1. 1. 4), whose pleas might have no merit. Justinian required barristers to throw up cases in which they had no faith (C. 3. 1. 14. 4); contrast Gell. 1. 6. 4 ('rhetori' = *causidico*: for *rhetor* synonymous with *orator* see 3. 13. lemma ∼ § 3; 18. 3. lemma ∼ § 1, cf. 1. 5. lemma; 1. 8. lemma, 2). In the Senate appointment had become the normal practice (Plin. *Ep.* 7. 6. 3). On advocates' ethics cf. Frier 131–3.

an inquiry into his undisguised corruption as president of a murder-court.[51] His contemporary Lucilius could make him a paradigmatic villain (1312–13 M), but Cicero had never heard of him when he composed the *Verrines*; by 54 BC he has discovered him to be reputed the wickedest man in history, yet seems to take him for a poisoner (*Scaur.* 2. 9 Olechowska = fr. k Clark). Nine years later he asks Atticus for details of the charge (*Att.* 12. 5b), then deploys the information in *De finibus* and *De natura deorum*. 'Cui Tubuli nomen odio non est?' he asks at *Fin.* 5. 62, but only after taking care that we shall know it; Gellius, acquainted with both Lucilius and *De finibus* (see *NA* 15. 13. 9, cf. p. 208), can therefore affect to assume we do.

Antique and novel words are valued, as for surprise, so for variety; thus pr. 5 'uariam et miscellam et quasi confusaneam doctrinam', with one classical, one archaic, and one modern adjective.[52] Variation over a longer range appears in the three different expressions for 'tomorrow' and for 'at dawn' of 2. 29. 7–14: 'die crastini' (archaic), 'ubi primum diluculabit' (modern), 'luce oriente' (classical), 'crastino' (modern), 'cras' (classical), 'primo luci' (archaic). Furthermore, the same event, on three consecutive days, is narrated successively as 'ipsa iret cibum pullis quaesitum' (§ 6), 'mater in pabulum uolat' (§ 10), 'auis in pastum profecta est' (§ 13). At 17. 9. 7 the two rods of equal length and thickness that served as Spartan message-sticks are described as 'pari crassamento eiusdemque longitudinis'.[53] The notion of using a noun in the singular appears at 19. 8. 11–17 in a new guise every time: 'includi in singularis numeri unitatem', 'singulari numero dicta', 'singulariter dicto', 'ἑνικῶς dicatur', 'singulari numero appellauerint', 'numero singulari dictam';[54] that of visiting the sick elicits, in the whole work, six different constructions: 'cum ad M. Frontonem ... uisum iret' (2. 26. 1), 'ad quendam aegrum cum isset uisere' (16. 3. 2); 'quod ad se aegrotum non uiseret' (18. 8. 2), 'cum ... uisendi mei gratia uenissent' (18. 10. 3), 'ad Frontonem Cornelium ... ire et uisere' (19. 10. 1).[55] Singular

51. Cic. *Fin.* 2. 54; Ascon. 23 C states that he was brought back for execution, but took poison. Tubulus does not appear in our evidence for Livy 53, nor in Val. Max. (who is also silent on Verres, for Cicero sufficed). For another use of unexpected names see ch. 10 n. 41.

52. *Miscellus* occurs in Cato and Varro; *confusaneus* is found nowhere else, though conjectured by Haupt at Fronto, *Orat.* 2. For other such combinations see Faider ad loc.

53. For abl. and gen. of quality juxtaposed see G. Edwards and E. Wölfflin, *ALL* xi. 469–90 (on Gellius, pp. 484–5); with *par* only the ablative is used (ibid. 203–4). *Crassamentum* is found in this sense only here; Columella uses it and *crassamen* for 'sediment'.

54. For Gellian *uariatio* in grammatical nomenclature see Klinkers 10–14; Fraenkel, *Kl. Beitr.* ii. 336–8; in use of particles Müller 27–30.

55. Plain 'uisere' with neither preposition nor verb of motion is left to Lucil. 184 M (18. 8. 2); Cn. Piso fr. 27 P (7. 9. 5) has 'ad collegam uenisse uisere aegrotum'. Cf. too 12. 1. 2, if we read 'eamus ... puerperam visum'; with the variant *puerum*, 'visum' may come from *videre*. Mother (cf. Jac. Gronovius) or child alike might have been disturbed by the intrusion; §4 concerns the mother, and 'puerpera' is the rarer word. At 12. 5. 2 'pergit eum propere uidere' Thysius' *uisere* deserves consideration: *uidere* denotes enjoying the friend's company for its own sake, irrespective of illness (cf. Cic. *Fam.* 9. 23). *Visere* transitive of other visits 2. 2. 1; 19. 8. 1; of tourism 12. 5. 1; 16. 19. 5; cf. 'reuise(s) ad me' (6. 17. 11; 13. 31. 10), from Plaut. *Truc.* 433. Note too 2. 26. 1 'pedibus aegrum' ~ 19. 10. 1 'pedes ... aegrum'.

nouns are paired with plural: 'a uocabulis non a uerbo' (3. 12. 3), 'ingenio ...
atque doctrinis' (13. 5. 3), 'tabemque et morbos' (19. 5. 3).[56]

Gellius likes to group synonyms or near-synonyms in pairs, triads, or even
foursomes, sometimes joined by conjunctions, sometimes in asyndeton. At 14.
4. 3 Chrysippus requires a judge to be 'grauem sanctum seuerum,
incorruptum inadulabilem, contraque improbos nocentesque inmisericordem
atque inexorabilem, erectumque et arduum ac potentem, ui et maiestate
aequitatis ueritatisque terrificum'; we may add at random 'Cloatius Verus ...
non pauca hercle dicit curiose et sagaciter conquisita, neque non tamen
quaedam futtilia et friuola' (16. 12. 1), and the opening sentence of 1. 1 '...
scite subtiliterque ratiocinatum ... in reperienda modulandaque status
longitudinisque eius praestantia'. A familiar word may accompany a rare or
new one: 'argutae admodum et gestuosae' (1. 5. 2), 'excitarentur atque
euibrarentur' (1. 11. 1), 'lubrica atque ambagiosa coniectatione' (14. 1. 33).
Synonymy, less favoured by the early Empire than by the Republic,
flourished again in the mannerists, but neither Cato nor Cicero is more
addicted to it than Gellius, who far outstrips his colleagues.

Recounting the tale of Protagoras' law-suit in *Flor.* 18 Apuleius pairs the
near-synonyms 'acriter et inuincibiliter'; Gellius, in 5. 10, couples 'referri
contra conuertique', 'auditor adsectatorque', 'coniciendae consistendaeque
causae gratia', 'dubiosum hoc inexplicabileque esse'. Fronto's declamation on
Arion offers 'cognitus acceptusque'; Gellius, in 16. 19, displays 'amicum
amatumque', 'uoluptatibus amoribusque', 'grandi pecunia et re bona multa',
'praedae pecuniaeque', 'feros et inmanes', 'cinctus, amictus, ornatus', 'studiis
delectationibusque', 'opulentum fortunatumque'. Contrariwise, the con-
ceptual partitions favoured by Apuleius ('cuncta illa exorabula iudicantium
et decipula aduersantium et artificia dicentium', 'paribus utrimque aculeis,
simili penetratione, mutuo uolnere') and Fronto ('et homo et uestis et cithara
ac uox incolumis', 'amore atque lucro et laudibus retineri') are paralleled in
the Gellian chapters only by the leptology 'induere ... indumenta et fides
capere et canere carmen' (16. 19. 12).[57]

56. Wasse 402–3 (Lat. tr. 433), cf. Müller 28, 34. Joseph Wasse, the 'uir doctus' of our
apparatūs at 6. 3. 55; 19. 12. 3, is identified by Oudendorp on Apul. 8. 6. 1 'defuncto [*immo
definito*] iuuene' and by Saxius i. 311, who also states that 'A.', the annotator of the Latin
version, was Burman, not (as Hertz on 17. 10. 7; 19. 1. 1) Abresch.

57. Their rarity (despite exx. in the preface) is noted by Marache, 'Préface' 789–90.
Synonym-groups (for which in Gellius see Gorges 58–61, Ebert 582, Hache 21–2) occur in
Apuleius' oratory (*Apol.* 25. 9 'nosse atque scire atque callere', *Flor.* 9. 30 'non singillatim ac
disertim sed cunctim et coaceruatim'), as in Fronto's speech on transmarine wills ('fingo haec et
comminiscor?', *Ep. M. Caes.* 1. 6. 4), but are not the most prominent figures of their rhetoric.
Portalupi, *Ricerca* 69–106, examining our three authors' use of multiplied adjectives and adverbs,
finds in them intense concern with the exactness of personal statement; they are more frequent in
the discursive than the narrative passages of the *Nights*, and in Lucius' own adventures than in
the tale of Cupid and Psyche. But if all parts of speech are taken on an equal footing, free use of
groupings appears in Gellius' set-piece narratives 3. 7. 3–17 ('fraudi et perniciei', 'imperes
horterisque', 'ad occursandum pugnandumque in eos', 'gratias laudesque'), 9. 11. 3–8 ('uasta et
ardua proceritate', 'perque contemptum et superbiam', 'uenire iubet et congredi'), and 16. 19; in

Nor does Gellius compete in brevity and neatness. Apuleius' *Protagoras* concludes 'Ita si uincis, in condicionem incidisti, si uinceris, in damnationem', his Euathlus 'Ita me omni modo liberat, si uincor condicio, si uinco sententia'; Fronto displays the antithesis 'Rex homini credere, miraculo addubitare'; Gellius' narratives yield nothing similar. Apuleius absolves the sophistic law-suit in 231 words, Gellius takes 318; Fronto tells the story of Arion in 306 words, Herodotus in 332, Gellius in 392.[58]

In describing the moment of Arion's rescue, Herodotus, narrating a folk-tale,[59] takes the miracle in his stride: καὶ τοὺς μὲν ἀποπλέειν ἐς Κόρινθον, τὸν δὲ δελφῖνα λέγουσι ὑπολαβόντα ἐξενεῖκαι ἐπὶ Ταίναρον (1. 24. 6). Fronto, declaiming on a well-known theme, omits the first clause, attaching the rescue directly to the singer's leap, but elaborates his account by dividing the action into stages, set forth in a series of short clauses with like verb-endings, the last expanded to round off the section and add a comment, as if limiting the strain on our credulity: 'Carminis fine cum uerbo in mare desilit, delphinus excipit, sublimem auehit, naui praeuortit, Taenaro exponit, quantum delphino fas erat, in extimo litore.' Gellius, zealous to show himself a stylist as well as a scholar, restores and amplifies the mention of the sailors, adds a comment, with three epithets, on the wondrous intervention, and (reverting to *oratio obliqua*) relates it in four clauses, the fourth roughly twice as long as each of the first three, all ending with tetrasyllabic perfect infinitives in *-isse*.

'Nauitae hautquaquam dubitantes quin perisset, cursum quem facere coeperant tenuerunt. Sed nouum et mirum et pium facinus contigit.' Delphinum repente inter undas adnauisse, fluitantique sese homini subdidisse, et dorso super fluctus edito uectauisse, incolumique eum corpore et ornatu Taenarum in terram Laconicam deuexisse.[60]

In 18. 8 Gellius expresses scorn for those who over-indulge in Isocratean figures, citing Lucilius' mockery of the rhyme (ὁμοιοτέλευτον) 'nolueris cum debueris' (184-5 M). A similar rhyme has already appeared in a tricolon (and isocolon) at 14. 1. 23: 'ire in balneas uolueris ac deinde nolueris atque id rursum uolueris', but not for mere show: the equal length of the clauses reflects the equal strength of the impulses, and the emphatic

2. 29. 3-16 there are only 'tremibundi trepiduli', 'cedendi et abeundi', but Aesopic fable demands a simpler style. Gellius' prose 'cherche l'abondance dans la forme plus que dans les subtilités de la pensée' (Marache, edn. i, p. lxiii).

58. Protagoras' statistics cover *Flor.* 18. 19-28, *NA* 5. 10 entire: counting only Apul. §§ 20-7, Gell. §§ 4-16, yields Apuleius 187, Gellius 258. For Arion, the limits are Hdt. 1. 23 ἐτυράννευε δέ-24 *fin.*, Gell. 16. 19. 23 excluding parenthetic *inquit* §§ 2, 12. If *-que* is reckoned as a word (like τε), Apuleius has 233 words (on the short count 189), Gellius 326 (265); Fronto 308, Gellius 412.

59. Stith Thompson B551.1.

60. *NA* 16. 19. 15-16; the sequence continues with 'petiuisse', 'optulisse', 'narrauisse', 'credidisse'. Cf. 17. 9. 16-17 'abscondisse ... accepisse ... incidisse ... conleuisse', followed by 'misisse ... derasisse ... legisse'.

recurrence of the termination serves to delineate their self-containment. At
11. 7. 3 'ut quod numquam didiceris, diu ignoraueris,[61] cum id aliquando
scire coeperis', the jingle seems rather an augmentation of the mockery: at 10.
3. 7 'quae ibi tunc miseratio! quae comploratio! quae totius rei sub oculos
subiectio!', Gellius is describing Ciceronian grandiloquence by demonstrating
one of its resources. Despite the lemma to 18. 8 and the literal sense of § 1,
Gellius does not in fact consider such devices inept and childish, but only
their inordinate and offensive use by the pretentiously inartistic ('quae isti
apirocali qui se Isocratios uideri uolunt in conlocandis uerbis immodice
faciunt et rancide').[62] Certainly he is not ashamed to make a modest use of
them himself.

Like other writers, Gellius has his favourite clausulae for sentences and
phrases, the commonest being ⏖ — — — ⏑ — (quite often as — | — — ⏑ —)
and ⏖ ⏑ ⏖ — (sometimes with preceding — ⏑ —); ⏖ ⏑ ⏖ ⏖ — (but
the pure form — ⏑ — — — is avoided at period-end); ⏖ ⏑ — — ⏑ — and
⏖ — ⏖ — are also frequent (the latter especially as — ⏑ — | — — — —), less so
— ⏑ ⏑ — ⏑ —, — ⏑ — ⏑ —, and the heroic ending — ⏑ ⏑ — — (generally
— | ⏑ ⏑ — —).[63] However, the true test of rhythmical prose is not the
clausula, observable in so low a work as the *Mulomedicina Chironis*, but the
natural articulation of the sentence into smaller segments and segments of segments in constant interplay, with peaks and troughs of emphasis, yet combining
into a whole.[64] Fronto and Apuleius pass this test, not only in their speeches;
but the *commentarii* of Gellius' *Attic Nights* are as little rhythmical as those
of Caesar's *Gallic Wars*. Fronto's account of Arion's rescue is easily delivered
like the narrative section of a speech; Gellius', despite its balanced composition, imposes the level tone of a lecture.[65] When Arion tells his tale to Periander, Fronto's neat antithesis finds resolution in a longer clause whose last
word expressing the king's decision, is the goal to which the entire sentence
is directed, the 'key or clasp' that the epideictic orator requires in this
position;[66] 'rex homini credere, miraculo addubitare, nauem et socios naualis
dum reciperent opperiri'. Gellius too produces a tricolon crescendo, but with
less concision; and, by adding a fourth member dependent on the verb that

61. For such asyndetic pairs of subordinate clauses see Leo, *Plaut. Forsch.* 272 n. 4, Fraenkel,
Elementi 390 n. 1.

62. For *apirocalus* 'tasteless' see ch. 11 n. 113; for *rancide* 'nauseatingly', 18. 11. 2, cf. 13. 21. 1,
Pers. 1. 33, Juv. 6. 185, Apul. *Met.* 1. 26. 7.

63. Marache, 'Prose métrique', analyses the clausulae in the preface (neglecting those with
Greek words, which in fact do not differ) and those ending periods in 1. 1; 1. 2; 1. 11; 9. 1;
14. 1; 20. 1. He observes the restricted use of unresolved — ⏑ — — — but misses the frequency of
— — — ⏑ — by recognizing *mol* + *cr* despite Fraenkel, *Leseproben* 195–6 (ibid. 79, 104, 187
would have saved him from taking '-que uariis feceramus' (pr. 3) as ⏑⏑ ⏑ — — ⏑ — — instead of
(⏑) ⏑⏑ — — ⏑ — —) and scans the 'o' of 'redolentia' (pr. 9) long.

64. Fraenkel, op. cit. 19–20, cf. *Kl. Beit.* ii. 493–6, 503–4. Not the smaller units' presence, but
their interplay, is decisive.

65. There is a like contrast between Fav. fr. 95. 1–4 B and Hdt. 1. 23–4 or Plut. *Mor.* 161
A–162 B. Cf. Demetr. *Eloc.* 193.

66. Fronto, *Laud. fum.* 2.

ends the third, negates any notion of a climax: 'regem istaec parum credidisse, Arionem quasi falleret custodiri iussisse, nauitas inquisitos[67] ablegato Arione dissimilanter interrogasse, ecquid audissent in his locis unde uenissent super Arione'. The structure of the sentence excludes rhetorical delivery.

At 5. 10. 7–8 Gellius skilfully adjusts the lengths of his cola to illustrate Euathus' time-wasting and Protagoras' impatience:

> Postea cum diutule
>   auditor adsectatorque Protagorae fuisset,
> et in studio quidem facundiae
>   abunde promouisset,
> causas tamen non reciperet,
> tempusque iam longum transcurreret,
> et facere id uideretur
>   ne relicum mercedis daret,
> capit consilium Protagoras
>   ut tum existimabat astutum:
> petere instituit ex pacto mercedem,
> litem cum Euathlo contestatur.

But the even tenor remains, in contrast with Apuleius' version:

> Igitur Euathlus,
>   postquam cuncta illa exorabula iudicantium
>   et decipula aduersantium
>   et artificia dicentium
>   uersutus alioqui
>   et ingeniatus ad astutiam
>   facile perdidicit,
>   contentus scire quod concupierat,
>   coepit nolle quod pepigerat,
> sed callide nectendis moris
>   frustrari magistrum
>   diutuleque
>   nec agere uelle
>   nec reddere
> usque dum Protagoras eum ad iudices prouocauit,
>   expositaque condicione
>   qua docendum receperat,
>   anceps argumentum ambifariam proposuit.

However, although Gellius does not couch his scholarship in rhythmical prose, he would have us know he can write it. When he blames C. Gracchus for not matching his style to his subject, he himself makes good the want (10. 3. 4):

---

67. *inquisitos* δ, *requisitos* Fγ; cf. 11. 17. 1 *quaerentibus* δ, *requirentibus* Fγ; *requiro*, a frequent verb in Gellius, is the *lectio facilior*.

In tam atroci re
 ac tam misera atque maesta
  iniuriae publicae contestatione
ecquid est,
 quod aut ampliter insigniterque
 aut lacrimose atque miseranter
 aut multa copiosaque inuidia
  grauique et penetrabili querimonia dixerit?

When he praises Cicero for rising to the occasion, he does so thus (§§ 7–8)

At cum in simili causa
 aput M. Tullium
  ciues Romani,
   innocentes uiri,
 contra ius contraque leges
  uirgis caeduntur
  aut supplicio extremo necantur,
quae ibi tunc miseratio!
quae comploratio!
quae totius rei sub oculos subiectio!
quod et quale
 inuidiae atque acerbitatis
  fretum efferuescit!
animum hercle meum,
 cum illa M. Ciceronis lego,
imago quaedam et sonus
 uerberum et uocum
  et eiulationum circumplectitur.[68]

Such passages are exceptional, and Gellius promptly lapses into his normal style after each of them;[69] a style, however, considerably more elaborate than is normal in Roman works of scholarship. Unlike the rough-hewn Varro, the over-compressed Pliny, and the businesslike Suetonius,[70] Gellius, loving words as gems even when treating them as flintstones,[71] consciously contributes to literature as well as learning.

---

68. For 'miseratio', 'comploratio', 'sub oculos subiectio' see ch. 11 n. 9; 'fretum efferuescit' is a pseudo-etymological allusion to Varro, *LL* 7. 22 (cit. Thysius), D.H. *Dem.* 22 demonstrates the corybantic effect of Demosthenes' eloquence in words that like the orator's 'themselves indicate how they should be delivered'.

69. Rhythmical passages are also found in the preface (see Marache, 'Recherche du rythme'), where any author seeks to shine, and in 18. 3, where a passage from Aeschines is recast in Latin.

70. 'Businesslike': e.g. J. C. Rolfe, LCL edn. i, p. xix; Wallace-Hadrill 19.

71. Cf. Fronto, *Ep. M. Caes.* 4. 3. 6.

Chapter 4

Presentation and Sources

THE variety of subject-matter between and within chapters, which defeats attempts to classify them under simple headings,[1] is matched by that of presentation, which juxtaposes direct exposition (with or without acknowledgement of a source), anecdotes of Gellius' own activities, reports of others' speech or writing, and dialogue in which Gellius plays a major part, a minor part, or none.[2] A single chapter may illustrate several modes: 18. 9, having begun with a quotation from Cato at once debated in a dialogue, moves to a statement of Gellius' opinion with successive support from evidence discovered by himself, argumentation in his own name, and other scholars' doctrine. This interplay of the third and first persons lends the *Nights* much charm; it may also mislead the modern reader.

In 2. 26 Favorinus, the Gaulish devotee of Greek culture, declares that Greek is richer in colour-names than Latin, but Fronto, the master of Latin who rebuked Marcus for composing in Greek (*Ep. M. Caes.* 3. 9. 2 ~ 1. 10), convinces him that Latin is superior in nuancing red and green. He quotes passages from Vergil, whom he commends for his care with words (§ 11);[3] this virtue stood high with the real Fronto, yet we find no trace of Vergil in his writings. Even Horace, though mainly dear to the landowner (*Ep. M. Caes.* 1. 9. 5), contributes the phrase 'post decisa negotia' (*Epist.* 1. 7. 59) to *Princ. hist.* 2. 13; but the remote or commonplace Vergilian parallels occasionally noted by editors are completely inconclusive.[4] It is therefore illegitimate to cite *NA* 2. 26. 11 as evidence for Fronto's own judgement; these well-selected champions are pitted against each other to enliven Gellius' erudition. Naturally the philosopher Favorinus did take his pupil Gellius to

---

1. So rightly Nettleship 258. Besides the conflicting classifications of translated chapters by Verteuil and Walterstern (App. n. 26), there is a statistical table, based on some eccentric attributions, at Vogel, 'De compositione' 4.

2. For another classification see Steinmetz 280–7, who proposes five types: the acknowledged *Lesefrucht*, the apophthegm, the report (*Bericht* or *Referat*) of a learned man's solution to a problem, the disputation, and the reminiscence, this last in the two subtypes authentic and fictitious. These types he finds in the opening chapters of the *Nights*: 1. 1 *Lesefrucht*, 1. 2 authentic reminiscence, 1. 3 disputation, 1. 4 report, 1. 5 apophthegm, 1. 6 fictitious reminiscence. Not all will agree that 1. 2 is authentic and 1. 6 fictitious; 1. 4 is a reminiscence, but fits less well with Steinmetz's definition of a report (p. 282) than 1. 1; similarly 1. 8 is both *Lesefrucht* and apophthegm.

3. 'Poeta uerborum diligentissimus'; cf. 1. 7. 17; 4. 11. 4; 13. 25. 4 for this typically Gellian structure, and in the positive degree 18. 5. 6.

4. See Gamberale, 'Autografi' 365–6; Holford-Strevens, 'Fact and Fiction' 65. Horace, quoted in the letter to Marcus, may be echoed again at *Princ. hist.* 2. 18 ~ *Carm.* 2. 10. 9–10.

see his gouty friend, and there were learned conversations; but we are not to take the imitation for reality.

When Gellius reports a declamation he has heard (9. 8. 3; 14. 1; 19. 12), he need not be disbelieved, though he will have used the written text. But the *mise en scène* of 12. 1, in which Favorinus addresses a Greek harangue to a Roman senator's mother-in-law, is rendered implausible by the citation in § 20 from 'our own Maro', as an Arelatensian, speaking Greek, could hardly call Vergil in Rome.[5] Moreover, as in some other chapters, the initial framework of the narrative is not completed afterwards;[6] similarly, in 19. 9 the Greeks who have run down Latin love-poetry make no comment on the verses Julianus cites against them.[7] At 2. 22. 30, after Favorinus has discoursed on wind-names, Gellius admits uncertainty on a point of detail: 'In saying above that etesians blew from different regions of the sky, I may have spoken incautiously through adopting a widespread opinion.' The first person, though doubtless inadvertent, indicates that the text brought back no memories of a real dinner-party and a real Favorinus holding forth upon the topic. This *conuiuium* is no more historical than the symposia of Plato, Xenophon, or Plutarch.

Gellius' story (2. 23. 4–6) that he and some friends, while reading Caecilius, decided to compare him with his original Menander, is in itself no less credible than Dio of Prusa's assertion (52. 1) that he read the three great tragedians' *Philoctetae* after breakfast on a midsummer's day, or Sidonius' parallel reading of Terence and Menander in *Ep.* 4. 12. 1–2; comparison of the two *Plocia* is confirmed by 3. 16. 3–4, where in a chapter on gestation-periods Caecilius is quoted as departing from Menander. But in 2. 23 the narrative is soon forgotten and Gellius' judgements on the passages 'recently' read (§ 4) are registered as habitual, in the present tense (§ 11 'in hoc equidem *soleo* animum attendere, quod ...', § 22 'cum haec Caecilii seorsim *lego*'); like the general principle of §§ 1–3. The structural similarity with 9. 9. 1–11 suggests rather artistic device than factual report.

Sometimes a literary origin can be demonstrated. In the debate between a Stoic and a Peripatetic in 18. 1 on whether virtue is a sufficient condition of perfect happiness, the Academic Favorinus is umpire ('tamquam apud arbitrum Fauorinum', § 15); Cicero states (*Tusc.* 5. 119–20) that another Academic, Carneades, used 'tamquam honorarius arbiter' to adjudicate this

---

5. In Latin, *noster Maro* would have raised no eyebrows (cf. 17. 10. 14; but note 2. 22. 8–15, 20; Macr. *Sat.* 5. 3. 2), but ὁ παρ' ἡμῖν Μάρων would have been sheer insolence. The passage must come from Gellius, who at 1. 15. 12 appends to a verse of Eupolis (probably derived from Favorinus) 'quod Sallustius noster imitari uolens sic scribit ...'. Cf. pp. 83, 86; Holford-Strevens, 'Fact and Fiction' 65.

6. 'Suasit' in the lemma need not mean 'persuasit', cf. 14. 2. 24; for the slip 'nobili feminae' see ch. 2 n. 24.

7. In real life they would have observed that Catulus' epigram (fr. 1 M–B) is an adaptation of Callim. *Epigr.* 41; the others too will have had Greek originals. (Porc. Lic. fr. 6 M–B was compared by Jacobs with *AP* 9. 15; see too *A. Plan.* 209, Luc. *Asin.* 6 ~ Apul. *Met.* 2. 7. 7, and perhaps cf. P. Köln V 203 A 3–4). That is not to deny the beauty especially of Aedituus' poems.

very contention between Stoics and Peripatetics. Gellius has taken the hint, set the debate in his own day, located it on the shore at Ostia (cf. Suet. *Rhet.* 25. 9), and found a few handbook arguments for the disputants to use.[8] At 1. 2. the pseudo-Stoic holding forth in the symposium at Herodes' villa, but silenced by a quotation from Epictetus 2. 19, seems derived from § 8 of that chapter (cf. p. 100).

However, Taurus' demolition of a young coxcomb in 10. 19 with a passage of Demosthenes that was the rhetors' stock example of the enthymema,[9] though easily invented, may be based on fact: it was a good text to cite at erring pupils, and his dislike for students whose main concern was rhetoric is exhibited elsewhere (pp. 66–7). In 17. 20 he considers Gellius himself, as a freshman, to be of this kidney. When a reading of Plato's *Symposium* reaches Pausanias' words on love at 180 E 4–181 A 6, Taurus addresses him as 'little rhetor': can he find so finely turned an argument in any of his orators? Nevertheless, he should regard its stylistic virtues as secondary and concentrate on the thought. But these remarks, far from suppressing Gellius' interest in the rhetorical merits of the passage, actually stimulated him to attempt their reproduction in Latin; his version follows. Little as he needs encouragement to translate Greek into Latin, the narrative appears to confirm Taurus' judgement. Yet Gellius, who is proud to have become one of his intimates, is not an open or consistent champion of rhetoric against philosophy;[10] he might ascribe his critical jargon to Taurus (p. 162), but not make up a story to show himself what his teacher thought he was (indeed, in § 4 he has implied that he was more). But naïve self-revelation is no less credible in Gellius than in Cicero, who reports his silencing by Servilia with no awareness that he looks a fool.[11] The *Symposium* passage, though not found in the rhetoricians, is quoted at Stob. 3. 5. 12; but a florilegium would not have told Gellius the speaker's name (§ 2).

No law of the genre prevented either Gellius or Clement (*Strom.* 1. 11. 1) from reporting his teachers' remarks: Favorinus' comment on Lysias and Plato (2. 5) and Taurus' jibe at Epicurus (9. 5. 8) will be genuine. But since the dialogue, even when purportedly a reminiscence as in Xenophon, was an established literary form with its own conventions, Gellius may put in their mouths things they did not say and would not have said, even as Cicero assigns to Roman statesmen philosophical discussions they would never have dreamt of.[12] Hence, although the frequency with which Favorinus is made to

8. Cf. 'exposita in libris' § 12.

9. Dem. 22. 7, cf. 23. 99; see Demetr. *Eloc.* 31, 248; Quint. 5. 14. 4; *Rhet. Gr.* iii. 111. 24–6 Sp; Apsin. 10 (i²/2. 288. 15–18 H); cf. id. 9 (285. 2–5); [Cornut.] 187; Theon, *Prog.* 1 (ii. 64. 9–17 Sp); [Hermog.] 179. 6 Rabe.

10. Nor vice versa (p. 193).

11. *Att.* 15. 11. 2. Who now would dare to say with Tert. *Nat.* 2. 10. 1 'ad foediora festino' except for fun?

12. *Att.* 13. 19. 5, cf. ibid. 13. 12. 3; 13. 16. 1, *Fam.* 9. 8. 1.

treat of Latin matters probably indicates that he did so in real life (pp. 82–9), no particular account need be authentic.

We shall not believe in every boastful ignoramus whom Gellius or another puts to shame, least of all when the scene is explicitly cast in the form of a Platonic dialogue (4. 1. lemma; 18. 4. 1),[13] or the sciolist takes refuge in demanding payment like Thrasymachus (13. 31. 13). But such persons certainly existed, the spiritual heirs of Aelius Melissus (p. 108); the unnamed opsimath of 15. 30. 2–3 and sophist of 17. 21. 1, both mentioned in passing with the allusive 'ille', may well be genuine. Like cooks and doctors, grammarians sought employment through self-advertisement; Apion, indeed, called himself Πλειστονίκης, 'Supreme Champion'.[14] Naturally promise might outrun performance: in 16. 6 a grammarian invited to Brundisium from Rome (where presumably he was in no demand) cannot read correctly (cf. 13. 31. 8–9) and avers that sheep have but two teeth. Since Paul the Deacon says the same of cattle (31. 21 L), absurdity does not prove fiction.

This grammarian was touting his ignorance when Gellius' ship put in after her stormy voyage (19. 1), entirely credible even if the pallid Stoic (p. 206) be inspired by Aristippus' *mot*.[15] In 9. 4 Gellius states that on disembarking he took a walk to regain his land-legs, and then caught sight of some books for sale, including Greek records of *miracula* by Aristeas of Proconnesus, Isigonus of Nicaea, Ctesias, Onesicritus, Polystephanus (meaning Philostephanus), and Hegesias, old and dirty, but also dirt-cheap. He spent the next two nights in reading them, and copied out statements about such strange peoples as the cannibal Scythians, one-eyed Arimaspi, and Sauromatae beyond the Dnepr who ate only every other day, together with matter he later found in the seventh book of Pliny's *Natural History*, such as the African tribe who could kill by uttering praise and Illyrians who cast the evil eye.

All these tales, according to Gellius largely ignored by Roman writers (§ 5), appear at Plin. *NH* 7. 9–26 in the same order, though interspersed with others: the sources acknowledged are 'Herodotus et Aristeas Proconnesius' (§ 10), 'Baeton' (§ 11, for a detail not in Gellius), 'Isigonus Nicaeensis' (§ 12), 'Isigonus et Nymphodorus' and again 'Isigonus' (§ 16), 'Megasthenes' (§ 22), 'Ctesias' (§ 23), 'Megasthenes' (§ 25); Both authors thus give ethnic qualifications to Aristeas and Isigonus alone, but Pliny cites authors Gellius ignores, while not mentioning Onesicritus till § 28 (by which time Gellius has

13. See Holford-Strevens, 'Fact and Fiction' 65–6; note too the Platonic motifs at 18. 4. 8 'ne sibi inuideret discere uolenti orabat' (cf. *Rep.* 338 A 3; *Lach.* 200 B 7–8; *Euth.* 297 B 5–6, etc.). Similarly Cic. *Rep.* 1. 16 (a passage that like D.H.'s discussion of Thucydides' speeches shows an ancient reader taking fiction in his stride) serves to warn us that, as Plato to Socrates, so Cicero has lent his learning (and opinions) to Scipio.

14. *I. Mem.* 71 (the edd. are hypersceptical), J. *Ap.* 2. 3, Plin. *NH* pr. 25, Gell. 5. 14. 3. So the sophist Varus (Philost. *VS* 540–1).

15. § 10 (fr. 87c Mannebach); for the theme, Epict. 2. 16. 22; 2. 19. 15; Luc. *Per.* 43. So frequent were storms on the Cassiope–Brundisium run that shippers refused to risk cargoes, only lives (D. 14. 1. 1. 12).

ceased to follow him), nor Philostephanus and Hegesias till § 207. In the list of authorities contained in *NH* 1, the *externi* for book 7 show Gellius' six authors, without ethnics, respectively 2nd, 4th, 14th, 17th, 41st, and 42nd. If Gellius has taken them from Pliny, he must have read and excerpted book 7 as a whole; there are two more quotations (of §§ 36 and 34) in this chapter, and two others, from §§ 40 and 42, tacked on at the end of *NA* 3. 16, but we are still well short of § 207.

That the order is the same is an argument for dependence, supported by linguistic similarities. At *NH* 7. 16, *NA* 9. 4. 7–8, and nowhere else till Symmachus, *Ep.* 6. 77, we find the verb *effascinare*: Pliny writes 'in eadem Africa familias quasdam effascinantium', Gellius 'quasdam in terra Africa hominum familias uoce atque lingua effascinantium'; to Pliny's 'effascinent interemantque' correspond in Gellius 'exitialem fascinationem' and 'interimant'. The similarity extends to 'pupillas binas in oculis singulis habeant' ~ 'pupillas in singulis oculis binas habere'; outside this passage, both authors write 'oculos in umeris habentes' (§ 23 ~ § 9).[16] Pliny is therefore a source, but not the only source: whereas at § 25 he states that the Astomi are clad in leaves, 'uestiri frondium lanugine', Gellius (§ 10) gives them feathers like the birds', 'auium ritu plumantibus'. An original πτέριον, it seems, has been diversely understood as 'fern' and 'little feather'.[17] Gellius thus wrote with one eye on Pliny and the other not on the grimy *bouquins* of §§ 3–4 but a collection, also used by Pliny, of *Strange Tales about Strange Tribes*.[18]

Although each case must be considered on its merits,[19] we should be slower to accept the historicity of the dialogues than the verisimilitude of their settings, which afford precious glimpses of second-century social life: visits to friends especially when sick, the crowds awaiting the imperial *salutatio*, lucky finds and lively conversations in bookshops and public libraries, learned banter even on an Aegean voyage underneath a starlit sky.[20] We may doubt the ascription of views, but not the description of personalities, at least as representing Gellius' teachers as he saw them; but he no more expected full faith and credit for his narratives than historians for their speeches or philosophers for their dialogues.[21]

* * *

16. But Gellius substitutes for Pliny's 'sine ceruice' the more classical plural 'nullis ceruicibus', cf. 5. 14. 9; 11. 9. 1 (vs. 3. 9. 3; 5. 2. 4). Cf. Varro, *LL* 8. 14, 10. 78; Quint. 8. 3. 35, but see Skutsch on Enn. *Ann.* 483. (Pl. in Fronto, *Ep. M. Caes.* 5. 27 etc., but sg. *Ant. P.* 5. 1 and usually in Apuleius.)

17. See M. L. West, *CR*² 14 (1964) 242; cf. Bolton 27–31.

18. Παραδοξολογούμενα περὶ ἐθνῶν (Bolton 31).

19. Cf. A. Barigazzi, *Gnomon* 42 (1970) 682; P. K. Marshall, *CPh* 74 (1979) 173–4; Holford-Strevens, 'Fact and Fiction'. Faith (Baldwin 83) has nothing to do with it.

20. Sick-visits (cf. p. 226): 2. 26; 12. 5; 16. 3; 19. 10 (cf. 12. 1). *Salutatio Caesaris* (cf. Millar 21–2, 209–10): 4. 1; 19. 13; 20. 1. Bookshops: 5. 4; 13. 31; 18. 4. Libraries: 11. 17; 13. 20. Starlit voyage: 2. 21.

21. Or than Politian, Crinitus, and Falster expected for theirs, composed in the Gellian manner and sometimes with Gellian matter.

In 1851 H. E. Dirksen established that many of the legal chapters were derived from single works themselves incorporating (in the manner familiar from extracts in the Digest) the citations of earlier writings that Gellius presents as if read independently.[22] Nine years later,[23] Ludwig Mercklin demonstrated that this held true of other chapters as well: he laid down as a general rule that a work quoted by title and book was likelier to have been directly consulted than one quoted by author alone. Almost at once Julius Kretzschmer published his Greifswald dissertation, based on the hypothesis that each chapter should if possible be ascribed to a single source: controversy ensued between the two scholars both on the validity of this rule, which Mercklin thought too sweeping, and on source-criticism of its author, whom Mercklin accused of plundering his work.[24]

The floodgates having been opened, studies of Gellius' sources poured forth for the next four decades,[25] till Hosius, in his Teubner edition of 1903, set out his own and others' conjectures on no fewer than 296 of the 398 known chapters, including nine out of fifteen in the lost book 8: he accepted Kretzschmer's thesis and assumed that Gellius used no author not named at least once in our extant text.[26] Furthermore, although he allowed that, having been referred to a text, Gellius might consult it for himself, he was most unwilling to let him read a text on his own initiative (at least in a critical spirit), refusing to believe that Gellius had himself detected Varro's error in 1. 18 or ventured to approach Cicero at his own risk in 2. 17. In the former passage, Gellius suspects Varro (one of his favourite authors) of the same error with which the latter had taxed Stilo: devising a Latin etymology for a word derived from Greek, namely *fur* < φώρ. Not only does Gellius specify the book ('in XIV rerum diuinarum libro' § 1) but he knows (§§ 3–4) that the criticisms of Stilo (fr. 89 Cardauns) came in the first half, the misderivation from *furuus* (fr. 194) in the second; and it was easy enough to bring the Greek word into relation with the Latin. Perhaps he did so for himself, perhaps he found this already done by some grammarian, perhaps the equation was common doctrine in his day; at all events, he prefers this etymology to Varro's, respectfully disagreeing as he does elsewhere.[27] Hosius posits a juristic source, because Paul (D. 47. 2. 1. pr.) offers alternative etymologies from *furuus* (so Labeo), from *fraus* (so Sabinus), and from *fero* or

---

22. Cited from the revised reprint of 1871 in his *Hinterlassene Schriften*.

23. 'Citiermethode', cited here as Mercklin.

24. Mercklin, who would not ('Beglaubigung' 440) be convinced even by the assurances of Kretzschmer's teacher Hertz; cf. Hertz ii, p. cxxxvii n. **. Less acrimonious is his reply in 'Capita', which Hosius sought in vain, but of which there is a copy in the University Library, Cambridge.

25. See Hosius i, p. xxi n.

26. This rule of method was first enunciated by Ruske 1, 58; for Froehde 533 it is 'oberster Grundsatz der Quellenanalyse' to admit only *works* named by Gellius; Hosius i, pp. xviii f. restricts the principle once more to authors, but seems inclined to regard it as binding on Gellius' own practice.

27. Cf. p. 116; Maselli 21.

φώρ (no source named). Certainly, jurists like to flaunt their etymological learning, but they will normally have acquired it from grammarians.[28] In the latter instance, 2. 17, Hosius assembles, mainly out of a treatise once misascribed to Probus, passages that do indeed bear on the subject of the chapter, but at no point offer any similarity of treatment, in order to show that Probus was the source; this absurdity, refuted by his own proof-texts, is caused by supposing Gellius unable to read Cicero and reflect. Such nonsense, and the many contradictory conjectures, provoked Georg Wissowa in his review not only to confute particular proposals, but to deny outright (p. 740) the source-critics' assumption that Gellius, who wrote when authors were still read, should be reduced to the level of a Nonius, a Macrobius, or an Isidore.

It is as perverse to doubt that the references to Q. Mucius and Ser. Sulpicius in 4. 1 are taken from Sabinus[29] as to suppose that Gellius did not read Cicero for himself. But when in 9. 9 he first claims to have noticed, in a comparative reading at table, good replacements in Vergil's *Bucolics* for untranslatable passages in Theocritus, and then states that Probus, according to his pupils, held *Aen.* 1. 498–502 to be very ill adapted from *Od.* 6. 102–8, the critic who makes Probus the source for the whole chapter should specify whether the favourable judgements were his too, or only the parallels themselves. The pedantic Probus of §§ 12–17, though not on the evidence of *NA* 13. 21. 1–8 entirely without taste, seems less likely to perceive new beauties than to miss old ones.[30] Gellius himself takes a keen interest in translation; there is no reason why the comments cannot be his own.[31] Even if they are not, neither they nor the parallels need come from Probus; did no one else read Theocritus? Must Probus also be the source of Servius on *Buc.* 9. 23, where the same translation considered in §§ 10–11 is differently judged?

Yet some scholars have sought to make him responsible for *NA* 13. 27, on the grounds that there too Vergil is found successfully translating a Hellenistic poet but falling short of Homer; that Parthenius, the author there cited, is named at 9. 9. 3; and that Gellius, like Probus ap. D.S. on *Aen.* 12. 605, makes use of the pejorative epithet *neotericus*, 'new fangled, post-Homeric, Alexandrian, pretty-pretty, sentimental, over-bold'.[32] That Parthenius was among the authors imitated by Vergil, his pupil in Greek (Macr. *Sat.* 5. 17. 18), will have been plain to contemporaries such as

---

28. Labeo was a keen etymologist (*NA* 13. 10. 1–3; cf. Plut. *QR* 46, J. A. C. Thomas in Watson (ed.) 324 n. 14), but his *fur* > *furuus* comes from Varro. See Kunkel, *Herkunft* 203 n. 379; cf. Ulp. D. 29. 1. 1. 1, *NA* 4. 9. 8; 7. 12 (where Trebatius' etymology of *sacellum* is likewise from Varro, fr. 453 Fun.).

29. Dirksen i. 35–9.

30. Cf. Jocelyn II 160–1, if whose scepticism (ch. 9 n. 31) towards reports of Probus' opinions be justified, we have even less right to invoke him as a source.

31. In the lemma Gellius writes 'uertisse . . . bene apteque . . . existimatus est'; but by then he may have forgotten which judgements were his own (such lapses of memory do not always work in our favour; cf. ch. 9 n. 43). Cf. Berthold 128: 'beide Kapitelhälften kaum aus einer Quelle'.

32. Hosius i, p. xlviii; Aistermann 143–4; Gamberale 132–3.

Hyginus, and to anyone who had read him in the public libraries (Suet. *Tib.* 70. 2), perhaps to please his imperial admirer by writing on him; Hadrian too may have encouraged interest in this disparager of Homer, if *SH* 605(*b*), (*d*) are rightly interpreted. Even if we knew for sure that 9. 9. 3 came from Probus, this would prove nothing for 13. 27. 1–2. That Gellius shares a critical term with him indicates at most that he shared his taste; it was a standard piece of jargon found elsewhere.[33] There remains the unsupported assumption that the source of *NA* 9. 9. 12–17 must be the source of §§ 1–11 and 13. 27. In the surviving commentaries, Probus is not represented as teaching that Vergil could match or surpass the Hellenistic poets but botched his imitations of Homer[34]—which suits ill with the doctrine of 9. 9. 3 that Vergil was wise to omit untranslatable passages in various Greek poets, Homer among them. To be sure, competition with Homer was recognized— by Vergil himself, according to Don. *Verg. uit.* § 46—as an exceptionally difficult task, in which critical opinion as transmitted by Macrobius held that he did not always succeed; but for that very reason, such judgements do not bear the hallmark of any one critic.

We should therefore take *NA* 9. 9. 12–17 at face value as a postscript, one of many in the *Nights*,[35] appended 'while we are on the subject' ('et quoniam de transferendis sententiis loquor') attached to matter independent of it. The resulting diptych may have been imitated, in miniature, at 13. 27; but this proves nothing about the sources.

Even when a critic had found good arguments for deriving one chapter from a particular author, he could rarely leave well alone, but had to charge him with others in addition. Nettleship concluded (p. 256) from the similarity between *NA* 2. 21. 8–9 and Festus 454. 36–456. 11 L that Gellius' source was Verrius Flaccus; certainly it was not Varro *LL* 7. 74, but either some other work of Varro's or (as the lack of a specific reference suggests without proving) a quotation in Verrius. But, noting that the word *penus* is discussed by Festus 296. 12–14 L, Nettleship (p. 268) hints that Verrius was also used in 4. 1, though even the non-juristic matter in this chapter has nothing in common with Festus, who mentions only the *locus intimus* in the temple of Vesta usually concealed by mats. Not even PF 231. 8–9 L, where 'penora' are defined as things necessary for daily life, is close enough to prove kinship.

Although the one-source theory is frequently delusive, Kretzschmer rightly observes that 'et plerique alii' and the like need not mean Gellius has used these other authors, even if they exist: he draws attention (p. 7) to the variations in number at 10. 26. 4–5, on Asinius Pollio and others with malice

---

33. Serv. on *Aen.* 8. 731, 10. 192, 11. 590; [Asc.] on Cic. *In Caec.* 15; cf. Cameron 136–9.

34. Probus' punctuation of Ter. *Eun.* 46 and interpretation of *Phorm.* 49 (see Donatus ad locc.) tell against close observation of Greek originals; observe too his ignorance of Nicander (Macr. *Sat.* 5. 22. 9–10). Vergil's borrowings from other poets attracted widespread notice (and censure); Q. Octavius Avitus filled eight books of Ὁμοιότητες with them (Don. *Verg. uit.* § 45, cf. Nettleship 263).

35. Treated at length by Mercklin 701–4.

(*iniquis*) towards Sallust' (§ 1): 'aiunt ... inquit ... putauit ... negant'; Mercklin (pp. 663–4), assuming the literal truth of Gellius' words, had identified Sallust's other enemies with Probus and Castricius, in neither of whom does Gellius reprehend any such *iniquitas*.[36] However, he did sometimes find the same information in more than one author: in 3. 6 he cites both Aristotle and Plutarch, but quotes exclusively from the latter, who does not mention the former. What is true in some instances is not in others.

That the same applies to the argument from form of reference was admitted by Mercklin himself.[37] At 6. 9. 11–12 verbatim quotations explicitly lifted from an unnamed work by Probus carry full indications of source; so do other extracts in the chapter, all from authors Gellius knew. Most critics ascribe the whole to Probus; but Gellius could perfectly well have added examples from his own reading to those that Probus had collected even as we do to those we find in our grammars—a possibility all too often disregarded by the source-critics, as if only lost authors could see things for themselves.

If Gellius set out to name all his sources (standard commentaries apart), the carelessness of his redaction made successful execution unlikely. As a working hypothesis—theoretically invalidated by incomplete preservation of his work—it saves us from some wild speculations but weakens our defences against others;[38] and if, as Giovanni D'Anna has argued, one source for the chronographical chapter 17. 21 was Atticus' *Liber Annalis*, the principle must be abandoned.[39]

Like ourselves, Gellius would find in a scholarly text a quotation from an author he had read directly;[40] but verifying references in rolls, without our line- and section-numbers, was a task the ancients often shirked. He will therefore cite the same writer now at first, now at second hand. These categories have recently been refined by Marcos Mayer,[41] who distinguished (*a*) direct quotations made while reading the work concerned; (*b*) quotations from memory, which as he observes do not fit into Mercklin's system; (*c*) indirect quotations, (i) through Gellius' teachers, (ii) taken from a commentary on a text; (iii) found in a treatise or collection of extracts; (*d*) quotations checked against the original. It is one thing to devise classes, another to

36. Cf. Mercklin, review 721–2; Kretzschmer, 'Zu A. Gellius' 367–8.

37. Mercklin 651–2; against his proposed class of exceptions see Lebek, '*Pluria*' 346–7 and nn. 21–2.

38. As respectively Nettleship's notion (pp. 264–5) that 1. 23 and Macr. *Sat.* 1. 6. 18–25 were independently derived (complete with post-classical diction) from L. Cornelius L. et Fausti l. Epicadus, and Aistermann's ascription to Probus of any grammatical chapter not demonstrably another's.

39. G. D'Anna, *ArchClass* 25–6 (1973–4) 166–237, *StudUrb* 49/1 (1975) 331–46.

40. Cf. Hornsby, p. xxiv. Mignon i, p. xv, 'Certes, Aulu-Gelle a lu Virgile et Cicéron, mais ce ne sont pas ses lectures de Virgile et de Cicéron qui lui ont suggéré ses réflexions sur les textes qu'il cite d'eux', is wrong: for Cicero see e.g. 2. 17; 6. 11; 10. 3; 15. 3 (cf. K. Paulo de Silva, *Meander* 22 (1967) 450–1; Berthold, 'Aulus Gellius' 48 and n. 17); for Vergil see e.g. 3. 2. 14–15; 6. 20; 12. 1. 20; 20. 1. 54; for both writers 13. 1.

41. In *Roma en el siglo II* 103–7, with special reference to quotations from Nigidius.

apportion membership: Mayer's own examples are not all convincing.[42] But his schema may remind us that reality is complex; even more complex if Gellius did not always record his source when excerpting a quotation, and read some commentaries right through but consulted others only when puzzled by a text.

Even when Gellius does identify his source, he may not quote exactly. It was normal practice in antiquity to adjust for loss of context, as when Varro's 'eius disciplinae genera sunt tria' (*RR* 3. 3. 1) becomes 'uillaticae pastionis genera sunt tria' at *NA* 2. 20. 2; we should write 'Of this science [farmhouse stockbreeding] there are three branches'. Minor differences may reflect carelessness in Gellius, or in either of the traditions; they must be considered by the textual critics of the author cited. Kretzschmer (p. 21) accused Gellius of adding the words 'uiuebatque cum proderem haec' ('and is alive at the time of writing') to Plin. *NH* 7. 36 when citing the passage at *NA* 9. 4. 15; but since there is a lacuna at precisely this point in Pliny's text, the charge falls. However, when at 1. 3. 18 Gellius writes 'Contra patriam, inquit Cicero, arma pro amico sumenda non sunt', the sense of *Amic.* 36 is indeed given, but not the wording; we also find 'inquit' used with Gellius' free translations or paraphrases of Greek authors, as in this same chapter, § 23, and the great set-pieces such as 16. 19. Hence, when 'inquit' (as opposed to formulae with 'uerba' or 'haec') accompanies a sentence in pure Gellianese, cited for content not for form, we have to do with paraphrase, not quotation: Cicero's freedman, in requiring counsel for the defence to begin by soothing, not startling, the court, never wrote such a sentence as Gellius gives him (6. 3. 13):

> In principiis autem, inquit, patroni, qui pro reis dicunt, conciliare sibi et complacare iudices debent, sensusque eorum exspectatione causae suspensos rigentesque honorificis uerecundisque sententiis commulcere, non iniuris atque imperiosis minationibus confutare.

The compulsive congestion of synonyms, the threefold -*que*, and the unclassical *complacare* (not found again till the *Epistula Alexandri*, of the third or fourth century) and *commulcere* (used by Apuleius and Arnobius) are quite inconceivable in Tiro's day but just what we are used to in the *Nights*. When a Latin author is quoted for a point of grammar or the beauty of his style, the quotations may be trusted; but writers cited only for their information may

---

42. Of (*a*) 17. 7. 7–8, plainly right; of (*b*) 11. 11, perhaps rather from an unspecific note; of (*c*) (i) 2. 22. 31, which I take to be direct, and 2. 26. 19, as if this chapter came from Fronto (who never mentions Nigidius); of (*c*) (ii) 7. 6. 10–11, cf. 16. 6. 12–13, Hyginus appearing in both chapters, which is not conclusive; of (*c*) (iii) 6. 9. 5, assigned not to Probus but to Pliny with Beck 14; of (*d*) 18. 4. 10–11, the procedure being also employed at 12. 14. 3–4 and commended at 17. 13. 11. Mayer claims that his criterion is content; the published text, a summary of his paper, omits his arguments. Berthold, 'Aulus Gellius' 48 promises further analysis in his forthcoming Teubner edn.

be adapted to Gellius' taste, as may any Greek author whom he renders into Latin.[43]

He also demonstrates his creative skills in retelling a story from another author. In 12. 7 a woman from Smyrna kills her husband and their son to avenge her son by a former marriage, whom they had murdered; the proconsul of Asia, unwilling either to absolve or to condemn, refers the matter to the Areopagus at Athens, which in turn evades a decision by setting down the case for a hundred years later.[44] In § 8 Gellius cites the ninth book of Valerius Maximus (the true reference is 8. 1. amb. 2); Valerius calls the governor P. Dolabella, as against Cn. in Gellius, whose carelessness with names is amply evidenced.[45] Both authors describe his governorship in the same untechnical phrase;[46] thereafter the two accounts diverge, not only in language, but in substance. Gellius adds the details that the stepfather and half-brother had lain in ambush for their victim, that the bereaved mother had executed her vengeance by means of poison, that she confessed her crime, and that Dolabella consulted his *consilium*; whereas in Valerius he recognizes that her motive was a justified grief, in Gellius his advisers take note that the punishment was deserved. These divergences invite no doubt that Valerius was the source, for similar changes are made by three later writers all dependent on Gellius: Ammianus (29. 2. 19) notes that the Areopagites were said to have settled disputes among the gods; John of Salisbury (*Policraticus* 4. 11, i. 272–3 Webb) makes the woman claim the rights of not knowing the law[47] and of avenging a crime against herself, her kin, and the whole state; Rabelais (*Le Tiers Livre*, ch. 44, v. 314–15 Lefranc) states that the murderers had acted without provocation in order to seize the entire estate, and that the Areopagites' pretended purpose for summoning the parties was to put questions not covered by the pleadings. That is the way of good storytellers, including Gellius.[48]

43. Equally Gellian is the language of 4. 18. 3, which is not a verbatim extract from Scipio's alleged speech (cf. p. 143). *Nebulo*, frequent in Gellius, was also found in the speech (Liv. 38. 56. 6), but is post-Plautine.

44. Cf. 5. 19. 5, probably Gellius' own addition (not in other versions).

45. See p. 227. Gellius may have confused P. Dolabella, pr. 69 BC, proconsul of Asia 68/7 BC, and probably father of Cicero's son-in-law, with Cn. Dolabella, cos. 81 BC (15. 28. 3).

46. Valerius 'proconsulari imperio Asiam obtinentis' ∼ Gellius 'proconsulari imperio Asiam obtinentem' (cf. 5. 14. 17); *proconsulare imperium* (cf. Tac. *A.* 1. 14. 3 etc.) is not a term of art (Mommsen ii. 647–50, Syme, *RP* i. 184–90).

47. Allowed to women 'in quibusdam causis' (D. 22. 6. 9. pr., e.g. incest, PS 2. 19. 5, cf. D. 23. 2. 57a; 48. 5. 39. 4; but cf. C.Th. 3. 5. 3, C. 1. 18. 3, 13); John, the pupil of Vacarius and subject of Henry II, anticipates the objection, later made by the lawyer Thysius, that she should have gone to court. What her theoretical or practical chances of redress at Smyrna were neither John nor Thysius knew; Valerius and Gellius did not entertain the possibility. For self-help in matters of justice cf. F. Millar, *JRS* 71 (1981) 71.

48. Cf. Holford-Strevens, 'More Notes' 148–9; on Gellius' taste for adding pathos see Berthold 67–8, id., 'Interpretationsprobleme' 14. For all we know, he modified minor details in 2. 29 (from Ennius), 3. 7 (from Cato), 9. 11 (from Antias?); but 5. 14 will be closer to Apion than Aelian's *remaniement* at *N. An.* 7. 48, which imposes chronological sequence (like Diceto i. 40–1 St) on the Homeric scholar's ὕστερον πρότερον and the *soi-disant* eye-witness's order of experience.

When Gellius cites the text of the supposedly Solonian law against neutrality in time of stasis, the nineteen words of his source ('Arist.' *Ath. Pol.* 8. 5) are expanded to fifty-four at *NA* 2. 12. 1.[49] Although he employs his normal stylistic devices, he probably hints at the wordiness of early Roman laws; elsewhere too he Romanizes Greek material. At 2. 18. 9–10, in a story going back to Menippus and one Eubulus (D.L. 6. 29, 30, cf. 74), Diogenes is bought in the slave-market by Xeniades of Corinth; when Xeniades asks Diogenes about his skills, he replies 'noui hominibus liberis imperare', inspiring Xeniades to say 'accipe liberos meos quibus imperes'. This play on the two senses of *liberi*, 'free men' and 'children', cannot be expressed in Greek; but if a Roman poet could invent an ambiguous oracle for a Greek god to vouchsafe a Greek king,[50] a Roman miscellanist may devise an elegant reply for a Greek dandy to give a Greek philosopher. Likewise, when recounting the tale of Protagoras and Euathlus, he makes the latter observe that he could have pre-empted the dilemma by not conducting his own case but relying on an advocate (5. 10. 11); at Athens even the man assisted by a συνήγορος was obliged to speak in person.[51] Presumably Gellius was no less inventive where we cannot find him out.

---

49. Likewise πιέζῃς (= Plut. *Mor.* 724 E) becomes 'tam grauiter urgeas oneresque ut magnitudo oneris sustineri non queat' (*NA* 3. 6. 2). For a very free paraphrase of a cited text see 7. 2. 1 ~ § 3.

50. Cic. *Diu.* 2. 116 on Enn. *Ann.* 167 Sk. Note too the Latin point of *NA* 9. 2. 8 (p. 101). Apuleius likewise Romanizes the *fabula Graecanica* of *Met.* (Pricaeus, comm. 333; Helm, edn. of *Flor.*, pp. xviif.).

51. Euathlus will be the butt of Ar. *Ach.* 710, *Vesp.* 592, fr. 424 K–A; according to Arist. fr. 67 R he prosecuted Protagoras for impiety.

PART II

PRECEPTORS AND
ACQUAINTANCES

Chapter 5

Teachers

FIVE of Gellius' teachers appear in his work by name: one grammarian, two rhetors, and two philosophers, of whom one taught him in Rome, the other in Athens. Favorinus, the Rome-based philosopher, plays sufficient part in his life and writing to merit a separate chapter; the others are studied below.

The Eminent Grammarian

In his quest for higher education Gellius visited the bookshops of the Vicus Sandaliarius, where a braggart professing to understand the very blood and marrow of Sallust's style was trounced by Sulpicius Apollinaris even as the Sophists were by Socrates, with an apparently innocent question that he could not answer (18. 4). The Socratic allusion implies fiction (p. 50); we recall the Homeric expositor Ion (Plat. *Ion* 530 C, 533 C) and the self-styled Varronian expert of *NA* 13. 31; nor does Gellius round off the narrative by stating that he decided to become Apollinaris' pupil. His pupil, nevertheless, he became.

C. Sulpicius Apollinaris composed an elegant *periocha*, or summary, in twelve senarii for each of Terence's six comedies. To 'Sulpicius Carthaginiensis' Donatus ascribes an epigram, well worthy of Apollinaris, on the *Aeneid*'s preservation;[1] but the life prefixed to pseudo-Probus' commentary credits the poem, shorn of its final couplet, to one Servius Varus. The title 'Hexasticha Sulpicii Carthaginiensis' is also attached to careless summaries in six hexameters for each of the epic's twelve books, prefaced by a feeble imitation (elsewhere attributed to Phocas) of the epigram;[2] although these hexastichs, like the Terentian *periochae*, offer seventy-two verses in the metre of the parent work, they are too inept, in style and sense alike, for Apollinaris or indeed much lesser men. Either, therefore, he and the Carthaginian are two persons, and Donatus erred;[3] or, more probably, Apollinaris was the Carthaginian, 'Servius Varus' is a misnomer for Marius or Maurus Servius

---

1. *Verg. uit.* § 38.
2. *Anth. Lat.* 653 Riese, from Leiden, Cod. Voss. Lat. F 111, *c.* 800, also in a lost 11th-c. MS (L. Traube, *RhM²* 48 (1893) 284 n. 1). J. J. Scaliger, edn. of *App. Verg.* (Lyon, 1572), pp. 146, 154–5 found the derivative epigram ascribed to Phocas and vv. 1–15 of the summaries without a name. Condign scorn for the summaries in Heyne, edn.⁴ of Vergil, i, pp. cxlix–cli.
3. A. Mazzarino, *SIFC²* 22 (1947) 165–77.

the grammarian, through whom pseudo-Probus knew his poem, and both imitation and summaries are the work of later times.[4]

Gellius lauds his master's learning (4. 17. 11; 16. 5. 5; 18. 4. 1); it ranges over a host of Roman authors from Plautus to Vergil, besides Homer, Aristophanes, etymology, semantics, prosody, proverbs in both languages, and the lines of descent from old Cato. Here, we must understand, is no commonplace *grammaticus* (p. 126).

We may believe that his manner in reproof was gentle (13. 20. 5), and that he read 'obicibus' at Verg. *Georg.* 2. 480 with short *o*, 'sed ... I litteram ... paulo uberius largiusque pronuntiabat' (4. 17. 11), that is, rendered the word /objikibus/; this was correct, but to judge from Gellius, unusual.[5] Also correct is his statement in a letter to Erucius Clarus (13. 18. 3) that Cato's 'inter os et offam' (fr. 196 Sblendorio Cugusi = 217 Malcovati) refers to the slip 'twixt cup and lip;[6] his explanation of *praepes* as 'broad-winged' (7. 6. 12) is accepted by Norden on Verg. *Aen.* 6. 15, though others prefer 'flying ahead', therefore 'swift'.

However, Gellius is not always persuaded by Apollinaris' ingenuity. A difficulty is found in Verg. *Aen.* 6. 763–5, on Aeneas' son Silvius:

> tua postuma proles,
> quem tibi longaeuo serum Lauinia coniunx
> educet siluis regem regumque parentem.

If Silvius was Aeneas' posthumous offspring, how could Aeneas be called aged at his birth? Tradition had Silvius born in the shepherd Tyrrhus' cottage, where Aeneas' widow had found refuge from her stepson Ascanius. Caesellius Vindex, a grammarian of Hadrian's time, saw that 'postuma' bore its etymological sense of 'last', Aeneas being still alive but old—a version of events for which he failed to cite authority. Apollinaris argues in opposition that 'longaeuo' means not 'old', which is against history, but 'immortal', as the *indiges pater* Aeneas became after death (§ 8). Gellius is not convinced: a long time is not for ever, and the gods are called not long-lived but immortal. In fact, there are several places where 'long-lived' or the like is used by

4. O. Jahn, in Reifferscheid's Suetonius, p. 54, emended 'Varus' to 'Maurus'; E. Norden, *RhM*[2] 61 (1906) 174 supposed authorial error. Summarizers might make free, or be endowed, with the identities of Ovid and Augustus (*Anth. Lat.* 1 Shackleton Bailey, cf. 2. 1–4 app. crit.; 672 Riese); another epigram on the *Aeneid*'s near-destruction (*Anth. Lat.* 235 ShB) was attributed to Gallus; the name 'Sulpicius Carthaginiensis' could be dishonestly assumed, or carelessly transferred, by any reader of Donatus/Servius. Only one Sulpicius is known to Schol. Veron. *Aen.* 9. 369. (*NA* 19. 13, where Apollinaris converses with Fronto and Postumius Festus, does not prove him an African: their bond was scholarship, and they had met away from home at the Palatium. He does not appear in Fronto's correspondence.)

5. In Silver Latin, from 'ădice' Man. 1. 666, 4. 44 onwards, compounds of *iacio* dropped the /j/; in Gellius' day readers of classical poetry restored the metre by lengthening the vowel of the prefix.

6. Apollinaris cites the verse πολλὰ μεταξὺ πέλει κύλικος καὶ χείλεος ἄκρου (Arist. fr. 571 Rose; Zenob. 5. 71 with Leutsch–Schneidewin ad loc.); cf. *ODEP* 160, *GW* 140.

meiosis for 'immortal' or 'everlasting';[7] but the sense is always obvious, as it would not be here. Gellius' common sense told him Apollinaris was wrong, and he lacked the curious learning that might have overborne it. None of the three considers Vergil's motive for altering the story.[8]

He is again dissatisfied in 12. 13. Instructed to give judgement 'within the Kalends'—by the first of the next month—he asks if the phrase correctly includes the Kalends themselves;[9] Apollinaris argues that since only they can be within, that is inside, the Kalends, it must denote them alone, but Gellius cites Ciceronian examples of *intra* used for *citra*, 'this side of'. Nevertheless, having doubted the propriety of common usage, he had consulted the leading authority on the Latin language (§ 4)—in whose presence indeed another grammarian apologized for discussing either Latin or Greek (19. 13. 5). Unsurprisingly, he elsewhere follows him in error: at 11. 15. 8 Apollinaris derives the suffix -*bundus* from *abunde*; in 15. 5 he imagines that *profligare* 'nearly finish' is unclassical (p. 130); his interpretation of Sallust in 18. 4 is even worse than his victim's.[10]

In no passage does Apollinaris express a view on the literary merits of an author or a text, save that at 19. 13. 3 he speaks of 'low and undignified' terms given currency by Laberius.[11] He may not have played much part in forming Gellius' literary taste; he is given only one citation (20. 6. 11) from Quadrigarius, for whom Gellius has a peculiar predilection. Although the Veronese scholiast on Verg. *Aen.* 9. 369 ascribes an opinion to 'Probus et Sulpicius', i.e. Probus as reported by Apollinaris, we can no more tell how much of Probus' learning he passed on to his pupil than what other Sulpician matter lies hidden in the *Nights*; but perhaps his main influence lay in personal encouragement.

Rhetoricians, Genial and Grave

Having completed his grammatical studies with Sulpicius Apollinaris, Gellius progressed on to the next subject, rhetoric. For this he had two teachers,

7. A. *Sept.* 524, S. *Ant.* 978, *Carm. Epigr.* 960. 7, [Sen.] *Oct.* 14–15, Luc. *Demon.* 8, cf. Philost. *VS* 553 θεῶν μακροημερώτερος and the English 'long home', used by R. Mannyng, *Handlyng Synne* 9194 Furnivall, and M. Coverdale, Eccles. 12. 5, without support from their originals.

8. Because it was discreditable to Augustus' adoptive ancestors; cf. Norden, comm. 367. Liv. 1. 3. 6 found a different way out, but Vergil gives Aeneas a virile and felicitous old age. For 'contra historiae fidem' (§ 8) = παρ' ἱστορίαν see Jocelyn II 161 n. 157; add Lucill. *AP* 11. 254. 6.

9. See p. 223; Gellius knew well enough it did in practice.

10. Sall. *Hist.* 4, fr. 1 Maur. says of Cn. Lentulus Clodianus (*cos.* 72 BC) 'perincertum stolidior an uanior'. Apollinaris seeks to know the difference; the loudmouth declares that both denote stupidity, and scurries away on the plea of business. According to Apollinaris, however, *uanus* is used in its older sense of 'deceitful' and *stolidus* means 'unpleasant', 'crass', μοχθηρός (Stephanus to Vulcob 9 observes that ὀχληρός would have been somewhat less inappropriate), φορτικός. But Sallust meant there was no telling whether Lentulus was more thick-headed or thoughtless (cf. 'uanitas' *Cat.* 23. 2); note Fronto's echo at *Orat.* 1, and cf. Tac. *A.* 2. 30. 2.

11. Apollinaris cites Laberius at 20. 6. 6, but omits him from the recapitulation at § 11. Whether he was responsible for Gellius' reservations about him (ch. 10 n. 31) we cannot tell.

Antonius Julianus and T. Castricius, whom he presents in a contrast like that of the comic and the tragic masks.

Were it not for Gellius, Antonius Julianus would be no more than the ascriptive author of some *extemporaneae* or unprepared declamations promised but not delivered by a manuscript known in the fifteenth century but long since lost;[12] he appears, however, in seven chapters of the *Nights* that amply convey his personality.[13] Like Quintilian, he was a Spaniard (his speech bewrayed him);[14] he was a publicly appointed teacher of rhetoric, a good and eloquent man well versed in ancient literature, of acute judgement and sunny disposition, a charming conversationalist. He took his pupils on a summer holiday to Naples and Puteoli, centres of Greek culture; himself a welcome guest at the birthday-party of 19. 9, he called for musical entertainment and, after a show of embarrassment not for a moment to be taken seriously, patriotically defended Roman erotic poetry—of which he was a connoisseur—against the sneers of Greeks.[15] He gave a tactful but witty answer when asked his opinion of a young show-off,[16] went to great expense and trouble to check a reading in Ennius,[17] and cited Quadrigarius on missile-trajectories and fire-prevention, expressly approving of a practical question asked by Gellius.[18]

This wide range of interests did not distract Julianus from his duties. In 1. 4 he carefully analyses the craft with which Cicero, at *Planc.* 68, purporting to contrast debts of money with those of gratitude, switches from owing the one to having the other by the unobtrusive substitution of *habet* for *debet*: retention, to equate owing with repayment, would have been incongruous and false.[19]

T. Castricius, the 'Castricius noster' who bears letters between Fronto and Volumnius Quadratus at *Amic.* 2. 2, is an altogether sterner figure: approved by Hadrian for his learning and his character, 'summa uir auctoritate grauitateque' (13. 22. 1), of strong views, though appearing in only four chapters he leaves an indelible impression. He rebuked his senatorial pupils

12. Schanz–Hosius–Krüger iii. 153.

13. *NA* 1. 4; 9. 1; 9. 15; 15. 1; 18. 5; 19. 9; 20. 9.

14. *NA* 19. 9. 2, explained by Hosius, review of Rolfe, 1304 from 'facundia rabida iurgiosaque' (§ 7), which insults the profession, not the origin. *Nomen* (and even *cognomen*) suggest a *Hispanus* (like Quintilian and Martial), not a *Hispaniensis* (like the Annaei and Hadrian).

15. 'Pro lingua patria, tamquam pro aris et focis' (§ 8); to speak Latin is to be a Roman, though one come from Spain or Africa. Cf. § 9 'nos, id est nomen Latinum'; ch. 1 n. 9.

16. *NA* 9. 15. 11 (see p. 217).

17. *NA* 18. 5. 11, on Enn. *Ann.* 236. The interpretation of Verg. *Georg.* 3. 115–17 is not persuasive, though shared by other ancient commentators (misdivision of an early gloss 'et equum et rectorem', i.e. *equum cum rectore?*). For the purportedly Lampadionian MS see p. 139; for the *Ennianista*, R. J. Starr, *RhM* forthcoming.

18. Why, asks Gellius, does Quadrigarius say that stones and arrows are less effective when projected downwards? Julianus explains 'comprobato genere quaestionis' (9. 1. 3).

19. At *Post. red. Quir.* 23, *Off.* 2. 69, Cicero uses *habere* in both members of the enthymeme. For *debere* in both Beloe cites Milton, *Paradise Lost* 4. 55–7; but Cicero could afford neither to puzzle the jury nor to make it think. He himself explodes the conceit at *Fam.* 5. 11. 1 'nec enim tu mihi habuisti modo gratiam, uerum etiam cumulatissime rettulisti'.

for being informally dressed on a public holiday (13. 22; detail fictitious, but Hadrian thought likewise: *HA Hadr.* 22. 2), and was not afraid to find extravagance in Sallust (2. 27) and redundancy in Gracchus (11. 13), but praised Metellus for arguing honestly, as a censor should, and not with pleaderly evasions—especially when the fact he refused to conceal, the inconvenience of married life, was known to everyone (1. 6).[20] Not a man like Julianus, to be the life and soul of the party, but an authority to whose stern judgement one would mentally subject one's words and actions.

Marache has constructed from these data a partisan but posthumous upholder of the optimate cause determined to discredit the Whig dogs Gracchus and Sallust.[21] This would be most suprising: by this time the sentimentality attaching to the good old days as such did not comport the desire to restore the Republic, let alone to refight its factional dissensions.[22] Nor is that interpretation imposed by the texts.

In 2. 27 Castricius compares Demosthenes' famous description (18. 67) of Philip's readiness to surrender whatever part of his body fortune wished to take, that he might live in honour and glory with the rest, and its Sallustian echo (*Hist.* 1, fr. 88 Maurenbrecher) concerning Sertorius, who bore scars and had lost an eye: 'But indeed he thoroughly delighted in the disfigurement of his body and did not worry about these things, since he retained the rest with greater glory.' Is it not (he asks) beyond the bounds of human nature to delight in bodily disfigurement, given that delight is a kind of mental exultation, more vehement than joy, at the coming to pass of things desired?[23] He contrasts the 'unprecedented and unreasonable' concept of delight in bodily disfigurement with that, much truer to life, of despising loss of limbs 'quaestu atque compendio gloriarum'—as if glory were the profitable return on a corporal investment. In fact, Sallust's 'maxime laetabatur' conveys the sense 'was very proud of': the disfigurements were the badge of honour.[24] Other men, Sertorius boasted (Plut. *Sert.* 4. 4), took off their decorations; his always remained with him, and those who beheld his injuries also beheld his valour. Thus too Sallust: 'quae uiuus facie sua ostentabat'. Furthermore, like 'gaudens lumine perdito Metellus' (Sidon. *Carm.* 9. 200), who had lost his sight rescuing the Palladium from the burning

20. The Metellus concerned is Macedonicus, though Gellius miscalls him Numidicus (pp. 228–9). For Marache's comment on this chapter see ch. 11 n. 45. For 'rhetori' § 4 see ch. 3 n. 50.

21. 'Jugement'; cf. *REL* 36 (1958) 32–3.

22. 'To write of the Republic hardly touched anybody's interests or prejudices' (Syme, *Tacitus* i. 229); the Gracchi were paradigmatically seditious (Juv. 2. 24, Tac. *A.* 3. 27. 2, Flor. 2. 1–3; contrast what the Greeks could read in Appian), but Gaius' style was judged on its merits. (Likewise Cicero, who detested the tribune, respected the orator.)

23. Stoic doctrine in Ciceronian terminology; see Holford-Strevens, 'Five Notes' 144. 'Gaudio' means 'quam gaudium'.

24. Cf. Sen. *Prov.* 4. 4: 'militares uiri gloriantur uulneribus, laeti fluentem meliori casu sanguinem ostentant: idem licet fecerint qui integri reuertuntur ex acie, magis spectatur qui saucius redit.'

temple of Vesta,[25] he could surely delight in those feats that had caused his impairments,[26] and prefer disfigurement with achievements to intactitude without, which is precisely what Demosthenes says of Philip.[27]

Castricius reveals himself as a confirmed civilian, unable to understand the passions of a warrior;[28] this does not make him an optimate, much less his censure in 11. 13 of C. Gracchus, who, taking unusual care over verbal artistry, had slipped into virtual truism.[29] The criticism is entirely justified, and made in the mildest of tones: far be it from Castricius to find fault with so eloquent an orator, whose venerable antiquity atones for anything amiss, but let students take care in their speeches not to destroy the sense for the sake of the sound. If this be right-wing bigotry, what was unbiased moderation? Castricius defended Metellus as Gellius was to defend Cato,[30] but Gellius also admired the elder Scipio, to whom Cato was a persistent enemy; if Gellius did not judge orators by their politics, why should Castricius have done so?

The Dignified Philosopher

Of Gellius' teachers at Athens only one is known: the Berytian Middle Platonist L. Calvenus Taurus,[31] who according to Eusebius flourished in AD 145.[32] As befits a commentator on *Gorgias*, he had small love for pupils whose main interest lay in rhetoric; Gellius at first seemed one of their number (17. 20. 4). Indeed, the result of Taurus' injunction to perpend not form but content was an attempt to adumbrate Plato's style in Latin (§ 7, cf. p. 49); but there were worse offenders. In 10. 19 the philosopher sternly rebuked a student who excused a misdeed on the ground that others had committed it before him: if philosophy could not persuade him, might he not have recalled

25. Contrast Plin. *NH* 7. 141: 'quo fit ut infelix quidem dici non debeat, felix tamen non possit'. For the legend see Courtney on Juv. 6. 265.

26. Cf. Pfeiffer on Call. fr. 107. So Beloe: 'This is certainly an indefinite expression; but it may easily be imagined, that they whose characteristic is an ardent love of glory, can receive satisfaction, and even delight, from the incidental circumstances promoting that glory, though occasioned by wounds, loss of limbs, and such like accidents.'

27. No doubt Sertorius' condition made him seem the more Hannibalic to the Celtiberians (cf. App. *BC* 1. 112): in turn Civilis the Batavian likened himself to Sertorius and Hannibal (Tac. *Hist.* 4. 13. 2, using Sallust's *dehonestamentum*).

28. He thus demonstrates anew the gulf between antiquarianism and antiquity.

29. Fr. 32 M: 'quae uos cupide per hosce annos adpetistis atque uoluistis, ea si temere repudiaritis, abesse non potest quin aut olim cupide adpetisse aut nunc temere repudiasse dicamini'; on the artistry see Norden i. 172. The first 'cupide' and 'temere', as Castricius observes, detract from the sense; but for the Gellian context, the most superstitious devotee of MSS would have essayed an emendation.

30. *NA* 6. 3, cf. p. 151.

31. On Taurus' *nomen*, see p. 227.

32. Against Dillon 232–3, 237–8, who makes this the date of his appointment as head of a school, see Lynch 183, Glucker 142, who deny that such a school existed; note that Taurus taught at home (*NA* 2. 2. 2). Nor was he a διάδοχος (see Oliver 93).

how Demosthenes had scouted that defence?[33] If the story is fictitious, Gellius considered that such impudence would have exasperated a man whose reproofs were generally milder (18. 10. 5). At 1. 9. 10 Taurus is disgusted by those who read Plato for his style rather than his morality;[34] his remarks follow a complaint about pupils who presume to dictate the syllabus, in sad contrast to the discipline observed by neophytes in the school of Pythagoras. The same concern for the philosopher's dignity is shown at 7. 10. 5: whereas Eucleides of Megara had braved the Athenian embargo to hear Socrates, visiting him at night in woman's garb though living over twenty miles away, modern youth expects the philosopher to wait at its door till it shall have slept off its hangover. The theme was commonplace: Marcus' tutor Apollonius of Chalcedon maintained that the pupil should come to the master, not the master to the pupil (*HA Pius* 10. 4).[35] Taurus took his profession seriously, and with it his pupils' moral conduct: in 20. 4 he sends a rich young man who spends his time with actors and musicians an Aristotelian problem, 'Why do most artists of Dionysus have low morals?', with the injunction to read it daily.[36] This concern was accompanied by interest in the health of students and friends alike: when Gellius falls ill in Herodes' villa, Taurus comes to visit him (18. 10), as he does a sick Stoic friend at Lebadeia, even though hurrying to reach Delphi for the Pythian Games (12. 5. 1-2); Gellius is in attendance as a philosopher's pupils ought to be even when Socrates is visiting the beautiful Theodote (X. *Mem.* 3. 11).

Some pupils, indeed, he treated as friends, inviting them to dinner; this inner circle of συνήθεις ('qui erant philosopho Tauro iunctiores', 7. 13. 1) included Gellius, who must have overcome the earlier suspicions. As one would expect, the fare was simple (17. 8. 2), the relish intellectual (7. 13. 2), light discussions resembling those at the Roman students' Saturnalia, or Plutarch's symposia;[37] Taurus good-humouredly bandied words with a pert slave-boy (17. 8. 7-8).[38] On another occasion (2. 2), having kept Gellius back for a chat after his other pupils had departed, he settles the point of etiquette that arises when the proconsul of Crete and Cyrene calls together with his father: which should have the only chair, the magistrate or the *paterfamilias*? At least in Gellius' account, he discusses the matter in Roman terms ('priuata actio', § 10): but a Roman citizen should do no otherwise. His

33. Cf. p. 49. 'Demosthenis uestri' (10. 19. 2) resembles 'rhetorum uestrorum' (17. 20. 5), but Gellius would tell even a true story in his own words.

34. Cf. Sen. *Ep.* 108. 6, Plut. *Mor.* 42 C–F, 79 D, Epict. 3. 23. 20–1, *AP* 9. 203. 7–10, and contrast Aug. *Conf.* 3. 4. 7; 5. 14. 24. Dörrie 321 suggests that Taurus was taking aim at Gellius, whose thick Roman skin did not feel the blow; but had Taurus always considered him a ῥητορίσκος, he would not have admitted him among his intimates.

35. See too Aristippus fr. 28a Mannebach; Ael. *VH* 7. 21; cf. Philost. *VS* 535.

36. This passage should be added to those in Rabbow 218–22, cf. I. Hadot 16–17, P. Hadot 18–19, 23 n. 50, 58. It is a pleasure to acknowledge the help given especially on this topic by the Revd Professor Henry Chadwick.

37. At § 12, Carrio's 'symbolae taliaque' was anticipated by Politian, *Misc. II*, ch. 43, p. 74.

38. But see p. 171.

tact is also displayed in 18. 10, when a doctor's slipshod terminology arouses general disgust,[39] but Taurus is sure it shows no ignorance. In 8. 6 he warns against rehearsing grievances when composing quarrels.

We are thus shown an amiable and kindly man, but one zealous for the dignity of his discipline and severe in the face of frivolity; all qualities of a good teacher. What, then, did he teach?

Like other philosophers,[40] he frequently let his pupils put questions after the lecture (1. 26. 2). Gellius, less than originally, asks whether the wise man becomes angry;[41] Taurus gives his own answer, a defence of the golden mean, and then tells an anecdote about Plutarch, who, when a slave he had ordered to be flogged taxed him with violating the precepts of his treatise *On Not Being Angry*, asked what made him think that he was angry when he showed none of the normal symptoms such as blazing eyes or shouting;[42] then bade the overseer, 'Carry on while we argue.' Taurus knew how to round off his disquisitions with a joke; unfortunately, the joke interests Gellius far more than the serious doctrine, which is attached in précis form ('summa autem totius sententiae Tauri haec fuit', § 10). The view that anger, like other passions, should be moderated but not eliminated, will be directed at the Stoics, against whom Taurus had published a polemical treatise (12. 5. 5).

Yet after the visit to the Stoic, seen bearing up against pain,[43] Taurus is cheered when a follower asks how a Stoic can be compelled to groan; his answer, despite its Stoic language, is compatible with such a Platonism as Antiochus',[44] and the natural attraction to pleasure asserted at § 8, cf. Plat. *Leg.* 732 E, is denied by Chrysippus (*SVF* iii. 178). Taurus rejects the Stoic ideal of indolentia (ἀναλγησία) and impassibility (ἀπάθεια), adding that it had been abandoned by Panaetius[45]—that great revisionist who by

39. See p. 224.

40. See Clarke 90–2; and note Cic. *Fam.* 9. 26. 3.

41. That the wise man will not be angry is a Stoic principle on which the Platonist Taurus is invited to comment; Gellius has probably copied from his anti-Stoic treatise, the enquiry being fictitious.

42. Cf. Caelius fr. 25 M; see too ch. 14 n. 96.

43. 'Vidistis ... congredientes conpugnantesque philosophum et dolorem' (12. 5. 3), cf. Epict. 3. 22. 58, Jerome, *Adu. Iouin.* 2. 14 (PL 23. 305 D), and Gell. 15. 2. 8, ultimately from Plato. *Leg.* 647 C). Gellius' phrase is imitated by Min. Fel. *Oct.* 37. 1, cf. L. A. Holford-Strevens, *RAC* ix. 1051–2; add 'equitis' = *equi* 7. 3 ~ *NA* 18. 5. 8.

44. Dillon 240–1, Inwood, 'Hierocles' 171 and n. 23, on Antiochus 169–71, 173–7; for his Stoicizing see Cic. *Luc.* 69, 132, S.E. *PH* 1. 235, Tarrant 90–3.

45. M. Schäfer, *Gymnasium* 62 (1956) 349–50 derives both 12. 5 and 19. 12 from Panaetius, with unconvincing parallels from Cicero. As regards 12. 5, Panaetius, in the very treatise Schäfer takes to be Gellius' source, did not bother to state that pain was not an evil (Cic. *Fin.* 4. 23), which Taurus does at some length. The definition of courage in § 13, though Stoic, not Platonic, recurs at Iambl. *VP* 190; the sects had long been borrowing from one another, and the ascription to 'maiores nostri' (the founders of our school, cf. 19. 1. 13, Apul. *Apol.* 36. 3, *Flor.* 2. 1), will be Gellius' own inaccurate variation on 'a ueteribus philosophis' § 7 (i.e. οἱ παλαιοί, cf. *antiqui* Cic. *Fin.* 5. 14). The five πάθη of 19. 2. 3 should not be supported by Cic. *Off.* 1. 69, where 'animi et iracundia' is interpolated.

pruning away the more outrageous paradoxes had made Stoicism acceptable to the Roman ruling class as an underpinning of the *mos maiorum*. Nor was Taurus reluctant to quote his contemporary, the Stoic Hierocles, against Epicurus: 'Pleasure is the *summum bonum*: a strumpet's tenet. There's no Providence: a tenet too bad even for a strumpet'[46] (9. 5. 8). This was a matter on which Taurus felt strongly: according to Philoponus (*De aet. mundi*, p. 187. 3–14 Rabe), he declared in his commentary on *Timaeus* that Plato, though not supposing the cosmos created in time, wrote as if it had been, not only for ease of exposition—an idea he found in Aristotle and Theophrastus —but out of piety, in order to protect belief in Providence.

In a good cause Taurus was ready to borrow from either the Stoa or the Peripatos.[47] However, when in 19. 6 Gellius seeks his opinion of the Aristotelian problem why shame turns people red but fear pale, he replies that the explanation given, though correct as to *how*, says nothing of *why*, and that one might also ask why this difference should exist even though shame is a species of fear, being philosophically defined as the fear of justified reproach: αἰσχύνη ἐστὶν φόβος δικαίου ψόγου, a Stoic definition in Platonic garb.[48]

Physical problems are also aired in 17. 8: why olive-oil often freezes, wine seldom, vinegar hardly ever; why river- and spring-water freezes but not the sea. Despite this last absurdity, Gellius' source may well be Taurus; at all events, it was not a Peripatetic.[49] The discussions of sound—whether it is

46. Bentley 496–7 thus translates his emendation, which improves on Pearson, 'Prolegomena', sig. [*8]ᵛ, and which Hertz's successors adopt in silence.

47. Though he also wrote on the differences between Plato and Aristotle (*Suda T* 166); he disbelieved in the Fifth Element (Philoponus, *Aet.* 520. 20–3 R). In 8. 6 he may have cited Theophrastus, but see p. 201.

48. Plato had treated αἰδώς and αἰσχύνη as two names for the 'divine fear' (*Leg.* 671 D, cf. 647 A), making for obedience to the law; Aristotle, though distinguishing between reverence (αἰδώς) and fear (φόβος) as motives for it (*EN* 1116ᵃ31, 1179ᵇ11), defines αἰδώς as φόβος τις ἀδοξίας (1128ᵇ11) and throughout the section uses αἰδώς/αἰδεῖσθαι indiscriminately with αἰσχύνη/αἰσχύνεσθαι (cf. [Arist.] *Probl.* 11. 53). Chrysippus, however (*SVF* iii. 440), differentiated αἰδώς and αἰσχύνη in accordance with his antithesis between rational εὐπάθειαι and irrational πάθη; αἰδώς was defined as εὐλάβεια ὀρθοῦ ψόγου (iii. 423), αἰσχύνη as φόβος ἀδοξίας (iii. 407–9), ill fame being a matter of indifference to the sage (iii. 646). The definitions, like other Stoic formulae, find their way into the pseudo-Platonic Ὅροι (412 C 9–10, 416 A 9). Taurus, who like Plut. *Mor.* 449 A–B (cf. 529 D) and Gal. *Plac. Hipp. Plat.* 4. 4. 8 (i. 252 De Lacy) will have seen these distinctions as mere verbal shifts to escape from the absurdities of ἀπάθεια, accepts the formula of 'justified rebuke', since ill fame may be due to the ignorance and perversity of the many (cf. Plat. *Rep.* 473 C), but restores the φόβος of both Platonic and ordinary discourse; he uses αἰσχύνη because the point of departure is a text concerning αἰσχυνόμενοι. Against the doctrine of φόβος δοξίας see Alex. Aphr. *Eth. Prob.* 21.

49. Whereas [Alex. Aph.] *Prob.* 1. 128 states that water and (in extreme cold) olive-oil freeze, wine, vinegar, and garum do not (with a different explanation), Peripatetics like the real Alex. Aph. *In Meteor.* 208. 17–209. 23 Hayduck repeat Aristotle's dictum (*Meteor.* 383ᵇ23–4, *GA* 735ᵇ27–9; but cf. *PA* 648ᵇ30–2) that olive-oil thickens with the cold but does not freeze (so in other terms Plut. *Mor.* 950 C; *contra* Gal. xi. 510 Kühn); in fact it solidifies at -6°C. Frozen wine and vinegar were known to Aristotle (*Meteor.* 384ᵃ13; for wine cf. X. *An.* 7. 4. 3, on the south coast of the Euxine); although Taurus treats Hdt. 4. 28 as aberrant (§ 16, cf. p. 182),

corporeal or incorporeal (5. 15)—and vision (5. 16) come not from Taurus'
Περὶ σωμάτων καὶ ἀσωμάτων,[50] but from a doxography (cf. 'Aetius' 4.
19–20, 4. 13, respectively) that accorded Plato's view neither more nor less
respect than any other. Taurus might appear a likelier source for 9. 5
(philosophers' views on pleasure): he is cited directly and Plato receives the
most attention. But such potting of *placita* seems beneath him.

In 17. 20 Gellius is too busy translating the *Symposium* passage to report
how his master expounded it; at 1. 9. 9 we are told that Taurus detested
students who wanted to read that dialogue for Alcibiades' drunken entry, or
Phaedrus for Lysias' speech, but not what he had to say about these works. In
7. 13 he observes that the problem of defining the moment at which a process
is completed had elicited from Plato the concept of instantaneity (τὴν
ἐξαίφνης φύσιν, *Parm.* 156 D), but takes the matter no further. However,
the next chapter at last brings an explicit citation from one of Taurus'
Platonic commentaries, that on *Gorgias*. The discussion of punishment came
in the first book, therefore (as in other commentaries) during the debate with
Polus, not on the passage that Gellius quotes from the closing myth. Taurus
states three purposes that punishment may serve: κόλασις or νουθεσία, to
correct the offender; τιμωρία, to uphold the victim's standing; παράδειγμα,
to deter others by making an example.[51] Gellius observes that Plato, at 525
B, uses τιμωρία in the general sense of punishment and admits only the two
purposes of correction and deterrence; he is undecided whether Plato did not
accept the principle of maintaining the victim's status, or omitted it as
irrelevant to punishment in the afterlife, even as at 1. 18. 6 he wonders
whether Varro overlooked an etymology or rejected it. In fact (as Taurus
surely knew) Plato consistently declared correction and deterrence to be the
only two ends of punishment, except that at *Leg.* 862 E he justifies the
death-penalty for the incurably wicked not only by both these criteria,[52] but
as ridding the city of bad men.[53] Although the victim is entitled to
reparation (*Leg.* 933 E), retribution is beastly and irrational, since it cannot
make the deed undone (*Prot.* 324 A–B, *Leg.* 934 A–B). However, the τιμωρία
for which flesh-and-blood Greeks never ceased to thirst is not *only* vengeance
for past wrongs, but *also* a demonstration for the future that they are not
persons to be injured with impunity ('propter tuendam laesi hominis
auctoritatem' § 9). By respecting the man in the street's concern for status
within the community, Taurus has rehabilitated retribution and found three

Mithridates' general Neoptolemus won a cavalry-battle on the frozen Straits of Kerč' (Strabo
307 C, cf. 73 C).
    50. Mercklin, 'Capita' 11–12, hinting that 9. 5 too came thence (so Ruske 53). For the work
see *Suda* loc. cit.
    51. Compare and contrast Arist. *Rhet.* 1369[b]12–14.
    52. Cf. Sen. *De Ira* 1. 15. 1–2.
    53. Correction, deterrence, and security are the three ends of punishment at Sen. *Clem.* 20. 1.
Taurus ignores security, superfluous if the death-penalty either benefits the criminal or deters
others.

purposes where Plato gave only two.[54] The extended quotations in 10. 22 show that Gellius had read *Gorgias*, even if he did not understand it;[55] at 12. 9. 6 he refers to the doctrine repeatedly asserted there, that it is better to be wronged than to wrong. On coming to 525 B, after he had read Taurus' comments on the earlier passage, he noted the discrepancy, a feat requiring not the philosophical acumen he lacked, but the grammarian's ability to compare one sentence with another: a skill in which the unimaginative and literal-minded often have the advantage over those with one eye on their own thoughts, and the other on the accumulated doctrine of past ages.

But Taurus' greatest work was his commentary on *Timaeus*, perhaps known to Iamblichus, and certainly to Philoponus.[56] The descent of souls to earth and the non-creation of the cosmos will have engaged his attention far more acutely than the commonplace ethics, the snippets of natural history, the elementary anatomy that exhaust the wisdom his pupil took away with him. No doubt he was used to such limitations in his Roman students; at least Gellius was a modest youth, who did not tell him what to teach, and gained access to his table because he tried to learn. But despite the attractive portrait, we are not shown cause why Taurus' works should endure for four centuries: Gellius reveals the man, but Philoponus the mind.[57]

54. Is this a reason to make Taurus the source of 'Apul.' *Plat.* 1. 17 (so on other grounds Dillon 327), where again a dyad has become a triad?

55. The interpretation of Callicles' speech as a justified attack on ivory-tower intellectuals suits very well with 13. 8; Grilli suspects in both chapters (cf. ch. 11 n. 84) the direct or indirect influence of a polemic against philosophy *in angulis* by Hortensius in Cicero's dialogue (edn. 131 and n. 11, *Proemi* 59 n. 20, 'Echi' 194–6), combining Dicaearchus' advocacy of the πρακτικὸς βίος with a tendentious use of *Gorgias* by Antiochus of Ascalon (*Proemi* 68–70 cll. Them. *Or.* 34. 12) and affording later Roman authors a *locus communis*. Indeed, one might exploit the speech when urging the student of philosophy, as Antiochus urged Cicero (Plut. *Cic.* 4. 4), to take part in public life; but despite the resemblances between Antiochus and Taurus in 12. 5, the latter would have opposed to false philosophers not wise statesmen but persons who understood the cosmos. Even the view that Plato is warning against unworldliness falls foul of *Theaet.* 173 C–E.

56. See Koch 274–6, Dillon 242–6.

57. Dillon 244 notes that Gellius does not report any 'even vaguely dualist tendencies', such as Plutarch's pupil might be expected to display; but he would not have noticed them.

Chapter 6

Favorinus

OF NO contemporary does Gellius speak so often or so warmly as of Favorinus, a philosopher (or as others said a sophist) from Arelate, now Arles, in Gallia Narbonensis,[1] of Gaulish race and Hellenic education. To this pupil of Dio the Golden-mouthed and friend of Plutarch, Fronto, and Herodes Atticus, Gellius attached himself on leaving the schools of rhetoric; ever afterwards he loved him as a friend, and revered him as a teacher.

Gellius apart, our main sources for Favorinus' life and thought are three declamations,[2] the polemic against him in Galen's treatise *On the Best Education*, the brief biography in Philostratus (*VS* 489–92), and a hateful account by his rival sophist M. Antonius Polemo of Laodicea on the Lycus.[3] The scurrility of their mutual invective is deplored by Philostratus, who reports that for his part in it the normally arrogant Polemo feared the censure of the philosopher Timocrates (*VS* 536);[4] but in his treatise on physiognomy he included a physical portrait that in such a work may be presumed accurate (and is compatible with our other evidence) and a moral portrait, or rather character-assassination, that we shall not take for truth.[5]

Although other sources describe Favorinus as a eunuch or a hermaphrodite, Polemo expressly states that he was born without testicles; this should indicate cryptorchism, or undescended testicles, which condition would not

---

1. The bishop of Aleria undertook the *ed. pr.* of Gellius in order that the praise of the Gaul Favorinus might please his brother of Ostia, Guillaume d'Estouteville, who had made good resources sufficing 'ne ad ponendam quidem barbam' with a long loan of 100 gold ducats (letter to Paul II, fos. [1]ᵛ–[3]ʳ: Botfield 81–4). Cardinal d'Estouteville, a wealthy man, had reviewed the proceedings against Joan of Arc, and contended for the Papacy at the conclave of 1458.

2. Two (frr. 94–5 B) preserved as Dio Prus. 64 and 37 respectively; a third (fr. 96 B) in P. Vat. Gr. 11 (early iii AD).

3. Preserved in an Arabic translation ('Arabs') of whose five MSS (H. Hommel, *AAHG* 27 (1974) 205) one—Leiden, Cod. Or. 1206—was edited by G. Hoffmann at *Scriptores physiognomonici* i. 93–294 Förster; for Favorinus see i. 161–5. Hoffmann's Latin translation (= test. 3 B) incorporates several unjustified conjectures; the text must be read in Arabic with constant reference to the apparatus criticus. The original passage is summarized by a careless Latin Anonymus (§ 40, pp. 82–3 André = ii. 57–8 Förster), whose work is based on Polemo (called *Palemon auctor* throughout, though André alters); general remarks, without the individual instances, are preserved, with greater fidelity than by Arabs or Anonymus, at Adamantius i. 343. 1–5, 351. 10–352. 4 Förster. In what follows, Polemo is reconstructed out of all three.

4. Timocrates was a pupil of the Tyrian Stoic Euphrates, and no friend of the effeminate; nor of Favorinus (p. 73). Polemo had taken his part against Scopelian.

5. None of the scoundrels whose pen-portaits enliven the treatise is named, but the clues sufficed for Anonymus to identify Favorinus.

(and according to Polemo did not) prevent an active sex-life.[6] Persons of this nature, he declares, are generally savage, treacherous, and criminal; moreover, Favorinus' eyes (the chief indices of character in Polemo's system) were wide-open, dry, with a cheerful glint and a piercing gaze, betokening a shamelessness that shrank from nothing. His appearance, like his voice, was feminine, in particular his soft cheeks and long slender neck; he had a broad mouth, thin lips, thick legs, fleshy feet, loose joints, supple limbs, and a stooping gait.[7] He took great care of his person, dyeing his hair and rubbing his body with ointments and aphrodisiacs.[8] The description suits well with Philostratus' statements that he had no beard even in old age, that his voice was shrill, thin, and high-pitched,[9] and that together with his expressive eyes and his rhythmic diction it charmed even Greekless listeners in Rome, above all with the singsong delivery of his epilogues.[10] Lucian, however, makes Demonax find it ignoble, womanish, and unworthy of a philosopher, declare that his ears were not easily deceived, and mock Favorinus for possessing neither testicles nor beard (*Demon.* 12–13).

Gellius, who does not give physical descriptions, calls him very sweet of speech (16. 3. 1 'homo ille fandi dulcissimus'), meaning that his conversation was delightful. Timocrates might brand him a chatterbox, and Polemo reply 'Like every old woman' (*VS* 541), but he had the power to detain Gellius and his friends all day with his wit and charm (*NA* loc. cit.). Although Polemo had declaimed in Rome about the time that Gellius was studying with Apollinaris (M. Caes. *Ep.* 2. 7. 1, July or August 143), Gellius ignored him, unless the notion in 14. 3 that the rivalry between Plato and Xenophon was got up by their followers is derived from a feud assigned by Philostratus to that very cause (*VS* 490).

Polemo (no mean scorner himself) attributes to his enemy a sardonic sense of humour. Gellius portrays Favorinus' smiling charm, but the most biting jest that he puts in his mouth closely resembles one ascribed by Lucian to Demonax: Favorinus tells a young man who uses obsolete words that he

6. *Ex rel.* the late Dr K. Dewhurst, who observed that the physical description fits; for another case see Eus. *HE* 7. 32. 4. The condition was known to ancient doctors: Marganne 297–8.

7. The detailed physiognomy begins in the Leiden MS with baggy eyelids (i. 161. 12 app. crit., cf. i. 165. 17 (where Hoffmann's conjecture is based on a *uox nihili* in Freytag's lexicon)–167. 3 = Adamantius i. 343. 3–7), in Anonymus with a taut forehead (p. 83. 7 André = ii. 58. 4 Förster). Hoffmann's text yields a swollen or protuberant forehead; neither a prominent nor a taut one is so described elsewhere (see i. 231. 7, 17, 19), but in Arabic script the change from *'aynayn* 'two eyes' to *jabīn* 'forehead' is easy. If the text is sound, either one translator is in error or (far less probably) each left out a different item at the outset of the list. But we should neither emend nor defend till the other MSS of Arabs have been collated.

8. I owe this understanding of i. 161. 17–163. 2 to Professor A. F. L. Beeston (pers. comm.), who confirmed that Hoffmann's interpretation was ungrammatical, emended *ḥiṣb* 'luxuriance' to *ḥaḍb* 'dyeing', and restored the MS lection *'uḥar* 'other', rendering: 'He paid regular attention to his person, with the use of hair-dye, and he massaged his body with other drugs [sc. than the hair-dye]'.

9. Like Hadrian of Tyre's (Philost. *VS* 589).

10. For this affectation, much despised by critics and much admired by audiences, see Norden i. 55–7, 135, 161, 265, 294–5, 375–9, ii. 859–61; Heiberg ii. 90.

speaks as if addressing Evander's mother (1. 10. 2),[11] Demonax comments
that an archaist has answered like a contemporary of Agamemnon's (*Demon.*
26; cf. *Lexiph.* 20).

Warming to his theme, Polemo declares that Favorinus acted on his every
whim (which was mostly sexual); that he generally used Greek as his means
of expression, was a sophist, and toured the cities and market-places
gathering crowds in order to display his wickedness and pursue his
debauchery, which included homosexuality both active and passive; that he
was a charlatan who dealt in magic,[12] claiming powers to confer life or death
and to compel men and women into each other's arms, and gaining credence
for his claims by producing a hidden (that is, ventriloquial) voice, as of a
familiar spirit; and that he collected deadly poisons, in which he conducted a
clandestine trade.

Commonplaces of invective are only sometimes true; but Favorinus' sexual
energy is confirmed by Philostratus, who also reports that, having been
accused of adultery with a consular's wife, he used to state the three
paradoxes of his life as being a Gaul but speaking Greek, being a eunuch but
standing trial for adultery, and having quarrelled with an emperor but lived.
If Lucian's Bagoas, as seems probable, is in this respect Favorinus in disguise,
and if, as must be doubtful, the report is fair, he was caught in the
act—'members in members'—but achieved acquittal by pleading his condition, as making the crime impossible.[13] Evidently the court lacked medical
advice.

For this reason (observe the indignant denial at fr. 95. 33–4 Barigazzi), his
relations with Hadrian, at first good enough for Favorinus to dedicate a
philosophical book to him (fr. 29 B), broke down despite the tact that refused
to bandy grammar, even when in the right, with the lord of thirty legions
(test. 8 B). He had not helped his cause when, appointed to the high-
priesthood at home,[14] a highly expensive honour, he claimed exemption as a
philosopher; seeing Hadrian inclined to deny him the title, he avoided the
humiliation by opportunely dreaming that his master Dio told him men were
born for their fatherlands as well as for themselves—a sentence that not only
a philosopher should have heard before. Hadrian transferred his favour from
Favorinus to Polemo, and also from Ephesus, which cheered Favorinus, to
Polemo's supporter Smyrna (Philost. *VS* 531); the Athenians and Corinthians

11. Cf. p. 165. Carmentis becomes King Dan's great-grandam in Holberg, *Moralske
Tanker* 3. 85 (*Samlede Skrifter* xiv. 349).

12. As was said against Apuleius and Hadrian of Tyre, both unhealthily knowledgeable in
these arts (Hadrian's own argument at pp. 44–5 of Hinck's Polemo; cf. Philost. *VS* 590). 'Sophists'
had been coupled with such persons since the 4th c. BC: Plat. *Symp.* 203 D, Dem. 18. 276; note
too Euseb. *HE* 7. 30. 9). See too Philost. *VS* 619; but the theme is less frequent in the sophists
than in novels (Russell, *GD* 26 n. 38).

13. *Eun.* 10; although Favorinus appears under his own colours in § 7, a second real
philosophical eunuch charged with the same offence would seem unlikely. Russell *GD* 52 n. 42
sees another possible echo in Hermog. 60. 19–61. 3 R.

14. Not in Arelate, but as flamen of the Narbonensian *concilium* (Bowersock 35).

promptly threw down Favorinus' statues, the Corinthians' conduct provoking the discourse fr. 95 B. Philostratus states that Favorinus came to no harm, οὐδὲν ἔπαθεν, but since the declamation on exile locates the speaker—Favorinus himself—on Chios (fr. 96 xiv 39–41 B), the phrase must mean 'survived'.[15] Had he been convicted on the adultery charge, he would have suffered *relegatio in insulam* and the loss of half his property (PS 2. 26. 14); as it was, Hadrian, no longer enduring his presence, dismissed him without financial penalty to an island infinitely pleasanter than the likes of Gyaros.[16] His successor revoked the order; Favorinus returned to Rome, regained admission to the imperial *salutatio* (*NA* 4. 1. 1), and numbered consuls among his friends.[17]

The three preserved declamations may be compared with orations on like themes by Dio: fr. 94 on fortune with no. 65, fr. 95 on statues with no. 31, and fr. 96 on exile with no. 13. Philostratus detected no trace of Dio's influence; the contrast indeed could scarcely be more marked. Even Barigazzi, who does his best for his author, finds flaccidity and languor in his style (edn. 71); others, recalling Ael. Arist. 34. 48 Keil, would say that the unmanliness of Favorinus' body was matched by the effeminacy of his style. However, he declaimed not for us, but for the audiences of his own day, who clearly relished it; he travelled all over Italy and the Greek world, being particularly admired at Ephesus and highly successful at Rome, where Gellius witnessed the tumultuous applause (9. 8. 3); Herodes Atticus was not ashamed to call himself his pupil;[18] he taught, or influenced, other sophists; his works were sought after for two centuries, even by Libanius; and Phrynichus the Atticist felt obliged to record, with shock and shame, the un-Attic words that sullied the works of this notable man.[19] For although Favorinus claimed to Atticize (fr. 95. 26 B), he was by no means strict enough for Phrynichus, or even for Galen, who—despite his own harsh words for 'the practitioners of the accursed sham-scholarship' (vi. 633. 3–4 Kühn) and 'ultra-Atticists' (*Progn.* 5. 2, p. 94. 5–7 Nutton)—scolds him for using the Stoic and Hellenistic term καταληπτόν 'apprehensible' rather than the Platonic and Attic βεβαίως γνωστόν 'securely knowable'[20]—reasonably, since the Academic position he defended went back to polemic against the Porch. Barigazzi's lengthy

15. Cf. Arist. *Wasps* 385–7 ἥν τι πάθω 'γώ (bury me under the bar of the court)—οὐδὲν πείσει.

16. Philostratus ignores the exile as not a formal sentence: he denies that either Dio or Herodes was exiled (*VS* 488, 562), though the former says it himself (13. 2) and the latter, after Sirmium, avoided Athens till Marcus intervened (but cf. Ameling i. 150).

17. Herodes and Fronto; cf. also *NA* 13. 25. 2.

18. See testt. 6. 4; 11–12 B. Herodes said the same of Polemo; politeness and tact had their due.

19. See testt. 13–17, frr. 7–8, 25, 129–41 B.

20. Such fastidiousness is a commonplace of polemic: e.g. Aeschin. 3. 72, Cic. *Phil.* 3. 22, 13. 43.

analysis (edn. 29–68) confirms that his Atticism was neither strict nor consistent, and did not eschew the poetical.[21]

The content of the Greek declamations is not remarkable either for originality or for profundity: when all allowance is made for the difference between modern and ancient tastes—even between northern and southern Europe—it is hard to hear in them any more than the tinkling cymbal of a *Gallus*. We are not surprised that he particularly excelled in the paradoxical praise of 'things without honour' (ἄδοξοι ὑποθέσεις, *infames materiae*).[22] The declamation on astrology recorded in *NA* 14. 1 gives a more favourable impression of the speaker, partly because despite Gellius' warning (§ 2) that it may not have been serious,[23] we are in entire agreement with his arguments, and partly because his pupil, himself no ascetic in his style, has pruned the luxuriating verbiage. Naturally that is not how Gellius puts it: he professes to summarize 'sicca et incondita et propemodum ieiuna oratione' and states that Favorinus, by his own genius and the resources and charm of Greek eloquence, treated the subject 'latius ... et amoenius et splendidius et profluentius' (14. 1. 32). Although the disclaimer is subverted by the mode of its expression, Gellius sincerely admired his master's style. Likewise, when he reports Favorinus' plea for mothers to breast-feed their own babies, he declares that Latin can hardly do justice to the delightful abundance of the original, and certainly not his own stylistic poverty (12. 1. 24). Nevertheless, he has contrived to convey at least a hint of Favorinus' manner especially in its liking for rhetorical questions, but also in the use of balanced clauses, antitheses, and anaphorae: e.g. 12. 1. 6 'aluisse in utero sanguine suo nescioquid quod non uideret, non alere nunc suo lacte quod uideat, iam uiuentem, iam hominem, iam matris officia implorantem?', 14. 1. 9 'cur non euenta quoque rerum ac negotiorum alia efficiunt in Chaldaeis, alia in Gaetulis, alia aput Danuuium, alia aput Nilum?' But he does not let these devices run away with him as the real Favorinus continually does.

Favorinus is described by the *Suda* (Φ 4 = test. 13 M, 1 B) as 'full of philosophy, but given more to rhetoric';[24] conformably, in comparing Plato and Lysias, he observes that the slightest alteration to the language impairs Plato's elegance, but Lysias' meaning. Comparison between the two had been incited by Plato's *Phaedrus*; his unfavourable judgement on Lysias was reversed by Caecilius of Cale Acte, though with the concession that the orator's οἰκονομία (*dispositio*) was inferior to his εὕρεσις (*inuentio*);[25]

21. Polemo's vocabulary is no purer (Phryn., pp. 170, 271, 421 Lobeck; Schmid i. 48–66); his syntax shows plural verb with neuter subject (*A* 3), omission of ἄν (*B* 21), and constant misuse of μή.

22. *NA* 17. 12; Fronto, *Laud. neg.* 3; Philost. *VS* 491; see A. S. Pease, *CPh* 21 (1926) 27–42.

23. According to Synes. *Dio* 37 B–C one can always tell; and Gellius soon forgets his doubts.

24. His statement that Socrates taught rhetoric (fr. 30 M = 62 B) would have disgusted Plato, but Favorinus saw no harm in it.

25. Plat. *Phdr.* 235 E; Caec. Cal. fr. 110 Ofenloch; [Long.] 32. 8 (contrast 35. 1). Arethas praised Dio of Prusa for combining Plato's solemnity with Lysias' simplicity (H. von Arnim, edn. of Dio, ii. 538). For Favorinus' antithesis cf. Sen. *Contr.* 9. 1. 13.

Plato's complaint that Lysias' sentences exhibit no logical order is quoted by Fronto.[26] Favorinus' judgement concentrates on style, ignoring not only arrangement but content; it is a rhetorician's judgement, not a philosopher's. Indeed, although Favorinus was an Academic, he did not hold Plato in unquestioned esteem: he may include him together with Socrates, Pythagoras, and the very gods and goddesses, among those whom malicious tongues have slandered, but himself alleges that the *Republic* was largely borrowed from Protagoras.[27]

Favorinus and Plutarch were friends; they rivalled each other in the number of books they composed (*Suda* loc. cit.), though few would surrender a work of Plutarch's to revive one of Favorinus'. Plutarch quoted Favorinus in the *Roman Questions*, gave him a part in his *Table-talk*, dedicated to him his treatise *On the Principle of Cold*, and wrote him a philosophical letter on friendship; for his part Favorinus gave the alternative title *Plutarch* to his treatise *On the Academic Disposition*, and wrote another work in which Epictetus was confronted by Plutarch's slave Onesimus. But whereas Plutarch was essentially a Platonist, Favorinus was an Academic, a sceptic given to suspension of judgement (ἐποχή) and argument on both sides of the question (εἰς ἑκάτερα ἐπιχείρησις), which suited the sophist as it had suited Cicero. The Academic profession was itself an archaism: even if, as is doubtful, the Academy still existed, it had abandoned scepticism in the first century BC.[28] That doctrine, however, had found new adherents who invoked the shadowy name of Pyrrho; the new school differed from the Academy in refusing to claim certainty even for uncertainty, and in refusing to distinguish probable from improbable.[29] These 'Pyrrhonians' codified ten modes of argument (τρόποι) to undermine belief.[30]

Favorinus wrote several works on sceptical themes; besides *Plutarch* and *Against Epictetus* there was an *Alcibiades* and three books *On Cataleptic Phantasy* (the Stoic principle of cognition), but above all the books on the *Pyrrhonian Modes*, his finest work according to Philostratus, extremely subtle and ingenious according to Gellius, in which he set out the similarities and differences between Academic and Pyrrhonian sceptics.[31] The other books are known only through Galen's treatise *On the Best Education*, which is directed against them: it is alleged that Favorinus recommended argument on both sides of questions with the pupils left to make up their minds, and that in *Plutarch* he allowed the possibility of certain knowledge, but in

26. Plat. *Phdr.* 262 C–264 E; Fronto, *Laud. fum.* 4.
27. Fr. 23 M = 55 B; cf. Aristox. fr. 67 Wehrli. On Plato as plagiary see Riginos 165–6.
28. See in general Glucker (on Plutarch pp. 257–80).
29. *NA* 11. 5. 8, *PH* 1. 226–30; but see Frede, *Essays* 179–222.
30. The sources are translated and discussed by Annas–Barnes.
31. Barigazzi, edn. 172–5; according to Philostratus he rebutted the commonsense sneer that a Pyrrhonian would be no use as a judge (fr. 27 B). Plutarch also wrote on these matters, seeking to minimize the Academics' disagreements with Platonists like himself and (no doubt) to maximize those with the Pyrrhonians; he discussed the ten modes, and considered whether suspension of judgement entailed inaction ('Lamprias' nos. 63–4, 158, 210).

Alcibiades, a later work, he inclined to the view that nothing could be known. What Galen calls reprehensible inconsistency might rather be change of opinion with the years; more probably Favorinus, like a good Academic, chose to argue *in utramque partem*. Yet it was in Galen's interest—and his favourite polemical device—to find contradictions in the works attacked; we cannot say how fairly.

Gellius is aware that, with his school, Favorinus is wont 'inquirere potius quam decernere' (20. 1. 9), and reproduces his doctrine that Academics and Pyrrhonians differed on whether uncertainty was itself certain (11. 5. 8),[32] but offers no further evidence on his master's views. He himself tends towards Stoicism without adhering to it; he may owe to Favorinus a willingness to judge arguments on their merits, but struggles towards his own conclusions.

In 18. 1 Favorinus umpires a debate between a Stoic and a Peripatetic, disallowing an unfair argument from the latter; since the chapter is inspired by a passage of Cicero (pp. 48–9), we should not ascribe to Favorinus the words put in his mouth. In general, he inclined to Peripatetic opinions as the most persuasive;[33] sympathy with Stoicism is Gellius' own propensity, whereas Favorinus' opinion of the Academy's long-standing foe will not have been improved either by Stoic (and Cynic) mockery of his physical imperfections[34] or by the anti-Stoic arguments of his friend Plutarch. All the same, as Plutarch uses Stoic doctrines when they suit him, so Favorinus draws abundantly on Stoic and Cynic motifs in Περὶ φυγῆς; he made frequent and favourable reference to Demetrius the Cynic (fr. 98 B); and despite his epistemological dispute with Epictetus he quotes his scathing words on philosophers in name only and cites his commandment to bear and forbear (*NA* 17. 19). But there was no denying Epictetus' moral grandeur, and Favorinus was no less entitled to raid the enemy than Seneca to reconnoitre Epicurus. Not that he himself was either an ascetic or a rigorist; he could get expansively drunk after dinner (*NA* 2. 22. 25) and defined χάρις as a relaxation of strict standards when required by friendship (*NA* 1. 3. 27 = fr. 100 B).

It is as an Academic that Favorinus attacked the astrologers (*NA* 14. 1 = fr. 3 B),[35] demonstrating the folly of belief in them. Gellius' suspicion that he was speaking for mere show has disappeared by § 32, where Favorinus counsels his audience against trusting their prophecies because they are

32. No significance attaches to 'probabile' in Favorinus' mouth (3. 1. 4); the adjective is frequent in the *Nights*.

33. *Symp.* 8. 10: he revives a theory of Democritus' so absurd it seems intended to win support for Aristotle's view. See Glucker 287–90.

34. Luc. *Eun.* 7.

35. For the common stock of arguments against astrology laid down by Carneades see Fr. Boll, *JbClPh* Supp.² 21 (1894) 181–2 (whose stemma omits Basil. *Hex.* 6. 5–7), Bouché-Leclercq 570–627; cf. MacMullen, *Enemies* 328 n. 11.

occasionally right, and §§ 35–6, where he argues that we are better off without any predictions, favourable or unfavourable, true or false.[36]

The other full-length discourse, in *NA* 12. 1, on the superiority of the natural mother over wet-nurses,[37] may recall or rival Plutarch's Τιτθευτικός ('Lamprias', no. 114); the doctrine is implied in his essay *On Natural Affection*.[38] Besides the supposed ill-effects of the wrong person's milk,[39] and the moralistic desire that a woman be a total mother, we may discern (as elsewhere in that age) a high valuation of familial ties. Favorinus had been devoted to his sister, whom he mentions along with his parents at fr. 96 xi 22–4 B; in fr. 125 B he makes Solon describe fraternal concord (another of Plutarch's themes) as stronger than any rampart. It is brothers and friends whose quarrels he discusses in 2. 12. 5.

Favorinus wrote a work on Socrates and his art of love;[40] there is nothing of that in Gellius, except his deep affection for his teacher. On the other hand, the definition of χάρις cited above comes in a long chapter (1. 3) on how far one may breach strict morality to help a friend:[41] Chilo the Spartan sage, it is recalled, was troubled on his deathbed by nothing save his doubt whether he had been right in persuading his fellow judges to acquit a guilty friend, though himself voting for conviction; passages from Theophrastus and Cicero are adduced but found to give no useful answer, the quotation from Favorinus being inserted like a wedge into a sequence of extracts from the former. To Chilo, too, is attributed the advice 'so love as if one day to hate', and he is quoted out of Plutarch as saying that he who has no enemies has no friends.

Although Gellius quotes Theophrastus at length, either in Greek or in his own translation, his citation of the source as 'his first book *On Friendship*, if I remember rightly' induced Mercklin (p. 654) to suppose that though he had once read the work, his quotations come from somewhere else; but such

36. The Peripatetic Dicaearchus preferred not to know the future (Cic. *Diu.* 2. 105, cf. 22–3); Plutarch, the priest of Pythian Apollo, disagreed, even using Stoic arguments (Sandbach, LCL *Moralia* xv. 99), and sought to reconcile belief in prophecy with 'Academic' doctrine ('Lamprias' nos. 71, 131). Cf. Diogenian. Epicur. fr. 4. 39–65 Gercke, Luc. *Astr.* 28–9, Ach. Tat. 1. 3. 2–3, Hld. 2. 24. 6–7.

37. For the social context see ch. 2 n. 68. This ch.—not in the florilegia but quoted twice by Diceto (i. 43–6, 181 Stubbs)—was exploited in the Renaissance by medical and moral authors, and translated into French in 1534 (App. n. 19), into English by Wm. Painter, *The Palace of Pleasure* 1. 23, and into French again by the gynaecologist J.-L. Moreau, *Mémoires de la Soc. médicale d'émulation* 1 (V [1797/8]) 389–95 (at § 2 giving 'voir l'enfant', see ch. 3 n. 55), who compared it favourably with Rousseau's plea in bk. 1 of *Émile*.

38. Chrysippus had assumed the use of wet-nurses (*SVF* iii. 733–5); for protests see Tac. *Germ.* 20. 1, *Dial.* 28. 4, 29. 1, [Plut.] *Mor.* 5 C, [Quint.] *Decl. Mai.* 18. 3; cf. *CIL* vi. 19128. 5, and contrast M. Ant. *Med.* 5. 4, P. Lond. III 951 verso 2–5. See Gourevitch, *Mal* 233–59 and Bradley. Jerome, *Ep.* 107. 4. 7 (CSEL 55. 295), takes a nurse for granted. Gregory I ap. Bede *HE* 1. 27 complains.

39. Soranus 2. 18–20 had recently discussed the need to find the right nurse (for preference, but not always, the mother, p. 65. 14–20 Ilberg).

40. Barigazzi, edn. 161–9.

41. Cf. pp. 32, 200; *Cat. Dist.* 3. 3.

affectations are conventional.[42] One might well doubt if either Plutarch or Favorinus would have quoted Theophrastus verbatim at such length; that Favorinus is not the source is shown by the disruptive intrusion of § 27, a self-interpolation on Gellius' part,[43] but, as Mercklin saw, if it had been Plutarch, Pericles' dictum at § 20 'One should collaborate with one's friend, but stop short of the gods (ἀλλὰ μέχρι τῶν θεῶν)', would have run 'at the altar (μέχρι τοῦ βωμοῦ)' as it does whenever he quotes it. Gellius may therefore have read Theophrastus, as well as Plutarch, for himself; in any case he did read Cicero. The unattributed tales about Chilo, however, may well come either from Plutarch or from Favorinus, who like Gellius bestows on him (fr. 96 xviii 41–2 B) the advice on love that others ascribe to Bias of Priene. The story of his deathbed doubts recurs in Diogenes Laertius (1. 71), but with only two judges on the bench; we should not regard Favorinus as Diogenes' main source or ascribe to him whatever we also find in Gellius.[44] He certainly wrote about friendship; frr. 101–2 B concern flatterers, whom he will naturally, like Plutarch, have distinguished from true friends. At 2. 12. 5 he finds in Solon's supposed law against neutrality in stasis[45] the lesson that friends of quarrelling parties, instead of standing aside, should take over the dispute and resolve it in agreement. However, Plutarch wrote him an epistle Περὶ φιλίας ('Lamprias' no. 132), and others too will have treated of the subject.

Among several fragments in which Favorinus discusses Socrates is *NA* 2. 1. 3 (fr. 65 M = 97 B) alleging that he often stood stock-still from dawn to dawn. This is the incident of Plato, *Symp.* 220 C–D conflated with the habit of 175 B, and reinterpreted at § 1 as training for endurance;[46] as § 2, as in Plato, Socrates is lost in thought. Either Gellius or more likely Favorinus has combined intellectual concentration with physical askesis; Favorinus too is probably responsible for §§ 4–5, in which Socrates' healthy mode of life preserves him against the Great Plague of Athens.[47]

The source-critics frequently assume that, whenever Favorinus speaks in Greek, Gellius was quoting from a written work. This will be true of 12. 1, even of 14. 1; the words that Gellius remembers hearing delivered amid

42. See ch. 2 n. 27; or else Gellius' note was defective.

43. Wissowa 738: 'bei uns würde es eine Fußnote sein'. In theory, one Favorinian excerpt could have been injected into another (Mensching, edn. 55 n. 35), but nothing speaks for such a notion.

44. Wilamowitz, 'Epistula' 142–64; cf. Mensching, edn. 62.

45. Leaving aside Solon's own ὥσπερ ἐν μεταιχμίῳ (fr. 37. 9 W) and such traditions as as Plut. *Sol.* 29. 2, D.L. 1. 58, I cannot see how mass-participation in aristocratic faction-fights could have suited its ends as it did Peisistratus' and Cleisthenes', nor why Lysias (*Or.* 31) should not have treated departure from Athens as an aggravation of the offence; I prefer the view that the law was devised after Philon's case to cow hankerers after the Three Thousand. Suspect, Chaumette told the Paris sections, were 'Ceux qui, n'ayant rien fait contre la liberté, n'ont aussi rien fait pour elle.' For authenticity, Rhodes ad loc. 'Arist.', with bibliography.

46. Cf. X. *Mem.* 1. 2. 1, 4; 1. 5. 3–4; 1. 6. 7–10; 3. 12; 4. 7. 9; D.L. 2. 22.

47. Cf. Ael. *VH* 13. 27 (Socrates alone immune), D.L. 2. 25 (Socrates often immune).

universal applause (9. 8. 3)[48] are found at the end of a longer extract in Stobaeus (fr. 104 B). But Gellius spent whole days in Favorinus' company, imbibing such wisdom as that fierce invective does less harm than feeble praise;[49] nor will he have missed the declamations that even Greekless Romans flocked to hear. Granted that his memory was not so good as the elder Seneca's, he could remember (or write down) the odd *sententia*; but he also had access to his master's text.

If Favorinus vied with Plutarch in the number of books composed, he must have repeated himself no less often; nevertheless it is easy, perhaps too easy,[50] to suppose that Gellius made special use of his Ἀπομνημονεύματα and Παντοδαπὴ ἱστορία, the former a disorganized collection of anecdotes about philosophers in at least five books and the latter a work of miscellaneous information in twenty-four.

At 3. 17. 3 Gellius records that Aristotle paid three talents Attic for a few books of Speusippus'; D.L. 4. 5 relates that according to Favorinus' Ἀπομνημονεύματα (fr. 9 Mensching = 39 B) Aristotle paid this sum for Speusippus' books (τὰ βιβλία). This should denote his entire library, rather than the 'libros pauculos' in Gellius; Mensching baulks at the discrepancy (edn. 56–7), but either author may have misexpanded *libros* or βιβλία from his notes. No evidence links the rest of *NA* 3. 17 with Favorinus, but the allegation in §§ 4–6, launched by Timon of Phleious (*SH* 828),[51] that Plato borrowed the substance of his *Timaeus* from a Pythagorean tractate would have interested this dealer in tales of plagiarism (frr. 23, 43–4 M = 55, 75–6 B).[52] Moreover, as a sceptic and a philosophical anecdotist, Favorinus had a double motivation for reading Pyrrho's pupil, whose Σίλλοι[53] spared no philosopher except his master; most quotations from Timon come from Sextus Empiricus the sceptic, Diogenes Laertius the philosophers' biographer, and Athenaeus the sniffer-out of their sins.[54]

---

48. Cf. Barigazzi on fr. 104, *Epicurea* 471–4 Usener, Gow on Theoc. 16. 63, *Rh. Her.* 4. 24, [Sotad.] 8. 4–7, *GDK* VII ii 20–4, Housman on Man. 4. 6, Sen. ap. Gell. 12. 2. 13, Apul. *Apol.* 20. 3–6, Servas. 2. 11–14, Boeth. *Cons. phil.* 2. 5. 23, A. Otho 270. 'Much would have more' (*ODEP* 550).

49. *NA* 19. 3, cf. Cic. *Att.* 12. 21. 1. As both practitioner and victim, Favorinus ought to have known the futility of immoderate abuse.

50. For caution see Mensching 52–3, 56–7; cf. Wissowa 735–6. The Ἀπομνημονεύματα are at best alluded to by ἀπομνημονεύειν 13. 25. 12 (an entirely different context); Παντοδαπὴ ἱστορία is one of the fanciful titles cited at pr. 8.

51. For the opening words see Holford-Strevens, 'Two Notes'; for the story, Burkert 225–7.

52. Verses 2–3 are found in late writers on Platonic and Pythagorean matters (see Lloyd-Jones and Parsons ad loc.), but Taurus' commentary on *Timaeus* is less likely a source for Gellius than Favorinus' snippets.

53. 'Squint-eyes', hence lampoons that view askance. Gellius uses the singular Σίλλος; such variations are frequent in ancient titles, but the absence of book-number tells against direct use. No other Roman cites a single line of Timon's, though the Hellenized Tiberius accepted dedication of a commentary (D.L. 9. 109).

54. Quotations from Timon outnumber those for any other poet except Callimachus in *SH*, and any except Euphorion and Rhianus in *CA*.

In 16. 15 Gellius notes that Theophrastus attributed two hearts to the Paphlagonian partridge and Theopompus two livers to the Bisaltian hare;[55] Stephanus of Byzantium repeats the latter statement, 'as Theopompus reports, and Favorinus [fr. 61 M = 86 B]'. Although Mensching shows (edn. 53, cf. 25) that this need not mean 'as according to Favorinus Theopompus relates', it is not unreasonable to suppose that Favorinus was Gellius' source, and probably for both relations.

One certain quotation from Favorinus appears at 10. 12. 9–10, on the mechanical dove invented by Archytas of Tarentum (fr. 66 M = 93 B). The words 'Fauorinus philosophus memoriarum ueterum exsequentissimus' may suggest the Ἀπομνημονεύματα, the subject of discoveries the Παντοδαπὴ ἱστορία; both recent editors hedge their bets.

In 14. 6 Gellius relates that a friend with a literary reputation and a bookish way of life offered 'librum grandi uolumine, doctrinae omnigenus ut ipse dicebat praescatentem', which he first accepted gratefully 'tamquam si Copiae cornum nactus essem', but then, finding it to contain 'mera miracula' (cf. Varro, *Sat.* 286 Bücheler) of no moral value, returned to its owner. Nietzsche, in a study of Diogenes Laertius' sources, suggested that Gellius had borrowed the Παντοδαπὴ ἱστορία; Hertz's objection that he would not so mishandle the work of his beloved teacher found no favour with contemporary scholars.[56]

The words 'doctrinae omnigenus' resemble Favorinus' title; but how else should Gellius say 'all kinds of learning'? To translate Παντοδαπὴ ἱστορία, he could have anticipated Julius Valerius' 'Omnigenae historiae' (p. 13. 3 Kübler). Moreover, a *liber grandi uolumine* must be a single large volume;[57] but Favorinus' twenty-four books can hardly have been available in such an absurd and hippocentaur-like monstrosity as the one-volume Homer of D. 32. 52. 1. That Gellius ironically calls its author 'doctissime uirorum', and congratulates him with a Heracleitean double edge on his polymathy (§ 5), does not suffice to indicate Favorinus, even if the *Suda* describes him as a polymath in every branch of learning.

Despite Favorinus' concern in several fragments with inventions and inventors, nothing in Clement's report (*Strom.* 1. 79. 3) of authors who discussed the first grammarian (cf. Gell. § 3) need come from him. Nor, since among the many sources for Diogenes Laertius' lists of namesakes Favorinus

55. These items are cited, with the same authorities, in clearly separated treatments of the creatures in question by Athenaeus (390 C, 401 A–B) and Aelian (*N. An.* 10. 35, 5. 27), who depend on Alexander of Myndos (M. Wellmann, *Hermes* 26 (1891) 481–566).

56. Nietzsche, *RhM²* 23 (1893) 642–7 (*Werke* II. i. 91–6 Colli–Montinari); Hertz, *Opusc. Gell.* 72–85; Maass 49, 104; Wilamowitz, *Epistula* 145. The case for the theory is made anew by Barigazzi, pp. 215–16, that against by Mensching, pp. 29–30. To find criticism of Favorinus in the general complaint at pr. 11 is not fair. Those who with M. Pezzati, *ASNP* 3 (1973) 837–60, maintain that Gellius both returned Favorinus' work as unprofitable and made large use of its contents apparently find neither contradiction in their theory nor dishonesty in his conduct.

57. *Liber* here, as at 18. 9. 5, denotes the roll, not the work (contrast 16. 19. lemma; 17. 11. 6; Jul. Val. loc. cit.).

appears but once (fr. 1 M = 32 B), may he be held responsible for D.L. 8. 46–7, on persons called Pythagoras, and for Gellius' 'quot fuerint Pythagorae nobiles, quot Hippocratae', even though he is quoted immediately afterwards for something else (fr. 27 M = 59 B); Diogenes flits among authors like a bee among flowers. The Homeric disposition in books lettered *A* to *Ω* does not require Favorinus' work to treat of the Homeric problems Gellius disdains; although his author inquired whether Odysseus wandered the Mediterranean, as Aristarchus, or the Atlantic, as Crates argued (cf. Sen. *Ep.* 88. 7),[58] and although Favorinus' names for the latter waterway (frr. 50–50a M = 82 B) are known to be Cratetean, there is no evidence that he also considered the local habitation of Cimmerii and Laestrygones.[59]

Rather than posit an actual book, whether Favorinus' Παντοδαπὴ ἱστορία, Sotion's Κέρας Ἀμαλθείας,[60] or any other, one might surmise (p. 46) that Gellius draws on a moralistic tract, perhaps supplemented by his reading in Homeric scholarship; the ancient (or rather poetical) place-names in § 4 were added from another source. Some are found in Stephanus of Byzantium, an author who occasionally cites Favorinus; but that proves nothing. We learn from Photius (*Bibl.* 164, 103^b 4–6) that the Παντοδαπὴ ἱστορία included aetiologies of names, which Stephanus duly quotes: Argilos is so called from the Thracian word for 'mouse' (fr. 47 M = 79 B), Cremmyon from the mythological sow (fr. 63 M = 88 B); Acte, the old name for Attica, as Gellius records, from the locally born King Actaeus, as he does not (fr. 59 M = 84 B). Favorinus, in fact, wrote on the origins of names, not necessarily all place-names—though only these were of interest to Stephanus —and not all changed; Gellius notes certain places' change of name, but no derivations. Such μετονομασίαι had been collected by Callimachus and Nicanor of Cyrene; Gellius' source may in turn have drawn on them.

Favorinus delivered a discourse ἐπὶ τῶν λήρων, on the same subject as Plutarch's *De garrulitate*; it is highly praised by Philostratus (*VS* 491). Gellius preaches a learned sermon against idle talk (1. 15), citing Favorinus' reinterpretation of Eur. *Bacch.* 386–8 as aimed no less at chatter than at blasphemy (§ 17); the same view is implicit at Plut. *Mor.* 503 C (*Garr.* 3), where it is coupled with an allusion to the Homeric 'fence of teeth' similar to the moralizing interpretation in § 3. He also offers citations from Eupolis (§ 12) and Epicharmus (§ 15), who make no other appearance in the *Nights*. It is reasonable to see Favorinus' declamation as his source.[61]

There remains the problem of Favorinus as a student of Latin and exponent of Roman culture—even law. Although we have no evidence that

58. See Gem. 6. 10–12, 16–20; 16. 22–3 for Crates' theories.
59. Barigazzi's interpretation (p. 236, on fr. 82) of Fav. fr. 96 xix 35–43 is incomprehensible.
60. O. Regenbogen, *RE* xviii/3. 320, cll. 'Copiae cornum' § 2, but see 18. 6. lemma.
61. Cf. Barigazzi on fr. 6. I would also assign to Favorinus the quotation from Hesiod in § 14 (perhaps he used his friend Plutarch's commentary, cf. fr. 89 Sandbach); but that in § 19 from Aristophanes' *Frogs*, a play Gellius has clearly read, may be his own postscript (if so, the distortion of its sense shows that he had learnt the tricks of Favorinus' trade).

he wrote, or even declaimed, in Latin, he not only has Latin, as well as Greek, read at his table (2. 22. 1; 3. 19. 1), but frequently discusses the Latin language and Roman institutions. Modesty requires him to describe his Latin studies (apparently pursued with 'Probus noster', 3. 1. 6) as spare-time and haphazard (13. 25. 4), just as politeness makes the jurist Sex. Caecilius Africanus call him the supreme expert in Roman as well as Greek matters (20. 1. 20).[62] But Africanus vindicates the Twelve Tables against his strictures, as Fronto (2. 26) the Latin vocabulary of colour; in 18. 7 Favorinus, in ignorance whether *contio* is classical Latin for a public speech (δημηγορία), consults the bad-tempered grammarian Domitius, and then asks Gellius for examples, which he provides. Though Gellius can disagree with Apollinaris, the only occasions on which he actually teaches his teachers are this chapter and 8. 2, where in exchange for ten Greek words in common use but 'adulterina et barbara' (sc. non-Attic), he gives Favorinus ten Latin ones not found in ancient authors.

Allusions to early and Republican Rome being found in Favorinus' speeches, he could well, declaiming at Rome, contemplate a prediction whether King Pyrrhus or M'. Curius would win their battle (*NA* 14. 2. 24). At fr. 95. 26 B he calls himself a Roman; at *NA* 4. 1. 18 his citizenship imposes a linguistic obligation (p. 87). Interest in such matters seems therefore undeniable.

In Plutarch's *Roman Questions* (28 = test. 20 B) Favorinus' explanation is cited for the Roman custom of telling children to go out into the open air before they swore by Hercules: it was to prevent rash oaths. The conjecture, whether recalled from conversation or excerpted from a treatise against hasty speech ('Wisely therefore do the Romans bid their children ...'), did not require any knowledge of Latin, let alone the degree of acquaintance Favorinus shows in Gellius. The only assertion that he wrote on Latin words comes from Macrobius' discussion, *Sat.* 3. 18. 13, of a nut called *terentina* so soft that the slightest touch will break it, 'de qua in libro Fauorini sic reperitur: item quod quidam Tarentinas oues uel nuces dicunt, quae sunt terentinae a tereno, quod est Sabinorum lingua molle, unde Terentios quoque dictos putat Varro ad Libonem primo'. Favorinus writes that some people called this species of nut, and a breed of sheep, 'Tarentine', from Tarentum, but they were properly 'terentine', from the Sabine for 'soft', which Varro proposed as the etymology of his own gentile name Terentius.[63] The real Favorinus would have invoked the Greek τέρην 'tender', 'soft', without recourse to Sabine; but Varro of Sabine Reate is as ready to cite that

---

62. By a like politeness Favorinus tells the jurist that he reads the Twelve Tables with as much delight as Plato's *Laws* (§ 4), which no one is meant to believe. Cf. Caesar (for whose exquisite manners see Suet. *Iul.* 53) ap. Plin. *NH* 7. 117.

63. For Varro's fascination with his *nomen* cf. *NA* 11. 6. 4, where it is imposed even on a mulctee; *LL* 8. 7, 14, 36; 9. 38, 54–5, 59–60.

language as Gellius to quote him. Dismissing 'in libro Fauorini' as a blind,[64] Barigazzi (test. 48) supposes Macrobius' source to be *NA* 8. 14, where Favorinus has a 'most amusing argument' with a fool about verbal ambiguity (cf. 11. 12), unusual expressions in Naevius and Cn. Gellius are considered, and etymologies are listed—not from Varro, but from Nigidius, an unlikely source for Sabine origins. More probably Favorinus discussed *terentinae* in the mutilated book 20; perhaps he was given the last word in the *Nights*.

Until Constantine established a Latin-speaking capital in the East, a Hellene had little to gain among his fellows by parading knowledge of their masters' tongue,[65] especially after the Greek revival. Unlike Caecilius of Cale Acte, and professing a modesty that had not deterred pseudo-Longinus,[66] Plutarch, despite his knowledge of Roman literature, declines to compare Demosthenes and Cicero; his readers sought rivals to the Attic orators not at Rome but amongst themselves. Aristeides Quintilian (p. 61. 4–25 W-I) repels Cicero's unlooked-for attack on his art; that is no treason, and Aristeides may well belong to the Latinizing fourth century. A minor poet uses Vergil, Lucian's wage-slave intellectual speaks for Juvenal's hungry Greekling;[67] their sources are not confessed.

Greeks write freely on Latin in Latin, but in Greek only for historical aetiology or to claim the parentage of some expression.[68] Athenaeus, who quotes the obscurest Greeks, all but ignores writers in Latin; a reference to Sulla's farces apart,[69] only Varro (160 C) and L. Aurunculeius Cotta (273 B) are cited, both by the Roman Larensis, Varro's descendant, who observes that his ancestor had baffled Roman grammarians with a Greek proverb. Favorinus, writing in Greek, may have noted that a Greek word had yielded a Latin one, or, if his subject-matter was Roman, made fleeting mention of a Latin text (translated or paraphrased like *cedant arma togae* at Plut. *Cic.* 51. 1,

64. At *Sat.* 7. 13. 8 Dysarius claims to have heard a 'sermo' (λόγος) from Egypt, which he doubted but found confirmed 'libris anatomicorum'. Nothing of the kind: Macrobius has pillaged *NA* 10. 10. 'Apul.' *De mundo* 13 introduces a paraphrase of *NA* 2. 22. 3–29 with the words 'At Fauorinus, non ignobilis sapiens, haec de uentis refert', which if the *Nights* had perished we should understand as *scribit*.

65. See Egger 259–76; A. Gudeman, *TAPhA* 21 (1890) pp. vii–x; L. Hahn, *Philologus* Supp. 10 (1907) 675–718; Balsdon, *Rom. and Al.* 123–8, 131–5. As a self-made Hellene, Favorinus could afford such lapses even less than others.

66. Caec. Cal. fr. 153 Of, cf. Plut. *Dem.* 2. 4; [Long.] 12. 4. For Plutarch's less than perfect knowledge of Latin see Glucker 386–9.

67. On P. Bon. 4 see Lloyd-Jones–Parsons, 'Cat. Orph.' 88, Holford-Strevens, 'Two Notes'; for Lucian's use of Juvenal see now E. Courtney, comm. on Juvenal, pp. 624–9.

68. This is true even of most etymologies in Plutarch's *Roman Questions*, where the odd exception is justified by the subject. Crepereius Calpurnianus is pilloried by Lucian, *Hist. conscr.* 15 for unnecessary use of Latin words. The hostile six-book commentary on Cic. *Rep.* by Didymus (Claudius, despite Amm. 22. 16. 16, who knew only Chalcenterus; what was Cicero to Alexandria?) will have been in Latin. Even Claudius Aelianus of Praeneste is sparing of Roman subject-matter. (A disastrous Christian exception: Just. Mart. *Apol.* 1. 26. 2 ~ *CIL* vi. 567.)

69. Ath. 261 C: the source will be Nicolaus of Damascus, proving his assertion about Sulla's cheerful nature. Romans who write in Greek (the Quintilii, Rutilius Rufus) are acceptable if their Greek is good; Blaesus of Capreae will have been an Italiote.

or the fatal Vergilian quotation at Cass. Dio 75. 10. 2), but not determined whether *parcus* 'thrifty' came from *par arcae* 'like a strongbox' or *parum* 'too little' (3. 19), much less asserted that 'our' Vergil had improved on Homer, as he does in an illogical and easily detachable digression (12. 1. 20), as if there were no Greek poet he could have cited.[70] Nor will he have bespattered his Greek with Latin equivalents for scientific terms; it passes belief, even if he supplied the aberrant Greek wind-names of 2. 22, that he included the Latin nomenclature in his Greek miscellany. Gellius is following a different source, which like other Latin accounts related the sidewinds, even in the eight-wind system, to the solstitial risings and settings, and appended a discussion of various local winds.[71]

Favorinus is at times a mere lay-figure who has no more to do with the words put in his mouth than any other participant in an ancient dialogue. Yet it seems clear he sometimes talked of Latin matters; why else should he be the lay-figure rather than Fronto or Julianus or Apollinaris? Even if he normally spoke in Greek,[72] he will sometimes have used Latin, if only to accommodate less gifted pupils; he is explicitly portrayed as speaking it at 3. 16. 17–18, where in explaining the Homeric περιπλομένου ἐνιαυτοῦ (*Od.* 11. 248) as a twelvemonth near its end, he employs the choice Ciceronian *adfecto anno*.[73]

In 5. 11 Favorinus rebuts the Bachelor's Dilemma (as we may call it) propounded by Bias of Priene: 'You will marry (ἄξεις [*sic*]) either a pretty woman or an ugly one; if pretty, you will have a whore (κοινήν), if ugly, you will have a torment (ποινήν); neither is acceptable; *ergo*, you should not marry.' He escapes between the horns: the bride may be neither a beauty nor a fright, but present the intermediate appearance Ennius called *stata*, 'regular';[74] Favorinus himself neatly ('non mi hercule inscite') terms it *uxoria*, 'wifely'.[75] There is no Greek word that this can render: had Favorinus used

---

70. Cf. Theoc. 3. 15–16. The rock-born Aeneas' cruelty is reinforced by nurturing tigresses; but Favorinus has just been speaking of children made *unlike* their parents by their nurses' milk, 'Scite igitur ... ubera tigres' will be Gellius' interpolation; 'quoniam uidelicet ... indolem configurat' will come from Favorinus. See too ch. 4 n. 5.

71. Indeed, a third source seems needed for § 22, where Iapyx (N 60° W) blows 'exaduersum eurum', that is diametrically opposite the S 60° E wind: in § 7 Eurus was due E and in § 12 'aduersus' denoted opposition ἐπ' εὐθείας (contrast Arist. *Meteor.* 363ᵇ18–20). Masselink 145 notes that the local winds of §§ 19–24, all fitted by Timosthenes into his 12-wind system, are of another order than the *atabulus* of § 25; but the opening words of §§ 19 and 25, which say the same thing in different ways, do not assist his theory of a division by Favorinus (who cannot have cited Roman poets in a Greek text), rather than carelessness by Gellius.

72. Polemo i. 163. 5–7 Förster; at *NA* 2. 1. 3 Marshall's ⟨*Graece*⟩ improves the sense and sets up long-range *uariatio* with 1. 2. 6.

73. Discussed in 15. 5, from Apollinaris, and possibly put in Favorinus' mouth by Gellius himself (otherwise Hertz, *Op. Gell.* 82 n.); but that is not the point. For the interpretation 'non confecto esse anno sed adfecto' cf. Eust. 1682. 27–8.

74. *Sc.* CXVIII Jocelyn; such women, says the speaker, are generally chaste.

75. A familiar word in a new sense. '*Vxoriam* hanc dictam puto, ut differat a *Virginea*, uel forte *Meretricia*, quae praestantiores esse solent' (Falster, 'Noct. Rip.' 1020). Nor should wives be sexually skilful (Lucr. 4. 1277). See too Beroaldus on Apul. *Met.* 6. 24.

γαμική, the obvious equivalent was *coniugalis* or *conubialis*.[76] Nor, writing Greek, could he have quoted Ennius, though he might well have quoted Euripides: 'It is not safe to receive beauty beyond the mean' (fr. 928 Nauck); he would also (as at fr. 96 xxiv 26 B) have expressed the notion 'take to wife' by the middle ἄγομαι, not the active thrice used in this chapter. Gellius either invents or reconstructs a Latin conversation; if when he contemplated marriage, Favorinus was still alive, he surely sought his counsel.[77]

We are given, in any case, to understand that Favorinus spoke a Latin after Gellius' own heart, using recherché expressions, but within due bounds: in rebuking the youthful archaist of 1. 10 he reinterprets Caesar's warning against artificial analogy, to shun the unheard-of and unusual word like a rock.[78] There is no conflict with Fronto's pursuit of the unexpected and unlooked-for word, which was tempered by considerations of taste and perspicuity;[79] but although the Latin precept matches Favorinus' Greek practice, Gellius may have attached his name, and Fronto's in 19. 8 (p. 98), to a passage from a book that he himself admired.[80]

The narrative of 4. 1, though fictitious, is instructive. Among the crowd at the Palatium awaiting the *salutatio* is a grammarian airing his school-like knowledge with unbearable pomposity, who inflicts on Favorinus, a virtual stranger, a lecture on the different genders and declensions of *penus*, 'stored provisions', found in ancient writers.[81] Favorinus gently interrupts: he does not particularly wish to know all that; what difference does the gender or declension of *penus* make to speaker or to listener, provided one avoids a downright barbarism (§ 5)? But he does wish to know its definition. The grammarian does not know what a definition is; Favorinus, having humbled him for his ignorance of philosophy, and still more for his inability to define a word used by Vergil (here he tosses in the variant readings at *Aen.* 1. 703), explains the term himself, out of Gellius' second-favourite jurist Masurius Sabinus, adding that for a Roman citizen to call a thing by the wrong Latin word is as shameful as calling a man by the wrong name (§ 18). Thus, says Gellius, would Favorinus steer a conversation from trivialities to worthwhile

76. Both Beloe and Rolfe render 'conjugal'; 'conjugale' Marache, though Verteuil i. 378 has 'celle des épouses'. Were Gellius translating with conscious felicity, we should expect e.g. 'γαμικήν, quam non incommode dixeris uxoriam'. The *actio rei uxoriae* (abolished in C. 5. 13) is ἡ *reuxorías* in Byzantine jurists; the Basilica tr. of D. 32. 29. pr. is lost.

77. Cf. Callim. *epigr.* 1, Val. Max. 7. 2. ext. 1 (p. 327. 6–16 Kempf²). Since Favorinus, who was fond of revising well-known saws (Barigazzi on test. 34), elsewhere cites the Dilemma (fr. 122 B), albeit ascribed to Solon instead of Bias, we may believe that he repeated orally, in Latin, what he also included in a Greek treatise on marriage (once more emulating Plutarch), but not that Gellius worked from such a text. But Gellius may have made the chapter up himself, recalling the Dilemma from his schooldays (cf. [Hermog.] 193. 19–22 R). Perhaps ἄξεις is intended to avoid hiatus (which Favorinus did not eschew; Barigazzi, edn. 34–5).

78. See Funaioli, *GRF* 147; Lebek 348 n. 29; Holford-Strevens, 'Five Notes' 143; and for the youth's moral pretext p. 188. 79. *Ep. M. Caes.* 4. 3. 1, 3, cf. pp. 163–5.

80. This ch. underlies Macr. *Sat.* 1. 5. 1, whence perhaps Gir. Camb. *Exp. Hib.*, intro., ll. 26, 36–7 Scott–Martin.

81. A favourite theme with grammarians (cf. Hosius ad loc.).

subjects, without showing off or dragging them in by force. A few more legal quotations end the chapter.

That Favorinus, with his personal charm, his rhetor's invention, and his polyhistor's stock of themes and information, could take charge of the proceedings is entirely credible. He may have been more interested in semantics than in accidence; but the assertion in § 18 is meant to anticipate the charge of merely substituting one pedantry for another.[82] Gellius certainly does not despise the niceties of accidence (4. 16; 6. 9; 9. 14); wishing to tell us both that *penus* is variously treated in ancient authors and that the jurists have spent time discussing what it means, rather than lecture us in dry professorial tones he adopts (as in 14. 6. 4) a species of *praeteritio* to let us know what he only pretends is not worth knowing,[83] and then deploys his extracts from Sabinus. Having decided to speak through a mask, he cannot ascribe the view that grammar is unimportant to a grammarian (Domitius the Mad apart) or a rhetor; but a philosopher may say so, and Favorinus' value-judgements bear authority. He does not discuss accidence elsewhere, but cares for purity of diction (8. 2; 18. 7), against which might be urged the principle of 4. 1. 5, 'quid enim refert mea eiusque quicum loquor?'; and the etymological studies in 3. 19 and Macr. *Sat.* 3. 18. 13 are of no practical use at all. When in 18. 7 Domitius abuses him for being interested, although a philosopher, in nothing but petty words, he tolerantly ascribes his rudeness to 'melancholia' and likens the outburst to the sayings of Antisthenes and Diogenes (§ 4), but—like Gellius—does not ponder its justice or take it to heart. 'Sachant plaisanter,' observes Marache, 'il sait se montrer indulgent à l'égard des faiblesses d'autrui ... Favorinus goûte en artiste la verve du personnage';[84] this forbearing enjoyment implies a self-confidence that criticism cannot shake.[85] The only message of 4. 1. 5 is that if the ancients decline a word in several ways, any one of them is right—and the unintentional message of 18. 7. 4 that moral saws are for relish, not for guidance.

If Favorinus discussed the rhetorical function of tautology, it was not as in 13. 25, less because he cites Latin examples and echoes Gellius' view of Cato (§ 12) than because all the Greek instances come from Homer and the one Aristophanic play that Gellius has demonstrably read, the *Frogs*; there is nothing from the orators, not even ἀξιῶ καὶ δέομαι.[86] Who can say

---

82. But the forensic orator needs to know the term's extension (Quint. 7. 3. 13).

83. Note Fronto's interest in another variation, *Ep. M. Ant.* 1. 2. 11–12.

84. *Critique* 255.

85. The ancients' relish for rhetorical debate makes them readier than we to see the other side's point of view while maintaining their own: Critognatus declares that the Romans will enslave Gaul, but it is Caesar who makes him say so (*BG* 7. 77. 15). Gellius is not hinting at a fault in Favorinus, or in Antonine society, even if modern readers (like Beloe ad loc.) take Domitius' side.

86. Despite the interlocutor's comment in § 8. Contrast M. Caes. *Ep.* 5. 43. 1 (from Demosthenes, ch. 12 n. 75), and cf. D.H. *Dem.* 58.

whether he admired the vividness of Quadrigarius' battle-scene (9. 13. 5),[87] judged a verse of *Neruolaria* sufficient proof of Plautine authorship (3. 3. 6),[88] denied that his teacher Probus could suspect Sallust of periphrasis (3. 1. 6),[89] and justified Hyginus' wrong reading in Vergil by the wrong Lucretian parallel (1. 21. 5)?[90]

A more complex problem is posed by 17. 10. Favorinus, spending the summer with a friend at Antium, remarks that Vergil compared himself to a she-bear licking her cubs into shape, and besought his friends to burn the unfinished *Aeneid*. Since the resulting licence to fault the poem without dishonouring the poet had already been exploited by Hyginus (10. 16. 1, 11), Mercklin (p. 660) ascribed to him Favorinus' suggestion (17. 10. 8) that Vergil had not revised his picture (*Aen.* 3. 570–7) of Mt Etna in eruption,[91] unfavourably contrasted with its putative model Pi. *Pyth.* 1. 21–6; Kretzschmer (p. 106) preferred to invoke Probus. But Favorinus is likelier than any Roman to have supposed that Vergil (who even names a different foe of Zeus) was inspired by Pindar (cited at fr. 96 vi 31–2) rather than Lucretius;[92] the spirit of the criticism—hostility towards extravagance—is more happily expressed by Gellius himself in 2. 23 (where Caecilius appears coarse and bloated beside Menander), but conceivable in a master whose own speeches, however wordy, are at least free from the ludicrous excesses of a Polemo,[93] and who as a Greek might be disposed to find much Latin writing overblown.

---

87. With Favorinus' reaction in § 5 cf. Plut. *Mor.* 347 A on Thucydides' ἐνάργεια. Quadrigarius' simple, unadorned, almost conversational style (§ 4, cf. p. 184) might well seem elegant to a Greek taste, even Favorinus'—whereas Romano 61 finds the fragment 'una fredda narrazione' beside Livy.

88. See pp. 142–3.

89. The occasion is as much philosophical as philological (p. 186).

90. Cf. p. 140; but Gellius makes little use of Lucretius, p. 161.

91. Gamberale 150–1 denies that the criticisms in §§ 11–19 imply a want of *labor limae*; but Housman i. 349–50 finds in the *Aeneid*, but not the *Bucolics* or the *Georgics*, 'frigid hyperboles' inserted as stopgaps (*tibicines*), and cites from this very book passages where Vergil 'soars too near the stars' (vv. 423, 567, 619–20). The principle is the same, though the omission of v. 574 offers eloquent dissent on its application; but see Hardie 241–92.

92. Vergilian commentators occasionally cite Pindar, mainly for mythology; the 'Probus' who does so on *Buc.* 7. 61 is not the Berytian. On Vergil's independence of Pindar see Pontanus 67–73 (cf. Ascensius ad loc.); Turnebus, *Aduers.* 20. 18, citing Lucr. 6. 639–702. No doubt Vergil read all descriptions available, and depended on none. Favorinus merely asssumes that Pindar is scientifically correct in distinguishing smoke by day from flame by night, and Vergil wrong in deviating from him. Both Pontanus and Turnebus insist on Vergil's truth to fact; ancient evidence is collected by de la Cerda ad loc. Verg. In J. C. Scaliger's counter-attack (*Poet.* 245bD–247bB, cf. *Probl.* CIX, pp. 33–4) comes the characteristic outburst, 'Quasi uero nos Graeculorum famuli simus, ac non emendatores.' Heinze 490 observes that for [Long.] 35. 4 Etna instances the sublime in nature. Berthold, 'Carmen Pindari', finds similarities between this and other Favorinus-chapters, but denies that Gellius could have incorporated *Fremdgut* in them (p. 290); in fact, 17. 10 contains misunderstandings of Gellius' own (ch. 12 n. 50). For the Etna episode see now Hardie 263–5.

93. e.g. the terrestrial shipwreck, *A* 29 (cf. Sen. *Contr.* 8. 9, Norden i. 386) and the repetition of conceits (esp. *A* 10–11).

Favorinus' discussion of a judge's duty in 14. 2 is purely Roman; no other treatment was appropriate, for the *iudex* in a suit between citizens must, at least in public, prefer the *mos maiorum* to peregrine speculations. In 1. 13 Gellius himself discusses a moral problem in Roman terms; but if he felt in need of guidance, he would have turned at once to Favorinus. Perhaps the answer received was not the one recorded; but Gellius perceives no incongruity in letting Favorinus speak of Roman judicial ethics, as elsewhere of Roman law.[94]

In 20. 1 Favorinus finds fault with certain provisions of the Twelve Tables:[95] the law on haling a sick defendant to court perched on a beast of burden (*iumentum*) was cruel; that prescribing a penalty of 25 asses for assault absurdly lenient (one L. Veratius had gone round hitting people in the face, accompanied by a slave doling out the legal damages); the *lex talionis* for personal injury was unworkable; and the dissection of judgement-debtors by their creditors inhuman. The jurist Africanus replies that the provision for sickness did not encompass grave illnesses, and *iumentum* denoted a cart; *iniuria* covered only minor assaults, and in the decemvirs' time the *as* still weighed a pound;[96] the *lex talionis* was aimed at ensuring timely compensation; the law on judgement-debtors was designed to protect *fides* by preventing default, nor was there any case on record of its application. Fierce deterrents worked; if perjurers were still flung from the Tarpeian rock, there would not be so much false witness borne on oath. Mettus Fufetius had been torn apart for breaking his treaty with the king of Rome: a novel punishment and harsh, but as Vergil said he should have kept his word (*Aen.* 8. 643). The assembled company, including Favorinus, is convinced.

The story of Veratius is explicitly derived from Labeo's commentary on the Twelve Tables, the last known to us or Tribonian apart from Gaius'. Rather than posit a lost work by Africanus,[97] we should probably ascribe the factual statements to Labeo, and perhaps the moral judgements to Gellius, Africanus appearing because Gellius knew him through Favorinus,[98] and Favorinus because, as in 2. 26, he was the obvious opponent for the Roman expert to refute. He could not be expected to know what *morbus* and *iumentum* had (actually or supposedly) mean six hundred years beforehand; as a Greek he could legitimately find Roman institutions harsh. We no more know that the real Favorinus would have disapproved of them—or if he had, would have been thus won round—than that the real Africanus would have defended them.

---

94. No profound knowledge was required at 14. 1. 4: such things were familiar to any landowner. Cf. Plat. *Leg.* 844 A–D; Dem. 55; *OGI* 483. 101.

95. See Nörr, 'Rechtskritik' *passim*; M. Ducos, *REL* 62 (1984) 288–300.

96. Being indeed not a coin but a weight. Veratius' conduct caused the praetors to issue the *edictum generale* (§ 13, Coll. 2. 6. 1), cf. Kaser, *Priv.* i. 623 n. 27 (with i. 207 on magistrates' overriding statutes); for a different view P. Birks in Watson (ed.) 39–48.

97. Even if he was old-fashioned (Honoré, 'Julian's Circle' 11–12).

98. But not well enough to learn judicial procedure from him (ch. 15 n. 21).

Labeo may well have noted the want of evidence that either *talio* or dissection had taken place, deducing thence that they were prescribed *in terrorem*.[99] The ensuing *declamatiuncula* in Gellius seems too high-flown for juristic writing; but Labeo, with his penchant for explaining legal principles,[100] might observe that nothing was dearer to the ancient Romans than *fides*: they had cast perjurers to their death, they had torn Fufetius in two, and in order to protect credit they had enacted this grim sanction. On such a base Gellius could erect his altar to severity.

Whereas Labeo's contemporaries Varro (*Vit. p. R.* fr. 6 Riposati) and Livy (1. 28. 11) had found Fufetius' end inhuman, for Gellius it is only unprecedented and harsh; the comment Vergil had made to quell distaste by fastening the blame entirely on the criminal (see Servius ad loc.) is cited in triumph as the last word on the subject. But Varro, Livy, and Vergil had supped full on horrors in half a century of civil strife; Gellius, under the gentle Antonines, not having yet seen a Roman emperor murder cripples with his club,[101] felt able to admire the rugged ways of times long past.

Favorinus was no profound thinker; but his Παντοδαπὴ ἱστορία would even now find more readers than Taurus' commentary on *Timaeus*. His speeches, though more enervated, are less absurd than Polemo's, and beyond question he was the more reasonable man. It was not Favorinus who treated cities as his inferiors, or lusted after wealth and power;[102] and whatever Polemo might allege about magic and poisons, the charms by which he

99. For the ancient evidence see *FIRA* i. 33–4; Cass. Dio fr. 17. 8 also denies that the law was put into practice. Clearly our sources had no evidence of its enforcement, and since it was not formally repealed no annalist needed to invent a pathetic scene like that of Livy 8. 28. But in England, where documentation is far superior, the *peine forte et dure*, or pressing to death the prisoner mute of malice, though likewise 'purposely ordained to be exquisitely severe, that by that very means it might rarely be put in execution' (Blackstone, *Commentaries*, edn.¹ iv. 320), was certainly inflicted, and on persons who, unlike poor debtors, could have avoided it at will. It would be rash to believe what the ancients wished to think.

100. P. Stein, *Cambridge Law Journal* 31 (1972) 10–11. But Gellius' 'sic clientem ... censuit' echoes 5. 13. 2, 4.

101. Cass. Dio 72. 20. 3; Grosso 338–9 explains, and would gladly doubt, the fact. On the other hand, when brutality in the name of religion and taxation has become a matter of routine, Claudian can make the ghost of a Christian emperor declare that, if alive, he would have followed King Tullus' precedent in a like case (*Bell. Gild.* 1. 253–5). Ennius may have allowed himself nothing more than the rhetorical expression of pity at *Ann.* 125–6 Sk (cf. v. 158 with n.), which no more implies criticism of Tullus than Dionysius' ὁ δείλαιος and οἰκτρᾶς καὶ ἀσχήμονος τελευτῆς (*Ant.* 3. 30. 6–7; Dionysius is more Roman than the Romans, ibid. 2. 26); the nation that can portray weeping captives on coins celebrating conquest is little afflicted by guilt-feelings. Other authors relate the Alban's end without comment. To the mind that launched this legend, being torn in two was the fitting punishment for waiting to see who won.

102. Not even Polemo makes such allegations. Favorinus did not meddle with affairs of state; nor did he seek, or require, the huge fees that Polemo levied, not always justly, for the maintenance of his equipage (*AP* 11. 180–1, Philost. *VS* 533, 535, 538). It was no mark of especial meanness to decline the flamonium. See too frr. 104–5 B on wealth, 108 B on ambition (men are ridiculous when they aspire to things too great for them, detestable when they attain them, and pitiful when they fail, but enviable never).

attracted audiences and pupils were those of speech and personality.[103]
Punctilious in visiting his friends in sickness or at their children's birth (2. 26.
1; 12. 1. 2; 16. 3. 2), aware even when drunk that he must not monopolize the
conversation (2. 22. 25–6), calm under the assault of rudeness (4. 1. 4; 18. 7.
4), he imparted social grace along with intellectual curiosity. True, he was
full of himself, and in all the praise of Favorinus' style, instruction, and
personality the virtue of *grauitas* is not accorded him; yet he was a kindly man
and the best of company, the delight of the friends and followers whom he led
as if tethered to his tongue, 'ita sermonibus usquequaque amoenissimis
demulcebat'.[104]

103. 'A French gentleman expressed some surprise at the immense influence which Fox, a
man of pleasure, ruined by the dice-box and the turf, exercised over the English nation. "You
have not," said Pitt, "been under the wand of the magician"' (Macaulay, 'William Pitt', *Works*
x. 509).
104. Herodes longed for the honey of Favorinus' lips (Philost. *VS* 490, cf. ch. 7 n. 10).
Wilamowitz, 'Epistula' 146 makes Favorinus the pattern of an age 'cuius deus est exoletus,
decora Graecae linguae Aristides comitiali morbo, Latinae Fronto podagra enecati', as if
Antinous did any harm, or the rhetors' sickness indicated want of moral fibre. Indeed,
Wilamowitz likened the era to a corpse on the point of rotting; but if Favorinus died in 154, the
Antonine order had as long to run before the death of Commodus as the society in which
Wilamowitz was writing, *anno* 1880, before its collapse in 1918.

Chapter 7

Honoured Orators

THE consular orators Cornelius Fronto and Herodes Atticus did not take fees from Gellius, but admitted him to their company and spread before him the treasures of their minds. He was not their pupil as he was Apollinaris' or even Favorinus'; yet in a broader sense the term is well in place.

Fronto

The life and career of M. Cornelius T. f. Quir. Fronto is well set out in Champlin's recent study:[1] he came from Cirta in the province of Africa,[2] was born *c.*95, moved early to Rome (where he acquired Maecenas' former mansion on the Esquiline), becoming the foremost orator and advocate of his day. After some years of strained relations with Hadrian, he was appointed by Pius as tutor in Latin rhetoric to his adoptive heir M. Caesar, and held the suffect consulate of July and August 143, the year in which Herodes Atticus was *ordinarius*;[3] he continued as a writer into the reign of the *diui fratres*, preparing a panegyric on Verus' campaign in Parthia, till death, perhaps from the plague brought back thence by the army,[4] released him from old age and a life of sickness.

Fronto's eloquence was unreservedly praised by later writers:[5] the panegyrist of Constantius Chlorus ranks him equal with Cicero, in whose company he is also named by Jerome, Macrobius, and Sidonius. The critics, however, could not agree how to classify his style: Macrobius makes him the

---

1. Champlin, *Fronto*; for the tribe see *ILS* 2928. There is still no palaeographically reliable edition of the Corpus Frontonianum, no commentary beyond translators' notes, and no concordance, only word-indexes for certain works used as the raw material for number-games (cf. R. Marache, *Gnomon* 56 (1984) 660–2).

2. Specifically Numidia (cf. *Ep. M. Caes.* 1. 10. 5), not yet formally a separate province, but governed by the legate at Lambaesis rather than the proconsul at Carthage. Cirta, a highly Romanized city, had provided the first two African consuls, the brothers Pactumeii, under Vespasian.

3. Cf. Birley, *Marcus Aurelius* 80. Ausonius, *Grat. Act.* 32, applies to Fronto's consulate the same jest ('quibus consulibus gesserit consulatum') that Macrobius ascribes to Cicero apropos of C. Caninius Rebilus' (*Sat.* 2. 3. 6).

4. Smallpox, according to R. J. and M. L. Littman, *AJPh* 94 (1973) 243–55. For the date of Fronto's death cf. p. 23.

5. *Paneg. Lat.* 8. 14. 2; Eutr. 8. 12. 1; Auson. *Grat. Act.* 32–4; Jerome *Ep.* 125. 12; Macr. *Sat.* 5. 1. 7; Mart. Cap. 5. 432; Sidon. *Ep.* 4. 3. 1; 8. 10. 3; Claud. Mam. CSEL 11. 206. 2. Mai, edn.[2] 197 n. 1 suggested that *Ver.* 1. 3. 1 was imitated by Symm. *Ep.* 4. 21. 1–2; but cf. Men. fr. 744 K–Th, Apul. *Flor.* 17. 5. *Princ. hist.* 2. 10 probably underlies the common source of Eutrop. 8. 8. 1, *Epit. Caes.* 15. 3, *HA Pius* 2. 2. 13. 4; § 14 was used by Nazarius, *Paneg. Lat.* 4. 24. 6–7.

master of the *genus siccum*, Jerome and Sidonius accord him *grauitas*, Claudianus Mamertus singles out his *pompa*.[6] A reading of the speech imperfectly preserved at *Ep. M. Caes.* 1. 6. 2–6 may suggest how these three diverse qualities could be ascribed to him: there is no extravagance of diction, but the phrases pile up, hammering the message home and also displaying, even flaunting, the author's care in composition, the labour spent in choosing every word.

> Siue maria naufragos deuorent siue flumina praecipites trahant siue harenae obruant siue ferae lacerent sive uolucres discerpant, corpus humanum satis sepelitur ubicumque consumitur; at ubi testamentum naufragio submersum est, illa demum et res et domus et familia naufraga atque insepulta est (§ 5).

> Whether the seas swallow men in shipwreck or rivers sweep them headlong away or sands entomb them or wild beasts rend them or birds peck them apart, the human body is well enough buried wherever it is destroyed; but when the will has sunk in shipwreck, that property, that house, that household lies shipwrecked and unburied.[7]

And yet, once works of Fronto's had been rediscovered, the extravagant laudations of Mai and Leopardi[8] were opposed by venomous invective from beyond the Alps; the great orator was deemed contemptible in doctrine, style, and content.[9] In part this was due to disappointment at not finding in a prince's tutor those sage counsels that idealizers of antiquity had expected; in part to the contrast between his stylistic principles and those acceptable to his critics; in part to lamentations about illness that in cumulation soon disgust the strong and healthy. By contrast, postwar distaste for gravity and grandeur, ready even to regard the second-century emotionalism manifested in the letters of master and pupil as a moral advance and not a mark of

6. Not 'grandeur' but 'display'; cf. *OLD* s.v. At *Ep. M. Caes.* 3. 17. 3 Fronto warns Marcus he is not yet ready to imitate the 'ornatas et pompaticas orationes' he has begun to read.

7. To disagree with the thought, one must be either superstitious about death or philosophical about wealth; and what of the slaves the will might free (§ 6)? For the content cf. Lucr. 3. 888–93 with commentators; for the expression Sen. *Ep.* 92. 34, *Rem. fort.* 5. 2–4, Min. Fel. *Oct.* 11. 4. See too the fine appreciation of this speech by Steinmetz 211–15, and of *Nep. am.* by A. Ramírez de Verger, *Faventia* 5/1 (1983) 65–78. The apparent contradictions in the ancient critics were considered at length, but inconclusively, by Leopardi, *Scr. fil.* 52–69, 78–82, 85–8 (cf. Timpanaro, *Filologia* 41–2); Norden i. 365 n. 1 relates the judgements to different works (cf. Timpanaro, *Contributi* 346 n. 2) and strangely describes the speech on transmarine wills as 'schmucklos'. At *Eloq.* 2. 7 Fronto commends both the grand and the simple style (for the 'genera diuersa' of Menelaus and Odysseus see p. 162).

8. Mai, edn.[1], i, pp. xxxvii–xlii, Leopardi, *Opere inedite* i. 325–51 Cugnoni (repr. without final section, *Opere* i/2. 639–56 Flora), cf. Timpanaro, *Filologia* 23, 41–2, *Contributi* 346–7.

9. Niebuhr, edn., pp. vii f. *et passim*, cf. *Vort.* iii. 232, Naber, edn., p. iii. Dorothy Brock, however, ably defended him; and condemnation was never absolute outside Germany, where even the greatest Roman writers could scarcely hold their own against the obsession with an ideal Hellas.

decadence,[10] proclaimed the merits of Fronto's style, though not always without misconception:[11] in particular, since Fronto did not proclaim an *elocutio nouella*,[12] he did not see it as a tender shoot that would flourish in the future.[13] There is much beauty in his writings, above all in the prose-poem of *Fer. Als.* 3. 9–13 (the fable of Sleep), and his lament for his grandson displays both dignity and pathos; but seekers after greatness must look elsewhere.

Fronto's stylistic theory holds that the orator must attend above all to the choice of words, not being content with good ones but seeking out the best—even if the choice turns on a single syllable—and prefer the unexpected to the commonplace;[14] they should not be invented, but found out from constant study of approved authors, excerpted for this purpose.[15] Yet the words selected must not be obscure or jarring, least of all in an official speech, and must be disposed in the best order.[16] Adornments will come from the traditional figures of rhetoric, nor is the γνώμη or *sententia* neglected; but the favoured device is the εἰκών or *imago*.[17]

Among prose-writers Cato is the most careful with his words, and his follower Sallust, among the poets Plautus and Ennius; other authors commended are Coelius, Naevius, Lucretius, Accius, Caecilius, and Laberius, besides others in specialized fields.[18] Cicero is the greatest of Roman orators and the most skilful at embellishing his theme, but too proud, too lazy, or too diffident to search out the unlooked-for and unexpected word; his letters, however, are unsurpassed.[19] Seneca is to be torn out by the roots, a writer in

10. This is the view of Fronto's champion Portalupi (for a parallel see Sherwin-White on Plin. *Ep.* 5. 16. 10); others may find the warmth of these letters as charming, yet also as disconcerting, as Egyptian art of the Amarna period. It was not peculiar to Fronto and Marcus; observe how Herodes addresses Favorinus, *VS* 490 (palliated, it is true, by its literary origin, Ar. fr. 598 K–A). Gellius, by contrast, retains his dignity.

11. Portalupi confuses neologism with vulgarism: at *MCF* 104, though not in her edition, she misunderstands *Eloq.* 2. 2 as denoting the language of the people as as whole. See in general Timpanaro, *Contributi*, 364–9.

12. On *Eloq.* 5. 1 see pp. 163–4.

13. So Portalupi, *MCF* 38.

14. *Ep. M. Caes.* 1. 5. 3; 3. 17. 5, 4. 3; *M. Ant.* 1. 2. 4, 7; *Eloq.* 4. 7; *Orat.* 11–12. Contrast Quint. 6. 3. 107, 8. pr. 25–7, 31.

15. *Ep. M. Caes.* 4. 3. 3; *Eloq.* 2. 4 m^2 d; *Orat.* 18. For excerpting see ch. 2 n. 26. But Fronto's condemnation of *dictio* (*Ep. M. Caes.* 5. 3), a Republican word, seems uncalled-for (and Marcus was ready to defend it, *Ep.* 5. 4). At *M. Ant.* 1. 2. 9 he forgets Plaut. *Rud.* 694; for *obsecro* with the gods as object cf. Fest. 206. 17–18 L.

16. *Ep. M. Caes.* 3. 1; 4. 3. 3, 7; *Ver.* 2. 1. 29 (§ 5 v.d.H.); *Eloq.* 2. 1; 5. 3.

17. Figures: *Ep. M. Caes.* 1. 9. 3; 3. 16; *M. Ant.* 1. 2. 6, 11–12; 3. 1; *Eloq.* 4. 7; *Amic.* 1. 11. γνῶμαι: *Ep. M. Caes.* 3. 12–13; 5. 74; *M. Ant.* 4. 2. 5 m^2 d. εἰκόνες: *Ep. M. Caes.* 1. 10; 4. 12. 2; *M. Ant.* 1. 2. 5; *Eloq.* 4. 7. As McCall 243–51 observes, the εἰκών is not a comparison, but an 'imagistic description' used for comparative purposes. In fact, Fronto abounds in comparisons (see Schmitt, and for the three 2nd-c. mannerists Portalupi, *Ricerca* 22–68).

18. Even Lucilius appears only in this catalogue, for terms of crafts and trades. On Cato's careful diction cf. Gell. 11. 1. 7. In a different spirit, cf. Quint. 1. 4. 4.

19. *Ep. M. Caes.* 4. 3. 3 (cf. 1. 9. 5 as a reply to 2. 7. 1); *M. Ant.* 3. 1. 1 *fin.* (cf. *M. Caes.* 1. 9. 4); 3. 10. 2; *Ver.* 2. 1. 18 (§ 17 m^2 c v.d.H.); *Amic.* 1. 14. 2; *Bell. Parth.* 10.

the worst taste who says the same thing over and over again (Lucan is just as bad) and whose vocabulary is incorrect.[20]

Far from dilating on the moral virtues of the ancients, Fronto complains that Romans lack affection, φιλοστοργία.[21] His imperial pupil was to recall that observation, and also his insight into 'the malice and caprice and hypocrisy of absolutism';[22] he pays no tribute to the rhetorical teachings of a master who failed to curb his taste for oddity.[23] Nor did Fronto respect the Stoicism to which Marcus was addicted: the man whose body was racked with constant pain found the Stoic moralist who proscribed the desire for good health as insufferable as the Stoic logician who informed his drowsy pupils that 'if it is day there is light' with the windows wide open—besides, the school employed such an execrable style. It might be fit for gods, but not for human beings.[24]

Gellius makes no mention of Fronto the orator; his fame did not require it. He is free to praise the learning that Fronto revealed in private conversation, but the only adequate compliment he can bestow on his eloquence is to borrow certain phrases from *Arion* when he himself relates the story at *NA* 16. 19.[25] Gellius allows himself more ornamentation than Fronto does, a difference in taste that returns in their remarks on C. Gracchus: for Fronto he and Cato are almost the only grand orators among the ancients, but Gellius finds him too pedestrian.[26] Furthermore, Gellius admires Vergil, whom Fronto ignores, and praises Cicero for that care in the choice of words which Fronto, because it was not his own care, denies him.[27] Gellius was no mere *Famulusnatur*, or *âme seconde*,[28] a congenital disciple lost without a master; his

---

20. *Orat.* 2–7, *Fer. Als.* 3. 2.

21. *Ep. Ver.* 2. 7. 7, *Amic.* 1. 3 m^2 f, cf. Marcus at *Fer. Als.* 4. 2; Champlin 90. See too M. P. J. van den Hout, *Mnem.*[4] 3 (1950) 330–5.

22. M. Ant. *Med.* 1. 11 (tr. Farquharson); want of affection is here predicated of the patriciate. For Fronto as a teacher of truthfulness cf. Marcus, *Ep. M. Caes.* 3. 13. 1, Verus, *Ver.* 2.2. 1; on the reluctant courtier, Champlin, *Fronto* 94–117. He proclaims his own openness and honesty at *Amic.* 1. 12. 3, *Nep. am.* 2. 9; readers of *Princ. hist.* will have their reservations.

23. Fronto, *Orat.* 17, 19; Cass. Dio 71. 5. 3 (iii. 256 Boissevain); Herodian 1. 2. 3.

24. *Eloq.* 2. 10, 16; 5. 4; *Amic.* 1. 2; 1. 15. 2. By 'philosopher' Fronto generally means 'Stoic'; contrast the respect shown a Platonist, *Amic.* 1. 4. 1; but Plato was a stylist, *Eloq.* 1. 16; 4. 4.

25. § 4 Periander described as *rex* (but so is 'Pyranthes' in Hyginus' version); § 5 'Siciliam atque Italiam', Fronto 'Siciliae atque Italiae', Herodotus Ἰταλίην τε καὶ Σικελίην; § 7 'grandi pecunia et re bona multa copiosus' combining Herodotus' χρήματα μεγάλα with Fronto's 're bona'; § 8 'Corinthios delegit', Fronto 'Corinthios potissimum delegit'; § 10 'haberent'; § 16 'incolumique eum corpore et ornatu', Fronto 'et homo et uestis et cithara ac uox incolumis'; § 20 'super Arione', Fronto 'super Arione Lesbio' ; § 23 'atque esse fabulae argumentum quod simulacra duo ... uiserentur', Fronto 'uisitur ... atque rei argumento magis quam simulacro'.

26. *Ep. M. Caes.* 3. 17. 3 ∼ *NA* 10. 3.

27. *Ep. M. Caes.* 4. 3. 3 ∼ *NA* 10. 21; 13. 25. 4; that it was anti-archaistic is recognized at 13. 21. 22—but at § 15 'uetustius' was true of *fretus*, not *fretum*; read '(crassius) inuenustiusque' (Wakefield, L. Mueller), of the repeated -*tō* ('perangusto freto').

28. Teuffel–Kroll–Skutsch iii. 97; Marache, *Critique* 313.

judgement is influenced, but not governed, by Fronto, the greatest, not the only, orator in Rome.[29]

Nevertheless, their acquaintance began in Gellius' student days at Rome, before he went to Athens: when he had time to spare from formal instruction, he visited Fronto and enjoyed his refined and learned conversation (19. 8. 1). This conversation, as reported in the *Nights*,[30] is entirely concerned with the niceties of Latin usage: in 2. 26 he maintains against Favorinus (who had probably introduced Gellius to him) that Latin is richer than Greek in colour-words within the ranges of 'red' and 'green'; in 13. 29 he examines Quadrigarius' use of *(cum) mortalibus (multis)* for *hominibus*;[31] in 19. 8 he insists that in good Latin *quadrigae* is always plural and *harena* singular; in 19. 10 he establishes that *praeterpropter* is no mere vulgarism but occurs in ancient authors; in 19. 13 he doubts the Latinity of *nanus* ('dwarf'). The first four scenes, set in Fronto's own home, show him in command: he can even tell his audience (for there is always a considerable company) to seek examples of *quadriga* or *harenae* in a reputable ancient author ('id est classicus adsiduusque aliquis scriptor, non proletarius', 19. 8. 15),[32] just as if he were their teacher, in order to train them in the search for rare words. He is not infallible, however, for Gellius can find *quadriga* in Varro (§ 17)—while taking less trouble over *harenae* because he recalls no other learned man who has used it (§ 18).[33] On the other hand, in 19. 13, whose setting is tactfully removed to the Palatium, Fronto is no longer sure of himself, but asks Apollinaris whether he was right to avoid saying *nani* for *pumiliones*. In fact he had been over-scrupulous, since the word is found in Aristophanes; Apollinaris, however, acknowledges in him the right that Pomponius Marcellus had denied the emperor Tiberius,[34] of conferring citizenship upon a word.

29. Champlin, *Fronto* 52, like many others, makes Fronto 'virtually [the] progenitor' of mannerism (whose exponents were *Frontoniani* for Sidon. *Ep.* 1. 1. 2); but cf. Intro. n. 29. At *M. Ant.* 1. 2. 2 'nostrae sectae' need not claim, and cannot prove, originality (*m²* paraphrases 'facundiae suae'); *Ep. M. Caes.* 1. 9. 4, if not mere flattery, may mean that Fronto came late to the fashion). By Gellius' day mannerism was so much the norm as to embrace a variety of tastes and judgements.

30. Of the five chapters, three are in a single book, and that the last but one, as if to leave an impression of greater warmth and intimacy than there was in fact.

31. For which see Fraenkel, *Kl. Beit.* ii. 135; Lebek 255–6; Ronconi 133–5; Skutsch on Enn. *Ann.* 366.

32. Cf. 6. 13 on *classici*, 16. 10 on *assidui* and *proletarii*, Plaut. *Mil.* 752 'proletario sermone'. This passage is the first known instance of 'classic' in a literary context; cf. Curtius 249–50.

33. Gellius fails to remember that *harenae* is frequent in Vergil; it slips from his own pen at 5. 14. 7; 16. 11. 7 (cf. ch. 3 n. 22). The real Fronto uses it ap. M. Caes. *Ep.* 1. 6. 5. Some translators misunderstand 'id' of the condemnation, and Tränkle 112 obtains this sense by writing *denegauit* for 'dedit'; but in Republican Latin *harena* is a *singulare tantum*, and grammatical tradition did not forget the fact (Charis. 131. 25–6 B). To be sure, neither interpretation excuses failure to seek examples.

34. See Suet. *Gram.* 22. 2, Cass. Dio 57. 12. 2; cf. the modern saying *Caesar non supra grammaticos* (*GW* 344). What was servility in Capito—and to a master who, in this matter, brooked dissent—is politeness in Apollinaris; for similar compliments see p. 84.

The zeal for pure diction and the observance of nice distinctions suit well with the Fronto of the letters, as do the warning at *NA* 13. 29. 5 that choice words must be used with discretion,[35] the minute study of ancient authors, and the gout that confined him to a Grecian pallet (19. 10. 1, cf. 2. 26. 1).[36] True to life too will be the presence in 19. 13 of another distinguished African orator, M. Postumius Festus, who takes part in the conversation,[37] and the contemplation of a new bath-house costing some 300,000 sesterces in 19. 10. 4;[38] the ensuing discussion of *praeterpropter*, even if fictitious, adheres to Fronto's and Gellius' principle, that words found in approved authors cannot be low.[39] But although in 2. 26 Fronto's role as the champion of Latin seems to accord with his disapproval when Marcus writes in Greek,[40] the citation of Vergil is out of character; at 13. 29. 3, when he admits that his judgement may be blinded by his love for Quadrigarius and all old Latin, the love of old Latin is indeed Frontonian, but it is Gellius, not Fronto, who displays a particular interest in Quadrigarius.[41] Caesar's *De analogia*, another of Gellius' favourites despite discrepancies with early usage, is quoted in 19. 8; the real Fronto, though he commends to Marcus, now emperor, Caesar's example in writing it 'atrocissimo bello Gallico', does not, like Gellius, cite it as an authority.[42] Unless, therefore, our Frontonian remains are seriously misleading in their defectiveness, Gellius presents his own learning in the great man's name and belies the show of modesty that makes him a silent listener to the five discussions, not even informing Fronto that he has turned up *quadriga* in Varro. As an obscure young man, no doubt he knew his place; but maintenance of contact, not perhaps without friction, is suggested by Fronto's letter to Claudius Julianus, governor of Lower Germany in 160, dated by Champlin to that year or soon afterwards:[43]

FRONTO CL. IVLIANO SALVTEM

Non agnoui ista mea ab Gellio pessime [*m²* aptissime] quaeri: credideris admonuisse se edere. Ego epistulas inuitissime scribo. Aetate sic aspera mea senis cupere tantum est; eo peruenit [*m²* peruenisti] ut non tantum mihi carissimus sis sed etiam paene solus, ita solitario uteris [*rest illegible*]

---

35. Cf. *Ep. M. Caes.* 4. 3. 3 *fin.*
36. Besides the correspondence, see Artem. 4. 22 (257. 13–15 Pack). On gout in 2nd-c. society see Gourevich, *Triangle* 217–47.
37. *Amic.* 2. 11. 1, cf. p. 110.
38. Cf. Champlin, *Fronto* 24.
39. Observe the references to Atellan farces, etc., *Ep. M. Caes.* 2. 5. 2; 3. 17. 3; 4. 3. 2; *M. Ant.* 4. 2. 5 *m²* d; *Laud. fum.* 2. See too ch. 11 n. 85.
40. *Ep. M. Caes.* 3. 9. 2, cf. Champlin, *Fronto* 58.
41. If Hosius' reconstruction of 8. 6 is correct (see pp. 208–9), 'amor atque ueneratio caeco esse iudicio facit' recalls Cicero as quoted there. However, Fronto affects to fear he may judge Marcus too leniently from excess of love (*Ep. M. Caes.* 3. 17. 1).
42. *Bell. Parth.* 9; *NA* 4. 16. 9; 9. 14. 25, cf. 1. 10. 4 (p. 87).
43. 'Chronology' 152. Julianus was still in his province when the *diui fratres* succeeded (*Amic.* 1. 20. 2).

Fronto, in the agony of impotent old age, believes that all the world has deserted him save Julianus; he hates writing letters (so too *Amic.* 1. 21. 1)—and therefore does not dwell on what his friend has told him, namely that Gellius is doing something in relation to matter of Fronto's, and has not informed him of his intention to publish.[44] 'Pessime quaeri' might mean 'were wanted very badly (= much)'[45] or 'were being sought in a most improper way';[46] but Edmund Hauler, who first descried this sentence in the palimpsest, interpreted 'ista mea ... quaeri' as *de istis meis quaeri*—so that Gellius was botching his research on Fronto's ideas, aimed at unauthorized publication—and further suggested that Fronto altered 'pessime' to 'aptissime' when the quarrel was made up.[47] The verb could indeed, on this hypothesis, be modified by either adverb without a change of sense; but if Fronto wrote 'pessime quaeri', he was not, in the midst of his woes, considering what he might wish to say once reconciled. Although the second hand, besides linguistic trivializations, offers some good readings,[48] 'pessime' seems more appropriate, especially to Fronto's black mood; we shall most naturally understand that Gellius was making a nuisance of himself in his quest for Frontonian writings to publish, whether as such or in his own work. But we do not know what Julianus said Gellius was publishing, or how soon;[49] whether he actually published it, then or later; whether Julianus (at Cologne?) was well informed; and whether Fronto, in his depression, read more into his letter than was there.

Herodes Atticus

The vastly rich and abundantly eloquent Herodes Atticus; the friend of Fronto and legatee of Favorinus; Athenian archon in 126/7 and Roman *consul ordinarius* in 143; *corrector* of the Asian cities when Antoninus was proconsul, and Greek tutor to his sons when he was emperor; the lifelong intimate of Marcus, who toyed with making him his Eleusinian mystagogue and entrusted him with filling his new chairs of philosophy; the builder of the Athenian theatre that bears his name, of the Olympic aqueduct that met a need unsatisfied for nine centuries, and of many other fine and useful

44. There is no more need to doubt that this Gellius is our Aulus than that 'Castricius noster' (*Amic.* 2. 2) is his teacher: the L. Gellius to whom Arrian dedicated his Epictetus, suggested by Marshall, 'Date' 152, was the Corinthian aristocrat L. Gellius Menander (G. W. Bowersock, *GRBS* 8 (1967) 280). No assistance is derived from *m*[2mg]: 'sauiata arte uiribus humanis eo peruenisti ut tu mihi non tantum carissimus sis, sed paene solus'.

45. Cf. fr. III 'male me, Marce, praeteritae uitae meae paenitet', from another low-spirited letter describing his life as wasted (*not* wicked, cf. *Nep. am.* 2. 9).

46. Cf. Portalupi: 'che Gellio cercasse di procurarsi queste mie cose tanto malamente'.

47. E. Hauler, *WS* 46 (1928) 244–5; on illicit publication cf. A. Kappelmacher, *WS* 48 (1930) 120.

48. Timpanaro, *Contributi* 349–50, 378–84.

49. 'Edere' implies that Gellius' project was already under way; but it need not have gone according to plan. Even if it was the *Nights*, I have suggested in ch. 2 that they took many years to compose.

buildings in his own and other cities: was widely regarded in Athens as a swindler, a murderer, and a tyrant, hated by the common people for defrauding them of his father's legacy, prosecuted by his brother-in-law for the killing of his wife, and resented by his fellow oligarchs as an engrosser of their power; but always protected by his wealth and twice by Marcus, who before his accession persuaded Fronto to moderate his zeal when defending the sophist's foremost enemy, and who, distracted in the midst of a grievous war by the culmination of these quarrels, refused to condemn him and soon compelled the Athenians to take him back.[50] An American scholar has styled him a 'World Citizen';[51] perhaps his closest modern analogue would be the son of an oil-magnate and an heiress, cultured, munificent, and a friend of Presidents, with far more power than many governments, but detested by his family, subordinates, and neighbours.

He invited Roman students to his suburban villas;[52] it was at Cephisia—still a favourite resort in summer-time, and together with Marathon dearest of demes to Herodes[53]—that Gellius spent the height of summer and the Dog-days, enjoying the shade of vast woods, long and gentle footpaths, a cool situation, well-kept, abundant, and gleaming pools, everywhere delightful with the prattle of water and the song of birds.[54] A young man also staying there, who claimed to be the world's greatest authority on Stoic doctrine, was put down by Herodes with a quotation from Epictetus that set at nought all book-learnt principles not taken to heart. Observing that the chapter from which Herodes quotes (Epict. 2. 19) also contains an account of a logical problem the young man flaunted, and exhibits an empty-headed person preparing to astonish party-guests by enumerating those who have written on it, one suspects that Gellius owes rather more to Epictetus than he admits; the appearance in 15. 2 of another sham philosopher at dinner shows that he found the motif congenial.

In 9. 2 Herodes again encounters a self-styled philosopher, a street-corner Cynic who demands money for bread. 'Who are you?' 'A philosopher, can't

---

50. For his life see Ameling and Graindor. His style as a Roman citizen was L. Vibullius Hipparchus Ti. Claudius Ti. f. Quir. Atticus Herodes, as an Athenian Ἡρώδης Ἀττικοῦ Μαραθώνιος.

51. So Rutledge; how changed from Diogenes! Contrast Syme, *Tacitus* 505: 'a millionaire, and a very nasty fellow'; it was not only the honey of Herodes' eloquence that subjugated the Greek cities (Philost. *VS* 561). But nasty fellows have their uses; and art-lovers even now forgive both tyranny and treason (cf. Philost. *VS* 560).

52. *NA* 1. 2. 1 'accersebat saepenumero [G. Bernardi Perini, *Živa Antika* 22 (1972) 131–3, 'Revisione' 258; *saepe nos* codd.] cum apud magistros Athenis essemus' implies that the Roman students were not Herodes' pupils; Gellius, who portrays Herodes as a dabbler in philosophy, not a teacher of rhetoric, was not studying to be a Greek sophist, but, insofar as he was in Athens 'eloquentiae … extundendae gratia' (17. 20. 4), to acquire a general competence in Greek impartible by hacks unworthy of commemoration alongside Castricius and Julianus. But he may have been influenced by the form or the content of Herodes' writings (cf. p. 22).

53. Philost. *VS* 562; archaeology confirms (Ameling ii *passim*).

54. *NA* 1. 2. 2 (*ecphrasis* of a *locus amoenus*, as suited the taste of the time); cf. 18. 10, where Gellius falls ill at the villa, Herodes playing no further part in the chapter.

you see?' 'I can see the beard and the cloak, but not the philosopher.'[55] Informed that the fellow is a dissolute vagabond, who rails against those who do not give him money, Herodes, whom Gellius describes as famous for his pleasant nature, answers 'Let us give him some money, whatever his character, as men, not as to a man'. After the beggar has been sent away with enough for a month's supply of bread, Herodes recalls that Musonius, told that a like scoundrel deserved nothing good, replied 'Then he deserves money'; but how sad it is that such filthy beasts should usurp the sacred name of philosopher! His Athenian ancestors had decreed that the names of the tyrannicides Harmodius and Aristogeiton should never be bestowed on slaves;[56] and he had heard that in ancient Rome some patrician state criminals' *praenomina* had been forbidden to their *gentes*.[57]

Herodes must have often faced such pests, whether or not Gellius was of the company; his contemptuous generosity recalls his no less contemptuous tolerance of Peregrinus: 'Insult me if you must, but why in such bad Greek?'; 'You have grown old in abusing me and I in listening' (Philost. *VS* 563–4). 'Tamquam homines non tamquam homini'—harsher than Aristotle's reported comments, respecting humanity even in so vile a specimen[58]—may render Herodes' formula on such occasions; the Athenian decree is credible in his mouth, the Roman prohibition addressed to Roman students not impossible, in view of Favorinus' practice; but in its present form the Musonius anecdote seems to require Gellius' 'nulla re bona dignum', from Cic. *Rep.* 1. 9, not the normal Greek οὐδενὸς ἄξιος.[59] At the very least, Gellius has embroidered the facts.

Certainly authentic is Herodes' last appearance in 19. 12, rebutting a Stoic's attack for unmanly and unphilosophical grief at the death of a boy he

55. See 13. 8. 5, A. Otho 53 n., Quint. 12. 3. 12, Luc. *Demon.* 13, *Eun.* 9, Apul. *Flor.* 7. 10, 9. 9, Ath. 211 E, Apostol. 6. 93e with Leutsch ad loc. *Habitus non facit monachum*; the contempt for such philosophers in ancient literature resembles that for idle monks and friars in mediaeval. For the form of Herodes' remark cf. Sceptus on Alexander the Clay-Plato (Philost. *VS* 573).

56. 'Hippiam tyrannum interficere adorsi erant' (§ 10) is perfectly correct (Thuc. 6. 54. 3, 57. 1–3, 'Arist.' *Ath. Pol.* 18. 3), though it was Hipparchus whom they killed (as Gellius knows, *NA* 17. 21. 7). For the decree cf. Liban. *Decl.* 1. 71; nor did other Greeks so name their slaves (M. Lambertz, *JB d. k. k. Staatsgymn. im VIII. Bez. Wiens 1906/1907* 24). At Suet. *Dom.* 10. 3 a man is punished for calling his slaves Mago and Hannibal; but that was because his military daydreams alarmed Domitian's paranoia.

57. Gellius' language implies a decree or a law, as against the plebeian Antonii (Plut. *Cic.* 49. 4, Cass. Dio 51. 19. 3), not by the *gens* itself (e.g. Cic. *Phil.* 1. 32); does this, like 'audio', indicate a Greek's imperfect information, in contrast to the recondite correctness of § 10? If so, we have either a masterly piece of characterization, or (more plausibly) a translation from a Greek attack (perhaps by Herodes) on false philosophers. For a similar exercise see Apul. *Flor.* 7.

58. D.L. 5. 17, 21 (cf. Sen. *Ben.* 4. 29. 3); the motif is reinterpreted in Molière, *Dom Juan* III. ii *fin.*, 'pour l'amour de l'humanité' (sc. not of God).

59. Musonius might have been told ἀλλ' οὐκ ἄξιός ἐστιν ἀγαθῶν παρὰ σοῦ τυχεῖν, but Gellius' expression is more pointed, since *res bona* may, as at 16. 19. 7, mean 'wealth'. Is he adding a Latin twist as at 2. 18. 9 (p. 58)? Of course for Musonius money is not a good; but perhaps in the original version the man was described only as an evil-doer, so that Musonius' meaning was, as Verteuil i. 317 puts it, 'l'argent est donc fait pour lui' (cf. Epict. 3. 17. 2).

had loved. Gellius praises his Greek eloquence elsewhere (1. 2. 1; 9. 2. 1), but reserves for this chapter his declaration that Herodes far excelled virtually all his contemporaries' 'grauitate atque copia et elegantia uocum'.[60] The description, though applied to his oratory in general, is evoked by an occasion on which he needed all those qualities.

Even in the sentimental second century, when the younger Pliny could encourage in Fundanus that unworthy woe which Ser. Sulpicius had reproved in Cicero,[61] Herodes' grief at the deaths of his loved ones passed all bounds: Marcus, deeply struck as he was by Fronto's complaint of Roman coldness, found Herodes' sorrow for his stillborn son excessive.[62] Members of his family, including his three foster-sons Achilleus, Polydeucion,[63] and Memnon the black, whom he mourned as much as if he had been their father, he honoured in death not only with ostentatious lamentation but with numerous and expensive monuments, which survive in sufficient quantity to confirm Philostratus' reports at *VS* 556–60:[64] Herodes was rebuked by Plutarch's Stoic nephew Sextus;[65] apt comments were also made by Demonax, if we may believe anything that Lucian tells us of that walking joke-book (*Demon.* 24–5). In particular, seeing Herodes preparing gifts for Polydeucion, untimely dead, he affected to bear a message from the departed: why did Herodes not come and join him?

Indeed, the greatest display was lavished on this youth, who having died in the lifetime of Herodes' mother (born in the early 80s), was accorded a hero's cult precisely at Cephisia[66] and turned into a new Antinous. The inviting identification with the boy of *NA* 19. 12 (d. *c.*147) would fail if, as is currently asserted, the foster-sons died in the 160s (perhaps of the plague) or early 170s; but the case is not conclusive.[67] In any event, Gellius could

60. So at much greater length Philost. *VS* 565–6; Philostratus' dedicatee claimed (intellectual?) descent from the sophist (*VS* 479; Anderson 297–8). Herodes did not strain after effect, but allowed his diction to follow from his subject-matter; he was also a better Atticist than most in style and language (indeed, his letters were too Attic and too ornate for the genre: Philost. *Dial.* 1, ii. 258 Kayser). The oration miscalled Περὶ πολιτείας preserved in his name is in plausible but imperfect Attic (see Schmid 195–200, but note the sudden run on ὀρρωδεῖν towards the end, a sure sign that the author has just remembered another γλῶσσα, and the Latinisms πολιτικὸν πόλεμον § 11, συντιθέασιν = *componunt*, 'compare' § 27); it is also confused in thought and tediously flat. Russell, *GD* 111, though mistrustful of stylistic arguments against Herodes' authorship, suggests it may be by Hippodromus of Larisa (Philost. *VS* 615–20).

61. Contrast Plin. *Ep.* 5. 16 with Ser. Sulpicius ap. Cic. *Fam.* 4. 5, Sen. *Ep.* 99; but even Pliny was unimpressed when the mourner was his *bête noire* Regulus (*Ep.* 4. 2), cf. Polyb. 15. 17. 2.

62. *Ep. M. Caes.* 1. 6. 8; cf. Fronto's *consolatio* ibid. 1. 8. When Fronto lamented his lost grandson, he was a sick old man; Herodes was in the prime of life and fortune.

63. Polydeuces in our literary sources, but Vibullius Polydeucion on the monuments.

64. Graindor 90–118; Ameling ii, nos. 132–82, some erected by others who 'ran along with his passion' (Luc. *Demon.* 24).

65. From whom Marcus learnt to be impassible but affectionate (*Med.* 1. 9. 9).

66. Ameling ii, nos. 174, 177–9 (also at Marathon, no. 175).

67. Polydeucion died no later than the archonship of Dionysius (Ameling ii, no. 172), previously dated to 147/8 × 153/4 (excl. 150/1) but brought down to 173/4 by Follet, *Athènes* 6–7, *REG* 90 (1977) 43–54, cf. L. Robert, *AJP* 100 (1979) 160–5, to fit the mission of the Quintilii in the early 170s (cf. Philost. *VS* 580–9). If the τρόφιμοι, having compensated Herodes

observe Herodes' grief, and no doubt heard harsh words from the much-admired Peregrinus;[68] yet he appears to take Herodes' side, not only praising his eloquence, but stating that he spoke 'lacessitus a quodam Stoico' (§ 2), a phrase not sympathetic to the critic. Herodes replied *ad hominem*, or rather *ad sectam*, with a polemic against the Stoic doctrine that the wise man will feel no passion, culminating in the apologue of the Thracian who pruned and weeded till he had no crop.[69] But Herodes' precept that the passions should be controlled and wisely purged of their excess was precisely the ground on which his practice was to be condemned; he did not live up to his Olympic oration on the golden mean (Philost. *VS* 556–7). Fine words so captivate Gellius that, for all his theorectical dislike of preaching without practice (13. 8. 4–5; 13. 24. 2), he does not see through them to the truth that they conceal.[70]

for his lost children (ibid. 560), died in the 160s (Ameling) or 170s (Follet), the *puer* of *NA* 19. 12. 2 was not Polydeucion (cf. ch. 1 n. 26), but a boy of whom we have no other notice. Had Herodes followed Fronto's advice, *Ep. M. Caes.* 1. 8. 3? was the boy such as the Philetos of Stat. *Silu.* 2. 6? (Gellius' language excludes Regillus, proposed by Astarita 428, or any other son.) However, Philost. *VS* 558 does not impose a chronology on the boys' deaths, but contrasts Herodes' love for them with his indifference towards his stupid son Bradua; § 559 shows that Herodes was still erecting statues to them, not that he had only just begun; since Lucian's *Demonax*, though written after 170 (§ 30), reaches back into Epictetus' lifetime (§ 55), § 24 need not be topical; the grotesqueness of Herodes' grief was manifest long before his old age. A normal person would not have mourned Polydeucion for thirty years; but rich men of Herodes' stamp do not practise self-control. Cf. Holford-Strevens, 'More Notes' 150.

68. See p. 104. Lucian does not say that Peregrinus rebuked Herodes on this score, since it would have been to his villain's credit; when Peregrinus finds fault with Herodes' benefaction at Olympia (*Per.* 19–20), Lucian, taking Herodes' side, suppresses the name he readily records when Demonax is the assailant and in the right.

69. Whence La Fontaine, *Fables* 12. 20 ('Le Philosophe scythe'). On a misguided derivation from Panaetius see ch. 5 n. 45.

70. Gellius was Herodes' guest, confirmed in his good opinion by Favorinus and (despite *Pro Demostrato*) by Fronto; Herodes was a bestower of private and public munificence, and a millionaire is seldom short of admirers. But other friends and admirers found his mourning excessive, nor need Gellius, had he concurred, have stated the occasion of the speech. As it is, the reader who knows only this chapter, and others in which ἀπάθεια is attacked, must suppose that Herodes' critic was a flinty-hearted dogmatist. (Contrast *NA* 15. 24, where no one who has read the *Nights* will imagine that Gellius agrees with Volcacius' preference for Caecilius over Plautus.) Gellius alone was not offended by what was too much for Marcus and Philostratus.

Chapter 8

Miscellaneous Contemporaries

Peregrinus Proteus

WHILE in Athens, Gellius often visited a hut outside the city inhabited by the Cynic philosopher Peregrinus, later called Proteus, 'uirum grauem atque constantem' (12. 11. 1), who uttered many valuable and noble sentiments: for example, that the wise man would not do wrong even though gods and men should never know, but others ought to recognize that nothing could be concealed for ever, and repeat Sophocles' injunction 'Hide naught, for Time discovers all.' Another old poet, adds Gellius on his own account, called Truth the child of Time; by thus abandoning Peregrinus' sermon, he incurs suspicion of inventing it.[1] When Peregrinus rebukes a young man of equestrian birth for yawning (8. 3), we recall the *aduocatus* with the gapes[2] who narrowly escaped censorial punishment (4. 20. 8–9, from Scipio). Yet a fashionable youth, having come to see a sight, would find the preaching prosy; whereas Gellius is so taken with moral sternness as to praise the reviler of Herodes Atticus. The harangue on the Olympic aqueduct had not yet been delivered,[3] but the outspoken critic of the great, whose banishment from Rome conferred a reputation to maintain,[4] must already have attacked this tempting target.[5] Gellius, who admired the high-handed plutocrat, admires no less the cur that barked against him.

This same Peregrinus is represented by Lucian as a demented charlatan, guilty of monstrous crimes; the traits are those of Lucian's other villains,[6] but

1. Cf. pp. 24, 48. Both theme (cf. 'Gyges' Ring') and quotation (Soph. fr. 301 R) were commonplaces that Gellius might no less easily incorporate in a fictitious homily than Peregrinus in a real one.

2. For Beloe's rendering of *oscedo* cf. Jane Austen, *Persuasion*, ii, ch. 8 (p. 397 Davie); 'Gähnsucht' Walterstern, 'zevotoju' Afanasij.

3. See Harmon on Luc. *Per.* 19, Ameling ii. 137–8 (who would date Gellius' visit later, but see ch. 1 n. 26).

4. Cf. Luc. *Per.* 4. He vilified the mild and gentle Pius, till the City prefect, ἀνὴρ σοφός (either Bruttius Praesens, in whom Syme, *RP* ii. 774 detects an Epicurean, or Erucius Clarus), brooked no more (§ 18). It was harder to be banished under Pius than Domitian; but his want of Hadrian's common touch (cf. M. Ant. *Med.* 1. 16. 15) perhaps caused disaffection (cf. *Epit. Caes.* 15. 9) for Peregrinus to exploit. Away from Rome he was harmless: the authorities found nothing subversive in the 'insurrectionary' speech of *Per.* 19.

5. e.g. for the legacy swindle, or his ostentatious mourning.

6. Robinson 18–19. Wieland in his tr. of Lucian paired Peregrinus the *Schwärmer* with Alexander the *Betrüger* (iii. 45 n.) and defended Lucian's portrait of one whose whole life 'eine fortdaurende Lüge und aus Selbstbetrug erzeugter Betrug anderer Leute ist' (ibid. 99); but his novel *Geheime Geschichte des Philosophen Peregrinus Proteus* (Leipzig, 1790–1) presents a misguided but sincere Peregrinus (a Cerinthian heretic) modelled on the Christian charlatan

his suicide by fire at the Olympic Games of 165 sufficiently demonstrates a mental flaw. He was given to religious speculation, having even for a time been a Christian; his last days blend Christian pastorship,[7] Indian asceticism,[8] and Neopythagorean miracles,[9] with visions of Zeus and Stoico-Cynic *imitatio Herculis.* No doubt this religiosity infused his teaching, and underlay his fling with Christianity. Lucian has him converted while on the run in Palestine after, as 'you all know',[10] murdering his father (*Per.* 10–11); he becomes a leading theologian, courts martyrdom, exploits the Christians' charity, but is excommunicated, already living like a Cynic,[11] when—'I think'—seen eating forbidden meats (§ 16), presumably the leavings of a sacrifice. It is implied that his hypocrisy had been unmasked;[12] those who allow him sincerity may see instead a formal token of apostasy: perhaps rejection of the god who had refused the offer of his death (*Per.* 14), perhaps a stern moralist's disgust with the doctrine of divine forgiveness.[13] But fraudulent, sincere, or deceived deceiver, Peregrinus was more complex than Gellius knew.[14]

Lavater ('Der Prophet' in Goethe's and Schiller's *Xenien*). Sincerity was also allowed by Zeller, 'Alexander und Peregrinus, ein Betrüger und ein Schwärmer' (*Vort.* ii. 154–88; cf. *Phil.* iii/1. 801–3), by whose day *Schwärmer* was less pejorative than in Wieland's; others went further (Bompaire 478 n. 2)—but even Alexander the False Prophet (honoured, like Peregrinus, at Parium: Athenag. *Leg.* 26. 3) finds defenders (Bompaire 480 with n. 3). A Catholic represented a Montanist as a convicted criminal who battened on innocent Christians (Eus. *HE* 5. 18. 6–10); cf. *Did.* 11–13 on true and false prophets.

7. The letters to Greek cities (Luc. *Per.* 41) recall Ignatius' missives before the martyrdom he, like Peregrinus (§ 14), craved; Pearson, *Vindiciae* i. 5–6 saw in ἐχειροτόνησεν Peregrinus' echo of Ign. *Smyrn.* 11. 2, *Polyc.* 7. 2, *Phil.* 10. 1, but cf. Luc. *Philops.* 12. He could now achieve the martyrdom he had missed with the Church, and demonstrate that a Greek philosopher could die as bravely as a Polycarp (*c.*155–7: T. D. Barnes, *JTS²* 18 (1967) 433–7; Birley, *Marcus Aurelius* 261), but the death-wish came before the choice of purpose.

8. Luc. *Per.* 27, 39. Cf. Calanus (Luc. *Per.* 25, Syncellus 430 Mosshammer) and Zarmanochegas, on whose tomb at Athens Peregrinus could read the boast of self-immortalization (Strabo 720–1 C). 9. With Luc. *Per.* 39–40 cf. Philost. *VA* 8. 30–1.

10. Meaning there was no proof, cf. [Dem.] 40. 53–4 (despite e.g. § 23). For the motif of flight cf. Apul. *Met.* 1. 19. 12.

11. Cf. Dodds, *Pagan and Christian* 60 n. 3, Benko 46–50 on the affinities between Cynicism and Christianity.

12. Although Egypt, where the apostate next went, swarmed with Gnostics of all kinds (one sect even revered the Cynic favourite Heracles: Hippol. *Ref.* 5. 23–7, 10. 15), and Gnostics freely ate εἰδωλόθυτα, Peregrinus did not join them: he had not been influenced by their ideas, and most sects were too small to attract an adventurer (H. Chadwick, pers. comm.). G. Bagnani, *Historia* 4 (1955) 108–9, suggests that Peregrinus, having joined the Judaizing church at Pella, was excommunicated, in the anti-Jewish reaction after Bar Kokhba's defeat, for *refusing* to eat food proscribed by the Mosaic law; but Judaizers had not yet been put to the ban (Chadwick, *Early Church* 22–3), and if modern Christianity was too neglectful of the Torah, Cynicism showed even greater disrespect for laws and ceremonies. (Nor does Lucian mock the circumcision that would have been revealed by the Cynic exercise of *Per.* 17.)

13. Orig. *C. Cels.* 3. 59–71; Jul. *Caes.* 336 A–B (cf. Soz. 1. 5. 1, Zos. 2. 29. 4).

14. Cf. Wieland, tr. iii. 105; 'Ein solcher Mann [as Gellius] kommt nun freylich, wo es auf Urtheile von Menschen, die nicht ganz leicht zu beurtheilen sind, ankömmt, gegen einen Lucian in gar keine Betrachtung' (cf. ibid. 106–7). For confirmation see 14. 3 (pp. 198–9). Schettino 79 sees in *constans* (used of no other contemporary) a riposte to Lucian, but Gellius may have heard ill reports in Athens.

Poets

Gellius' lifetime, his children's, and their children's abounded in writers of pleasant and skilful verse, often in new or unfamiliar metres; in Latin at least, they rarely attempted the grander genres,[15] but are not contemptible in the lesser. No Greek, but four Latin poets, make personal appearances in the *Nights*, two anonymous, two named. Of the former, one is the youth of 19. 11 plausibly identified with Apuleius, the other the friend of Fronto's who in 19. 8 employs, and attempts to defend, the plural *harenae*; the incident may be fictitious, but Fronto's guests undoubtedly included dilettante versifiers, than which *poeta* need imply no more.[16]

Fronto's friend was 'a learned man and at the time a well-known poet' (§ 3); if this means that the fame of his verse had already perished, the same fate soon befell the work of Julius Paulus, whom Gellius describes as the most learned man (and poet) he had known and as a good man much learned in antiquity.[17] On this occasion (19. 7), Gellius tells of his visits to the poet's small property in the *ager Vaticanus*, and the vegetarian but unstinted fare that he enjoyed; it was there that he and a companion heard a reading of Laevius' *Alcestis*, full of striking words and phrases they discussed on their way home in the autumn evening. Laevius, who is also quoted by Fronto and Apuleius, may well have served the poets of the second and early third centuries as a model.[18] In other chapters Paulus brings his learning to bear on the correct use of *superesse*, on a wrongly impugned reading in a manuscript, and on ancient legal terms with which a lawyer cannot be bothered. This learning was not forgotten, if he is the Paulus whom Charisius quotes as an authority on Coelius and Afranius.[19]

The remaining poet is Annianus, who entertained Gellius and other friends to the festivities of the wine-harvest on his Faliscan estate, with oysters on the table sent from Rome: a more sumptuous meal than one got at Paulus'.[20] On the strength of this report some pleasant little verses recorded by the metricians Terentianus Maurus and Apthonius have been ascribed to him; but of the four fragments so assigned only two, quoted by Terentianus

---

15. In Greek the 2nd c. exhibits Oppian's *Halieutica*, and Marcellus' *Iatrica*, the Severan age ps.-Oppian's *Cynegetica*; but the efflorescence of late-imperial epic is still to come. In Latin, Apuleius' friend Clemens wrote an epic on Alexander (*Flor.* 7. 4), from which the three hexameters of *Flor.* 6. 3 are thought to be taken; we bear its loss bravely. Some have assigned the *Ciris* to the 2nd c., whose reactionary spirit might have favoured a return to Catullan structures.

16. Champlin, *Fronto* 54; cf. 158 n. 56 for metrical inscriptions by senators and *equites*.

17. 1. 22. 9; 5. 4. 1; 16. 10. 9; 19. 7. 1.

18. The iambic dimeter, frequent in Laevius, is used by Hadrian, Alfius, Marianus, Serenus, and Gellius' friend; Laevius' anacreontics reappear in Hadrian and Florus. The main resemblance, however, lies in the cultivation of the light, the smooth, and the pretty.

19. See now F. Della Corte, *Studi noniani* 7 (1982) 89–96; but there is no proof.

20. *NA* 20. 8. 1–2; but the oysters were thin, allegedly because the moon was waning (cf. ch. 14 n. 93).

from 'ille poeta Faliscus', are universally accepted as his work.[21] They are, as our source calls them, light verse ('ludicra carmina'); the first celebrates the prolific Falernian grape, the second describes an immigrant, or more probably a luxurious import, from the East.[22]

Ausonius records that Annianus wrote Fescennine verses, ribald poetry in honour of a wedding; he couples them with Laevius' work to defend by their example his own indecent *Cento nuptialis*.[23] When, therefore, Gellius states at 9. 10. 1 that Annianus and most others 'of the same Muse' admired the delicacy with which Vergil had described the marital intercourse of Venus and Vulcan, the praise comes not from a mere critic cataloguing tropes but from a practising erotic poet who knew from experience how difficult a task the master had performed.[24]

We also learn from Gellius that Annianus was a connoisseur of ancient literature and a delightful conversationalist on anything from the correct pronunciation of compound adverbs (6. 7) to the effect of the moon's phases on oysters, onions, and cats' eyes (20. 8). But of his poetry, as of Paulus', we are told no more, since like Fronto's speeches it stood above the need for praise; it is the human beings whom Gellius must commend, in order that we may know he was their intimate.

Grammarians

At *NA* 2. 3. 5 Gellius reports that a renowned Roman grammarian, Fidus Optatus, showed him a copy of *Aeneid* 2 thought to be Vergil's own (cf. p. 140); the two *cognomina* both suggest African origin.[25] He was not, as Hertz conjectured, Fronto's friend Caelius Optatus (*Amic.* 1. 9), a man of far higher

---

21. Cameron 142–3, following Apthonius and Servius, assigns fr. 3 M–B to Serenus' *Opuscula ruralia*, well known in late antiquity; id. 166–7 doubts the modern ascription of fr. 4. S. Mattiacci, edn. of the so-called *poetae nouelli*, pp. 92–104, allows Annianus' authorship of both frr.; her interpretation of Ter. Maur. 1991 (pp. 94–6) is plainly right.

22. Fr. 1: 'uua, uua sum et uua Falerna / et ter feror et quater anno'; fr. 2: 'unde, unde colonus Eoae? / a flumine uenit Oronti' (*undae unde* Camerarius; or is 'Eoae' subst., cf. ἡ Ἐῴα, e.g. 'Apul.' *Mund.* 13, Philost. *VS* 563, Porph. *Antr.* 23, p. 72. 14 Nauck?).

23. P. 169 Prete; cf. Annianus fr. 4, if it be his.

24. Cameron, who refutes the theory of a self-conscious poetic school with Annianus its doyen, takes the men 'eiusdem Musae' for fellow critics (pp. 162–3; cf. Gellius' fellow scholars at pr. 19), not fellow love-poets. Yet the reference to difficulty (§§ 3–4) suggests practical experience; and the ancient critics, even if they do not do dirt on the passage like Probus and Cornutus, merely record it as a periphrasis to avoid obscenity (cit. Hosius ad loc.). In any case, Annianus was (though not exclusively) an erotic poet, and there is nothing in Gellius' text to suggest that he did not speak as such, repeating the view of other erotic poets from Vergil's day onwards. Ausonius' self-defence adduces the same passage, and also *Georg.* 3. 123–37; his 'honesta uerborum translatione uelauit' recalls *NA* 9. 10. 1 'uerecunda quadam translatione uerborum ... protexit'. At *Protr.* 48, *Epigr.* 26. 2 Ausonius imitates respectively *Epigr. Plauti* 3 (*NA* 1. 24. 3) and Cn. Matius fr. 3 M–B (*NA* 7. 6. 5).

25. Syme, *RP* iii. 1109–10.

social status, who was to command Legio III Augusta at Lambaesis;[26] no more can be said.

In 18. 6 one Aelius Melissus is described as the leading Roman grammarian of Gellius' day, but owing his prominence more to self-advertisement and showmanship than to achievement ('sed maiore in litteris erat iactantia et σοφιστείᾳ quam opera' § 1); his book on correct usage, *De loquendi proprietate*, whose title would make it seem essential reading for anyone concerned to speak good Latin, is found to contain an absurd distinction between *matrona* and *materfamilias* as having borne respectively one child and more. Gellius prefers the alternative account that makes the *matrona* any married woman, the *materfamilias* one married *cum manu*, as at Cic. *Top.* 14;[27] he includes the wife *in manu* of a husband himself *in potestate*, which is contradicted by PF 112. 27–30 L.[28] In fact, since *manus* hardly existed by this time except for certain priestly households in which marriage had to be solemnized by the special rite of *confarreatio*, the term *materfamilias* had become equivalent to *matrona*; the synonyms invited the ingenious to invent a distinction like those discussed in 11. 11 and 13. 3, or by such writers as Ammonius and pseudo-Fronto.

The next chapter introduces us to Domitius, called Insanus because of his bad temper ('cui cognomentum Insano factum est, quoniam erat natura intractabilior et morosior' 18. 7. 1), ascribed to the 'melancholy', or excess of black bile, believed to afflict outstanding minds.[29] When Favorinus asks him whether *contio* is good Latin for a public speech, Domitius glowers, and lets loose a tirade:[30] the world is indeed going to the dogs if even philosophers care only about words; still, he will send him a book with the answer. He, the grammarian, seeks rules for living life, but the grammarians, as Cato put it, are nothing but cerements, collecting wordlets and dictiuncules as pointless as the dirges of hired mourning-women.[31] If only the human race were dumb! Wickedness would be out of a tool (and grammarians, he neglects to notice, out of a job). Favorinus tolerantly concludes that Domitius is having

---

26. *CIL* vii. 2736, 17958. Pflaum 547 suggests that the legate was the son of Fronto's friend; but see Bowersock 125.

27. D.S. on *Aen.* 11. 476, Serv. ibid. 581, Boethius ad loc. Cic. (v. 299 Orelli), further restrict the title to a woman married *per coemptionem*. Boethius, however, treats *usus, confarreatio,* and *coemptio*, not as the three forms of marriage conferring *manus*, but as the three forms of marriage in general, only the last doing so; which does not inspire confidence in this tradition.

28. Cf. [Suet.] p. 280 R: 'matrona filios ampliat, materfamilias quae patri familiae nupsit'; PF denies the title to widows and the childless. Gellius' exposition is conceptually archaic (cf. ch. 15 n. 40).

29. [Arist.] *Probl.* 30. 1. Unsociable behaviour is a mark of doubtful sanity in Pliny *Ep.* 6. 15.

30. 'Voce atque uultu atrociore' (§ 3); cf. 19. 10. 10 'iam uoce atque uultu intentiore'.

31. 'Vos philosophi mera estis, ut M. Cato ait, mortualia; glosaria [= γλωσσάρια, diminutive of γλῶσσα 'hard word'] namque colligitis et lexidia [= λεξείδια, as in Epictetus and Galen, dim. of λέξις 'id.'], res taetras et inanes et friuolas tamquam mulierum uoces praeficarum [a periphrasis for *nenias* 'dirges' or 'screeds of nonsense']'. For the sentiment cf. Sen. *Ep.* 108. 23 'itaque quae philosophia fuit facta philologia est'. See too Tränkle 110–11.

one of his turns.[32] Domitius sends the book; by Verrius Flaccus as Gellius thinks and as we may well believe: similar discussions of words relating to public life and bearing several senses are found at PF 36. 21–7, 74. 15–27 L.[33] The grammarian who despises mere words has put on a show of verbal bravura, and Favorinus, when discussing Insanus' ailment, drops repeatedly into Greek with every sign of quoting from a treatise. We may well suspect that these are Gellian embellishments, but it is hard to believe that he gratuitously concocted an encounter of which Favorinus had the worst. Rather, Favorinus did have his head bitten off; whether he retained his composure as well as Gellius makes out, or Domitius betrayed himself with such a display of strange words, is as open to doubt as any other partisan report, but the former, at least, is not incredible.

The Westphalian jurist Everhard Otto[34] suggested that Mad Domitius was the Domitius Labeo whose question on a point of law to his friend Juventius Celsus provoked the crushing reply: 'I don't understand your problem, or else your question is a very silly one: it is more than ridiculous to doubt whether a person is lawfully a witness because he has also written out the will' (D. 28. 1. 27).[35] Following him, Paul Kretschmar appended to his masterly elucidation of the question and its answer the conjecture that Domitius, embittered at the humiliating rebuff, thereafter refused to answer any questions remotely touching the law—even one on public speeches, since it presupposed acquaintance with constitutional law—dear as its study remained to him:[36] Insanus' statement 'uitae iam atque morum disciplinas quaero' (18. 7. 3) is here interpreted in the light of *moribus receptum*, used of Roman institutions at D. 1. 6. 8. pr., 24. 1. 1.[37] On top of this Kretschmar supposed that Domitius—no longer Labeo, a *cognomen* the frustrated amateur refused to share with M. Antistius, but Insanus because the iron that had entered his soul had corroded his temper—was also the unnamed grammarian of *NA* 20. 10, likewise a man of renown, who rebuffs a question about a legal phrase with the words 'you are either mistaken, young man, or not in earnest', an echo of Celsus' rudeness to himself.

32. 'Videtur enim mihi ἐπισημαίνεσθαι', to display the symptoms (Salmasius i. 734ªE–ᵇA, P. K. Marshall, *CQ*² 10 (1960) 180).

33. 'Exempla in eo libro scripta non erant' (§ 8) suggests that their absence in Paulus is not due to successive abridgements; Gellius would hardly have told a lie so easily exposed. He himself produces examples, one from Cic. *Orat.* 168 preceding a sentence quoted at 13. 21. 24 (p. 26); for Gellius instructing Favorinus, see p. 84.

34. 'De vita Servii Sulpicii' 1578.

35. Celsus was fond of calling an idea ridiculous (D. 41. 2. 18. 1; 47. 2. 68. 2; cf. 3. 5. 9. 1); even Sabinus' view could be dismissed as 'stolida' (FV 75. 5). Other jurists were no less forthright (E. Otto 1578–9).

36. P. Kretschmar, *ZSS* 57 (1937) 52–75; on Insanus, pp. 71–5. Either Domitius Labeo was confusing the requirements of civil and praetorian law, or the apparently stupid question concealed a fraud that Celsus was to be trapped into legitimating.

37. Namely *patria potestas*, whose origin is lost in the mists of time and the *leges regiae*, and invalidation of gifts between spouses, which took place unrecordedly after 204 BC (FV 302) but before the late Republic (Watson, *Property* 229–30).

A touching picture, but it must remain a dream. Domitius is not a rare *nomen*, there is nothing in 'the discipline of life and morals' to suggest the law, Favorinus' question could be answered without 'staatsrechtliche Kenntnisse', and if mere mention of a *contio* were enough to violate forbidden ground, what subject would be safe? As for 20. 10, there are plenty of anonymous, famous, and probably fictitious grammarians in Gellius; as elsewhere, he is waging war on narrow specialists. Having thus rejected Otto's and Kretschmar's theory, we must admit that but for Gellius the fame of Optatus, Melissus, and Domitius would have perished;[38] a warning for whoever shall write the long-desired history of Roman scholarship.

Other prominent persons

Gellius reports his teacher Apollinaris' oral and written replies to enquiries from Sex. Erucius Clarus (*cos. II* 146, cf. p. 12), a former protégé of the younger Pliny's, a man of great learning and keen interest in the ancient writers, suffect consul in 117 after his capture of Seleuceia; eclipsed under Hadrian, he found new favour from Pius, being made City prefect and receiving the second consulate that post comported.[39] He appears on familiar terms with Apollinaris; Gellius was merely an observer, as he is in 19. 13. 1, when 'Fronto Cornelius et Festus Postumius et Apollinaris Sulpicius' are among those waiting to pay the emperor their respects. Festus, who asks about the Latinity of *nanus* in the sense 'dwarf mule' or 'pony' (§ 4), is the suffect consul of 160 M. Postumius Festus, owner of a house on the Quirinal, an orator in Greek and Latin whose consular great-grandsons proclaimed him for their master,[40] one of three men Fronto commended to act in his stead as *patroni* of Cirta, declaring him suitable in character and eloquence, from a nearby *ciuitas* in Africa.[41]

In 19. 7 Gellius and Julius Celsinus, having dined with Paulus, on the way home discuss the poet Laevius. Three chapters later Celsinus, now called *Numida*, is again at Gellius' side visiting the sick Fronto; he recalls a passage of Ennius that supports his host's contention. Champlin identifies him with P. Iulius Proculus [Cel]sinus, *cos. des.*, honoured at Cirta and a member of its

38. The reference to 'Melissus grammaticus' and his doctrine at Isid. *Diff.* 1. 373 (PL 83. 48B) is derived (at whatever remove) from Gellius. Some fragments ascribed to an undifferentiated 'Melissus' may be from Aelius rather than Maecenas' freedman (Funaioli, *GRF* 538).

39. See Plin. *Ep.* 2. 9 with Sherwin-White's nn.; Syme, *RP* 488–9, who notes that 'A predilection for archaism in literature ought not to have alienated a man from Hadrian.' Kinship with Septicius Clarus may have done (Sherwin-White); but his rise under Trajan is slow for a military man (Syme), and Pliny's letter suggests abnormal effort to rescue his career. Fronto, however, can assume that Pius will think the better of his friendship with Censorius Niger for the latter's friendship with Erucius, the foremost senator (*Ep. Ant. P.* 3. 3).

40. *Fasti Ostienses* s.a. 160 (see Vidman, edn.² 135–6). Though designated proconsul of Asia, probably for 174/5 (Alföldy 122), he did not serve; perhaps Gellius accords him a posthumous commemoration, but considers him too eminent to need his praise.

41. *Amic.* 2. 11; *c.*158, Champlin, 'Chronology' 153–4. The *ciuitas* remains undetermined.

tribe, Quirina;[42] but in the late 170s the city of Cuicul, one of the IIII Coloniae Cirtenses, erected a monument to Iulia Celsina C. f., wife of its patron A. Iulius Pompilius Piso Laeuillus, legate at Lambaesis and consul designate.[43] Perhaps Gellius' companion was her father, C. Iulius (presumably Pap.) Celsinus, from a Cuicul family that married another daughter to a Iulius Proculus of Cirta.

Herodes' guests in 1. 2. 1 include 'me et clarissimum uirum Seruilianum compluresque alios nostrates', studying at Athens. As a senator, Servilianus seems out of place amongst these young students; but if his title be proleptic, he could have returned to Rome, entered the vigintivirate, married in his early twenties,[44] and begotten a son whose career peaked under Commodus; perhaps Caecilius Servilianus, legate of Thrace in the 180s.[45] Although a Reverend may be scandalous, an Honourable blackguardly, and a *uir clarissimus* obscure, we are meant to recognize the bare *cognomen* dropped with such casual care.

Servilianus, Celsinus, Postumius Festus, and Erucius Clarus testify by their presence that Gellius, in his youth, had rubbed shoulders with the great and famous; thus might a modern memoirist mention the future Cabinet ministers he had known at college.[46] These apart, Gellius can name only the jurist Africanus, not the greatest of his day,[47] and the philosopher Macedo, 'a good man and my friend', otherwise unknown.[48]

42. *IL Alg.* ii. 638; Champlin, *Fronto* 14, 147 n. 61; but see *PIR²* I 155.

43. *AE* 1911, 103; cf. Alföldy 191 n. 213. Other Iuliae Celsinae in Africa (*CIL* viii, index) are of purely local interest.

44. See Sherwin-White on Plin. *Ep.* 7. 24. 3.

45. *PIR²* C 82.

46. The 'praeses Cretae prouinciae' in 2. 2. 1 is not named; a praetorian with little hope of further promotion, long forgotten by the time of publication, would have lent no lustre. It is enough that Gellius was suffered to remain in a proconsul's presence. Our *fasti* for Crete and Cyrene under Pius are almost blank (Alföldy 263).

47. *NA* 20. 1; not cited in the Digest as frequently as Gaius, let alone Cervidius Scaevola, and not known to have held even equestrian office, though kinsmen may have done better (Kunkel, *Herkunft* 172–3).

48. *NA* 13. 8. 4; Mosellanus, sig. K7ʳ states that 'Suidas' mentions a philosopher of this name who flourished under Hadrian, but our texts of the *Suda* contain no such entry. Unknown, too, are the targets of pr. 20, 'quorundam male doctorum hominum scaeuitas et inuidentia', whom he defies by bidding the vulgar herd depart; Gellius could have said with the fabulist, 'Hoc quo pertineat dicet qui me nouerit', but we are completely in the dark (rival miscellanists as envisaged at 1. 25. 18?), though 'quorundam' should imply more specific opponents than those scorned by Greek poets.

PART III

SCHOLARSHIP AND STUDY

Chapter 9

Scholarly Reading

GELLIUS read few learned writers in Greek except philosophers. He is acquainted with Homeric scholarship,[1] but the one problem discussed at length, the σπάρτα of *Il.* 2. 135, comes from Varro (17. 3. 4); Apion, who wrote a major work on Homer's vocabulary, provides only marvels. No first-hand knowledge need be supposed of Aristarchus and Crates (2. 25. 4; 14. 6. 3), Alexander Aetolus (15. 20. 8), or Apollodorus (17. 4. 5–6). The miscellanies of Sotion (1. 8) and Pamphila (15. 17; 15. 23) may contribute more than we can recognize; others too of those listed at pr. 6–9 may have been of service, despite the disdain of § 11. But grammar in its broad ancient sense,[2] Gellius pursued in Latin.[3]

The poet Accius' views on authentic Plautine comedies, like others cited in 3. 3, are known to Gellius through Varro (§ 9); so, presumably, his assertion that Hesiod was older than Homer (3. 11. 2), and perhaps his reasons (§ 5),[4] but the contemptuous comment on his feeble arguments (§ 4, cf. lemma) may be Gellius' own. Of the other authorities in 3. 3. 1, 'non indicibus Aelii nec Sedigiti nec Claudii nec Aurelii nec Accii nec Manilii', from Varro's treatise on Plautus' plays, L. Aelius Stilo Praeconinus is described as the most learned Roman of his day (1. 18. 1; 10. 21. 2). He was Varro's teacher (16. 8. 2, cf. Cic. *Brut.* 205); all knowledge of him in the *Nights* is likely to come from Varro[5] except the treatise on propositional logic that Gellius turned up in the

1. *NA* 2. 6. 11 ~ Schol. *Il.* 4. 223–4, Eust. 465. 24 (but cf. Hermog. 306. 8–10 R); *NA* 3. 16. 17 ~ Eust. 1682. 27–8 (unless really from Favorinus); *NA* 6. 20. 5 ~ Schol. T *Il.* 22. 152, Schol. *Od.* 11. 596, Eust. 1702. 19–22 (cf. Holford-Strevens, 'Nola', 393 n. 1); *NA* 13. 21. 15 ~ Schol. T *Il.* 16. 583, 21. 345; *NA* 13. 25. 21 ~ Schol. T *Il.* 2. 8; *NA* 18. 9. 9 ~ Schol. T *Il.* 2. 484, Eust. 1381. 28 (the equation of *inseque* and ἔννεπε probably came from a commentary on Ennius). The moralistic comment at 1. 15. 3 on ἕρκος ὀδόντων (cf. Schol. T *Il.* 4. 350) will be due to Favorinus, the interpretation of αἴθοπα οἶνον at 17. 8. 10 (cf. Eust. 135. 34–6, 1449. 20–2, 1854. 63–4) to Taurus.

2. That is, the study of literary texts and all things necessary to their understanding: e.g. 'Dion. Thrax', § 1 with Schol., Quint. 1. 4. 2, S.E. *Math.* 1. 91–3.

3. Knowledge of Greek technical terms, e.g. ἀπαρέμφατον 'infinitive' 1. 7. 6, came with the study of Greek; they were the more necessary since Latin usage was not yet fixed (note 'per infinitum modum' 15. 13. 9 of the impersonal indicative 'est ueritum'; *modus infinitiuus* in our sense not till Char. 216. 3 B). Occasional reference to Attic usage, real or supposed (pp. 170–1), shows the fashion of the day but not a serious study of the Attic authors.

4. 'inuolgatum esset', from a verb never found before Gellius, scarcely after him, but used at five other places in the *Nights*, indicates the wording is his own; 'itidem' is common in Early Latin, but also characteristic of Gellius, and 'procul dubio' is unlikely for Accius (ch. 13 n. 28).

5. Explicitly in 1. 18; 10. 21; perhaps through the additional filter of Verrius 2. 21. 8 and of Sinnius Capito 5. 21. 6. At 12. 4. 5 the citation is confessedly indirect, presumably through Varro

Bibliotheca Pacis but found unhelpful (16. 8. 2–3).[6] Volcacius Sedigitus, a noted poet (Pliny *NH* 11. 244), delivers a versified ranking-list of comic dramatists in 15. 24. At 13. 23. 19 Stilo's son-in-law Ser. Claudius or Clodius derives *Nerio* from *ne* and *ira*; the notice, in postscript form, does not (despite Hosius i, p. xlvii) come from Varro—who, had he mentioned this conjecture, would have refuted it as he refutes Stilo's etymologies at 1. 18. 2—but from Claudius himself: 'in commentario quodam [cf. 6. 20. 1] Seruii Claudii scriptum inuenimus'. Gellius quotes it for what it is worth ('cuicuimodi est'); he makes no further reference to Claudius, and does not know that he practised the very mode of Plautine criticism advocated in 3. 3.[7] Aurelius Opillus[8] is cited in another postscript (1. 25. 17–18) for an etymology that Gellius mentions, as we might in a footnote, to forestall the charge of ignorance. There is no other mention of Manilius.

All these writers belong to Varro's boyhood or his youth: Stilo followed the unbending Numidicus into exile in 100 BC, Aurelius the upright Rutilius Rufus eight years later. The aged Accius conversed with the youthful Cicero; Manilius may be the proconsul of Gallia Transalpina, L. Manlius, defeated by the Sertorian Hirtuleius;[9] Claudius left his library to his brother (or cousin?) L. Papirius Paetius, who gave it to Cicero in 60 BC. To this period belongs Hypsicrates, cited by Cloatius Verus for an absurd etymology (p. 133).

Far more attention is devoted to the varied learning of Varro and Nigidius, the greatest scholars of their age (4. 16. 1; 19. 14. 1); Varro was even greater than Nigidius (4. 9. 1).[10] Neither is infallible: Varro falls into the same error as his teacher (1. 18. 5), gives a definition of a truce more amusing than sound (1. 25. 3),[11] and includes some trivial items in his disquisition on the number seven (3. 10. 16); Nigidius' etymologies of *auarus*

(Kretzschmer 52–3), through whom comes too Stilo's judgement (Quint. 10. 1. 99) that if the Muses spoke Latin they would speak like Plautus.

6. For his comment that Stilo had written it 'rather to remind himself than to teach others' (16. 8. 3) cf. 17. 7. 5 on Nigidius.

7. Cic. *Fam.* 9. 16. 4. Ritschl 92 n. 1 allowed, and Mercklin 643–4 asserted, that Gellius had access to Claudius' *index*; the mode of reference, as an item in a list, suggests otherwise, nor is there reason to suppose that Claudius wrote after Varro (cf. Kretzschmer 43 n. 1).

8. The correct form of the *cognomen*, despite 'Opilius' in Gellius' MSS: see Suet. *Gram.* 6. 4, Funaioli, *GRF* 86. Gellius does not remark that *stribiligo*, said at 5. 20. 1 to be an old word for *soloecismus*, was Opillus' term (fr. 17).

9. See Schanz–Hosius i⁴. 605–6, cf. Rawson 273 n. 43.

10. Cf. Serv. on *Aen.* 10. 175; perhaps from a common source (the Suetonian life posited by Della Casa, ch. 1?), but Gellius knew both well enough to form his own judgement, even if it confirmed another's. It proves nothing that only here and at 7. 6. 10 does he write 'Nigidius Figulus' insted of 'P. Nigidius'.

11. Stephanus to Vulcob 16 states that Gellius expresses 'tribus elegantissimis modis' the notion *se non è vero è ben trovato*; he does not cite the instances, of which there are five (1. 25. 3; 12. 14. 7; 15. 3. 5; 18. 1. 12; 20. 1. 35; cf. also 1. 23. 8; 3. 19. 4; 7. 8. 5; 15. 9. 7). So e.g. Arist. *Cael.* 290ᵇ14, 295ᵇ16, *Pol.* 1291ᵃ11; Satyrus, P. Oxy. IX 1176 fr. 39 xviii 17–20.

and *autumo* are unconvincing (10. 5. 3; 15. 3. 5), his view of -*osus* as always pejorative is wrong (4. 9. 12).[12]

Varro is cited for every field of knowledge in which Gellius takes an interest, and from a wide range of his writings: he tells of Sallust in love and Naevius in war, he inveighs against gluttony and prescribes for a banquet, he defines terms of geometry and logic and comments on the caesura of hexameter and trimeter.[13] He is quoted nearly eighty times, in over seventy chapters, and is the likely source for much else;[14] full examination must await a comprehensive modern edition of his fragments.[15] Furthermore, he is an authority on Latin usage not only as a grammarian but also as a stylist, which conflicts with the judgements of Quintilian (10. 1. 95), of Gellius' own admirer Augustine (*CD* 6. 2), and of modern readers disgusted by the diction of *De lingua Latina*. The remnants of the satires show that Varro could write more skilfully when he tried; in any case Gellius admired the pre-classical tradition to which he belonged, anacolutha and all.[16] A play on words is described as witty ('lepide ... composita sunt', 1. 17. 5);[17] the use of *mutare* 'to change' as an intransitive is praised at 18. 12. 8 ('inquit elgantissime'). Varro also gave it the sense 'to differ', not only illustrated in the next sentence but adopted at 2. 23. 7 and 13. 3. 1;[18] it is otherwise found only at Catullus 22. 11. At 1. 4. 1 and 20. 1. 34 Gellius uses 'ad amussim', found at Varro, *RR* 2. 1. 26, *Sat.* fr. 555 Bücheler, in preference to the Plautine 'examussim'; it has been plausibly restored in Apuleius (*Met.* 2. 2. 8)—who also read Varro (*Apol.* 42. 6)—and is otherwise confined to Gellius' own imitators Ammianus and Macrobius. It may indeed have been used by other late Republican

12. See O. Schönwerth and C. Weyman, *ALL* v. 212–13 (and p. 203 on Nigidius' *bibosus*, cf. *NA* 3. 12).

13. Sallust 17. 18 (cf. pp. 186–7), Naevius 17. 21. 45. Gluttony 4. 19, banquets 13. 11 (cf. 6. 16; 13. 31). Geometry 1. 20, logic 16. 6, caesura 18. 15 (cf. Aug. *Mus.* 5. 26 = PL 32. 1060–1; Weil 142–4; but the Ennian term for hexameters, 'longis versibus', cf. Enn. *Op. inc.* 20 Sk, may be Gellius' own touch). The caesura presupposed is penthemimeral; contrast the third trochee (increasingly prevalent in Greek) at Arist. *Metaph.* 1093ᵃ28–31.

14. Most obviously at 18. 13, which will come from Varro, *De disciplinis*; in general see Kretzschmer 44–54, Ruske 21–33.

15. For some frr. cited by Gellius reference is still made to the Bipontine edn. of 1788, which drew (not without error) on Ausonius Popma's edn. (Leiden, 1601) and the Berewout *Opera omnia* (Dordrecht, 1619).

16. Varro was not an archaizer, using old expressions for effect, but a stick-in-the-mud, writing as Romans had written in his youth; cf. Lebek 331 n. 96. In his defence, and emphasizing his variety of styles, H. D. Jocelyn, *RFIC* 108 (1980) 121–2.

17. 'Vitium uxoris aut tollendum aut ferendum est' (Rolfe: 'A wife's faults must be either put down or put up with'). The literal meanings of *tollere* and *ferre* overlap, the figurative are in contrast.

18. In Early Latin *mutare* is intransitive only in the sense 'to change one's mind' (Plaut. *Rud.* 865, cf. Cic. *Fam.* 16. 1. 1, and 'non demutabo' Plaut. *Pseud.* 555, 566, cf. *Stich.* 725); in the general sense of changing it is frequent in Livy, present in the Senecas and Tacitus, and a mannerism of Tertullian's (the influence of μεταλλάττειν may be suspected). At Lucr. 1. 787 'mutare' means 'to change places', cf. *mutitare* at *NA* 2. 24. 2, 18. 2. 11 in connection with the Megalensia (the only attested instances; though Verrius Flaccus in the same context has *mutitationes* at *Fast. Praen.* for 4 April). Of course, 'quantumque mutare' (2. 23. 7) alludes to Verg. *Aen.* 2. 274–5; but the poet had employed the normal passive.

writers; but Gellius was always likely to imitate an author he admired.[19] No such sentiment is found in Fronto.[20]

Nor does Fronto take any notice of Nigidius Figulus, mentioned by Apuleius (*Apol.* 42. 7, from Varro) for his proficiency in divination. Although Gellius occasionally cites his treatises on augury and entrails, and quotes one passage each from those on winds and animals,[21] he is mostly concerned with his grammatical writings, which unlike Varro's are exclusively linguistic with no concern for literature. They were (says Gellius) far less familiar than Varro's, being more abstruse (19. 14. 2–3): examples follow on Latin phonology, which the reader is left to work out for himself. In 17. 7, on the temporal import of the future perfect, Gellius finds it necessary to explain the argument. Elsewhere Nigidius discusses the accentual contrast, in his day, between *Valéri* genitive and *Váleri* vocative (13. 26. 1),[22] and the articulation of personal pronouns (cf. *SVF* ii. 895) as evidence for the natural origin of language (10. 4. 4). He provides etymologies, and those who seek the origin and basic sense of *quin* are referred to him at 17. 13. 11; he was clearly a more philosophical linguist than Varro. Although his skill in saying the same thing three times over is observed at 11. 11. 4,[23] he is not a model stylist,[24] and only his technical vocabulary is of interest.[25]

Nepos, a major source of the chronological chapter, occasionally contributes anecdotes. In 15. 28 Gellius notes that neither his scholarship nor his friendship with Cicero saved him from mis-stating the latter's age when he defended Sex. Roscius, and suggests, without disapprobation, that he was improving on the truth for his friend's sake (§ 5),[26] Despite his date, Nepos is

---

19. On other echoes of Varronian usage see ch. 3 n. 20, p. 82, Hache *passim*, Knapp 159 (on *paupertinus*), Foster 42 (*ruminor*). Aper mocks those who prefer Sisenna and Varro to Aufidius Bassus and Servilius Nonianus (Tac. *Dial.* 23. 2).

20. At *Nep. am.* 2. 3 'fata a fando appellata aiunt' Fronto is repeating what everyone knew, not specifically citing Varro, *LL* 6. 52.

21. At 6. 9. 5 the paradosis is *deligitur* CPR; V's *diligitur*, ably championed by Timpanaro, *Contributi* 120–3, will be error correcting error.

22. Cf. pp. 132–3. See Mariner; Leumann 425; and on the whole chapter Bernardi Perini, 'Sistema'.

23. The Annaei, who had the misfortune to be born in an unfavoured age, reap harsher words from Fronto (*Orat.* 5–7).

24. In 3. 12 his form *bibosus*, 'boozy', is 'noua et prope absurda' (lemma), irregularly derived and supported only by Laberius (cf. ch. 10 n. 31); despite the lemma, his offence was to recognize rather than to use it.

25. He calls planets *errones* (3. 10. 2 from Varro, 14. 1. 11), barbarous language rustic (13. 6—for Greeks corrected foreigners, Romans polished the country cousin), accents *uoculationes* (13. 26. 3, cf. 13. 6. 1), and the genitive the *casus interrogandi* (13. 26. 3; cf. 20. 6. 8); the bibliography on this term (see Della Casa 83–5, Bernardi Perini, 'Sistema' 2 n. 4) is long and depressing. The style of the extracts in 13. 26 is not Gellian; fr. 12 Fun. = 38 Sw excludes misunderstanding. Least bad of explanations is that alone among the cases properly so called the genitive may by itself constitute the predicate in a question about ownership or other relations (J. C. Scaliger, *Probl.* C, pp. 31–2). See too ch. 2 n. 33.

26. Cf. 1. 3. Mercklin's rule, and the representation of Asconius as correcting only Fenestella (whom in the surviving commentaries he cites five times, thrice in disagreement), suggest that Nepos (whom Asconius is not known to mention) was used directly.

never cited for his language or his literary merit as at Fronto, *Ver.* 2. 1. 20 (§ 18 v.d.H.).

The chief Triumviral and Augustan scholars to appear are Tullius Tiro, Gavius Bassus, Verrius Flaccus, and Julius Hyginus. Bassus' etymology of *persona* is praised at 5. 7. 1 ('lepide mi hercules et scite'), but when that of *parcus* finds no favour at 3. 19. 3 Favorinus has harsh words for 'your friend Gavius Bassus'.[27] Gellius disagrees quite sharply with Tiro (6. 3, cf. 13. 9) and Hyginus (7. 6. 1, cf. 5. 18. 2), and describes a Verrian etymology as 'too forced and absurd' (16. 14. 4). Indeed, of the six chapters in which Verrius is cited, his opinion is rejected in three; nor is he ever accorded the respectful qualifications that Gellius bestows on other writers, even when he differs.[28] Although Verrius' dictionary, like any other, might well be used without acknowledgement, Gellius does not follow the common ancient practice of citing his source only in dissent; we should be slow to suppose use of Verrius unless Festus or Paul exhibits the same doctrine and no common or intermediate source is plausible.[29] Seemingly Gellius held him in no high regard.[30]

Of post-Augustan writers, Cornutus is cited in only two chapters, and only to be refuted (pp. 155–6): that he is 'not in general unlearned' (9. 10. 5, cf. 2. 6. 1) does not save him in specific instances. An 'ancient' grammarian whose name is irretrievably corrupted (*Elydis*, gen. sing.) records the emperor Claudius' inclusion of the Aventine within the *pomerium* (13. 14. 7). The illustrious and infamous Q. Remmius Palaemon is not mentioned.

The greatest grammarian of the first century AD was Probus, whose writings Gellius assiduously collected and whose opinions were reported to

---

27. 'Superstitiose ... et nimis moleste atque odiose confabricatus commolitusque magis est originem uocabuli Gauius iste Bassus quam enarrauit'. With 5. 7. 2 (fr. 8 Fun.) cf. Boeth. *Eutych.* 3 (Chadwick, *Boethius* 193), *GLK* viii. 202. 2–4, 248. 33–249. 2 and n.

28. *NA* 5. 18. 1–2 (but Verrius has his doubts); 16. 14. 4; 17. 6, where Gellius' view is widely accepted (e.g. Kaser, *Priv.* i. 330 n. 7, Sblendorio Cugusi on Cato fr. 113 = 158 M; H. Kornhardt, *ZSS* 58 (1938) 162–4, for whom Gellius is only nearer the truth than Verrius, has lost favour). Courtesy in dissent: 2. 6. 1; 6. 3. 8; 9. 10. 5; 18. 11. 1; cf. [Long.] 4. 6; Quint. 9. 1. 18; Macr. *Sat.* 5. 19. 2–3. Similar compliments are bestowed on *anonymi* at 13. 29. 2; 14. 6. 1; 18. 5. 2.

29. For alleged parallels see Mercklin 701 n. 1, 'Capita' 4–11, review of Kretzschmer 723–4. The most convincing is 10. 3. 10 ~ PF 28. 19–21 L; the connection between 2. 21. 8–10 and Fest. 454. 36–456. 11 L may be use of Varro, between 4. 6. 8 and Fest. 242. 11–19 L of Capito (but see Strzelecki's edn. of Capito, p. xxiv n. 6). (Is Festus the source of Aldhelm, *Ep.* 4 at MGH Auct. Ant. xv. 483. 7?) Although Ser. Sulpicius will be cited at 4. 3. 1–2 through Neratius, § 3, tacked on with little relevance, conceivably comes from Verrius, cf. Fest. 248. 2–6 L. Dr John Pinsent (pers. comm.) believes that Festus supplemented Verrius from Severan sources, who could have used Gellius. L. Gamberale, *RFIC* 90 (1970) 194–8 derives 'profestum et profanum' (pr. 20) from Verrius (cf. Fest. 298. 31 L), but the collocation came readily to the ear (cf. 2. 17. 5). For divergence from Verrius cf. chs. 11 n. 114, 16 n. 30.

30. Kretzschmer 69 (yet even he strains to derive 5. 18. 6–9 from Verrius, pp. 70–1, along with notices in Servius and Isidore), cf. 'Zu A. Gellius' 368. But 'si qui sunt' (17. 6. 4) is not contemptuous; cf. 12. 3. 4.

him by former associates such as Annianus.[31] He is described as a man eminent in his age for learning (4. 7. 1), and skilful in the study of ancient authors (9. 9. 12).[32] On no occasion does Gellius disagree with him, though Favorinus is made to disbelieve a report as out of character (3. 1. 6), and Gellius himself denies that a certain absurd opinion was found in his works (15. 30. 5; cf. 12. 14. 3–4 for false ascription to Nigidius).

In 13. 21 Probus is said to have stated that the choice between the accusatives plural *urbis* and *urbes* should be made not by following pedantic rules but by consulting one's ear, as Vergil had done.[33] At *Georg.* 1. 25 he had found, in a manuscript corrected (he said) by the poet's own hand, 'urbisne inuisere', where *urbes* would sound crass; but at *Aen.* 3. 106 'centum urbes habitant magnas', *urbis* would be thin and bloodless. Whereas the questioner's inability to appreciate the difference roused Probus' disdain, Gellius not only understands the principle but applies it to other instances.[34] Contempt for school grammar, use of allegedly autograph manuscripts, and considerations of sound, are all found elsewhere in Gellius; scorn for 'finitiones illas praerancidas' and 'fetutinas grammaticas' sits easier with Probus and Gellius, in their different circumstances, than with those who taught such stale and stinking rules for their living; and although euphony was not invented by Probus, such discussions are not found in Fronto.

Probus has frequently been debited by modern scholars with a taste for textual conjecture,[35] in reading e.g. 'infusum' for 'infusus' at *Aen.* 8. 406 to

---

31. I do not assert against Jocelyn I 465 that Gellius' accounts of the oral tradition accurately represent Probus' opinions, nor against id. I 471, III 472–4 that Donatus' and Servius' explanations of his readings are authentic; but, finding in those accounts and explanations a coherent quasi-personality, I treat it as the Probus in whom Gellius believed and by whom he was influenced. The quest of the historical Probus I leave to others.

32. Against Zetzel's suggestion (pp. 41–54) that Probus touched no author older than Terence see *NA* 4. 7, Don. on Ter. *Phorm.* 372 (though Plaut. *Truc.* 265 is missed).

33. Cf. J. S. Th. Hanssen, *SO* 22 (1942) 80–106. But each instance was decided by the poet as it arose, not always with the like care or by the same considerations; rational analysis is not always possible (Quint. 9. 4. 119).

34. 'Nos autem aliud quoque postea' § 10 recalls 3. 3. 7–8, where Gellius interrupts his summary of Varro (for self-interpolation cf. chs. 6 n. 43, 11 n. 4, p. 187) and 1. 7. 18, where Gellius reports finding other accusatives for ablatives than those adduced by his friend (see 17. 2. 11, cf. Caec. 170 R at 2. 23. 21, Enn. *Scen.* 12 V at 19. 8. 6); he then passes from the legitimacy of the construction to its rhythmical motivation in Cicero, and that of the verb-form *explicauit*, citing the same speech by title twice (§§ 16–20) without adverting to the fact. Various notes have been tacked together; the friend, having linked the accusatives of §§ 16–17 with the infinitives of §§ 1–15 as usages wrongly impugned, is discharged when Gellius changes theme. Yet the source-critics assign the whole chapter to Probus!

35. Suetonius says nothing of such alterations (Jocelyn I 466); Probus' readings cannot be proved conjectures (id. III 472). Timpanaro, *Stor. fil. virg.* 87, 122–6 allows that 'infusum' was one, but regards 'loquentiae' as an error of transcription. Gellius, however, seems—rightly or wrongly—to take it as conjectural; at least nothing is said of MSS, *pace* Timpanaro, op. cit. 123. It is interpolated in some Sallustian MSS, but not known to Plin. *Ep.* 5. 20. 5 (who credits another with the coinage), Fronto, *Ep. M. Ant.* 3. 1. 1, *Orat.* 1, Sidon. *Ep.* 9. 9. 2, Grillius 11. 27–8 Martin, Prisc. *GLK* iii. 85. 4.

avoid an obscenity perceptible only to the filthy mind,[36] and 'loquentiae' for 'eloquentiae' at Sall. *Cat.* 5. 4. This last fancy is reported by Gellius (1. 15. 18): late in life Probus had so read the statement that Catiline had eloquence enough but little wisdom ('satis eloquentiae, sapientiae parum') because the former was inconceivable without the latter. Gellius is too much in thrall to philosophical piety, as well as Probus' authority, to detect the flaw in the argument; but whatever a Cicero might prescribe for the ideal orator, the clear-eyed Sallust could have flirted with no such fatuity.[37] However, even if some Probian readings were conjectures and not variants (a matter of debate), Gellius does not venture to play such games himself: his own textual suggestions are always based on at least the report of a manuscript reading.

Probus' conception of grammar extended to writing a monograph on Caesar's use of code (17. 9. 5); but for the broad range of scholarship, Varro's heir was Pliny, whose remarks on his own and others' titles Gellius ironically echoes (pp. 20–1). The implication that he can do better is supported by the ensuing contrast between his predecessors' indiscriminate accumulation and his own rigorous selection (pr. 11–12). Gellius artfully ascribes the fault especially to the Greeks, but the Roman reader will have associated unselective bulk first and foremost with the *Naturalis Historia*. Pliny had complained (*NH* pr. 24) that though the Greek books had marvellous titles, there was nothing in them; Gellius adopts and adapts this same complaint, saying in effect that there is both nothing in the other miscellanies and far too much. In § 12 he claims to have spent every stolen moment of leisure in reading; Pliny (pr. 18) had written his book in his spare time. This was a commonplace of Roman literary life; Pliny's 'subsiciuis(que) temporibus', which Gellius later resumes and refreshes with a coinage of his own ('subsiciua et subsecundaria tempora', pr. 23), can be traced back to Cicero (*Leg.* 1. 9). But the limitation reinforces Gellius' contrast between the industrious but uncritical compiler—what better summation of the man than Heracleitus' dictum?—and himself, the judicious and discriminating collector whose work was worth reading.[38]

It is in this spirit that Gellius uses Pliny's information. He cites him for facts (3. 16. 22–4; 17. 15. 6), but affects disgust at his talk of wonders (10. 12. 6, cf. 9. 4. 12), denying that Democritus wrote the account of the chameleon from which they are taken. One is left to conclude that Pliny not only filled his pages with rubbish, but did not realize it was rubbish. In fact, Pliny, though uncritical enough to accept the text as authentic, was not stupid enough to suppose it true; but even now authors are often debited with

36. For Probus' prudery cf. Don. on Ter. *Phorm.* 1005. Despite R. Hanslik, *RE*² viiiA. 200–1, silliness is no ground for doubting Servius' report, nor does 'infusus' in Gellius and the artigraphers disprove it.

37. Probus adds that Sallust was a word-coiner—which does not prove him the source of *NA* 4. 15.

38. In turn, some 250 years later, Macrobius would appropriate Gellius' language for a preface promising order and completeness: Macr. *Sat.* pr. 2–3 ~ Gell. *NA* pr. 2–3, 12.

opinions they rebut.[39] Whereas Pliny had enjoyed a good laugh at the lies of the Greeks (*NH* 28. 112 'non sine magna uoluptate nostra cognitis proditisque mendaciis Graecae uanitatis', cf. 'derídiculae uanitatis' *NA* 10. 12. 4), Gellius has to assure us—with the high moral tone of one who would touch pitch and not be defiled—that he finds this matter utterly boring (§ 1 'ex quibus pauca haec inuiti meminimus quia pertaesum est') but reproduces it as a public service, to demonstrate the harm such things do to those who love knowledge (§ 4).

At 9. 4. 13 he observes that Pliny supports one marvel with his eye-witness—as Apion had the tale of Androclus and the Lion (5. 14. 4; cf. 6. 8. 4–5),[40] describing him as a man of great authority for his intellect and rank; at 10. 12. 4 he implicitly includes him among 'the cleverest minds, especially those intent on learning'; at 9. 16. 1 he states that Pliny was considered the greatest scholar of his age, but promptly takes him to task for missing a counter-argument in a *controuersia*. He never denies his erudition, but insinuates that the great polymath would have done better to learn less and think more.[41]

Suetonius is quoted by name only twice,[42] but will also be the source for Augustus' 'Hasten slowly' (*Aug.* 25. 4, *NA* 10. 11. 5)[43] and the measures taken against philosophers and rhetors (*Gram.* 25. 1, *NA* 15. 11. 1–2). Other ascriptions by Ruske (p. 44) rest on Reifferscheid's over-ambitious collection of the fragments[44] and the source-critic's calculus, in which two and two make fifteen. Indeed, Gellius may have used him oftener than we can tell;[45]

39. Gellius himself so suffers at D.S. on *Georg.* 1. 260 ~ *NA* 10. 11. 1, Rabelais, *Gargantua*, ch. 3 (i. 40 Lefranc) ~ *NA* 3. 16. 16; cf. Jac. Gronovius on 2. 6. 5 (p. 135 n. 8). Moreover, Democritus' book 'de ui et natura chamaeleontis' is a not unnatural misreading on Gellius' part of Pliny's 'peculiari uolumine' (DK ii. 214. 12 n.); with less excuse Proust, edn. sig. CCcc1ᵛ was to extract a book by Messalla 'de minoribus magistratibus' from 13. 16. 1.

40. *Pluris est oculatus testis unus quam auriti decem*, and Gellius does not like to give the lie direct; but whereas Pliny's attestation of a sex-change (cf. Phlegon, *Mir.* 9, dated to 116) does not pass belief, Apion is telling a well-known folk-tale (Thiele, edn. of 'Romulus', pp. xxiv f.; Stith Thompson B381; yet cf. Sen. *Ben.* 2. 19).

41. It makes no difference that Gellius owes Pliny more than he admits (e.g. 17. 15 comes from *NH* 25. 48–52, 61; cf. Mercklin 670, but see ch. 13 n. 22). Beck's hypotheses are unconvincing; J. Avilés, *Helmantica* 29 (1978) 91–8 advances us no further.

42. *NA* 9. 7. 3 (see ch. 16 n. 48), 15. 4. 4.

43. But not for Augustus' letters; Gellius' elaboration (cf. § 87) or—despite his *oratio obliqua*— discovery (cf. 15. 7. 3, and see also 10. 24. 2; Gascou 501–2)?

44. Cf. Wallace-Hadrill 41–2.

45. Reifferscheid's argument (edn. 424–5, cf. Wallace-Hadrill 58) for making him the source of 15. 28—that since Jerome, whose *Chronica* took Roman dates from Suetonius' *De uiris illustribus*, concurs as to Cicero's age (Ol. 174. 2 'XXVI anno aetatis suae Cicero Quintium defendit') despite the misdating to 83 BC (and of *Pro Sex. Roscio* to Ol. 175. 2 = 79 BC; cf. Helm 28–9) with Asconius, whom Suetonius/Donatus cites in the *Vita Vergilii*, against Nepos and Fenestella, who appear in Suetonius' life of Terence, therefore Gellius too used Suetonius, not Nepos (cf. n. 26) and Asconius—is at any rate better than Della Casa's (p. 35 n. 52) for deriving 19. 14. 3 from Suetonius because *in uulgus exire* (cf. *NA* 12. 12. 3; 14. 3. 3; Fronto, *Amic.* 2. 2) and *obscuritas* (Ciceronian; cf. *NA* 19. 10. 8) are found in that author. To be sure, Asconius is cited without specific reference; but if the place was his preface to *Sex. Rosc.*, it hardly needed stating. However, Gellius' sources may be Nepos and Suetonius. *NA* 13. 2. 1 may suggest Suetonius

yet Suetonius (whom Fronto cites at *Amic.* 1. 13) was perhaps too well-known for frequent copying to be prudent.

His contemporary Caesellius Vindex[46] was much criticized by later authors: both the Hadrianic grammarian Terentius Scaurus and Gellius' teacher Apollinaris had joined in the sport, which was not always conducted fairly (6. 2. 2). Against Caesellius' statement that verbal adjectives in -*bundus* were simply equivalent to present participles (11. 15. 2), Scaurus maintained that they denoted simulation of the action,[47] which Gellius saw to be absurd ('What was meant by acting or imitating one at play, I would rather appear not to understand than suggest that Scaurus himself did not understand', § 4). Instead, he should have blamed Caesellius for not examining whether the suffix conveyed a nuance of its own: remembering a passage of Sisenna in which *populabundus*, 'laying waste', is used with a direct object, he consults Apollinaris, who derives -*bundus* from *abundantia*. Gellius applauds ('εὐεπιβόλως hercle'); by contrast, in 2. 16, despite repeating his teacher's criticism of Caesellius, he is not convinced by his alternative theory (pp. 62–3).

Yet despite their eagerness to do down Caesellius, many scholars had failed to notice that he had taken *cor* in a line of Ennius' for a masculine through not connecting it with what followed. In *NA* 6. 2 Gellius sets out Caesellius' discussion and refutes it;[48] he throws in an absurd defence that does not merit a reply, thus bolting the door against all foreseeable objections.[49] He need not depend on Scaurus or Apollinaris either here or at 3. 16. 11, where Caesellius wrongly takes Livius Andronicus' 'Morta' for the name of an individual Fate and not generically 'quasi Moeram';[50] Gellius could observe that the original had Μοῖρα, perhaps even that Homer never names his Μοῖραι. This error earns Caesellius the contemptuous qualification

rather than Varro; the story is noted by Jerome, *Chron.* Ol. 160. 2. Suetonius may underlie the 'plerique alii' of 3. 3. 14, cf. Jerome, *Chron.* Ol. 145. 1 (whence, not from Gellius, Boccaccio, *Geneal. deor. gent.* 14. 4, ii. 690. 9–14 Romano).

46. Whose other fragments confirm both his interest in the ancient authors and (if *GLK* vii. 206. 26–7 is authentic) his capacity for misunderstanding them. M. T. Vitale, *SRIL* 1 (1977) 221–58 is more than fair to him; she discusses the Gellian references on pp. 224–40. Cf. A. M. Tempesti, ibid. 179–84.

47. So too the pack of Latin grammarians; Hosius ad loc. omits Serv. on *Aen.* 4. 646, against whom Beroaldus, *Ann. Seru.*, sig. [b5]ᵛ–[b6]ʳ cites 'moribundo similis' (Val. Max. 5. 7. ext. 1; Q. Curt. 9. 5. 10); see too Valla, *De linguae Latinae elegantia* 1. 9 (*Opera* i. 13), Pianezzola 18–21.

48. *Ann.* 371–3 Sk: 'Hannibal audaci cum pectore de me hortatur / ne bellum faciam, quem credidit esse meum cor / suasorem summum et studiosum robore belli': Hannibal, whom Antiochus had thought the keenest advocate of war, counsels against it. Caesellius, ignoring 373, and taking 'cum' for a conjunction, understood a question 'quem credidit esse meum cor?', 'what did he believe my [heart =] intelligence to be?', i.e. 'what kind of fool does he take me for?' Nonius, whose use of Gellius is documented by Mercerus (edn.², comm. 89–90 *et passim*) and Hertz, *Opusc. Gell.* 85–146 (cf. Lindsay 104 n. f), copies the wrong interpretation at 287. 17–20.

49. Cf. 1. 25. 18; 9. 14. 26; 17. 13. 7–9.

50. Fr. 23 B (from *Od.* 2. 99–100 and parallels or 10. 175, not 3. 237–8, where the subjunctive is generic). Whether Caesellius had some right on his side is disputed (Latte 53 n. 1; G. Radke, *KlP* iii. 1431 and literature there cited). '... men set up the Deity of *Morta*', Sir Thomas Browne, *Hydriotaphia*, ch. 4 (p. 115 Martin).

'homo minime malus';[51] at 20. 2. 2 he is 'homo ingenuae ueritatis' for admitting that he does not know what instrument a *siticen* played.[52] At 18. 11. 1 he is 'by no means unlearned'; but prompt rebuke follows for wantonly and ignorantly ('petulanter insciteque') censuring the verbal coinages of Furius Antias. Only once is he vindicated outright: at 9. 14. 6 he states that Cicero, at *Sest.* 28, used the genitive singular *dies*, which Gellius confirmed from ancient manuscripts. For all Caesellius' faults, he had a pair of eyes.

Scaurus does not appear in any other chapter; his contemporary Velius Longus is cited only at 18. 9. 4. A schoolmaster and a scholar are arguing over a word in Cato: the former maintains that it should be *insequenda*,[53] and that Ennius had written *inseque* in the imperative. The latter answers that Velius should be believed when he says that Ennius had written *insece*; that was why the ancients had called narratives *insectiones* (our only evidence for this word); and Varro, reading *sectius* at Plaut. *Men.* 1047, had interpreted it as 'worthy to be narrated'.[54] It is formally uncertain whether the references to *insectiones* and *sectius* belong to the quotation or the narrative,[55] but probable that Velius is the source.[56]

Gellius himself settles the argument to his own satisfaction in § 5 by citing *insece* from a 'really old' manuscript of Livius Andronicus he had seen at Patrae, no doubt taken there by one of Augustus' colonists. He adds that *sectius* proves nothing (§ 6),[57] that *insece*, though smoother and lighter ('lenius leuiusque', cf. Cat. 84. 8) than *inseque* (§ 7), was derived from the same root, that of *sequor*, just as *secta* was (§ 8), and that experts in Greek took Homer's ἔννεπε and ἔσπετε for its kindred, as also ἔπη 'words, verses' from ἕπεσθαι 'to follow' and εἰπεῖν 'to say' (§§ 9–11).[58] We need neither deny that Gellius personally inspected the manuscript of Livius and devised the

51. i.e. 'uir simplex' (Proust). See Cic. *In Caec.* 45, *Rep.* 3. 26, *Off.* 3. 39; for the notion of *naïveté* (already implicit at Plaut. *Mil.* 356) cf. ἄκακος, εὐήθης, *bonus* (e.g. *NA* 7. 16. 3), German *harmlos, treuherzig,* and English 'innocent'. Cf. Liv. 40. 14. 5 'minime malus ac suspicax' (ironical).

52. Cf. Cic. *Orat.* 230 'o uirum simplicem, qui nos nihil celet'.

53. Since the beginning of this chapter is known only from the corrupt (and now vanished) β, we do not know the context of the word, missing from what remains of the citation: but it should mean 'to be narrated'.

54. The direct tradition exhibits *setius*, used as at *Capt.* 417, which makes better sense. (β's *minus*, not supported by the paraphrase, must be a post-Gellian corruption for *mihi*).

55. 'Velio Longo ... fidem esse habendam qui ... scripserit non inseque apud Ennium legendum sed insece, ideoque a ueteribus quas narrationes dicimus insectiones esse appellatas, Varronem quoque uersum hunc ... sic enarrasse': are 'esse appellatas' and 'enarrasse' parallel to 'esse habendam' or 'legendum'?

56. If Gellius took the whole of § 9 from Velius for the starting-point of his story, he would have been less conscious of the ambiguity, which could have been avoided by *quod*-clauses (ch. 3 n. 34). Cf. Kretzschmer 93.

57. 'Nihil in alteras partes [Hertz: β *plus*] argumenti habet'; for *alter* after a negative = 'either' cf. Liv. 25. 28. 4; 28. 18. 4; 40. 20. 4. See Holford-Strevens, 'Aduersaria' 112.

58. *insece/inseque* is the same word as ἔννεπε (< *enseqᵘe), pl. ἔσπετε (< *ensqᵘete), related to *sequi*/ἕπεσθαι, 'say', and 'see'; but εἰπεῖν (Ϝειπεῖν) and ἔπος are related to *uox*. Gellius' 'sequo [cf. Prisc. *GLK* ii. 396. 21; ἔπω Schol. Hom. *Il.* 2. 484] ... et sectio' suggests a link with *secare*, cf. Non. 649. 7–9, Serv. on *Aen.* 10. 107, Isid. *Orig.* 19. 19. 8.

arguments of §§ 6–8 for himself, nor make Velius the source of §§ 9–11;[59] much less, with Mercklin 660–1, invoke Verrius Flaccus on the not strength but weakness of PF 99. 10 'inseque apud Ennium dic. insexit dixerit'.

Since Gellius' pin-pricks against Pliny are not always justified, we may suspect unfairness or sleight of hand in his dealings with other authors; but we are not entitled to suppose it in any given case merely because it is requisite for our speculations, only to deduce it from solid evidence for what stood in his source. This is not a presumption of innocence (scholarship is not a lawcourt), but a precaution against wild theorizing. He is capable of independence even towards Varro and his teachers; if any grammarian holds him in subjection it is Probus.[60]

59. Indeed, the source of § 9 read *inseque*, not Velius' *insece*.

60. If in 6. 7 Annianus were a mere lay-figure permitting Gellius to disagree with Probus yet not say so, the enthralment would be less than total; but there is no proof. By whatever routes Probus' real or supposed opinions reached Gellius (P. Wessner, *RE*² ivA. 741–3 suggested transmission through Caesellius and Apollinaris, cf. p. 63, but there were other sources), they made a deep impression on him. But others—and why not Gellius?—will have attempted to apply the master's methods for themselves; not everything of a Probian spirit need come from Probus (cf. p. 120).

Chapter 10

The Latin Language

GELLIUS, purveyor of much grammatical information,[1] despises professional *grammatici* both intellectually and socially. He prides himself on not providing elementary instruction ('neque in scholis decantata neque in commentariis protrita' pr. 15); the bumptious bore of a grammaticaster in 4. 1 proffers 'scholica quaedam nugalia' (§ 1). At 18. 9. 2 a schoolmaster and a scholar are distinguished as 'alter litterator ... alter litteras sciens, id est alter docens, alter doctus';[2] the grammarian is shown to be dogmatic and wrong, and 'alter ... ille eruditior' is vindicated. A well-known *grammaticus*, engaged to check a manuscript for its prospective purchaser, is refuted by the poet Paulus in 5. 4; others are exposed by Gellius himself. True, the word is also used of the great Valerius Probus and the expert in ancient literature who quotes two haunting lines from Cinna the Poet to authorize the use of *nanus* 'pony' (19. 13. 5); yet whereas Favorinus constantly appears as *Fauorinus philosophus*, Apollinaris—in whose presence the grammarian of 19. 13 is reluctant to express an opinion—is never described as *grammaticus* except by implication at 7. 6. 12, but as a man of great learning ('uirum praestanti litterarum scientia' 4. 17. 11; cf. 13. 18. 2; 16. 5. 5; 18. 4. 1), whom one might suppose to be of a different order from the professionals who peddled their learning for pelf, though that is exactly what he did. Gellius was not obliged to earn his living, nor did he write for those who were; himself pursuing a gentlemanly breadth of erudition, he despised the specialist ignorant of philosophy and law.[3]

Moreover, Gellius had views on language that set him at variance with the preceptors. Grammar included a prescriptive element ('recte loquendi scientiam' Quint. 1. 4. 2); Gellius considers that this part was treated mechanically, with too much reliance on arbitrary rules (so said the Probus of 13. 21. 1, a *grammaticus* but not a schoolmaster) and insufficient knowledge of the early writers. This contempt for school prescriptions should not be

---

1. This chapter is much indebted to the excellent study by Maselli; treatments of individual words are considered by L. Dalmasso, *AAT* 58 (1922–3) 88–100, *RFIC* 51 (1923) 195–216, 468–84; *Ath* 3 (1925) 26–32. Klinkers (whose Greek leaves much to be desired) compares Gellius' statements with those in modern handbooks.

2. Although a *litterator* is properly a γραμματιστής or elementary master (Suet. *Gram.* 4. 4–5, Apul. *Flor.* 20. 3), Gellius distinguishes not primary from secondary education, but instruction as such from erudition. For the schoolmaster's low standing see Marrou 401; and note Cic. *Orat.* 144. Suetonius, who treats the rise in grammarians' prestige, 'wrote as such professors wrote' (Wallace-Hadrill 30); Gellius does not.

3. *NA* 4. 1; 20. 10.

called anomalism:[4] the debate between analogy and anomaly conducted by Greek grammarians in the second century BC, and echoed at Rome in the first, did not continue as a two-party contest ever afterwards.[5] Varro, who adhered exclusively to neither side (*LL* 8. 23), reportedly recognized four principles: *natura* (the constituent words of the language), *analogia*, *consuetudo* (normal speech), and as a last resort *auctoritas* (the usage of early writers).[6] Quintilian, in whose day the early writers' status was controversial, propounds *ratio* (analogy and etymology), *auctoritas* (use by approved authors), *uetustas* (use by the ancients), and *consuetudo*.[7] Gellius assigns the bilateral dispute to the past ('putauerunt' 2. 25. 1); his statement that Varro affords *loci communes* for and against analogy may indicate that there were still upholders of analogy before all else, choosing (perhaps even creating) word-forms for regularity of paradigm, but not that their opponents still deployed the banner of anomaly, content to deny that language would fit such Procrustean norms. Quintilian had championed *consuetudo*, 'the agreement of the educated';[8] Gellius appeals to the uncorrupted language in use before Augustus.[9]

In consequence, Gellius treats the normative grammarians as modernistic and half-educated.[10] At 17. 2. 15 he sees no reason why *opus esse* must take the ablative 'unless one observes the grammarians' new-fangled rules like the rites of holy places'; Quadrigarius had written (fr. 26 P) 'nihil sibi diuitias opus esse', with the predicative construction common in Early Latin and not unknown in classical (Cic. *Rep.* 5. 4). At 15. 9. 3 a grammarian objecting to Caecilius' use of *frons* 'forehead' in the masculine (v. 79 R) merits the epithet

4. Marache, *AFLT Pallas* 2 (1954) 32–8; but see Fischer, p. xliii n. 1, Maselli 11–20, Cavazza, edn. i. 33 n. 30. Moreover, Gellius admired Caesar's *De analogia*. Abstract and systematic intellectualism is a mark of the mediaeval and the modern, not the ancient, Latin mind; Gellius was the last man to possess a comprehensive and coherent theory.

5. See in general A. Dihle, *Hermes* 85 (1957) 170–205; Pfeiffer 202–3; Maselli 88 n. 21; Cavazza, *Studio* 106–53; Rawson 121–3; Frede, *Essays* 335–7. Wilamowitz, 'Asianismus' 269 n. 2 observes that anomalism did not outlast the Augustan age. S.E. *Math.* 1. 176–240, attacking analogy, upholds not 'anomaly' (though ἀνωμάλου is used casually at § 240 and ἀνομοίως at § 237) but usage.

6. Fr. 260 Fun.; cf. Cavazza, *Studio* 143–52 for this and other systems (guiding principles or ritual obeisance to method?).

7. *Inst.* 1. 6; 9. 3. 3; equation with Varro's tetrad is a misuse of ingenuity.

8. *Inst.* 1. 6. 45; cf. *SVF* iii, p. 214 (Diog. Bab. fr. 24), S.E. *Math.* 1. 235.

9. *NA* 13. 6. 4. The time-limit is relaxed to admit Vergil (who oftener supports than establishes usage, but cf. 15. 13. 10) and Augustus himself, a man well versed in the Latin language who imitated his adoptive father's elegance of speech (10. 24. 2; 15. 7. 3; cf. 10. 11. 5). Suetonius judged likewise (*Aug.* 86. 1); Fronto found in him rather the elegance and purity of his age than copiousness of diction (*Ver.* 2. 1. 13 = § 8 v.d.H.; contrast Tac. *A.* 13. 3. 2). Hadrian, in belittling his erudition (Intro. n. 14), implies that Augustan *usus* was already corrupt.

10. Cf. 'isti nouicii semidocti' (16. 7. 13), who use *emplastrus* fem. as in Greek (see n. 14). For *nouicius* see 11. 1. 5; cf. 1. 9. 11 (of arrogant modern students), Fronto, *Orat.* 13; for *semidoctus* cf. id. *Ep. M. Caes.* 4. 3. 1, 3. Note too the 'reprehensor audaculus uerborum' of 5. 21. 4 who casts his incomplete or unsound 'disciplinae grammaticae inauditiunculas' (overheard smatterings; cf. p. 168) like dust in his hearers' eyes (the first attested instance of this image, but cf. 1. 2. 7; Plin. *NH* 10. 17, Plut. *Sert.* 17), and despises the ancient writers (§ 7).

'semidoctus' by his inability either to dispute with Gellius on ancient usage or to find the flaw in his analogical argument, explicitly fallacious, that all nouns in *-ons -ontis* are masculine. Like a judgement-debtor under the Twelve Tables (*NA* 15. 13. 11; 20. 1. 45) he is given thirty days' grace to produce a counter-example,[11] and that is the last we hear of him.

It is not only the common herd, but the Roman bar, that adopts the 'unlearned and ignorant' use of *superesse* 'exceed' for *adesse*, 'represent a client' (1. 22. 1–2, 12);[12] when Gellius states that the *uulgus* or *multitudo imperitorum* uses *mathematici* 'savants'[13] for *Chaldaei* 'astrologers' (1. 9. 6), *dies nefasti* 'days on which the praetor may not pronounce the Three Words' for *d. religiosi* or *atri*, 'ill-omened days' (4. 9. 5; 5. 17. 1), *humanitas* 'learning' for φιλανθρωπία 'kindness' (13. 17. 1, cf. p. 130), *candens* 'shining white' for *feruens* 'boiling hot' (17. 10. 8), *uanus* 'dishonest' for *desipiens* 'silly' (18. 4. 10), *obesus* 'worn thin' for *uber* and *pinguis* 'fat' (19. 7. 3), he means not that only the lower classes spoke thus, but that the usages are not found in pre-Augustan writers. He is sometimes wrong, overlooking the familiar in searching for the rare.[14] Yet Gellius and the normative grammarians were confronting the same problem —the drift of the *consuetudo* away from the classical standard—though by different means: Gellius by studying older authors, the grammarians by imposing rules. For inculcating a basic modicum of *Latinitas* into school-children the latter method had its merits, but Gellius, not compelled by hunger to cram indifferent youth with the rudiments of written Latin, could afford to scorn the shifts of those who were.[15]

However, Gellius' basic grievance is not that the grammarians theorize without regard to the facts, but that they are moderns confining themselves to modern usage. He rightly scouts Aelius Melissus' absurd distinction between *matrona* and *materfamilias* (18. 6; cf. p. 108), but accepts a no less arbitrary one from Nigidius (11. 11) between *mentiri* 'to tell a deliberate lie' and *mendacium dicere* 'to make a false statement, believing it to be true';[16]

---

11. [*Spons*] *spontis* is feminine, but not *frons* before Cicero and Lucretius. For analogy as a debating-trick cf. Quint. 1. 6. 10–11.

12. In § 12 Falster's 'indoctum' ('Specimen' 140, *Am. phil.* iii. 224, cll. 19. 8. 12) should be read even against A; *indictum* makes no sense either as 'unsaid' or 'unsayable'.

13. For the broad sense cf. Vitr. 1. 1. 17, and Sextus Empiricus' title Πρὸς μαθηματικούς.

14. On *superesse* see n. 26, on *uanus* ch. 5 n. 10. *Mathematicus, nefastus, candens* are not used in the disapproved manner till Augustan times or later; *humanitas* of kindness is Ciceronian (*humanus* 'kind' Plautine); *obesus* = 'fat' at Cat. 39. 11. But without our dictionaries and concordances even Varro could err in such matters (Skutsch on Enn. *Ann.* 483, cf. 549); so do Probus (ch. 9 n. 32) and Fronto (ch. 7 n. 15). The 'uulgus' that reads *amaro* at Verg. *Georg.* 2. 247 (1. 21. lemma) cannot be the teeming masses; cf. the *uulgus grammaticorum* of 2. 21. 6; 15. 9. 3. On the other hand, at 16. 7. 13 the term denotes the common people; but their usage (*emplastrum* neut.) happens to concide with good authors' (Gellius could have cited e.g. Cato, *Agr.* 39. 2).

15. The grammarian who scorned *praeterpropter* as vulgar (19. 10. 9) was battling (like Serv. on *Aen.* 7. 289) against a rising tide of compound prepositions and adverbs (Hofmann–Szantyr 282–4); but this one is protected by early use.

16. Sir Thomas More, *The debellacyon of Salem and Bizance* (London, 1533), pt. ii, fo. clxvi[v] renders '... betwene hym that wyttyngly lyeth, and hym that telleth a lye wenyng that it were trewe' (cf. Schoeck 128); cf. too Boccaccio, *Geneal. deor. gent.* 14. 13 (ii. 720. 18–23 Romano).

mentiri 'err' is not found till Prop. 4. 1. 122, but *mendacium dicere* denotes intentional lying at Plaut. *Bacch.* 525, 957.[17] But Gellius, who greatly admires Nigidius' learning (cf. p. 116), also draws from it a definition of *mature* 'in good time' (10. 11. 2) that entails its distinction from *propere* 'quickly'; he observes the opposition of *properanda* and *maturare* at Verg. *Georg.* 1. 260–1 (but not 'maturate fugam' at *Aen.* 1. 137) and quotes Augustus' σπεῦδε βραδέως.[18] By contrast, finding counter-examples in Caesar and Asellio, he is scathing ('risu prorsus atque ludo res digna est' 13. 3. 1) about the doctrine of 'plerique grammaticorum' that *necessitudo* denotes the tie of kin or friendship and *necessitas* compulsion, which is generally true even in Republican writers.[19] It is the same with technical terms: whereas in 16. 13 Gellius first states that *colonia* and *municipium* are commonly confused, and then cites Hadrian discoursing 'peritissime' on the difference, in 10. 20 he first defines the different forms of Roman legislation, and then observes that approved authors use *lex* promiscuously.[20]

Gellius is aware that Latin had changed between Cato and Cicero: *elegans* had lost its pejorative force (11. 2. 4) and *gallica* of a slipper was a recent word when Cicero employed it (13. 22. 6). Cicero is distinguished from the 'ancient' writers at 13. 21. 22; 15. 13. 9, though in other places (e.g. 1. 4. 8; 1. 22. 14–15; 2. 6. 6–8; 16. 5. 11)[21] not only he but Sallust and Vergil are

---

17. At Plaut. *Trin.* 362, the sense is 'Come on, you know that isn't true.' 'Apul.' Π. ἑρμ. 5 uses 'mentiuntur' of false propositions (cf. Arist. *Interp.* 16ᵇ3, 5). Gellius normally has the strong sense, but at 14. 1. 33, 36, though seers are reckless of the truth, 'mentiuntur' implies only falsehood, not deception; cf. 'ementitus' 15. 30. 3. Dr Johnson gave 'to lie' the weak sense (Boswell, *Life* iv. 49 H–P). For *mendacium dicere* 'lie' cf. Nep. *Att.* 15. 1, Quint. 12. 1. 38. Of reckless statements Plaut. *Amph.* 198, 'Q. Cic.' *Comm. pet.* 47; *mendacium* of a false proposition *NA* 16. 8. 11, 14; of falsity 7. 1. 15; elsewhere in Gellius of deliberate lies. The distinction is otherwise expressed by Apul. *Apol.* 33, 2, Symm, *Ep.* 9. 87, Aug. *De mendacio* 3. 3 (*CSEL* 41. 414), Isid. *Diff.* 1. 381 (PL 83. 49B); different again is Cato fr. 240 SbC = 244 M. For the two senses of ψεύδεσθαι see 'Plat.' *Hipp. min.* 370E, M. Ant. *Med.* 9. 1. 4; of ψεῦδος, Polyb. 12. 12. 4–5. Modern English self-corrective 'I tell a lie' displays Nigidius' doctrine better than anything in Latin (the nearest is Plaut. *Persa* 102, but 'atque hau te decet' pretends otherwise).

18. Ascensius ad loc. over-subtly finds the Nigidian sense in *Aen.* 1. 137: see Ter. *Phorm.* 716, Cic. *Cluent.* 171, *Att.* 4. 1. 8, *Fam.* 2. 17. 1, etc. But *maturare* implies that time is ripe, or pressing. In 16. 14 Gellius follows Verrius Flaccus (cf. Festus 268. 3–7 L, [Suet.] p. 285 R) in accepting Cato's distinction (fr. 96 SbC = 131 M) between *properare* 'to do one thing quickly' and *festinare* 'to start many things at once and not see them through'. This is not borne out by usage (e.g. Cic. *Phil.* 9. 6, though *festinare* is used for 'bustle' by Plautus and Terence; closest to Cato is Sall. *Cat.* 42. 2), not even in Nigidius (see fr. 29 Fun. = 47 Sw at *NA* 9. 12. 6) and Gellius (10. 11. 4, 8; 17. 16. 5). In defining *properare* ('qui unus quid mature transigit, id properat'), Cato used *mature* in the sense given it by 'uolgus hominum improprie' (*NA* 10. 11. lemma); at 12. 5. 2 Gellius himself uses *maturare* for hastening. On Erasmus' 'festina lente' (*Adagia* 2. 1. 1) see Wind 97–112, 203, 208 n. 58, 215, pls. 52–5.

19. *Necessitudo* of compulsion is, however, not uncommon in Early Latin; *necessitas* of personal ties is rare, but recurs at Caes. fr. 44 M, cited for its content at *NA* 5. 13. 6.

20. If the ancients observe a distinction, they spoke correctly (3. 14. 20); if not, they were not fussy or pedantic (20. 6. 12).

21. With 9. 12. 4 'et ueteres plerique … et M. Tullius' cf. 10. 12. 9 'et plerique nobilium Graecorum et Fauorinus philosophus'; no contrast is intended. So 18. 7. 8 'et apud Ciceronem … et apud elegantissimos ueterum' (cf. 3. 16. 9).

counted with the *ueteres*.[22] Furthermore, it is noticed that Cicero rejected certain words in common contemporary use (10. 21. 1): the example is given of *nouissimus/-e*, freely employed by 'et M. Cato [sc. Uticensis][23] et Sallustius et alii quoque aetatis eiusdem', but condemned by Stilo for an improper neologism, as his pupil Varro reported (Gellius cites *LL* 6. 59). Charisius' statement (269. 15 B) that 'Tiro in Pandecte' called *nouissime* an incorrect innovation of his own day makes the probable source for Cicero's abstention his freedman's Πανδέκται, cited by Gellius in 13. 9.[24]

Normally, however, Cicero's language is contrasted, not always rightly, with the Antonine *consuetudo*. In 13. 17 he and Varro are said to have meant by *humanitas* not 'quod uolgus existimat', benevolence towards one's fellows, but a liberal education;[25] however, Cicero freely employs the word in the sense denied him (e.g. *Sex. Rosc.* 46, *Q. Fr.* 1. 1. 27), as also *superesse* for 'remain to do' (e.g. *De or.* 3. 31), despite *NA* 1. 22. 14–17,[26] *leuis* for 'fickle' (e.g. *Sull.* 10) despite *NA* 6. 11. 1–2,[27] *profligare* for 'nearly finish' (e.g. *Prov. cons.* 35, *Tusc.* 5. 15; *Fam.* 12. 30. 2; so the admired Augustus, *RG* 20. 3), condemned at *NA* 15. 5. 2 on the authority of Apollinaris. Similarly Gellius states at 19. 8. 18 that, to the best of his memory, 'nemo ... doctorum hominum' used the plural *harenae*, frequent in Vergil, the 'poeta uerborum diligentissimus' of 2. 26. 11. However, when the singular *quadriga* is produced as an extreme rarity ('unum ... rarissimum', 19. 8. 17) from a satire of Varro's, there is no oversight: neither Livy, who implies the singular,[28] nor Propertius, who uses it directly, is accorded any recognition in the *Nights*, and such authors as Valerius Maximus, the elder Pliny, and Suetonius, who all show it, are for Gellius mere conduits of information, whose language and style are not regarded.

Auctoritas is the highest principle in Gellius' eye; neither *ratio* nor *consuetudo* can take its place. In *NA* 14. 5 he reports with amused disdain a debate between two grammarians on whether the vocative of *egregius* is *egregi* or

22. For Sen. *Ep.* 108. 32 as in Tac. *Dial.*, Cicero is among the *antiqui*; cf. Cousin 437–8. For later usage see Cameron 137, A. C. Dionisotti, *JRS* 74 (1984) 207.

23. Not Censorius: see ch. 16 n. 14.

24. In fact Cicero admits the word once, at *Q. Rosc.* 30; it is used by Plancus, D. Brutus, and Cassius in letters of 43 BC, and appears in the spurious *Ep. Oct.* 3 (f.l. for 'leuissima' *Orat.* 237). It is not eschewed by Catullus and Caesar.

25. From this ch. sprang the Renaissance use of *humanitas* for classical studies (Baron 197 n. 2).

26. Gellius allows *superesse* the senses 'abound', 'be superfluous', and 'survive', but not 'remain'; at Enn. *Ann.* 514 Sk he reads 'super escit' as two words, Verg. *Georg.* 3. 10 is censured, and Caesarian usage (e.g. *BG* 5. 22. 4) neglected; yet at 15. 7. 3 Gellius cites from his admired Augustus the words 'mihi quantumcumque superest temporis'. He roundly condemns the sense 'appear for' a client, as at Suet. *Aug.* 56. 3 (Augustus himself?)

27. For Gellius it must mean 'worthless' (cf. 1. 15. 1). He also condemns the colloquial use of *nequam* = Fr. *malin* clear at Mart. 2. 27. 3, and in several other places combined with the sense of Eng. 'naughty'; Quint. 8. 3. 48 finds it too weak for a *parricida*, but implicitly appropriate for a man in a harlot's thrall.

28. Livy 1. 28. 10 'duabus admotis quadrigis' ~ *NA* 20. 1. 54 'binis quadrigis' of the same event: cf. Varro, *LL* 10. 24, 66–7.

egregie: neither cites an example, but *egregi* is supported by the analogy of proper names such as *Caeli*,[29] *egregie* (which its champion uses at § 3) by the impossibility of forming -*i* vocatives from such adjectives as *inscius*. Although adjectives in -*ius* (other than Greek loan-words) are not freely used in the vocative singular masculine till the third century, the discussion shows that *egregie* would have been acceptable, *egregi* abnormal;[30] but Gellius despises both parties alike. There is nothing intrinsically more absurd about determining the vocative of *egregius* than the genitive of *facies* (9. 14); but the discussion proceeds without reference to authority.[31]

Ratio is not repudiated altogether, if it supports ancient usage: in 5. 21 the *ratio* demanding *plura* by analogy with *meliora* and other such comparatives is capped by a reference to Sinnius Capito's 'rationes grammaticas', making *pluria* the only correct form (and not comparative), though Gellius' spokesman does not himself consider *plura* incorrect;[32] in 1. 16 *mille* with genitive plural and singular verb is rightly defended as the singular of *milia*. In both chapters, however, reason supports an ancient, not a modern, usage.[33] *Consuetudo*, too, can be respectable, provided it is that not of Gellius' day but of the ancients, the *ueterum consuetudo* illustrated at 10. 24. 3 by the praetor's formula for proclaiming moveable feasts (*feriae conceptiuae*). Whereas at 13. 30. 1 Gellius states that many words have departed from their original sense through the ignorant custom ('consuetudine et inscitia') of those who

29. MODI and TERTI ahould belong to the *nomen* Modius and *cognomen* Tertius: *terti* in the ordinal is implausible, *modi* in the measure, though correct, falls foul of artigraphic doctrine (n. 30), so that the question would be begged (Holford-Strevens, 'More Notes' 149–50).

30. Despite Varro fr. 252 Fun. most grammarians prescribed -*i* in proper names and *fili*, otherwise -*i*, but without exx. In fact substantives always take -*i*, except 'filie' Liv. Andr. 2. M–B, 'Gaie' *CGL* ii. 647. Greek or Hellenizing vocatives in -*ie* are found in Early Latin and in Silver poetry; they are joined by pure Latin adjj. from the 3rd c. AD (but Housman's '⟨conscie⟩' at Ticidas fr. 1. 2 M–B (*CP* ii. 695) would sit well beside 'sole'). Forms in -*i* are extremely rare, but note 'Arcadi' Apul. *Met.* 6. 7. 3.

31. Maselli 65. *Auctoritas* and *uetustas* are not distinguished; the partitive 'ueterum' (3. 16. 19; 6. 11. 2; 18. 7. 2, 8) should imply two classes of *ueteres*, one with and one without *auctoritas*, but in practice the only candidate for the second class is Laberius (3. 12. 2; 16. 7. 1–12; 19. 13. 3, but cf. 17. 2. 21).

32. The reference to Quadrigarius (fr. 90 P) is the only one in Gellius without book-number. Lebek, 'Pluria' 340–5, observing that in fact *pluria* was a vulgarism of Gellius' own day, suggests that Sinnius (and Plin. fr. 62 Mazz.) had merely deduced it by analogy from the well-attested Early Latin *compluria* [and justified it from the gen. *plurium*? Cf. Jul. Mod. frr. 3–3a Mazz.]; he also denies that a grammarian of Sinnius' date would have paid attention to prose historians (as Hertz, *Sinn. Cap.* 12, had supposed in assigning the entire discussion to him). But he does not trust § 6 even as evidence that Gellius had found *compluria* in the authors cited, since only *complura* is found in Varro—sc. in *LL*, written when he was eighty, as if he could never have used the other form in all his long life—and believes that Gellius simply invented his *auctoritates*, a notion for which there is no more warrant than for Maselli's assertion (pp. 37–8) that *NA* 6. 9. 15—'Cicero and Caesar used *memordi*, *pepugi*, and *spepondi*'—is an a priori inference. We ourselves have MSS offering *pepugisset* at Sex. *Rosc.* 60 (not incredible in an early work; some editors print it); Gellius knew of others with archaic readings (see pp. 139–41), right or wrong is not the point. Or was he, as in §§ 11–12, using the laconic Probus (Suet. *Gram.* 24. 5), chary of examples (cf. 4. 7. 3)?

33. But at 12. 13. 29 Gellius defends *intra Kalendas* 'by the Kalends' not 'quasi priuilegio inscitae consuetudinis, sed certa rationis obseruatione'.

use words they do not understand, at 15. 5. 1 he casts the same thought in another mould: the words have been corrupted 'a ratione recta et consuetudine', from their etymological sense and traditional usage.

This does not mean that Gellius either practised or preached a wholesale return to ancient usage: he knew, no less than Apollinaris, that meanings change with time, even as laws lapse by desuetude, and that custom is the mistress of all things, especially of words (12. 13. 5, 16). He may hope that his readers will not misuse *superesse* or *profligare*, but in 10. 24, although he observes that even in Augustus' letters the standard expression for 'in three/four days' time' was *die quarti/quinti(-e)* and that Cn. Matius, 'homo impense doctus', had written (*nuper*) *die quarto* for 'three days ago', he also observes that in his own day even the learned use *die quarto* for 'in three days' time' and 'we' say *nudius quartus* for 'three days ago', with no suggestion that 'we' should revive the older usage. He reports in 4. 16 that Varro and Nigidius adopted the fourth-declension genitive in *-uis* 'contra cotidiani sermonis consuetudinem' (lemma), but nowhere uses it himself.[34] In 9. 14 he discusses various forms of this case in the fifth declension, but admits that 'nunc propter rationem grammaticam faciei dicitur', the form he regularly employs;[35] even in the dative, although 'qui purissime locuti sunt' used *facie* and not *faciei* 'uti nunc dicitur',[36] he has *perniciei* at 3. 7. 4. According to 11. 2 *elegantia* was applied by the 'antiquiores' not to intellectual polish but to personal grooming, yet he himself freely employs it (even in § 3, as in the preceding chapter, 11. 1. 7) 'de amoeniore ingenio'.[37] He also uses the condemned *harenae* and *soloecismus*.[38] It is quite normal for theoretical purists to let their guard slip; Julius Pollux, for all his lexicography, was but a mediocre Atticist.[39] But Gellius was not trying to write in the language of the ancients, nor to defy the *consuetudo* at all costs.

In particular, he will not fly in the face of received pronunciation: at 13. 26. 2, having cited Nigidius' distinction between vocative *Váleri* and genitive

34. Nor has he the heteroclite form in *-i*, common in the older writers and used in Quadr. fr. 10[b] P (*NA* 9. 13. 17) and (despite 4. 16. 1) by Varro, *Sat.* fr. 62 Cèbe (52 Bücheler); he does admit the dative in *-u* ('usu' 4. 1. 23), discussed at 4. 16. 5–9, which though rare in prose was not exclusively Republican (Neue–Wagener i. 541–6).

35. Enn. *Ann.* 270 Sk at 12. 4. 4 could have shown him that *diēī* gen. sg. was good Early Latin; but in Republican times it was a solemn archaism like *-āī* in the first declension.

36. *NA* 9. 14. 21: Marshall's deletion makes the passage less coherent, not more (Holford-Strevens, 'Aduersaria' 112, where for 'confidence' read 'coherence'). Fronto has *diei* dat. at *Fer. Als.* 3. 9; so Apuleius at *Met.* 3. 1. 1, and *pauperiei* 11. 28. 4.

37. For *elegans* as a term of stylistic commendation see p. 157.

38. For *harenae* see ch. 7 n. 33; *soloecismus* occurs four times in 1. 7 and also at 15. 9. 3. In *NA* 5. 20. 3–4 Gellius states that good Greek (i.e. Attic) writers did not use either σολοικισμός or βαρβαρισμός (we first find them in Aristotle; Choeroboscus condemns them at *EM* 722. 8–12, but uses them at *In Theod.* i. 104. 6, 8–9, ii. 2. 6–7 Hilgard); ibid. § 6 and in 13. 6. 4 he has not yet found them in good Roman (pre-Augustan) writers (but see *Rhet. Her.* 4. 17 and the genitive plural 'soloecismon' at Lucil. 1100 M). He does not use the cited Latin equivalents *stribiligo* and *imparilitas* (the latter occurs in its proper sense at 14. 1. 22); but nor does he use *barbarismus*, as Fronto does (*Ep. M. Caes.* 1. 9. 8).

39. Philost. *VS* 592.

Valéri, he observes that anyone in his own day accenting the vocative on the first syllable would infallibly be laughed at,[40] and in 7. 15 his sympathies plainly lie with the man who for all his learning preferred to make the *e* of *quiesco* short, despite the reproaches of a linguistic precisian ('homo in doctrinis quasi in praestigiis mirificus communiumque uocum respuens nimis et fastidiens'), declaring that he would not follow the grammarians 'contra perpetuam Latinae linguae consuetudinem' or speak with distinction at the cost of abnormality ('neque se tam insignite locuturum, ut absona inauditaque diceret').[41] However surprising the change of quantity,[42] we must accept that in Gellius' day *quiĕsco* was the norm, as also that *adfatim* was stressed on the penultimate (6. 7. 2).[43] Here, however, Annianus alleged, besides arguments, the authority of Probus for accenting the first syllable like the ancients;[44] similarly, Apollinaris used to pronounce *obices* and *obicibus* with /obji/ (4. 17. 11). In rare or literary words correct pronunciation may be insisted on (so *succīdaneae* 4. 6. 6);[45] in everyday words one may hold out for it (as Gellius does for *āctito* in 9. 6, rightly arguing that the quantity of the root syllable in frequentatives is governed by the principal verb's past participle and not its present); but where learned and unlearned all pronounce a word alike, the man who knows better is well advised to keep his learning to himself.[46] One may, when reading classical verse, pronounce dactylic *inice* as

40. Cf. Serv. on *Aen.* 3. 451, Prisc. *GLK* ii. 302. 19. Despite Gellius' 'praecipit', Nigidius does not prescribe but describe (Mariner 158–60, Bernardi Perini, 'Sistema' 27).

41. Cf. the *bon mot* at Quint. 1. 6. 27 'aliud esse Latine, aliud grammatice loqui'. (Note the recondite names of *NA* 7. 15. 5 'ne si Aelii quidem Cincii et Santrae' rather than, say, *Verrii, Probi, Scauri*; cf. pp. 70–1. Santra is mentioned nowhere else in the *Nights*.)

42. The long vowel required by analogy (as the fastidious friend observes) is attested at *CIL* vi. 25531. 3 QVIÉSCERE; but in Vulgar Latin **quescere* (see Väänänen, § 79 with addendum, p. 221; Sursilvan *quescher*) *ĕ* is suggested by the British development *que* > **cu* (e.g. Welsh *cwsg* 'sleep'), since Latin *ē* would have retained its length, though **cu* is itself irregular (Jackson 402–3, cf. 330–5). Another unexpected quantity is the *ā* of *ususcāpio* (6. 10. 1), which modern writers ignore; but cf. *suspīcio*. Klinkers, who states (p. 31) that Gellius' observations on accent and quantity should not be overlooked, himself overlooks this one. Mistake is inconceivable in a word that Gellius the judge was used to hearing spoken.

43. The two elements, said Annianus, had coalesced into one, as in *admodum*, and *ad-* intensive bore the stress. Gellius himself observes that the latter argument is false; the former indicates that preposition and regimen, which in Early Latin had been subjected *en bloc* to the Law of the Penultimate, were by the end of the classical period pronounced—as the grammarians prescribe—with the accent proper to the regimen unless felt to form one word. (Contrast Enn. *Sc.* 187 J 'anté pedes' with Ov. *AA* 1. 184 'ante díem'; in this poem all pentameters end in a disyllable). *Ádmodum* still held together (though eventually, as Romance indicates, even *dénuo* was reconstituted as **de nóuo*; so too compound verbs), but not *ádfatim*, even though there was no noun *fatis* in actual use (cf. Serv. *Aen.* 1. 123). Against assimilation to *-ātim* is Gellius' 'prima acuta, non media' (§ 2): *affátim* would have been described as 'media circumflexa' (*affâtim* like προφῆτιν). Was there influence from **ad sátis* > Fr. *assez*, It. *assai?*

44. Probus so read Plaut. *Cist.* 231; at Ter. *Phorm.* 88 Annianus demanded *exáduersum* (Thysius compares *éxinde* Serv. on *Aen.* 6. 743, *síquando* Don. on Ter. *Eun.* 437, which show the same accentual pattern — — ×, but stress the first element of the compound.)

45. Cf. Fest. 242. 11–12 '⟨praecidanea porca prod⟩ucta syllaba ⟨secunda pronuntianda est', as plausibly restored by Müller.

46. Cic. *Or.* 160. Velius Longus allows learned spellings, but not pronunciations (*GLK* vii. 50. 4–6).

'injice' not 'ĭnice' (4. 17. 9), but Gellius does not propose to banish the tribrach 'ĭnice' from daily life.

Besides 'ratio proportionis quae analogia appellatur' (15. 9. 4) there is the *ratio* of etymology at 15. 5. 1; so too at 1. 18. 1 'ratione etymologica falsa'. By ancient standards, Gellius' etymological judgement is quite sober, especially concerning word-formation:[47] he knows that *testamentum* contains a common suffix (Ser. Sulpicius had taken it for a compound, 'a mentis contestatione') and that *sacellum*, which Trebatius Testa had derived form *sacer* and *cella*, is a diminutive of *sacrum* (7. 12); even Nigidius fails to persuade him in 10. 5 that *auarus* comes from *auidus aeris* rather than from *aueo* with the suffix of *amarus*, and Varro in 1. 18 that *fur* is from *furuus* rather than φώρ.

Gellius displays no less independence in discussing foreign etymologies. In 16. 12 he holds that Cloatius Verus, who wrote in the early Augustan age, was right to derive *errare* from ἔρρειν, *alucinari* from ἀλύειν, and *fascinum* from βάσκανον. The last two are certainly related, the middle pair probably: the first proposal, which must have seemed obvious, is in fact wrong, but neither Cloatius nor Gellius knew that ἔρρω was originally Ϝέρρω. Cloatius, however, had also followed Hypsicrates in deriving *faenerator* from φαίνεσθαι ἐπὶ τὸ χρηστότερον, because the moneylender puts on a show of kindness to the poor man in distress; Gellius declares that whether Cloatius or some other nincompoop was responsible for this nonsense, nothing could be sillier ('siue hoc autem ipse Cloatius siue nescioquis alius nebulo effutiuit, nihil potest dici insulsius', § 6), and adopts instead Varro's etymology of *fenerator* (the older form as used by Cato)[48] from *fetus*, interest being the offspring of money. (The obvious parallel of Greek τόκος (PF 76. 9–13 L) is not cited.) Modern scholarship confirms the derivation of *fenus* 'interest' (and *fenum* 'hay', cited by Paul), *fetus*, and *fecundus* from the root of *felix*, *femina*, *fello*, and θῆλυς; the original idea of 'suck(l)ing' developed by way of the female to the fertile.

At 15. 3. 8 Gellius suggests that the *au-* in *aufugio* and *aufero* is derived from the αὐ- of Homeric αὐέρυσαν and αὐίαχοι; again we know better,[49] but give him credit for seeing that it was no mere by-form of *ab*.[50] Of course, he sometimes offers wild etymologies: 1. 25. 17 *indutiae* 'truce' from *inde uti iam* ('that from then on', sc. fighting shall resume), 16. 16. 1 *Agrippa*, originally the *praenomen* of one born feet first,[51] from *aegritudo* (since such births are difficult and painful for the mother) and *pes*, a notion he takes from Varro;

---

47. See Maselli 71.

48. So Varro, who observes the same fluctuation in *f(a)enum* (*LL* 7. 96; Fr. *foin*, Sp. *heno* < *fenum*, It. *fieno* < *faenum*).

49. They are from *ἀνϜερύω and *ἀϜίϜαχοι respectively.

50. Other foreign etymologies at 4. 3. 3 (*paelex* 'concubine' correctly related to πάλλαξ and παλλακίς), 8. 13 (see pp. 11–12), 15. 30 (*petorritum* 'four-wheeler' rightly derived by Varro from Gaulish).

51. e.g. Agrippa Menenius Lanatus, who ended the First Secession with the fable of the Belly and the Members. (Despite Schoeck 127, the source of More, *Hist. Rich.* (Lat.) 7. 20–1 Sylvester is not *NA* 16. 16 but Plin. *NH* 7. 45.)

but he finds too artificial the theory that *saltem* ('at least', of a last resort) comes from *salutem* (since when all else is refused we beg that our lives be spared; 12. 14. 7). He devoted thought to these matters, puzzling over the force of *re-* in the verb *rescire*, 'to find out matters unwelcome or concealed' (2. 19).[52] There are some strikingly good guesses in his etymological chapters, and when he chooses between alternatives he never picks the worse. Quintilian gives us robust common sense (1. 6. 28–38), Gellius at times is acute.

He is not only acute, but so far as we can see a pioneer among his countrymen, in the attention he devotes to syntax. Although Greek grammarians had long had less to say on it than on morphology, in Gellius' day Apollonius Dyscolus wrote his masterpiece Περὶ συντάξεως. Roman *grammatici*, however, discussed little but tropes and solecisms—except for Arusianus Messius' collection of *exempla elocutionum* from the school authors Vergil, Sallust, Terence, and Cicero, made at the end of the fourth century— till Priscian, in the Constantinople of Anastasius I, treated syntax at length, with large use of Apollonius. However, Gellius is not to be deemed Apollonius' pupil even in the loosest sense:[53] other Greeks were seised of the topic, and Apollonius would not have taught him to reserve *particula*, as opposed to *pars orationis*, for indeclinables and formantia.[54]

Moreover, whereas Apollonius argues from first principles, Gellius generally starts from a specific phrase in an author, especially an early one. Cato, for instance, had said (fr. 171 SbC = 176 M) 'in hac contumelia quae mihi per huiusce petulantiam factum itur', the insult that is going to be inflicted on me; Gellius observes that the normal construction *contumeliam factum iri* may be rendered 'iri ad contumeliam faciendam'—that one is going (*iri* impersonal passive) to inflict an insult (10. 14. 3)—and states that *contumelia factum itur* amounts to the same thing by change of case. Here he has fallen into the same trap as Cato. In *contumeliam factum iri* the noun is the object (a category unknown to the ancients) of the supine *factum*, but the analogy of *contumeliam factam esse* and *c. fieri* induced its reinterpretation as the subject of a future infinitive passive. The nominative therefore appears as the subject of *uideor ... -tum iri* (Plaut. *Rud.* 1242 (?), Quint. 9. 2. 83): this is no different in principle from 'contumelia quae ... factum itur', but its

---

52. The semantic discussion is far superior to Donatus on Ter. *Hec.* 189, 285, 518, 868. Gellius does not know that the correct present is *resciscere*; neither does Donatus when his lemma is perfect or Pompon. D. 8. 16. 9. 1; cf. Publil. 230 Meyer (but Ribbeck's 'reus est' is more pointed).

53. As by J. Collart, *REL* 43 (1965) 384–95.

54. For Apollonius μέρος λόγου and μόριον are synonymous (e.g. τῶν μερῶν τοῦ λόγου *Synt.* 13. 12 Uhlig ~ τῶν μορίων 14. 2); for Gellius, *particula* may denote a prefix (2. 17. 6, 9; 2. 19. 3; 4. 17. lemma, 8; 5. 12. 9, 10; 6. 7. 6, 7; 16. 5. 5, 6), the suffix *-bundus* (11. 15. 5, 6, 9), or the indeclinables *atque* (10. 29. lemma, 1, 4), *pro* (11. 3. lemma, cf. § 1), and *quin* (17. 13. lemma, 1, 5, 10), but not a part of speech in general as in Priscian (*GLK* iii. 127. 2–3) and Sergius (Supp. 158. 28). The Byzantine *Et. Mag.* differentiates μόριον 'affix' from μέρος 'word' (141. 47–52, 809. 8–9); Cornut. *ND* 13 (p. 13. 15 Lang) τοῦ στερητικοῦ μορίου, wrongly adduced by LSJ, does not prove the distinction, cf. *SVF* ii. 204.

perversity is less patent. Cato could have said *fiet*, but preferred a more explicitly passive form,[55] and sought a more immediate future, a passive not to *faciet* but to *factum it* or *facturus est*, for which, in post-classical times, an expedient would be found in *facienda est*.

In the preceding chapter (10. 13), Gellius examines certain oddities in the use of *partim* 'some', which he describes as an adverb: from the common *partim hominum uenerunt* he moves to Cato's 'cum partim illorum' (fr. 192 SbC = 213 M), altered by the ignorant ('inperitiores') to *parti*; cites a remarkably confused piece of syntax in Quadrigarius (fr. 87 P), 'cum partim copiis hominum adulescentium placentem sibi', which seems to mean 'with some of the troops, consisting of young men he found attractive'; and finally quotes from the same author (fr. 89 P) 'neglegentia partim magistratum', by the negligence of some of the magistrates. Properly *partim* is the accusative of *pars* used adverbially, which does not preclude the attachment of a genitive;[56] but it was assimilated to a pronoun, and used either with a genitive or in apposition. It normally serves as nominative or accusative; the passages cited are exceptions. In one of them Quadrigarius has constructed *partim* with an appositional ablative, but successively qualified it by an appositive genitive and by a participle in the accusative: 'insolentius paulo', says Gellius, but Quadrigarius is capable of other oddities, like the two abnormal instances of *quin* where one might have expected *ut* in 17. 13.[57] Gellius is contemptuous of those who merely say that *quin* stands for *ut*; he asserts that this and other uses (some of which he also cites) can be understood only through recognition that *quin* is a compound with its own definite sense,[58] but for further details refers the reader to Nigidius' *commentarii grammatici*.[59]

That Gellius is not wholly opposed to analogical reasoning is shown again in 15. 29, where the account in Piso's *Annales* of the consul L. Brutus' request for his colleague's resignation in the first year of the Republic, 'quia Tarquinio nomine esset', is cited as evidence for a construction *mihi nomen est Iulium*: the *gentilicium* is rightly understood as an adjective (cf. *Lex Iulia, Via Flaminia, Aqua Claudia*), and the predicative ablative of quality is transformed into the subject of a possessive sentence. There is no evidence for Gellius' construction, nor indeed any parallel for Piso's, an unusual turn devised to

---

55. Observe 'fiebantur', 'fitur' (frr. 64, 156 SbC = 65, 77 M).

56. Ter. *Hec.* 14–15 'in is quas primum Caecili didici nouas / partim sum earum exactus, partim uix steti'; as subject Cic. *Part.* 86; Nep. *Att.* 7. 2; *NA* 3. 16. 16; 6. 3. 7.

57. Fr. 58 P 'paene factum est, quin castra relinquerent atque cederent hosti' (cf. *paulum afuit quin*); fr. 70 P 'Romam uenit, uix superat quin triumphus decernatur', meaning that he only just *obtained*, not prevented, the triumph: as it were, *senatus paucis sententiis non recusat quin triumphus decernatur*. Cf. Sen. *Ben.* 6. 7. 2 'quin nos non obliget manifestius est'; Draeger ii. 663–4; Kühner–Stegmann ii. 262.

58. Presumably Nigidius, who was much given to positing compounds (Della Casa 95–8), rightly analysed it as *qui* instrumental + *nĕ*: 'whereby not'. For his part in this chapter see Lebek, '*Pluria*' 345–8; there is no need to credit him with Gellius' examples.

59. One glossator copies Gellius' discussion (A. Reifferscheid, *RhM*² 16 (1861) 10–11); other grammarians do not advance beyond substitutive explanations (Maselli 103 n. 79); so Prisc. *GLK* iii. 467. 34–5 'quin, quod significat qui non et cur non et ut non et nec non'.

indicate the suspicions that the name was no mere accident, but a sign of the man's nature ('nimium Tarquinios regno adsuesse ... non placere nomen, periculosum libertati esse', Liv. 2. 2. 3). Professional grammarians, by contrast, absurdly extract an accusative predicate with *nomen est* from Verg. *Aen.* 3. 18 'Aeneadasque meo nomen de nomine fingo'.[60]

Greek analogies are invoked at 15. 14, *exigor* with retained accusative in Early Latin as the passive of *exigo* with two accusatives modelled on εἰσπράττομαι,[61] and 1. 7. 17; 17. 2. 11, where unusual accusatives with *in*—Cic. *Imp. Pomp.* 33 'in praedonum fuisse potestatem sciatis', Quadr. fr. 25 P 'nos in medium relinquemus'—are justified as semantically correct and corresponding to Greek usage; for the latter Gellius cites θεῖναι εἰς μέσον.[62]

Cicero's 'in ... potestatem' (for which Gellius is our only witness) is also justified on rhythmical grounds: *potestatem sciatis* is more pleasing to the ear and fuller, *potestate sciatis* unpleasant and incomplete (1. 7. 20). Indeed, although either would yield a ditrochee, at period-end we expect the former; *Verr.* 1. 131 'mortuum esse sciebat', *Phil.* 13. 19 'consedisse sciebat' end only internal cola.[63] For the same reason, says Gellius, Cicero (*Imp. Pomp.* 30) used *explicauit* rather than *explicuit*, 'which had already begun to be more usual' (not entirely true).[64] Again, *explicauit* affords a ditrochee, *celeritate explicuit* presents a rhythm found indeed at the end of cola and occasionally of periods (*Sex. Rosc.* 72, cf. *Cluent.* 30),[65] but less round and less grand than the stirring context seems to require.

Gellius does not state these observations in technical language, but gives them as the perceptions of a trained and sensitive ear ('si modo ita explorata aure homo sit, non surda nec iacenti')—like those in 13. 21, on euphonic choices between such equally legitimate forms as -$\bar{e}s$ and -$\bar{i}s$ in the accusative plural of *i*-stems, where only the ear can decide.[66] Similar principles are

60. Serv. on *Aen.* 1. 267, cf. Prisc. *GLK* iii. 360. 12; Arus. Mess. *GLK* vii. 494. 14–23 is sound. As in *NA* 10. 14, error was the easier for the ancients' ignorance of the grammatical categories 'subject' and 'object'.

61. *Exigo* active with double acc. is not attested till the 4th c.; the passive with retained acc. is a mannerism of Dominate constitutions (Cramer 84–7). The double accusative, as with *rogo* and *posco*, is an Indo-European construction also found in Sanskrit.

62. Pregnant εἰς (e.g. Hdt. 6. 1. 1, Thuc. 1. 109. 4) shades in later Greek to stative εἰς (cf. LSJ s.v. I. 2); whereas Greek says τίθημι εἰς, *pono in* normally takes the ablative (cf. *NA* 17. 2. 11). Gellius uses *in medium relinquere* at 7. 14. 9; cf. perhaps 'in ordinem [*QB*, ordine *rell.*] scriptum' 9. 14. 3. Cf. Prisc. *GLK* iii. 294. 5–295. 2. On use of Greek analogies see pp. 167–8.

63. Zielinski 199 notes Gellius' failure to recognize that impure *s* in Ciceronian clausulae always makes position (id. 174–5); but Cicero rarely relies on it, and chose not to do so here.

64. Against Cicero's preferred -*plicaui*, -*plicatum*, the MSS give *applicuisti* at *Flacc.* 82, *implicuisses* at *Dom.* 105 (cf. Fraenkel, *Leseproben* 198–200); at *Hortensius*, fr. 115 Grilli 'admiscuerint atque implicuerint' is guaranteed by the homoeoteleuton. But all these are later than *Imp. Pomp.* of 66 BC.

65. For different analyses see Zielinski 149–50, Fraenkel, *Leseproben* 30. Each separate 'testis' in *Imp. Pomp.* 30 concludes with a clausula regular at period-end.

66. Cf. Stanford 77. At Quint. 1. 5. 4 'uocalitas, quae εὐφωνία dicitur' gives 'quod melius sonet' the edge over its synonymous competitor. Cf. ch. 9 n. 33.

deemed to be inherent in the language: according to 16. 6. 13; 18. 9. 7 words were modified for ease of pronunciation. At 2. 3. 1 the *ueteres* insert *h* in various words to strengthen them and make them sound more forceful, following in this the precedent of Attic. Neither the general statement nor the particular instances hold water, but Greek grammarians both asserted Attic love of aspiration and appealed to the ear.[67] Among Gellius' examples is *ahenus* for *aenus* 'made of bronze' (where the *h* may be a mere graphy for hiatus);[68] this leads him to discuss readings found in Vergilian manuscripts, for his interests extend to textual criticism. Here, too, the aural argument is used in 6. 20. 6, where the pleasant effect of identical vowels in hiatus, as used by Homer, justifies a reading *ebria acina ebriosioris* at Catullus 27. 4. This will not do,[69] not least because the effect in question belongs specifically to the grand style (Demetr. *Eloc.* 72–4); but for that very reason Gellius is right in §§ 1–5 in preferring the sound of Verg. *Georg.* 2. 224–5, as transmitted by the manuscripts, 'uicina Ves(a)euo / ora iugo', to the 'Nola iugo' alleged 'in quodam commentario' to have been altered when the Nolans would not let Vergil irrigate his farm from their water-supply, a silly tale, yet apparently resting on the town's genuine reluctance—as its future bishop Paulinus would complain—to make its water available for newcomers.[70]

More normally, however, Gellius chooses either the unusual expression or the ancient manuscript. By the former principle he prefers *dii* (genitive singular of *dies*) at Vergil, *Aen.* 1. 636, where the 'imperitiores' read *dei*, recoiling before the abnormal form ('ab insolentia scilicet uocis istius abhorrentes'); the ancients, however, had declined *dies dii* (9. 14. 8–9). Similarly, the 'inperitiores' alter Cato's 'cum partim illorum' (p. 136) and *stetisses* is substituted at Cato fr. 184 SbC = 202 M 'quid si uadimonium capite obuoluto stitisses?' by those unaware that 'stitisses' comes from *sisto* (2. 14. 2–3).[71] Gellius has approached the recognition that *difficilior lectio potior*; if at times he takes the principle too far, he offends no more than modern

---

67. On aspiration see ch. 12 n. 40; on Greek euphonic theory see, apart from Stanford's full-length study, Plato. *Crat.* 404 D (etymology), Demetr. *Eloc.* 68–70 (style); D.H. *Comp.*, esp. 23; Pfeiffer 243. Gellius' assorted Latin exx. include *lachruma* and *sepulchrum*, illustrating the late Republic's taste for aspirated consonants.

68. So used in Umbrian (cf. **ahesnes** 'ahenis') and Oscan; cf. Fr. *envahir*.

69. See Fordyce ad loc.

70. See Holford-Strevens, 'Nola'; for the poet avenging want of hospitality cf. D.S. on *Aen.* 2. 197. (For a frigid attempt at grandeur by means of such hiatus see Paconianus fr. 1. 3 M–B.)

71. Historically, *steti* is the perfect corresponding to both *sto* and *sisto*, -*stiti* to their compounds; but when *sisto* acquired transitive sense in legal usage (*uadimonium sistere*; also with personal object 'produce in court'), *stiti* was promoted to be its perfect. In MSS it was corrupted either to *steti* or to *praestiti* (Cic. *Fam.* 16. 9. 4, Nepos, *Att.* 9. 4); by contrast, *stiti* is sometimes wrongly given by modern editors for *steti* perfect of *sto* 'appear in court' (e.g. Cic. *Quinct.* 25). As usual, Gellius knows better than the *Grammatici Latini* (Maselli 68), in this case from his forensic experience.

scholars have done on occasion.[72] Moreover, Gellius expects old manuscripts to offer correct readings corrupted in later ones, a reasonable though rebuttable presumption. In 9. 14. 2–3, 20 Gellius has confirmed the reading *facies*, gen. sing., at Quadrigarius fr. 10[b] P in several old manuscripts, but found other copies whose original reading had been obliterated and replaced by the modern *faciei*, and one in the library at Tibur with *facies* in the text and *facii*, which was also an ancient form, in the margin ('contra'); no old manuscript gave *facie*. His conclusion is that one should therefore read either *facies* or *facii*. We should wish to determine the relations between the various manuscripts, and prefer *facies* to *facii* not as the majority reading but as that more easily altered to the other, being more archaic and ambiguous of case, but as far as they go we can have no quarrel with Gellius' researches or his reasoning.[73]

At several places Gellius adduces manuscripts of allegedly superior authority—autograph Vergils, a Cicero overseen by Tiro, an Ennius believed to have been checked by Lampadio[74]—in support of variant readings. There was of course no way that Gellius or his contemporaries could ascertain the history of a manuscript; but when he tells us that a copy of *Aeneid* 2 believed to have been Vergil's own fetched twenty aurei, a hundred times the price of Martial, book 1 (which is slightly longer than *Aeneid* 2 without the Helen episode) in a de luxe edition,[75] we begin to smell a rat, and when we examine the readings themselves the stench is overpowering. In 1. 7 Cicero is made, in a manuscript allegedly 'Tironiana cura atque disciplina facto', to use the old invariable future infinitive in -*urum* at *Verr*. 5. 167; this is hard to believe, and crass errors in this 'libro spectatae fidei' destroy the credit of its provenance.[76] At 9. 14. 7 certain people produce from a Vergilian autograph

72. Galen too recognizes the superiority of the harder reading; but neither he nor Gellius separates this principle from that of preferring the older manuscript. See Timpanaro, *Genesi* 27 n. 28; on ancient use of MSS Lehrs 344–50, on Galen (who invokes both number and age) L. D. Bröcker, *RhM*[2] 40 (1885) 417; on trivialization of archaisms, Quint. 9. 4. 39.

73. Gellius no doubt took his examples of 5th-decl. gen. sg. in -*ii* from an earlier writer, as we should from Neue–Wagener; but he personally inspected the MSS he mentions.

74. C. Octauius Lampadio, who divided Naevius' *Bellum Punicum* into seven books (Suet. *Gramm*. 2. 4), hence the sort of man who might have taken, or been credited with, an interest in the text of Ennius.

75. *NA* 2. 3. 5; Mart. 1. 117. 16–17 (but 6–10 HS for a normal copy, 1. 66. 4); Luc. *Pseudol*. 30 has a purported text of Teisias' *Rhetoric* sell for 30 aurei = 750 denarii, thus confirming the gold–silver parity of Cass. Dio 55. 12. 4, 72. 32. 1 (contrast P. Baden 37. 1–10 for Trajanic Egypt). Fronto speaks of the value conferred on a MS by a Lampadio's or Tiro's hand (*Ep. M. Caes*. 1. 7. 4); it cost Julianus much trouble and money to check a reading in the 'Lampadio' of Ennius (*NA* 18. 5. 11). See Reynolds–Wilson 27–8, Kleberg 56–61.

76. That the construction was already obsolescent is suggested by the hybrid -*urum esse* without concord at Sulla fr. 20 P, Val. Ant. fr. 59 P; the original usage appears in the old-fashioned Varro (*RR* 1. 68) and at *NA* 3. 3. 1. (At Liv. 26. 45. 5 *daturum* will have been induced by *tempus*.) The 'Tironian' text gives *adierant, periculum* for *uiderunt, periculo*, and omits *ubi*. For such MSS cf. 13. 21. 16 'in uno atque in altero antiquissimae fidei libro Tironiano'; their reading *peccatu* at *Verr*. 2. 191 is more credible, but even if right does not prove Tiro's involvement. Moreover, the *subscriptio* of a true *Tironianus* might be copied into a non-Tironian text.

the reading *dies*, gen. sing., at *Georg.* 1. 208, 'Libra dies somnique pares ubi fecerit horas', replacing the everyday *die* or *dii* with an ambiguous archaism.[77] Worst of all—and most striking in that it shows how soon such texts were current—in 1. 21 Augustus' freedman, the Palatine librarian Julius Hyginus, professes to have found in a manuscript from Vergil's own household the reading *sensus . . . amaror* for *sensu . . . amaro* at *Georg.* 2. 247. The passage runs:

> at sapor indicium faciet manifestus et ora
> tristia temptantum sensu torquebit amaro.

'But the taste will reveal [salty soil] quite clearly, and twist the pained mouths of those who try it with a bitter sensation.' It was objected that since the taste *was* the sensation, the expression was tautologous; but such tautologies are frequent in Imperial poetry,[78] and the structure of the lines, with one subject predicated of two verbs linked by *et*, the second modified by an adjectivally qualified ablative, is thoroughly Vergilian.[79] *Amaror*, by contrast, imports a needless change of subject (with *sensus* a prosaic line-filler); though 'Favorinus' supports it as imitating Lucr. 4. 223–4, that is probably what suggested the interpolation in the first place. In fact, as Macrobius observes (*Sat.* 6. 1. 47), Vergil is imitating Lucr. 2. 401 'foedo pertorquent ora sapore'.

It follows that the readings quoted from the manuscripts must be accorded no greater authority than that of age; the variations between *-ēs* and *-īs* quoted in *NA* 13. 21 as showing Vergil's care for euphony, persuasive as they are, must be accepted on their merits irrespective of Probus' claim to have found *urbis* at *Georg.* 1. 25 in a copy corrected by the poet.[80] The spelling *ahena* at *Aen.* 2. 469 attested as a correction in the twenty-aureus manuscript at *NA* 2. 3. 5 stands only on a par with the *aheni* Gellius discovers 'in optimis libris' at *Georg.* 1. 296 (§ 6); sporadic insertion of *h* in this word is found in the direct tradition, but the vulgate spelling was without it.

The manuscripts' existence need not be doubted; likewise, we may as readily believe that Gellius found *insece* 'tell' in a Livius Andronicus preserved at Patrae (p. 124) as that Probus was stirred to study the early writers by manuscripts at that other veteran colony Berytus (Suet. *Gram.* 24. 2).[81] No

---

77. Is *dies* gen. sg. or acc. pl.? The corruption will be dittographic.

78. Housman on Man. 1. 539, 3. 496, 4. 472, 644, Lucan 1. 102, *CP* iii 1200–1; Shackleton Bailey 33–4; A. La Penna, *RFIC* 107 (1979) 1–11; A. Ronconi, ibid. 11–14. Add [Ov.] *Nux* 128. In Vergil, cf. *Aen.* 1. 246, 2. 206–8. At § 4 only *illius 'sensu torquebit amaro' risit et*, produced by Carrio from β (comm. 98; 'in uetustioribus codicibus' *Ant. lect.* 3. 12, p. 135), gives tolerable sense: with *amaroris* = *illius 'amaror'* either Favorinus lightly retracts his solemn oath or Gellius coolly contradicts it; cf. now Holford-Strevens, review of Cavazza, 37–8.

79. e.g. *Aen.* 1. 246; 3. 45–6; 4. 2.

80. Quint. 1. 7. 20 cites Cicero and Vergil's 'manus'; alleged literary autographs, or letters? Cf. Plin *NH.* 13. 83 (Suetonius saw Augustus' letters, Wallace-Hadrill 91–5).

81. Forgers and hoaxers equip their figments with a provenance (Speyer 69–70); but one must, as always, *die Geister unterscheiden*.

doubt he did seek out ancient copies to check the reading *dies*, gen. sing., at Cic. *Sest.* 28 (*NA* 9. 14. 6) and find *die*, gen. sing., in a venerable text of Sallust (*Jug.* 97. 3; *NA* § 26). His evidence must be taken into account, like the readings of papyri; but no store should be set by claims that brought the bookseller a better price.[82]

82. So Holford-Strevens, comm. 82–4, written independently of G. P. Goold, *HSCP* 74 (1970) 161–2, J. E. G. Zetzel, ibid. 77 (1973) 235–43, Gamberale, 'Autografi'. Then as now the trade had to cater for collectors as well as scholars (Luc. *Adu. ind.*, Gal. xviiiB. 630. 12–16 Kühn), but some of the MSS may have been old without being authentic; I see no reason to suppose they were commissioned to support conjectures. (Timpanaro, *Stor. fil. virg.* 51–8, 203–4 takes *sensus* … *amaror* for Vergil's first attempt, and *futurum* for Cicero's text; his arguments merit fuller consideration than they can receive here.)

Chapter 11

Roman Orators and Poets

DIONYSIUS THRAX, or one writing in his name, describes the criticism of poetry, κρίσις ποιημάτων, as the finest part of grammar. One commentator interprets 'judging whether metrical texts (i.e. poems) are composed correctly or incorrectly, well or badly, at this place or that, and knowing and explaining the reasons'; others repudiate this view and understand adjudging questions of disputed authorship, such as the theory that Sophocles' *Antigone* was written by Iophon.[1] Gellius—who does not confine himself to poetry—offers criticism of both types, but is chiefly concerned with qualitative judgements; looming large among them are comparisons, especially of Latin adaptations with their Greek originals.[2]

The chief discussion of authenticity is *NA* 3. 3, on plays ascribed to Plautus, some 130 altogether. Accius and others had attempted to distinguish the genuine from the spurious; Stilo had recognized only twenty-five. Varro registered twenty-one undoubtedly Plautus' work, presumably those surviving in our manuscripts; he also admitted Plautine authorship of certain others on stylistic grounds, including *Boeotia*, which others had attributed to Aquilius. Concurring with him, Gellius cites a passage from this play as enough to convince any connoisseur of Plautus that he wrote it;[3] he and Favorinus are thus emboldened to claim other plays for the poet, even on the strength of a single line.[4] Yet Gellius also states that comedies not composed by Plautus were revised by him, and therefore smack of his style—which

---

1. See 'Dion. Thrax', p. 6. 2–3 Uhlig; Schol. pp. 15. 26–9, 471. 34–47 2. 1 Hilgard (cf. ibid. 170. 25, 304. 2–3, 568. 13–31).

2. Throughout this chapter the reader should compare Marache, *Critique*, and to understand Gellius' criticisms consult Ernesti's lexica (the references to Gellius in the Latin volume are collected in the *index scriptorum*).

3. At *LL* 6. 89 Varro cites this play with a corrupt reference to its uncertain authorship; on the stylistic argument see Speyer 124–5. Wright 83–5 (but Gellius, let alone Varro, was better placed than we to tell one poet from another). On the passage cited (vv. 21–9 Lindsay) see A. S. Gratwick, *CQ²* 29 (1979) 308–23.

4. V. 97 Lindsay. Since neither *Neruolaria* nor *Fretum* is mentioned in § 9, Gellius' account of his own and Favorinus' experience breaks the thread of argument, 'Varro ascribed *Boeotia* and other comedies to Plautus on stylistic grounds, though Accius had rejected several plays including *Boeotia*'; it is a self-interpolation, not a fiction based on Varro (cf. Froehde 531–2). But it supports his judgements (Ritschl 129–30; *Neruolaria* is cited as Plautine by Varro, Festus, and Nonius), which conditioned Gellius' and Favorinus' responses. The non-canonical *Trigemini* is cited at 6. 9. 7, which breaks the sequence of *e*-reduplications; M. Caesar quotes *Colax* at *Ep.* 2. 5. 1. Apparently other plays were known besides the 21 *Varronianae*. Varro had ascribed some to 'Plautius', see A. S. Gratwick, *CQ²* 23 (1973) 83; the coincident genitive *Plauti* is noted at *LL* 8. 36.

would invalidate judgements based on one line or one passage; even if the stylistic sense be sound, there is no more care in the reasoning than Ritschl found in the report.[5]

At 4. 18. 6 Gellius, having cited the elder Scipio's purported defence to the charge of taking a bribe from Antiochus the Great, notes that even those who consider the speech spurious accept as genuine the passage quoted at § 3, in which Scipio, reminding the people that it is the anniversary of Zama, invites them to accompany him and give thanks to Jupiter on the Capitol. A literal interpretation of 'non eunt infitias quin haec quidem uerba fuerint quae dixi Scipionis' would imply that 'memoria, inquit, Quirites, repeto ... eamus hinc protinus Ioui Optimo Maximo gratulatum' was quoted verbatim from Scipio; but Cicero (*Brut.* 77) knew no sample of his oratory, and in Polybius' account (23. 14. 3) he said only that it ill beseemed the Roman people to hear anyone prosecuting P. Cornelius Scipio, through whom the prosecutors had their power to speak, whereupon the multitude at once dispersed. Even this seems to be an exaggeration; but the embellishing annalists invented the coincidence with Zama Day and converted the pride of Scipio's answer into deliberate disruption of a *iudicium populi*. The use of 'inquit' proves no more than at Liv. 38. 51. 7 or Val. Max. 3. 7. 1e, where the same sentiment is expressed in other, respectively more and fewer words; and the language of our extract better suits Gellius' own elaboration of the annalistic theme than a passage in the circulating speech.[6]

Whereas Favorinus' contrast between the effect of the slightest change on Plato and on Lysias (2. 5, cf. pp. 76–7) remains an *aperçu* not substantiated by examples, Gellius, maintaining in 10. 3 that as an orator C. Gracchus is inferior to Cicero and Cato, argues like a true critic from passages in which they treat of the same topic, the arrogance of Roman magistrates. The two extracts from Gracchus (frr. 48–9 M) narrate the outrages without any ornamentation: at best they show the 'breuitas ... et uenustas et mundities' of comedy, at worst they are on the level of everyday conversation. Indeed, Gellius feels obliged to show that he himself can write more ornately and prove himself at home in the art he judges.[7] The narratives are as plain as Gellius says; earlier generations of archaists had admired Gracchus for that very reason, in revulsion at Ciceronian pomp and Senecan cleverness, regarding the early writers as the Roman counterparts of Lysias and not admitting that what is simple in Greek may be jejune in Latin.[8]

For contrast Gellius turns to the fifth Verrine, in which the last and culminating crime to be narrated at length is the flogging and crucifixion of a

5. Ritschl 106–13, 119–22.
6. See Liv. 38. 56. 5–6, cf. ch. 4 n. 43; Scullard 298–310; Speyer 139; Walbank on Polyb. 23. 14. 1–4. For what it is worth, 'eamus ... gratulatum' is used at *NA* 12. 1. 2.
7. See pp. 44, 45–6.
8. 'Nos plerumque maioribus uelis mouemur', Quint. 12. 10. 37; cf. Hor. *Carm.* 2. 16. 38 'spiritum Graiae tenuem Camenae'.

Roman citizen. P. Gavius of Consa. Gellius omits all reference to the cross, and concentrates on the flogging: not merely narrated, but represented as if before our eyes[9] both by the detailing of the preparations ('nudari ac deligari et uirgas expediri iubet') and by the use of the imperfect 'caedebatur' as opposed to Gracchus' 'caesus est'. The observations are sound: and again Gellius displays his mastery of the grand style in expressing them.

However, he continues, some people may have ears too uncultured to appreciate such brilliance, yet may admire the unadorned, brief, unlaboured older style for its naïve charm and antique patina;[10] let them consider an older orator, Cato, to whose force and abundance Gracchus did not even aspire, and who, not content with the eloquence of his day, already sought to achieve what Cicero later accomplished (§ 16, cf. 13. 25. 12). The text quoted (fr. 42 SbC = 58 M) bears him out: Cato's indignation is raised through rhetoric to emotional heights that Gracchus does not try to scale. Indeed, as Cicero knew, the advance made by classical oratory over archaic was not in individual ornaments, or in the attention to rhythm within the clause, but in the construction of the period.[11] Accordingly, at 6. 3. 52–3, though conceding possible defects of structure and rhythm, in structure and rhythm, Gellius asserts that Cato used every device of rhetoric in his speech *Pro Rodiensibus*—a judgement fully compatible with that of 10. 3. 16, and on all fours with Cicero's at *Brutus* 65 'omnes oratoriae uirtutes in eis reperientur.'

Cicero had preached Cato at the Atticists in a show of patriotic indignation; if they rejected his own achievement, let it at least be for a Roman model.[12] Some in the next generation took him at his word, even as Sallust accepted Cato for the Roman Thucydides;[13] but they seem, like the Atticus of the dialogue, to have regarded him as 'hominem Tusculanum nondum suspicantem quale esset copiose et ornate dicere' (§ 294), only for praise rather than blame. Later critics were content with this verdict: Quintilian regularly couples 'Cato and the Gracchi' as the typical ancient orators, complaining at 2. 5. 21 that excessive study of them will impair boys' style, 'fient enim horridi atque ieiuni'; they reappear together at Plin. *Ep.* 1. 20. 4. Tacitus' aggressive modernist borrows Cicero's comment that no one had a fuller or richer style than C. Gracchus (*Brut.* 125) to declare that Gracchus was fuller and richer than old Cato (*Dial.* 18. 2); the assertion is

---

9. Cf. ch. 6 n. 87. For *sub oculos subiectio* see Cic. *De or.* 3. 202, *Orat.* 139; so Arist. *Rhet.* 1386^{b}33 etc. At § 12 the same notion is expressed by 'repraesentatione', cf. Quint. 8. 3. 61. Gellius' 'miseratio' is also technical (e.g. Cic. *De or.* 2. 196); for 'comploratio' (σχετλιασμός) cf. Don. on Ter. *Ad.* 237, 555, [Quint.] *Decl. mai.* 8. 22, 16. 1.

10. 'umbra et color quasi opacae uetustatis', cf. Intro. n. 12.

11. See Fraenkel, *Leseproben* 157, citing Cic. *De or.* 3. 198; for Cato see ibid. 125–56 (fr. 42 SbC is analysed at pp. 135–7).

12. His real motive was more personal (Lebek 176–92).

13. Syme, *Sallust* 53–6; Lebek 332–5 is sceptical, but allows *Brutus* 'anregende Bedeutung'. To be sure Cic. *Brut.* 66 does not say that Cato's historical style resembles Thucydides', but the comparison might be thence inferred (as of Cato with Lysias at Plin. *Ep.* 1. 20. 4), especially by a creative writer reinterpreting what he reads.

needed for his argument that oratory advances with the years, but dissent is neither expected nor expressed.[14]

Modernism palled, classicism failed: Cato and Gracchus were held in high esteem. For Fronto they are the only two ancient orators who wind the trumpet; the others merely moo or hiss ('mugiunt uel stridunt potius', *Ep. M. Caes.* 3. 17. 3, sc. like an unskilful player). Together with Cicero, they are the orators *par excellence* (*Eloq.* 2. 15).[15] In lieu of critical comparison, however, Fronto offers one-word descriptions (*Eloq.* 1. 2): 'Contionatur autem Cato infeste, Gracchus turbulente, Tullius copiose. Iam in iudiciis saeuit idem Cato, triumphat Cicero, tumultuatur Gracchus, Caluus rixatur'; animosity and ferocity on the one hand, rabble-rousing and trouble-making on the other, are exactly what one would expect from the πανδακέτης Cato and the *popularis* Gracchus, though not a word of their speeches had survived.

Although Fronto recommends Gracchus to his pupil, who developed a lasting taste for him (*Ep. M. Caes.* 3. 19. 1, *M. Ant.* 4. 1. 3), he receives far fewer mentions in their correspondence than Cato, the peer of Demosthenes (*Ep. M. Caes.* 2. 3. 1), and Cicero, the master of grandiloquence (ibid. 4. 3. 3), nor is he quoted. Yet the fashion for exalting the older authors caused not only Cato to be ranked above Cicero but Gracchus too, which Gellius finds intolerable: granted he is powerful and vehement,[16] he is certainly not sterner, sharper, and ampler than Cicero.[17]

The famous 'quo me miser conferam ...' (fr. 61 M) shows that Gracchus could command the higher strain, and fr. 32 M displays an ill-starred attempt at artistry (cf. p. 66) that Gellius at first relished all the more for finding the 'illustrious and severe' Gracchus already cultivating ornament (11. 13. 4). But the fragments as a whole suggest that he normally preferred a plainer style, which by no means eschewed barbed humour[18] or naked hostility,[19] and doubtless commended him to the people as their honest friend; the vehemence of which our sources speak consisted of bald statement vigorously delivered, so vigorously indeed that he needed a slave to moderate his excitement with a timely note from his pipe.[20] Gellius, however, like most critics, judges only the written text.

Comparison is also made between Greek literature and its Latin imitations. In 2. 23, Roman comedies are said to be enjoyable in themselves,

14. At Cic. *De or.* 1. 154 Gracchus, not Cato, is on a par with Ennius, the supreme orator besides the supreme poet; at § 171 Cato is the greatest orator of his day only. This is Cicero's consistent view.

15. But note *Eloq.* 4. 3 'Catonis et Sallustii et Tulli tuba'.

16. 'Fortis et uehemens': cf. Cic. *Har. resp.* 41, Tac. *Dial.* 26. 1, Gell. *NA* 1. 11. 14.

17. 'Seuerior, acrior, ampliorque': at 11. 13. 4 Gellius allows that he is *seuerus* in the positive degree; a reputation for *acrimonia* survived into late antiquity (Claud. Mam. CSEL 11. 206. 1–2).

18. Fr. 44 M, accusing his opponents of corrupt motives, at *NA* 11. 10. 2–6.

19. Fr. 38 M 'eo exemplo instituto dignus fuit, qui malo cruce periret'.

20. *NA* 1. 11. 1–16 with parallels in Hosius; and note Plut. *Ti. Gracch.* 2. 2 ἔντονος δὲ καὶ σφοδρὸς ὁ Γάιος, the first Roman to walk about on the rostra and pull at his toga, paralleling Cleon.

but to pall beside the Greek originals; three pairs of proof-texts are adduced
from Menander's *Plocion* and Caecilius' adaptation. Gellius finds (§§ 11–13)
that Menander's straightforward and delightful imitation of human life has
been omitted,[21] and replaced by the vulgarities of mime, the lowest form of
farce;[22] Caecilius was out to raise a laugh rather than to suit the character.
These comments are made on the following pair of extracts, in which a
hen-pecked husband (A; in Menander 'Laches') describes his wife to a
neighbour (B):

Menander fr. 334 Körte–Thierfelder

A. ἔχω δ' ἐπίκληρον Λάμιαν· οὐκ εἴρηκά σοι
    τουτὶ γάρ;[23]
B.   οὐχί.
A.   κυρίαν τῆς οἰκίας
    καὶ τῶν ἀγρῶν καὶ τῶν ἁπάντων ἄντικρυς
    ἔχομεν.
B.   "Απολλον, ὡς χαλεπόν.
A.   χαλεπώτατον.
    ἅπασι δ' ἀργαλέα 'στίν, οὐκ ἐμοὶ μόνῳ·
    υἱῷ, πολὺ μᾶλλον θυγατρί.
B.   πρᾶγμ' ἄμαχον λέγεις.
A. εὖ οἶδα.

A. My heiress wife's an ogre; haven't I
    Told you about it?
B.   No.
A.   She rules the house,
    The farm, and absolutely everything
    Completely.
B.   God, how awful!
A.   Horrible.
    She's beastly to us all, not just to me—
    My son, still more my daughter.
B.   Sounds a terror.
A. Too true.

Caecilius vv. 158–62 Ribbeck

B. sed tua morosane uxor quaeso est?
A.   ua, rogas?
B. qui tandem?
A.   taedet mentionis, quae mihi
    ubi domum adueni adsedi, extemplo sauium
    dat ieiuna anima.
A.   nil peccat de sauio:
    ut deuomas uolt quod foris potaueris.

---

21. See Housman on Man. 5. 476.
22. Demetr. *Eloc.* 151, Cic. *Or.* 88, Quint. 6. 1. 47, Diom. *GLK* i. 491. 12–16, J. Lyd. *Mag.* 1.
40. Cf. 'Caecilio ... mimico' at Volcacius Sedigitus fr. 1. 5 M–B (*NA* 15. 24, corr. Jac.
Gronovius). For the mimic and the tragic (§ 21) as faults in comedy cf. Euanth. 3. 5 ap. Don.
23. So punctuated by Professor Hugh Lloyd-Jones (pers. comm.).

B. But tell me, is your wife a Tartar?
A.   Is she?!
B. Well, how?
A.   I don't like saying. Straight away
    When I come home and settle down, she gives me
    A kiss that stinks of hunger.
B.   Quite right too—
    So you'll throw up the booze you've drunk while out.

The contrast bears out Gellius' comment: it is truly bronze for gold (§ 7).[24] Above all, Caecilius' coarse jest ill fits a downtrodden wretch no more capable of drowning his sorrows in drink than of sleeping with the slave-girl his termagant wife has bullied him by that accusation into selling.[25] The lover of Plautus and Pacuvius, reading Caecilius in isolation, no doubt enjoyed the vigorous *canticum* in which the husband bewails his fate (vv. 142–56 R), even the 'tragic bombast' (§ 21) of the slave's comment (vv. 169–72 R); but comparing them with the speeches they replace (frr. 333, 335 K.–Th), he saw that both elegance and humanity had departed.[26] Those tempted to consider Gellius—like Plutarch disparaging Aristophanes or Voltaire damning Shakespeare—a cultural élitist scorning a playwright who pleased all classes in a less precious age should recollect that Caecilius was no Aristophanes and no Shakespeare; nor does Gellius find fault but by comparison.[27] If he judges as if his criteria were rightly those of all times and all places, so do we all, though some do not admit it.

It is more serious that he approaches Caecilius' dramaturgy as nothing but an exercise in translation, complaining that he has not even tried to render what is best in Menander (§ 12) and concluding that he ought not to

24. In the land that long rejected Mozart, Menander's scene is called 'insipida' by Marchesi i. 93, *probante* Traina 50. For Arnaldi ii. 77–9 Gellius' criticisms are correct (so too Romano 69–71) but he lacks the historical sense to understand the inevitable nature of 'la commedia, meglio l'opera buffa di Plauto e di Cecilio', and had lost the taste for the primitive still shared by Cicero. The discussion by Leo, *Röm. Lit.* 221–3 remains unsurpassed.

25. The inappropriateness of the bad-breath joke, old stand-by that it was (Plaut. *Asin.* 893–5, 902–3, *Merc.* 574–6) and a comic reversal of the custom mentioned at *NA* 10. 23. 1, is asserted by Gellius, who knew the play and judged its characterization by ancient standards— namely Menander's, to which Caecilius did not even aspire (§ 11). One may enjoy both kinds of comedy in isolation, and the rope-walker besides Terence; but to *prefer* Caecilius' vulgarity is best excused as a patriotic reaction against the sneers of *Deutschhellenentum*.

26. Eduard Fraenkel, than whom none loved Plautus more, found him uninterested in 'il puro βίος, il quotidiano e tipico', which had never ceased to attract the Attic poets (a judgement borne out by our new knowledge of Δὶς ἐξαπατῶν; see Handley's essay); as the best description he cites *NA* 2. 23. 11 (*Elementi* 369–70). Cf. Wright 120–6.

27. Revisionism, as usual, misses the wood for the trees: the Roman spectators were indeed no mere bumpkins, and had seen tragedies (Wright 130–1); but glorious as the Latin tragic language is, and powerful its grasp on the emotions, we shall not place Roman tragedians on a par with Greek. The grotesque concert of Polyb. 30. 22, Terence's failures, and Mummius' offhand treatment of his priceless plunder like any common cargo (Vell. Pat. 1. 13. 4; see too Fav. fr. 95. 42 B) amply bear out Gellius' comment on those times (15. 11. 3).

have attempted the piece (§ 22).[28] Whenever Gellius discusses a Roman imitation, it is always in this same schoolmasterly spirit, shared by the Probus of 9. 9. 12–17 and evident again in Macrobius. A criticism that concentrates on language and style, examines a text word by word, and reads it against its original, can hardly avoid this approach; but Gellius was particularly interested in translation, as performed by both others and himself.[29] His methods and principles have been studied by Gamberale, who, reviewing the places where Gellius either renders Greek himself or judges versions made by other hands, finds throughout the same concern for semantic accuracy and the reproduction of Greek beauties in a less pliable language.

Only once are the extracts related to their contexts, in Probus' complaint that the simile of Artemis and her nymphs out hunting in the mountains, appropriate to Nausicaa and her maidens, did not suit Dido at her court (9. 9. 14)—which is immediately followed by the further complaint that Vergil had left out the hunting! One might have thought it obvious that Dido is equated with Nausicaa, not merely because both are royal ladies about to welcome the hero on his wanderings, or even because Carthage is Vergil's Scheria as well as his Ogygia, but to convey her guileless hospitality and unsuspecting happiness. 'Talem se laeta ferebat'—νηπίη, οὐδ' ἐνόησεν. The poet thinks ahead: 'felix, heu nimium felix ...'. Since she is not a lithe princess, but a majestic queen, the chase is suppressed as unsuited to her stately progress;[30] later, she will hunt, with a fatal outcome. But the pedant, seeing none of this, even misunderstands his own language, taking 'pertemptant' (v. 502) to mean that Latona's pleasure is slight and superficial.[31] No criticism that Gellius offers in his own name is so thoroughly and philistinically misconceived; nor indeed is he ever as wrong-headed as

28. For 'sequi ... assequi' cf. Cic. *Or.* 104; *Off.* 1. 110 (also *Fam.* 15. 21. 4), Vell. Pat. 1. 17. 7: see too ch. 2 n. 5; for *assequi* 'match' see Lebek 92 n. 42.

29. For translation cf. Sen. *Contr.* 9. 1. 13, Quint. 10. 5. 2–3. Fronto complains that the student of (Stoic) philosophy has no occasion to render Greek into Latin (*Eloq.* 5. 4; as at 4. 5 he seeks to shame Marcus back to rhetoric by representing philosophy as the soft option). Gellius' translation are praised by Stephanus (letter to Vulcob 10–11), but some individual glosses censured (ibid. 8–9).

30. A hint remains in the quiver, an attribute even a statue may bear (cf. Marache, *Critique* 307: 'La déesse n'est plus la vierge chassant, c'est la statue porte-carquois'); the wretched Probus thought of a shoulder-bag. His criticisms of the passage, already rebutted by Servius on v. 497 (similes do not apply in every detail), were answered by Ascensius ad loc. (citing v. 336 for the quiver), J. C. Scaliger, *Poet.* 219ᵇC–220ᵃD (who censures Homer no less carpingly), Carolus 389–90; Pope commented (*Works*, Twickenham edn., ix. 211–12 n.) that Leto's joy, in both poets, 'may be judg'd superfluous'! Romano 99 valiantly denies that Gellius accepted Probus' view. Austin ad loc. is excellent; cf. L. Schley, *WZ Leipzig* 1/3 (1952–3) 95–6 (who, however, echoes Probus' complaint that Vergil has omitted v. 108, the loveliest line in Homer's simile but, as Ascensius observes, irrelevant to his own), Knauer 153 n. 3. Vergil offers formal echoes of A.R. 3. 876–86 (Clausen 18–20)—and a total contrast to his hurtling chariot and cowed commons. With a subtlety worthy of Macrobius or Porphyry, M. K. Thornton, *Latomus* 44 (1985) 614–22 argues that Dido is likened nominally to Diana, but really to Venus, *tout entière à sa proie attachée*.

31. But see Lucr. 6. 287, Verg. *Georg.* 3. 250–1, Serv. on *Aen.* 1. 502; again Austin should be consulted.

Castricius in censuring Sallust's adaptation of Demosthenes (2. 27, pp. 65–6) or Favorinus in condemning Vergil's lines on Etna (17. 10, p. 89).

To be sure, he can be quibblesome. In 11. 4 he examines Ennius' version (*Sc.* 172–4 Jocelyn) of Eur. *Hec.* 293–5, where Hecuba beseeches Odysseus to dissuade the Greeks from sacrificing Polyxena at Achilles' tomb:

> τὸ δ' ἀξίωμα, κἂν κακῶς λέγῃς, τὸ σόν
> πείσει·³² λόγος γὰρ ἔκ τ' ἀδοξούντων ἰών
> κἀκ τῶν δοκούντων αὑτὸς οὐ ταὐτὸν σθένει.

> Thy reputation, though thou speak amiss,
> Shall sway them; as the speakers lack renown
> Or bear good fame, like words have not like power.

Ennius wrote:

> haec tu etsi peruerse dices, facile Achiuos flexeris;
> nam opulenti cum locuntur pariter atque ignobiles,³³
> eadem dicta eademque oratio aequa non aeque ualet.

Although Gellius in general praises the translation for its neatness, he objects that the second verse, 'for when alike the mighty speak, and men of low degree',³⁴ does not correspond to the original: not all men of humble station lack, or all rich and powerful men possess, a good name. We need not consider the differences, or similarities, between the relation of social status to moral standing in Euripides' Athens and Ennius' Rome (let alone Homeric and Antonine society), though Gellius might have remembered the power of wealth to shore up reputation from the much-abused Caecilius;³⁵ he was no more concerned with comparative sociology than with the significance of the change for Ennius' play. The words do not mean the same thing, and verbal accuracy is an end in itself. Likewise, at 9. 9. 9–10 he complains that the billygoat of Theoc. 3. 4–5 has been castrated in Vergil's translation (*Buc.* 9. 25); the meaning of *caper* he has learnt not on the farm but from Varro. He is not worried that the operation has unfitted the beast for the context, but only that Vergil seems guilty of a verbal slip.³⁶

At the beginning of the same chapter, Gellius states as an accepted rule that when outstanding passages of Greek poetry are to be translated and adapted, not everything must be exactly rendered at all costs, since many phrases lose their charm if forcibly translated against their will and struggling

---

32. πείσει Euripides, νικᾷ Gellius.

33. *Cum opulenti* codd., long since corrected (*dubitante* Jocelyn); see Hertz ad loc. (though the corruption may well be pre-Gellian).

34. *Opulentus* denotes not only wealth, but power and status (Jocelyn on v. 173, *TLL* ix/2. 838. 42–69); Gellius accepts *ignobilis* as its antonym.

35. 'Nam opulenti famam facile occultat factio' (v. 172 R ap. Gell. 2. 23. 21): *factio* is a synonym for *opulentia*, denoting the influence conferred by money (Non. 473. 24–36; R. Seager, *JRS* 62 (1972) 53). On Ennius' tr. and Gellius' criticism see Jocelyn's comm.; Traina 130–3; Gamberale 119–22.

36. But cf. *Buc.* 7. 7 'uir gregis ipse caper'. Horace and Ovid agree with Vergil, Martial with Varro; the narrower sense, as of 'ox' and 'wether', is secondary.

('si quasi inuita et recusantia uiolentius transferantur'). Vergil was therefore right to omit what he could not render; at *Buc.* 3. 65 he substitutes for Theocritus' untranslatable καὶ ἁδύ τι ποππυλιάζει (5. 89)[37] the even more delightful 'et fugit ad salices et se cupit ante uideri'.[38] Word-for-word translation Gellius has discovered to be often impossible, as when he finds no Latin for Plutarch's title Περὶ πολυπραγμοσύνης (*NA* 11. 16; cf. p. 168). Unfortunately, the loss of book 8 has denied us 'my experience when trying to translate some passages of Plato into Latin' (8. 8. lemma); in 17. 20 he offers his version of a passage from *Symposium*, but in 10. 22 does not attempt to render the long extracts from *Gorgias*.

Not everything said in Greek is expressible in Latin, but when the Roman poet does imitate a Greek model, he may vary the phrase but not without good cause the sense. He may add matter of his own—Vergil is praised for subjoining nurture by Hyrcanian tigers (*Aen.* 4. 367) to a motif from Homer (*NA* 12. 1. 20)—but even then must remain faithful to the original spirit. Gellius takes no heed that the poet may be writing a different kind of poetry for a different audience; a defence available both to Caecilius adapting Menander for the boisterous Romans, and to Vergil imitating Homer's

ταῦρον δ' Ἀλφειῷ, ταῦρον δὲ Ποσειδάωνι (*Il.* 11. 728)

with

Taurum Neptuno, taurum tibi, pulcher Apollo (*Aen.* 3. 119).

Homer's verse, says Gellius (*NA* 13. 27. 3), is simpler and more natural ('simplicior et sincerior'),[39] Vergil's decadent with ornamentation soldered on ('νεωτερικώτερος et quodam quasi ferumine inmisso fucatior').[40] Certainly Vergil here imitates not Homeric directness but Hellenistic prettiness; as Gellius knew (*NA* 9. 9. 3), he was the heir, not merely of Homer and Hesiod, but of Callimachus, Apollonius, Theocritus, and Parthenius, living in a more sophisticated society than archaic Greece. Noble simplicity was no longer to be expected, however much a cloyed Antonine might prefer it. Vergil, who uses epic apostrophe—itself not unknown to Homer—far less wantonly than later poets, distinguishes Apollo, who has just vouchsafed an oracle, from the surrounding deities; but Gellius' eyes are fixed on the single lines. Concentration on detail is not confined to criticism of translations, nor peculiar to Gellius: it is common to his teachers (e.g. in 1. 4; 11. 13) and to less favoured critics. Cornutus, for instance, had misunderstood Vergil's

37. Literally 'and sweetly makes a little *psst*-sound'; 'pout' and 'moue' are the visual, πόππυσμα the auditory component of this behaviour.

38. 'And to the willows flees, and hopes I've seen her', a realism delightful to the Romans.

39. For 'sincerior' cf. 2. 27. 4. Others (see D.S. ad loc.) complained that *pulcher*, an epithet Lucilius' Apollo had rejected (fr. 23 M), was fit only for catamites; yet it is frequently applied to deities.

40. See Ernesti, s.vv. κόλλησις (not itself pejorative), κομμωτικόν (cf. Wiseman, *Clio's Cosmetics* 4–5).

'uexasse', which Gellius explains out of Cato and Cicero;[41] other censures of individual words are rebutted in this chapter (2. 6) and many others.

A broader approach is taken in 6. 3, where Cato's speech on behalf of the Rhodians—who had sympathized with Perseus of Macedon against Rome— is vindicated against the criticisms of Cicero's freedman Tiro: failing to conciliate the audience, confessing the charge, and employing captious arguments. Gellius' defence is sound, piecemeal and overall: Cato was neither a declaimer (§ 52) nor an advocate (§ 17), but a statesman urging the policy he believed most beneficial with every available device of the orator's art; the speech might perhaps have been better organized and more rhythmical,[42] but hardly more forceful and vivid (§ 53). Castricius too had made the elementary distinction between forensic and deliberative speaking in 1. 6, when Metellus, urging the Romans to marry, shocks certain readers by admitting the disadvantages; but whereas Metellus frankly confesses what is common knowledge, and Castricius holds fallacious arguments unworthy of a censor, Cato admits only that he thinks the Rhodians harboured disloyal sentiments, and Gellius allows him to deem permissible any means of preserving valued allies, even by constantly shifting ground—but also by casting in the Romans' own teeth the pride they reprehended in the Rhodians, a noble passage Tiro had omitted; tactical astuteness no more compromises his moral grandeur than (so Jerome would urge in self-defence) that of philosophers, the Fathers, and St Paul himself.[43]

By Gellius' day, Cato was unassailable; Cicero faced attack from extreme reactionaries and cheapjack critics.[44] This was not new: in 17. 1. 1 Gellius, comparing such folk to blasphemers against the gods,[45] specifies Asinius

---

41. At *Buc.* 6. 76 Scylla is said 'Dulichias uexasse rates', with the sense we learnt at school (cf. Judg. 10. 8 Coverdale, AV); but in Cornutus' day *uexare* was moving towards our 'vex' or 'disturb' (cf. Mart. 1. 117. 5, Juv. 1. 2, 126). A reader knowing only modern English would be similarly puzzled by Milton, *Samson Agonistes* 577-8 'Wilt thou then serve the *Philistines* with that gift / Which was expressly giv'n thee to annoy them?', for Samson was a warrior, not a wasp. Probus too had felt the need to defend 'uexasse' (see Servius ad loc.), likewise taking *uexare* for the intensive of *uehere*; but he supposes Vergil to mean that Scylla carried off the ships and capsized them, which is παρ' ἱστορίαν. Gellius' parallels, like much else from him, reappear in D.S. (not from Gellius himself, as A. Van Hoye, *PhS* 5 (1933-4) 188-97, but from D.S.'s source Donatus).

42. Not so, says Fraenkel, *Leseproben* 157 n. 1; all Cicero's rhythms may be found in Cato's speeches. But Gellius means that Cato did not compose in Ciceronian periods. He ignores the context of Tiro's criticisms (G. Calboli, edn. of *Pro Rod.*, pp. 80–90; above, Intro. n. 21).

43. *Ep.* 49. 13 (CSEL 54. 368–70).

44. The persons 'durae auris' (13. 25. 22) who mislike the *congeries* 'decepit, fefellit, induxit' (*Pis.* 1; cf. Quint. 9. 3. 47, citing the same speech) recall the hypothetical archaizer 'tam agresti aure ac tam hispida' (10. 3. 15) who prefers the inartistic Gracchus; for the pedant of 17. 5 see ch. 14 n. 76 (with 'inlotis quod aiunt pedibus' § 14 cf. 1. 9. 8, Dio Prus. 12. 43, A. Otto 275).

45. Marache, *Critique* 293, 297 takes both this passage and 17. 1. 1 to be ironical, as if what a modern scholar cannot say with a straight face an ancient writer could not mean, or the Antonines felt the detachment from the past that has marked the 20th-c. cultural élite. Gellius praises Cicero with his own ornaments; and if Homer can be called a god (θεὸς οὐδ' ἄνθρωπος Ὅμηρος, Ziebarth no. 26; cf. Fronto, *Eloq.* 2. 15) and worshipped at Homereia, if Vergil can be deified at Calp. Sic. 4. 70 and his tomb made a shrine by Silius Italicus, it is

Gallus and Larcius Licinus. The former, son of Cicero's vindictive detractor Pollio, wrote to exalt the father who overshadowed him above the classic orator;[46] the latter, who began the fashion for treating the centumviral court as a theatre of eloquence, and offered the elder Pliny 400,000 sesterces for his notebooks, gave his polemic the 'infamous' title of *Ciceromastix*.[47] Only one of their criticisms does Gellius deign to answer, that of 'paeniteat' at *Cael*. 6: Caelius will never take the allegations about his younger years so hard 'ut eum paeniteat non deformem esse natum'; this is silly, for we cannot repent of things like good looks that are not of our causation. Modern scholars understand *paenitere* in its earlier sense of 'be dissatisfied', still available for Cicero (e.g. *Sen*. 19) and even the younger Pliny (*Ep*. 6. 19. 6);[48] Gellius, though apparently aware of this usage (§ 9: the ancients derived *paenitet* from *paene* and *paenuria*), dismisses it as irrelevant ('aliorsum pertinet'). Cicero did mean 'repent', and his critics have failed to see the joke of making the prosecution absurdly blame Caelius for what he could not help. This seems to be right:[49] in context, we expect a reference to Caelius' youthful conduct, but hear instead that he is handsome. Yet the surprise depends on the ambiguity of *paenitere*: Cicero relies on the earlier usage to support the subtlety here explained.

Further dexterity was observed by Julianus at *Planc*. 68 (*NA* 1. 4, cf. p. 64); Gellius himself (12. 12) finds in the tale of Cicero's unblushing but urbane admission he had told a lie the paradigm for laughing off what cannot be denied.[50] However, forensic technique is not his chief preoccupation. He relishes the invective of the Verrines and Philippics (to him *Antonianae*) above the legerdemain of *Pro Cluentio* and *Pro Milone*, which yield only one

scarcely unreasonable to say that defamation of Cicero is *like* blasphemy against the gods. But at edn. 1. 6. 5 n. Marache supposes 'la candeur d'Aulu-Gelle' unable to see the humour in Metellus' and Castricius' remarks on marriage, as if they were anticipating such masterpieces as *Les Quinze Joyes de mariage* and Panurge's consultations: in fact, Metellus was deploying traditional wisdom (cf. Ar. *Lys*. 1038, Men. fr. 578 K–Th, and the famous fragment of 'Susarion') to overcome a real and unwelcome reluctance in Roman males.

46. Sen. *Contr*. 4. pr. 4 (on Pollio, *Suas*. 6. 14–15, 24, 27); Quint. 12. 1. 22; Plin. *Ep*. 7. 4. 3, 6; Claudius wrote a learned reply (Suet. *Claud*. 41. 3).

47. Plin. *Ep*. 2. 14. 9, 11; 3. 5. 17. Cf. Ὁμηρομάστιξ, *Vergiliomastix*, *Aeneomastix*.

48. Cf. Fraenkel, *Horace* 5 n. 6.

49. Cf. Scipio Gentilis on Apul. *Apol*. 4. 6 (comm. 39 n. 79); 'quem locum A. Gellius lepidissime explicauit'. The verb recurs with its normal sense at *Cael*. 14. At Apul. *Met*. 4. 30. 3; 5. 30. 2 Venus uses the same formula 'iam faxo ... paeniteat' of Psyche's 'unlawful' beauty and Cupid's misconduct.

50. When P. Sulla was accused of complicity with Catiline, Cicero, needing money to buy the house on the Palatium later demolished by Clodius, took his case in return for a secret loan of 2m. HS. The story got out; Cicero denied all interest in the house. When he bought it, the lie was cast in his teeth; he made light of it as normal prudence. For the tale cf. [Sall.] *In Cic*. 2. 3–4; for Cicero's skill in humorous self-extrication cf. *Clu*. 138–42. The rhetorical device is called διασυρμός or *eleuatio* (Mart. Cap. 5. 525, Phoebammon, *Rhet. Gr*. iii. 54. 18–26 Sp; cf. Cic. *De or*. 2. 230, Quint. 6. 3. 75).

quotation apiece;[51] in Quintilian, by contrast, they vie for frequency of citation with the entire *actio secunda*.

Cicero's letters, admired throughout antiquity and judged by Fronto, who excerpted them for style and content, more rewarding even than the speeches to read in their entirety (*Ep. M. Ant.* 3. 10. 2), yield only three quotations in the *Nights*, one of them from Pollio,[52] all for lexical illustration. Being no historian, Gellius ignored their information on the late Republic; caring more for books than people, he neglects their portrait of Cicero's personality. His one anecdote about him, in 12. 12, comes from a secondary source; it is not the man that interests him but the orator, most careful in his diction (13. 25. 4) and undoubtedly the most eloquent of all (17. 13. 2).

The age of Cicero and Caesar, writes Gellius (19. 14. 1), saw many learned men but few great orators; so much for Hortensius, Cato Uticensis, Caelius, and the *salaputium disertum* Calvus. Gellius does not one-sidedly prefer the archaic to the classical: he admires the purity of Caesar's style,[53] and insists on Cicero's supremacy. But Calvus, an orator of uneven merit, had taken the first steps towards modernism (Tac. *Dial.* 21. 2); the others were overshadowed by Cicero.[54] Even Caelius, with one foot in each stylistic camp (ibid. §§ 3–4), and much admired—with seven verbatim quotations— by Quintilian, is, as an orator, ignored along with Messalla, Pollio (letters apart), and later figures. By contrast, Cicero and Cato Censorius, who overall are cited almost as often as Vergil and Varro, stand on their speeches alone in frequency of quotation far ahead of Gracchus, who is followed by Numidicus and Aemilianus. The Corpus Frontonianum yields similar results; to Marcus, Pollio was as dead as Horace (*Ep.* 2. 5. 3).[55]

Vergil is cited over twice as often as any of his Latin predecessors; next come Plautus, Lucilius, and Ennius. But apart from fleeting hints of Horace,[56] and

51. *Pro Milone* is cited for a construction, and a textual variant, at 1. 16. 15; *Pro Cluentio*, still much quoted by the later rhetoricians, Cicero's finest speech at Sidon. *Ep.* 8. 10. 3, contributes one solitary word (16. 7. 10).

52. *NA* 1. 22. 19 ('et' specifies as at Liv. 27. 1. 10; cf. J. F. Gronovius ad loc.); 4. 9. 6; 12. 13. 21–2; at 16. 7. 4 Gellius misses *Fam.* 7. 25. 1. *Obiurgatorius* (1. 26. 7; 6. 3. 12; 9. 2. 3), anticipated at *Att.* 13. 6. 3, could be formed at will.

53. *NA* 10. 24. 2; 19. 8. 3; cf. 4. 16. 8. Gellius cites *De analogia*, *Anticato*, and three speeches, mentions the ciphered letters, but ignores the *commentarii* (as others do: Syme, *Sallust* 50), cf. ch. 10 n. 26; in 10. 26 Sallust's *transgredi* of ships is defended by *cursus* and Cato's *ambulare*, but not by Caesar's *progredi* (*BG* 7. 60. 1, *BC* 3. 24. 2).

54. Hortensius and Calvus are known to be poets (19. 9. 7); Hortensius is the most illustrious orator of his day after Cicero (1. 5. 2), but yields only a joke against L. Torquatus, whose description as 'subagresti homo ingenio et infestiuo', contradicting Cic. *Brut.* 265 (cf. ch. 15 n. 17), must come from his opponent's ἄμουσος ἀναφρόδιτος. See too Wiseman, *Cinna the Poet* 105, and for ἀπροσδιόνυσος 'irrelevant, out of place, mal à propos' Lambecius 34.

55. The *grammaticus* Pollio in printed texts of *HA Marcus* 2. 3, invoked by Mai, edn.¹ i. 20 n. 2, is an editorial ghost; see A. R. Birley, *Bonner HAC 1966/1967* (1968) 40–1.

56. Cited for *atabulus* at 2. 22. 25 and possibly for *Iapyx* in § 1; but Gellius has spoken of 'uetus carmen', which should in a literary context—as opposed to the looser usage of 13. 14. 7 (an 'ancient' grammarian mentions the emperor Claudius) and 18. 10. 11 ('ancient' doctors of

one apparent reminiscence of Ovid,[57] no other Augustan or Silver poet leaves a trace; not even Lucan, whom Fronto had deemed worthy of his censure while completely ignoring Vergil.

In neglecting Vergil, Fronto stood alone. Apuleius knew him well; the grammarian of *NA* 20. 10. 2 invites questions on Vergil, Plautus, and Ennius. But though greatly admired, he is not beyond reproach; his dissatisfaction with the unfinished *Aeneid* encouraged the suggestion that any passage one disliked would have been revised had he lived. This device, employed by Hyginus soon after the poet's death, is still not out of favour;[58] it would be legitimate if one knew what (half-lines apart) Vergil would have regarded as faulty or defective.

According to Gellius, in *NA* 10. 16, Hyginus surmised that Vergil would have corrected three passages in book 6. At v. 366 he objected that Aeneas would not understand Palinurus' injunction to seek the harbour of Velia ('portusque require Velinos'), since the town was founded over six hundred years later, by exiles 'ex terra Phocide'. The anachronism could not be defended by 'Lauinia' at 1. 2 or 'Chalcidica' at 6. 17, where the poet, in his own person, was speaking proleptically:[59] Palinurus could not know about Velia, or even if, without support from the text, one credited him, in death, with prophetic powers, the living Aeneas would not recognize the name.[60] Sad souls offended by the mention of Milford Haven in *Cymbeline* or bull-bearing Milo in *Troilus and Cressida* may tell themselves that the Sibyl explained the matter afterwards, or that Velia lay in territory that 'Oenotri coluere uiri' long before Aeneas, let alone the Greeks, arrived;[61] others will

---

Gellius' own century, p. 224, if he knew)—exclude the Augustan who scorned the early poets. (At 6. 8. 1 'recentes ... memoriae' denotes Apion's account of an alleged event under Augustus.) Could Laevius have used the word? 'Profanum et profestum uolgus' (pr. 20) echoes *Carm*. 3. 1. 1, 'male feriati' 10. 22. 24 recalls *Carm*. 4. 6. 14 (but the sense differs); at 17. 10. 8 'aemulari', a favourite word for translation (Gamberale 120 n. 111), may also reflect *Carm*. 4. 2. 1. Cf. Heraeus 1170. *Epist*. 1. 17. 36, 59 are not cited at 1. 8. 4 (contrast Sallust and Cicero at 1. 15. 13, 15); 16. 7. 10. For Fronto see p. 47; Marcus may recall *Serm*. 2. 6. 90 at *Med*. 11. 22 (I ignore *HA AC* 11. 8); Apuleius has two certain and two likely allusions in *Apol*. alone (Owen, edn., p. lxiii). Horace violates some Gellian prescriptions: *Carm*. 2. 13. 1 ∼ *NA* 4. 9. 5; 5. 17. 1; *Epist*. 1. 1. 79 ∼ *NA* 2. 20. 14; *Epist*. 2. 1. 227 ∼ *NA* 2. 19. 4.

57. *NA* 12. 1. 19 'inter ipsas artificis naturae manus' ∼ *Met*. 15. 218 (v. 227 is used at Apul. *Apol*. 36. 2); but in Gellius 'artificis' will be gen. sing. At § 8 the link with *Am*. 2. 14. 7 is probably life: for wrinkles see Mart. 3. 42; 3. 72. 4, for cosmetic abortions *Nux* 23–4, Sen. *Helu*. 16. 3, Juv. 6. 597–9. Both Ovid (several times) and Gellius (19. 9. 7) use *deliciae* of love-poetry; connection is no less tenuous than between *Met*. 1. 687–8 and 'recens repertis fistulis'. Fronto, *Eloq*. 4. 2. *NA* 2. 7. 12 need owe nothing to *Met*. 2. 137; for the commonplace see Nisbet–Hubbard on Hor. *Carm*. 2. 10. 5, [Thgn.] 335, Liv. 32. 21. 33; for 'optima et tutissima' cf. Cic. *Verr*. 5. 69.

58. e.g. E. Courtney, *BICS* 28 (1981) 13–29. Observe the use of this topos by Petrarch, *Res fam*. 24. 12. 22–5.

59. 'κατὰ πρόληψιν historiae'; editors wrongly give πρόληψιν (see Schulze, *Orthog*. 17–18). Cf. ch. 12 n. 40.

60. So Serv. on *Aen*. 6. 359. Cf. Vell. Pat. 1. 3. 2; the theme is a favourite with Servius as with Greek scholiasts (Norden, comm. 113, cf. Mühmelt 124).

61. Hdt. 1. 167. 3, cf. *Aen*. 1. 532 = 3. 165. Both Ὑελῆ (Schulze, *Kl. Schr*. 395–6) and Ἐλέα come from the Oscan equivalent of *Velia*.

dismiss with contempt these petty cavils of petty minds, and observe with delight that Phocis has been put for Phocaea.[62]

Hyginus next complains that whereas at v. 122 Theseus is counted among those who returned from the underworld, he is eternally confined there at vv. 617–18; the discrepancy is real, but that does not mean the poet would have removed it.[63] Finally, Vergil is taxed with confusing, at vv. 838–40, the war against Pyrrhus ('Aeaciden') with Mummius' campaign over a century later; here it is Hyginus who has confused Pyrrhus with Perseus and Mummius with Paullus.

We have already seen this same Hyginus, with 'Favorinus'' approbation, producing a textual variant at *Georg.* 2. 247 to eliminate a construction found elsewhere in Vergil, and frequent in Propertius, whom an Augustan critic might be expected to have read.[64] But when he airs his skill in sacral law (acknowledged at 16. 6. 14), Gellius springs to the poet's defence: well in 7. 6, where he upholds Vergil's right to use *praepes* according to its etymology ('uim ... naturamque uerbi' § 7) rather than as the augurs do, badly in 5. 8, where the syllepsis 'ipse Quirinali lituo paruaque sedebat / subcinctus trabea' (*Aen.* 7. 187–8)[65]—as legitimate as ἔδουσί τε πίονα μῆλα / οἶνόν τ' ἔξαιτον (Hom. *Il.* 12. 319–20),[66] however defective it seemed to Hyginus with his precise knowledge of the *lituus*—is explained as an ablative of quality with *erat* understood. But at least Gellius is not afraid to put Hyginus in his place: 'immo ipse Hyginus parum animaduertit' (5. 8. 3), answering the objection that Vergil had failed to notice the inappropriateness of *lituo subcinctus*; 'sed Hyginus nimis hercle ineptus fuit' (7. 6. 5).

Even worse is in store for Persius' tutor Annaeus Cornutus (notorious for the assertion that tonsure of the dying was Vergil's own invention, Macr. *Sat.* 5. 19. 2), who had soiled *Aen.* 8. 404–6 with filthy and offensive criticism ('reprehensione spurca et odiosa inquinauit' 9. 10. lemma), accusing Vergil of carelessness in using the word 'membra'. Gellius, taught by Annianus to admire the delicacy of these verses (p. 107), comments admirably 'egregiam totius istius uerecundiae laudem insulsa nimis et odiosa scrutatione uiolauit' (§ 5); 'odiosa scrutatione' exactly hits off a pedant peering underneath the bedclothes.[67] In *NA* 2. 6 Cornutus knows too little of Latin usage before his own day to recognize the strong sense of 'uexasse' ('to have ravaged') at *Buc.* 6. 76, disapproves of the litotes 'inlaudati' ('unpraised') for the loathsome Busiris at *Georg.* 3. 5, and misunderstands the etymological use of

---

62. So Sen. *Helu.* 7. 8, Lucan 3. 340, 5. 53, Sidon. *Carm.* 23. 13 (the reverse error Ov. *Met.* 2, 569, Lucan 3. 172, 5. 144); cf. Housman on Man. 4. 767. Plut. *QR* 53, *Rom.* 25. 7 takes *Sardi* for Σαρδιανοί instead of Σαρδόνιοι.

63. See Norden, comm. 214, 291–2, Austin on vv. 122–3.

64. Prop. 1. 11. 11–12 etc., cf. ch. 10 n. 78.

65. 'Picus himself sat girt with an augur's wand and a short robe, like Romulus'.' On the anachronism *ex propria persona* see Servius.

66. 'They eat fat sheep and choice honey-sweet wine'; cf. Eust. 907. 53–61.

67. Cf. ch. 8 n. 10. On the obscenities found by Cornutus and Probus in *Aen.* 8. 406 and by eager moderns elsewhere the best comment is Quint. 8. 3. 47.

'squalentem' ('encrusted') at *Aen.* 10. 314. Gellius refutes the first and third objections from his knowledge of Republican authors, but makes heavy weather of the second, a matter of style: he struggles to find a logical defence—Busiris was so wicked as to do nothing laudable all his life—and even drags in as an alternative the legal expression *auctorem laudare*, to name, or vouch to warranty, the person who had mancipated to oneself a *res mancipi* the plaintiff sought to evict, so that *inlaudatus* may mean 'unworthy to be named'.[68]

In lacking comprehension of a poem as a whole, to which each passage, line, and word is subordinate, Gellius is at one with the despised *grammatici*, who must perforce direct their attention to difficulties and details, but also the true son of an age that judged an author on his words. Nevertheless, Vergil's minor blemishes do not diminish Gellius' admiration of one who is not only careful in his use of language (2. 26. 11)[69] but an expert in antiquity, though discreet in revealing his knowledge (3. 2. 14; 5. 12. 13). Here already we catch the supposition, familiar from Macrobius and not without its modern counterparts, that apparently innocent texts in reality hint at some hobby-horse of the critic's: at 3. 2. 14–16 the parting words of Anchises' ghost to his dreaming son at *Aen.* 5. 738–9 are referred to the start of the Roman civil day at midnight.[70] With more reason at 13. 1. 5 'nec fato' (*Aen.* 4. 696) is cited to show that violent death thwarts the decree of fate.[71]

Of the earlier poets, Livius and Naevius are occasionally cited, the former only for his *Odyssia*, the latter mainly for his plays; his jibes against great men are noted (3. 3. 15; 7. 8. 5), and his purported epitaph (1. 24. 2),[72] just praise in another's mouth. But Gellius does not literally believe that at Naevius' death Latin was forgotten: Ennius, the ostensible target, is admired (despite metrical irregularity, 13. 23. 18)[73] for beautiful verses (2. 26. 21, 23; cf. 20. 10. 4), correct usage (3. 14. 5), and pleasantness of sound (13. 21. 14), being

---

68. On *uexare* see n. 41. At *Georg.* 3. 5 (and *Aen.* 7. 11) Servius observes that since Isocrates did praise Busiris, *inlaudati* means 'undeserving of praise'; his standing comment on *squalens* is that when used for *splendens* it comes from *squamae*, but when meaning *sordidus* from *squalor*. Gellius' comment (§ 11) that 'Homerus non uirtutibus appellandis, sed uitiis detrahendis laudare ampliter solet' applies to himself (see Müller 21–2 on Gellius' fondness for *non in-*) as to other ancient authors.

69. Despite odd lapses: *Georg.* 3. 10 'modo uita supersit' (*NA* 1. 22. 12; at most an innovation in this precise sense, cf. ch. 10 n. 26 and Carrio ad loc.); *Aen.* 3. 573 'turbine fumantem piceo et candente fauilla' (a syllepsis less harsh than 7. 187–8), where Favorinus (17. 10. 17–18) suspects Vergil of using *candens* of mere heat without glow (as e.g. Col. 6. 5. 2; at Man. 1. 587 'candentem … aestum' may be understood as *solis candentis aestum*). No fault is found with 'prorupit ad aethera nubem' (v. 572), censured by D.S.; cf. 'se prorupit' *NA* 15. 22. 6.

70. 'torquet medios nox umida cursus / et me saeuus equis oriens afflauit anhelis', i.e. 'Nox ad altissimum mediumque caeli culmen euecta iam decliui uia fertur' (Heyne). Gellius and Conington make dawn follow hard on midnight; cf. Serv. here and on 6. 255.

71. See Schulze, *Kl. Schr.* 131–48, 159–60; cf. Plin. 1. 12. 1–2, Courtney on Juv. 14. 248.

72. See H. Dahlmann, *AAWM* 1962, 617–52; Suerbaum 31–41 fails to compare the epitaphs composed for Greek poets, but wrongly stumbles at 'itaque' *Epit. Naeu.* 3 (see *TLL* vii/2. 529. 43–65).

73. But see Skutsch on *Ann.* 99.

cited some forty times. Fronto too honours Ennius while ignoring Livius and mentioning Naevius only once (though Marcus has two quotations); Cicero, who praises Naevius (*Brut.* 75–6; but not Livius, ibid. 71), pays Ennius far more attention, nor did Hadrian reverse the ranking. So well loved was Ennius that an 'Ennianista' read his works in public (*NA* 18. 5) and Gellius could frustrate modern scholars by citing two verses 'in that most famous book' (19. 8. 6), which we cannot identify. He is, like Cato, a pillar of sound morality. The fable of the Lark and her Young, which Ennius versified and Gellius retells,[74] agrees with the teachings of (Stoic) philosophy (2. 29. 18–19), which are matched for value by his description of Servilius Geminus' client, a model for friendship with men of higher rank, and according to Stilo a self-portrait (12. 4).[75] Yet we miss the mighty pathos that had enthralled a Cicero: Ilia and Cassandra cannot breathe Antonine air.

Plautus, cited almost as often, is relished as a master of Latin, the glory of the language (19. 8. 6), 'elegantissimus' in diction (1. 7. 17, cf. 6. 17. 4), that is, choosing his words with care;[76] what Cicero's Crassus had called 'incomptam antiquitatem' (*De or.* 3. 45) is for Gellius studied art—as for Fronto, *Ep. M. Caes.* 4. 3. 2 it is in Cato. He is frequently cited as a grammatical authority, but also savoured for his gusto. Fronto, as if imitating Cicero's epistolary hybrid 'flocci facteon' (*Att.* 1. 16. 13), writes in a letter to Marcus 'Plautinotato uerbo' (*Orat.* 2), but Gellius finds verses in a disputed play 'ut de illius Plauti more dicam, Plautinissimi' (*NA* 3. 3. 4): Plautus does indeed love the superlative, which combines colloquial emphasis with a

---

74. This ch., used by Av. *Fab.* 21 (but not included in Steinhöwel's collection), was added in some edns. and trs. of Aesop; it was the source of La Fontaine, *Fables* 4. 22. In the 19th c. scholars presented 2. 29. 3–16, hacked into *uersus (pessime) quadrati*, as reconstituted Ennius; but see Vahlen, edn.², p. ccxii. (G. Faernus' tetrameters, *Fabulae*, no. 96, are far better.) There are indeed trochaic rhythms present, but they cannot vindicate for Ennius 'ubi primum diluculabit' (§ 7, cf. 6. 1. 6; Marache, *Mots* 200–1; hexameter-poets would not have scorned *diluculat*), or 'fiet nunc dubio procul' (§ 15, cf. ch. 13 n. 17). Note too the post-classical 'crastino' (§ 9) and 'dicto oboediant' (§ 82, cf. Vulg. Tit. 3. 1; Early Latin only *dicto oboediens*). Gellius, who conceivably altered minor details of the narrative (ch. 4 n. 48), could easily introduce trochees of his own to hint at his original ('dubio procul' recalls 'patria procul', *Scaen.* 219 J, but cf. 'factis procul' *NA* 17. 19. 1), being in any case much given to them: whole septenarii can be found in him (e.g. 'contra perpetuam Latinae linguae consuetudinem' 7. 15. 5; 'stricta ... feris' 15. 16. 4; 'rerum ... inopinabilis' 17. 9. 18) or easily recovered ('Italia ad regem descisset, tum Ambraciensis quispiam' < 3. 8. 1, 'et cum eo potitus esset, ipsum uictum postea' < 3. 9. 5), half-lines abound, and for clausulae see p. 44. We must beware of pecking at painted fruit.

75. *Ann.* 268–86 Sk; despite Suerbaum 142 n. 455, Badian at *EFHE* 173–7, it is hard not to transfer these lines from book 7 to book 8 and Cannae. (Gellius' MSS exhibit 'septimo' spelt out, but his *annotatio pristina* will have used figures.) On the portrait and the tradition that Ennius (not a modest man) had himself in mind, see Skutsch, *Stud.* 92–4, and the discussion at *EFHE* 206–7; Rawson 270. In his edn. Skutsch takes the length of the description to imply a personal interest. For Gellius' quotations from Ennius see Skutsch, edn. 30. Vergil's use of him is noted only at 12. 2. 10, by Seneca; but it hardly needed stating.

76. See Krebs i. 498–9, and cf. Fronto, *Ep. M. Caes.* 4. 3. 2, 4; on Plautus cf. Claud. Mam. CSEL 11. 205. 30–206. 1 (from Cic. *De or.* 3. 45?), and note Fronto, *Fer Als.* 3. 1 'aut te Plauto expolires aut Accio expleres aut Lucretio delenires aut Ennio incenderes'.

convenient ending for the line.[77] Nor is he without his share of learning (13. 23. 12–16): when at *Truc.* 515 the soldier Stratophanes addresses Phronesium as Mars greeting 'Nerienem uxorem suam', this is not a joke, as if the ignorant and uncouth warrior had misunderstood the prayer-formula 'Nerienemque Martis' as designating a wife instead of an abstract quality,[78] because Cn. Gellius and Licinius Imbrex show the same interpretation; this is taken to prove, not that the error was widespread, but that Plautus was erudite enough to know another version.

The experiment of comparative reading that turned out so disastrously for Caecilius is not made with Plautus; its result might have proved disconcerting. But despite his disgrace, Caecilius is quoted several times; even in the unhappy *Plocium*, another departure from the original is justified at 3. 16. 5–6 on scientific grounds,[79] and elsewhere the observation that the worst enemies are those who conceal their malice ('fronte hilaro, corde tristi') is praised for its truth and its skilful expression ('uere ac diserte Caecilius ... scripsit' 15. 9. 1) before being subjected to grammatical debate. But there is no sign that Gellius could have agreed with Volcacius Sedigitus in preferring him to Plautus himself (*NA* 15. 24).[80] Terence, who approached the Menandrean virtues, but lacked *uis* and offered fewer stunning words, occasionally contributes to Gellius' as to Fronto's language,[81] but is rarely cited even for parallels to usages discussed.[82]

Of other comic quotations, the most notable is one from L. Afranius, the supreme exponent of the *fabula togata* or comedy in a Roman setting: vv. 298–9 R (*NA* 13. 8. 3), in which Wisdom is said to be the child of Experience

---

77. e.g. 'exclusissumus' (*Men.* 698), 'inuictissumis' (*Mil.* 57). 'Plautinotato' in Fronto is a conjecture, but palmary.

78. Correctly understood at § 10. Roman deities had no spouses till equated with the Olympians; the *comprecatio* includes two attributes for Quirinus, and 'Heriem Iunonis'. See Latte 5 n. 2, Skutsch on Enn. *Ann.* 99; for the misunderstanding Varro, *RD* fr. 28 Cardauns, Sen. *De superst.* fr. 39 Haase, Serv. on *Aen.* 1. 144, D.S. *Aen.* 10. 76 (who abuses Salacia even worse at *Aen.* 1. 720).

79. Ancient doctors disagreed on the existence of eighth-month births; Caec. 164–5 R adds the eighth month to Men. fr. 343 K–Th.

80. Despite stylistic disapproval (*Brut.* 258, *Att.* 7. 3. 10), Cicero mentions Caecilius, not Plautus, in the same breath as Terence (*Fin.* 1. 4; frequency of citation confirms), cf. Vell. Pat. 1. 17. 1; he is tentatively put first at [Cic.] *Opt. gen.* 2, awarded the prize for plots at Varro fr. 99 Fun. (cf. fr. 40), and deemed to excel in *grauitas* by the public opinion assailed at Hor. *Ep.* 2. 1. 59 (cf. *Ep. Pis.* 54). Seneca ignores all three; Quintilian quotes only Terence, whom he regards as the least inadequate (10. 1. 99), though at 11. 1. 39 he mentions the *Caecilianus pater* of Cic. *Cael.* 37. Plautus comes into his own in the Corpus Frontonianum, where Caecilius is barely noticed.

81. Echoes are collected by Hosius (edn. i, p. xi n., F. Skutsch contributing 2. 22. 25 'plus paulo adbibi' ∼ *HT* 220), Heraeus 1070: e.g. *NA* 2. 23. 18 'uitium esse oblatum' ∼ *Hec.* 383, *Ad.* 296 (unless anticipated by Caecilius). *NA* 7. 13. 1 'asymboli ueniremus' ∼ *Phorm.* 339 (but no doubt the participants used ἀσύμβολοι). For Fronto, see van den Hout on *Ver.* 1. 3. 1, *Amic.* 1. 5. 2; Terence is never named.

82. Thus Terence offers three examples of *liberi* denoting a single child (*NA* 2. 13), and 33 of *resciscere* (cf. *NA* 2. 19); 'compluria' (*NA* 5. 21) appears at *Phorm.* 611, 'tui carendum' (19. 7. 7) at *HT* 400.

and Memory.[83] On this moral text Gellius preaches a fine Roman sermon on the superiority of practical experience, submitted to intelligent reflection, over theories derived from books and schoolmasters, conveyed through empty words and fantasies, as in a mime or dream (§ 2). This outburst gives vent to endemic impatience and incomprehension in the face of Greek word-spinning, and pandemic suspicion that philosophers are scoundrels under their cloaks.[84] In a lower genre, Publilius' mimes abound in moral sentences (17. 14. 3–4); Laberius, narrowly the better playwright (§ 1), took liberties with the language (3. 12. 2–4; 16. 7. 1–12; 19. 13. 3), but his riposte to Caesar was cited in 8. 15, and his lines on Democritus are praised in 10. 17.[85]

Individual quotations apart, the tragedians Accius and Pacuvius appear in the anecdote of 13. 2. The young Accius calls on the old and sick Pacuvius at Tarentum with a tragedy his host finds resounding and grandiloquent, but somewhat hard and harsh. Accius unrepentantly agrees: so young minds, like young fruit, should be, maturing into pleasant ripeness; those that are wrinkled and soft and juicy at the outset do not ripen but rot. The distrust of precocious maturity in orators displayed by Cicero (*De or.* 2. 88) and Quintilian (2. 4. 4–8) is extended here to poets.[86] Pacuvius is characterized at 1. 24. 4 by 'elegantissima grauitate', extreme refinement and dignity of style, with which the modesty and purity of his purported epitaph are in keeping.[87]

Lucilius—who won fame by attacking the other poets' works (17. 21. 49), possessed a thorough knowledge of Latin (18. 5. 10), and took care with his diction (3. 14. 12)—is constantly cited for grammar and occasionally for

83. 'Vsus me genuit, mater peperit Memoria; / Sophiam uocant me Grai, uos Sapientiam.' Cf. Enn. *Ann.* 211–12 Sk, Cic. *Off.* 1. 153, Sen. *Ep.* 89. 7.

84. Gellius' friend Macedo, inveighing against such hypocrites, wished to see Pacuv. 348 R inscribed on temple-doors. Grilli, 'Echi' 194 n. 13 (cf. ch. 5 n. 55 above) derives the entire chapter from Cicero's *Hortensius*. The Pacuvian verse is frequently assigned to *Antiopa* (so now D'Anna's edn.), whose original is cited in Callicles' speech (Plat. *Gorg.* 484 E, 485 E-486 D), the ultimate source of these invectives; but it paraphrases Eur. fr. 61 N, apparently from *Alexandros*. For 'intercutibus ipsi uitiis madentes' cf. Cato fr. 44 SbC = 60 M.

85. This view of Publilius, shared with schoolmasters, the Senecas, and the anonymous collector of his *sententiae*, was so unoriginal that Trimalchio could propound it as his own (Petr. *Sat.* 55. 5). For Laberius see ch. 10 n. 23, pp. 189–90; Gellius does not himself use the words cited in 16. 7. Fronto and Marcus have a higher regard for 'noster Laberius' (*Ep. M. Caes.* 1. 7. 3, cf. 2. 8. 1; 4. 3. 2; *Orat.* 2).

86. Carolus 475–6 compares Alexis fr. 45 K, *SVF* i. 388, Plut. *Them.* 2. 7. The play was *Atreus*, third in number and extent of surviving fragments to *Eurysaces* and *Philocteta*, including 'oderint dum metuant' (203–4 R), notorious long before Caligula. Sen. *De ira* 1. 20. 4 states (on what authority?) that it was written in the Sullan period, when Accius was about as old as the Sophocles of *OC*; Gellius' story would then originate not in reminiscence by Accius to Varro but in Roman *aemulatio* of the fictions concerning Greek tragedians. But Accius' latest known play is *Tereus*, of 104 BC; comparison suggests that the poet's prophecy had been fulfilled, especially in the absence (if we may trust our quotations) of the *grand guignol* emphases in which *Atreus* abounds and to which this plot lent itself no less. Cf. Leo, *Röm. Lit.* 399 n. 3.

87. Other views of the tragedians: Lucil. 875 M; Varro ap. Gell. 6. 14. 6; Cic. *Brut.* 258, *Orat.* 36; Hor. *Ep.* 2. 1. 55–6; Vell. Pat. 2. 9. 3; Col. 1. pr. 30; Quint. 10. 1. 97; Pers. 1. 76–8; Tac. *Dial.* 20. 5, 21. 7; Mart. 11. 90. 6; Fronto, *Eloq.* 1. 2, 4. 3, *Fer. Als.* 3. 1.

fact;[88] Annianus affectionately calls him 'nostrum' (20. 8. 4). But Gellius shows no interest in the life portrayed in his poetry *uotiua ueluti depicta tabella*; as among the Greeks, literature is admired for representing life in general (Menander, Ennius' Good Companion, love-poetry), not a particular life (Lucilius, Cicero's letters).

In 18. 11 five fragments, comprising six verses, are cited from the *uetus poeta* Furius of Antium,[89] whose coinage of new words (all denominative verbs) had been criticized by Caesellius Vindex; 'wantonly and ignorantly' in Gellius' opinion, since they are well within a poet's rights[90] and do not sound harsh or unpleasant. Four of them are formed in -*escere*; the exception is *purpurat*, used of the wind that curls the sea and makes it gleam ('crispicans nitefacit': Gellius demonstrates that he can coin words with the best). The chapter attests the long-standing Roman inhibition against neologism; but in practice the mannerists do create new words, and a poet is entitled to greater freedom.[91] Gellius praises Cn. Matius for coining the verb *recentatur* 'is renewed', reasonably and euphoniously ('non absurde neque absone'), and also *edulcare* 'to sweeten' (15. 25); Antonius Julianus took delight in the same poet's *columbulatim* 'like little doves' and *uenenatur* 'is dyed' (20. 9). Matius composed a Latin *Iliad*, and *mimiambi* in scazons; both works are cited in the *Nights*, but only the latter receives critical appreciation, and that for individual words. Yet doubtless Julianus and Gellius, with their enjoyment of love-poetry, relished the verses (fr. 12 M–B):

> sinuque amicam refice frigidam caldo,
> columbulatim labra conserens labris.

> And thy cold love revive on thy warm breast;
> In dovish wise be lips to lips close prest.

Certainly they relished the early poems cited in 19. 9 (p. 16; Porcius Licinus had already been quoted for Roman literary history, 17. 21. 45) after the Greek guests had condemned all Latin love-poets except Catullus and Calvus in a few pieces. Catullus is 'elegantissimus poetarum' at 6. 20. 6, in an inept discussion of his text; at 7. 16. 2 Gellius judges the four lines of poem 92 ('Lesbia mi dicit semper male') to be the most delightful of all,[92] though a would-be

---

88. Gellius specifies only bks. 1–20, which were in hexameters; all his full quotations are in this metre, not exclusive to those books. But v. 952 M, to which he alludes at 1. 3. 19, was probably a septenarius (cf. ch. 12 n. 49), and vv. 830–1 M, which underlie *pr.* 11, are senarii from bk. 29. Fronto knew a hexameter from bk. 30 (*Orat.* 17 ~ 982 M).

89. Probably Catulus' friend A. Furius (Cic. *Brut.* 132). The verses cited by Macrobius from 'Furius' *Annales*' seem too modern for a *uetus poeta*, not least in their relatively frequent *enjambement*: are they by the Furius Alpinus mocked at Hor. *Serm.* 2. 5. 40–1?

90. See Fronto, *Ep. M. Caes.* 3. 14. 1; but also Cic. *Or.* 68, Hor. *Ep. Pis.* 48–59, Mart. Cap. 5. 511, Kroll 52–3. Cf. for freedom of metaphor *NA* 7. 6. 7; of periphrasis 3. 1. 6.

91. Laberius in his mimes 'oppido quam uerba finxit praelicenter' (16. 7. 1; cf. 'licentius petulantiusque' in the lemma); Gellius quotes a goodly number. In prose he admires Sallust's coinages (p. 186); note too 17. 2. 3 on a word in Quadrigarius: 'Inlatebrant uerbum poeticum uisum est sed non absurdum neque asperum'. Cf. Marache, *Critique* 263, and Intro. n. 28 above.

92. 'omnium meo [C: *om.* V] quidem iudicio uenustissimos'; cf. 20. 1. 24 and 6. 3. 25; 12. 4. 3.

orator without a sound knowledge of Latin had condemned them as utterly pointless ('frigidissimos') through not understanding that 'deprecor illam' in v. 3 means 'I pray to be rid of her'. In the spoken *consuetudo*, which alone he knew, *deprecor* meant only 'plead with'.[93]

Although Lucretius is praised for his outstanding intellect and eloquence (1. 21. 5), Gellius gives only five quotations: Vergil's frequent use of him is noted at 1. 21. 7, but parallels are missed, one in this very chapter.[94] At 13. 21. 21 he makes *funis* feminine (2. 1154) for euphony's sake.[95] Fronto and Marcus take more notice; Apuleius cites him in *De deo Socratis* and borrows from him elsewhere; a later mannerist, Arnobius, was to be his ape. But since Lucretius, despite Aper's sneer (Tac. *Dial.* 23. 2) at those who preferred him to Vergil, had not been forgotten by modernists or neoclassicists, the second century could not rediscover him. Cicero's verse (scorned by Seneca at 12. 2. 5) is ignored, apart from the slip observed in 15. 6; Antonine zeal for rehabilitation had its limits.

Some texts are recorded for their moral value, others for their literary excellence. At 12. 9. 6 Gellius professes to have cited a passage from Numidicus for ethical precept as well as grammatical example; at 2. 26. 13 his Fronto quotes Pacuvius (244–6 R) not merely to demonstrate *flauus* qualifying water and *fuluus* dust,[96] but also because the verses are delightful, as indeed they are:

> cedo tuum pedem mi lumpis flauis fuluum ut puluerem
> manibus isdem quibus Vlixi saepe permulsi abluam
> lassitudinemque minuam manuum mollitudine.
>
> Give me thy foot, in water fair that I the brown dust may,
> With these same hands that oft did soothe Ulysses, wash away
> And with the softness of my hands thy weariness allay.

The sweetness of the sense is supported by an abundance of liquid consonants and narrow vowels,[97] joined together by alliteration, assonance, and rhyme; the rhythm of the resolutions hints at lapping water; Eurycleia, by fine

93. Gellius himself uses the verb in several of its other senses: 2. 23. 12; 6. 3. 5; 11. 8. 4; 12. 2. 8. Although they are found in Silver writers (cf. Apul. *Flor.* 9. 6), the awful warning of Cornutus' comment on 'uexasse' should deter us from echoing Rutgersius 295 (on 18. 4. 10): 'Sed non est inusitatum Gellio tritissima quaeque obtrudere pro reconditis'.

94. See ch. 6 n. 92; p. 257; n. 31 above. Jac. Gronovius on 2. 6. 8 aptly defends Vergil's 'uexasse' by Lucr. 6. 429–30.

95. 'Aurea de caelo demisit funis in arua'; Gellius observes that he could have written *aureus e caelo*. True, *de* suits better with *demisit* (cf. 6. 426–7, 433), but at 6. 257 'ut picis e caelo demissum flumen' is preferred to *pici' de* (final *s* is cut off at this point only in 1. 978; 2. 462 is corrupt). At 2. 1154, however, Lucretius prefers the feminine of Homer's σειρὴν χρυσείην (*Il.* 8. 19), perhaps assisted by the variable gender of *finis*; though *funis* fem. and *funicula* are found sporadically in later authors, Quint. 1. 6. 6 uses *funiculus* to prove *funis* masc. Cf. Wiseman, *Clio's Cosmetics* 167–9.

96. *Flauus* is often used of the silty Italian watercourses (André, *Étude* 331, 361), but here the sense is 'brightly gleaming', as in Enn. *Ann.* 377–8 Sk cited in § 21.

97. Pacuvius probably wrote *mei lumpeis flaueis, eisdem, Vlixei, permulsei*, representing a narrow monophthong [ẹ:] (Allen 53–5) like Danish long *e*; cf. the *i* of Southern English *bid*.

dramatic irony, addresses these lines, in ignorance, to him of whom she speaks.[98] But although Gellius perceives their beauty, he does not explain it; at 20. 10. 4 he professes to have remembered certain verses from Ennius (*Ann.* 248–53 Sk) because they were outstandingly well written, but does not specify their merits (a rude vigour, and deliberate disharmony, evoking the oubreak of war). Gellius' poetic taste seems to encompass forcefulness, musicality, simplicity, delicacy, verve, intricacy,[99] noble thoughts, and precise diction; but grandeur is sought in prose, and the overpowering sound and emotion of the older poets are little better represented than the pointed compression of the Silver Age.

Gellius' technical language, mainly for prose, is somewhat repetitious. At 16. 1. 1 Musonius' 'truly and eloquently stated' apophthegm is linked together in brief and well-turned phrases, 'uerbisque est breuibus et rotundis uinctum';[100] 'uincta' is used at 10. 19. 2 by Taurus, who at 17. 20. 4 calls Plat. *Symp.* 180 E 4–181 A 6 a compact, brilliant, rounded argument, bonded with short and well-turned rhythmical cola into a balanced periodic structure.[101] Julianus says much the same of Cic. *Planc.* 68.[102]

The theoretical chapter 6. 14 on the three styles (rich, lean, and middle) with their respective virtues and adjacent vices, a traditional theme, is entirely derived from Varro even in its examples: Pacuvius, Lucilius, and Terence; Odysseus, Menelaus, and Nestor; Carneades, Diogenes, and Critolaus. No one could reassess the final triad (the philosophical diplomats of 155 BC), and the Homeric heroes were classified not on what Homer makes them say but on what he says about them;[103] the comment on the

---

98. For Cicero's 'Anticlea' (*Tusc.* 5. 45) see S. Lundström, *Eranos* 58 (1960) 73–4.

99. In the word-play of *Sat.* 59–62 V (*NA* 18. 2. 7), cf. *Sc.* 195–202 J (*NA* 19. 10. 12).

100. 'Verbis' *sensu composito*: length of individual vocables is no more in point than at § 3 'laxioribus paulo longioribusque uerbis', in diffuser clauses. For περιφερής, στρογγύλος, *rotundus* 'elegantly concise, yet as complete in rhythm as in sense', see Ernesti s.vv., Brink on Hor. *Ep. Pis.* 323, D.H. *Dem.* 43 *sub fin.* (periods 'round as if from the lathe' contrasted with 'flat and straggling' ones; for the image cf. Plat. *Phdr.* 234 E, Prop. 2. 34. 43, Hor. *Ep. Pis.* 441, *Laus Pis.* 96, Gell. *NA* 9. 8. 3). Cicero understands rather completeness (*Or.* 40) and neat construction (combined with *aptus*: *Brut.* 272, where see Douglas; *Fin.* 4. 7); so, yet not without the sense of concision, *NA* 11. 13. 4, cf. §§ 5, 10 (see Ernesti s.v. *cursus*, p. 101).

101. ἐνθύμημα crebrum et coruscum et conuexum breuibusque et rotundis numeris cum quadam aequabili circumactione deuinctum'. ἐνθύμημα, a favourite word (1. 4. 2; 6. 3. 27 unless from Tiro; 7. 13. 4 dim.; 12. 2. 14; 16. 1. 1 dim.), here means generally 'argument' (cf. Isocr. 9. 10, 12. 2; Fronto, *Eloq.* 4. 10, *Add. ep.* 5. 1, 6), 'crebrum' = πυκνόν (cf. Quint. 2. 5. 8, Plin. *Ep.* 1. 20. 22), 'coruscum' = γοργόν; 'conuexum' = *rotundum* (στρυγγύλον ἐνθύμημα *Rh. Gr.* iii. 111. 19–112. 2 Sp; cf. Juv. 6. 449–50), but qualifying the whole; the following 'rotundis' refers to the individual clauses; *circumactio* = περιαγωγή (Demetr. *Eloc.* 19).

102. 1. 4. 3 'crispum sane ... agmen orationis rotundumque ac modulo ipsorum numerorum uenustum'; 'crispum' here means 'concise' (cf. Ernesti, *Lex. tech. Lat.* 56, Lion ad loc., οὖλα Plut. *Mor.* 510 E) and 'elegant' (Mart. Cap. 5. 511), not 'affected' (as 'crispulum' Fronto, *Orat.* 13; cf. *calamistri*).

103. *Il.* 3. 212–24, 1. 247–9; cf. *Laus Pis.* 57–64, Quint. 12.10. 64–5, Auson. *Prof. Burdig.* 21. 16–24, *Rhet. Gr.* iii. 152. 12–153. 15 Sp; for Menelaus and Odysseus cf. Plin. *Ep.* 1. 20. 22, Fronto, *Eloq.* 2. 7. On the three styles, D. A. Russell, edn. of ps.-Long., pp. xxxiv–xxxvi, *Criticism* 137–9, Calboli Montefusco, edn. of Fortunatianus, pp. 446–52, cf. Wiseman, *Clio's Cosmetics* 4–5.

early Roman poets, which could have been reviewed or exemplified, is left to speak for itself. Gellius ignores the tripartition even in 10. 3, where C. Gracchus might have represented the counterfeit leanness of jejunity (6. 14. 5); but only *Systemzwang* would assign Cato to the middle style. The doctrine could have prevented error at 6. 20. 6 (cf. p. 138); but Gellius judged by no theory, only by his tastes, and not by utility to the orator—the primary concern of Fronto, as of Quintilian—but by pleasure to the reader.

Nevertheless, he excerpts early authors for suitable expressions to employ himself (17. 2. 1; 19. 7. 2, 13), distinguishing, when the author is the poet Laevius, between those admissible in prose and others exclusively poetic.[104] Persons who use archaic words with less discrimination are mocked in 11. 7, a chapter best understood in the light of Fronto's letters.

In *Ep. M. Caes.* 4. 3 Fronto deems total ignorance of any art superior to a smattering: 'Omnium artium, ut ego arbitror, imperitum et indoctum omnino esse praestat quam semiperitum ac semidoctum' (§ 1). Above all this is true in the choice and disposition of words, which allows no room for bluffing: it is therefore necessary to study ancient authors with great care. Several writers are considered from this standpoint: Cicero's inattention to the matter is deplored. The ideal is the *insperatum atque inopinatum uerbum* which the reader could not have supplied if called upon to guess it. However, there is great danger one will use the word inapppropriately, obscurely, or inelegantly, like a *semidoctus*; it is far better to use common, trite words than unusual, recherché ones, if they cannot be understood ('si parum significent' § 3).[105] After illustrating his theory, Fronto considers Ennius' dictum that an orator should be bold;[106] let him indeed be bold, but nowhere stray from expressing ('a significando' § 7) what he means. Clarity, he writes elsewhere (*Ep. M. Caes.* 3. 1), is particularly important in an official speech, which should resemble the trumpet,[107] not the less sonorous and more difficult double aulos; Marcus is praised for not using any out-of-the-way word, any obscure or unusual figure. Consequently, at *Eloq.* 5. 1 'non nihil interdum elocutione nouella parum signatum', *parum signatum* should mean *obscurius*:

---

104. *NA* 19. 7. 13. The poetic words, apart from *onychinus* (cf. ch. 12 n. 3 for Greek words in Roman poetry), are compounds, some (e.g. *trisaeclisenex, subductisupercilicarptores*) recalling Old Comedy; but *foedifragus* is accepted as usable in prose (cf. Skutsch, edn. of Enn. *Ann.*, pp. 781–2; interpolated at Cic. *Off.* 1. 38).

105. So Orelli for 'significet', which lacks a subject.

106. In Enn. *Fr. inc.* 21 V *orator* may have denoted an envoy (cf. Skutsch on *Ann.* 202), who must boldly state his country's case, however unwelcome to his audience; but Fronto takes it of a speech-maker.

107. The trumpet is the recognized symbol for the grand style (W. Bühler, *ZPE* 31 (1978) 57; *OLD* s.v. 'tuba'); for contrast with the aulos cf. Prop. 2. 7. 12, Luc. *Rh. Pr.* 13. See too *Ep. M. Caes.* 3. 17. 3, *Eloq.* 2. 16 ('clangere'), 4. 4, and on the special requirements of clarity in Caesar cf. Philostr. *VS* 628 and n. 117 below.

some parts of Marcus' recent speech were unclear for their new-fangled diction.[108]

In 11. 7, Gellius states that, whereas it is considered an equal fault to use excessively worn-out[109] and well-trodden words or unusual ones of harsh and unpleasant novelty, he holds it a worse offence to use new, unknown, unheard-of words than commonplace and undistinguished ones; such novelty may attach even to the unfamiliar and obsolete, although old.[110] This is the characteristic vice of those persons, much despised in ancient writers, who make up late in life for lack of early studies and are wont to air their new-won knowledge.[111] Gellius illustrates his thesis with two purported anecdotes from his forensic experience. A barrister of rough and ready education, averring before the City prefect that a certain *eques* lived on bran-bread and stale wine, declared 'hic eques Romanus apludam edit et flocces bibit' (§ 3),[112] using words from early comedies that no one understood; the reaction was at first astonishment, then laughter. Another man of skimpy reading and poor taste ('apirocalus' § 7),[113] when the other side sought an adjournment, asked the praetor how long this *bouinator* was to delay proceedings, and exclaimed several times 'bouinator est'. Murmurings were heard in court; the advocate enquired if they had not read Lucilius, who so described a *tergiuersator*.[114]

108. See Holford-Strevens, '*Elocutio nouella*'; for 'nouella' (not a term of praise, cf. Ter. Maur. 1973) cf. 'nouicium' *Orat.* 13 (a fault, cf. ch. 10, n. 10; 'néologique' Cassan, 'new-fangled' Haines, better than 'novello' Leopardi, Portalupi); the abl. of cause is no harsher than 'laetissimo caelo' (*Amic.* 1. 3. 5). Leopardi and Cassan confuse *parum* with *paulum*; Haines gives 'not sufficiently marked with novelty of expression' (cf. id. i, p. xxxii, Cameron 157–8), as advocated at *Eloq.* 2. 4 *m*² d (cf. 4. 7), where old words are to receive new life, a different notion. Portalupi follows the tradition that Fronto blended the archaic and the vulgar in a style called *elocutio nouella* (which would have damned it): 'a volte qualche parte è poco improntata al nostro stile novello'. Marache, *Critique* 135 opines that Fronto advocates a small dose of 1st-c. modernism; *Orat.* 2 refutes.

109. 'Obsoletis' is not 'obsolete' but 'trite' (Holford-Strevens, '*Elocutio nouella*' 140 n. 3).

110. See Cic. *Or.* 12; cf. Quint. 1. 6. 39, Fronto, *Eloq.* 2. 4 *m*² d; Don. on Ter. *Ad.* 259; Sidon. *Ep.* 4. 3. 3.

111. The opsimath is the intellectual counterpart of the *nouveau riche*, and no less offensively ostentatious.

112. For the City prefect see Kunkel, *RR* 68–9; for bran-bread (normally dog-food) André, *Alim.* 69. To Gellius, the terms were bookish archaisms; to us they are rustic, *apluda* for chaff (locally restricted, Plin. *NH* 18. 99, cf. PF 10. 14), *flocces*, or rather *flōces* (Non. 164. 15–16; Meyer-Lübke no. 3376; *DEI* iii. 1649), for grape-skins (Lucchese *fiogia*, cf. It. *fiocine*), marc-wine (τρύγες στεμφυλίτιδες, 'uini faecem e uinaceis expressam' Gell.), or wine-lees (Non., citing Caec. 190 R, presumed to underlie Gell. § 6). The speaker's post-classical 'edit' for *ēst* has no ironic point; cf. 19. 2. 7, ch. 3 n. 23.

113. ἀπειρόκαλος, a regular term of critical disapprobation, is used of would-be Isocrateans at *NA* 18. 8. 1 and of ill-judged Atticizing at Philost. *VS* 503.

114. A backer-out; specifically one who, having laid a criminal charge, withdraws without leave of the court (D. 48. 16. 1. 1), but here more generally of a party anxious to delay the hearing, perhaps a slow payer like old L. Cotta (Lucil. 413–15 M) or Heracleidas of Temnos (Cic. *Flacc.* 47); although one adjournment was admissible for cause (D. 2. 12. 10), the other side put its own construction on the request. G. Landgraf, *Philologus* 72 (1913) 156–7, showed that *tricosus* in the verse cited (Lucil. 417 M, cf. *trico* vv. 414. 416, *tricari* Col. 11. 1. 16) denotes an excuse-monger, and explained a *bouinator* as one too lazy for anything but watching cattle (better

The mannerists who revived archaic words were in danger of neglecting the distinction between those disused but comprehensible and those not only relinquished but forgotten.[115] This was particularly unfortunate, as in political and forensic utterance (Marcus himself did not always avoid the pitfall), so in daily conversation: hence Favorinus' advice to shun the abnormal,[116] the 'inauditum atque insolens uerbum' (1. 10. 4), echoed by 'insolentibus' and 'inaudita' (11. 7. 1). To be 'insperatum atque inopinatum' as Fronto desired, a word need not be 'inauditum atque insolens';[117] in practice, although he and Gellius exhibit many words outside the *consuetudo* and not used by more recent authors, they do not perplex the reader.

'as sluggish as an ox', cf. Petr. 62. 13?). 'ore improbus duro' = 'shameless [Ter. *Eun.* 806, Cic. *Quinct.* 77, Ov. *Met.* 5. 451; cf. Spanish *caradura*] and unscrupulous', as such a shifter must be; PF 27. 26 L 'bouin{i}atur conuiciatur' may derive from misinterpretation of 'ore duro' as 'abusive, rough-tongued' (so 'durae buccae' Petr. 43. 3?). Falster, 'Noct. Rip.' 145 renders 'En grov eller plump Oxe' (a coarse or boorish oaf), but no such sense attaches to *bos* or its derivatives. If Paul is true to his source's source, Gellius, as in 17. 6, has resisted one of Verrius' less happy notions. Non. 112. 27–9 follows Gellius; for the two interpretations see *CGL* vi. 150, cf. vii. 366. Mart. 3. 63. 14 gives 'pertricosa' its etymological sense of *tricarum* ('difficulties', but also 'trifles') *plenissima*; the *tricones* of *HA Verus* 4. 6 are idlers with nothing better to do than get drunk. At *Carm. epigr.* 870. 2 (deemed a Renaissance forgery at *CIL* vi. 3623*) the deified Hercules is called 'tricosus' for deserting his earthly labours.

115. Luc. *Lexiph.*, cf. Gal. vi. 633 Kühn, Ath. 97 C–99 E.

116. Cf. p. 87.

117. Fronto, praising Verus' dispatches from the front, asks: 'Numquod uerbum insolens aut intempestiuum?', *Ver.* 2. 1. 29 (§ 5 v.d.H.).

Chapter 12

Greek: Language, Poets, Orators

THE currency of Greek expressions in rough colloquial speech at Rome is attested by Plautine comedy;[1] when to this is added an openness towards Greek culture among the social élite, the satires of Lucilius display an equal willingness to use the Greek of Homer and of whores. A like bilingualism *sans gêne* marks the intimate private letters of Cicero, Augustus, and Fronto;[2] but the language of public affairs and high literature stood aloof.[3] The Rome of the late Republic was not content with reading the literature of the Greeks, but aimed to match it, genre for genre, in its own: Greek might enrich the Latin language by offering new senses for familiar words (so that *mundus*, a collective term for ornaments, is used, like κόσμος, for the universe); it might stimulate translations of its technicalities, and offer models for the construction both of phrases and of sentences; but Greek words, unless unavoidable in context, or no longer counted foreign, were not acceptable, and quotations from Greek literature must be translated—the more occasion for Cicero to parade his poetry. This was so even in that most Greek of subjects, philosophy, which Cicero set out to make Roman, defending the project in a dialogue against the doubtful Varro.[4]

Varro, indeed, whose style belongs to an older age, admits Greek not only into his work on the Latin language, where it could not be avoided, but into his satires, in the manner of Lucilius, and even into *De re rustica*, a work of literary pretensions although technical: a Greek epigram is cited in the original (3. 16. 4). In the Augustan age, the prohibition on unnecessary Greek is extended to satire (Horace, *Serm.* 1. 10. 20–34); if the technical writer Vitruvius uses Greek terms in abundance, many were required by his subject,[5] and no one would call him a master stylist.

Yet as Greeks flocked into Rome to make their fortunes, and the cities especially of Asia recovered from the ruinations of the Civil Wars, not even the imperial pride that banished from a decree of the Senate a Greek word

1. For the Republican *plebs*'s interest in things Greek see Momigliano 13–14. Terence uses less Greek than Plautus, being freest in the earthy *Eunuchus*: R. Maltby, *CQ*² 35 (1985) 110–23.

2. The younger Pliny is far more restrained; Seneca's *Epistulae morales* follow the practice of philosphical treatises.

3. Poetry was not so strict as prose: see e.g. Macr. *Sat.* 6. 4. 17–22; T. Oksala, *Arctos* 16 (1982) 99–119; C. Bailey, *ed. mai.* of Lucretius, i. 139 (incomplete).

4. *Acad.* 1. 4–12.

5. Cf. Varro, *RR* 2. pr. 3, despite the pose of disapproval.

not disdained by Cicero himself,[6] and withdrew the Roman citizenship from a man who failed to understand a Latin question,[7] could hope to maintain the barriers for ever. Silver prose accommodates Greek inflexions previously admitted only by the poets;[8] Silver verse of the lighter kinds even offers a few Greek phrases.[9] The technical but elegant Quintilian, besides abundant terms of art, exhibits a few untranslated Greek examples; the bilingual scholar Suetonius goes further, admitting Greek with no little freedom to his Latin writing, by means only, as in the elder Pliny,[10] for names and technicalities. To be sure he eschews fine style;[11] but by now Rome has reverted to the archaic practice that confined the insistence on pure Latin to the higher genres. Apuleius indeed is to violate even that restriction, flinging Greek at the head of a proconsul throughout the course of a forensic speech, but one designed to dismay the burghers of a provincial town; when he declaims on the god of Socrates he translates a line of Homer into Latin, with a more than Ciceronian panache.

In use of Greek within Latin, Gellius far exceeds both Suetonius and Apuleius. If Greek has a word that Latin lacks, he will employ it either with remark (e.g. 1. 15. 17 'quod genus homines a Graecis significantissimo [= 'highly expressive'] uocabulo κατάγλωσσοι appellantur',[12] chatterboxes who are all over tongue) or without (e.g. 13. 29. 4 ἐμφατικώτερον); he may provide a Latin gloss (e.g. 1. 26. 10 ἀνάλγητον et ἀναίσθητον, id est hebetem et stupentem', 6. 7. 5 'ἐπίτασιν, quam intentionem nos dicimus').[13] Yet Greek may also explain a Latin expression (10. 24. 1, 'die quarto et die quinto, quod Graeci εἰς τετάρτην καὶ εἰς πέμπτην dicunt';[14] 13. 31. 17 'refrigerare id dicit, quod Graece ψύχειν dicitur'), especially a coinage (15. 25. 1 'Cn. Matius ... finxit recentatur pro eo quod Graeci dicunt

---

6. Suet. *Tib.* 71, cf. Cass. Dio 57. 15. 2–3. *Emblema* could scarcely be avoided in the fourth Verrine. For a like purism in Marcus see W. Williams, *JRS* 66 (1976) 81.

7. Cass. Dio 60. 17. 4 (Claudius). Cf. Balsdon, *Rom. und Al.* 132.

8. Cicero reproaches himself at *Att.* 7. 3. 10 for writing 'Piraeea' (6. 9. 1, contrast 7. 1. 1). Even in poetry, Horace in his satires, and Vergil everywhere, are charier of Greek endings than Silver writers in the same genres. Manilius, writing under Tiberius, allows himself the Homerism 'syboten' of Eumaeus and 'onus' for the undignified *asinos* (5. 126, 350; Housman, *CP* ii. 1164–5).

9. Martial, who abounds in Greek words and Greek inflexions, quotes Greek endearments at 10. 68. 5; Juvenal uses Greek at 5. 121, 6. 195, 9. 37, 11. 27 (see Courtney, comm. 44).

10. The inscription of *NH* 7. 210 is cited for the similarity of early Greek letter-forms with Latin; but Ἀπελλῆς ἐποίει is translated (and misunderstood) at pr. 26.

11. So Wallace-Hadrill 20. On Suetonius' use of Greek see G. B. Townend, *Hermes* 88 (1960) 98–120; with *Galba* 4. 1 contrast Tac. *A.* 6. 20. 2, upholding (unlike Vell. Pat. 1. 5. 3) the dignity of historical writing (even *Soter*, admitted by Cicero, is avoided at *A.* 15. 71. 1).

12. Cf. Epict. 2. 16. 20 (Gellius follows Favorinus, cf. p. 83).

13. Such glosses are a literary device, not implying ignorance in the reader: cf. Timpanaro, *Contributi* 376–8.

14. For καί where logic requires *et* cf. 1. 20. 2; 10. 1. 11 (MSS vary at 13. 25. 20; 17. 19. 6; 18. 4. 10; 18. 9. 9); Col. 8. 1. 4; Vel. Long. *GLK* vii. 51. 6, (12?); R. A. B. Mynors ap. Timpanaro, *Contributi* 343 n. 15. At 11. 4. 4. ἀντὶ ἀδοξούντων καὶ δοκούντων the Greek conjunction is entailed by the Greek preposition, which preserves Euripides' genitives and avoids the pseudo-ablatival dative needed after *pro*; cf. the regular ἀπὸ τοῦ in etymologies.

ἀνανεοῦται', in turn glosed 'id est denuo nascitur atque iterum fit recens';[15] justify syntax (1. 16. 8 *mille* + gen. like χιλιάς), morphology (6. 9. 13, reduplicative *e*), or vocabulary (in 19. 13 the Atticism of νᾶνος vindicates the Latinity of *nanus*); and supply technical terms (e.g. 1. 7. 6 ἀπαρέμφατον, 'infinitive', 6. 9. 13 παρακείμενος, 'perfect', 17. 5. 3 ἀμφισβητούμενον ἀντὶ ὁμολογουμένου, 'begging the question',[16] 18. 10. 9 ἀγγεῖον 'blood-vessel'). But it may be employed gratuitously (p. 39).

Although Greek is discussed for its own sake in *NA* 17. 3—where Gellius adopts Varro's theory that σπάρτα at Hom. *Il.* 2. 135 means not 'esparto cords' but '(cords from) things sown (e.g. hemp, tow)'—and in consequence proposes the accentuation σπαρτά,[17] it is normally brought into relation with Latin, especially as a model for translation or imitation. Gellius' interest in finding Latin equivalents for individual Greek words generates such dissertations as 1. 20, on the geometrical terms σχῆμα/*figura*, ἐπίπεδον/*planum*, στερεόν/*solidum*, etc.,[18] and such neologisms as 'inpuluerea, ut dici solet, incruentaque uictoria' (5. 6. 21) from ἀκονιτί, 'by a walkover',[19] and 'inauditiunculas' (5. 21. 4) for casual smatterings ('rudiments appris par ouï-dire' Marache), reproducing παρακουσμάτια.[20] The task of augmenting the Latin language, despite Cicero's patriotic and personal vaunts,[21] had still to be shouldered by Priscian and Boethius; it was made no easier by Roman distaste for new formations,[22] and the grammatical stiffness of Latin when compared with Greek.[23] Sometimes Gellius does not try—the armillary sphere remains κρικωτή (3. 10. 3)[24]—or admits defeat: by πολυπραγμοσύνη (11. 16),[25] by ἡμιόλιος and ἐπίτριτος (18. 14).[26]

15. In 8. 12 *plerique omnes* was derived from Greek: presumably πλεῖστοι πάντες (even if Don. on Ter. *And.* 55 implies πάμπολλοι).

16. Cf. Fronto, *Add. ep.* 5. 2, S.E. *Math.* 1. 223, *Comm. in Arist. Soph. El.* ii. 262, 325 Ebbesen; see too Alex. Aphr. *In Anal. Pr.* 44. 14–15 Wallies, Ernst 15–25.

17. Varro is misled by Lat. *spartum*; Homer's σπάρτα are simply cords. For the etymology from σπείρω cf. Pacuv. 251 R; were it true, Gellius would be right on the accent (ξυστόν and ῥυτόν rebut his reservation that the specialized sense may entail a shift). At § 4 write Σπαρτούς. Plin. *NH* 19. 25, 24. 65 combines Varro with notions of his own; on the whole subject see Salmasius i. 261ᵇA–266ᵇC.

18. See also 1. 26. 11; 5. 10. 2; 9. 15. 6; 13. 6. 1; 16. 9. 3; 20. 5. 13.

19. 'ut dici solet', sc. *a Graecis*; cf. 12. 5. 6 'indoctius ut aiunt et apertius', from Ar. *Frogs* 1445.

20. Plut. *Mor.* 354 A, cf. Falster, *Am. phil.* iii. 245; but *inaudire* lacks the implication of mishearing conveyed by παρακούειν.

21. *Fin.* 1. 10 (but see 3. 3), *ND* 1. 8. Cf. *Caec.* 51, *Leg.* 1. 27, *Tusc.* 2. 35, Lucr. 1. 832–4, Quint. 12. 10. 34, Fronto, *Eloq.* 4. 9.

22. Cicero must justify *moralis*, excuse *beatitudo*, and smuggle *medietas* through the back door (*Fat.* 1, *ND* 1. 95, *Tim.* 23); Sen. *Ep.* 58. 6, 'Apul.' *Plat.* 1. 9 apologize for words not even new.

23. Sen. *Ep.* 58. 7 must render τὸ ὄν *quod est*; Caesar's *ens* (fr. 28 Fun.) remained theoretical (cf. fr. 2) till the Middle Ages.

24. From Varro; still *cricote* for Mart. Cap. 8. 815.

25. In Plutarch's title. 'De negotiositate', rejected as unsuitable, would suggest 'on being busy', like a good Roman (cf. § 7; to rest is to rust, said Cato, 11. 2. 6); Laurentius' and Erasmus' 'De curiositate' (cf. Apul. *Met.* 1. 12. 8 etc.; Tert. *passim*) would to Gellius mean 'on taking pains': *curiosus*/-*e* in the *Nights* denotes care in considering a text or problem (at 19. 13. 1 'curiosius captabam' does not imply eavesdropping). A πολυπράγμων is *multus homo* in Plautus, Catullus, and Cicero, *ardalio* in Phaedrus and Martial, colloquialisms that would not serve

To render the Stoic definition of an ἀξίωμα (proposition), λεκτὸν αὐτοτελὲς ἀποφαντὸν ὅσον ἐφ' αὑτῷ (an utterable complete by itself and capable in itself of being asserted),[27] would, says Gellius, require new, uncouth, and hardly bearable words (16. 8. 4–5). Not every writer found it so;[28] if Gellius, who cites with approval a slapdash formula from Varro,[29] forbore to translate what he did not understand,[30] he showed more prudence than at 1. 11. 7, where he mistook Herodotus' ὑπὸ ... αὐλοῦ γυναικηίου τε καὶ ἀνδρηίου (1. 17. 1, 'to treble and base auloi') to mean that Alyattes' band included women ('atque feminas etiam tibicinas'),[31] but perhaps, studying philosophy for the most part in Greek, he flinched from the effort of thinking the matter through in Latin. Less forgivably in 2. 9 he does not recognize the idiomatic use of neuter article and participle for abstract noun (p. 202), and at 2. 26. 20 he makes Favorinus of all people overlook the counterfactual force of κεν and say καί νύ κεν ἢ παρέλασσας ἢ ἀμφήριστον ἔθηκας[32]—which should mean, as Beloe renders it, 'Thou wouldst have either won, or made it doubtful', like Diomedes in the third-person original, Hom. *Il.* 23. 382, had he not lost his whip—in order to state what Fronto has actually done.[33]

No Roman writer can be expected to be perfect in his Greek. Livy's shortcomings are well known;[34] Pliny, besides confusing names of species, takes σπανίαν 'rare' at Thphr. *HP* 4. 5. 6 for the proper noun Σπανίαν

Gellius' turn. Cf. Seneca's difficulty in rendering ἀπάθεια (*Ep.* 9. 2); Gell. 12. 5. 10; 19. 12. 2, 10 does not try. (Cf. Aug. *CD* 14. 9 'quae si Latine posset inpassibilitas diceretur'; elsewhere he uses the word without qualms. John of Salisbury, *Ep.* 276 (ii. 584. 5 Millor–Brooke) gives *insensibilitas*, properly ἀναισθησία; whence?)

26. But see Cic. *Tim.* 22–3 (Arnob. 2. 24, Mart. Cap. 1. 11, Boeth. *saepe*), *Or.* 188, 193 (Plin. *NH* 2. 84, Quint. 9. 4. 47, Ter. Maur. 556 etc., Apthon. *GLK* vi. 40. 29 etc.), Vitr. 3. 1. 6, Cens. 10. 8–11.

27. See Frede, *Logik* 32–7; the definition recurs at S.E. *PH* 2. 104, cf. D.L. 7. 65 (ὅσον ἐφ' αὑτῷ means *quantum in ipso est*, Frede, op. cit. 36–7).

28. 'Apul.' Π. ἑρμ. 1 (p. 176. 13–14 Thomas): 'quae pronuntiabilis appellatur, absolutam sententiam comprehendens'; *pronuntiabilis* (cf. 'enuntiabile' Gaza ap. Bussi) is no more uncouth than Gellius' own adjectives of this formation.

29. 'Proloquium est sententia, in qua nihil desideratur' (cf. Mart. Cap. 4. 341); for similar looseness on Varro's part see 1. 20. 8 (ch. 16 n. 45), 1. 25. 1–7 (where Gellius' common sense detects the flaws that in more intellectual disciplines escape him).

30. So Frede, *Logik* 33. But Aristotle's definition of the syllogism is translated at least as well (if freely: Huetius 198, Gamberale 142–3) at *NA* 15. 26. 2 as at Π. ἑρμ. 7 (p. 184. 13–16 Thomas), Mart. Cap. 4. 406, or by Boethius and the Schoolmen.

31. Either Gellius wrote 'fidicines ⟨et tibicines⟩ atque' or he has committed two errors and not one; 'fidicinas' in the lemma will then be the third.

32. The text was restored (and the neglect of κεν observed) by Stephanus, *Noct. Par.* 181–2, before J. F. Gronovius confirmed it from P and his son printed it, rendering 'Et certe aut praeuenisti aut ambiguum fecisti'.

33. At 16. 3. 9 'cum serenum atque placidum est' Gellius misses the rarer sense 'in warm weather' of ἐν ταῖς εὐδίαις (opp. ἐν τοῖς ψύχεσιν): cf. Arist. *Met.* 347ᵃ22–4, and perhaps [Hipp.] *Vict.* 4. 89. 13 (224. 19–21 Byl). See H. Magius, *Misc.* 2. 1 *fin.* (Gruter ii. 1314–16); Jac. Gronovius' defence is unavailing. But Gamberale 203 is wrong to allege error at 3. 6. 3, a paraphrase not a translation.

34. P. G. Walsh, *G&R* 5 (1958) 83–8, cf. Briscoe 6.

('Hispania', *NH* 12. 7);[35] not even Cicero is infallible,[36] Terence associated γαλεώτης 'gecko' with γαλῆ 'weasel';[37] Vergil apparently took ἔναλλα 'confused' (v.l. Theoc. 1. 134) for ἐνάλια 'marine';[38] Catullus, translating Callimachus' *Lock of Berenice*, made nonsense of

ἧς ἄπο, παρθενίη μὲν ὅτ' ἦν ἔτι, πολλὰ πέπωκα
λιτά, γυναικείων δ' οὐκ ἀπέλαυσα μύρων.

from which [*sc.* Berenice's head], while her girlhood lasted, I drank many frugal perfumes, but had no chance to enjoy those she wore as a woman (fr. 110. 77–8 Pfeiffer)

by not attending to his particles:

quicum ego, dum uirgo quondam fuit, omnibus expers
unguentis, una uilia multa bibi,

together with whom, when of old she was a girl, untouched by any unguents, I drank many cheap things (66. 77–8).

This is what one might expect of a careless schoolboy who has failed to observe the antithesis between παρθενίη μέν and γυναικείων δέ.[39]

The habit of deriving Latin from Greek was well entrenched (p. 134); Gellius even explains an alleged Early Latin fondness for the aspirate by the precedent of Attic.[40] Two examples of the latter are offered, ἰχθύς, which is as strange to Attic as to all other Greek,[41] and ἵππος, in which aspiration

---

35. Meiggs 24; and see e.g. ibid. 24–5, 420–2, André 16 nn. 16–17, Bonniec on *ateramum* and *teramum* (18. 155).

36. Thus at *Oecon.* fr. 13 Garbarino 'in duas partes diuisimus' mistranslates X. *Oec.* 9. 8 δίχα ... κατέθεμεν ('stored separately'); at *Rep.* 2. 8 he forgot that the inhabitants of Φλειοῦς were Φλειάσιοι (*Att.* 6. 2. 3). Notorious since Turnebus, *Aduers.* 23. 32 is his misapprehension of Arat. 319–21 at *Ph.* 96–101.

37. *Eun.* 689 with Don. ad loc., citing Men. fr. 163 K–Th.

38. *Buc.* 8. 58 'omnia uel medium fiat mare'; Gow ad loc. Theoc. is doubtful, but offers no other explanation.

39. Critics who attempt emendation (beyond Lobel's *uilia* for *milia* codd.) correct the author, not his copyists. Observe too the Roman mistranslation of λαβὴν παρέχειν/ἐνδιδόναι 'to allow a hold' (a wrestling metaphor) as *ansam praebere* 'to afford a handle' (as we still say), and among Christians of διαθήκη 'covenant' as *testamentum*. Enn. *Ann.* 184 Sk seems a creative misinterpretation of A. *Sept.* 545; but see Skutsch ad loc.

40. *NA* 2. 3. 1–2, cf. A. Lentz, *Philologus*, Supp. 1 (1860) 703–6: see esp. Ael. Dion. fr. 219 Schwabe, Apoll. Dysc. *Pron.* 56. 4 Schneider. In fact all aspirating dialects, including the Koine, show inorganic aspirations of their own (Buck 54, Mayser–Schmoll i/1. 173–6, Gignac i. 134–8, Schulze, *Kl. Schr.* 517 and n. 2); genuine Attic exx. are ὅρος and ἔχω (Meisterhans 87 n. 737, Threatte 457–8). For Gellius' interest in Attic cf. 5. 20. 4–5; 8. 2; 19. 13. 3; but the grammatical terms πρόλημψις (ch. 11 n. 59; contrast ἐπιλημψίαν 19. 2. 8), οὐθετέρως (16. 7. 13: in non-grammatical context 11. 5. 4, though Favorinus will have written οὐδ-) remain in the Koine. In τρίτον καὶ τέταρτον 10. 1. 11 '"for the third" and "fourth time"' Attic prose, despite Plat. *Laws* 659 C 9, had preferred the article. Note too ἀφηλιώτην 2. 22. 8 (Attic ἀπ-, Latin often *aph-*).

41. Eustathius, who at 437. 13, 928. 16 records an etymology from ἱκέσθαι and θύω (= θυίω), does not posit aspiration; elsewhere he cites Ar. fr. 586 K–A with ἀπίχθυς.

is not confined to it.[42] This speaks ill for his knowledge; indeed, whereas Suetonius cast whole treatises in Greek, Apuleius declamations, and Fronto letters, Gellius affords no evidence of Greek composition, once his student days were over, apart from the snippets ὄναιό σου ταύτης τῆς πολυμαθίας (14. 6. 5) and the stylized and incorrect Attic he ascribes at 17. 8. 7 to a pert slave-boy: μὴ γελᾶτε· ἔνι τοὔλαιον. ἀλλ᾽ οὐκ ἴστε οἷα φρίκη περὶ τὸν ὄρθρον γέγονε τήμερον; κεκρυστάλλωται. 'Don't laugh: the oil is there. Don't you know what a shivering [φρίκη used for ψῦχος 'frost'] has occurred [γέγονε used for ἦν 'was'] this morning? It's frozen solid.'[43]

Gellius read Greek philosophers, technical writers, and miscellanists like Apion and Pamphila; but what knowledge does he show of literature in the narrow sense?[44]

Homer, 'that wisest and oldest of poets' (7. 2. 14),[45] the fountainhead of culture and the first Greek author read at school, whom not only the erudite will know (15. 6. 1), is freely cited by Gellius and his sources: this is no more surprising in ancient literature than biblical quotation in Christian. He depicts the silent courage of the Achaeans (1. 11. 8); makes speech proceed from the breast over the rampart of teeth (1. 15. 3–4); sets the example of praise by negation (2. 6. 11–12); explains, if attentively read, the different actions of north and south winds on the waves (2. 30. 6–10); demonstrates that the most deeply affecting speech evokes not applause but silence (5. 1. 5–6); declares that men's troubles are their own fault, not the gods' (7. 2. 14); respects euphony (13. 21. 25), illustrates the effective use of synonyms (13. 25. 16–21); provides Socrates with a motto (14. 6. 5); alludes to the warming power of wine (17. 8. 10); and perhaps shaped Cicero's view of fate (13. 1. 2). So universal is his authority that Gellius is worried by a disagreement with Herodotus (13. 7. 6). He is also cited to account for Latin usages,[46] and yields problems for discussion, though some are dismissed as paltry (14. 6. 3–5); Gellius shows some knowledge of his commentators.[47]

Hesiod, 'poetarum prudentissimus', as he is called as *NA* 1. 15. 14, is quoted not only there (probably by way of Favorinus' discourse on twaddle) but at 4. 5. 7 and 18. 2. 13, albeit (as in Favorinus' declamation at 17. 12. 4) for well-known tags from the *Works and Days*. Fronto, *Add. ep.* 5. 8 vaguely

---

42. e.g. *Il.* 5. 13, *IG* v/1. 213. Or was the proper name Λεύκιππος contrasted with Attic ἄφιππος and ἔφιππος? (Gellius' MSS offer *IPPON*, correctly interpreted by F. Skutsch in Hosius' edn.)

43. φρίκη was suggested by *frigus*, the tense of γέγονε either by *fuerit* or by contemporary usage (e.g. [Plut.] *Mor.* 572 C). Cf. ἄγω = *duco* for ἄγομαι in 5. 11 (pp. 86–7). Fronto, *Add. ep.* 5. 8 writes Ὁμήρῳ μάρτυρι = *Homero teste* for κατὰ τὸν Ὅμηρον.

44. Cf. Marache, *Critique* 117–19, 183–200, 322–5; Gamberale 173–209.

45. Cf. 1. 15. 3; 5. 1. 6; Apul. *Apol.* 31. 5; etc. etc. etc.

46. *NA* 7. 6. 12; 15. 3. 8; 18. 9. 9; cf. 13. 21. 14.

47. See ch. 9 n. 1.

echoes *Op.* 350, but the verse is cited at Cic. *Att.* 13. 12. 3.[48] Marcus cites Hesiod more than once in the *Meditations*; Favorinus occasionally mentions him, Apuleius never.

Of the iambic and elegiac poets, Solon, who supplies the well-known pederastic verse fr. 25. 2 West at Apul. *Apol.* 9. 9, is to Gellius, as to Fronto and Favorinus (Marcus is silent), not a poet but a legislator and a sage (2. 12; 11. 18. 5; 17. 21. 3–4). Archilochus appears for his date at *NA* 17. 21. 8 and Theognis by way of Lucil. 952 M at 1. 3. 19;[49] our other authors have nothing.

The entertainment at the dinner-party of 19. 9 included poems by Sappho and Anacreon. The custom is attested by Plutarch (*Mor.* 622 C, 711 D), and singing the songs of Sappho is a courtesan's accomplishment for whose want Philodemus' mistress compensated by sheer sexuality (XII Gow–Page = *AP* 5. 132). The only specific instance is the poem attributed to Anacreon at 19. 9. 5–6, which Gellius quotes to relieve his scholarly labours; it is one of those Anacreontea (4.i West) that imposed on most readers till the nineteenth century. He is our first witness to their existence, though Luc. *Trag.* 30–53 has been speculatively derived from *Anacr.* 12 W. The comparison between Vergil and Pindar in 17. 10 comes from Favorinus (p. 89),[50] in whose writings the lyric poets are not seldom mentioned and at whose table their works were sung (2. 22. 1); their only other trace in Gellius outside the doxography of 20. 7 is the derivative citation of Alcaeus at 17. 11. 1.[51] Apuleius alludes to Anacreon, Alcman, Simonides, and Sappho, praising the 'mulier Lesbia' for the charm of her love-poems, which commends the abnormal dialect (*Apol.* 9.

48. He also, in a lost work, asserted that Hesiod was made a poet while asleep, an interpretation not supported by the text (cf. West on *Theog.* 22–34), but refuted by Marcus (*Ep. M. Caes.* 1. 4. 6) not from Hesiod himself but from Callim. fr. 2. 1–2 Pf, taken as showing that the Muses came to meet him while he was tending his flocks. Fronto may have read Hesiod in the darkness of a theory, and Marcus may have thought Callimachus more explicit.

49. 'hoc profecto nemo ignorauit et priusquam Theognis ut Lucilius ait nasceretur': Lucilius wrote e.g. 'hoc quidem prius sciebam quam Theognis natus est', cf. *Com. inc.* fr. 461 K τουτὶ μὲν ᾔδειν πρὶν Θέογνιν γεγονέναι. For the subjunctive, impossible in Lucilius outside *oratio obliqua*, cf. 5. 10. 6; 6. 18. 3; 12. 12. 3; 16. 5. 9; 19. 5. 8; 19. 8. 1; Holford-Strevens, 'Aduersaria' 111.

50. Since *carmen* may denote a short passage within a poem (Cic. *Sen.* 16. Tac. *A.* 15. 70. 1), its use at §§ 8–9, where only the second strophe is at issue, need be neither a characterization of the entire ode (so Berthold, 'Carmen Pindari' 286) nor a sign that he did not know the rest of it; but probably he copied out only those lines that Favorinus marked for him and by reading them out of context misunderstood κεῖνο δ' Ἀφαίστοιο κρουνοὺς ἑρπετόν / δεινοτάτους ἀναπέμπει as signifying 'quasi quosdam igneos angues' (§ 13). That his text lacked πέτρας in v. 23 is shown not only by § 19 and by Macr. *Sat.* 5. 17. 9 (Timpanaro, *Contributi* 551–2), but by its failure to leave a trace in § 13 (cf. Tränkle 109); Gellius, faced with corrupt Greek, has extracted from the next sentence an object for φέρει (his 'ferre'). Favorinus, we may suppose, took φέρει as intransitive, and gave Ἀφαίστοιο κρουνούς its obvious meaning; only thus can the contrast in § 15 with Vergil's 'globos flammarum' make sense. But the paraphrase in § 13 is poor floundering Gellius' own.

51. The doxography will not be further mentioned since it proves no knowledge of the poets cited. Note that Gellius prefers the choice term *melicus* (2. 22. 1); cf. Pfeiffer 182–3. Conceivably 12. 11. 7 owes something to Pi. *Ol.* 2. 17; v. 16 is cited at Fav. fr. 96 vi 32 B, but v. 18 is not to the purpose.

6–7). Fronto has nothing. Marcus' one quotation from Pindar (*Med.* 2. 13. 1) is indirect. Little else could be expected when even Cicero had made no time for the lyric Muse.[52]

Aeschylus, who after his eclipse by Euripides in the early fourth century BC did not fully return to favour till the Romantic era,[53] is ignored by Fronto, Marcus, and Apuleius; Favorinus possibly cites him once.[54] He appears in Gellius' chronography (17. 21. 10); at 13. 19. 4 the similarity is noted between fr. 208 Radt and Eur. fr. 413 Nauck. This does not mean that Gellius knew the plays; the resemblance, and the identity of Soph. fr. 695 R with Eur. *Bacch.* 193 (§ 3), will ultimately come from a compiler of echoes such as Ptolemaeus or Aretades. Plato's misascription to Euripides of Soph. fr. 14 R (§§ 1–2) was common knowledge to the Greeks.[55] The story of Polus in 6. 5, who when playing Electra wept over his own son's ashes, concerns the actor rather than the playwright; the explanation of Sophocles' plot at § 6 suggests that Gellius' public could not be expected to have read the play. The Sophoclean text (fr. 301 R) reportedly adduced by Peregrinus (12. 11. 6), and the few others from Euripides, are good anthology material, reappearing in Stobaeus: the single exception (Eur. fr. 451 N) at 6. 3. 28 is taken from Tiro—who furthermore names speaker and interlocutors, otherwise identified only at 11. 4. 2, where Eur. *Hecuba* 293–5 is quoted for Ennius' adaptation. This may be the fruit of comparative reading;[56] but if Gellius found Euripides' lines in an anthology, he could easily have recognized in them Ennius' source. In any case, he is concerned not with plays but with verses, above all as moral saws;[57] in these, as Quint. 10. 1. 68 remarks, Euripides is supreme. A purported life is retailed in 15. 20; like a good tourist, Gellius inspected the grim cave on Salamis in which he allegedly wrote his plays (§ 5). His poor competitive record is noted at 17. 4. 3.

Fronto ignores these poets; Apuleius merely relates that Sophocles dispelled a charge of senility by reading from *Oedipus at Colonus*;[58] Marcus quotes only *sententiae*, but regards the main value of tragedy as teaching us to bear misfortune on the greater stage of life (*Med.* 11. 6. 1–3). Favorinus, by contrast, sometimes locates the cited passage in its dramatic context: in

---

52. Sen. *Ep.* 49. 5; cf. Grilli on *Hortensius* fr. 12 (comm. 66–7). No doubt Calvisius Sabinus thought his vicarious knowledge of the *nouem lyrici* a mark of singular refinement (Sen. *Ep.* 27. 6–7).

53. Dio of Prusa, who admires him, must defend him against those who do not (*Or.* 52. 5); cf. Quint. 10. 1. 66, *Vita Aeschyli* 333. 17–21 Page.

54. For us fr. 96 ix 42 B κατακαφαὶ δόμων recalls *Cho.* 50; but perhaps Euripides, who several times approaches the phrase (*HF* 566, *Hel.* 196, *Phoen.* 1196), used it outright like Timotheus (*Pers.* 191, cf. Janssen ad loc. = *PMG* 791. 179).

55. See Radt ad loc. Gellius' 'legimus' is present, *on lit.* Cf. pp. 197–8; Gellius parades Greek commonplaces before impressionable Romans.

56. Not necessarily by Gellius himself; but we hear of no ancient commentaries on Ennius' plays. For scholarly comparison of an early Latin tragedy with its Attic original see Apthon. *GLK* vi. 77. 7–13.

57. Cf. Marache, *Critique* 189.

58. *Apol.* 37. 1–3, cf. Lefkowitz 85.

particular, he has obviously read *Phoenissae*.[59] Acquaintance with Attic tragedy, essential to Hellenic culture, was not conferred by Roman schooling;[60] nor did educated Romans still feel impelled to read it for themselves, being content to know a handful of preselected verses, mostly from Euripides, the fixed point to which the other two must be referred.[61]

On the other hand, Gellius has clearly read two Greek comedies: Aristophanes' *Frogs*, which he quotes in several chapters,[62] and Menander's *Plocion*, which he compares with Caecilius' adaptation (pp. 146–8, 158);[63] but the quotations from Eupolis and Epicharmus in 1. 15 probably come from Favorinus, that from Aristophanes' *Thesmophoriazusae* (specified as *First*) at 15. 20. 7 from a life of Euripides; his use of ναῦος in *Merchantmen* (fr. 441 Kassel–Austin; *NA* 19. 13. 3) is known at second hand, like the animal diet in Alexis' *Pythagorizusa* at 4. 11. 8. In 17. 4 some biographical information is offered on Menander, including the rivalry with Philemon prefixed by Apuleius in *Flor.* 16. 6 to one of the many conflicting stories about the latter poet's death; the comments on his plays (§§ 7–9) indicate that Apuleius has read, if not Philemon, at least a critic. This exhausts his interest in comedy; Fronto has none—for there is no more reason to identify him with the author of the epigram *AP* 12. 233, headed Φρόντωνος, naming five Menandrean plays (not necessarily read) than with the eponym of *pullus Frontonianus* (Apic. § 248 André).[64] Favorinus cites Menander at fr. 96 xxiii 29–30 B and an unidentified poet at fr. 94. 15–16 B. Marcus quotes Aristophanes twice in the *Meditations* (4. 23. 5; 7. 66. 2), Menander once (5. 12. 4); at 11. 6. 4–6 he prefers the Cynic frankness of Old Comedy to the technical virtuosity of New, a reversal of established opinion (but Atticism too raised Aristophanes above Menander, whose diction no longer passed for pure).

59. The misattribution at fr. 96 xviii 4 B is a mere slip.

60. Cf. Dionisotti 122. In the 3rd c. (Keil, *GLK* vi. 323) Ter. Maur. 1960–4 knows the context of Eur. *Or.* 1369–72, and (despite 1971) can cite v. 1287 of that play at 963 (em. Dawes).

61. Apul. *Apol.* 37. 1 'Sophocles poeta Euripidi aemulus et superstes'; but *NA* 13. 19. 2 'prior autem natus fuit Sophocles quam Euripides' may be an illicit argument that even if Euripides does use the verse, the credit is Sophocles'; at § 4 'fuit autem Aeschylus non breui antiquior' the point is that Euripides must be the borrower.

62. At 1. 15. 19, vv. 837–9 are wrenched out of context, cf. ch. 6 n. 61. Here and at 13. 25. 7 Aristophanes is *facetissimus* as at Cic. *Leg.* 2. 37 (and *festuissimus* pr. 20, cf. 17. 1. 10 'festuissimum adeo et facetissimum'); though the adjective implies elegance (Quint. 6. 3. 20), and the superlative frequently recurs in Gellius, Menander must make do with the positive (2. 23. 11). C. Pascal's notion, *AR* 11 (1908) 20–2, that the Plato of 8. 8 is the comic poet because the saying ascribed to 'Agellius' by Petrus Cantor (cf. ch. 2 n. 17) goes back to fr. 22 K may serve as a monument to perverse ingenuity.

63. At 3. 16. 3 Menander, 'humanarum opinionum uel peritissimus', is cited in a medical controversy.

64. *AP* 12. 174, also ascribed to 'Fronto', and alluding to X. *Cyrop.* 1. 4. 6, exhibits a 3rd- and 4th-c. licence in v. 4 (σῦν || αἱ); lateness seems also indicated by Σάκας (v. 3), which, though exhibiting by accident the quantity of Aramaic *šāqē* 'cupbearer', conflicts with Σάκας in the ethnic name for which Greeks will have taken it. Warning against identifying unspecified Frontones with M. Cornelius is afforded by the error of Schol. Juv. 1. 12, cf. J. Salis. *Polic.* 8. 13 (ii. 320 W).

Other poets cited in the *Nights* are Empedocles and Callimachus in 4. 11, probably from Plutarch (p. 110); Timon of Phleious, almost certainly from Favorinus (p. 81); Alexander Aetolus (fr. 7 Powell) at 15. 20. 8, no doubt from the same source as other matter on Euripides; Theocritus in 9. 9, reportedly read together with Vergil's *Bucolics*, but possibly taken from a Vergilian commentary, as Parthenius will be at 13. 27. 1; Apollodorus' *Chronica*, quoted in 17. 4. 5 (but without book-number), from a source concerned with Menander. Also Hellenistic is the distich in 19. 11 attributed by 'several ancient writers' to Plato,[65] and translated by Gellius' friend; of the elegies by more modern poets ('recentiorum') sung with the works of Sappho and Anacreon at 19. 9. 4 we hear no more. Nor does Hellenistic poetry much engage our other authors, though Marcus cites Callimachus at *Ep. M. Caes.* 1. 4. 6 and the moral Crates at *Medit.* 6. 13. 5. Altogether exceptional is Fronto's commendation of Apollonius' proem above even Homer's, canonical for Horace and Quintilian, at *Orat.* 8.

We shall see (chs. 13–14) that Gellius has read Herodotus for style and stories, cites Thucydides once, and studies Greek philosophy in the original. Fronto, too, admires Herodotus' style and retells stories from him;[66] in correspondence about the Parthian War and its projected history Fronto mentions Nicias' letter in Thucydides, Verus the Pentecontaetia.[67] Apuleius and the *Meditations* do not cite the Greek historians; Favorinus (at whose table both Greek and Latin histories were read) speaks only of Herodotus (following Plutarch for his injustice towards Corinth at fr. 95. 18–19 B), though his language shows Atticizing echoes from Thucydides and Xenophon.[68] In philosophy, Marcus, Apuleius, and Favorinus had read more widely; Fronto knows *Phaedrus* (as a rhetor should) and the context of *Phaedo* 60 B–C (*Ep. M. Caes.* 4. 9. 1), ignores Aristotle, makes superficial comments on philosophers' styles at *Eloq.* 1. 3–4, but shows some acquaintance with Chrysippus (*Eloq.* 2. 17) and Stoic teaching (*Eloq.* 2. 5. 9–10; 5. 4).

Among the orators, it is Aeschines whom Gellius describes as 'most incisive and intelligent' (18. 3. 1). His invective against Timarchus, of which §§ 180–1 are paraphrased at 18. 3. 2–8,[69] is the only speech by any of the classic Ten that Gellius has demonstrably read apart from *De corona*;[70] it supplies barbs

---

65. *AP* 5. 78; see now Page 62–3.

66. *Laud. fum.* 5 m^2 e; *Bell. Parth.* 4–6; *Arion*; cf. *Ver.* 2. 1. 8 (§ 15 m^2 a v.d.H.).

67. *Ver.* 2. 1. 19 (§ 17 v.d.H.); 2. 3. 2. There are occasional references to Xenophon both as philosopher and historian. Marcus knows Theopompus to be reputed 'disertissimum' at *Ep. M. Caes.* 2. 8. 2; for the false ascription ibid. 3. 18. 1 see ch. 14 n. 78.

68. Barigazzi, edn. 47–8, 51–2.

69. Nothing in Aeschines corresponds to 'quod si proba istaec ... turpissimi auctoris contagio' or 'sic bona sententia mansit, turpis auctor mutatus est' but τὰς δὲ τῶν ἀποδεδειλιακότων ... μηδὲ τοῖς ὠσὶ προσδέχωνται has been replaced by 'nulla prioris mentione habita'. In § 5 it is not clear that Spartan γέροντες are not merely old men but Elders.

70. For which see 2. 27. 1; 13. 1. 6; in any case Gellius surely read the acknowledged masterpiece of all Greek oratory. At 10. 19. 3 the source is either Taurus or a handbook (cf. p. 49).

against Demosthenes' unmanly dress that Gellius cites at 1. 5. 1, where allegations of pathic practices are noted.[71] (These especially recall Aeschin. 2. 88, but the speech is not cited.) We also hear that Demosthenes refused to pay Lais' fee,[72] broke down before King Philip, took a bribe, and ran away from Chaeronea.[73] But Gellius never censures him, and often gives him the merry last word.[74] His *Philippics* are praised at 9. 3. 1, but so is Philip's greatness; the man who abstains from taking sides between Cato and the elder Scipio is under no compulsion, as a citizen of Rome, to decide between an Athenian democrat and a Macedonian monarch. Demosthenes' primacy among Greek orators is too secure to want stating, except implicitly in the observation that both he and Cicero made brilliant speeches at a like age, and lived about as long (15. 28. 6–7). Aeschines, whom he overshadowed, stood in more need of praise; perhaps Gellius learnt to appreciate him in Greece from a teacher who (like Philost. *VS* 507) saw in him the founder of modern Sophistic. Fronto says nothing about Demosthenes, but Apuleius bestows the conventional laudation in relating anecdotes at *Apol.* 15. 8–9. Marcus, who in the *Meditations* ignores the orators, pairs Demosthenes with Cato at *Ep.* 2. 3. 1 and cites him ibid. 5. 43. 1;[75] Favorinus alludes to his fortitude (fr. 96 xxi 15 B). None of the four notices Aeschines.

Gellius cites no speech by any other orator, though Lysias' style is praised by Favorinus in 2. 5 and a grammatical example at 17. 13. 2 states that Isocrates did not abstain from advocacy on moral grounds; the sneer at his would-be imitators in 18. 8 is not aimed at him in person.[76] Demades appears in 11. 10, but only because C. Gracchus had transferred to him a tale about Demosthenes. Fronto cites Plato's criticism of Lysias, and offers his own version of the ἐρωτικὸς λόγος;[77] Apuleius is silent, and likewise Favorinus, *NA* 2. 5 apart.

Although Gellius may have read more than he quotes, the evidence of other mannerists suggests that while the Romans of the day could not dispense with Greek learning, they were no longer steeped in Greek literature. They did not discard it, but read less of it; they still cite it for

---

71. 'parum uir et ore quoque polluto', a *cinaedus* abaft and afore (cf. 3. 5. 2). Triller 3–4 (cf. Falster, *Am. Phil.* iii. 278) wrongly supposed oral services (of which he confuses two kinds) bestowed on women, even baser in ancient eyes.

72. *NA* 1. 8. Was the 'absolutely shameless' demand (so Hornsby) for 10,000 dr. a reflection on Demosthenes' corrupt gains or a means of sending him away? The sum Demosthenes refused to spend on pleasure Plato spent on books, but not of his own money (3. 17. 1–2). At Philodemus, XXV Gow-Page = *AP* 5. 126. 1–2 a matron charges only thrice as much.

73. *NA* 8. 9; 11. 9; 17. 21. 31.

74. *NA* 1. 8. 6; 11. 9. 2; 17. 21. 31 (cf. Men. *Monost.* 56 Jäkel, Tert. *Fug.* 10. 1, *ODEP* 256). For laughing off one's fault cf. Cicero in 12. 12; for Demosthenes' cowardice Aeschin. 3. 159, 181, etc.; Nesselrath on Luc. *Paras.* 42 (comm. 419).

75. From Dem. 27. 68 rather than Lys. 18. 27, 21. 21, Isae. 2. 2, 44; the faulty order is Marcus' own (cf. Fronto, *Ep. M. Caes.* 4. 3. 7).

76. Contrast D.H. *Isoc.* 12–14, Hermog. 299. 9–10 R, Roman. 3. 4; more favourably Cic. *Or.* 174, cf. Quint. 9. 3. 74, Aquila, *RCM* 29. 26–7 Halm.

77. *Laud. fum.* 4, *Add. ep.* 8.

examples, but no longer—except when judging Latin imitations—take it for their point of reference.[78] The Silver Age did not neglect the Greeks, but could find models and foils among the Golden writers;[79] the mannerists, rejecting their immediate predecessors, looked with one eye at the contemporary sophists, with the other at the early Romans. These *ueteres*, relished and exploited for their language, were appreciated for their own sake and not as mediators of Greek culture; Caecilius' mangling of Menander does not incite the systematic comparison of stages and societies that modern scholars have attempted on far less evidence. We expect no more of a dilettante, but there is no sign that anyone else did as much. By the standards of so recent a scholar as Suetonius, Gellius' knowledge of Greek literature is not impressive; yet through his own inclination or Favorinus' inspiration he is perhaps not too ill versed in it for a Roman of his age.

78. So too J. Styka, *Meander* 37 (1982) 146 (omitted in the Latin summary).
79. Cf. Ogilvie 259.

Chapter 13

History

'Aulus Gelius, that noble historiar', as John Skelton calls him,[1] will not be so described by modern writers; nor will any other Latin author between Tacitus and Ammianus Marcellinus. History was not being written because the Latin reading public had no interest in true historiography: it either conned compendia of events (whether penny plain from Granius Licinianus or twopence coloured from Florus) or regaled itself with anecdotes, *exempla*, and preferably scandalous biography.[2]

Under the Republic, history had been written to justify Roman rule in Greek eyes, to match Greek literary achievements, to inculcate moral values or political opinions into the educated classes, to glorify a great house, or to outdo a previous author in elegance of style or clarity of arrangement. By Tiberius' day the Greeks had acquiesced in their subjection to Rome, literary emulation had been accomplished, political principles were either dangerous or subversive, the noble houses were in terminal decline, and no one could compete with Livy even as a moralist. That he was not a critical historian was known,[3] even to Quintilian, whose preference for Sallust owes nothing to any taste for archaism,[4] but who would devote his life to correcting sundry errors in a hundred and forty-two books? To condense them was another matter, since few would be undaunted by the thought of reading or even storing them (Mart. 14. 190. 2); and a Velleius or a Florus could trick out his compendium with sentiments inoffensive to the ruler.

Serious history was still possible, but only on recent events, on which the truth might be hard to discover and dangerous to publish. In the first century, such works were written; they were superseded by Tacitus, after whom historical writing is confined to Greek—ranging from Appian and Arrian to the twaddlers mocked by Lucian; Fronto's *Principia historiae* is not a

1. *Garlande or Chapelet of Laurell* 351 (p. 322 Scattergood); cf. vv. 328–9 'Esiodus, the iconomicar / And Homerus, the fresshe historiar'. Gellius' historical chapters are reviewed by M. T. Schettino, *Latomus* 45 (1986) 341–66; 46 (1987) 123–45.
2. Observe the all but total neglect of Tacitus; if Florus filched the odd phrase from him, it is no matter (see Jal, edn. i, p. xxx n. 3). That Fronto, *Eloq.* 2. 12 is not derived from *Hist.* 4. 6. 1 is shown by the reference to Plato; a common origin in Sallust may be suspected. (For the theme cf. ch. 14 n. 26.) Tertullian alludes to the opening chapters of *Hist.* 5 in the *Apologeticum* and *Ad Nationes*; a Gentile account of the Jews was of especial interest to Christians once the daughter religion had turned against the mother. The Emperor Tacitus' claim to descent from the historian (*HA Tac.* 10. 3) is an agreeable fiction of the late 4th c. Ammianus began his narrative where the *Historiae* left off.
3. Cf. Syme, *Tacitus* i. 201–2.
4. Quint. 2. 5. 19 (cf. 10. 1. 32, 101); 8. 3. 29–30. He cites Sallust twice as often as Livy.

history, but a Velleian panegyric in Sallustian garb.[5] Not even the upheavals that followed could stimulate a Latin writer to compose a history: there was no Latin Dio, nor even a Latin Herodian, only two successors to Suetonius Tranquillus.[6] The Romans, never as intellectual as the Greeks, had turned against profundity. Gellius narrates stirring, improving, or warning anecdotes, but never undertakes a critical scrutiny of their truth or historical significance;[7] he relies on the pre-Livian writers, not for any greater accuracy or penetration, but for their style.

To learn a jumble of anecdotes rather than a sequence of events is to risk confusion in chronology: one declaimer had made Carneades receive a purse from Alexander the Great and Panaetius consort with the elder Africanus (17. 21. 1). Gellius' remedy is a list of Graeco-Roman synchronisms, compiled out of Varro and Nepos,[8] with no reflections on the facts related; far from comparing the political histories of Rome and the Greek cities, he does not even mention the approximate synchronism between the expulsions of Hippias and Tarquin.[9] He displays, rather, a love of facts for their own sake, as in the chapter on the Porcii Catones (13. 20). The relative dates of Greek historians (15. 23), like those of Greek poets (3. 11), are mere curiosities.

In 17. 2 Gellius reads Claudius Quadrigarius and notes down not events (he does not record the contexts of his quotations) but words and phrases. In 9. 13 Quadrigarius' account of the single combat between T. Manlius and the Gaul from whose torque he took the *cognomen* of Torquatus is reproduced verbatim with praise of its style. Two chapters earlier, Gellius had retold a similar tale, of the challenge through which M. Valerius acquired the name Corvinus from the raven that settled on his helmet.[10] A scholar who has analysed these two narratives, and the corresponding accounts in Livy (7. 10, 7. 26), finds that whereas Quadrigarius aims at inspiring confidence, and

5. Cf. Champlin, *Fronto* 55. Cova demonstrates Fronto's lack of interest in the historical *genus*, but however little attention Fronto pays narrative in his rhetorical precepts (Cova 99), he was compelled to practise it in his forensic speeches; cf. *Bell. Parth.* 4–6, *Fer. Als.* 3. 9–13, *Arion*. Less persuasive is Cova's interpretation of *Princ. hist.* as a *recusatio* inviting Verus to be his own historian like the great figures of the past with whom the ensuing panegyric ranges him.

6. Marius Maximus and *Ignotus* (Syme, *Emperors* 30–53, Barnes 99–107); only Maximus for Birley *Sept.* 308–26, *Marcus Aurelius* 230.

7. Despite e.g. Leuze, *Jahrzählung* 48–55, the debate in 5. 4 concerns language, not history; the supremely learned Paulus routs the grammarian with the exx. preserved at Non. 142. 9–14 (cf. ch. 2 n. 40).

8. See Leuze, 'Synchr. Kap.' (vainly contested by Castorina 111–12); cf. pp. 55, 187. No trace of any annalist, not even Quadrigarius.

9. Though he does note that Hipparchus was murdered about the time of Pythagoras' voyage to Italy while Tarquin the Proud reigned at Rome (§§ 6–7). Following Varro for the date of the Gaulish siege (§ 25), Gellius neglects the firmest synchronism in early Roman history (Polyb. 1. 6. 1–2).

10. The Latin of *NA* 9. 11, wrongly reckoned by Peter as Quadr. fr. 12, belongs (despite Lebek 213 n. 14) to the 2nd c. AD (cf. J. Marouzeau, *RPh* 47 (1921) 163–5; Sypniewska; Schibel 9–10, 96–8), though the odd phrase (e.g. 'tali genere' § 3, in any case a redactional carelessness) may come from the source, probably Antias (p. 185); cf. S. Cavallin, *Eranos* 35 (1937) 98 n. 3; Heurgon 163–5; Holford-Strevens, 'More Notes' 147–8).

Livy at exciting emotional appreciation of the great events, in Gellius one word merely mirrors another, and the tale does no more than 'display, as in a looking-glass, the extraneous image of a Valerius with his raven',[11] being told, not as an example for the reader to emulate, but as a commentary on a *cognomen*.[12]

In 5. 18. 8–9 Gellius quotes from Sempronius Asellio (frr. 1–2 P) a distinction between *annales* and *historiae* or *res gestae*: annals are a bare chronicle of events, of no moral value, mere tales told to children, but serious history explains not only what happened but why, and includes political as well as military events. This does not evince any interest on Gellius' part in historiographical method, but merely concludes a discussion on the difference between *historiae* and *annales* as stated by Verrius Flaccus and others: his concern is with the words and not the thing. He cites Asellio's Latin translation of a Greek term: 'qui diarium scribunt, quam Graeci ἐφημερίδα uocant' , denoting not (as Gellius' paraphrase in § 7 might suggest) journals like those of Alexander's campaign, but diaries like Trimalchio's or day-books like Chaerea's.[13] At *NA* 2. 28. 6 Cato's refusal (fr. 77 P) to record eclipses and high grain-prices does not interest Gellius as a statement of the historian's proper concerns, only for the offhand phrase, 'darkness or something obstructed the light of moon or sun' (§ 7). Even here he misses the significance of Cato's knowing that eclipses had a rational cause (as Paullus informed his men before Pydna), and therefore were not portentous, despite his anti-intellectual and traditionalistic pose.

Some, however, ascribe to Gellius interest in historians' programmatic statements on the strength of these two extracts and of 4. 15, where he explains Sallust's 'arduum uidetur res gestas scribere' (*Cat.* 3. 2); 11. 8, where Cato takes A. Postumius Albinus to task for confessedly writing in bad Greek instead of good Latin; 12. 15. 2, where Sisenna justifies his continuous narrative of a summer's events in Greece and Asia (no doubt running ahead of those at Rome) 'ne uellicatim aut saltuatim scribendo lectorum animos impediremus' (fr. 127 P), so as not to confuse the reader by picking at one subject and then leaping to another; and finally 16. 9. 5, where a sentence is quoted from Varro's *Sisenna uel de historia*.[14] But these texts afford no evidence for serious interest in historiographic theory.

Sallust had said that writing history is *arduum* both because one must match events with one's style and because any criticisms one makes will be

---

11. Schibel 118–19.

12. Ibid. 94. The Celtic motif of the supernatural fighting raven (the Gaul's own battle-godhead siding with the enemy) precludes a simple theft by Antias of a Manlian exploit. S. P. Oakley, *CQ*[2] 35 (1985) 392–410, insisting on the place of single combat in Republican warfare, accepts both duels as historical without regard to historiographical considerations.

13. Petr. 53; Cic. *Q. Rosc.* 5–9; cf. Prop. 3. 23. 19–20.

14. Romano 55–7, Berthold 8, 126–7. I do not deny that Gellius found the matter of interest besides the manner; but it was a fleeting, not a systematic, interest.

ascribed to personal bias; but why, pedants asked, should other people's misinterpretation or disbelief make it *arduum*, which indicates a difficulty inherent in the task itself? Gellius explains that *arduum* here means χαλεπόν, not only difficult but disagreeable. The discussion turns on words, not content; the passage itself is not a programmatic statement but a *captatio beneuolentiae*, and tells us nothing about Sallust's aims or methods. At 11. 8 interest centres not on Albinus but Cato; Gellius neither seeks the reason for Albinus' choice of language, nor observes that Cato thought Roman rule sufficiently justified by the legions.[15] Anyone who savours Latin word-formation must enjoy the *-atim* adverbs, of which Gellius has just cited another from the same author; anyone interested in historiography would have examined whether Sisenna had adopted the continuous method elsewhere in his work or was merely compelled to use it here by the complexity of his subject.[16] The Varronian passage, exemplifying the expression *susque deque*, runs

> quod si non horum omnium similia essent principia ac postprincipia, susque deque esset.

> But if the beginning and the further courses of all these things were not alike, it would be all one.

Gellius does not see fit to explain whether the events have no place in serious historiography, or the words are uttered in order to be refuted; if he was ever interested in the point of principle, he is not so now. Moreover, had he cared enough about historians' aims and methods to record their programmatic statements, we might have expected something from his favourite historian Quadrigarius.

Historians

The only Greek historian to make frequent appearance in the *Attic Nights* is Herodotus, the charm of whose diction delighted Gellius as it did the Atticists. Fronto couples his unaffected elegance with Cato's: *Laud. fum.* 5 m^2 e 'modo dulce illud incorruptum sit et pudicum, Tusculanum ac Ionicum, id est Catonis et Herodoti', and in retelling the tale of Arion adopts the naïve Catonian manner of beginning sentences: 'id ... ille ... tum ... ibi'. Gellius, in his own narration of the story, follows suit: 'is ... eum Arionem ... is inde ... ubi eo uenit ... is tum postea ... sed eos Corinthios'; although Herodotus had related the event 'in very swift and concise style, with smooth and elegant diction' (16. 19. 1), an excellent description of his manner, Gellius

15. There is no warrant for supposing a Frontonian shot across the bows of Romans who wrote on Verus' war in Greek.

16. Namely the events of 88 BC, when Sulla marched on Rome, Mithridates overran Asia, and much of Greece, including Athens, rallied to his cause.

does not seek to imitate it, but rather to substitute for it a Latin style that shall likewise recall the noble simplicities of ancient days.[17]

It is not, however, for the Persian Wars that Herodotus is cited, but for the unusual and the marvellous: Alyattes' band (1. 11. 7), Croesus' son cured of aphasia (5. 9), the extirpation of the Psylli (16, 11. 3–8). At 17. 8. 16 Taurus, who absurdly maintains 'mare omne incongelabile', notes as conflicting with other evidence Herodotus' report (4. 28. 1) that the Straits of Kerč' and adjacent sea freeze over;[18] however, the discussion is curtailed by dinner, leaving Herodotus' credibility in the balance. In 8. 4 certain statements by the 'scriptor historiae memoratissimus' are said to be false or rash;[19] at 3. 10. 11 Herodotus is characterized, in an Aristotelian phrase, as 'homo fabulator'.[20] Had Gellius read him more attentively, he would have learnt that Histiaeus of Miletus was not a barbarian (17. 9. 18–19) and that the device ascribed to 'Hasdrubal or another Carthaginian' (ibid. §§ 16–17) had been used by the Spartan Demaratus (Hdt. 7. 239. 3–4).

Herodotus is not commended as he was to the Greeks by his glorious subject-matter, but by his style, his incidental assertions, and the legends he reports. Nor do his qualities as a historian concern one who, despite Sallust's notorious emulation,[21] cites even 'auctor historiae Graecae grauissimus Thucydides' (1. 11. 1) only once, for the Spartans' marching to the aulos.

Other historians occasionally appear, never demonstrably at first hand; Polybius' and Timaeus' accounts of Roman matters are known only through Varro (6. 14. 10;[22] 11. 1. 1). At 5. 6. 27 we miss the Greek name for the *ouatio*, ὁ πεζὸς θρίαμβος, which might have supported Sabinus' statement (5. 6. 27) that the commander entered the city on foot, not as others said on horseback. At 17. 9. 16, however, Gellius claims to have read a history of Carthage.[23]

*   *   *

17. Gellius' version was added to some reprs. and trs. of Steinhöwel's Aesop; it found a place in L'Estrange, *Fables*⁴, no. 382.

18. Cf. ch. 5 n. 49, and see Chr. M. Danoff, *RE* Suppl. ix. 944.

19. Namely 6. 37. 2, on the pine-tree, and (as Lion saw) 2. 22. 3 on rain after snow.

20. For Orestes' seven-cubit corpse (reckoned as 12¼ feet: see ch. 16 n. 46) at 1. 68. 3. Though the chapter summarizes Varro, Gellius comments here in his own name ('arbitramur'), cf. Mercklin 700; *fabulator* is not attested before Seneca but also found at *NA* 2. 29. 2; for the echo of Arist. *GA* 756ᵇ6–7 see ch. 14 n. 33.

21. Vell. Pat. 2. 36. 2, cf. Quint. 10. 1. 101; 10. 2. 17. On Sen. *Contr.* 9. 1. 13 see D. Guilbert OSB, *LEC* 25 (1957) 296–9.

22. Mercklin 651, Kretzschmer 49; cf. Falster, *Mem. obsc.* 198. At 17. 15. 2 'in historia Graeca' conceivably denotes Favorinus' Παντοδαπὴ ἱστορία; one may suspect a blind for Plin. *NH* 25. 51, but how much stood in the lacuna there? Or did Gellius find the report in his Greek source and turn to Pliny for elucidation?

23. *Prima facie*, 'in uetere historia rerum Punicarum' should denote Καρχηδονικά (Falster, loc. cit.); such a work (even when by a Roman emperor, Suet. *Claud.* 42. 2) would be in Greek. There is no knowing what Gellius might have chanced upon; but Peter suggests the source was Coelius (fr. 67, *dub.*), who perhaps found the tale in Silenus of Cale Acte. But Trogus had told it of Hamilcar Rodanus (Justin 21. 6. 6).

Gellius' knowledge of the *annales maximi* is confined to a citation in Verrius Flaccus (4. 5. 6); the annalists who wrote in Greek are represented only by Cato's butt Albinus, for 'Fabii annales' (5. 4. 1) are the Latin version. But several Latin historians from Cato to Sallust appear in the *Nights*:[24] these two are the most frequently cited apart from Claudius Quadrigarius, almost half whose preserved fragments come from Gellius.[25] Coelius Antipater, whom Hadrian exalted above Sallust (*HA Hadr.* 16. 6), is quoted only twice.

At least one explicit quotation is given from each of the seven books in Cato's *Origines*: nearly always, however, Gellius' interest is exclusively linguistic. The only exceptions[26] are fr. 77 Peter = *NA* 2. 28. 6 discussed above, and the story of the military tribune, Q. Caedicius, who led a forlorn hope (fr. 83 P = *NA* 3. 7). Much as he admires Cato, Gellius related the bulk of the story in his own words: he incorporates Cato's military slang *uerruca* 'wart' for a wooded hill,[27] but also writes 'procul dubio' (§ 6), a favourite phrase not attested till long after Cato,[28] and 'demirantur' (§ 12), from a verb hitherto defective.[29] If the famous *sententia* that the troops were to go whence they did not expect to return (Cic. *Tusc.* 1. 101, *Sen.* 75; Sen. *Ep.* 82. 22) has been rightly referred to this narrative by modern scholars, Gellius omits it, writing instead more starkly that they marched out to die (§ 11 'Tribunus et quadringenti ad moriendum proficiscuntur'). But having demonstrated his ability to tell a story—in simpler language than his normal style, but more polished than Cato's—on reaching the climax he copies out verbatim Cato's sublime passage on the hero's miraculous escape and the small fame he won in comparison with Leonidas.

There follows a brief note, a typical Gellian postscript, that Quadrigarius calls the tribune not Caedicius but Laberius; this deepens the pathos of Cato's comment, for so small indeed was the tribune's fame that not even his name was certain.[30] Gellius, however, does not make that point, nor even remark that naming the tribune at all was contrary to Cato's normal practice.

---

24. But not Livy or later authors; the Patavine seer of 15. 18 will ultimately come from his compatriot (cf. Plut. *Caes.* 47; not known to Caes. *BC* 3. 105), but not directly. There is no reason to derive *dexteritas* 'kindness' (13. 17. 1) from Livy 37. 7. 15 (cf. 28. 17. 6)—let alone through misunderstanding as supposed by A. P. MacGregor, *CPh* 77 (1982) 42–8: it is a calque on δεξιότης (e.g. Paus. 7. 7. 5). For disregard of Livy cf. n. 40.

25. Contrast the faint praise at Cic. *Leg.* 1. 6.

26. Apart from *Orig.* fr. 95 P = *Pro Rodiensibus* at 6. 3.

27. Cf. Quint. 8. 3. 48, 8. 6. 14.

28. Affected by Lucretius, but not found in prose before Livy (even 'sine dubio' is no older than Terence); used (Knapp, 'Prepositions' 29) on 11 other occasions in Gellius besides the paraphrase of Accius at 3. 11. 5 (ch. 9 n. 5), paraphrases or quotations from Hyginus (10. 16. 18) and Apollinaris (15. 5. 4), and 'dubio procul' 2. 29. 15 in honour of Ennius' trochees (ch. 11 n. 74). It would be a strange coincidence if all these authors had used the phrase so dear to Gellius in passages adduced for other purposes.

29. See ch. 3 n. 31.

30. Livy's divergent account calls him M. Calpurnius Flamma (*Per.* 17; 22. 60. 11); but all three versions refer to the same incident of 258 BC (Frontin. *Strat.* 1. 5. 15). If the name were not in Cato, Gellius must have said whence he got it.

Comparing two historians' accounts of the same events (e.g. 3. 8. 5; 6. 19. 8; 7. 8. 6) does not make him a critical student of the past.[31]

The other passages of Cato the historian are brief extracts strictly confined to illustrating the word or phrase under discussion; only at 2. 22. 28, where the point at issue is the form *cercius* (Spanish *cierzo*) for what others call *circius*,[32] has Cato a longer say (fr. 93 P), on the mineral wealth of north-eastern Spain and the salt-mountain near Cardona, said to repair its losses.[33] This is not history but marvel-mongering.

L. Calpurnius Piso is praised for his pure and delightful style (7. 9. 1; 11. 14. 1); an unusual construction appears in 15. 29 (fr. 19 P). Asellio is cited six times, only at 1. 13. 10–13 (fr. 8 P) for events. But the most fragments, forty-four,[34] all but one with book-number, come from Claudius Quadrigarius, an authority both historical and linguistic nearly always quoted in his own words. Unreserved admiration of his language is expressed at 9. 13. 4–6: Quadrigarius has narrated T. Manlius' combat with the Gaul in the purest and most vivid manner, with the simple, unadorned sweetness of ancient style, and to such effect that Favorinus felt all the excitement of a spectator on the spot. The 'almost conversational' style that Gellius found inadequate in Gracchus is accepted from a historian (13. 29. 2).[35] When Quadrigarius uses *quin*, in Gellius' own word, 'obscurissime' (*NA* 17. 13. 5),[36] this means, not that he is a bad writer, but that the force of the particle must be traced back to its etymology of *qui* and *ně*. Quadrigarius is also Gellius' chief informant on Roman history, contributing for instance Fabius Cunctator's deference to his son the consul (2. 2. 13 = fr. 57 P),[37] the date of Cannae (5. 17. 5 = fr. 53 P), and the six-hour truce requested by the Samnite commander (1. 25. 6 = fr. 21 P)—refuting Varro's definition of a truce as a few days' peace in the field.

This admiration for Quadrigarius[38] is apparently Gellius' own: although, in a summary catalogue of Roman authors, Fronto declares it to be general knowledge that Quadrigarius wrote attractively (*Eloq.* 1. 2: 'Claudius lepide') he does not allude to him again, nor is he on Marcus' reading-list. We need

---

31. Nor will *NA* 7. 8. 6; 10. 24. 7 count as source-criticism.

32. Probably from a Celtic root meaning 'violent' (E. P. Hamp, *Bulletin of the Board of Celtic Studies* 27 (1976–8) 215–16).

33. The interior of the mountain, on which mining has been concentrated (though attention is now paid mainly to potash), yields clear crystals like those described at Sidon. *Ep.* 9. 12. 1. (Plin. *NH* 31. 80 has been compared, but Tarraconensis, in Sidonius' day, no longer extended to Egelasta, cf. *CIL* ii. 5091.) For the motif of self-renewal cf. Plin. *NH* 31. 73, 77; more reasonably X. *Vect.* 4. 3, 25–7.

34. Including 20 disordered frr. of bk. 1 in 17. 2, but not the story of Valerius Corvinus (n. 10).

35. For Quadrigarius' colloquialism cf. Lebek 261.

36. See ch. 10 nn. 57–8.

37. Where Fabius is wrongly made proconsul instead of legate; simple anachronism? or from Cn. Mallius Maximus' defence in 103 BC (Holford-Strevens, 'Five Notes' 143)?

38. Though Varro's learning and authority are greater (10. 1. 4).

not doubt that, as the book-numbers suggest, most of Gellius' quotations are direct.

Fronto's next words are 'Antias inuenuste'; Gellius' concurrence is implicit in the lack of long quotations. Valerius Antias makes only nine appearances, five for archaic word-forms and four for substance, these last always in disagreement with other authorities. Nor are all the references first-hand: at 6. 9. 12 a quotation from book 22 is explicitly copied from Probus; suspicion must therefore fall on the other two quotations in this chapter, despite their book-numbers.[39] Gellius perhaps did not struggle through seventy-five books by a poor stylist; that he also thought him a poor historian is suggested by 6. 19. 8, where his version of events is said to conflict with documentary evidence and the authority of ancient writers.[40] All the same, he is cited, and is probably the source for *NA* 9. 11, bestowing on a Valerius' exploit the same *exornatio* that Quadrigarius had on Torquatus'.[41] The initial account of the Gaul's enormous stature, his overweening arrogance, and the unostentatious courage of the Roman would enhance the glorious deed; there is no disproof in their absence from Livy, who does not repeat in 7. 26 the motifs of 7. 10. 7–8, and Dionysius, who was used to pruning Antias' tales about Valerii.[42] Gellius, wishing to present the two stories as a pair, was happy to let Quadrigarius speak for himself, but rather than reproduce Antias' unpleasing prose, exhibited his own facility for narrative.

Latest among the cited historians—as opposed to chronographers and excerptors—is Sallust, 'primus Romana Crispus in historia', as Martial calls him (14. 191. 2) in the very next epigram after that on Livy. Quintilian concurred, despite reservations about the archaism that in the second century would make Sallust a general favourite.[43] Fronto's correspondence is full of references and quotations; Sallust, a close follower of Cato, shares his supremacy in the choice of words (*Ep. M. Caes.* 4. 3. 2), skilful at palliating the obscure or obscene (*Orat.* 19, *Eloq.* 5. 3, cf. ibid. 3. 1), and powerful in description (*Ep. M. Ant.* 3. 1).[44] But well as these virtues beseem

---

39. But the source-critics' assumption that at 7. 7. 6 he is cited only through Sabinus seems unsafe: the phrase 'ut in Antiatis historia scriptum est' recalls 3. 8. 4, where knowledge of his version cannot be owed to the author next cited, Quadrigarius. (For Antias' presence in this chapter see too Peter, *HRR* i, pp. cccxxx f.)

40. Typically, Gellius does not remark that Antias' version was followed by Livy.

41. Quadrigarius will have related the later story, and Antias the earlier, in few words: the former hardly had room for two set pieces on a like theme in a book running from the sack of Rome to at least the Caudine Forks, the latter would not wish to anticipate the splendour of Valerius' achievement.

42. See *Ant.* 15. 1; Peter, *HRR* i, p. cccxxvii.

43. Cf. n. 4. If the *Epistulae ad Caesarem senem* were composed in this age, 'Sallustian' style no longer seemed incongruous to their genre (see Fraenkel, *Kl. Beit.* ii. 132, 136–7; contrast the pre-Quintilianic *inuectiua in Ciceronem*).

44. One ex. (§ 8) is *Jug.* 44 on Metellus' restoration of discipline to an army out of control, applied at *Ver.* 2. 1. 22–3, *Princ. Hist.* 2. 12–13 to Verus' alleged emulation. Cf. Tac. *A.* 4. 20. 2; 'comperior' Gell. 3. 3. 1; Apul. 6× (at *Apol.* 37. 3 from *Jug.* 108. 3).

Ventidius' speech-writer,[45] Fronto, in praising the stylist, disregards the historian.

Gellius occasionally uses Sallust's information (10. 7. 1, the length of the Danube; 16. 10. 14, 16, Marius' enrolment of the *capite censi*), but is mainly interested in his language: he is one of his regular authorities (e.g. for *obnoxius* 6. 17. 7–8, *metus* with objective genitive 9. 12. 14);[46] since he is 'proprietatum in uerbis retinentissimus' (10. 20. 10), his putting *lex* for *priuilegium* was a reasonable concession to normal usage, not mere carelessness. His malevolent detractors (4. 15; 10. 26) dislike his 'elegantia orationis' and zeal for forging new words; he is also a master of concision (3. 1. 6), hence (says Favorinus) cannot have used 'corpus animumque' at *Cat.* 11. 3 as a poetical periphrasis for 'hominem'. This conversation turns on the assertion that avarice unmans body and mind; Favorinus asking how it can thus affect the body, one participant explains that it drives a man to sedentary and enfeebling occupations. An objection having been countered, Favorinus concludes that either his companion is right or Sallust, 'odio auaritiae',[47] has exaggerated the case against it.

In fact Sallust is thinking of effeminate luxury; no happier is Castricius' criticism in *NA* 2. 27 of *Hist.* 1, fr. 88 Maur. (pp. 65–6), yet another text deemed inferior to its Greek original. Marache, having accused Castricius of political motivation, supposes that Gellius disapproved of Sallust because, for all his high moral tone, he had been caught in adultery with Milo's wife, soundly thrashed, and made to purchase his release (17. 18). But moralists exposed are a stock of mirth, as are persons found in the wrong bed;[48] other writers' comments that Sallust's life invalidated his judgements[49] have no echo in Gellius. Sallust was no more diminished in his eyes by this alleged adventure than the elder Scipio by that of 7. 8. 5,[50] or Demosthenes and Cicero by their foibles; it is bad literary taste, not a life discordant with

---

45. *Ver.* 2. 1. 12 (§ 7 v. d. H.).

46. But at 11. 15. 7 he does not record 'uitabundus classem hostium' (*Hist.* 3. 37 Maur.) For the construction see Kühner–Stegmann i. 260, Pianezzola 99–103, 135, 180.

47. Cf. G. 44 (= J. 4. 6. 14): the illogical *condictio furtiua*, requiring the thief to 'give' what he did not legally own to the person who had not ceased to do so, was instituted 'odio furum'; Cass. Dio, fr. 87. 2: the Romans punished even the unconvicted suspects in the Vestal scandal of 114 BC μίσει τοῦ συμβεβηκότος.

48. Even for the staid Quintilian (6. 3. 87); and note the colloquial ring of Gellius' 'loris bene caesum'.

49. So Lact. *Inst.* 2. 12. 12–14 (contrasting *Cat.* 4. 11 with Sallust's life), Symm. *Ep.* 5. 68. 2 (offended by his scorn for hunting); cf. Macr. *Sat.* 3. 13. 9 (but see Syme, *Sallust* 283 on confusion with Augustus' friend). Cass. Dio 43. 9. 3 accuses Sallust of rapacity as proconsul of Africa Nova in 46–45 BC, after writing so pungently against extortioners; here it is the works that damn the life, though Sallust did not take up writing till his political career was over. Since Sallust supported Milo's enemy Clodius, Varro had a motive for defaming him (a point lost on Gellius, who emphasizes Varro's *fides*), and a fling with the notorious Fausta might be believed of any man. Cf. Syme, op. cit. 26–7, 278–80; for other such tales see Val. Max. 6. 1. 13. (B. Katz, *C&M* 36 (1985) 127–52 identifies the eponym of Varro's *Pius aut de pace* as Magnus Pius, alias Sex. Pompeius, the son of Varro's friend and Sallust's target; cf. Lenaeus test. 4 Fun.)

50. Observe the unbounded admiration in 4. 18; 6. 1; 12. 8. 1.

precept, that makes Seneca unsuitable for educating youth (p. 205). In sexual matters, Gellius was a man of the world.

The critics against whom Sallust is defended, including Pollio (10. 26. 1), are concerned not with veracity but with style; in 2. 27, where he is not defended, the question is not whether Sertorius was such a man as Sallust makes him, but whether any man could be. It belongs to ethics on the ancient view, to psychology on ours, but not to history, for which Gellius cares little.

His interest in chronology is amateurish. By switching sources in 17. 21. 16, 19 he sets the outbreak of the Peloponnesian War (431 BC) in AUC 323, on Varro's chronology, but the installation of the Thirty (404 BC) in AUC 347, on Nepos'; at § 44 he dates the first divorce in Rome, that by Sp. Carvilius Ruga of a loved but sterile wife, to AUC 519, but at 4. 3. 2 to AUC 523—yet with the consuls of 227 BC, which is AUC 527 on Varro's system, 526 in the Capitoline era, but not 523 by any reckoning known to either Dionysius (*Ant.* 1. 74) or ourselves.[51] At § 3 he forgets that, as he himself had recorded in 3. 11, some writers made Hesiod older than Homer. Self-interpolation at § 48 puts the embassy of 155 BC before the heyday of Ennius, Caecilius, and Terence. At 3. 4. 2 the statement that Scipio was under forty when prosecuted by the tribune Claudius Asellus,[52] though purporting to be established fact, is simply false.[53]

Such information as Gellius offers on the past is derived in the main not from historians but from antiquarians, miscellanists, and lawyers. It is neither the sweep of events that matters, nor their deeper causes and significance,[54] but isolated facts, connected by nothing but their relative dates to avoid a social gaffe, and proffered for their piquancy, or at most to cap another man's story and adorn a speech with an *exemplum*. Truth hardly matters: Gellius' words at 7. 8. 5 on the scabrous tale about the elder Scipio, 'uerone an falso incertum, fama tamen', are a world away from the deadly Tacitean *incertum an*. It is amusing, and a fragment of Naevius can be hung on it; beyond that

---

51. This was not the first divorce, nor does Gellius' source Ser. Sulpicius say it was (Watson, *Tijdschr.* 33 (1965) 38–50, *Rome of the XII Tables* 32–4). The event is firmly dated by year of the City, Olympiad, and consuls to 231 BC (D.H. 2. 35. 7), which on Varro's chronology is AUC 523, on Nepos' 520, but 519 on none we know; Leuze, 'Synchr. Kap.' 258–63 proposes a solution that raises further problems. Carvilius was consul in 234 and 228. Other accounts augment confusion: Val. Max. 2. 1. 4 has AUC 150 (500 Kempf, *cl* > *d*); Plut. *Comp. Thes. Rom.* 6. 4, *Comp. Lyc. Num.* 3. 7 gives AUC 230 (sc. under Tarquin the Proud, an appropriate season for moral laxity; according to the second passage, under that king Thalaea Pinari became the first woman in Rome to quarrel with her mother-in-law); Tert. *Apol.* 6. 6, *Monog.* 9. 8 allows the City pagans 600 years before their first divorce.

52. Hence (Gellius had thought) would not have been in the habit of shaving; see Plin. *NH* 7. 211, Marquart 600–1, A. Mau, *RE* iii. 33.

53. Scipio was born in 185 BC (rather than 184; cf. Astin, *Scipio* 246–7), Asellus was tribune in 140 BC; 'minorem' is guaranteed by the context, which requires the age not yet attained. Jac. Gronovius' *L*, translated by Walterstern, corrects the author.

54. The significance of the Second Punic War (10. 27. 2) was a commonplace (e.g. Polyb. 1. 3. 7; 15. 9. 5, Lucr. 3. 836–7).

who cares? It amused the Roman of the second century AD to hear that King Romulus stayed sober at a party[55] as it amuses us to hear that King Alfred burnt the cakes; but whereas we wish to know the truth about King Alfred and even King Arthur, the Roman of Gellius' day wanted nothing but the story, whether about Romulus or even Scipio. Only in Greek was there a market for anything more; the Latins read and relished Suetonius, who does not aim at writing history, but abounds in anecdotes, in letters, and in jokes. Gellius too abounds in anecdotes, is happy to offer letters (mostly fictitious),[56] and enjoys good jokes: Hannibal telling Antiochus that his richly bedizened army will be enough for the Romans despite their greed (5. 5. 5), the heckler's apt riposte to Demosthenes (11. 9. 1), Demosthenes' own jest upon the same shady transaction (ibid. § 2), and Cicero's defence of his double dealing (12. 12).[57]

Gellius' Attitude to Antiquity

Admiration for the stern and sturdy virtue of old Rome, abundantly attested in Gellius, is a constant theme in Roman writing. It might encourage—or at least be used to justify—imitation of her speech; thus Favorinus, rebuking the inopportune archaizer, anticipates his defence that he admires antiquity because it was honourable and good and sober and restrained: 'Then live by the ways of the past, but speak in the words of the present.'[58] However, this admiration for the frugal elders had been shared by generations that would no sooner have dreamt of speaking than of living like them; even Seneca, who indulges in self-denial (*Ep.* 108. 15–16) and takes a trip to the country with only one cart-load of slaves (*Ep.* 87. 2),[59] is as free with the *exempla* of the ancients as with the tenets of the philosophers, but is the dearest foe of antiquarian writing. To be sure, rich men under the Antonines wore their wealth with less vulgarity of ostentation than the freedmen of Claudius or the boon companions of Nero; but they had no wish to see Fabricius rise from the dead and expel them from the Senate for owning ten pounds of silverware (*NA* 4. 8. 7; 17. 21. 39), or to curtail the pleasures of their table in accordance

---

55. *NA* 11. 14. 2 = Piso fr. 8 P. He drank little because he had affairs of state to ponder in the morning; when someone said that wine would be cheap if everyone followed his example, he replied that on the contrary it would be dear, since he had drunk as much as he wanted.

56. Augustus' to his adopted son C. Caesar at 15. 7. 2 is undoubtedly genuine; but Gellius has drawn on a collection of letters fathered on members of the Macedonian royal family (9. 3. 13. 4, 20. 5). The consuls' letter to Pyrrhus in 3. 8. 8 comes from Quadrigarius. Public demand for letters by historical or imaginary persons may be gauged from the proliferation of such artefacts, whose authors range from pseudo-Phalaris to Alciphron.

57. See pp. 152, 176; for other exx. see Berthold 68–9.

58. *NA* 1. 10. 3; cf. pp. 87, 165.

59. Cf. *Ep.* 123. 1–2; such 'non incompta frugalitas' (*Ep.* 5. 5) reminds us that Fabricius and M'. Curius are not to be equated with the ragged *hidalgos* of Spain or the clog and moccassin nobility of Poland and Hungary (Gelzer 23 n. 166).

with a sumptuary law like those enacted in the late Republic (*NA* 2. 24).[60] If neverthelesss they enjoyed hearing such things read as they munched their thrushes and their truffles, it was certainly not because their desire to imitate antiquity was any more serious than Alfius' to be a countryman;[61] it is improbable that they ever felt any guilt about their wealth, but if they did, these tales did not implant such feelings, but rather assuaged them.[62] Unlike those moral orators who had refused the adornments of art in supposed imitation of the ancients, the mannerists neither rejected art nor revived the archaic style, but tricked out their Brass Age diction with antique words. Beyond a municipal moralism already fashionable under Vespasian there was no desire to emulate the early Romans, only a purely passive admiration, as of Ennius' poetry or the temples at Anagnia, whose like one would not write or build.

Nor did interest in the older literature instil any genuine sympathy for the culture that produced it: Gellius is firm that the early comedy, though enjoyable in itself, falls sadly short of its Greek originals (2. 23). Such a judgement would be impossible for a taste that genuinely preferred the primitive gusto of a society in the ascendant to the long-refined sophistication of one on the decline; but Antonine culture, itself the product of long sophistication and sliding towards decline, could hardly fail to value Menandrean simplicity and fidelity to life above the bombast and vulgarity that pleased the early Roman groundlings.[63] Not even respect for antique morality revived the political republicanism that had lasted for over a century after Actium. The sturdy independence of Laberius and Labeo is not admired; in the former it is called 'maledicentia et adrogantia' (17. 14. 2), in the latter seen through the eyes of his pliant rival Capito as 'libertas quaedam nimia atque uecors' (13. 12. 2).[64] Even thus had Valerius Maximus treated

60. At 11. 5. 2 Cato, having stated that of old horses cost more than cooks, continues 'poeticae artis honos non erat'; Gellius would no more wish such times to return than the rude days of 15. 11. 3.

61. Tac. *Dial.* 8. 4, 'diuitiae et opes, quas facilius inuenies qui uituperet quam qui fastidiat'; cf. Fav. fr. 96 v 24–8 B; Griffin 312.

62. Cf. those who applauded noble sentiments in the theatre (Sen. *Ep.* 108. 8–9, see Plaut. *Rud.* 1249–53) or paid a railing Cynic, and the *jeunesse dorée* who declaimed on the virtues of the poor and the vices of the rich (Russell, *GD* 27–30). Not only the oppressed and their sympathizers enjoy tales in which the virtuous underdog prevails; others relish the thought that 'die Gerechtigkeit ist nur auf der Bühne'.

63. Why, then, did it not appreciate these virtues in the half-Menander Terence? Because in language he was only a half-Plautus; but what was missed in Terence was not sought in Menander.

64. *Maledicentia* is also ascribed to Naevius (3. 2. 16), but free speech was not for one of low birth; Laberius was an *eques Romanus*. Labeo is not admired for adhering to ancient punctilio against common sense (§§ 7–8)—or as he saw it, defending established law against encroachment —even though the rule was laid down by Varro in the very book cited by Gellius in the next chapter to settle a similar question of procedure: ancient practice is to be studied because it is ancient, but adopted only if it is useful.

'libere dicta aut facta' with reserve or disapproval (6. 2. 1–12);[65] the same
deference to authority that admires the arrogance of the elder Scipio (*NA* 4.
18)[66] and Metellus Numidicus (7. 11) when challenged by low-born tribunes
is as readily shown to the *dictator perpetuus* and the emperor, with no
Republican abhorrence for living at one man's nod.

On the other hand, at 8. 15 Gellius recounted Caesar's humiliation of
Laberius and the latter's riposte: the chapter is reproduced by Macrobius
(*Sat.* 2. 7. 1–8). Unfortunately, since neither 'sed potestas non solum si inuitet
sed et si supplicet cogit' (§ 2) nor 'notantes impotentiam eius hac dicacitate
lapidatam' (§ 5) can safely be ascribed to Gellius,[67] we cannot tell whether
he portrayed Caesar in darker colours than at 17. 14. 2.[68] Nowhere do the
Nights show preference between Caesar and Pompey; even the younger
Cato's suicide in 13. 20 is purely a cold fact with no hint of *nobile letum*.[69] At
4. 10. 8 Gellius impartially recounts Cato's filibuster in defiance of the consul
Caesar in 59 BC. Sallust had called them the two outstanding men of their
day (*Cat.* 53. 6); so were the elder Cato and the elder Scipio in the early
second century BC, whom not only Gellius but Cicero and Seneca (*Ep.* 87. 9)
can equally admire. Gellius loves rather to honour great men than to judge
their principles. Numidicus' disdain for a Marian tribune is a model of not
descending to one's opponents' level (7. 11. 1), but the nobly born and
eloquent *popularis* C. Gracchus is treated with respect. His oratory may be
criticized, but his moral character is extolled (15. 12); of his political activities
not a word is said in praise or blame. It is the speeches themselves that
matter: for all the interest taken in their context, they might as well have
been declamations from the schools.[70] The Republic afforded opportunities
for oratory, and for displays of *magnitudo animi*, but as a political system it
means nothing to Gellius for good or ill except a body of constitutional law
and practice (3. 18; 4. 10; 14. 7; 15. 27), some of it still theoretically in
force.[71] He can admire the second century BC for its language and its *uirtus*,
but does not understand its principles: that Cato could be an enemy of

---

65. The Greek *exempla* that follow (ext. 1–3) are narrated with more sympathy: no Roman
need respect foreign kings or tyrants.

66. So already the Scipios' client Polybius (23. 14. 2), followed by other narrators; for
republican sentiment see D.Sic. 29. 21 *init.*, Liv. 38. 50. 8–9.

67. Of the two comments, the former seems too concise for Gellius, and *lapidare* as used in the
latter is not found till the 4th c.

68. For the events, see G. Hoffmann, *RhM*[2] 39 (1884) 471–6, J. Schwarz, *REA* 50 (1948)
264–71, Cic. *Fam.* 12. 18. 2 with Shackleton Bailey ad loc. (edn. ii. 365), Pollio ibid. 10. 32. 2.
Laberius, who had stood up to Clodius (Macr. *Sat.* 2. 6. 6), gave Cicero as good as he got (ibid.
2. 3. 10; 7. 3. 8); at *NA* 10. 17. 3; 16. 7. 12 Gellius ignores the political allusions (cf. Wiseman,
Catullus 188 nn. 19–20).

69. Cassius appears once, coming to grief after seizing the ill-fated *equus Seianus* (3. 9. 5),
Brutus never.

70. Other than at 6. 3. 1–7, no doubt from Cato's narrative in *Origines* leading up to the
speech.

71. The rules on consular seniority in 2. 15 are imperial, not Republican (not even § 8): see L.
R. Taylor and T. R. S. Broughton, *MAAR* 19 (1949) 3–14, eid. *Historia* 17 (1968) 168–72. See
FV 197–9; *Lex. Malac.* 56; D. Nörr in Watson (ed.) 240–1.

Scipio's is not beyond his comprehension, but he cannot see, in tales he lovingly relates of the latter's high-handedness, that it was precisely such arrogant impatience with convention and even law that angered the former; let alone that the conflict between individual ambition and oligarchic levelling, like the relentless pursuit of personal feuds in political trials, was an early symptom of the tensions that were to rend the ruling class. Such are the limitations of his view, surprising at first in so eager a student of Sallust; but it was not for history that he read the great historian.[72]

72. The same is true of Fronto (p. 186; Cova 79–82); but cf. Gran. Lic. 36. 31 'nam Sallustium non ut historicum aiunt, sed ut oratorem legendum' (since he goes beyond bare narrative), Justin, 38. 3. 11 (Trogus fr. 152 Seel); Syme, *Sallust* 289; Steinmetz 139–45.

Chapter 14

Philosophy

GELLIUS' attitude to philosophy is expressed in two verses from early Latin tragedy: one by Ennius, whose Neoptolemus declares (*Sc.* 95 J) 'I must philosophize, but briefly; to be thorough I have no mind',[1] quoted with approval to conclude a doxography on sound (5. 15. 9) and mentioned again after one on sight (5. 16. 5); the other by Pacuvius (v. 348 R), 'I hate the man of dastard deeds and philosophic words', which Gellius' philosopher-friend Macedo had recommended for inscription on all temple-doors (13. 8. 4). Again and again Gellius dismisses all philosophy not directed to improving human life as a waste of time, at best to be dabbled in, not dwelt on, and inveighs against philosophers whose beards and cloaks and moral saws are belied by their behaviour, or who use philosophy as a pretext for their vanity and vices. Ennius, old Cato, Numidicus, even Aesop, are at least as good as the best philosophers in moral guidance;[2] and too great an interest in the niceties of logic will lead one onto the Sirens' rocks.[3]

Yet Seneca or Epictetus would have damned as useless most of the learned or curious information that Gellius dispenses; and his warning that logic is perilous to one who has overcome initial repugnance and discovered the pleasures of its study recalls his assertion that tall stories entrap the intelligent and inquiring mind (10. 12. 4), which does not prevent his purveying them. Optics and musical theory, too, as Varro had said, seem boring and pointless at the outset, but afterwards turn out to be pleasant and useful (16. 18. 6); no warning is appended, and their utility is not explained. Despite his ethical pose, if Gellius takes less notice of dialectic and natural science, this is less from disapproval than incomprehension: they were not beneath his cognizance but above his head. Even the most philhellenic of Romans found it

---

1. Both Cicero (who held that one should know the philosophers' precepts but live by civil custom, *Epp.* fr. VIII. 4 Watt) and Gellius so interpret 'omnino haud placet' (see ch. 1 n. 63), not 'I do not like it at all'. At *NA* 5. 16. 5 'non diutius muginandum' confirms 'muginamur' (Politian, *Misc. II*, ch. 11, p. 24; Popma, edn. of Varro 442 = i. 337 *ed. Bip.*) at Plin. *NH* pr. 18 (cf. Dr Jean Chiflet the Elder *ap.* Dalecampius, cll. Cic. *Att.* 16. 12).

2. e.g. 2. 29. 18–19; 7. 11. 1 (cf. Fronto, *Ep. M. Caes.* 3. 3. 2); 12. 4. 2; 13. 24. 2; cf. 'Quint.' *Decl.* 268. 7–8, *Anth. Lat.* 243 ShB (Flor. *Carm.* 8. 1–3 M–J); a Greek riposte: Epict. 3. 8. 7. On immoral philosophers Cic. *Tusc.* 2. 11, Nep. fr. 39 Marshall, Sen. *Exhort.* fr. 18 Haase (not that Greeks are silent); they abounded under Marcus (Cass. Dio 71. 35. 2, cf. P. A. Brunt, *JRS* 64 (1974) 12).

3. *NA* 16. 8. 15–17. Beloe compares Sen. *Ep.* 111. 5 on the insidious charm of sophisms; see too Quint. 1. 7. 35 on grammar.

hard to follow the Greeks in all their subtleties, and the patriot in him rebelled against the attempt: Rome had conquered them without such arts, and Roman morality had nothing to learn from Greek examples. The theme of the hypocrite is all the more congenial: Gellius presents no fewer than three specimens (1. 2; 9. 2; 15. 2). But many Athenians would have directed like strictures at Herodes, and some at Peregrinus.

Furthermore, not even sound morality saves Seneca from proscription for his modernistic taste; and although Gellius does not, like Fronto or Aelius Aristeides, openly couch a lance for rhetoric against philosophy, he cites Favorinus' judgement on Lysias and Plato, which tells in the orator's favour, and relates Demosthenes' abandonment of Plato for Callistratus, of philosophy for rhetoric.[4] Even the assertions that Latin poets and orators can match the best of Greek philosophers express, besides national pride, a defence of literary culture against the exclusive claims of philosophy. Ever since Isocrates' dispute with Plato, most educated men had taken the former's side against a view that could appeal only to a would-be élite within the élite; Gellius was at least more sympathetic to philosophy than Fronto, and not less than many of his readers. He belongs to no school; he can even be fair, for a while, to Epicurus. For the metaphysical and the mystical he has neither taste nor aptitude; neither is he an intellectual anti-intellectual, like the contemporary Sceptic philosophers and Empiric doctors.[5] He readily cites tenets and more readily tells stories; Platonic dialogue and Stoico-Cynic preaching afforded literary devices.[6]

Sages, Pythagoreans, and Other Presocratics

Of the seven sages who constitute one of Varro's more trivial septets (3. 10. 16), Chilo contributes a case of conscience and a piece of worldly wisdom (1. 3), Bias the Bachelor's Dilemma (5. 11), and Solon laws on stasis (2. 12) and theft (11. 18. 5); his code is misdated to the thirty-third year of the elder Tarquin's reign (17. 21. 4). Periander appears only as Arion's patron (16. 19).

The mid first century BC saw not only a return from Academic scepticism to Platonism, but a revival of interest in the real or pretended doctrines of Pythagoras, which often foreshadowed Plato's. This interest continued: Apollonius of Tyana and Nicomachus of Gerasa wrote his life; Plutarch abounds in references; Apuleius devotes *Flor.* 15 to him, noting that Plato

---

4. *NA* 3. 13, from Hermippus, cited at Plut. *Dem.* 5. 7 for the benefit Demosthenes' oratory derived from Plato (but see Austin on Quint. 12. 2. 22).

5. Cf. Annas–Barnes 16–17; Frede, *Essays* 243–60; and see W. R. Schoedel, *JTS*[2] 35 (1984) 31–49 on the attraction of this approach for such Christians as Irenaeus.

6. See p. 198, Hirzel 259–60, Marache, *AFLT* Pallas 1 (1953) 84–95, edn. i, pp. xxxi–xxxvi (but the concept of 'the diatribe' is questionable). Despite Dewaule's and Gassner's studies, the philosophical chapters have received little attention.

generally 'pythagorissat' (§ 26); he is regularly named in illustrious company.[7]

Gellius too pays tribute, but to the mathematician and the moralist, not the magician or the speculator. In 1. 1 Plutarch relates how Pythagoras calculated Heracles' human height: since the running-track at Olympia was 600 of his feet in length, and those in other cities, though all reckoned at 600 feet, were shorter than the Olympic prototype, Heracles' foot was longer than common mortals' in proportion as the Olympic stade exceeded others; but since there was a settled ratio between length of foot and height of body, he was also taller than other people in the proportion just established. Read in the light of Vitruvius 3. 1. 2, 7 (foot : stature :: 1 : 6), this makes Heracles' height 1.9227 m, striking but not superhuman,[8] which suits well with the ancients' unquestioning belief in the heroes' historicity, if supernatural tales were discounted.[9] In 1. 9. 1–8 Taurus describes the discipline imposed by Pythagoras on his pupils; his account, from a late source, differs from others, themselves inconsistent.[10] At 1. 20. 6 Pythagoras makes the cube of three represent the moon's orbit of twenty-seven days;[11] no deep mystery.

In 4. 11 Gellius denies, on Aristotle's and Aristoxenus' authority, that the Pythagoreans were vegetarians or abstained from eating beans; the latter belief is ascribed to misunderstanding of Empedocles' line 'Wretches, all-wretched, keep your hands from beans' (31 B 141 DK), in which 'beans' allegedly stood for the testicles. Aristotle indeed is reported (fr. 195 Rose) to have adduced the resemblance of *Vicia faba* to the genitals as one among many possible explanations; yet more are found in other sources.[12] The short step from interpretation to reinterpretation was easy for one anxious like Aristoxenus—who declares (fr. 25 Wehrli) that Pythagoras thought beans excellent food, being emollient and diuretic—to rescue the Pythagoreans' memory from the comic picture of ragged and superstitious starvelings.[13] This tendency will have appealed to Gellius, who could take for granted the

---

7. Particularly in the triad Pythagoras, Socrates, Plato (Plut. *Mor.* [2 C], 331 A, Fav. fr. 95. 82 B, Apul. *Soc.* 22); but he appears in several other groupings with such men as Homer, Solon, Heracleitus, Anaxagoras, Archytas, Plato, and Chrysippus.

8. Apollod. *Bibl.* 2. 4. 9 makes Heracles six foot tall, Herodorus (*FGrH* 31 F 19) seven; cf. Sol. 1. 88 with Salmasius i. 42^bB–D. (He is μορφὰν βραχύς beside Antaeus at Pi. *I.* 3–4. 71, an ode in praise of an ill-favoured victor; the two-cubit footprint by the Dnestr, Hdt. 4. 82, would imply a height of 18 feet; Luc. *VH* 1. 7 is a joke. For the competing conceptions of heroes as human and superhuman in stature see S. Eitrem, *SO* 8 (1929) 53–6; the seven-cubit Orestes appears at *NA* 3. 10. 11.) Pythagoras gave Heracles 4.89 cm more than the six Byzantine feet allotted Jesus Christ by Epiphanius Monachus, *De uita B. Virg.* 15 (PG 120, 204 C; only 5¼ feet Nicephorus Callistus, *Eccl. hist.* 1. 40 = PG 145. 748 C; Mr Joseph Rykwert (pers. comm.) adduces the six-foot *mensura Christi* in the basilica of St John Lateran).

9. Veyne 52–3.

10. See Hosius ad loc., Gassner 224–31. Burkert 192–208 (on §§ 4–5, p. 193 n. 6).

11. Pythagoras rounded down (cf. Cens. 11. 11), Aristarchus up (*NA* 3. 10. 6, cf. p. 227; 'integris' is wrong). The sidereal month lasts 27 d. 7 h. 43 m. 11.5 s.; Thysius gives ancient estimates.

12. See Guthrie i. 184–5, Burkert 183–5, André, *Alim.* 228 n. 2.

13. Burkert 200–1; Wehrli, edn. 55.

similar *religio* constraining the *flamen Dialis* (10. 15. 12) but in matters of human determination kept his feet firmly planted on the ground: a warning against sexual indulgence made far more sense than a prohibition on eating the harmless bean. Yet his overriding concern was to correct a vulgar error with a curious fact; in § 14 he happily enumerates the lesser-known transmigrations of Pythagoras' soul.

Beyond these chapters we have only Plato's purchase of Pythagorean books (3. 17), and Archytas' aerodynamic wooden dove (10. 12. 9–10). Archytas—a friend of Aristoxenus' father—represented the highest point of Pythagorean science; that was of interest to Gellius, not the tetractys and the arcane wisdom. The only other Pythagoreans mentioned are Philolaus as the source of the books that Plato bought,[14] and Xenophilus as Aristoxenus' informant (4. 11. 7). All in all, Gellius did not pay the sect the same attention that it received from many of his contemporaries.

Gellius implausibly claims Heracleitus' famous sentence (fr. 16 Marcovich, DK 22 B 40) 'Much learning does not impart intelligence' for a lifelong motto (pr. 12); he alludes to it again at 14. 6. 5. Other remarks about pre-Socratics are biographical: Anaxagoras and Prodicus taught Euripides physics (15. 20. 4), Protagoras was a bearer till Democritus, seeing how scientifically he had disposed his burden, persuaded him to be his pupil (5. 3), but became a sophist who charged huge fees (cf. Plat. *Meno* 91 D) for teaching how to make the worse cause seem the better (§ 7, cf. Arist. *Rhet.* 1402^{a}24–6) till he was outwitted by Euathlus (5. 10). Democritus features in three other chapters: his alleged self-blinding is recounted at 10. 17, and two spurious works are cited. Whereas in 10. 12 Gellius refuses to believe that Democritus could write such rubbish,[15] at 4. 13. 3, apparently accepting that the aulos cures adder-bites (for a like report from Theophrastus see p. 200), he does not question authenticity. At 19. 2. 8 he credits Hippocrates with a saying normally ascribed to Democritus (DK 68 B 32 and n.), that sexual intercourse is a minor epilepsy.

Socrates

At 12. 9. 6 Socrates holds it better to be wronged than to wrong (cf. pp. 71, 198); at 14. 6. 5 he admires the verse Hom. *Od.* 4. 392 (cf. p. 29); at 19. 2. 9 he declares (another doxographic commonplace) that whereas others live to eat, he eats to live. His manner of exposing the sophists is employed against ignorant grammarians by Favorinus (4. 1. lemma) and Apollinaris (18. 4. 1). He appears in the chronography (17. 21. 18–19) and in various anecdotes,

14. 'Tris Philolai Pythagorici libros' § 1 may denote the author, not as in the original story the owner (Burkert 223–5). Cf. Riginos 169–74.
15. For Gellius' use of Pliny here see pp. 121–2. He misinterprets Plin. *NH* 28. 112 as indicating a separate book (ch. 9 n. 39). For the forgery cf. Speyer 132–3. R. Burton recalls those 'absurd and insolent fictions' in the preface of 'Democritus Junior to the Reader' (*Anat. Mel.* i. 15 Jackson).

two about his unhappy marriage (1. 17. 1; 8. 11); at 15. 20. 4 he is Euripides'
teacher in ethics, but when reporting in § 6 that the poet had two wives at
once, Gellius does not record the similar fable about the philosopher.

Plato

Plato, like other philosophers, often features in passing references and trivial
stories: he goes to Syracuse (17. 21. 28), buys Pythagorean books (3. 17. 1–2)
and is accused of plagiarism (ibid. §§ 4–5); Demosthenes deserts him for
Callistratus (3. 13). He is included in derivative doxographies on sound,
sight, and pleasure (5. 15. 7; 5. 16. 4; 9. 5. 7). His dialogues are praised:
'librum illum diuinum' of *Phaedo* (2. 18. 2), 'Timaeum nobilem illum
dialogum' (3. 17. 5), 'libro suo illi incluto' of *Protagoras* (5. 3. 1), 'inclito illi
operi' of *Republic* (14. 3. 3); but there is no further reference to *Protagoras*,
Phaedo is cited only through Chrysippus (7. 1. 6), *Republic* only for the sexual
prescriptions cheerfully discussed at Saturnalia (18. 2. 8).[16] Two of the
Timaeus passages adduced by Gellius' editors appear in the doxographies, the
anatomical assertions in 17. 11. 1 are reported at best from Erasistratus,[17]
and the statement in Favorinus' show-declamation at 17. 12. 3 that
according to Plato the patient who recovered from a quartan fever was all the
healthier afterwards, which is not said at *Tim.* 86 A, represents the licence of
the genre.[18] Perhaps Taurus reserved *Timaeus* (and his commentary) for the
more advanced students.

At 19. 9. 9 Julianus recalls a story that Socrates covered his head with his
cloak in some indelicate conversation; the loose and vague allusion to
Phaedrus 237 A (where Socrates is about to improve on Lysias' erotic *suasoria*)
makes a light irony not unlike Julianus' seem mere prudery. *Parmenides* 156 D
is cited by Taurus at 7. 13. 10–11 for the concept of instantaneity; the
examples in Gellius' chapter tell against direct use. Despite Taurus'
complaint that some students demanded to read *Phaedrus* or *Symposium* for the
wrong reasons (1. 9. 9, cf. p. 67); *Symposium* was read (17. 20) and
Gellius ignored Alcibiades to concentrate not on substance but on style and
even translate a passage; the same exercise was attempted in 8. 8.

At 15. 2. 3 a young man from Crete, on his own showing eloquent and a
Platonist, but in fact a drunken sot, justifies his inebriation on the ground
that Plato, in his *Laws*, had praised that condition as useful for good and

16. Fronto knows the context of the *Phaedo* passage (p. 175). For the down-to-earth view of
Guardians' sex-life cf. Epict. 2. 4. 8–10, fr. 15; Luc. *Symp.* 39, *V. Auct.* 17, *Fug.* 18.

17. See p. 210, cf. ch. 15 n. 56.

18. Fr. 2 B with n. [Hipp.] *Hebd.* 28 Toul states that those who recover from quartan fever do
not succumb again; at *Epid. I* 24 (i. 200 Kühlewein) the quartan is said to cure other maladies
(Gal. xviiA. 364 Kühn specifies epilepsy). Oiselius' tale that Plato was all the better for a
quartan comes from Ficinus' *Vita*, elaborating silly anecdotes from late antiquity (Riginos 121–3,
cf. Huit i. 206–7).

brave men, an 'ignitabulum' for intellect and virtue.[19] Gellius does not shame him as Herodes shamed the pseudo-Stoic of 1. 2, but tells the reader that in *Laws* 1 and 2 Plato had recommended cheerful yet well-regulated drinking-parties under sober controllers as a relaxing refreshment of the mind, a relatively safe means of detecting improper desires, and training not to be overcome by wine like those unused to it. In book 1 Plato does regard wine-drinking as a discoverer of latent vices (649 D–650 B), and as an exercise in resistance, even amid pleasures, against improper desires (647 C–D, cf. 634 A–B, 635 B–C), but in book 2 the well-regulated drinking-parties encourage the men aged between thirty and sixty to perform in the 'chorus of Dionysus' and reinforce the moral lessons of the city, by making them feel younger than their years and less inhibited (666 B–C, cf. 665 D–E, 671 B–C); however, boys under eighteen are not to drink at all, youths between eighteen and thirty only in moderation and never passing the bounds of sobriety (666 A–B)—which would have been decisive *ad hominem* —and mature men with various restrictions of Carthaginian inspiration (674 A–B).[20] Gellius has replaced the Dionysian choir, which has relevance only to the projected city, with the relaxation that refreshes us for serious matters; Plato says merely that the gods have instituted festivals as intermissions of our toils (652 D), and the Carthaginian requirement that magistrates, slaves, and generals on campaign drink only water would deny relaxation to those who need it most. Either Gellius, who at 14. 3. 2 quotes—or rather misquotes—a text from *Leg.* 3 as 'quodam in libro', had not dug deep into book 2, or he was expanding a summary; but although the *Laws* were little read even among Greeks (Plut. *Mor.* 328 E), some knowledge of the text is suggested by the speaker, and perhaps the occasion, of §§ 1–3.[21]

At 2. 8. 9 Gellius observes that many syllogisms in Plato are set out otherwise than in the technical handbooks with a fine disregard for criticism ('cum eleganti quadam reprehensionis contemptione'). If modern scholars can judge Greek tragedy by the *Poetics*, we should not blame Gellius for writing as though Plato knew the *Analytics*. The statement that *Theaetetus* falsely ascribes a Sophoclean verse to Euripides (13. 19. 2) itself confuses that

19. Wine indeed makes the soul διάπυρος (671 B; hence younger, cf. 665 E), but so that it can be moulded (*Leg.* 666 B–C, 671 B–C). See too Antig. Car. (p. 85 Wil) ap. Ath. 547 F–548 A, Plut. *Mor.* 645 B–C, Fronto, *Fer. Als.* 3. 6, Gal. *Scr. min.* ii. 67–71 Müller, D.L. 3. 39; and note the gentle irony of Hor. *Carm.* 3. 21. 9–10.

20. Note too *Leg.* 775 B–D.

21. Although Cretan mendacity was proverbial, there would be an ironic contrast with Cleinias of Cnossos and the Cretan sobriety celebrated in the dialogue. Apollo's festival (which god could young men more aptly worship?) on the 7th day of the lunar month (Mikalson 19, cf. West on Hes. *Op.* 770) would recall the young men in the Chorus of Apollo (664 B) if 'hebdomadibus lunae' (§ 3) represents the Koine use found in MSS of Thphr. *Char.* 16. 10, Herod. 3. 53[sl], cf. Harp. 102. 15, E.M. 308. 41; neither '7th, 17th, 24th' nor 'at the moon's quarters' makes good sense (even though later authors use *hebdomas lunae* for the week between two quarters), for no rites linked either of these sets and Apollo permitted no other god to share his 7th. Marin. *Procl.* 11 (cit. Jac. Gronovius), on Neoplatonist veneration of the moon, does not help.

dialogue with the pseudo-Platonic *Theages* (125 B), which follows *Rep.* 568 A; Plato's error, if new to Roman readers, was familiar to the Greeks, from one of whom Gellius has derived it.

Taurus' commentary on *Gorgias* is compared with the original, but Gellius ignores the parallel passages in other dialogues, including the 'famous' *Protagoras* (p. 124). In 12. 9. 6 the central doctrine on injustice is quoted from memory (with ἢ τὸ for τοῦ); in 10. 22 two long extracts from Callicles' tirade against philosophers are transcribed and misinterpreted.[22] Nowhere does Gellius breathe a word about the Forms, though Favorinus had written about them.

Plato, however, contributes literary motifs: the 'recent' dialogue, the boastful, money-grubbing ignoramus begged by the ironist not to begrudge one who wished to learn.[23] As always, it is the writer, not the thinker, whom Gellius follows.

In 14. 3 Gellius—like Ath. 504 E–505 B, D.L. 3. 34—rehearses evidence for jealousy between Xenophon and Plato: neither mentions the other,[24] Xenophon answered two books of the *Republic* with his *Cyropaedia*, Plato riposted that Cyrus had no proper education;[25] Xenophon denied that Socrates had ever discoursed on the nature of the universe as he sometimes did in Plato. In fact, several of Socrates' pupils wrote dialogues, each claiming to be his true follower; personal rivalries ensued. Gellius, however, is reluctant to believe such things 'de uiris optimis et grauissimis' (§ 7); if they did happen, it was not because Plato and Xenophon disliked or envied each other or sought a greater renown, since such sentiments are alien to philosophy, but their supporters ('fauisores' § 9) got up a rivalry that then infected the principals. As a result they seemed to be rivals because their adherents so treated them. Observe Gellius' embarrassment: he does not wish to believe in the rivalry, yet faced with the evidence, real and supposed, can only invoke a phenomenon not unknown in his day (Philost. *VS* 490 blames it for the feud between Polemo and Favorinus), but quite inappropriate to the case in hand (who were Xenophon's *fauisores?*); then, by drawing back from the conclusion that the partisans actually succeeded in setting their principals by the ears, he fails to explain the very phenomena initially recorded. Had he

22. See ch. 5 n. 55.

23. Cf. p. 12, ch. 4 n. 13.

24. Diogenes notes that at X. *Mem.* 3. 6. 1 Socrates is well disposed towards the younger Glaucon for the sake of Charmides (his uncle) and Plato (his brother); in this context Xenophon could not ignore him, but whereas in the very next memoir the interlocutor is Charmides, there is no further mention of Plato.

25. *Leg.* 694 C. Diogenes names the work, Athenaeus specifies bk. 3; Gellius does neither, and quotes inaccurately. His 'uirum ... gnauum et strenuum' hardly reproduces στρατηγόν τε ἀγαθὸν εἶναι καὶ φιλόπολιν (but φιλόπονον Athenaeus; was there a common source?). In context, Plato means that Cyrus did nothing to educate his sons; but that itself implies a want of παιδεία in him, which the words παιδείας δὲ ὀρθῆς οὐχ ἧφθαι τὸ παράπαν would appear to mean in isolation. Why should not Plato, writing after Xenophon had published, use this phrase to put down a work unworthy of more detailed refutation?

posited that each man, regarding the other as gravely in error, took suitable opportunities of making his opinion clear—which would neither exclude nor entail personal jealousies—Gellius could still retain his rose-tinted view of philosophers;[26] instead, he resorts to a perverse ingenuity that is not even allowed to solve the problem, because it would still have been unworthy of philosophers to be caught up in enthusiasms they should have curbed. A judge should have seen deeper;[27] but sentimental piety is not absent from modern treatments of Socrates and Plato.

Academics

Although Favorinus was an Academic philosopher, and discussed the difference between Academic and Pyrrhonian sceptics,[28] Gellius has very little to say about the Academy after Plato. Speusippus is noted for for his views on pleasure (9. 5. 5) and Aristotle's book-purchase (3. 17. 3); Arcesilaus for a piece of repartee (3. 5); even Carneades, the champion of Academic scepticism, whose arguments against astrology will underlie 14. 2, appears only at 17. 21. 1, where the uneducated sophist gets his date wrong, in 17. 15, where this 'uir ingenio praestanti' purges himself of peccant humours before writing against Zeno the Stoic, and at 6. 14. 8–10 (cf. 17. 21. 48), where he, the Stoic Diogenes, and the Peripatetic Critolaus represent Athens in an embassy to Rome. This was the notorious occasion in 155 BC when, to Cato's horror, Carneades, having expounded Plato's and Aristotle's views of justice, spoke again the next day to refute them;[29] Gellius, however, notes only their modes of oratory—Carneades forceful and torrential,[30] Critolaus elegant and smooth, Diogenes restrained and sober—included (by Varro) in a discussion of the three styles (pp. 162–3).

Aristotle and the Peripatetics

Aristotle, whose great renown and experience in all the affairs of mankind are duly praised at 19. 2. 5 and 19. 5. 3, is frequently cited, sometimes directly, for facts and curiosities: it is to him that Gellius means (but fails) to turn for authoritative information on the lioness's litter (13. 7. 6). The greatest number of quotations come from the *Problems*, whose authenticity was not yet doubted, and which Gellius excerpted for himself (2. 30. 11); a collection of

26. See Riginos 108–10, cf. Lefkowitz 127–8: the stories were mere inferences from the texts. But we too may infer, nor will the Socratics have been less quarrelsome than Christians or Marxists. For sophists' quarrels see Bowersock 89–93. On philosophers' love of fame see Cic. *Arch.* 26; cf. P. Wendland, *Hermes* 51 (1916) 481–5. Nothing in X. *Mem.* 1. 1. 11–16 corresponds to 'idcircoque . . . attribuerent' § 5.

27. A like *naïveté*, the vice of a happy age, is displayed by Arrian, whose model is Xenophon and who trusts the word of kings (*Anab.* 1. pr. 2).

28. *NA* 11. 5; cf. P. Oxy. LII 3658, Annas–Barnes 96–8.

29. See Astin, *Cato* 174–5.

30. As suited his very loud voice (D.L. 4. 63), which no doubt increased dismay.

physical problems is praised for its charm at 19. 4. 1. The passages cited include *Probl.* 30. 10, sent by Taurus to a young man who consorts with stage-performers (20. 4, cf. p. 67); it is with Taurus too that Gellius reads a problem on the changes of colour caused by fear and shame (19. 6).[31] These two, and *Probl.* 28. 7 on sensual pleasure (19. 2. 5), are the only texts cited touching ethical questions; but 17. 5. 13 makes the familiar distinction between action and habit, though untechnically expressed.[32] At 3. 15. 1 Gellius briefly alludes to an interesting tale, told at length by Plutarch.[33] Exoteric and acroatic works are wrongly distinguished, and spurious letters cited, in 20. 5.[34] Science and history apart, Gellius quotes (and translates) the definition of the syllogism (15. 26), his only glance at Aristotle's logic, and reports such anecdotes as his buying a few of Speusippus' books (3. 17. 3) and his elegant means of designating Theophrastus his successor (13. 5). In sum, Aristotle is treated even more scrappily than Plato; although Gellius studied him with both Taurus and Favorinus (who in 2. 12. justifies the alleged Solonic law of *Ath. Pol.* 8. 5), and held him in very high regard, he conceived of him less as a thinker than as a more venerable version of himself.

In 1. 3. Gellius, debating how far one may stretch morality to help a friend, cites 'that most sober and learned Peripatetic' Theophrastus' long and intricate discussion; it reaches no specific conclusion but finds the question too complex to admit of rules. In 8. 6, however, Theophrastus says firmly that when quarrels are composed grievances should not be rehearsed, a sound piece of practical advice such as Gellius relished. Elsewhere, like his master, he is a purveyor of strange facts: aulos-music relieves sciatica (4. 13. 2), a dolphin fell in love with a handsome boy from Naupactus (6. 8. 2–3), the partridge of Paphlagonia has two hearts (16. 15). The second relation apparently comes from Apion (cited verbatim for a similar incident at Puteoli), the third from Favorinus (see p. 82); the first, which Gellius claims to have found 'in libro Theophrasti',[35] was in fact common property. However, it seems probable that Περὶ φιλίας was directly used in 1. 3 (pp.

31. But *Probl.* 8. 9 is not cited at 16. 3. 9–10 (p. 211). At 19. 4. 4 'quod timor omnis sit algificus, quem ille appellat ψυχροποιός' Gellius is probably citing a problem not in our corpus, as in 19. 5–6, rather than a secondary source: it is evident that he knew the *Problems* in a different editorial disposition from ours.

32. 'per ipsam perpetuae benignitatis constantiam', not 'ipsum habitum'; deliberate variation for *adnominatio* with 'circumstantiam'? (But even at 8. 7. lemma *habitus* is a mere synonym for *natura*, cf. 17. 11. lemma.) In § 12, 'aliis enim longe nominibus appellandus est' may recall ἄλλος τις ῥηθήσεται *EN* 1120ᵃ29, but the doctrine that liberality excludes self-seeking was especially Stoic (e.g. Cic. *Off.* 3. 118; Sen. *Ben.* 1. 7. 1, 2. 31. 3). See too n. 76.

33. *Mor.* 254 F (Arist. fr. 559 R). *NA* 10. 2. 1 seems to be a distorted version of *HA* 584ᵇ33–5, like others in ancient writers (see Thysius and Hertz ad loc.; cf. Seel on Trogus fr. 3): Phlegon, *Mir.* 28 locates the story (relayed through Antig. *Mir.* 110. 1) in Alexandria, Gellius' 'in Aegypto' reflects *HA* 584ᵇ31, *GA* 770ᵃ35, on polygony περὶ Αἴγυπτον. But 'Herodotus, homo fabulator', not in Varro (ch. 13 n. 20), translates Arist. *GA* 756ᵇ6–7 Ἡρόδοτος ὁ μυθολόγος.

34. See Düring 432–4; Gellius' source is Andronicus.

35. The title is omitted, at least in our MSS; Hosius supplied περὶ ἐνθουσιασμοῦ from Ath. 624 A (fr. 87 Wimmer, cf. fr. 88).

79–80); in the lost 8. 6 the work may have been cited through Taurus or, like Cicero's adaptation, independently. In 8. 9 Theophrastus is too much overawed, for all his eloquence, to say a few words in the Athenian assembly; Aelian, *VH* 8. 12, makes him break down in the Areopagus, a different elaboration of the same tale. At 2. 18. 8 he has a philosophical slave by the name of Pompylus.

Aristoxenus is cited in 4. 11. 4–7 for Pythagoras' diet. He is described, after his main work, as 'Aristoxenus musicus', but not quoted on that subject; he cannot be the source of 1. 9. 1–8, with its late and artificial distinction between ἀκουστικοί and μαθηματικοί (cf. p. 194). Various adherents of the Peripatos contribute minor facts and anecdotes; the figment of 18. 1 states its doctrine at greater length than all his post-Theophrastean colleagues put together. In compensation, both Taurus (1. 26. 11) and Herodes Atticus (19. 12) assert the Peripatetic ideal of moderation against the Stoics' impassibility.

Epicurus

Most of Gellius' references to Epicurus are summary: items in doxographies, a chronological notice, his man Mys as a noted philosopher-slave (2. 18. 8). The normal hostility is expressed by Taurus at 9. 5. 8 in a Stoic contemporary's words: his views were too bad for a whore (cf. p. 69). Yet in 2. 8–9 Gellius defends Epicurus against Plutarch's objections to his second and third *Chief Opinions*.

The former runs: 'Death is nothing to us; for that which has been broken up has no feeling, but that which has no feeling is nothing to us.' Plutarch complains that Epicurus has neglected to state 'Death is the breaking-up of soul and body'; Gellius replies that this was too obvious to need saying,[36] that Epicurus was not interested in such formalism, and that Plato, too, often negelcts scholastic niceties.[37] Plutarch's cavil had been anticipated by Cicero, *Fin.* 2. 100; in itself it may seem trivial, but when the syllogism is set out 'in text-book fashion' as at *NA* 2. 8. 5, 'Death is the breaking-up of soul and body; that which has been broken up has no feeling; that which has no feeling is nothing to us', a sharper mind than Gellius' will observe that the breaking-up is not the same as the thing broken up. The point was soon to be made by Alexander of Aphrodisias, who adds that 'death' has two senses, dying and being dead; the latter might not concern us, but the former does.[38]

36. Quint. 5. 14. 13 objects that the permanent or temporary survival of the disembodied soul is 'in dubio'; not for Epicurus.

37. Rappolt's citations (sigg. F2ᵛ, F3ᵛ) from Quint. 5. 14. 27–32 on avoiding dialectic pedantry and Arist. *Rhet.* 1357ᵃ17–21 on omitting what is already known may remind us that Epicurus issued these κύριαι δόξαι for persuasion rather than proof.

38. *In Top.* 14. 7–17 Wallies; his first objection is cited by Muretus, *Var. lect.* 11. 16 (Gruter ii. 1079–80), who supposes it also made by Plutarch; for the second cf. Lact. *Inst.* 3. 17. 31–2. Less rigorously Tert. *An.* 42. 1 'dissoluitur autem et caret sensu non ipsa mors, sed homo qui eam

In 2. 9 the theme is Epicurus' equation of extremity in pleasure with removal of all pain, ἡ παντὸς τοῦ ἀλγοῦντος ὑπεξαίρεσις (*Sent.* 3); Plutarch objects that Epicurus should have said not ἀλγοῦντος but ἀλγεινοῦ, since it is not the thing in pain but the pain itself that must be removed.[39] Gellius retorts impatiently that this is mere quibbling; Epicurus has no time for such verbal exactitude.[40] He would have done better to say, first, that τὸ ἀλγοῦν for 'pain' is a good classical construction, secondly, that Plutarch uses the same device himself, and thirdly, since ἀλγεινός is not 'pain' but 'arousing pain', that cause, even when sufficient, is not effect— unless 'doloris' be Gellius' own mistranslation.[41] Bluff commonsense has served as a substitute for thought and knowledge.

All the same, Gellius stands up for an author it was generally thought respectable to denigrate by any means;[42] he even cites this definition of maximum pleasure to defend the Vergilian litotes *inlaudati* 'unpraised' as not too weak for Busiris' wickedness (2. 6. 12). Gellius lacks the commitment to be biased; and when he reads Plutarch's nit-pickings, the Roman makes common cause with the foe of pedantry.[43]

Stoics and Cynics

Whereas Zeno, despite a doxographic appearance at 9. 5. 5, is little more than a name—the owner of a philosophical slave called Persaeus (2. 18. 8), an author requiring Carneades' best alertness to refute him (19. 15. 2)—Chrysippus engages more attention. In 7. 1–2 he is quoted at length justifying the doctrine of Providence against the Argument from Evil (7. 1. 1) and reconciling fate with free will (though not, it is observed, to Cicero's

patitur' (he should have said 'dissoluitur qui mortem patitur, caret sensu qui passus est'). In fact there are three stages, the process of dying, the moment of expiry, and the state of being dead, though contrasts are typically by pair, Epich. DK 23 B 11, *Trag. inc. inc.* 203 R, Plaut. *Capt.* 741, Sen. *Tro.* 397; cf. Eur. *Alc.* 541. For the logical problems caused by the instant of death see *NA* 7. 13. 5 (cf. 6. 21. 1, 3), S.E. *PH* 3. 110–11, *Dogm.* 3. 269, 4. 346–7; on the whole topic Sen. *Ep.* 30.

39. At *Mor.* 1088 C Plutarch accepts τοῦ ἀλγοῦντος without comment, but paraphrases it as ἀλγεινόν, cf. μήτε ἀλγεινὸν μήτε λυπηρόν 1091 A. (At Soph. *OC* 1664 ἀλγεινός has its normal sense: Oedipus arouses neither lamentation nor pain, but admiration.)

40. The *adnominatio* 'non modo non sectatur ... sed etiam insectatur' ensures we do not think the same of Gellius (cf. pp. 19, 76).

41. On the 'Thucydidean' participle see J. D. Denniston, *CR* 45 (1931) 7. Cf. Ephippus fr. 6. 6–7 K–A, Epicurus, *Sent.* 4; Plutarch himself uses it, *Mor.* 446 C, though at 447 F τὸ ἡδόμενον καὶ τὸ ἀλγοῦν is the part of the soul feeling pleasure and pain. The dialectical error of cause put for effect escaped Muretus and other commentators; one might also maintain that pain outlasts its stimulus, though Diog. Oen. fr. 28 vi–vii Chilton states that once we have removed the passions that disturb the soul the things that please it will replace them.

42. Cicero, who treats Epicurus as a philosophical Verres or Vatinius, pours scorn on the faulty *diuisio* of *Sent.* 29, setting out the approved form (*Fin.* 2. 26)—precisely that of *Ep. Men.* (D.L. 10. 127). Epicurus did not entirely despise such matters (Long 30).

43. The objection Chrysippus meets at 7. 2. 4 (fate excludes moral responsibility) is Epicurean (A. Grilli, *Riv. crit. stor. filos.* 3 (1948) 237–48; cf. P. M. Huby, *Phronesis* 15 (1970) 83–5). With § 14 cf. Diogenian. Epicur. fr. 1. 11–20 Gercke.

satisfaction, 7. 2. 15).[44] In 14. 4 he describes Justice in stern and awful terms; that adherents of softer schools had taken the portrait not for Justice but for Cruelty is all the more reason, says Gellius, to ponder and adjudge it. Such moral austerity appealed to Romans, especially in books: having cited a mouth-watering list of delicacies from Varro, Gellius adds that we shall feel a greater indignation against the world-wide search for dainties on recalling Eur. fr. 892 N, often quoted by Chrysippus (6. 16. 6, cf. Plut. *Mor.* 1044 B). Such commonplaces by no means imply that their authors lived on Epicurean bread and cheese: we find them in Nero's crony Lucan (4. 373–81) and his arbiter of elegance Petronius (*Sat.* 119. 33–8), who used to upbraid his meanness (Plut. *Mor.* 60 E). Indeed, if one reasoned the need so nicely one would be obliged to become a Cynic, a most disagreeable conclusion; the man who admired Peregrinus had no desire to emulate him. It was sufficient tribute to frugality if one occasionally declaimed on the vice of luxury and relished the occasional anecdote about Diogenes: Gellius duly tells of his conduct in the slave-market and his riposte to a Platonic debater (2. 18. 9–10; 18. 13. 7–8). Since Gellius could not afford to keep the best table in Rome, the sumptuary laws he lists in 2. 24 would have some appeal for him besides their aim of restoring antique virtue; there are other chapters reproving gluttony.[45] Such things do not make him either a self-denier or a kill-joy.

Panaetius, the grave and learned man,[46] is said at 12. 5. 10 to have repudiated the Stoic doctrine of ἀπάθεια or impassibility: he is the source of 13. 28, where the man in active life who wishes to be of use to himself and his own is compared with the pancratiast constantly on guard.[47] The passage, rendered in some of Gellius' finest Latin, sets out the need for constant vigilance as well as it has ever been expressed, but the image too may have apppealed to Gellius, who retained from his visit to the Pythian Games with Taurus sufficient interest in athletics to record the stories of Diagoras and Echeclus, Milo's end, and Euripides' boyhood prizes;[48] he never displays either the Roman disapprobation of such events, with their flagitious nudity, expressed by his beloved Ennius and shared by Cicero,[49] or the dismal

---

44. On 7. 2 cf. Inwood, *Ethics* 48–50.

45. 15. 8; 15. 19; 19. 2; cf. 4. 19; 11. 2. 5. From 15. 8. 2 we learn that the late Republican gourmet refused to eat the breast of poultry; André, *Alim.* 129 n. 24 cites Plin. *NH* 10. 140, Mart. 2. 37. 5, but omits this passage. Not that Gellius subsisted on humble fare; at 16. 7. 11 he mistakes the lowly *botulus* (black pudding) for a synonym of *farcimen* (sausage); cf. App. n. 39; André, *Alim.* 137–8, 147–8; and for ignorance of the simple life cf. Sherwin-White on Plin. *Ep.* 1. 15. 2.

46. Cf. Cic. *Off.* 2. 51 'grauissimo Stoicorum Panaetio', likewise to justify retreat from rigour.

47. With 'qui aetatem in medio rerum agunt' (§ 3) cf. 'in medio rerum et hominum uitam qui colunt' (20. 10. 6).

48. 3. 15. 3; 5. 9. 5–6; 15. 16; 15. 20. 3; cf. 1. 1; 3. 6. At 5. 9. 6 read 'ipsum' (*C recc.*): 'ipsos' (*VPR*) makes no sense (Greeks did not compete in teams), and before 'aduersarios' the corruption was easy.

49. *Tusc.* 4. 70, quoting Enn. *Sc.* 241 J; cf. Sherwin-White on Plin. *Ep.* 9. 5. 1. Roman games are taken for granted (5. 14; 6. 3. 30–1; 12. 5. 13), with no sermons against their cruelty; the gladiator of 12. 5. 13 is the typical ἀναίσθητος, as at *Rhet. Her.* 3. 6, 4. 35 (contemptuous too 3.

contempt for sport and sportsmen affected by many intellectuals and moralists, not least by Stoics and Cynics.[50]

The one chapter Gellius accords a Silver Latin author (scholars apart) is 12. 2, the critique of Seneca. His great vogue was past; he was still read, but it had become fashionable to find fault. Both Quintilian and Suetonius insinuate that he disparaged the classics for fear of comparison;[51] a like jealousy was read by Niebuhr into the adverse judgement of Fronto[52]—whose pretended imitations of Senecan catachresis (*Fer. Als.* 3. 2) are not a patch on Seneca's hit at Sallust (*Ep.* 114. 17). It is this irreverence towards his favourites that Gellius does not forgive.

Some say (he reports in § 1) that Annaeus Seneca is a writer of no value, his vocabulary undistinguished, his style full of empty vehemence and shallow cleverness, his learning commonplace with neither the grace nor the dignity that could have been imparted by ancient writings; others that, although no stylist, he knows his subject and his morality is laudable and attractive. Gellius declines to give a general judgement (§ 2), but reviews with disgust Seneca's jibes at Ennius, and at the homage paid him by Cicero and Vergil; they are branded the work of a trifler ('homo nugator', § 8), silly and tasteless ('inepti et insubidi hominis', § 11),[53] unworthy to be read by studious youth (§ 12). Granted there are some good things (§ 13),[54] such as the rebuke to a miser—however much money he has, there is more that he has not[55]—yet things well said ('quae bene dicta sunt') in an author do the young less good than things very badly said ('quae pessime') do harm, especially when they are more numerous and proffer not arguments on trivialities but advice on doubtful questions (§ 14). 'Well' may connote either wisdom, as in § 13, or elegance; 'advice' would most naturally be understood as moral, but no example of bad morality is given, only of bad taste. Gellius has after all delivered a general judgement: Seneca the moralist cannot atone for Seneca the modernist.

Here speaks (despite 14. 6. 5) the worthy follower of Fronto, who in an impassioned plea to Marcus, by now emperor, to give up reading Seneca declares that even when the thought is grave, the style is as disgusting as the

14); contrast Cic. *Tusc.* 2. 41. Marcus prefers the pancratiast to the gladiator as using no extraneous weapon (*Med.* 12. 9).

50. The theme (cf. Xenophanes DK 21 B 2, Eur. fr. 284 N) is found in Sen. *Ep.* 15. 2–3, Dio Prus. 9. 11, Epict. 2. 18. 22, M. Ant. *Med.* 11. 2; see also Sherwin-White on Pliny, *Ep.* 9. 6. 1. But Stoics and Cynics (especially Epictetus) also put athletics to moral use: in particular Panaetius' image recurs at Sen. *Ep.* 80. 3 (cf. *SVF* iii. 569, Epict. 3. 10. 6, 3. 25. 2–3).

51. Quint. 10. 1. 125–31 (Bacon, *Essays*, no. 26, ascribes to Gellius a distorted version of § 130), Tac. *A.* 13. 3. 1, Suet. *Cal.* 53. 2, *Nero* 52; cf. Trillitzsch i. 69–75 on Fronto and Gellius. His decline, however, was not precipitate (Zwierlein 339–41).

52. Niebuhr I. iii. 232: 'Fronto's Haß gegen Seneca kommt eigentlich daher daß er fühlt wie er zu einer solchen Feinheit ganz unfähig ist.' Cf. id., edn. 134 n. 2; Cic. *Or.* 24 'nunc enim tantum quisque laudat quantum se posse sperat imitari'.

53. Cf. Macaulay, *Letters* iii. 180 Pinney: 'an affected empty scribbler'.

54. So Seneca had allowed Ennius a few good lines (§ 11).

55. See ch. 6 n. 48.

table-manners of a guest who juggles with his olives (*Orat.* 3): the ocasional good lines no more justify reading him than the slivers of silver sometimes found in sewers would commend a contract for their cleansing (§ 4).[56] This exaltation of manner over matter had not been foreign to his pupil in his youth: in the summer of 143 he had written (*Ep. M. Caes.* 2. 7. 1) that the sophist Polemo reminded him of a sturdy and hard-working peasant whose farm yielded corn and grapes in abundance, but nothing for delight, to be praised but not loved.[57] Although it is over-simple to speak of Marcus' conversion to philosophy,[58] the unrhetorical starkness of his *Meditations*, written for—or as if for—his eyes only, drew from Winckelmann the verdict that, sound morality apart, the thoughts and style were vulgar and unworthy of a prince.[59] The view that noble doctrine does not excuse bad writing is not peculiar to pedants in an age of decadence.

Musonius Rufus, exiled to Gyaros by Nero and to Syria by Vespasian, always willing to speak his mind whether or not it was wanted—he displayed 'untimely wisdom' on an abortive peace-mission (Tac. *Hist.* 3. 81. 1)[60]—held a number of unconventional opinions, as that both sexes should be educated in philosophy, that men should observe the same rules of chastity as women, and that sexual intercourse should be confined to marriage, for the sole purpose of procreation;[61] Gellius does not allude to these notions. At 18. 2. 1 he cites Musonius' disapproval of relaxation 'remittere animum quasi amittere est',[62] but at pr. 1 and 15. 2. 5 Gellius has no objection to relaxations of the mind; his moral enthusiasms are at best a kind of catharsis for the conscience, which does not interfere with his day-to-day judgement. In 5. 1 Musonius condemns the custom of applauding philosophical lectures, contrasting it with the silence that followed Odysseus' narration of his

56. The plea was in vain: see *Med.* 4. 19. 1 ~ Sen. *Ep.* 54. 5, *Med.* 11. 25 ~ Sen. *Ben.* 5. 2. 2, 6 (in both places Seneca is closer than the Greek parallels), *Med.* 11. 26 ~ Sen. *Ep.* 11. 8–10. Fronto's 'dictabolaria, immo dicteria potius eum quam dicta confingere' (*Orat.* 2) vindicates the paradosis at Gell. 12. 2. 1 'leui et quasi dicaci argutia' against Th. Vogel, *JbChPh* 111 (1875) 574.

57. The modern reader who finds the extant declamations full of rank weeds intended for exotic blooms, but nothing fit for human consumption, will wonder at this judgement no less than one who relied on Philostratus. But Polemo was close to his final illness, and Marcus never quite lost a penchant for the outlandish and obscure (ch. 7 n. 23). With the image contrast Quint. 8. 3. 8.

58. Champlin, *Fronto* 121–2, but see Birley, *Marcus Aurelius* 94, 226, 275 n. 13.

59. Winckelmann ii. IV. K. f, p. 416 (*Sämtliche Werke* vi. 309), cit. Friedländer, *Kunstsinn* 24 n. 2.

60. The Roman philosopher run out of Athens for preaching against gladiators (Dio Prus. 31. 122) is generally identified with Musonius, since no one else is known to fit the description; resistance to such Roman cruelties in Ἑλλάδος Ἑλλάς was in time attributed to other preachers (Luc. *Demon.* 57, Philost. *VA* 4. 22).

61. See frr. 3–4, 12, 13 Hense. But note the importance of male chastity in the Greek novel.

62. The original will have played on ἀνιέναι and ἀφιέναι (cf. Hense on fr. 52). Even other Stoics knew better (Sen. *Tranq.* 17. 5, M. Ant. *Med.* 1. 8. 4, cf. Epict. fr. C 24 Schenkl); and see Val. Max. 8. 8, Dio Prus. fr. 5, Fronto, *Fer. Als.* 3. 1–7, Balsdon, *Life and Leisure* 147.

wanderings;[63] but in 9. 8. 3 Gellius records that Favorinus delivered a
well-turned moral sentiment 'inter ingentes omnium clamores'. The remaining quotations are a jest that the man who was fit for nothing good was
therefore fit for money (9. 2. 8, see p. 101), repeated by Herodes (the last
man to take it seriously), and the *sententia* that as the exertion of a noble deed
soon departs, but its nobility remains, so the pleasure of a base one soon
departs, but its baseness remains (16. 1. 2), a thought already expressed by
Cato and therefore more venerable in his version despite its lack of elegance.
As at 13. 24. 2 the Roman prefers the wisdom of the Tusculan to anything in
Greek; that C. Musonius Rufus was no Greek, but an *eques Romanus* from
Etruscan Volsinii, makes no moment. Yet his sentence was a joy to remember
for its truth and eloquence (§ 1); and Musonius is accorded the honour of first
appearance in two books of the *Nights*.

That the 'famous philosopher' Epictetus' had been a slave is a thing of
recent memory (2. 18. 10); his banishment is noted (15. 11. 5). His sermons
against false philosophers whose intellectual pursuits are not combined with
sound morality are quoted in 1. 2. 7–12 and 17. 19. 1–4, his advice to bear
and forbear at 17. 19. 5–6 (cf. *Diss.* 4. 8. 20). He is also cited in the famous
chapter 19. 1.

The ship carrying Gellius home from Greece was buffeted by wind and
wave; a well-known Stoic whom he had met in Athens with an attentive flock
of pupils displayed the same symptoms of fear in his face, though not his
bearing, as the other passengers. Vulgar notions of Stoicism, such as the
offensive youth of 1. 2. 5 proclaimed, did not allow for this; after the storm
was over, a rich Greek from Asia bade him justify this manifestation of a fear
he himself had neither felt nor shown. The Stoic dispatched him with
Aristippus' reply in the like circumstance; '*You* are not much worried about
the life of a worthless ne'er-do-well; *I* fear for that of Aristippus.' As the ship
approached Brundisium, however, Gellius ventured to ask him the true
reason, and was given the fifth book of Arrian's Epictetus, which presented a
highly technical account of the matter: the wise man cannot determine his
perceptions but can withhold assent from them.[64]

A similar doctrine is expounded by Taurus in 12. 5 to explain why his
Stoic friend in Lebadeia had been obliged to sigh in pain: however, despite
the reference to things indifferent but preferable or dispreferable, it expresses
not Stoicism but Stoicizing Platonism (cf. p. 68). Both Taurus and Gellius
cite the Stoic Hierocles on Providence (p. 69); though the word occurs at
Plat. *Tim.* 30 C 1, it was the Stoics who had elaborated the doctrine.

---

63. Fr. 49 Hense, cf. fr. 48 (Epict. 3. 23. 29), Plut. *Mor.* 46 A–C, Eus. *HE* 7. 30. 9; see A.
Stuiber, *RAC* ii. 92–103. Odysseus among the Phaeacians recurs in Muson. fr. 9 (p. 46. 3–7
Hense); with 'nisi ille est plane deperditus' (*NA* 5. 1. 3) Hense compares οἵ γε μὴ τελέως
ἀπερρωγότες fr. 12 (p. 64. 7). See too Luc. *Nigr.* 4, 35, cf. Th. Reinach, *RhM*² 64 (1909) 102.
64. Inwood, *Ethics* 177 compares Sen. *Ir.* 1. 16. 7; see too K. Abel, *Hermes* 111 (1983) 78–97.

Stoicism, intellectually moribund and destined to succumb before the *soi-disant* heirs of Plato, was still the most fashionable philosophy to profess, if not to follow;[65] it also possessed a large literature on moral duties (καθήκοντα, *officia*). It is in Stoic terms that Gellius discusses filial obedience (1. 7),[66] defines pleasure (2. 27. 3) and proof (17. 5. 5),[67] and moralizes a fable (2. 29. 18–19); Stoic too is the propositional logic of 16. 8.[68] But in 11. 12 Chrysippus' view of ambiguity receives less space than Diodorus the Eristic's; none of Gellius' known teachers was a Stoic; the famous paradoxes are not mentioned; despite 19. 1, Taurus and Herodes attack impassibility. No doubt Gellius did not appreciate its subtleties;[69] only at 2. 27. 3 can we trace the distinction (to non-Stoics a mere smokescreen covering retreat) between irrational πάθη and rational εὐπάθειαι. Gellius was no more unfair in equating impassibility with torpor than Chrysippus in dismissing as absurd the Platonic concept of injustice to oneself,[70] or nearly everyone in representing Epicurus as a *viveur*.

Although in the debate on virtue and happiness, a Peripatetic objection to the Stoic case is disallowed (18. 1. 12–14), to Stoic impassibility Gellius' authorities prefer Peripatetic moderation: considering himself sufficiently virtuous and sufficiently happy, he could afford to lean towards the Stoics, but where anger, pain, and grief were concerned, his feelings would not submit to an inhuman theory. Nor would he put off the toga for the pallium; in 1. 13, despite an initial reference to writings on καθήκοντα, the discussion is purely Roman, and the traditionally desirable attributes ascribed to Crassus Mucianus are accepted as goods without regard to Stoic definitions (§ 10). Gellius is a Stoic only when Romanity and common sense allow.

65. Cf. Hertz, *R. und R.* 36: 'im Sinne des damaligen, etwas verwaschenen Modestoicismus'. But Hierocles displays some powers of thought (Inwood, 'Hierocles' 183).

66. Far more so than Muson. fr. 16 (cf. 15 n. 16); the topic had been treated by Arist. *EN* 1164^{b}22–1165^{a}35 and many others. With Gell. § 13 cf. Hierocles Stoicus (a possible source for this and other Stoic matter in Gellius) ap. Stob. 4. 25. 53, *Cat. Dist.* br. sent. 46.

67. See ch. 5 n. 23 and *SVF* ii. 266 respectively.

68. With § 8 cf. 'Apul.' Π. ἑρμ. (pp. 176. 12–177. 2 Thomas); but Sergius Plautus' *effatum* (cf. Cic. *Luc.* 95) is not in Gellius. For the misleading treatment of subdisjunction see Frede, *Logik* 98–100. Yes-or-no catches (16. 2; cf. 18. 2. 9; 18. 13. 7–8, reappearing at Aug. *Doct. Christ.* 2. 31. 48, Alcuin, *Rhet.* 948–57 Howell) and the Liar Paradox (18. 2. 10) were not original or exclusive to the Stoics (see Zeller, *Phil.* ii/1. 294–6), nor need 'disciplinae dialecticae' indicate that school despite e.g. Cic. *Top.* 56, Fronto, *Eloq.* 2. 18–20, *NA* 1. 22. 7; 16. 8 (so rightly Falster, 'Noct. Rip.' 289, against Oiselius, and see 18. 13. 7); but it was with the Porch that they were most associated (Cic. *De or.* 1. 43, *SVF* ii. 270–87, Mart. Cap. 4. 327. 7–8), and the rider at 16. 2. 13 recalls Chrysippus at Cic. *Luc.* 94.

69. See van Straaten 182–90 (at 183 n. 1 for 'A. Gellius' read 'Taurus').

70. *SVF* iii. 288. He even used the phrase himself (ibid. 289).

Cicero

Gellius both cites Cicero's equivalents for Greek philosophical terms and adopts them unacknowledged: so respectively 16. 8. 8 and 2. 27. 3.[71] *Hortensius* apparently underlies his misrepresentation of Plato in 10. 22;[72] the *Tusculans* provide the inspiration for 18. 1 (pp. 48–9) and a scholarly note at 10. 18. 2;[73] there is curious information from *De diuinatione* at 4. 11. 3; from *Fin.* 3. 15, on Latin paraphrase of Greek terms 'pluribus uerbis', comes the confession of 11. 16. 9, 'ne pluribus quidem uerbis'. False memory of Homer in *De gloria* is detected in 15. 6;[74] use of Theophrastus in *De amicitia* is observed at 1. 3. 11, as of Panaetius in *De officiis* at 13. 28. 1. However, Gellius finds that Cicero, having skated over Theophrastus' hardest passage, is even less helpful on the problem under discussion (*Am.* 61; *NA* 1. 3. 12, 21);[75] the more rigorous treatment at *Off.* 3. 43–6 is not mentioned. On the other hand, *Am.* 31 is defended against pettifogging objection in 17. 5.[76] In 8. 6 Gellius reported Cicero's opinion 'de amore amicitiae'; perhaps *Am.* 85 'One should love after judging, not judge after loving.'[77] Hosius proposed the fragment 'amantium caeca iudicia sunt', from a Platonic dictum that Theophrastus may have cited in this context;[78] there is an apparent echo at

71. See Cic. *Tusc.* 4. 13–14; the actual definition of delight comes from elsewhere. But at 6. 3. 12 'gaudio atque laetitia ... deturbati', even if 'atque' meant καὶ δὴ καί, 'gaudio ... deturbati' would still be un-Stoic; Gellius has relapsed into ordinary language—and Cato's own usage (§ 14)—which made no distinction.

72. See ch. 5 n. 55. Cf. *Rep.* 1. 2 (dialogue cited at 1. 22. 8; 7. 16. 11, and echoed at 9. 2. 8).

73. 'Rhetorum epilogis' 14. 2. 1 probably comes from *Tusc.* 1. 112 (p. 218).

74. This is the one mistake in Cicero that Gellius admits; even here he shifts the blame onto Tiro for not detecting it. But as Jac. Gronovius observes (edn. 902) correction entailed rewriting the whole passage.

75. S. Jannacone, *Ciceroniana* 3–6 (1961–3) 197 complains that Gellius ignores Cicero's references (§ 61) to reputation and public approval; neither was relevant to Chilo's conduct, known only to himself.

76. Cicero argues that as we are generous not for investment but by natural propensity so we seek friendship not for reward's sake but its own. A rhetorician complains that the protasis has not been proved; one could just as well argue that as we seek friendship for its own sake, so we should be generous without thought of return. Gellius answers that philosophers call only him generous who expects no profit; Cicero had spoken not of acting generously, as an ungenerous man might for some chance reason, but of generous people (cf. n. 32 above). He does not deploy *Leg.* 1. 48–9.

77. 'cum iudicaris diligere oportet, non cum dilexeris iudicare' ~ Thphr. fr. 74 W οὐ φιλοῦντα δεῖ κρίνειν ἀλλὰ κρίναντα φιλεῖν. Cicero goes on to discuss broken friendships; Gellius has just cited Theophrastus on reconciliation. Maserius suggested §§ 59–60, attacking the dictum approved at *NA* 1. 3. 30 (cf. Publil. 245 Meyer at *NA* 17. 14. 4); Falster, *Vig. pr.* 36 adduces *Pro Gabinio* fr. 2 Schoell. Other possibilities are *Leg.* 1. 34 'ut nihilo sepse plus quam alterum diligat' and 1. 49 'ubi illa sancta amicitia, si non ipse amicus per se amatur toto pectore, ut dicitur?'; despite the silence of 17. 5, knowledge of this dialogue is suggested by the standing epithet 'facetissimus' for Aristophanes (ch. 12 n. 62).

78. Jerome, *In Os.* 3 pr. (CCSL 76. 109), *C. Ioh.* 3 (PL 23. 357 B), cf. Plat. *Leg.* 731 E τυφλοῦται γὰρ περὶ τὸ φιλούμενον ὁ φιλῶν widely misquoted (Plut. 4×, M. Caes. *Ep.* 3. 18. 1, Jerome, *In Os.* 3) as τυφλοῦται (γὰρ) τὸ φιλοῦν περὶ τὸ φιλούμενον (cf. Gal. *Scr. min.* i. 4. 17–18 Marquardt). I suppose an intermediate source; perhaps Theophrastus, to whom Jerome ascribes the saying, so cited it in Περὶ φιλίας (Marcus, 'puto Thucydides' being then one *Th-* for another). It is applied to friends at Plut. *Mor.* 90 A.

13. 29. 3 (p. 98). But the phrase 'amor amicitiae', so frequent in Aquinas, seems to occur in ancient writers, outside *NA* 8. 6. lemma, only at Cic. *Tusc.* 4. 70, as philosophers' palliation of their pederastic vice; this seems irrelevant to a chapter on reconciliation, yet no more so than the servile origin of Caecilius Statius to the censorial severities of 4. 20, with which it is linked through the mention of a slave called Statius. Never citing *De natura deorum*, Gellius does not know that an opinion he scouts in Tiro (13. 9) was also Cicero's (*ND* 2. 111). In 7. 2 Chrysippus' argument, despite the quotation from *De fato* at § 15 on its complexities, is derived directly from its author; even the image of the cylinder, given in Latin at *Fat.* 43, is translated anew at § 11.[79] For all Cicero's literary assistance,[80] Gellius read his philosophy in Greek.[81]

Plutarch

Plutarch of Chaeronea, Favorinus' friend and Taurus' teacher,[82] whom the latter is made to call 'uir doctissimus ac prudentissimus' (1. 26. 4), interests Gellius as a source of information and a teacher of morality. His standing in Antonine culture is demonstrated, as by Apul. *Met.* 1. 2. 1, where Lucius claims descent 'a Plutarcho illo inclito', so by Gellius' choice of him as source, and his name as first word, of his opening chapter. His *Table-talk*, with its light-hearted learning and engaging variety, contributes not a little to the *Nights*.

In 3. 6 Gellius paraphrases *Symp.* 8. 4. 5 (*Mor.* 724 E–F): palm-wood does not bend under a weight but bears up against it;[83] for this reason, the palm is

---

79. P. L. Donini, *AAT* 109 (1975) 196–203; R. W. Sharples, *SO* 56 (1981) 84–7. Gellius has not read *De fato* closely enough to observe with 'Apul.' *Π. ἑρμ.* 1, p. 176. 15–16 Thomas, Boeth. *De diff. top.* 1 (PL 64. 1174 C) that ἀξίωμα is generally *enuntiatum* or *enuntiatio*, not (as *Tusc.* 1. 14, cf. *NA* 16. 8. 8) *pronuntiatum*, though *pronuntiatio* occurs at § 26.

80. As Miriam Griffin observes (pers. comm.) apropos of 1. 2. 1–2, the settings of Gellius' dialogues, even in Greece, recall Cicero's Roman care to show that the participants are legitimately enjoying *otium* (a word frequent in the *Nights*).

81. At 15. 5. 8 Gellius does not compare Cic. *Oec.* fr. 24 Garbarino with X. *Oec.* 19. 19, where nothing corresponds to 'adfecta iam prope aestate' unless Cicero misconstrued τὴν ὀπώραν; but only the word 'adfecta' concerned him, and the ex. will come from Apollinaris.

82. 'Plutarchus noster' 1. 26. 4 need mean only 'my friend Plutarch'; but (*pace* Glucker 143) the much younger Taurus regarded Plutarch as his teacher, however informal the relationship. Vegetarianism (17. 8. 2) may show Plutarch's influence, but cf. 19. 7. 1.

83. Plutarch's οὐ κάτω θλιβόμενον ἐνδίδωσιν becomes 'non deorsum palma cedit nec intra flectitur'. The reading *in terram*, exhibited in witnesess to the Valerio-Gellian florilegium (*in terram* S, *in terra* TY) and the φ anthology (*in terram* Wm. Malmes. *Polyh.* 66. 8 Ou., J. Salis. *Polic.* 5. 6 = i. 306. 16 W.; *iter* K), was translated by Afanasij and Mignon; it is palaeographically plausible (*intrā*, cf. J. H. Onions, *JPhil* 11 (1882) 78), but would be appropriate only to the living bough. *Intra* (so too MS B of Diceto, i. 51–2 n. 3 St, where for 'ejusdem' read 'eiusmodi'; *ipse contuli*) is explained by J. F. Gronovius as 'in sese' (Rolfe: 'made concave') in contrast to the following 'recuruatur'; this seems better than Weiss's gloss 'inwendig (abwärts)' (cf. *TLL* vii/2. 44. 50), for which we should expect *infra* (mooted by Triller 7, printed by Marache; cf. Plin. *NH* 16. 223 'in inferiora pandantur').

a prize for athletes, who must resist pressure.[84] In 17. 11 he repeats the anatomist Erasistratus' objection to Plato's theory (*Tim.* 91 A) on ingested liquids,[85] as recorded by 'et Plutarchus et alii quidam docti uiri' (§ 1), adding that 'Plutarchus in libro symposiacorum' (§ 6) had cited Hippocrates and other physicians in the philosopher's defence. At *Symp.* 7. 1 (*Mor.* 699 C–D) Plutarch also notes Erasistratus' comments and, like Gellius but with a better text, quotes Alcaeus' injunction (347 Voigt) 'drench your lungs with wine'.[86] However, he does not record the suggestion that Plato followed Alcaeus into error, and gives rather less detail: neither Plato's reference to the bladder (*NA* § 1) nor Erasistratus' to the colon (§ 2) appears in Plutarch, and Erasistratus' doctrine of the two vessels, set out methodically in Gellius ('duas esse quasi canaliculas quasdam uel fistulas ...'), is taken as read in Plutarch. This is no rhetorical amplification;[87] Gellius must have used a second source.[88]

The remaining reference to the *Table-talk* comes at 4. 11. 13:[89] 'Sed et piscibus mullis abstinere Pythagoricos Plutarchus in symposiacis dicit'; Pythagorean abstinence from mullet, which Gellius' editors have vainly sought in *Symp.* 8. 8, is recorded at 4. 5. 2 (*Mor.* 670 D).[90] Gellius' statement is appended to a quotation from the first book of Plutarch's *Homeric Studies*, citing Aristotle (fr. 194 R) on the sect's readiness to eat most forms of meat; Aristoxenus' assertion on beans precedes. It is natural to see the *Homeric Studies* as the source for Gellius' knowledge of Aristoxenus, as of Callimachus, Xenophilus, and Alexis.[91] From the second book of this work come the criticisms of Epicurus that Gellius rejects in *NA* 2. 8–9.[92]

At 20. 7. 7 Annianus cites the fourth book of Plutarch's commentary on Hesiod's *Works and Days* for the inverse relationship between the phases of the moon and the life-cycle of the onion, which caused the inhabitants of Pelusium to refrain from eating it. In the previous sentence cats' eyes are said to grow larger and smaller as the moon waxes and wanes; this too will come from the commentary, being reproduced by Proclus on *Op.* 765–6. Both

---

84. Aristotle, cited as a parallel authority, is not mentioned by Plutarch.

85. Plato held that ingested liquids passed through the lungs to the bladder; Erasistratus stated the true function of trachea and oesophagus.

86. Plutarch has rightly πλεύμονας, Gellius πνεύμονα; Macrobius, who in *Sat.* 7. 15 works mainly from Gellius and Plutarch, exhibits a further corruption, and an explanation, due to neither (§ 13).

87. As at § 6 ~ *Mor.* 699 C–D.

88. Although even Hosius (i, p. li) allows the quotations in 16. 3 to come from Erasistratus, if he is used directly in 17. 11 Gellius has for once exaggerated that dependence on secondary sources he frequently conceals.

89. The Sapphic and Anacreontic poetry at dinner (19. 9. 4) need not come from *Mor.* 711 D, even though the conversation is fictitious; Gellius ate real dinners and enjoyed real entertainments.

90. A. Barigazzi, *Gnomon* 42 (1970) 684–5; Holford-Strevens, 'More Notes' 147.

91. For the Homeric connection see *Mor.* 730 C–D. Schrader 7. The taboo on beans is stated as a fact at *Mor.* 286 D, 729 A, but so is Pythagorean vegetarianism at 993 A.

92. Cf. S.E. *Math.* 1. 273, Schrader 8.

statements, widely separated and in slightly different form, are found in *Isis and Osiris*,[93] but speculative religion is not to Gellius' taste: for him, these are curious facts and no more.

On the Soul is represented by two quotations from book 1: *NA* 1. 3. 31, the anecdote (also told at *Mor.* 86 A, cf. 96 A) that Chilo asked the man who boasted of having no enemies whether he also had no friends, and 15. 10, the suicide-wave among the maidens of Miletus, ended when the city decreed they should be laid out naked with the noose still on.[94] The story appears again at *Mor.* 249 B–D, where the lesson is drawn that those who would endure death could not bear the thought of shame; Gellius contents himself with the hint 'pudore solo deterritas tam inhonesti funeris'.

Plutarch the moralist is not entirely neglected: in 11. 16 his attack on busybodies is discussed, though Gellius' main concern is translating the title Περὶ πολυπραγμοσύνης into Latin.[95] In 1. 26 Taurus tells of the slave who quoted *On Not Being Angry* back at Plutarch when under the lash (see p. 68); in a society that took slavery for granted, it does not detract from his benevolence.[96]

There is much in Plutarch that might have been of interest to Gellius, even if he did not choose to read about Roman affairs in Greek and was impervious to religious thought:[97] but he had other people to read, and does not sow with the whole sack. At 16. 3. 9–10 he quotes Erasistratus' statement that research is needed on why bulimia chiefly occurs in cold weather; that question was discussed at [Arist.] *Probl.* 8. 9 and Plut. *Symp.* 6. 8, but if Gellius had read either passage he did not recall it. However, he appreciated Plutarch as a source of interesting information and found his philosophy quite deep enough.

---

93. *Mor.* 353 F (onions thrive in the waning moon; they are not said to wither as it waxes), 376 F (cats' *pupils* dilate and contract; more accurate, but Proclus' ὄμματα vindicates Gellius' 'oculi'). On the substance see A. S. Pease, edn. of Cic. *Diu.*, pp. 406–7.

94. Cf. King 118.

95. See ch. 12 n. 25.

96. Cf. Finley 121–2. No doubt the slave relied on *Mor.* 459 C (many slaves are shamed into reformation by forbearing masters); but this fellow was unshameable. Montaigne, *Essais* 2. 31 (ii. 765–6 Villey²) translates the tale with approval; it reflects far better on Plutarch than *Cat. min.* 68 on the hero of Utica, or *Mor.* 70 E on Ammonius; however, his absence of remark in these places shows him less solicitous of slaves than animals, and in deprecating angry violence (for which see Gal. *Scr. min.* i. 13–16 Marquardt) he seeks the master's advantage, not the slave's. For the theme cf. Plat. *Leg.* 777 D–E, X. *Hell.* 5. 3. 7, Aristox. fr. 30 Wehrli, Sen. *De ira* 3. 12. 5–7, Plut. *Mor.* 551 B with De Lacy–Einarson; the tale falls into the pattern of *SVF* i. 298, but is perfectly credible. (Gellius' view of slavery is utterly conventional: Berthold 163–6; cf. ch. 2 n. 75).

97. *NA* 12. 11. 7 is perhaps a confused reminiscence of Plut. *QR* 12 (cf. ch. 8 n. 1). I find no demonstrable borrowing from the *Lives*. Oiselius derived 17. 9. 6–15 from Plut. *Lys.* 19. 8–12; but the information was widely available (cf. Hosius ad loc.), and Gellius speaks of a 'lorum', not a βιβλίον ὥσπερ ἱμάντα. Marcus may have a confused reminiscence of *Ages.* 30. 6 at *Ep.* 4. 13. 3 (but such tales may float from name to name) and intend *Phoc.* 36. 5 at *Med.* 11. 13. 2 (but G. Heilbut, *RhM*² 39 (1884) 310 cites Muson. fr. 10, p. 55. 2–9 Hense).

EXCURSUS:
RELIGION, SUPERSTITION, AND THE SUPERNATURAL

At 17. 1. 1 an indignant Gellius likens Cicero's detractors to those unnatural persons ('monstra hominum') who have delivered false and impious opinions concerning the immortal gods; his own are declared at 1. 6. 7 by his praise, as no less worthy of constant reading than the gravest philosophers' writings, for Metellus' words in his speech on marriage:

> The gods have the greatest power over us, but cannot be expected to care more for us than our parents do: but parents disinherit children who persist in going wrong; what else can we expect from the gods if we do not mend our ways? It is those who are not their own enemies for whom divine favour is meet; the gods should show approval of our virtue, not confer virtue on us in the first place.[98]

These, in a pre-Augustinian world, are normal views; but neither here nor elsewhere does Gellius display the religious emotions of an Aristeides or an Apuleius,[99] and when recording such matters of ritual as the taboos imposed on the *flamen Dialis*, he does not, like Plutarch, attempt an explanation[100]—other than the philological comment that the newly inducted Vestal Virgin is called Amata because that was the first Vestal's name (1. 12. 19). He shares the religious antiquarianism of Marcus, who toured the temples at Anagnia and revived the fetial rite, without his inward piety.

The verse quoted from Nigidius commending piety and discouraging superstition (4. 9. 1),[101] though called 'well worth remembering', leads only to discussion of adjectives in *-osus*. Admittedly Nigidius had cited it without source in a grammatical work for the pejorative use of the suffix; but the—wholly linguistic—treatment of *religiosus* is not derived from him. By itself the verse offers no more guidance than the injunctions in *NA* 1. 3; yet Gellius does not discuss the distinction between honour to the gods and enslavement to a bugbear.

At 6. 1. 6 we read that the elder Scipio used to enter the *cella Iouis* on the Capitol, just before dawn, as if conversing with Jupiter on state affairs, with no reaction from the guard-dogs; at 12. 8. 3 that he became reconciled with

---

98. Q. Metellus Macedonicus, fr. 7 M freely translated; see for discussion G. Bernardi Perini, *BStudLat* 9 (1979) 65–70. Cf. Cic. *ND* 3. 86–7 (but see Mayor's and Pease's nn.).

99. Fronto too is free of them (Brock 87–8); *Ver.* 2. 6. 1 expresses devotion to Verus, not the religious warmth suggested by P. Frassinetti, *GIF* 2 (1949) 249–50. His portrayal of Christian orgies, though echoing Cato's denunciation of the Bacchanalian scandals, may have been closer in purpose to Cicero's account of Piso's private life (Champlin, *Fronto* 64–6 assigns it to *In Pelopem*); Brock 92–5 displays her usual good sense.

100. Contrast *NA* 10. 15 (barring § 32, taken straight from Varro, *RD* fr. 51 Cardauns) with *QR* 40, 44, 50, 109–13. Ritual is quite frequently discussed (Berthold 182–3), but as a bundle of facts. Reverence for temples (4. 9. 9) is normal social decency, and serves to interpret Masurius.

101. See M. Mayer, *CFC* 9 (1975) 319–28.

Ti. Gracchus (*cos.* 177 BC) at the Capitoline banquet as if the gods had brought their hands together. These are stories about great Romans rather than the gods, of whom Gellius' 'quasi' avoids asserting more than was acknowledged by the City.[102]

The storm at sea of 19. 1 caused fear and wailing, yet nothing is said of prayers or vows, which many a passenger must have offered. In calling the use of *superesse* for *adesse*, 'appear for', not only incorrect but ill-omened, if the advocate be older than the client (1. 22. 21), Gellius displays neither superstition nor enlightenment in his own person: it is elementary that an advocate should not give offence. He does indeed credit things that presage: he relates the Sibyl's visit to Tarquin with her nine books (1. 19) and the augur Cornelius' second sight during the battle of Pharsalus (15. 18);[103] the first book of Cicero's *De diuinatione* is quoted, not the sceptical second. Etruscan haruspices are villainous (4. 5), but in asserting the opposite of the truth their art descried; it is therefore not the fraud old Cato took it for.[104]

The oracle that in the ancient *Vita* (ll. 5–6 Nauck)[105] foretold victory in contests for Euripides had been transmuted before reaching Gellius into an astrological prediction impossible (as he did not know) for fifth-century Athens. Such prophecies were easily taken as inspired when events fell out accordingly; but Favorinus had answered such apparent vindications in his demolition of astrology (14. 1. 33). At 1. 9. 6 astrologers are said to be correctly termed not *mathematici* but *Chaldaei*;[106] although this prescription would follow from Gellius' distaste for Silver usage, it is presented as a contrast between the noble $\mu\alpha\theta\dot{\eta}\mu\alpha\tau\alpha$, like geometry or music, and the low barbarian trade to which the vulgar apply it. To the Chaldaeans is ascribed at 3. 10. 9 (though not in 15. 7) the theory of the climacteric, during Varro's discourse on the hebdomad; in contrast to Philo. *Opif.* 113, Lact. *Inst.* 7. 14. 8, planetary influence, even on the seasons, is not mentioned.

102. Whereas Polyb. 10. 2. 8–13 (cf. Val. Max. 1. 2. 1) treats all Scipio's show of divine inspiration as a device to impress the people, Liv. 26. 19. 4 allows that he may have believed it; App. *Hisp.* 23 accepts that he did; with Gellius' 'quasi' cf. Liv. 'uelut sorte oraculi missa', App. ὥσπερ τι παρὰ τοῦ θεοῦ, *Vir. ill.* 49. 3 'quasi diuinam mentem acciperet'. Scipio and Gracchus were reconciled by the Senate (Livy 38. 57. 5, Val. Max. 4. 2. 3). On *Iouis epulum* see Latte 377, on Roman reserve towards the gods, id. 61–3; for *quasi* cf. e.g. Cic. *Har.* 6, *Phil.* 4. 7. Scipio's superhuman qualities were demonstrated above all by his deeds, *NA* 6. 1. 5, rather than the snake-prodigy transferred from Alexander.

103. The transmitted *remigis* of the lemma inopportunely recalls Cic. *Diu.* 1. 68 (Madvig ii. 605 n. 1).

104. Cic. *Diu.* 2. 52. Cato (who at *Diu.* 1. 28 complains that augurs did not take their duties seriously enough) was no rationalist, but a patriot suspicious of the *Etrusca disciplina*. The *augures* attacked with Gellius' approval (14. 1. 34) at Acc. 169–70 R no doubt represent μάντεις, a disreputable tribe.

105. See Lefkowitz 91.

106. Cf. Cic. *Div.* 1. 2, S.E. *Math* 5. 2, ch. 16 n. 21.

Greek myths are noted as poetical fables at 15. 21 and 20. 7;[107] the one barbarian observance recorded is the Pelusiotes' refusal to eat onions (20. 8. 7), derived from Plutarch. The Graeco-Egyptian cult of Serapis, Isis, and Osiris that could capture Apuleius no more engages Gellius than Judaism, Christianity, or the blood-chilling worship of Mithras;[108] he cares for the old religion, and that alone. He grants no space to magic, nor to other notions that in his day were not confined to the vulgar: in this contemporary of Aristeides and Artemidorus no one is cured by incubation and not a single dream is read. Large as the claim may seem that a humble compiler was less superstitious than Hadrian, Marcus, and Galen,[109] it cannot be disproved.

Gellius may have aimed at redirecting attention away from Oriental deities to the ancestral religion of the Roman People;[110] in any case, taking for granted the religious notions he was reared in, Gellius gives them little thought, and adds nothing to them either from Taurus' Platonic speculations or from the exotic cults attractive to many of his contemporaries. The world and his life made sense enough; he was immune to *Angst*;[111] whether he concurred with Plato, whose *Phaedo* he praises, or with Epicurus, whose argument against the afterlife he defends, he did not crave fleshly resurrection; the offer of forgiveness for his sins he would have taken as an insult.[112] He gave the Roman gods as much as they demanded—and as much as many a Christian has given their supplanter.

107. Gellius reports a grammatical discussion at Eleusis (8–10); initiation is not proved by pr. 21, but conceivable (cf. Cic. *Leg.* 2. 36; it would betoken respectable piety, not eccentric superstition). Falster, *Vig. pr.* 54–6 reviews the possibilities, aptly citing Plut. *Mor.* 635 A. Varro's reference to the mysteries at 11. 6. 5 (p. 472 Popma = i. 375 *ed. Bip.*) throws no light on this question.

108. The quotation at 4. 11. 13 from Plutarch's chapter on Jewish abstention from pork (p. 210) merely shows that Gellius had been browsing through the *Table-talk*; at most that the pork-loving Roman wondered how anyone could spurn such delicious food (Juv. 6. 160, 14. 98, Tac. *Hist.* 5. 4. 1, cf. Rut. Nam. 1. 384). No one will suppose that Peregrinus' Christian period was mentioned in 8. 3.

109. See e.g. Brock 95–6; MacMullen, *Paganism* 178 n. 25; add Cass. Dio 69. 11. 3; PGM i. 148; Syme, *HAP* 84–7; Luc. *Alex.* 48; F. Kudlien in Nutton (ed.) 117–30.

110. Fischer, p. lxiv. MacMullen, *Paganism* combats the view that 'traditional' paganism was wilting in face of 'Oriental' cults; but even if this was not in fact the case, an antiquarian might think it so (cf. too Luc. *Iupp. conf.* 13, *Deor. conc.* 9–10).

111. Pagans too could suffer from the death-wish (Dodds, *Pagan and Christian* 135 n. 4); Gellius notes only that the city of Miletus put a stop to such nonsense (p. 211).

112. Fronto consoles himself in his darkest hour with the contemplation of his virtue (*Nep. am.* 2. 9); cf. H. Chadwick (tr. H. Brakmann), *RAC* x. 1037. (Even the wretch of Plut. *Mor.* 168 D, cited by Dodds, *The Greeks and the Irrational* 253, is worried about ritual, not ethical, misconduct.) Celsus ap. Orig. *C. Cels.* 3. 62 complains that the Christians' god is not interested in the sinless; his concession (3. 63) merely grants that to err is human—but man may rise above his nature (Cic. *Tusc.* 4. 80, Alex. Aphr. *Fat.* 6, p. 171. 11–16 Bruns) without divine grace (Metellus Macedonicus, cited above). Observe too *NA* 17. 19. 6, a formula for being 'pleraque inpeccabilis'.

Chapter 15

Other Sciences: Rhetoric, Law, Medicine

Rhetoric

IMPERVIOUS to the attacks of early imperial writers, rhetorical education flourished in Gellius' day as it did long afterwards: Gellius, despite his occasional jibes at theoreticians, has no general objection. In 15. 11 he cites (from Suetonius) a *senatusconsultum* of 161 BC banning philosophers and rhetors (in those days Greek)[1] from Rome, and a censorial edict of 92 BC suppressing *rhetores Latini*; he comments that the expulsion of philosophers was not confined to those uncultured and unhellenized times, but took place again under Domitian: even Epictetus had left Rome for Nicopolis. To expel philosophers is the mark of the boor (so much for old Cato) and the tyrant; to expel rhetors at least of the boor. No consideration is given to the moral pretext or the political motive.[2]

Occasionally Gellius discusses rhetorical *controuersiae*; he is particularly interested in ἀντιστρέφοντα, or *reciproca*, as 'some' have called them in Latin (5. 10. 2), dilemmas that can be turned against their author.[3] The classic example is Protagoras' claim against his pupil Euathlus, who had undertaken to pay the balance of his fee after winning his first case,[4] but then not practised: Protagoras took him to law, arguing 'Either way you must pay: if I win, by judgement of the court; if you win, under the terms of our contract'; but Euathlus retorted 'Either way I don't pay: if I win, the court will award you nothing; if you win, I shall owe nothing under the contract.' The court in

---

1. In § 1, without support from Suetonius or the SC, Gellius' MSS read 'de rhetoribus Latinis': the adjective is plainly inappropriate despite Jac. Gronovius' defence (see Cic. *De or.* 3. 93, Suet. *Gram.* 26), an untimely anticipation of § 2; cf. Hertz ad loc.

2. Cf. Rawson 78. One of the censors in 92 BC was the great orator L. Crassus.

3. *Conuersio* is similarly used at Cic. *Inv.* 1. 83 (cf. *Rhet. Her.* 2. 38, Victorinus, *RLM* 253. 9–19 Halm); but Hermog. 32. 17–133. 3 Rabe (cf. Fortunat. 69. 13–19 CM, Grillius 7. 7–13, 53. 17–24 Martin) uses κατὰ τὸ ἀντιστρέφον of a case in which the two parties exchange ground halfway through. A claims repayment of a debt, with interest, from B, who avers that the transaction was a deposit, therefore interest-free; the people pass a law to cancel all existing debts (red revolution in the ancient world, but a sophist can take it in his stride); A demands the return of his deposit, B pleads the statute in bar of his debt. To this Sopater (*Rh.* iv. 154. 25) appends as similar the present dispute, under the names of Corax and Teisias (cf. ch. 1 n. 62).

4. In other authors, *if* he won his first case; but cf. D.L. 9. 56 ἀλλ' οὐδέπω νίκην νενίκηκα. Quint. 3. 1. 10 names the fee as 10,000 dr.; cf. D.L. 9. 52.

its perplexity postponed the case 'in diem longissimam'.[5] The next chapter,
5. 11, presents the Bachelor's Dilemma: a pretty wife will be frolicsome, a
plain one plaguesome; to say that in either case she will lack the other vice is
not enough (a fair point, and no less valid against Euathlus), but—as
Favorinus observed—the disjunctive premiss, 'you will marry either a pretty
woman or a plain one', is false (p. 86). In 9. 16 Gellius returns to the theme:
in discussing a *controuersia*, the elder Pliny had failed to notice an ἀντιστρέφον.
The hypothetical law permits war-heroes to choose their reward; a war-hero
demands, and gets, another man's wife; the former husband, distinguishing
himself in turn, reclaims her. Pliny applauds the argument 'If the law is good,
restore her; if it is bad, restore her'; Gellius objects that the opponent could
reply 'If the law is good, I need not restore her; if it is bad, I need not restore
her.'[6] As usual in declamations, concern is not with the legally correct or
philosophically just solution, but with something to say on the other side.[7]

In the previous chapter a young declaimer at Naples, after an
introductory talk[8] too boastful for his years, had (as usual at impromptu
performances) asked for a theme. One of Julianus' pupils, offended at such
presumption in the great man's presence, proposed 'temptamenti gratia' (9.
15. 6) the *controuersia*: 'Seven judges shall decide by a majority: two are for
exile, two for a fine, three for death; the prosecution demands the
death-penalty; defendant to reply.' The question is debated in surviving
declamations;[9] analogous situations could occur in both fiction[10] and real
life.[11] Gellius, however, calls it 'controuersiam parum consistentem' (from
the Greek for a faulty question, ἀσύστατος) of the kind known as ἄπορον,
'insoluble' (he suggests as a Latin equivalent 'inexplicabile').[12] The

5. Perhaps Gellius takes this detail from the Areopagitic finesse in 12. 7. The version making
Corax the teacher allows the judicial jest ἐκ κακοῦ κόρακος κακὸν ᾠόν. But if Euathlus had
undertaken to practise within a stated time of finishing the course (cf. Sopat. *Rh*. iv. 155. 7), he
was liable after its expiry for breach of contract; if not, then victory would expose him to a *second*
action if he did not pay. At Syrian. ii. 42. 2–8 R he argues: 'If I win, I am not liable under the
contract [i.e. the court will have rejected Protagoras' construction]; if I lose, I cannot have learnt
the art and ought not to be pressed for payment [cf. Plat. *Prot*. 328 B].' The Romanian writer I.
L. Caragiale, in 'Logica baroului' (cited by Fischer), makes the court dismiss the plaintiff's suit
and order the defendant to pay his debt (at *Opere* (1960) ii. 386. 5 read '⟨nu⟩ trebuie'?).

6. Cf. Quint. 7. 1. 24–5; 7. 5. 4; for the ἀριστεύς or *uir fortis* see Russell, *GD* 24–5, Bonner
88.

7. Pliny's case was sustained by J. C. Scaliger, *Probl*. LXXIII, pp. 23–4, Carolus 397–8 (cf.
Thysius ad loc.), Gellius' by Jac. Gronovius.

8. See Russell, *GD* 77–9, Bonner 51–2. For shamelessness and unreflective fluency (§ 9) cf.
Luc. *Rh. Pr.* 15, 18.

9. See n. 12 below; Russell, *GD* 23 and n. 1.

10. Hld. 1. 14. 1 makes 1,000 votes for exile prevail over 1,700 for death divided between
stoning and the pit.

11. Plin. *Ep*. 8. 14, recounts how he (irregularly) argued for a three-way vote in the senate: it
is taken for granted that the plurality would have prevailed. (It has not always done in Scottish
courts, where each of 15 jurors may give one of three verdicts.)

12. The προθεωρία to [Liban.] *Decl*. 45 states (§ 4) τὸ πρᾶγμα παντάπασιν ἄπορον, yet
claims precedent for adopting the στάσις of ποιότης (the nature of exile, for which three of the
judges have opted and the defendant pleads). Fortunat. 96. 17–23 CM calls it a *status negotialis*,

declaimer ought (we infer) to have declined it; instead, without pausing either to reflect on it or to hear alternatives, he jabbered away in a welter of words to loud applause from his friends, while Julianus grew red in the face and sweated with embarrassment. When he had finished, rhetor and pupils made their escape; Julianus, asked his opinion, replied 'adulescens hic sine controuersia disertus est' (§ 11), 'this young man's fluent, there's no argument'. 'Sine controuersia' here means both 'incontrovertibly' and 'without a *controuersia*'; an old joke, one suspects, but good and possibly used by Julianus on another occasion if not this.

At 7. 8. 3–4 Gellius suggests as a topic for declamation the relative chastity of the elder Scipio, who returned a beautiful Spanish girl to her father untouched, and Alexander, who refused even to set eyes on Darius III's sister-wife. Historical *controuersiae* are characteristic of Greek rather than Roman declamation, although a Greek would hardly declaim on Scipio;[13] Gellius, however, is thinking of Graeco-Roman comparison.[14] Though not taking it too seriously ('lepide igitur agitari potest', § 3, 'declamatiunculam', § 4), he reveals the hold of declamation over educated minds. Even the merits of grammatical analogy become a *controuersia* at 2. 25. 11: Varro's discussions are 'loci quidam communes' for both sides. The limits on a son's obedience to his father, treated in Stoic terms by Gellius (2. 7) but already considered by Aristotle, were an ancient topic of the rhetors';[15] the dilemma dismissed as 'argutiola ... friuola et inanis' (§ 9), that one need never obey one's father, since what he commands is either right (therefore to be done anyway) or wrong (therefore not to be done), suggests the brainchild of some declaimer, deliberately confusing 'must' with 'may', though the sophistry recalls the playfully bad arguments with which the Platonic Socrates confounds the dealers in unexamined platitude.[16]

specifically *quantitatum comparatio* in the numerical mode (whether the three who vote for death outweigh the four who do not; so 'Quint.' *Decl.* 365, arguing for the death-penalty); the language is Hermagorean (see Quint. 3. 6. 57; Hermogenes applied πραγματικὴ στάσις to deliberative speeches). It is not clear how the apory arises, unless the majority must be absolute and no judge may change his vote (a bold defendant might then argue that since there was a majority against each penalty, he ought to suffer none). Hermagoras' school used ἄπορον for the loan/deposit case (I fr. 19 b, c Matthes), and for two men each accusing the other of murdering a third (I fr. 19 a = Fortunat. 69. 3–8 CM; in an English case of 1946 both were hanged); Hermog. 33. 3–8 R applies it to a logically self-defeating problem (should Alexander trust a dream bidding him trust no dreams?); Grillius 53. 23–54. 2 M, rendering *inops*, adds an ex. concerning war-heroes, Syrian. ii. 42. 1–10 R Protagoras' suit (for Gell. 5. 10. 15 'dubiosum ... inexplicabileque' in the non-technical sense). Sulp. Vict. *RLM* 315. 26–8 Halm applies the term to such insoluble questions as whether the stars are odd or even in number.

13. Russell, *GD* 106–7; but both Romans and pre-Atticist Greeks debated the atrocious conduct of L. Quinctius Flamininus (Sen. *Contr.* 9. 2 with Winterbottom ad loc., Russell, *GD* 107).

14. Plutarch apart, see Cato, *Orig.* fr. 83 P (*NA* 3. 7. 19), Cic. *Brut.* 43, Liv. 9. 17–19. For arguments on Gellius' theme see P. Mejía, *Silva de varia lección* 2. 30.

15. Bonner 6; cf. Sen. *Contr.* 2. 1. 20, 'Quint.' *Decl.* 257, 271, 283; Hermog. 38. 15 R; ch. 14 n. 66.

16. Similarly Muson. fr. 16 argues from the τέχναι and redefines obedience as Plato redefines many other moral concepts.

In 17. 5 Gellius defends Cicero against a petty teacher of rhetoric, pedantic in two languages, who professed a systematic doctrine (such is the implication of τεχνικός and *artifex*, §§ 3, 9); the generally educated gentleman once more puts down the narrow professional, in this case (as in 4. 1) for ignorance of philosophy. Although Gellius and his masters give careful scrutiny to words and phrases, they recognize (1. 6; 6. 3) that serious oratory cannot be reduced to the formulae of schools and handbooks.

Indeed, no handbooks are cited by name, not even Cicero's *De inuentione*; his maturer discussions are quoted, but not primarily for their theoretical insights, even his insistence on understanding one's topic (*De or.* 1. 51, 3. 142) being presented in *NA* 1. 15. 5–7 as an ethical, not a rhetorical, precept. *De oratore* is otherwise adduced for anecdotes (1. 11. 15–16; 4. 8. 8), *Brutus* for the word *elegans* (11. 2. 4).[17] Two extracts are quoted from the treatment of euphony at *Or.* 168: one (13. 21. 24) in a chapter mainly devoted to the poets, the other (18. 7. 8) to illustrate *contio* 'audience at a public meeting'. The comments on prefixes (*Or.* 158–9 ~ *NA* 17. 1–2, 15. 3. 1–3) belong to grammar. However, although the use of 'rhetorum epilogis' (14. 2. 1) is closer to *Tusc.* 1. 112 than to *Or.* 57, the conceit that obsolete terms are new by reason of their strangeness (11. 7. 2) goes back to *Or.* 12, and the friend who did not trouble about words (5. 21. 2) echoes *Or.* 77.[18]

Law

The interest in law that was a part of Roman culture was not abated by the growth of specialist legal science;[19] Lucan and Apuleius found legal phrases no less suited to literature than Plautus or Lucretius. Gellius was a legal dilettante, but though a judge, no jurist. Under the normal procedure in private suits (e.g. in *NA* 14. 2) the parties or the praetor chose, normally from the official *album*, a *iudex* to try the case according to the praetor's *formula*, which stated the legal issues as conditional instructions to condemn, absolve, or assess.[20] Neither praetor nor *iudex* was typically a lawyer, but both had professional advice. A newer procedure *extra ordinem*, which ultimately drove the other from the field, committed the entire case to a magistrate or his

17. In Gellius' comment on Cato, *NA* 10. 3. 16, 'intelleget' conceivably echoes 'intelleges' *Brut.* 298, and the identification of Albinus at *NA* 11. 8. 2 resembles *Brut.* 81 (unless from Nepos); but *Brut.* 265 is not recalled at 1. 5. 2 (see ch. 11 n. 54), nor *De or.* 2. 260 at 4. 20. 1–6.

18. Cic. 'de re hominis magis quam de uerbis laborantis', Gell. 'doctrina ... nihil de uerbis laborante'. *Conuertere* = ἀντιστρέφειν (5. 10. 3; 5. 11. 3, 4, 6; 9. 16. 7) may reflect the passages cit. n. 3 (cf. in another sense *conuersio* = ἀντιστροφή *Rhet. Her.* 4. 19, Cic. *De or.* 3. 206); but cf. Grillius 53. 19 M ~ formal *retorquens, retortum.* At 14. 2. 8 'non apud censores de moribus' need not, especially in one so fond of censorial proceedings, echo *Rhet. Her.* 2. 5 (cf. n. 24); it was probably a commonplace of practice. Conceivably 'acerrimus prudentissimusque' of Aeschines (18. 3. 1) follows [Cic.] *Opt. gen.* 17 'acer et doctus'.

19. Although a gentleman advocate was expected to understand the law (Champlin, *Fronto* 74), its formal study was not part of a liberal education (Suet. *Galba* 5. 1).

20. Kaser, *Zivilpr.* 273, qualifies the conventional statement that the *iudex* merely found the facts. For *formulae* see especially G. 4. 34–47.

delegate, called from the third century a *iudex pedaneus* and in the later Empire appointed from the by then legally educated bar; but in the second century a Gellius could still be chosen, with expert advisers to guide him in the law (12. 13. 1–2). He possibly performed no worse than a Victorian Justice of the Peace who relied on his Blackstone, his clerk, and a strong conventional sense of right and wrong.

In 14. 2. 1 Gellius states that on enrolment he had, in the absence of living instructors,[21] sought out texts in Greek as well as Latin on the duties of a judge. Procedure was set forth in Augustus' law *de iudiciis priuatis* and in standard commentaries; but the reference to Greek suggests concern not only with law but with moral philosophy,[22] presumably in Stoic texts amplifying Chrysippus' view of justice (14. 4). At any rate, the problem reportedly confronting him in an *actio certae creditae pecuniae* was moral and not legal.

A plaintiff of known integrity, but lacking witnesses or documents, claimed repayment of a loan from a notorious scoundrel, who denied the transaction;[23] as formerly in England, neither party was allowed to testify (D. 22. 5. 10). The defence, urging the ancient as well as modern commonplace that the court was one of law not morals,[24] demanded that the suit be dismissed for want of evidence and the plaintiff mulcted for *calumnia*.[25] Gellius' advisers state firmly that, since the plaintiff has failed to prove his case, the court must find for the defendant; this was the view of busy and experienced professionals (§ 9),[26] no doubt *causidici* and *leguleii* whom a Fronto or a Julian would have barely deigned to notice, but quite competent to advise Gellius on standard practice. Roman law did not deal in palm-tree justice: the plaintiff, not the defendant, had to prove his case (D. 22. 3. 2),[27] and this he had not done ('nulla probatione sollemni', *NA* loc. cit.).

The young, however, are liable to heady notions of a justice that overrides the narrow law, and the inexperienced are prone to scruples. Gellius could

21. We are amazed to read, in that age, 'uocis ut dicitur uiuae penuria erat'; but Gellius means that he numbered no jurists among his acquaintance, though in due course he gathered some round him (§ 9); and Favorinus secured him the passing attention of Africanus. Besides, his concerns were not the same as theirs, cf. 16. 10. 3.

22. Even if D. 14. 2. 9; 43. 10. 1 attest (as is doubtful) Greek juristic texts before the *Constitutio Antoniana*, such works will have been few, and Gellius did not need them.

23. No doubt the plaintiff was a man of pecuniary, not only moral substance (cf. Arist. *An. post.* 89^{b}13–14); but in a defendant who could engage several *patroni* (§ 7), 'non bonae rei' (§ 6) will describe character (so 'nulla re bona dignum' 9. 2. 8, 'nulli rei' 9. 2. 6; 13. 31. 3; 15. 9. 11; cf. 6. 11. 2) rather than (as e.g. Garnsey 210–11) fortune and status: the loan, if loan there was, supplied not lasting indigence but a temporary need of ready cash.

24. *Rhet. Her.* 2. 5. cf. Cic. *Inv.* 2. 37, [Cornutus] 45; but a man's life is his best witness (Gorg. 82 B 11a. 15 DK, Cic. *Sull.* 78–9, Apul. *Apol.* 90. 2–3). See too Quint. 5. 7. 34; cf. Plin. *Pan.* 80.

25. i.e. bringing a suit he knew to be baseless; the penalty was one-tenth of the sum at issue (G. 4. 178).

26. For the barrister with more commitments than time (still a hazard to the modern litigant) see 'Q. Cic.' *Comm. pet.* 47, Tac. *Dial.* 3. 4; for orators in a judge's *consilium* cf. Plin. *Ep.* 1. 20. 12, Fronto, *Ep. M. Caes.* 4. 13. 1.

27. Kaser, *Zivilpr.* 278 and n. 15 injects common sense into a discussion no little marred by anachronistic scholasticism.

not bring himself to find for a scoundrel, subjecting a pillar of society to a
iudicium calumniae, merely because the formal requirements had not been
satisfied.[28] It was law that the judge must decide for himself whom to believe
(so Hadrian had insisted when asked for a rule of thumb: D. 22. 5. 3. 1–2)
and pronounce 'prout religio suggerit' (D. 5. 1. 79. 1; cf. Plin. *Ep.* 6. 2. 8);
Gellius had a *religio* (§ 12) against finding for the defendant and his filthy life.
This was a moral question, and therefore the philosopher's province.[29]
However, Favorinus, on whom he duly calls, invokes no philosophical
doctrine, but, after airing several questions raised in the younger Tubero's
handbook for lay *iudices*,[30] refers to the elder Cato's declaration that by the
mos maiorum, when plaintiff and defendant are of like moral standing, the
defendant should be believed. Favorinus draws the inference that when the
parties are of unlike moral standing, the court should believe the better man;
but Gellius, young and obscure, lacks the confidence to give judgement in
such terms. Being still unable to find for the defendant, he takes refuge in a
non liquet.

Psychoanalysts assert that conclusions drawn from a dream are valid even
if it was made up to mislead them; Gellius' qualities as a judge would be no
less clear if the narrative were a total fiction, based on a rhetorical theme and
his own reading.[31] Yet it seems strange that he should, in an invented
incident, allow himself so unheroic a role as pronouncing a *non liquet*; youthful
diffidence is not a quality he displays in grammatical dispute.[32] On the other
hand, the real Favorinus would have answered his pupil's question out of
Greek philosophy rather than—as the published chapter required (p.
159)—of Roman antiquity: it is easier to believe in the case than the
consultation, at least as Gellius relates it.

In order to understand the older literature, it was necessary to understand
the older law, the *ius ciuile* of the Twelve Tables. Although in *NA* 20. 1 the
jurist Sex. Caecilius Africanus is made to defend certain clauses against

---

28. Status, reputation, and wealth are among Callistratus' criteria for credibility (D. 22. 5. 3.
pr.); said of a witness, *locuples* means 'reliable' (Cic. *Flacc.* 40, *Off.* 3. 10). So, in 1963, the
would-be gentleman Stephen Ward was indignant when a prostitute gave evidence against him;
cf. Suet. *Claud.* 15. 4. A man of substance will be more readily believed even now than one who
lives from hand to mouth. Callistratus repeats the ancient commonplace that the poor will do
anything for gain; British soldiers have insisted on payment by an officer (sc. a gentleman) lest
one of their own kind should cheat them. Despite Kelly 174, the Romans believed no less than
we in *suum cuique*, but their ideology, taken for granted even in the schoolbooks (Dionisotti 105,
122–3), differed from ours (or what is said to be ours) in its view of *suum*; the more respect for
status, the more justice. For love of justice Gellius overrode the lawyers; cf. Frier 213–15.

29. Cf. Friedländer–Wissowa iii. 289–90.

30. Whether a judge should be swayed by private knowledge of the facts; whether he should
attempt to reconcile the parties if that seems possible; whether he should repair omissions in the
conduct of the case; whether he should indicate the direction in which his mind is moving. See
Frier 217–18. (Some would assign authorship to the elder Tubero: Frier 217 n. 79.)

31. Cf. 'Quint.' *Decl.* 312; but this is a deposit case, for which in Athens witnesses had not
been usual (Isoc. 17. 2; 21 *passim*).

32. Cf. 15. 9. 7 'atque ego his eius uerbis ut tum ferebat aetas inritatior'. Indeed, he is surer of
himself in such matters than in judicial practice; but fiction need not thereby be constrained.

Favorinus' objections (pp. 90–1), some of his colleagues concentrated on the law of their own day:[33] when in 16. 10 Gellius asks a legal friend what is meant by the term *proletarius*, taken by Ennius (*Ann.* 170 Sk) from the Twelve Tables, he replies (§ 7) that he ought indeed to explain it if he had learnt the law of the Fauni and Aborigines, those primeval inhabitants of Italy—as it were, 'in Kronos' time' or 'before the Flood'—also invoked by the arrogant anti-archaist of 5. 2. 7.[34] What the specialist does not know, the poet Paulus explains.

Another specialist, the grammarian of 20. 10, cannot see why he should understand another legal expression in Ennius, *ex iure manum consertum*.[35] Although Gellius protests that a man active in the world ought to know the main terms of civil procedure, 'uerba actionum ciuilium celebriora' (§ 6),[36] the *legis actiones* had long been obsolete, except for *sacramentum* in centumviral cases (16. 10. 8, cf. G. 4. 30–1); the phrase in question was still used there (20. 10. 1), but the practical man no more needed to understand it than in eighteenth-century England to know the origin of the casual ejector.[37] Yet for a gentleman there is more to life than practicality; the man of books must understand the phrase in Ennius and terms of sacral law used by the poets (e.g. 4. 6; 7, 6). But the *ius ciuile* and the *ius sacrum* interested Gellius for themselves and their antiquity.

Whereas the *Nights* include chapters on the induction of Vestals (1. 12),[38] the constraints on the *flamen Dialis* (10. 15), and the extension of the *pomerium* (13. 14), the last jurist to treat of sacral law was Masurius Sabinus, who celebrated his fiftieth birthday under Tiberius; he is the latest authority whom Gellius regularly cites, being used in ten chapters besides Pliny's citation at 3. 16. 23. Capito is quoted in eleven, his rival Labeo in four (and indirectly in three others); their political dissension is noticed (p. 189), but not their inverse disagreement in private law (D. 1. 2. 2. 47: Capito the conservative, Labeo the innovator), nor the disputes between Sabinians and Proculians. Indeed, jurists later than Masurius appear in only six chapters:

---

33. Not all of them (Nörr, 'Der Jurist', cf. id. *ANRW* II. xv. 553–62); but to know legal antiquity might not be to admire it (id., 'Rechtskritik' 145 and n. 9). The Gellian Africanus disclaims wide reading in general history, *NA* 20. 1. 54).

34. Cf. *NA* 1. 10. 1.

35. Cf. Cic. *Mur.* 26, 30, Nörr, 'Der Jurist' 88. Skutsch on *Ann.* 247–53 takes the antithesis 'ex iure ... ferro' to refute Gellius' account; but the contrast *in iure ... ex iure* belongs to legal history, not textual exposition.

36. Observe the opposition of *actio ciuilis* and *honoraria* (praetorian) at D. 30. 28.

37. Cf. Blackstone, *Commentaries* 3. 11. It was precisely the antecedents of existing institutions that moved Roman (like English) lawyers to play the antiquary (Nörr 87 with n. 93).

38. At § 14 'uti quae optima lege fuit', which baffles commentators and translators, means 'on the same terms as her who was a Vestal on the best terms', i.e., 'with all a Vestal's entitlements'; see Fest. 216. 11–20 L, cf. *CIL* i. 585. 27, Cic. *Har.* 14, and *eodem iure quo qui optimo*, 'with perfect title'.

Caelius Sabinus in two, Neratius Priscus, Titius Aristo, Laelius Felix,[39] and (in person) Africanus in one each. Neratius writes on Latin marriage-law before 90 BC (4. 4), Aristo on ancient Egypt (11. 18. 16, see pp. 230–1), Laelius on Roman assemblies (15. 27), whose only relic was the formality of the *comitia curiata*; Africanus justifies the Twelve Tables. Neglecting the modern law, Gellius concentrates on legal history: his authorities include Cato but not Cicero, though the latter's treatise on systematizing the civil law is cited at 1. 22. 7 for the verb *superesse*.

The praetorian edict is quoted in its final form (10. 15. 31), but the aedilician in an older state (4. 2. 1 ~ D. 21. 1. 1. 1); Gellius archaically subjects the *filius*' wife to the *pater*'s *manus* (18. 6. 9),[40] and blithely cites from Sabinus doctrines disputed by subsequent writers (the definition of *furtum manifestum*, 11. 18. 11 ~ G. 2. 184), discredited (that *furtum* could be committed in respect of land, 11. 18. 13 ~ G. 2. 51), or reversed by legislation (the impossibility of adrogating *pupilli*, 5. 19. 7, 10 ~ G. 1. 102). He knows that the provisions of the *Lex Voconia* preventing a testator in the richest census-class from instituting a female heir has become a dead letter (20. 1. 23), a fact not recorded by Gaius (2. 274)—who, however, notes that the woman may take by *fideicommissum*, which will have frustrated the law—but since the census had long since lapsed, since the lower limit of the first class, 125,000 asses (*NA* 6. 13. 1, but cf. Cass. Dio 56. 10. 2, PF 100. 22–3 L), would have seemed abject poverty even to a man of such modest wealth as Gellius, and since testamentary dispositions were of constant interest in Roman social life, he must have observed the fact for himself, like the disuse of sortition for Vestal virgins (1. 12. 12).[41] By contrast, his outdated notions on *furtum* indicate that he rarely heard cases of this delict, the criminal procedure, which excluded the civil (D. 47. 2. 57. 1), being preferred by the victims.[42]

39. If, as is commonly supposed, he be the Hadrianic Laelius; but though he is later than Labeo, whom he cites, he writes as if Republican procedures were in full vigour (cf. Conradi, edn. i. 575–6).

40. Watson, 'Two Notes' 197–201, cf. id., *Rome of the XII Tables* 9 n. 1. Gellius equates *manus*, *mancipium*, and *potestas* (cf. 4. 3. 3), which the jurists distinguished (but note Ulp. D. 1. 1. 4); cf. E. Volterra, *MAL*[8] 12/4 (1966) 281.

41. The last known census was taken by Vespasian and Titus; the *Lex Voconia* was still enforced under Domitian (Plin. *Pan.* 42. 1), but did not inhibit Agricola or Curtilius Mancia (Tac. *Agr.* 43. 4; Plin. *Ep.* 8. 18. 4), nor later Domitius Tullus (Plin. § 2) or the testator of Juv. 10. 237–8. On 'Quint.' *Decl.* 264 tit. see Watson, *Succession* 170. Sortition was used to select a Vestal in AD 5 (Cass. Dio 55. 22. 5), but not in AD 19 (Tac. *A.* 2. 86).

42. Kaser, *Priv.* i. 617–18. The explicit statement at D. 47. 2. 93 (Ulpian, *Edict.* 38) that criminal procedure is more normal has been suspected of interpolation, but its opening phrase is typical of Ulpian (Honoré, *Ulpian* 58 n. 135; Professor Honoré (pers. comm.) accepts the entire *lex* as Ulpianic). With 'non ideo tamen minus, si qui uelit, poterit ciuiliter agere' cf. Gell. § 10 'si qui super manifesto furto iure et ordine experiri uelit'. The civil action, worth while against the owner of a thieving slave, was useless against the increasingly numerous free poor, and execution of the judgement was not provided for. If, as P. Garnsey, *JRS* 57 (1967) 56–60 argues, the *quaestiones* were obsolete by Severan times, *NA* 2. 4 is the last apparent evidence for their survival; but it may be a blind anachronism like 13. 14. 4 (corrected in § 7, cf. Tac. *A.* 12. 23–4, *CIL* vi.

The combination of legal and grammatical interest demanded in 16. 10 and 20. 10 was exhibited by Labeo (13. 10), and also by two of Cicero's juristic friends, Ser. Sulpicius Rufus and C. Trebatius Testa, who are taken to task for false etymologies (7. 12). Gellius himself, ordered in 12. 13 by the consuls to pronounce by the first of the month,[43] 'intra Kalendas', knew quite well that in legal parlance this meant 'on or before the Kalends' (§ 29, cf. D. 38. 9. 1. 9; 50. 16. 133), but for his own satisfaction enquired of Apollinaris what it ought to mean.[44] Law without grammar no more suffices Gellius than grammar without at least a gentlemanly tincture of the law, as of medicine (p. 224). But this is not the same as relating law to life, or the ancient to the modern: while lovingly collecting the grammatical and historical trinkets with which the jurists adorned their expositions, Gellius takes little notice of the contrast between their doctrines and current practice.

Reading Varro (he boasts in 13. 13) enabled him to resolve a problem of constitutional law that had arisen in real life: whether a quaestor could be summoned before the praetor by a private citizen (he could).[45] On the other hand, he never discusses points of law that had arisen in the course of his judicial duties: of the two cases he mentions, in 12. 13 the law is clear and in 14. 2 it does not help him. Nor does he tell of bizarre events narrated in his court, or of shrewd interrogations that exposed the truth; no matter how humdrum the majority of his cases, there must have been some of interest to a better lawyer or a keener student of mankind, but to Gellius they were tiresome distractions from reading Ennius or contemplating the preposition *pro*.

Gellius is a scholar-gentleman who dabbles in the law, more especially in its antiquities; Romanists, while complaining of his misconceptions,[46] gladly cite his evidence, knowing it has not undergone the interpolation that brought the texts in the Digest abreast of the times.[47] But he also reveals the gulf that existed between the great jurists and their lay coevals.

31537*a–b*), or *diuinatio* may have been applied in Gellius' day to the choice of prosecutor by the magistrate (D. 48. 2. 16; 48. 5. 2. 9; the term is not found in the jurists, but cf. Fortunat. 96. 1–6, 115. 6–12 CM).

43. For the consuls' jurisdiction see Kaser, *Zivilpr.* 363–4, cf. *NA* 13. 25. 2.

44. See p. 63. Sulpicius answers only on condition that Gellius follow normal practice (§ 5).

45. The anecdote is built round a quotation from the same book of Varro's quoted in the previous chapter; the young Gellius puts to rights the public professors of law.

46. e.g. Kaser, *Zivilpr.* 91 n. 21; with the professional's unfairness to the amateur Schulz 580 understands 'definitum sit' (11. 18. 19) of definitions by genus and difference, which he easily proves that Sabinus' dicta are not. Gellius, who himself indicates their incompleteness (§§ 23–4), knew perfectly well what a definition at logic was (4. 1. 10–12), but that is not the only use of the word (1. 25 *passim*, cf. Quint. 7. 3), and *definire = constituere* is excellent Latin, even in the jurists (*TLL* v/1. 345. 42–68).

47. Likewise, the appearance of 'tacito consensu' at *NA* 20. 10. 9, cf. 11. 18. 4; 12. 13. 5 concerning the repeal of laws by desuetude (recognized at J. 1. 2. 11 and in Scots law for statutes of the Three Estates) vindicates the phrase for Julian at D. 1. 3. 32. 1 despite attempts to delete it as post-classical.

Medicine

In the first century BC, the Pneumatic physician Athenaeus of Attaleia maintained that from the age of fourteen all children should receive instruction in medicine, to help them look after themselves: 'for there is hardly any time by night or day when we have no need of the art, but in walking and sitting, at the gymnasium and the baths, eating and drinking, sleeping and waking and in every activity, throughout our lives and our entire existence, we require advice on its safe and advantageous use; but to have recourse always and on everything to doctors is laborious and indeed impossible.'[48] His proposal was not taken up; but in the second century AD the Graeco-Roman world extended its extreme sensitivity to the care of its health. It flocked to doctors, gods, and charlatans; it devoured treatises of medicine as no other age had done before.[49] The art flourished: Archigenes is thrice named by Juvenal in metonymy for a physician; the quality of Rufus and Soranus is vindicated by their writings; but all are eclipsed in fame, in merit, and in versatility by Galen.

Correspondingly, laymen write about their illnesses (Aelius Aristeides is the worst offender), or themselves, like Plutarch, offer hints on keeping well. Gellius relates (18. 10) that he had gone down at Cephisia with a feverish diarrhoea; when Taurus came to see him with his pupils, the doctor declared him on the mend, as the pulse would show if Taurus cared to touch the vein. The company was scandalized, till Taurus pointed out that the use of 'vein' for artery was a common error of speech, and did not prove the doctor ignorant.[50] Gellius, deciding that a liberal education ought to include simple knowledge of the human body, such as nature had made easily available for the sake of our health, devoted some of his spare time to reading medical books; from them he offers definitions of veins, arteries, and the pulse, which correspond quite well to those in the pseudo-Galenic *Definitiones*.[51] This book, a work of the Pneumatic school, was probably written in Gellius' lifetime; the qualification of the pulse as natural and involuntary—despite Gellius' claim to be quoting the definition of the ancients—went back only to Archigenes. Rather to our surprise, Gellius is almost up to date.[52]

48. ap. Oreib. *Coll. Med.* lib. inc. 39. 5 Raeder.

49. Cf. Bowersock, *Sophists* 74–5 on the link between preciosity and hypochondria (of which, as of *Angst* in general, Gellius is free); that between heightened affluence and medical obsession may be illustrated by the USA.

50. φλέψ of an artery is regular, as in Aristotle, so in the Hippocratic corpus (as Galen more than once observes), apart from the late text *Nutr.* 31; it remains frequent in lay parlance, especially, as Gellius' doctor uses it, of the pulse, since this was the context best known to the layman (so too *uena*, cf. ch. 1 n. 65, even in Celsus; at *NA* 3. 10. 13 *uenas* is amended to *arterias*). Cf. J. Longrigg, *LCM* 10 (1985) 149–50.

51. Nos. 73–4, 110 (xix. 365–6, 375–6 Kühn).

52. For Archigenes see Gal. viii. 754 Kühn, cf. Marcell. *Puls.* 82 Schöne, [Sor.] *Q. med.* 147 Rose. In Gellius' lifetime Galen, who wrote extensively about the pulse, established the full and regular presence of blood in the arteries. At 'Hipp.' *Nat. oss.* 13, the ἀρτηρίη said to be ὀλίγαιμός τε καὶ πνευματώδης is the trachea.

According to *NA* 18. 10, veins contain blood mixed with a little pneuma (*spiritus naturalis*), arteries pneuma mixed with a little blood; the hitherto dominant view, taken over from Praxagoras by Erasistratus in the third century BC, was that blood, in a sound and healthy body, was confined to the veins and pneuma (not innate, but drawn in from the air) to the arteries.[53] Erasistratus, however, is cited in 16. 3 for his observations on the appetite, and again in 17. 11 for his refutation of Plato's theory that ingested liquid passed to the bladder through the lungs; but in the latter chapter, having offered detail not found in Plutarch, Gellius allows the last word to the defence of Plato in *Symp.* 7. 1 (p. 210). Since his theory, firmly denied by Arist. *PA* 664^{b}4–19 and [Hipp.] *Morb. IV* 56, survived with the help of another Hippocratic treatise, *Cord.* 2; only a small portion is said to take this route), to impose on Galen[54] and stir Vesalius to attempt its proof,[55] Gellius is not to be blamed for believing it; but a reader of medical books should not have been dependent on Plutarch's *Table-talk.*

Gellius has read the odd work by Erasistratus;[56] something on veins and arteries; something perhaps on 'melancholia', discussed at 18. 7. 4 (but a philosophical source is no less probable); and Sabinus' exposition of the pseudo-Hippocratic work *On Nourishment*,[57] in which eight-month pregnancies are considered.[58] Nothing else appears, not even the Hippocratic text *On Eighth-month Births.*

That philosophy and medicine should be linked was affirmed at the beginning of our period by Plutarch and at its end by Galen.[59] Philosophy provides Gellius with a number of medical items: Aristotle on the senses (6. 6), memory (8. 7), and multiple births (10. 2. 1);[60] the *Problems* on sensation, micturition stimulated by warmth, the unhealthiness of drinking melted snow, and the physical effects of shame and fear (19. 2; 19. 4–6); above all Favorinus on mother's milk (12. 1). Other topics (the properties of hellebore, Mithridates' antidote, 17. 15–16) come from Pliny, who states at 3. 16. 24 that 'yawning in childbirth is fatal, just as sneezing after intercourse is

---

53. Gal. viii. 716 Kühn, cf. Harris 185 n. 6. This, not Gellius' formula, was the 'ancient' view (though Herophilus' opinion was different again, Harris 180–1).

54. *Us. part.* 7. 17 (i. 428–9 Helmreich), *Simp.* 2. 17 (xi. 502 Kühn), *Plac. Hipp. Plat.* 8. 9 (ii. 532–8 de Lacy, q.v.); cf. Harris 170 n. 1. Contrast Cels. 4. 1. 3.

55. See *De corporis humani fabrica* 7. 19 *fin.* (*Opera* i. 572 Boerhave–Albinus): 'Dein, si animali ante sectionem potum colore aliquo infectum porreximus, ... cuiusmodi humor in pulmonis asperae arteriae ramis occurrat ... perquiro ...'.

56. Erasistratus' works were still available (Harris 195; Gal. xi. 221 Kühn is counterfactual).

57. Mercklin's theory (pp. 665–6) that quotations in §§ 1–11 come from Hadrian's *decretum* would require the emperor to outdo Claudius in public pedantry.

58. His text diverges widely from that in our MSS (see Heiberg in *CMG* i/1. 83): the cryptic statement ἔστιν δὲ καὶ οὐκ ἔστιν τὰ ὀκτάμηνα becomes in the direct tradition the even more cryptic οὐκ ἔστι καὶ ἔστι.

59. Cf. Bowersock 66–9, Frede, *Essays* 225–42; but see J. Kollesch in Nutton (ed.) 1–11, and for Galen as a philosopher M. Frede, ibid. 65–86 (= *Essays* 279–98), P. Moraux, ibid. 87–116. At a lower level, observe the medical interests of the philosopher Apuleius.

60. Misquoted: see ch. 14 n. 33.

abortifacient' (*NH* 7. 42) Further interest in child-rearing is suggested by 4. 19, on the dangers of over-feeding; but in 16. 16, on babies born feet-first, the emphasis is linguistic (on the name Agrippa) and religious (the Carmentes' altars).

Several items straddle the line between medicine and marvel: music as a cure for sciatica and snake-bite (4. 13), sex-changes (9. 4. 15), the alleged nerve linking heart and ring-finger (10. 10), the suicide-wave at Miletus (15. 10). But there is no concession to divine agency, and no trace, in the treatment of gestation in 3. 16, of the zodiacal speculations recorded by Censorinus (*Nat.* 8. 13). The law too may be concerned with questions of health: the return of an unfit slave to the vendor involves the definitions of *uitium* and·*morbus* (4. 2); the Twelve Tables' provision for a sick defendant does not envisage grave illness (20. 1. 11, 24–8).

Another social fact, the visit to a sick friend,[61] provides the starting-point for discussions both medical (16. 3, 18. 10) and non-medical (2. 26; 12. 5; 19, 10): the grammatical dispute in Fronto's house over the Latinity of *harenae* is set off by a guest's report (19. 8. 3) that he has been cured of dropsy by the application of hot sands.[62] Indeed, although such visits are normal and natural, it is remarkable that so many should occur in Gellius; and when at 13. 2. 2 Pacuvius, visited by his fellow poet Accius, is called old and chronically sick ('grandi iam aetate et morbo corporis diutino adfectus'), his age is relevant to the story, for the contrast with Accius' youth, but not his illness. It was, however, a detail to interest Gellius' readers, as also, at 17. 9. 22, in a narrative otherwise starved of the specific, the statement that Histiaeus' pretext for shaving his slave's head (in order to tattoo a message on his scalp) was the treatment of long-standing eye-trouble.[63]

Although Gellius inflicts his medical history on us only once (perhaps he was seldom ill), he shares his age's fascination with the healing art; but while remaining the veriest amateur, he is no further removed from Galen than from Aelius Aristeides.

---

61. Berthold 52–3; Gellius takes such visits seriously enough to vary his mode of expression (p. 41 above).

62. Oiselius ad loc. cites Cels. 3. 21. 6 and other passages.

63. Mentioned by Cels. 6. 6. 8 E, 15 A; 7. 7. 15 D, Aet. 7. 92–3, and Paul. Aeg. 6. 2. 1; 6. 4–7 as a preliminary to various procedures on or underneath the scalp to cure eye-troubles.

Chapter 16

Weak Spots and Blind Spots

Names

SOME people like to boast that they never forget a name or a face; Cyrus the Great was alleged to have known every man in his army by name.[1] Gellius, by contrast, though making Favorinus find disgrace in giving people the wrong names (4. 1. 18), stands rather in the tradition of Augustus' forgetful *nomenclator*.[2]

In an age when most Romans (though not Gellius himself) were known by *nomen* and *cognomen* to the neglect of the *praenomen*, it may not seem grave that at 7. 11. 2 T. Manlius (*tr. pl.* 107 BC) becomes 'C.' and at 15. 28. 3 C. Serranus (*cos.* 106 BC) is called 'Q.' like his colleague Caepio.[3] But in 12. 7, expanding Val. Max. 8. 1. amb. 2, Gellius transforms P. Dolabella into 'Cn.',[4] and at 18. 10. 3 he even calls one of his own teachers by the wrong *nomen*, for 'Caluisius Taurus philosophus' was L. Calvenus Taurus, with a *nomen* highly suitable for the veteran *colonia* of Berytus.[5]

Doubtless Gellius thought of the philosopher as Taurus, and spoke of him as ὁ Ταῦρος when in Athens; furthermore, Calvisii had achieved eminence at Rome.[6] There is no such excuse for calling the great Samian astronomer Aristarchus 'Aristidem ... Samium' (3. 10. 6). At 9. 4. 3 the polymath and

1. Val. Max. 8. 7. ext. 16, Plin. *NH* 7. 88, Quint. 11. 2. 50, and perhaps Gell. 8. 7; X. *Cyrop.* 5. 3. 46–50 more reasonably makes him remember his officers. Cf. Fronto, *Princ. hist.* 2. 7 (Trajan); *Epit. Caes.* 14. 3, *HA Hadr.* 20. 9–10 (Hadrian).

2. Macr. *Sat.* 2. 4. 15.

3. For Manlius, Sall. *Jug.* 73. 7 prevails over Prisc. *GLK* ii. 382. 6. At *NA* 1. 22. 19 'M. [instead of 'C.'] Asini Pollionis' Carrio, alleging MS support, deleted 'M.' (*Emend.* 1. 18; comm. 108); later editors concurred until the 20th c. The corruption is plausible (see Hertz ad loc.), and deletion reduces Pollio to two names, like Cicero and Plancus, and as at 10. 26. 1. The historian of 10. 28. 1 is called 'K. [*Fγ; om. δ recc.*] Tubero' (cf. G. F. Unger, *JbClPh* 143 (1891) 320–1); it is as hard to believe he was K. as to account for corruption (before or after Gellius) from L. or Q., yet it is a strange lapse of memory that falls on *Caeso* except for a Fabius or a Quinctius. D.H. *Thuc.* is dedicated to Q. Aelius Tubero.

4. See ch. 4 n. 45. For the false reference 'in libro ... nono' cf. 1. 2. 6 (see Holford-Strevens, review of Cavazza, 37); 1. 22. 8 (Patricius' assignation of the fr. is unassailable); 7. 16. 13 (refuting E. Badian at *EFHE* 176 n. 1); 12. 4. 1 (see ch. 11 n. 75); Skutsch, edn. of Enn. *Ann.*, p. 30 n. 22 adds 9. 14. 15, but J. J. Scaliger, *Coniectanea* 185 easily restored 'X⟨X⟩III'; 17. 21. 43 (Skutsch, edn. 675–6) is second-hand. The wrong Aristotelian title (Περὶ μνήμης for Περὶ ὕπνου) is cited at 6. 6. 2.

5. *SIG* 868a; Holford-Strevens, 'Chronology' 94 n. 6.

6. Beginning with Caesar's legate, the triumphator of 28 BC; they abound in the 1st c. AD. See too Holford-Strevens, loc. cit.

paradoxographer Philostephanus of Cyrene is registered as Polystephanus;[7] in 13. 5 Eudemus of Rhodes, the losing contender for the succession to Aristotle, is throughout called Menedemus;[8] at 13. 19. 2, even as Gellius accuses Plato of a false reference, he commits one himself by writing 'in Theaeteto' instead of 'in Theage'.[9] In turn, the Gellian florilegium used by William of Malmesbury and John of Salisbury puts Pythagoras for Protagoras (5. 10),[10] and the *Nights'* first translator changed the Sallust of 18. 4 into Seneca (p. 245).

No error, however, is made in 5. 11, where the Bachelor's Dilemma is ascribed to Bias the wise instead of Bion the witty, its author at D.L. 4. 48; it was also fathered on Solon, Pittacus, Aristippus, Antisthenes, and Theocritus of Chios.[11] The first two were Bias' colleagues in the septemvirate of sages; as in Callimachus, *Epigr.* 1, a sage was the obvious counsellor. But a mistake of prosopography is generally recognized in 1. 6, where the speech on marriage ascribed to Metellus Numidicus is that delivered by his uncle Macedonicus, censor 131 BC, and read out to the Senate by Augustus in 17 BC 'as if written for the hour' (Liv. *Per.* 59).[12] Numidicus was, through Sall. *Jug.* 43–5, known to Antonine Rome as an upright and able man;[13] in consequence his oratory, which Cicero had been content to describe as adequate (*Brut.* 135)—whereas Macedonicus 'in primis est habitus eloquens' (ibid. 81)—attracted the mannerists' attention. Fronto includes Numidicus among the great orators and poets never honoured by having Marcus for a scribe (*Ep.*

---

7. The correct name appears in Pliny, but at some distance from the passage used by Gellius (p. 51).

8. Gellius conflated Eudemus of Rhodes either with Menedemus of Eretria or with Menedemus of Pyrrha, who narrowly failed to succeed Speusippus (*Acad. Phil. Ind. Hercul.* vii 2–5, pp. 38–9 Mekler; hardly with the seaman of D.Sic. 20. 93. 3–4). The right name is found as a variant in the Valerio-Gellian florilegium (§ 3 *menedemus*[1,2] T, [2] SY; *eudemus*[1] SY, [1,2] T[2]; cf. *eudemius*[1,2] MS Bonn UB 218), which, being no later than the 11th c. (S was written *c.*1100), will derive it not from the *Eudemian Ethics* but Boethius: Aristotle, Theophrastus, and Eudemus appear together at *De syll. cat.* 2 (PL 64. 813 B–C, 814 D), *De syll. hyp.* 1. 1. 3 (p. 206 Obertello), cf. J. Salis. *Metalog.* 4. 4 (p. 168. 13–15 Webb); Apul. *Apol.* 36. 3 is less likely. ('Eudemus' also Petrarch, *Res mem.* 3. 74. 11, but 'Menedemus' Diceto i. 42 St.) The story (like that in *Suda A* 927, making Aristoxenus the bitter loser) is fictitious: Aristotle was not a scholarch (Düring 346).

9. Seleucus Nicator > Nicanor *NA* 7. 17. 2, cf. Isid. *Orig.* 6. 3. 3. 'Dioxippum' (17. 11. 6) for 'Dexippum' comes from Plut. *Mor.* 699 C; 'Flaccus' (12. 8. 5) for 'Nobilior' probably from Val. Max. 4. 2. 1 (cf. Skutsch, op. cit. 573). 'Phocide' (10. 16. 4, cf. pp. 154–5) for 'Phocaea' may be either Hyginus' or Gellius' error, but 'ex terra Phocide' is in Gellius' style (p. 36).

10. Marshall *et al.* 392; cf. Diceto i. 39 St, Thos. Wilson, *The Rule of Reason* (London, 1551), sig. [V7]ᵛ–X1ʳ, cf. Schoeck 233. John, *Polic.* 5. 12 (i. 338. 14–17 W), having copied Pythagoras from φ, finds Protagoras in Quintilian and Gellius. Androclus (*NA* 5. 14; so Diceto i. 40–1 St) > Andronicus (Androcus *K*) and Andromachus in φ, Androdus in late MSS and early edns.; so Painter 1. 22, Montaigne 2. 12 (ii. 288–90 Villey[2]), H. W. Kirchhof, *Wendunmuth* 1. 203, but *Andrónico* (from J. Salis.?) A. de Guevara, *Ep. fam.* 1. 28. Laelius > Laevius in the MSS at *NA* 2. 24. 8–9, Apul. *Apol.* 30. 12.

11. See Barigazzi on Fav. fr. 122.

12. Cima 97–8; the passage is Macedonicus fr. 6 M. The speech was probably preserved as *Oratio Q. Metelli de prole augenda* (cf. Suet. *Aug.* 89. 2). M. McDonnell, *AJPh* 108 (1987) 81–94, who defends Gellius' ascription, overstates his inerrancy.

13. For Fronto's use of this passage see ch. 13 n. 44.

M. Caes. 1. 7. 4); three of the four verbatim quotations to survive are supplied by Gellius, for whom it was all too easy to blend the two Metelli with geographical *agnomina*.[14]

Foreigners

Gellius shows little interest in peoples other than the Greeks and Romans; when he does speak of them, it is generally for their part in Roman wars.[15] The frequently mentioned Carthaginians were, it is admitted (10. 27), once equal rivals with Rome for the mastery of the world; but only once are their customs mentioned, and then for the scorn their linen tunics apparently aroused in Ennius (6. 12. 7; *Ann.* 303 Sk). Hannibal, whom the Romans could not help respecting,[16] delivers a fine rebuke to Antiochus, proud of his show-army (5. 5), and appears in model propositions (16. 8. 7, 11); but he was a contributor to Roman glory. Although at 17. 9. 16–17 a Carthaginian invents a means of sending secret messages,[17] the theme of the chapter is not Carthage but clandestine letters, and barbarians are allowed to be cunning: 'barbarico astu' (§ 18), unfortunately said of the good Greek Histiaeus.[18]

The Gauls, too, make frequent appearances, but always as enemies except for the detail at 17. 15. 7, in a Plinian chapter on the properties of hellebore, that they smear it on their hunting-arrows; Gellius is no more concerned with ethnography for its own sake than when he states, apropos of appetite, that the Scythians, in time of dearth, bind up their bellies (16. 3. 4). A moralist would have rodomontaded on the noble savage (*campestres melius Scythae*) and invented an apt remark for the wise Anacharsis; but Gellius feels no urge to criticize his own society, and does not doubt the superiority of Graeco-Roman civilization. Mausolus' widow Artemisia is presented not as a Carian princess who married her brother after the barbarian custom but as the

14. Modern scholars err likewise at 10. 21. 2 'cum et M. Cato et Sallustius et alii quoque aetatis eiusdem uerbo isto [sc. *novissimus/-e*] promisce usitati sint', taking 'M. Cato' for the Censor (fr. 51 Jordan). A word that he used freely would not have been a neologism to Stilo or Tiro (p. 130), nor would Caper have had to cite Antias for it (Charis. 269. 16–20 B), and Gellius knew the Censor was not contemporary with Sallust. (*NA* 19. 10. 10 'et M. Cato et M. Varro et pleraque aetas superior' = *et ueterum plerique* is not parallel; the *aetas* is that of pure Latin.) 'M. Cato' must be Uticensis, whom Tiro, like Capito (paraphrased at *NA* 4. 10. 8, fr. 4 Strz), will have intended by this name. (G. Bernardi Perini, *AAP* 91–3 (1978–9) 5–13 sees that 'M. Cato' cannot be the Censor, but unnecessarily emends.)

15. The Parthians provide Ventidius with his triumph (15. 4); the Germans launch the *bellum Cimbricum* (16. 10. 14); similarly the Persians are noticed only in relation to Greek history. There are no Britons.

16. Cic. *Sest.* 142, *Off.* 1. 108 (*Am.* 28 is too crude), *De or.* 1. 210, 2. 75–6 (where as in *NA* 5. 5 he is a foil against the Greeks); Nepos, *Hann.* 1. 1–2; Liv. 21. 4. 2–8 (despite 'ingentia uitia' § 9); Val. Max. 5. 1. ext. 6; Plin. *NH* 34. 32; Sil. 1. 185–8; Fronto, *Ver.* 2. 1. 23; Cass. Dio 13 fr. 54.

17. Demaratus' device (p. 182; already noted by Ascensius).

18. Nor does Gellius know the identity of Aristagoras or the contents of the message (§ 21). His source, compiling στρατηγήματα, may have thought such details irrelevant; contrariwise, the medical pretext (p. 226) is not in Herodotus (who offers a Carian Histiaeus, son of Tymnes; but did Gellius know him well enough to confuse the two?).

organizer of a poetry competition, an event as Greek as her name.[19] When the king of Lydia wages war to the sound of strings and woodwind, Gellius adds a reprobation not found in Herodotus: Alyattes, 'more atque luxu barbarico praeditus', has in his array 'lasciuientium delicias conuiuiorum' (1. 11. 7).[20] Mithridates, by contrast, commands respect (17. 16–17), but appears only for *faits divers*.

Gellius makes a point of calling astrologers not *mathematici* but *Chaldaei* (1. 9. 6), thus restoring the language of Cato and Cicero for that of Tacitus and Juvenal; if the name implies that astrology is not a fit concern for civilized persons, that will not distress the man who quotes Favorinus' refutation, even though the planets were discovered 'a Chaldaeis et Babyloniis siue Aegyptiis' (14. 1. 11).[21] At 3. 2. 5 he states that the Babylonians reckon the day from sunrise.[22] A people so doing was structurally required to balance the Athenians, who start it at sunset (§ 4), even as, in the longer arm of the chiasmus, the Umbrian midday (§ 6) balances the Roman midnight (§§ 1–3); and the Babylonians' achievement in astronomy entitles them to a hearing. But the entire discussion in this portion of the chapter is explicitly taken from Varro; and Gellius' real concern is with the Roman usages that follow in §§ 7–16.

The references in the *Attic Nights* to Egypt display an interest slight indeed in comparison with other writers', but rather more considerable for Gellius. He had read Apion's *Aegyptiaca*, which, however, ranged far beyond Egypt (being the source for Androclus and the Lion, 5. 14, and the Boy and the Dolphin, 6. 8); they informed him that rings were worn on the third finger of the left hand because Egyptian anatomists had discovered a very fine nerve running from it to the heart (10. 10).[23] At 11. 18. 16 the ancient Egyptians, renowned as they are for their inventiveness and intelligence, are said by the jurist Aristo to have had no law against theft, a fable that might inspire one

19. See Hornblower 332–51 (Hellenization), 359–63 (sibling marriage).

20. Gellius' disapproval was heightened by the delusion that the band contained 'feminas etiam tibicinas', whose services at symposia were not confined to music. Cf. Poseidonius' comment on an even less military turnout, *FGrH* 87 F 2 (cit. Hornsby).

21. The Egyptians of old were astronomers enough to know the planets, but no more astrologers than the classical Greeks; their lore of lucky and unlucky days, like Hesiod's, was grounded on mythology (L. von Beckerath, *LdÄ* i. 511–14). But once the Chaldaean art had conquered Egypt and her masters, her ancient sages, already ranked with the Babylonians in astronomy (e.g. Arist. *Cael.* 292ᵃ7–9), were accorded a like honour in astrology (e.g. Firm. *Math.* 1. pr. 6; 2. pr. 3). The spread of μαθηματικός/mathematicus in Imperial usage reflects the increasing participation of non-Orientals.

22. In fact from sunset in Seleucid times: O. Neugebauer, *PAPhS* 107 (1963) 529 (but see too K. Sethe, *NGG* 1920, 121).

23. This is not borne out by the Ebers Papyrus of Dyn. XVIII (Grapow 11–12, 15–19), admittedly over a dozen centuries before Apion. The third finger of the left hand is by no means the only Egyptian ring-finger; for other ancient cultures cf. Plin. *NH* 33. 24–5. A taboo is indicated by the term 'nameless' in several languages (e.g. Sanskrit, Russian, Turkish, Chinese) for the third finger. Macr. *Sat.* 7. 13. 9–16 gives an incomplete mystical interpretation (taking the hieroglyph for 10,000 to mean 6), and a rationalistic one from Capito (fr. 12 Strz).

man to moralize, and be critically rejected by another;[24] but Gellius, whose subject is the law of *furtum*, passes straight on to the Spartan ἀγωγή that encouraged boys to steal and punished them for being caught. Sparta being closer to home than Egypt, the truth is more easily ascertained (§ 17); Gellius does not necessarily disbelieve Aristo's report, but takes the matter no further. At 20. 8. 7 the Pelusiotes' taboo on eating onions is cited from Plutarch because the explanation is relevant to Gellius' theme, the effects of the moon's phases.

Nothing else of any interest is said about barbarians, unless we count the fabulous tribes of 9. 4 and the equally fabulous extinction of the Psylli at 16. 11. 3–8. The latter follows an account of magical powers among the Marsi (whose descendants in the Abruzzi were to retain that reputation), allegedly inherited from Circe.[25] But the peoples of Italy, so dear to Vergil's heart, are of scant interest to Gellius: the Latin cousins indeed afford the matter of 4. 4 (on their marriage-law), but the Samnites appear in unflattering or hostile contexts (barring the etymological remarks at 11. 1. 5, where they are said to be descended from the Sabines).[26] The only Etruscans are the villainous *haruspices* of 4. 5; at 3. 2. 6 Varro's contemptuous comment on the Umbrian custom of reckoning the day from noon—that a man born at midday in Umbria would have two half-days for a birthday—does not provoke the reflection that an Umbrian could say the same of a Roman born at midnight.[27] The Roman way is the right way; if we bear that principle in mind we shall not find Gellius' references to other peoples too few or too fleeting.

In 17. 17 Gellius records 17 that, whereas Ennius credited himself with three hearts for knowing Greek, Oscan, and Latin,[28] Mithridates, king of over twenty peoples, possessed all their languages like a native speaker;[29] by contrast, his own interest in tongues other than Latin and Greek is purely etymological. His information comes mostly from Varro: *multa* and *Nerio* are derived from Sabine (11. 1. 5; 13. 23. 7), *petorritum* from Gaulish (15. 30. 6),

24. Completely false, but perhaps a looser version of the fable at D.Sic. 1. 80. 1–2 that all stolen goods were deposited with the Head Thief, who restored them to their owners for a quarter of their value; had some lawless city known its Jonathan Wild? And note Drimacus (Nymphod. *FGrH* 572 F 4, Finley 113–14).

25. Marsi and Psylli are linked by such powers as snake-charming (cf. Cinna, fr. 10 M–B at *NA* 9. 12. 12).

26. *NA* 1. 14 (present offered to Fabricius); 17. 21. 36 (Caudine Forks). Also in grammatical chapters at 2. 19. 8; 17. 2. 21 (Caudine Forks) and (unnamed) 2. 19. 7; 6. 11. 7 (fraud on the Lucanians in 326 BC.).

27. There is no more intrinsic absurdity in reckoning the day from noon than the year from midsummer, or in dividing one natural day between two civil than in disallowing the *trinoctium* 27 Dec. (pre-Julian)–1 Jan. (Q. Mucius ap. Gell. §§ 12–13). However, neither astronomy nor astrology had yet adopted this system.

28. See Skutsch, edn. 749–50.

29. Twenty-five in most MSS: 22 in G π V *pars alt.* and *ed. pr.*, as in other sources (see Hertz and Hosius ad loc.). Reports of linguistic competence are commonly exaggerated, but Cleopatra too allegedly dispensed with interpreters (Plut. *Ant.* 27. 3–4). The monarchs may have been flattered at the time or later, but perhaps made genuine efforts to learn their subjects' languages.

lancea from a Hispanic language (ibid. § 7), but *cupsones* not from Punic (8. 13).[30] When in 4. 7 Probus claims the early poets' authority for pronouncing *Hannibālem, Hasdrubālem,* and *Hamilcārem,* but adduces only one example, this is a matter of Latin, not Punic, grammar; neither Probus nor Gellius asks which pronunciation is truer to the original,[31] or wonders why *Hannibal, Hasdrubal,* and *Hamilcar* are Ἀννίβας, Ἀσδρούβας, and Ἀμίλκας in Greek. Such indifference was the norm.

The Arts other than Literature

Gellius' indifference to painting and sculpure is well-nigh total.[32] Only one picture is mentioned, Protogenes' *Ialysos* (15. 31), which was indeed 'memoratissima' (§ 3) and had been admired by Cicero (*Or.* 5), but had perished in Nero's fire (Plut. *Demetr.* 22. 7). It had taken the artist seven years to complete (Plut. § 5); or eleven, even though he had no other work in hand (Fronto, *Ep. M. Caes.* 1. 10. 4); Apelles admired the painter's pains, but missed the charm of his own work (Plut. § 6; Ael. *VH* 12. 41). None of this does Gellius tell us, only a highly aberrant version of its part in the siege of Rhodes,[33] in which Protogenes is already dead, and Demetrius, far from respecting it, has to be shamed out of destroying it by an embassy: this is one of Gellius' many stories about *legationes.*[34] The iconography of Justice is discussed at 14. 4, but purely for its moral symbolism; Gellius even turns Chrysippus' γράφεται ('is painted') into portrayal by painters *and* orators (§ 2).[35] Though commemorative statues are mentioned (4. 5. 1; 9. 11. 10), no sculpture is discussed for its artistic merit; the image of Vediovis at 5. 12. 11 is

---

30. *Multa* is peculiar to the Italic languages. The Sabine origin of *Nerio* (and *Nero*) is certain (though Gellius'—or Varro's—ulterior derivation from νεῦρον is false; cf. ἀνήρ and Welsh *nerth,* 'strength'). *Petorritum* is Gaulish, and likewise *lancea* according to D.Sic. 5. 30. 4 (but did Cato report it from Celtiberia? Gauls fight with *lanceae* at Sis. frr. 21, 29, 71), with an unclear relation to λόγχη; again Gellius ignores Verrius, see PF 105. 17 L. For *cupsones* see pp. 11–12.

31. Length appears at Plaut. *Poen.* 997 (*Mytthumbālis* < *mtnbᶜl,* 'Gift of Baal'). Varro, *Sat.* 216 Cèbe (213 Bücheler). 1; [Prob.] *GLK* iv. 127. 3–8, 128. 35–9, invoking Latin analogies, prescribes *Hannibālis* but *Bomilcāris.* The early Romans simplified the final consonant-clusters ᶜl and *rt,* but lengthened the vowel to preserve the original syllabic weight (and in oblique cases stress, once initial accentuation had been abandoned) and match the declension of *animāl calcār,* as they were still pronounced. The rise of the Iulii Caesares (a praetorship in 208 BC) offered a masc. stem in -*ār*; the hexameter could not accommodate *Hannibālis,* cf. Skutsch on Enn. *Ann.* 371. Presumably Ennius' *Scipio,* the source of Probus' citation (*Var.* fr. 13 V), contained other exx.; Probus' reference to Plautus may envisage *Poen.* 997 or a non-Varronian play. No doubt the names were also found in *praetextatae.*

32. Friedländer, *Kunstsinn* 25.

33. Plin. *NH* 35. 104–5; Plut. *Demet.* 22. 4, *Mor.* 183 A–B; nothing in D.Sic. 20. 82–8, 91–100.

34. See *NA* 1. 14; 3. 8; 6. 14. 8–10 (17. 21. 48); 6. 18; 7. 4; 10. 27; 11. 9–10; 15. 20. 10 (cf. 4. 18. 8; 6. 3; 10. 3. 5).

35. For 'rhetoribus' see ch. 3 n. 50. To praise Chrysippus' description, Gellius uses (trite) pictorial metaphor (lemma, § 1). This shows that he could match his language to his subject, even that words made a deeper impression on him than pictures, not that he was at all interested in the literal denotations of his terms. 'Graphice' (12. 4. 1) is a Plautine reminiscence; the portrait of the Good Companion is moral, not visual.

of interest purely for its evidence about the god's nature, the gilded statues in Trajan's forum only for the inscription *ex manubiis* (13. 25. 1). No painter or sculptor is noticed among the eminent persons in the chronological chapter 17. 21, nor do such names as Pheidias or Apelles appear in Gellius' text.

Praxiteles does, an exception that proves the rule. In 13. 17 Gellius will have it that *humanitas*, in classical Latin, denotes not kindness, but education (p. 130); as an example he quotes Varro's words 'Praxiteles qui propter artificium egregium nemini est paulum modo humaniori ignotus', is known to anyone with a modicum of culture. Obviously, says Gellius, this does not mean a kindly person, who might be 'rudis litterarum', but an educated one, who will have read and heard about Praxiteles (§ 4). It does not occur to him that the educated person ought to know the statues; whereas for Varro, a connoisseur of the visual arts,[36] *humanitas* required that even a cup be beautiful (*LL* 8. 31).

The Roman property-owner might be expected to take some interest in architecture; but Gellius cares nothing for the λαύρη of Odysseus' palace (14. 6. 3) and says nothing of the designs for Fronto's bath-house (19. 10. 2–3)—as opposed to the estimated cost (§ 4), which stimulates a grammatical debate. In 2. 10 Catulus' wish to improve the proportions of the Capitoline temple serves only to introduce a little-known word;[37] the temple of Artemis burnt down at Ephesus (2. 6. 18) no more interests Gellius as a building than the Mausoleum (10. 18. 5), acknowledged to be among the Seven Wonders of the World (so, as Gellius does not say, was the rebuilt temple at Ephesus) but mentioned for the poetical contest at its dedication. At 10. 1. 6–9 Pompey's theatre appears only for its inscription.

Gellius' grasp of musical theory may be judged from the slapdash definition (16. 18. 4): 'The longer measure of sound is called rhythm, the higher melody.'[38] A marvel is alleged at 9. 7. 3, that at the winter solstice the strings struck on the cithara are not the strings that sound;[39] the aulos is said to relieve sciatica (4. 13) but to have become unfashionable at Athens because Alcibiades disliked the faces pulled in playing it (15. 17).[40] The use

36. See Plin. *NH* 35. 11, 173, and for his favourite statue 36. 17. Gellius knew Varro's work *De imaginibus*, in which seven hundred biographies were accompanied by portraits, but is interested only in the introductory remarks about the number seven (*NA* 3. 10) and in the biographies of poets (3. 11, perhaps also 13. 2 (but cf. ch. 9 n. 45); 17. 4): the portrait of Homer (3. 11. 7) is mentioned only to locate an epigram.

37. Catulus' temple, like Protogenes' *Ialysos*, had long since perished by fire.

38. Weiss and Rolfe rightly take the comparatives as polar, length being opposed to height; but the definitions are still crude. Quint. 1. 10. 22 at least avoids absurdity.

39. Proust understands like-tuned strings in different instruments (cf. Falster, *Am. phil.* iii. 257, whose alternative 'aut chordis in uno organo supra chordas positis' anachronistically envisages sympathetic strings as in the newly fashionable viola d'amore or the Norwegian *hardangerfele*), but admits that they would resonate every day. Or, since cold sharpens strings, did Suetonius mean that one emitted the note proper to another? Professor M. L. West (pers. comm.) recalls the Pythagorean cosmic lyre (Burkert 320 n. 107, 355–6).

40. For Athenian repudiation of the aulos (generally out of tune: Aristox. *Harm.* 2. 42. 7–15, 43. 22–4) see Arist. *Pol.* 1341^{a}37–^{b}8; the tale was commonly attached to Athena.

of musical instruments in war and oratory is discussed in 1. 11; a technicality is misunderstood (p. 169). Various kinds of trumpet are considered (5. 8. 8–11; 20. 2).[41] Naturally there is musical entertainment at the party in 19. 9, but the notice on *sicinnistae* (20. 3), whose song-and-dance had been reduced to song, soon becomes a commentary on Accius.[42] Gellius liked a good tune, but took no deeper interest.[43] In 18. 14 he does not remark that the ratios 3 : 2 and 4 : 3 constitute rhythmical γένη (the latter not recognized by Aristoxenus) and on the Pythagorean system yield the respective intervals of perfect fifth and perfect fourth; the obscure pseudo-medical assertion about the fourth at 3. 10. 13 is embedded in Varro's discussion of the number seven.[44] We are spared the music of the spheres.

Miscellaneous

Gellius defines, mostly from Varro, a few terms of mathematics (1. 20; 16. 18; 18. 14);[45] he lists textbook *placita* on sound (5. 15) and sight (5. 16); he records paradoxes of optics (16. 18. 2). Astronomy is confined to occasional facts from Varro (1. 20. 6; 3. 10. 6) and general knowledge blended with

41. For trumpets as musical instruments see ch. 11 n. 107; Ar. Quint. 62. 6–19 W-I discusses the music of Roman military signals, τοῖς πλείστοις ἄδηλον, cf. Quint. 1. 10. 14, [Plut.] *Mus.* 1140 C, Wille 75–104 on Roman 'Militärmusik'. The phrase is launched at *NA* 1. 11. 4 'ad quandam quasi militaris musicae disciplinam' as a doubly qualified μεταφορά describing the Spartans' use of the aulos, which others freely call music (cf. S.E. *Math.* 6. 9, 24) and link with Platonic μουσική (Quint. 1. 10. 14–15) or the king's sacrifice before battle to the Muses (Plut. *Lyc.* 21. 4–7, *Mor.* 238 B, 458 E, Mart. Cap. 9. 925).

42. The σίκιννις ('sicinnium' Gell.) was a wild dance performed in satyr-plays and elsewhere (cf. Seaford on E. *Cycl.* 37); for Rome see D.H. *Ant.* 7. 72. 10–12.

43. Against appreciating music only 'hac communi uoluptate aurium', Quint. 1. 10. 4, 9–33, Ar. Quint. 3. 6–8 W-I; for, S.E. *Math.* 6. 32–3. The great Antigeneidas, celebrated by Apul. *Flor.* 4. 1–2 in a virtuoso display of musico-ethical erudition, is for Gellius an incidental name in Pamphila (15. 17. 1). The proverb 'hidden music has no worth' (13. 31. 3; A. Otto 236) is cited as apt to the occasion and demonstrative of Greek learning; it proves no more interest in music than the tale of Arion (16. 19).

44. 'Venas etiam in hominibus uel potius arterias medicos musicos dicere ait numero moueri septenario, quod ipsi appellant τὴν διὰ τεσσάρων συμφωνίαν, quae fit in collatione quaternarii ⟨et ternarii⟩ numeri' (em. Bernardi Perini, 'Revisione' 264: cf. Philo, *Opif.* 96): 'He states that doctors who concern themselves with music say that the veins, or rather arteries [cf. 18. 10], beat by the number seven, which beating they call the consonance of the fourth, which is produced by the proportion of four to three.' Well may Fischer ask how the pulse can be called an interval; a misunderstanding of δι' ἐπιτρίτου λόγου 'in 4 : 3 rhythm' = 7/4 time at one crotchet to the mora (cf. W. H. Roscher, *Abh. K. Sächs. Ges. Wiss.*, phil.-hist. Kl. 24/6 (1906) 139)? But Herophilus did not recognize this rhythm, and assigned the healthy adult an even, spondaic pulse (2/2 time; Ruf. 224–5, Gal. ix. 278, 462–4, 499 Kühn, Ar. Quint. 32. 25–8 W-I). Thysius, invoking Cens. 14. 13, understands doctors who cure by music to say that the pulse is quickened by the playing of fourths, as if 'numero' were the antecedent of 'quod'; de Chaumont (see App. n. 39) absurdly takes 'septenario' to render ἑπτάχορδος, whence at length Wille 445. Professor M. L. West (pers. comm.) supposes mere number-mysticism without empirical intention.

45. At 1. 20. 8 he does not see that Varro's 'et altitudine' is superfluous; his own definitions of 'plane' and 'solid' (§§ 2–3) make a poor showing beside Eucl. *El.* 1. def. 7; 11. def. 1. In 16. 18 geometry includes optics and canonics, itself comprising musical theory and metrics; but Varro's geometrical explication of the penthemimeral caesura is not set out (18. 15. 2, see ch. 9 n. 13; cf. 16. 18. 5).

philology (2. 21; 13. 9); the causes of winds are not considered with their names (2. 22), those of earthquakes are said to be unknown (2. 28. 1), those of eclipses were dismissed by Cato as unimportant (ibid. §§ 5–7). But the practical Roman discusses ballistics (9. 1) and fire-prevention (15. 1); Greek money and measures are converted into those which with his readers are familiar.[46]

Cato's *De agri cultura* is cited twice for its language (3. 14. 17,[47] 10. 26. 8); Varro's *De re rustica* in 2. 20 not for parks and bee-houses but for their names. Gellius has seen oak fences on his travels in Italy (ibid. § 5), and looked at olive-leaves to confirm a reputed marvel (9. 7. 1–2);[48] he knows that sheep have more than two teeth (16. 6. 10), and has read that only a castrated goat should be called a *caper* (9. 9. 10, cf. p. 149). Although in olden days neglect of one's land was punishable (4. 12), agriculture above subsistence level had long since become a task for slaves.[49] Antonine moralism knew its bounds, and Gellius was a townsman.

46. In § 11 Orestes' seven-cubit corpse makes 12¼ feet, not the expected 10½; is Gellius reckoning with royal cubits (cf. Hultsch 94–5, 96 n. 3, 525, 529, 567 n. 1; a different explanation ibid. 76–7 n. 1)? He converts Greek money to Roman at the standard rate of 1 drachma to 1 denarius (cf. Hultsch 250–2); his practice is consistent, his arithmetic correct. By contrast, commentators and translators who proffer contemporary equivalents disagree with each other and even with themselves, borrow from long-dead predecessors—Verteuil from Proust, Weiss from Walterstern—at one place but not another, and exhibit faults in calculation; in any case, those who profess such knowledge, as Falster, 'Noct. Rip.' 912 observes, 'docte nugantur'.

47. From Varro's discussion of *dimidium* and *dimidiatus*, or from Gellius' own reading? The latter on Lebek's assumption that Varro did not cite prose; but see ch. 10 n. 32.

48. Namely that they turn over at both solstices; he has looked more than once and found it roughly ('propemodum') so. See Meuli i. 506–7, 508 n. (to the parallels add Porph. *Antr.* 33); the inclusion of the winter solstice is absurd.

49. Sall. *Cat.* 4. 1; the same is said of hunting, which makes only incidental showings in the *Nights* (the capture of Androclus' lion, the Nausicaa simile).

Epilogue

IF IT is the salesman in Bussi who prefaces his *editio princeps* by informing the Pope that Gellius has always been reckoned with the greatest Latin authors, or even exalted above the rest as a master of all styles, not only one, who discusses every field of knowledge, is suitable for students of all ages, and has barely a word to be faulted,[1] it is the Spaniard in Vives who, to avenge his compatriot Seneca, reviles him as a mere compiler and show-off, an unlearned chatterbox with a disgusting style, whose semantic discussions are footling and mostly false.[2] Neither of these judgements is acceptable.

Admiration for the early writers does not lead us, like Gellius and Scaliger,[3] to despise those of the Silver Age; but Gellius, for his time, is a remarkably sound critic. His grammatical discussions, though fallible, display intelligence; and in grammar as in criticism, he often appears to greater advantage than the professionals. He is no philosopher, but no more unphilosophical than most of his, and our, contemporaries; he is no historian, but history was no longer being written except in Greek. His knowledge of that language and its literature, adequate by the standards of his age, is less than may be found in the late Republic; but it has rarely been his students' strongest suit. He has an interest, albeit superficial, in law and medicine; he is a skilful narrator with no small facility for invention; he can express his personal affection without embarrassing even an English reader; his laudatory superlatives are no more monotonous than Cicero's; his confessedly inexhaustive expositions are successfully designed to stimulate our own researches.[4] Few among the learned, if they attempted to write in Gellius' vein, could produce so attractive or wide-ranging a miscellany.

---

1. Letter to Paul II, fo. [1]ʳ, cf. fo. [5]ʳ (Botfield 80, 89).

2. Vives, *De tradendis disciplinis* 3. 8 (*Opera* vi. 337; cf. ibid. 340, '*Gellius* durissimarum elegantiarum affectator'); cf. *Opera* ii. 141, cit. ch. 3 n. 3, and n. on Aug. *CD* 9. 4, but contrast his *Praelectio* to Filelfo's *Conuiuia*, 'Aulus Gellius per se ipsum probatissimus' (*Opera* ii. 84). Stephanus, *Noct. Par.* II–III replies at length (on motive, pp. 30–1). Vives preferred the synthetic classicism of Petrus Crinitus' *De honesta disciplina*, a work permeated by Gellius, 'vir gravi consilio in rebus humanis' (*DHD* 8. 9; with the debate between Savonarola and Pico, *DHD* 3. 2, compare *NA* 2. 26; 20. 1), but less than perfect in its emulation: *DHD* 1. 1 (on Tamerlane's three tents, familiar from Marlowe, *Tamb.* 1421–35) begins with two ponderous *sententiae*, whereas Gellius, not obliged to strike up marble poses, tells his tale in *NA* 1. 1 without preamble; and neither the mystification nor the obscenity of *DHD* 11. 8 is conceivable in the *Nights*.

3. 'Ennius, Poëta eximius, magnifico ingenio. Vtinam totum haberemus & amisissemus Lucanum, Statium, Silium Italicum, & tous ces garçons-là' (*Scaligerana* 136).

4. *NA* pr. 17, cf. Berthold, 'Aulus Gellius' 48.

If the enterprise itself be maligned, we should remember what a fine and versatile scholar observed over sixty years ago: the worst faults of the Second Sophistic, such as 'the superficial "general education"' and 'the debasement of scholarship in face of the mass public', were common to his own day—and are to ours.[5] What the sophists may plead, that too may Gellius; amid our popular digests, Companions to tell us what a writer wrote or a thinker thought, and books of classified quotations to deck out a text with others' words, posssibly mistranslated and certainly out of context, it ill becomes us to sneer at the learned miscellanies, the collections of *placita*, the handbooks of *exempla*, in which Gellius' age times abounded.

The dogma that writers should have a moral purpose, asserted with more vehemence than authority, will not compel us either to blame Gellius for lacking one or to defend him by inventing it. His conventional morality, despite his protestations, is not his central theme. If women must be reminded of maternal duties, or the rise of superstition combated by refutation of astrology, or Rome's religious inheritance asserted against new cults,[6] these are incidental considerations beside the display of eloquence and learning.

For all his public service and his sermons on the active life, he is a bookish man, who has not even noticed the boundary-stones delimiting the *pomerium*,[7] Wagner the *Famulus* not Faust;[8] but since when has it been a sin for a scholar to be warmed on winter nights by what he reads, and on unrolling a noble manuscript to feel that all heaven has come down to him?[9] When one history of Roman literature finds Gellius devoted to the withered leaves and not the flourishing tree,[10] we should remember that to the lovers who lie beneath the flourishing tree, to the children who play in its branches, and to the lumberjack who chops it down, the greatest scholar is but a porer over withered leaves; when another states that Gellius portrays an era carried away by trivialities,[11] we should not forget that the man in the street, or the laboratory, thus belittles the study of dead languages and cultures not his own. In an age with less respect for learning than the second century, we should not throw stones from our glass house, nor assail our ancient colleague in displaced self-hatred. For all his limitations, he is a delightful companion,

---

5. Heiberg ii. 105: 'den overfladiske "almindelige Dannelse", Nedværdigelsen af Videnskaben overfor det store Publicum'.

6. *NA* 12. 1 (cf. ch. 2 n. 68), 14. 1; and see p. 214.

7. *NA* 13. 14. 7; see ch. 15 n. 42.

8. Niebuhr I. iii. 232; Friedländer, *Kunstsinn* 25; see Goethe, *Faust* 530–1. Hertz, *R. und R.* 35 adduces Matt. 15. 27 and Schiller, *Wallensteins Lager* 208–11; but Wagner was the normal whipping-boy for a would-be *faustisch* culture.

9. Goethe, *Faust* 1106–9, made into a reproach by Friedländer, loc. cit.

10. Schanz–Hosius–Krüger iii. 179: 'ein Mann, der die verdorrten Blätter, nicht den blühenden Baum mit seiner Liebe umfaßt'.

11. Teuffel–Kroll–Skutsch iii. 97 (and so, expressing the spirit of the *Reichsgründung*, Teuffel's edn.¹ (Leipzig, 1870) 749): 'ihre Verranntheit in Nichtigkeiten'; it is also accused of 'wichtigtuerische Geschäftigkeit ohne ernstes Ziel'.

full of charm and not without intelligence: 'one of the best writers of his kind', said Macaulay;[12] '[h]e compels our attention,' declares a modern critic, 'not only as a source of information, but in his own right ... we have in Gellius a helpful and congenial guide.'[13] How many scholars' work, ancient or modern, can be read for pleasure? Jealousy, masked in austerity, may disapprove; but he still defies his traducers as once he defied 'the gracelessness and envy of certain ill-educated persons',[14] while bidding the rest of us join in his festival of learning.

12. *Letters* iii. 181 Pinney, cf. iii. 237, iv. 49, v. 416.

13. Goodyear 680. For others so charmed see Hertz ii, pp. cxxxii–cxxxv; Vogel, 'De compositione' 8–9; Berthold 18–19; cf. P. K. Marshall, *OCD* 460: 'The work has a discreet charm of its own.'

14. *NA* pr. 20; see ch. 8 n. 48.

Appendix

Editions and Translations

Editions[1]

THE first edition of Gellius, as of Caesar, Lucan, and Apuleius, was published in 1469 by Giovanni Andrea (Giannandria) Bussi, bishop-designate of Aleria; Theodore Gaza's gloss is appended to the Greek. The books are unnumbered; the 600 feet of the stade in 1. 1 are reduced to 200; both 2. 8 and 2. 9 are numbered 'Caput .viii.'; the lemmata to book 8 are absent; Gellius' preface, relegated to the end with the late MSS, is set off as 'Autoris tanquam prefationis admonitio in operis totius summa. de noctium ordine. Caput .xi.'[2] Subsequent editions made good some deficiencies, and humanists from Beroaldus and Politian onwards contributed corrections,[3] but the first critical text was Ludovicus Carrio's of 1585, published (but not printed) by Henricus Stephanus; the projected commentary having fallen victim to personal quarrels (though some copies include 120 pages of *Castigationes et notae* down to 1. 25. 9), Stephanus appended *Noctes Parisinae* of his own.[4]

The numerous observations on Gellius in Claudius Salmasius' *Plinianae exercitationes* of 1629, many based on MS P in the Bibliothèque du roi, included the relocation of the preface and a great improvement in its text. Johannes Fredericus Gronovius, having procured Salmasius' annotated copy, drew on his work, and on Petrus Lambecius' reports of P and Q—both

---

1. See in general *ed. Bip.* i, pp. viii–xix, Lion i, pp. xix–xxxii, Schweiger ii/1. 375–80, Hertz ii, pp. cv–cxxxvi; but no one has thoroughly examined the pre-Carrio edns., in particular the Ascensianae. For the vulgate, and Guarino's part in its formation: Sabbadini, *Vita* 77–8, 86, 143, *Scuola* 118–19, 123, 204–5, 231, *Scoperte* 97, Baron 205–15, Marache i, p. liv.

2. Cf. Bussi, fo. [5]ʳ (Botfield 89); ch. 2 n. 20; Sabbadini, *Scoperte* 128, *Nuove ricerche* 24–5. Until Carrio's edn. (cf. *Emend.* 2. 8) 20. 2–3 formed a single chapter; hence 'Caput .xi.'

3. Beroaldus' edn. omits his own published corrections to 15. 1. 2 and 20. 8. 6 (*Annot.*, sig. [d4]ʳ⁻ᵛ); Ferrettus prints them in the margin, Connellus in the text. The nn. in Ascensius' later edns., and Petrus Mosellanus' comm., appear in several 16th-c. texts till Stephanus ejects them.

4. Thuanus 71, Stephanus to Paul Estienne 20–1. For Carrio's work on Gellius see Hertz ii, p. cxx. Stephanus (to Paul 19–20) complains of changes in the text; the ex. given, *clauderet* 1. 7. 21 (from β, comm. 43) tells in Carrio's favour but not e.g. *pluria* 5. 18. 7 (why not 2. 26. 3, 8; 4. 15. 1, etc.?), *beniuolentem* 15. 7. 3 (for 'bene ualentem' cf. *CIL* iii. 5815. 8, cit. Falster, 'Noct. Rip.' 141; for *ualens* 'healthy' Augustus fr. 2. 26 Malcovati). The *Noct. Par.* are numbered, without subdivision, II–III (reply to Vives), IV–V (impugning the lemmata), VI–VIII (textual); twenty had been envisaged (Stephanus to Vulcob). Reprints suppress all mention of Carrio and reject some of his readings, restored by Hieronymus de Vogel (Leiden, 1644) alongside casual errors (*quempiam* for *quemquam* [a vulgate interpolation after 'censeat' 6. 3. 36], *in* for *ex* 9. 15. 7).

designated 'MS. R(egius)'—in his *Prodromus lucubrationum* (Paris, 1647),[5] for his anonymous Elsevier edition of 1651.[6] On this text, with occasional alterations, Antonius Thysius based a commentary that by his death in 1665 had reached the end of book 12; the task was completed by Jacobus Oiselius and published in 1666. A few good conjectures are made; the notes are many and copious but often derivative and seldom incisive.[7] Fifteen years later Jacques Proust SJ produced a Delphin edition reactionary in text and superficial in annotation, but with Latin and Greek word-indexes that, though defective, have not been replaced.[8]

Gronovius, whom Bernhard Rottendorf gave the MS now known as R, continued all his life to work on Gellius, but died in 1671 having annotated no further than 9. 15. 5. Most of his comments were published in 1687, with a reprint of his edition, by his son Jacobus, who in 1706 brought out a revised text with his father's notes entire, readings recorded by Gaspar Scioppius, the bulk of Thysius–Oiselius' commentary, and remarks of his own often sharply critical of his predecessors; enjoyment of his invective is impaired by the badness of his Latin.[9] This 'Gronoviana' remained the standard Gellius for over a hundred years.[10] The eccentric recension by P. D. Longolius in 1741 introduced the section-numbers used by Albert Lion in his erratic, but sometimes acute, edition of 1824 and all its successors, including a Tauchnitz text (1835, reprinted 1870) that made an 'epilogus' of the preface.[11]

5. Lambecius is not always truthful or original; his account of accidentally finding P (sig. A2^r), disbelieved by Jac. Gronovius (1687 pr., sig. [a6]^v), is modelled on 11. 17. 1.

6. Publ. by L. Elsevier as 'Editio noua et prioribus omnibus docti hominis cura multo castigatior', set from an insufficiently corrected copy of de Vogel (cf. [6. 3. 36]; 9. 15. 7); reset (with light revision) by D. Elsevier in 1665.

7. The often unacknowledged sources include a fat comm. on bks. 1–14 by Phil. Carolus. At 2. 3. 5 Thysius steals from Mosellanus, sig. C1^v, the assertion that Vergil lived 300 years before Hadrian; but there is much valuable information too, which subsequent scholars have wrongly ascribed to Jac. Gronovius.

8. Proust, writing in Paris, relies on Lambecius for reports of P and Q; he rarely notices Salmasius, whose co-religionists' persecution is acclaimed at sig. [a3]^v–[a4]^r. Paraphrase and nn. (as usual in this series) recall a school edn.; they abound in errors, but occasionally Proust improves on his predecessors, as at 9. 7. 3 (ch. 16 n. 39), where Thysius had made strings resonate from mere proximity. At 17. 8. 14 he notes that vinegar exposed to the (Parisian) air on 17 Dec. 1673 NS had frozen solid. The word-indexes are cued by page and line, not without error; the pagination is ludicrously inaccurate, the sequence 279–88 even being repeated.

9. Cf. Beloe i, p. *xxiv; so, on his Cicero, Clericus in Locke, *Correspondence* iv. 528–9 de Beer. Triller i waxes pompous on his acrimony. Unsigned nn. are nearly all from Thysius–Oiselius; those signed 'Gronovius' (or various abbreviations) are the father's (presupposing Carrio's text) to 9. 15. 5, thereafter the son's.

10. Repr. in 1762 with legal excursūs by J. L. Conradi and a few good nn. by E. C. A. Otho. Text reissued by Societas Bipontina (Zweibrücken, 1784); A. J. Valpy (London, 1824) divided it into sections, subjoined Proust's paraphrase and nn., interspersed readings from de Vogel ('Lugd. Bat.') and Proust ('Delph.') among textual annotations from the Gronovii, and appended Falster's 'Libellus commentarius', Thysius–Oiselius' comm., bibliographical matter mostly from *ed. Bip.*, and revisions of Proust's indexes.

11. Longolius ignores the opening of 7. 1, available since 1712; his sections are uneven and ill-conceived, but smaller and more convenient than Valpy's. Some hard words are explained in the index, to which continual asterisks refer; Greek is rendered with grotesque quasi-literality (e.g. ἄν/κεν > si). The preface draws largely on Falster's 'Libellus Commentarius'. Lion

Editions had been projected by the Danish scholar, satirist, and schoolmaster Christian Falster, Abraham Gronovius Jacobi f., and the Strasburg goose Elias Stoeber. Falster, whose 'Specimen' of 1721 offered conjectures on books 1–4, and whose *Vigiliae primae Noctium Ripensium* of the same year prefixed a vindication of Gellius' lemmata to illustrative material on the topics of book 8, produced three folio volumes, comprising his 'Noctes Ripenses' and Latin and Greek lexica to Gellius, which despite support from Havercamp could find no publisher. He therefore included in his *Amoenitates philologicae* a 'Libellus Commentarius de uita et rebus A. Gellii' (ii. 243–72) and 'Admonitiones ad Interpretes A. Gellii' (iii. 211–344); the surviving 'Lexicon Latinum Gellianum', retitled 'Noctes Ripenses in Noctes Atticas A. [p. 561; om. p. 1] Gellii', donated to the University Library at Copenhagen and in 1938 transferred with the university's other manuscripts to the Royal Library, consists of two volumes bound into one, containing a detailed index of Latin words with ample notes on language, content, and text, compiled between 1722 and 1727.[12]

In a Teubner edition of 1853, Lachmann's devoted pupil and biographer Martin Julius Hertz presented a text based on the older manuscripts, including the recent discovery A, with few attempts at correction; he listed his many divergences from the Gronoviana, but gave no apparatus criticus. This provisional production was superseded by the two-volume *editio maior* of 1883–5, whose much-emended text is accompanied by a detailed apparatus; a long preface (ii, pp. iii–cli) sets forth the history of the *Attic Nights* from the second to the nineteenth century. Hertz's masterpiece (of which a lightly revised *editio minor* was issued by Teubner in 1886) remains indispensable for students of Gellius; although one may at times disagree with his choice of variant, or prefer other conjectures to awkward expressions supposed to have undergone haplography, neither correction of his apparatus[13] nor discovery of other MSS[14] has wrought more than a marginal improvement in the text. Carl Hosius' Teubner of 1903, despite some emendations by the editor and

adduces a bad Wolfenbüttel MS, but has flashes of insight; his nn. contain some useful matter along with readings of 16th-c. edns.

12. Falster, *Cog.* 136, 141–7, 151–6, *Vig. pr.*, sig.):(3ʳ, *Am. phil.* ii. 242, iii. 7–13, 214; Hansen 44, no. 418. At p. 976ᵐᵍ Falster notes (on *uerecundia* 8. 9) that 'hoc anno, 1727,' the French ambassador (Pierre Blouet, chevalier de Camilly, *ex rel.* Dr Rohan Butler) dried up in the presence of Frederik IV. He mentions a Greek lexicon 'infra' and 'Prolegomena' (apparently the basis of the 'Libellus Commentarius'). Textual and some other nn. were revised in his 'Admonitiones', including conjectures that range from the felicitous to the futile, and most of the comments he received from his friend the doctor and *littérateur* D. W. Triller in Merseburg (the emender of Suet. *Aug.* 80 and satirizer of Klopstock), whom silence had served better. Falster's marginalia in his Gronoviana (Copenhagen, University Library, Kl. 78212, 4°) include the gloss 'λιὰν [*sic*] meget' (very) on Asellio's 'nimis' (13. 3. 6), which had tied Jac. Gronovius in knots.

13. M. J. Hertz, *JbClPh* Supp.² 21 (1894) 1–48; (tacitly) Marshall's apparatus. Hertz also records countless conjectures by other scholars, with source; he misses little worth mention, though at 16. 4. 4 Aldobrandus' *denicales Kalendaeque* in the Juntine follows Crinitus, *DHD* 25. 11 (correct is *denicales* alone).

14. Or rather the discovery of one (C) too late for the OCT and the collation of another (F) known but unavailable to Hertz.

Franz Skutsch, is mainly of value for its plentiful though indiscriminate parallels;[15] the chief critical merits of P. K. Marshall's Oxford Classical Text (1968) and René Marache's unfinished Budé (1967–) are respectively thorough re-examination of the manuscripts and freedom from German punctuation;[16] Franco Cavazza (1985–) shows no awareness of the recently discovered Cambridge witness C; other bilingual editions are best considered simply as translations. Although individual corrections still accrue, no general advance seems possible unless an independent manuscript comes to light, or text and tradition are examined afresh by a critic who combines the insight of the elder Gronovius and the industry of Hertz. Great service would be rendered by a modern commentary to replace that in the Gronoviana: Hertz having abandoned the project of annotating his text,[17] we must make do with notes in bilingual editions and translations, which have to cater for less than learned readers, and with commentaries on the preface (by Paul Faider) and book 1 (by Hazel Hornsby).[18]

Translations

The first translation of the *Attic Nights* was a two-volume selection in French,[19] *Les Nuits Attiques d'Aulugelle traduites pour la premiere fois; accompagnées d'un Commentaire; & distribuées dans un nouvel Ordre. Par M. l'Abbé de V...*, published in 1776; a third volume was added the next year, ostensibly by popular request. Its perpetrator, the former Jesuit and future Jacobin François-Joseph-Ignace Donzé-Verteuil (1736–1818), would become in turn *substitut* to Fouquier-Tinville, a judge at the ex-queen's trial, and *accusateur*

15. Esp. in bks. 1–5, Hosius made use of Hertz's papers (i, p. xxi); his parallels are less full for Greek than Latin, are thinnest in philosophy, and jumble together the most disparate matter (cf. Wissowa 733–4). His review of Rolfe's tr. offers a few *retractationes*.

16. Marshall's text of bks. 9–20 presupposes that Fγδ form a three-branch tradition, and that δ (which less often agrees with F) deserves no preference over γ ; but see ch. 2 n. 18. At times, he refuses superior δ readings (e.g. 11. 17. 1; 16. 19. 19, cf. ch. 3 n. 67). Marache, who is too much taken by trivializations in the late MSS, includes frr. of Cn. Gellius among the testimonia (i, p. lviii) and constantly turns Breslau ('Vratislavia') into Bratislava; even thus was the dragon's neck for *Siegfried* at Bayreuth dispatched to Beirut ('Beyrouth'). On Marshall and Marache, vol. i see F. R. D. Goodyear, *CR*² 21 (1971) 385–90. New edns. are promised by Bernardi Perini ('Revisione' 257, cf. Cavazza, edn. i. 42) and Heinz Berthold (see ch. 4 n. 42).

17. Specimens appeared in 1868 (4. 14) and 1877 (pr.).

18. There are good nn. in Weiss, Fischer, and Marache (esp. vol. ii); Mignon is occasionally useful. The Panckoucke editors (n. 39) spill much ink. J. G. Kreyssig dedicated a comm. on 7. 1. 1–6 to the shade of Friedrich August the Just, by Napoleon's grace king of Saxony (Meissen, 1827); Iwan de Gloeden commented on the legal chapters of bks. 1–3 (Rostock, 1843). Unpublished comms. exist by me on bk. 2 (Oxford, 1971; uneven), by W. C. Kurth on bk. 13 (Chapel Hill, NC, 1964; doxographic).

19. In 1534 Guillaume Boulle (Boullé?) of Lyon appended a literal and Latinate version of *NA* 12. 1 to Geoffroy Tory's French translation, from Secundinus' Latin, of Plutarch's 'Politiques'; cf. ch. 6 n. 37. Falster, *Vig. pr.* 86–7, renders into Danish alexandrines Laber. 98–124 R, cited at Macr. *Sat.* 2. 7. 3 from *NA* 8. 15. Vernacular adaptations and renarrations (particularly frequent in the 16th c.) cannot be considered here. I have not seen W. L. Steinbrenner, *Erzählungen nach Aulus Gellius* (Zerbst, 1829).

public at Brest, where—having alleged in his Gellius (i. 320 n.) that Socrates' enemies had obtained his conviction by bribing the whole court—he exploited greedy judges, venal witnesses, and pliant juries to procure the death-sentences of which he had already notified the executioner.[20] His treatment of his author is no handsomer: omitting ninety-seven chapters, and rearranging the rest by subject-matter with a rebuke to Gellius' editors for having left the task undone,[21] he bases on the unsound text of his compatriot and confrater Proust[22] a translation equally remarkable for stale pomposities and childish errors. Gellius writes:

> 'Contra patriam' inquit Cicero 'arma pro amico sumenda non sunt.' Hoc profecto nemo ignorauit et priusquam Theognis, quod Lucilius ait, nasceretur (1. 3. 18–19).

The first sentence is too bald for our *soi-disant* abbé, who compels his Cicero to scream; he is punished in the second by a shameful blunder:

> *Malheur au Citoyen*, s'écrie Cicéron, *qui dans le dessein de servir son ami, tire l'épée contre la Patrie*; eh! qui est-ce qui l'ignoroit: c'est un axiome plus ancien que Theognis et Lucilius (ii. 36).

The Ennian Neoptolemus of 5. 15. 9; 5. 16. 5, becomes 'Ennianus Neoptolême' (iii. 97, i. 435; cf. iii. 419); from the 'indicibus' or lists of Plautine plays at 3. 3. 1 are extracted, to the ruin of the argument, 'certains traits caractéristiques' whereby the critics claim to detect the 'alliage impur' (ii. 297). The Sallustian phrase discussed in 18. 4 (iii. 405–8) is arbitrarily bestowed on Seneca; yet at ii. 254 n. (on 12. 2) the fellow has the face to say: 'Un des défauts de Séneque qu'on n'a pas assez remarqué, c'est qu'il manque de précision.' He boasts in his preface that his notes are not a learned commentary, and that the reader will find in them all he needs for the perfect understanding of the text; half his claim is true.[23]

20. The Brest tribunal continued to apply the *loi du 22 prairial* after its Thermidorian repeal. A rash jest against the new authorities led to Verteuil's arrest on 17 Feb. 1795; released under the amnesty of 16 Oct., he escapes from view, dying in the prudent seclusion of the Roman church at a seminary in Nancy. He is usually credited with *Derniers sentiments des plus illustres personnages condamnés à mort* (Paris, 1775); but see *Catalogue général des livres imprimés de la Bibliothèque nationale* clix. 681, ccvii. 237. His literary name was taken from his great-uncle the abbé Verteuil; the *particule* was his own embellishment. For his career see J. Joachim, *Revue d'Alsace* 98 (1959) 85–116.

21. See i, pp. xj f. The original selection contains 184 chs., grouped by subject into five books; the supplementary volume 101 in four books, I. xi (pp. 37–43) corresponding to Proust's 'XIII. xv', modern 13. 15–16. Gellius' lemmata are replaced by brief headings. Three decades earlier, J.-P. de Joly had imposed his own system on Marcus' *Meditations*, and R.-J. Pothier, with more excuse but less boldness, had rearranged the Digest—or rather the *leges* within each title—'in nouum ordinem'.

22. Extravagantly praised at i, p. vj, and said at i, p. xvj n. to be the first with Gellius' preface at the head.

23. At ii. 358 n. (on 15. 9) he avers: 'dans toute la langue latine il n'y a pas un seul mot en *ons* qui n'ait son génitif en *ontis*, comme celui de *frons, frontis*'; yet elsewhere he had translated oblique cases of *frons frondis*. At ii. 94 n. he confesses what his translation shows, that he cannot make head nor tail of 14. 1. 21. Pious obscurantism from Proust (at i. 157, n. *c* on 15. 18 Cornelius'

An even more selective German version was published in 1785 at Lemgo, in the county of Lippe: *Fragmente der alten Geschichte und Philosophie aus den Attischen Nächten des Aulus Gellius gesammlet*[24] *und übersetzt mit beigefügten Anmerkungen von A. H. W. v. W.*—namely Anton Heinrich Freiherr von Walterstern (1727–1802), who also translated Cicero's *De amicitia* (Altona, 1780) and extracts from Addison and Gibbon.[25] It contains Gellius' preface and 172 chapters, mostly in their original order,[26] translated from Conradi's reprint of the Gronoviana; it is less inaccurate than its predecessor,[27] but deserves no higher praise. At times long-winded, at others a précis,[28] it adopts from Verteuil mistakes and infelicities: at 3. 11. 7 Verteuil's 'petit Temple' (i. 26) for 'capella' reappears as 'Kapelle', and the noble simplicity of the verse 'flerent diuae Camenae Naeuium poetam' (1. 24. 2) yields place in both translations to a commonplace sentimentality: 'les Muses arroseroient de leurs larmes les cendres de Nævius' (ii. 305), 'so würden die Musen gewiß die Asche des Dichters Nævius mit ihren Thränen benetzen.' Walterstern's notes rather entertain than instruct, but at 12. 11. 7 (Truth the child of Time) he alone remembers Plut. *QR* 12.[29]

The first complete and faithful version was published anonymously at Moscow two years later, *Avla Gellija Afinskix nočej zapiski*, by the rector of the Slavonic–Greek–Latin Academy and archimandrite of the Zaikonospasskij

second sight is the devil's doing) vie in the Terrorist-to-be with a royalism that relates Blanche of Castile's insistence on suckling her son the future Louis IX (ii. 10 n. on 12. 1) and Frederick the Great's detection of forgery from a too recent watermark (ii. 233 n. on 14. 2). The author of *Derniers sentiments* (i, p. x n. 1) reproves in English republicans the notions that Verteuil was to derive from his reading of Roman history.

24. So in the two copies I have inspected, belonging to the Wessenberg-Bibliothek, Konstanz, and the Royal Library, Copenhagen: often modernized in bibliographies to 'gesammelt'. The Konstanz copy was kindly brought to my attention by Dr Helmuth Schneider (Freie Universität Berlin).

25. Hamberger–Meusel viii. 333–4, x. 788 (cf. xii. 371).

26. Renumbered continuously, with brief headings (some from Verteuil) and original numeration appended: 5. 3, 10 are juxtaposed as 49–50, 'XIII. xv' omitted, 17. 16–17 combined as 153, 9. 4 relegated to the end as 171. Walterstern censures Gellius' want of order (p. xxi) and provides a classified index of chapters (omitting 76 = 9. 2 and 171); although all but two (79 = 9. 8, 141 = 16. 3) had been translated by Verteuil, the classification is entirely different.

27. But see e.g. 16. 3. 7 'daß wegen der starken Zusammenpressung des Leibes der Hunger sehr groß seyn müsse' (Rolfe correctly 'that the ability to fast for a long time is caused by strong compression of the belly'); 16. 19. 8 'seinen Landsleuten' of the Corinthian crew with whom Arion of Methymna chose to sail.

28. With 16. 19. 19 'ablegato Arione' > 'und Ario mußte während der Unterredung, die der König mit ihnen hielt, sich heimlich in der Nähe aufhalten' contrast § 1 'celeri admodum et cohibili oratione uocumque filo tereti et candido' > 'sehr angenehm' (*angenehm* is a favourite word).

29. At 16. 3. 4 he notes that the 'Akanzas' (Quapaw) in America took the same precaution against hunger as the Scythians; he reports several chapters not included in the tr. and points out errors in natural science. Some nn. are taken from Verteuil (thus the anecdotes of n. 23 reappear); others show him a man of the Enlightenment. At 10. 23. 5 he deplores the harshness of Roman law towards women; at 14. 2. 16 he holds that in criminal cases the judge should take points overlooked by the defence, 'Ist es doch immer besser zehn Schuldige loszusprechen, als einen Unschuldigen zu verdammen'; 15. 10 suggests a principle—exploiting the offender's foible—that might be used to put down duelling.

monastery, Afanasij (Aleksej) Ivanov (1746–1805), a noted preacher who rose to be archbishop of Ekaterinoslav.[30] It is mainly, though not exclusively, based on the Gronoviana; the Greek is often rendered from the Latin gloss, and some readings, such as John of Salisbury's 'in terram' at 3. 6. 2 ('k zemle'), are derived from the commentary.[31] The style is heavy, the translation mostly literal and usually sound, but at 1. 1. 2 Heracles is made to run a stade from Olympia to the temple of Zeus Olympios,[32] and at 2. 27. 3 'čistoserdečnee' (purer-hearted, more sincere) for 'sincerius' compares unfavourably with Verteuil's 'plus naturel' (ii. 357; Walterstern omits the chapter). Occasionally it breaks free from slavishness into paraphrase: e.g. 2. 1. 2 'kakby v kakom nibud´ vostorge' (as if in a kind of ecstasy),[33] 2. 29. 10 'solnce uže na poludni, a ni prijatelej i ničego sovsem net' (the sun has reached noon, but no friends are to be seen, nothing at all).[34]

Eight years later, *The Attic Nights of Aulus Gellius* descended from the pen of the Revd William Beloe (1736–1817), who had translated Herodotus (London, 1791) and was later for a time Keeper of Printed Books at the British Museum, till in 1806 the caricaturist Robert Dighton, having wormed himself into his friendship, was found to have abstracted prints and drawings.[35] His translation is more elegant, but less accurate, than

30. Now Dnepropetrovsk. See Smirnov 310, 321, 332–6, 355–6, 363; Stroev (in chronological order) 212, 160, 1034, 839, 487, 312. He also publ. a book of his sermons (Moscow, 1787) and translated Tertullian's *Apologeticum* (Moscow, 1802). J. D. G. Seebode, *Krit. Bibl. für d. Schul- und Unterrichtswesen* 2 (1820) 255, after recording Russian trs. of Homer and Plutarch under way in 1820, adds 'Auch Cor. Nepos u. Gellii N. Att. sind Russisch übersetzt worden', whence via Lion i, p. xxxiii and Weiss i, p. xvi the ghostly 'translation into Russian of 1820' at Rolfe i, p. xxiii, Cavazza, edn. i. 42. Nepos had been translated by V. Lebedev (Spb., 1748, repr. 1785), named, unlike Afanasij, on the title-page; Schweiger ii/1. 312, 380 cites only anonymous 'St. Petersburg 1818' versions of Nepos and Gellius (not recorded by Naguevskij 13–14, 37–8), but with the same titles and octavo format as those already mentioned. (Nepos had appeared, under another title, in a bilingual edn. by N. F. Košanskij, Spb., 1816.) T. I. Kondakova, head of the 'Muzej knigi' at the Lenin State Library of the USSR, kindly informs me that these items are not known to Russian bibliography; she inclines to consider them *Titelauflagen*, for which the current projects made the time propitious.

31. Cf. ch. 14 n. 83. Sometimes he follows Thysius–Oiselius, or translates a reading promoted to the text by Longolius (from whom comes his prefatory life of Gellius: 'Atteja' i, p. iii < 'Atteium' Longolius, sig. b1ʳ ~ 'Atejum' Falster, *Am. phil.* ii. 254). At 18. 9. 9 he restores the then unpublished *v* and *s* for *n* and Carrio's *p* (om. Longolius; *s* Bussi, 6 [= σ] ref. Scioppius).

32. '... čto on iz Olimpii do xrama Jupitera Olimpijskago perebežal stadiju'. Note too 'ot retoričeskix sočinenij' (from rhetorical compositions) 14. 2. 1 ~ 'a rhetorum epilogis' (from rhetors' finales), and the wrong choice of sense at 2. 27. 1 etc. (*illustris*, brilliant, vivid > 'znamenityj' famous); 'fortunarum' (of fortunes) becomes 'blagopolučija' (of success) at 3. 10. 9 and 'bogatstva' (of wealth) at 14. 1. 21; proper names are confused at 2. 24. 6 ('Ennij' for Fannius), 3. 10. 7 n. ('Cicerona' for Thysius' Censorinus).

33. Cf. Walterstern: 'als ein Mensch, der in Entzückung gerathen'.

34. Cf. La Fontaine, *Fables* 4. 22. 41: 'L'aube du jour arrive; et d'amis point du tout.' The sense of 'inauditiunculas' is well brought out (see p. 168): 'nekotoryja naslyškoju perenjatyja grammatičeskija pravil´ca', a few petty rules of grammar picked up by hearsay.

35. *Dictionary of National Biography*[2] ii. 201–2, v. 979–80; Mr A. V. Griffiths, Deputy Keeper of Prints and Drawings, kindly refers me to his Department's *User's Guide*, p. 108. Douce noted in vol. iii of his Verteuil (now in the Bodleian Library, Oxford): 'Mr. Beloe has translated Aulus Gellius into English; to which translation, as he informed me, Dr. Parr wrote the Preface', sc.

Afanasij's: the 600 feet of 1. 1 become 'steps' or 'paces' (making the sprint a middle-distance, or in Greek a 'long', race); at 2. 27. 2 the *tribunus militum* Sertorius exchanges his sagum for a toga as a 'tribune of the people'; at 5. 17. 5 Sextilis is April; whole phrases are forgotten. The notes are full of quotations from Shakespeare, the Bible, Milton, Pope, and Gibbon, as well as ancient authors;[36] they also—as befits the co-founder of *The British Critic*, staunch for church and king—offer reflections on current affairs.[37] Archytas' artificial dove (10. 12. 9–10) recalls Turriano's like contrivances for Charles V, and accounts for alleged manifestations of the Holy Ghost to designate archbishops at Ravenna. (Cf. Eus. *HE* 6. 29. 2–4!) The prudery that abridges 12. 1. 8 and 19. 11 is matched by an archness that includes a Plautine obscenity in a note on *intestabilis* (15. 13. 11) and cites a faecal onomatopoeia from Aristophanes (assigned to the wrong play) in a comment—I defy the reader to guess—on 14. 6. 4.[38]

In the course of the nineteenth century more loose French versions appeared, one of which was turned into Spanish by a canon of Granada as a 'traducción directa del latín';[39] but the only significant translation was the German rendering by Georg Fritz Weiss (1822–93), who sang bass, and helped out with acting, at the Königlich Sächsisches Hoftheater in Dresden; having studied under Jan and Stallbaum at the Thomasschule in Leipzig, he was so devoted to the classics that he would read ancient authors in spare

Beloe's old schoolmaster Samuel Parr; 'he' is ambiguous. The preface speaks in Beloe's name, acknowledging Parr's help (i, pp. *xlvi f.).

36. On 13. 17 Beloe cites Varro, *RR* 1. 17. 4 with Scaliger's n. (bare reference in Jac. Gronovius) and Milton, *PL* 2. 108–9; the n. cited at ch. 5 n. 26 above continues with 'What is related of the Persians by Stobaeus' (i.e. Nic. Dam. *FGrH* 90 F 103 (x), cf. Carolus 167–8) and Matt. 5. 11–12 to illustrate the satisfactions of a good conscience. At 18. 11. 4 (Fur. Ant. 4) he proposes *sic fulica leuius*, perhaps rightly. In '6' [= 7]. 1 he incorporates the passage known only from Lactantius (ch. 2 n. 17).

37. The right to kill nocturnal thieves (Macr. *Sat.* 1. 4. 19 < *NA* 8. 1) leads by way of Beccaria, Blackstone, and Gibbon, to the contrast between the 'intended mildness and philanthropy' of the new French penal code and 'the unexampled and unprovoked barbarity, with which they treated their unhappy king'. When this was published, in the year of Verteuil's detention, Great Britain was at war with France (the singing Gaul of 9. 13. 16 evokes the Marseillaise). At 5. 18 he translates Luc. *Hist. conscr.* 2, turning τὸ ἐν Ἀρμενίᾳ τραῦμα into 'the overthrow received in America'; in vol. iii this is set down a misprint, one hopes falsely.

38. *Clouds* 390–1 quoted as from *Wasps* for 'a climax of a different kind' from that of the rhopalic hexameter. For *intestabilis* see Plaut. *Curc.* 30–1; cf. *detestatio* Apul. *Met.* 7. 23. 3.

39. Victor Verger (Paris, 1820, with Proust's text), is heavily dependent on Verteuil, 'cet estimable traducteur' (i, p. vii. *Un sot trouve toujours un plus sot qui l'admire*, but did the Restoration not identify 'l'abbé de Verteuil' with the Terrorist?). Many of his errors are retained; but at 16. 7. 11 n. Verger alone among commentators distinguishes 'botulum' (*boudin*; so Proust) from 'farcimine' (*saucisse*). Scarcely less free, but somewhat less inaccurate, is the paraphrase by P. Jacquinet (pr., bks. 1–10) and A.-V.-P.-D. Fabre (bks. 11–20) for Nisard (with Petronius and Apuleius, Paris, 1842, with Lion's text); often copied or adapted (with some use of Verger) by E. de Chaumont (bks. 1–'6'), Félix Flambard (bks. '7'–13), and E. Buisson (bks. 14–20, 'épilogue') for Panckoucke (Paris, 1845–6, with the Tauchnitz text), still more by their revisers J. P. Charpentier and J.-A. Blanchet for Garnier (Paris, 1863), who remove certain eccentricities and restore the preface to its rightful place. Jacquinet–Fabre are rendered into Spanish by Francisco Navarro y Calvo (Madrid, 1893), who appends the 'Sentencias de Publio Syro' from the Nisard Horace.

moments at rehearsals.[40] His translation, based on Hertz's first edition, won him a doctorate of philosophy from the University of Leipzig, but did not commend to a publisher either his Index Gellianus or his version of *The Golden Ass*. He is more scholarly in intention than his predecessors, and his notes are not without value; but his rendering is verbose and often wrong. Cicero's 'neque semper cum cognitoribus esse' (1. 7. 2) swells into 'noch immer Leute vorfinden, die gerichtlich bezeugen, dass sie die wirklich sind, (für die sie sich ausgeben)'; 'hebdomadibus lunae' (15. 2. 3) becomes 'an dem Monatsersten'. At 2. 27. 2 Sallust's nine words on Sertorius in Spain swell into forty, falsely stating that his prowess there brought promotion from the ranks.[41] The musician does not detect the mistake at 1. 11. 7, and like Proust, Verteuil (iii. 134), and Beloe interprets τὴν διὰ τεσσάρων συμφωνίαν (3. 10. 13; a perfect fourth) as a four-note chord. He makes frequent use of Walterstern, not always for the best:[42] at 1. 11. 5, where Thucydides' ὅπερ φιλεῖ τὰ μεγάλα στρατόπεδα ἐν ταῖς προσόδοις ποιεῖν (as great armies tend to do when attacking) is mistranslated 'welches immer die beste Art ist, einen Feind anzugreifen', only the comma is his own. This error, with many others, was taken over into a bad Hungarian version by two schoolmasters,[43] who turn Euripides' *Bacchae* (13. 19. 3) into his *Bacchi* ('Bacchusaiban'). Neither Gellius' 'Bacchis' nor Weiss's 'Bakchen' marks the gender, so how were they to know? The work was published by the Hungarian Academy of Sciences.

The twentieth century has seen versions in Catalan (curtailed by the Spanish Civil War),[44] Romanian (with an excellent introduction by Iancu

---

40. *Allgemeine Deutsche Biographie* xli. 569–71.

41. See Plut. *Sert.* 3. 5. Cf. 14. 2. 1 'ad iudicandas lites' ∼ 'zur Entscheidung von (ernsteren) Streitsachen (und Tagesfragen)', as if questions of the day concerned a *iudex priuatus*.

42. Faint praise for Walterstern ('stellenweise nicht ganz ohne Geschick verdeutscht', i, p. iii) masks Weiss's practice: his comments on Gellius' style (i, pp. xiv–xv) expand Walterstern, p. xix (who freely adapts Verteuil i, pp. xiv–xvi); he adopts his treatment of 1. 24. 2 (though 'Ruhstatt' replaces 'Asche'); at 7. 7. 3, like Walterstern and before him Verteuil i. 76, he takes 'contrarium' of a provision, as if 'inprobus' were fem.; at 9. 8. 1 he appropriates both 'Ausspruch weiser Männer' and the modal variation 'bedarf ... entspringe'; at 16. 3. 7; 16. 19. 8 he copies the errors cited in n. 27. A new German tr. is being prepared by Heinz Berthold.

43. By József Barcza (whose 10-ch. specimen had appeared in the report for 1897/8 of the Calvinist grammar-school at Kisújszállás, pp. 17–33) and József Soós (Budapest, 1905), based on Hertz's *ed. min.* of 1886. It abounds in errors: some original, e.g. 'hallották' (they heard; so specimen, p. 20) 1. 7. 2 for 'adierant', 'mariusi' (Marian) 2. 27. 2 for 'Marsico'; 'két' (two) 5. 6. 10 for 'secundo', 'himnemben' [= *hím*-] (in the masculine) 16. 7. 13 for οὐθετέρως; others from Weiss, e.g. 7. 7. 3; 15. 2. 3; 16. 3. 7; at 2. 27. 2 Sertorius 'Hispaniában katonai tribunná lőn' (became a military tribune in Spain), along with verbiage (at 1. 7. 2 only 'gerichtlich' is omitted), numerous nn., and the entire introduction; his ambiguous 'Pflaster' for 'emplastrum' (16. 7. 13) is rendered 'járda' (path). Verse-trs., often in the original quantitative metres, include some by Festus' editor Thewrewk.

44. Tr. Cebrià Montserrat, to bk. 5 only (Barcelona, 1930–4), generally sound, but at 2. 1. 2 Socrates' endurance is prolonged by twelve hours ('des de trenc d'alba fins a la posta de sol de l'endemà') and at 2. 27. 1 'illustria' becomes 'famoses' (cf. n. 32). The Catalonian salt-mountain of 2. 22. 29 provokes no comment; Carl Hosius is 'Carles Hos'.

Fischer),[45] and Italian;[46] the French paraphrastic tradition was continued by Maurice Mignon,[47] the only predecessor Marache professes to have consulted for his Budé version.[48] This last adheres in general to its text, not always without elegance: 'homme sans malice' well hits off 'homo minime malus' (3. 16. 11), an old metrical saw is admirably rendered by the *vers commun* 'Sois scrupuleux, pas superstitieux' (4. 9. 1); at other times fidelity impairs style, but a fidelity at which previous French translators had not even aimed. Errors, however, include 'il a trouvé' for 'inuentus est' (1. 21. 5),[49] 'le reste de sa vie' for τῷ λοιπῷ 'with the rest of him' (2. 27. 1),[50] and the equation of Sextilis with July at 5. 17. 5.

The Loeb edition by J. C. Rolfe,[51] though right in these places where Marache is wrong, is sometimes wrong where he is right. At 3. 16. 11 he gives 'though not a man without learning'; at 4. 9. 1 'ne fuas' ('be not') is taken as a final clause; at 3. 10. 13, where Marache correctly gives 'l'accord de quarte', Rolfe follows Weiss, on whom he repeatedly relies: finding 'apirocalus' (11. 7. 7) rendered '(geschmackloser) Einfaltspinsel', that is '(tasteless) simpleton', he picks out the wrong word: 'Another *Einfaltspinsel*', in a chapter directed against ostentation.[52] At 13. 7. 3 'sic enim feminas

45. Tr. David Popescu (Bucharest, 1965); Fischer also contributes useful nn. The version is as good as any, though at 2. 27. 1 ὑπὲρ ἀρχῆς καὶ δυναστείας is taken (as in pre-Hertzian texts, and also by Weiss and Barcza–Soós) with the preceding πρὸς ὃν ἦν ἡμῖν ὁ ἀγών, in disregard of sense and Dem. 18. 235. At 3. 1. 14 'plus quam potuit' (s.v.l. 'more than he fairly could') yields 'cit a putut mai mult' = *quantum potuit*.

46. Tr. Luigi Rusca (Milan, 1968), with numerous phrases from Rolfe (including the errors noted below at 14. 1. 32, 15. 2. 3; at 16. 7. 10 'sycophanta' receives its Attic sense of 'delatore') and the French paraphrasts. At 1. 1. 1 'quanto grande' implies a new reading *quantus*, and 'animi corporisque ingenio atque uirtutibus' is wrongly divided as 'per doti d'animo e di corpo e per valore'; in 2. 27 tenses go astray ('aveva sacrificato' §§ 1, 4 ~ προϊέμενον, 'apparve' § 5 ~ 'ostenditur') and Sallust's 'ignobilitatem' § 2 (i.e. Sertorius' low birth) becomes 'la pochezza', sc. of historians; 8. 9 n. asserts (like Thysius, refuted by Falster, *Vig. pr.* 49–53) that the stories are nowhere else attested. There is an interesting medical appendix (ii. 609–15) by Dr I. Della Rocca of Merate. Cavazza's edn. includes a deliberately literal tr.; but at pr. 2 'quae libitum erat' becomes 'le cose che mi erano piaciute', and at 3. 16. 11 he takes 'homo minime malus' for 'pur uomo niente affatto incapace', reversing the sense (ch. 9 n. 51).

47. For Garnier (Paris, 1934), with his own text; use is made of the previous Garnier version (e.g. 2. 27. 2 'C'est ce passage qu'a voulu imiter Salluste' ~ 'C'est ce passage ['cette éloquence nerveuse' de Chaumont] que Salluste a voulu imiter' Charpentier–Blanchet; Charpentier's introduction is cited at i. 341 n. 9, 342 n. 15). Mignon writes 'je me représente' 2. 27. 1 for ἑώρων and at 3. 6. 2 prints 'intra' but renders 'jusqu'à terre'. As a commentator, Mignon shows an interest in philosophical questions, and on 1. 20. 5 admirably explains the geometrical conception of number prevailing amongst the ancients.

48. Edn. i, pp. lxxii f.; debts include, at 1. 1. 2 'la piste du stade' and (as in de Chaumont and Charpentier–Blanchet) 'il lui avait donné une longueur de six cents pieds', at 2. 27. 5 'ce qui est invraisemblable et outré' (so Verger, de Chaumont, Charpentier–Blanchet; Jacquinet transposes the epithets; at § 2 both translators make Athens fight Philip for empire and lordship.

49. This is indeed what it would have to mean, but in the absence of a parallel for deponent use of this very common word other scholars have emended.

50. Noted by Gamberale 212; so too Montserrat ('d'aleshores endavant'), but Mignon 'avec le reste'. Pre-Hertzian texts read τὸ λοιπόν.

51. First published in 1927; the revision of 1946 takes some note of Hosius' review.

52. At 1. 5. 3 n. he follows Weiss in citing 'Luther' (probably J. H. Voss, see *GW* 69–70) on wine, women, and song, but ἀπροσδιόνυσος means 'irrelevant' (ch. 11 n. 54).

quoque uirili genere appellat, quod grammatici ἐπίκοινον uocant' (he so designates the females too in the masculine gender, which the grammarians call epicene), yields the utterly nonsensical 'using the masculine or "common" (epicene) gender, as the grammarians call it';[53] at 15. 2. 3 'at the beginning of each week' suggests confusion with *diebus Lunae* (not indeed that weeks begin on Monday); at 14. 1. 32; 16. 7. 10 *sycophanta* (cheat) becomes 'sycophant' (*adsentator*); at 17. 5. 3, 9 (again after Weiss) τεχνικοί (textbook-writers, teachers offering a system) turn into 'connoisseurs' and *artifex* (the Latin equivalent) into an 'artist'.

To render Gellius' style, to find archaisms, neologisms, and synonym-pairs wherever he exhibits them (or failing that, where he does not), and to reproduce his flashes of Greek by dropping into some other tongue, would tax the most skilful writer, and perhaps not please the reader; but plain accuracy, ever more incumbent on the translator as the need for his services grows greater, has all too often eluded the interpreters of the *Nights*, not only in difficult places. Put not your trust in translations![54] No doubt Gellius is read in the main by those who do not need them; but on this evidence we may well fear for authors who are not the preserve of scholars.

•

53. Substantives that may be either masculine or feminine (ὁ καὶ ἡ κύων, *hic et haec canis*) are of common gender, those with one gender for both sexes (ὁ ἀετός, *haec aquila*) epicene.

54. Gibbon vi. 518–19 n. 24. The worst failings, moral and intellectual, were displayed by clerics of a still Latinate church and schoolmasters of a lately Latinate nation.

Addenda

P. 12 l. 18. *Vrbi* 11. 7. 3; 13. 18. 2; 14. 7. 4; 14. 8. 1; cf. *aerario* 13. 25. 30.

P. 16 n. 48. Innocent II (1130–43) 'beate memorie' in 1131: D. Knowles, C. N. L. Brooke, and V. C. M. London, *The Heads of Religious Houses: England and Wales, 940–1216* (Cambridge, 1972) 10 n. 3.

P. 20 n. 5. *Inscriptionis* also London, BL MS Burney 175 (in France by Connellus' day; coincidence?).

P. 22 n. 17. William adapts Justin 44. 3. 8, and is Diceto's source; 516 is the Welsh annals' date for the battle of Badon.

P. 47 l. 19. Cf. Suet. *Vesp.* 21.

P. 79 n. 37. Over-literal Ancient Gk tr.: C. Reinhold, Γαληνός 1/2 (1879) 77–80.

P. 98 n. 41. The reference to Varro (§ 5) will be Gellius' own (p. 118).

P. 126 n. 1. Cf. F. Cavazza, *Historiographia linguistica* 13 (1986) 259–79; R. A. Kaster, ibid. 326–9.

P. 133 nn. 43–4. Ancient lore: Fr. Schoell, *Acta Soc. Phil. Lips.* 6 (1876) 177–93.

P. 154 n. 57. Cosmetic abortion: Soranus 1. 60. 3 (p. 45. 13 Ilberg).

P. 157 n. 74. But see M. J. Luzzatto, *Prometheus* 10 (1984) 82–4, who argues that Gellius paraphrased not Ennius but a Greek or Latin Aesop, the trochees being a device of unpretentious narrative (Hermog. 232. 11–233. 13 R).

P. 158 n. 80. The elder Pliny notices only Plautus; his nephew twice speaks of 'Plautus and Terence', but ignores Caecilius.

P. 168 n. 25. *De curiositate* already in Egnatius' Aldine gloss to Gellius (Gaza: 'De negotiatione et curiositate', § 7 'curiositatem').

P. 197 ll. 24–5. The *Laws* are poorly represented for their length in our *indices fontium*; the scholia are a little shorter than for the *Republic*.

P. 209 ll. 15–20. It takes an *opicus* not to have heard of him (11. 16. 7).

n. 83. Erasmus, *Adagia* 1. 3. 4 has 'infra'. The 12th-c. 'Excerpciones Roberti de Braci' have *cadit* for 'cedit' and *infra* for 'intra' (London, BL MS Royal 8 D. viii, fo. 119[rb]; top of *f* added later, but not *t*[ac] in this hand). Who are Marache's 'edd.'? This ch. was very popular in the Middle Ages (Marshall *et al.* 375).

P. 228 n. 10. Pythagoras in 5. 10: K; Wm. Malmes. *Polyh.* 65 Ou.; J. Salis. *Polic.* 5. 12 (i. 337 W), who contrasts the philosopher's failure with the authority attested at Cic. *ND* 1. 10; from § 6 P (a descendant of φ's source). In 5. 3 (not used in our φ texts), 5. 10; Diceto i. 37–8, 39 St; Oxford, Bodl. MS Canon. Class. Lat. 307. In 5. 3 only: London, BL MS Harley 2768. Wilson (later secretary of state to Elizabeth I) uses 1. 10, 5. 14, 17. 12 in *The Arte of Rhetorique* ([London], 'M.D.LIII. Mense Ianuarij'; 1553 not 1554 since Edward VI still alive), fos. 2[r], 103[r–v], 8[r].

P. 234 ll. 7–8. Aristox. *Rhyth.* 2. 35; Ar. Quint. 33. 29–30, 34. 13–15 W-I.

P. 243 n. 12. Triller's cj. on 14. 1. 18 also in his tr. of Grotius' *Christus patiens*, v. 1653 n. (²Hamburg, 1748, pp. 514–15), with abuse of '[d]er sonst überkluge, und alle Gelehrten gegen sich geringe haltende Jac. Gronovius'.

P. 244 l. 5. But see his vol. ii (bks. 4–5, 1987).

P. 247 n. 31. At 18. 9. 9 ν and σ (reported at second hand from Scioppius) are restored for n and g(*raecum*) in London, BL MSS Burney 174, Add. 16981; *s* for *g* MSS Burney 175, 176; Oxford, Bodl. MS E. D. Clarke 20[m̄iir] (*is* MS Harley 2768; correct is F's *ϛ*; sense is that ἔσπετε is metathetic for *σέπετε).

P. 249 n. 42. Now published (Leipzig, 1987): preface and 118 chs.

Bibliography

ONLY works cited above are included; for a fuller bibliography of nineteenth- and twentieth-century literature on Gellius see Cavazza, edn. i. 54–62. Editions and translations of the *Nights* are discussed at length in the Appendix; for a brief list see pp. xv f.

Aistermann, (W.) J. (F.), *De M. Valerio Probo Berytio capita quattuor* (Bonn, 1910).

Alföldy, G., *Konsulat und Senatorenstand unter den Antoninen: Prosopographische Untersuchungen zur senatorischen Führungsschicht* (Bonn, 1977).

Allen, W. S., *Vox Latina: A Guide to the Pronunciation of Classical Latin*² (Cambridge, 1978).

Ameling, W., *Herodes Atticus* (Hildesheim, 1983).

Anderson, G., *Philostratus: Biography and Belles-Lettres in the Third Century A.D.* (London, Sydney, and Dover, NH, 1986).

André, J., *Étude sur les termes de couleur dans la langue latine* (Paris, 1949).

—— *L'Alimentation et la cuisine à Rome*² (Paris, 1981).

Annas, J., and Barnes, J., *The Modes of Scepticism* (Cambridge, 1985).

Arnaldi, F., *Da Plauto a Terenzio* (Naples, 1946–7).

Astarita, M. L., 'Note di cronologia gelliana', *Orpheus*² 5 (1984) 422–32.

Astin, A. E., *Scipio Aemilianus* (Oxford, 1967).

—— *Cato the Censor* (Oxford, 1978).

Baldwin, B., *Studies in Aulus Gellius* (Lawrence, Kan., 1975).

Balsdon, J. P. V. D., *Life and Leisure in Ancient Rome* (London, 1969).

—— *Romans and Aliens* (London, 1979).

Baron, H., 'Aulus Gellius in the Renaissance: His Influence and a Manuscript from the School of Guarino', *From Petrarch to Leonardo Bruni: Studies in Humanistic and Political Literature* (Chicago and London, 1968) 196–215.

Barnes, T. D., *The Sources of the* Historia Augusta (Brussels, 1978).

Beck, J. W. 'Studia Gelliana et Pliniana', *JbClPh* Supp.² 19 (1892) 1–55.

Benko, S., *Pagan Rome and the Early Christians* (London, 1985).

Bentley, R., *Dissertations upon the Epistles of Phalaris* [etc.], ed. W. Wagner (London, 1883).

Bernardi Perini, G., 'Per una revisione del testo di Gellio, libri I–VIII', *AIV* 137 (1978–9) 257–68.

—— 'Il sistema eterografico di Nigidio Figulo (frr. 35–38 Swoboda)', *Orpheus*² 3 (1982) 1–33.

Beroaldus, P. (sen.), *Annotationes in commentarios Seruii Virgiliani commentatoris* (Bologna, 1482).

—— *Annotationes* (Bologna, 1488).

Berthold, H., *Aulus Gellius: Auswahl und Aufgliederung seiner Themen* (Diss. Leipzig, 1959) [Berthold].

—— 'Aulus Gellius: Seine Bedeutung als Vermittler antiker Bildungs- und Kulturtraditionen', *WZ Halle* 29/3 (1980) 45–50.

—— 'Carmen Pindari, quod est super monte Aetna (Pythia 1): Zur Dichtungskritik des 2. Jahrhunderts u. Z. (Gellius, *Noctes Atticae* XVII, 10)', in E. G. Schmidt (ed.), *Aischylos und Pindar: Studien zu Werk und Nachwirkung* (Berlin (DDR), 1981) 286–95.

—— 'Interpretationsprobleme im Miszellanwerk des Aulus Gellius', *WZ Rostock* 34/1 (1985) 12–15.

Birley, A. R., *Marcus Aurelius: A Biography*[2] (London, 1987).

—— *Septimius Severus: The African Emperor* (London, 1975).

Bolton, J. D. P., *Aristeas of Proconnesus* (Oxford, 1962).

Bompaire, J., *Lucien écrivain: imitation et création* (Paris, 1958).

Bonner, S. F., *Roman Declamation in the Late Republic and the Early Empire* (Liverpool, 1949).

Botfield, B., *Praefationes et epistolae editionibus principibus auctorum ueterum praepositae* (Cambridge, 1861).

Bouché-Leclercq, A., *L'Astrologie grecque* (Paris, 1899).

Bowersock, G. W., *Greek Sophists in the Roman Empire* (Oxford, 1969).

Bowie, E. L., 'Greeks and their Past in the Second Sophistic', in M. I. Finley (ed.), *Studies in Ancient Society* (London, 1974) 166–209.

Bradley, K. R., 'Wet-nursing at Rome: A Study in Social Relations', in B. Rawson (ed.), *The Family in Ancient Rome: New Perspectives* (London, 1986) 201–29.

Briscoe, J., *A Commentary on Livy, Books XXXI–XXXIII* (Oxford, 1973).

Broccia, G., *Enchiridion* (Rome, 1979).

Brock, M. D., *Studies in Fronto and his Age* (Cambridge, 1911).

Buck, C. D., *The Greek Dialects* (Chicago, 1955).

Burkert, W., *Lore and Science in Ancient Pythagoreanism*, tr. E. L. Minar, Jr. (Cambridge, Mass., 1972).

Cameron, Alan, '*Poetae nouelli*', *HSCP* 84 (1980) 128–75.

Carolus, P., *Animaduersiones historicae, philologicae, et criticae in Noctes Atticas Agellii, et Q. Curtii Historiam* (Nuremberg, 1663) [written 1628–9].

Carrio, L., *Antiquarum lectionum commentarii III* (Antwerp, 1576).

—— *Emendationum et obseruationum liber primus/secundus* (Paris, 1583).

Castorina, E., *Scritti minori* (Catania, 1979).

Cavazza, F., *Studio su Varrone etimologo e grammatico* (Bologna, 1981).

Chadwick, H., *The Early Church* (Harmondsworth, 1967).

—— *Boethius: The Consolations of Music, Logic, Theology, and Philosophy* (Oxford, 1981).

Champlin, E., 'The Chronology of Fronto', *JRS* 64 (1974) 136–59.

—— *Fronto and Antonine Rome* (Princeton, NJ, and London, 1980).

Cima, A., *L'eloquenza latina prima di Cicerone* (Rome, 1903).

Clarke, M. L., *Higher Education in the Ancient World* (London, 1971).

Clausen, W., *Virgil's* Aeneid *and the Tradition of Hellenistic Poetry* (Berkeley, Calif., 1987).

Cousin, J., review of Marache, *Critique: REL* 30 (1952) 436–45.

Cova, P. V., *I Principia Historiae e le idee storiografiche di Frontone* (Naples, 1970).

Cramer, A. W., *Kleine Schriften* (Leipzig, 1837).

Crinitus, P., *Pietro Crinito: De honesta disciplina*, ed. C. Angeleri (Rome, 1955).

Curtius, E. R., *European Literature and the Latin Middle Ages*, tr. W. R. Trask (London, 1953).

Della Casa, A., *Nigidio Figulo* (Rome, 1962).

Dewaule, L., *Aulus Gellius quatenus philosophiae studuerit* (Toulouse, 1891).

Dillon, J., *The Middle Platonists: A Study of Platonism, 80 B.C.–A.D. 220* (London, 1977).

Dionisotti, A. C., 'From Ausonius' Schooldays? A Schoolbook and its Relatives', *JRS* 72 (1982) 83–125.

Dirksen, H. E., 'Die Auszüge aus den Schriften der römischen Rechtsgelehrten in den Noctes Atticae des A. Gellius', *Hinterlassene Schriften* (Leipzig, 1871) i. 21–63 [rev. repr. of *Phil. u. hist. Abh. d. Kön. Akad. d. Wiss. zu Berlin*, 1851, 31–77].

Dodds, E. R., *The Greeks and the Irrational* (Berkeley, Calif., 1951).

––––– *Pagan and Christian in an Age of Anxiety* (Cambridge, 1965).

Dörrie, H. A., 'L. Kalbenos Tauros', *Platonica minora* (Munich, 1976) 310–23 [repr. from *Kairos²* 15 (1973) 24–35].

Draeger, A., *Historische Syntax der lateinischen Sprache²* (Leipzig, 1878–81).

Düring, I., *Aristotle in the Ancient Biographical Tradition* (Göteborg, 1957).

Ebert, A., review of Gorges: *Blätter f. d. bayer. Gymnasialschulwesen* 21 (1885) 574–84.

Egger, É., *Mémoires d'histoire ancienne et de philologie* (Paris, 1863).

Ernesti, J. C. T. [= G.], *Lexicon technologiae Graecorum rhetoricae* (Leipzig, 1795).

––––– *Lexicon technologiae Latinorum rhetoricae* (Leipzig, 1797).

Ernst, W., *De Clementis Alexandrini Stromatum libro VIII. qui fertur* (Göttingen, 1910).

Faider, P. (ed.), 'Auli Gellii Noctium Atticarum Praefatio', *Le Musée belge* 31 (1927) 189–216.

Falster, Chr., *Cogitationes uariae philologicae* (Leipzig and Flensborg [Flensburg], 1719).

––––– *Vigiliae primae Noctium Ripensium* (Copenhagen, 1721) [Falster's own interleaved copy is preserved in Copenhagen, University Library, Kl. 78268, 8°].

––––– 'Specimen Emendationum in *A. Gellii* Lib. I, II, III, & IIII. Edit. Gronov. 1706 in 4', in J. G. Krause (ed.), *Noua Litteraria anni M DCC XXI* 138–43.

––––– *Memoriae obscurae²* (Hamburg, 1722).

––––– 'Noctes Ripenses in Noctes Atticas A. Gellii' (1722–7), Copenhagen, Royal Library, MS E don. var. 4, fol.

––––– *Amoenitates philologicae* (Amsterdam, 1729–32; *Titelauflage* Utrecht, 1750).

Finley, M. I., *Ancient Slavery and Modern Ideology* (Cambridge, 1980).

Follet, S., *Athènes au IIᵉ et au IIIᵉ siècle* (Paris, 1976).

Foster, W. E., *Studies in Archaism in Aulus Gellius* (New York, 1912).

Fraenkel, E. D. M., *Horace* (Oxford, 1957).

––––– *Elementi plautini in Plauto*, tr. F. Munari (Florence, 1960).

––––– *Kleine Beiträge zur klassischen Philologie* (Rome, 1964).

––––– *Leseproben aus den Reden Ciceros und Cato* (Rome, 1968).

Frede, M., *Die stoische Logik* (Göttingen, 1974).

––––– *Essays in Ancient Philosophy* (Oxford, 1987).

Friedländer, L., *Über den Kunstsinn der Römer in der Kaiserzeit* (Königsberg, 1852).

––––– rev. Wissowa, G., *Darstellungen aus der Sittengeschichte Roms⁹/¹⁰* (Leipzig, 1920).

Frier, B. W., *The Rise of the Roman Jurists: Studies in Cicero's* pro Caecina (Princeton, NJ, 1985).

Froehde, O., 'Römische Dichtercitate bei Gellius', in *Festschrift Johannes Vahlen* (Berlin, 1900) 523–42.

Gamberale, L., *La traduzione in Gellio* (Rome, 1969) [Gamberale].

––––– 'Note sulla tradizione di Gellio', *RFIC* 103 (1975) 33–55.

––––– 'Autografi virgiliani e movimento arcaizzante', *Atti del Convegno Virgiliano sul bimillenario delle Georgiche* (Naples, 1977) 359–67.

Garnsey, P., *Social Status and Legal Privilege in the Roman Empire* (Oxford, 1970).

Gascou, J., *Suétone historien* (Rome, 1984).

Gassner, J., 'Philosophie und Moral bei Gellius', *Serta philologica Aenipontana* 2 (1972) 197–235.

Gebauer, G. C., *Anthologicarum dissertationum liber* (Leipzig, 1733).

Gelzer, M., *The Roman Nobility*, tr. R. Seager (Oxford, 1969).

Gibbon, E., *History of the Decline and Fall of the Roman Empire*, ed. J. B. Bury (London, ²1909–14).

Gignac, F. T., *A Grammar of the Greek Papyri of the Roman and Byzantine Periods* (Milan, 1976–81).

Glucker, J., *Antiochus and the Late Academy* (Göttingen, 1978).

Goodyear, F. R. D., 'Aulus Gellius', in *Cambridge History of Classical Literature* (Cambridge, 1982–5) ii. 678–80.

Gorges, O., *De quibusdam sermonis Gelliani proprietatibus obseruationes* (Halle, 1883).

Gourevitch, D., *Le Mal d'être femme: la femme et la médecine dans la Rome antique* (Paris, 1984).

——— *Le Triangle hippocratique dans le monde gréco-romain: le malade, sa maladie et le médecin* (Rome, 1984).

Graindor, P., *Un milliardaire antique: Hérode Atticus et sa famille* (Cairo, 1930).

Grapow, H., *Über die anatomischen Kenntnisse der altägyptischen Ärzte* (Leipzig, 1935).

Griffin, M. T., *Seneca: A Philosopher in Politics* (Oxford, 1976).

Grilli, A., *I proemi del De Republica di Cicerone* (Brescia, 1971).

——— 'Echi dell'"Hortensius"', *Helmantica* 28 (1977) 189–99.

Grosso, F., *La lotta politica al tempo di Commodo* (Turin, 1964).

Gruterus, J., *Lampas, siue fax artium* (Frankfurt, 1602–23).

Guthrie, W. K. C., *A History of Greek Philosophy* (Cambridge, 1962–81).

Hache, E., *Quaestiones archaicae* (Breslau, 1907).

Hadot, I., *Seneca und die griechisch-römische Tradition der Seelenleitung* (Berlin (West), 1969).

Hadot, P., *Exercices spirituels et philosophie antique* (Paris, 1981).

Hamberger, G. Chr., rev. Meusel, J. G., *Das gelehrte Teutschland*⁵ (Lemgo, 1796–1834).

Handley, E. W., *Menander and Plautus: A Study in Comparison* (London, 1968).

Hansen, P. A., *A Bibliography of Danish Contributions to Classical Scholarship from the Sixteenth Century to 1970* (Copenhagen, 1977).

Hardie, P. R., *Vergil's* Aeneid: Cosmos *and* Imperium (Oxford, 1986).

Harris, C. R. S., *The Heart and the Vascular System in Ancient Greek Medicine* (Oxford, 1973).

Heiberg, J. L., 'Græske Rhetorer i Kejsertiden', *Fra Hellas og Italien* (Copenhagen, 1929) ii. 71–105; first publ. separately (Copenhagen, 1920).

Heinze, R., *Virgils epische Technik*⁷ (Leipzig and Berlin, 1915; repr. Stuttgart, 1982).

Helm, R., 'Hieronymus' Zusätze in Eusebius' Chronik und ihr Wert für die Literaturgeschichte', *Philologus*, Supp. 21/2 (1929).

Henriksson, K.-E., *Griechische Büchertitel in der römischen Literatur* (Helsinki, 1956).

Heraeus, W., review of Hosius' edn.: *BPhW* 24 (1904) 1163–71.

Hertz, M. J., *De Luciis Cinciis* (Berlin, 1842).

——— *Sinnius Capito: Eine Abhandlung zur Geschichte der römischen Grammatik* (Berlin, 1844).

——— *Renaissance und Rococo in der römischen Litteratur* (Berlin, 1865).

——— 'A. Gellii quae ad ius pertinent capita quattuor (Lib. IV cap. 1–4) emendata et adnotata', in *Ind. schol. hib.* (Breslau, 1868) 3–20.

——— 'Vindiciae Gellianae alterae', *JbClPh* Supp.² 7 (1873–5) 1–91; also publ. separately (Leipzig, 1873) [reply to Madvig ii. 576–613; courtesy answers intemperance, informed talent fends off inexpert genius].

——— 'A. Gellii Noctium Atticarum praefatio recensa et adnotata', in *Ind. schol. aest.* (Breslau, 1877) 3–13.

Heurgon, J., *Recherches sur l'histoire, la religion et la civilisation de Capoue préromaine* (Paris, 1942, repr. 1970).

Hofmann, J. B., rev. Szantyr, A., *Lateinische Syntax und Stilistik* (Munich, 1965, corr. repr. 1972).

Holford-Strevens, L. A., 'Select Commentary on Aulus Gellius Book 2' (unpubl. D.Phil. thesis, Oxford, 1971).

——— 'Gellius', *RAC* ix. 1049–55.

——— '*Elocutio nouella*', *CQ²* 26 (1976) 140–1.

——— 'Towards a Chronology of Aulus Gellius', *Latomus* 36 (1977) 93–109.

——— 'Nola, Vergil, and Paulinus', *CR²* 29 (1979) 391–3.

——— 'Fact and Fiction in Aulus Gellius', *LCM* 7 (1982) 65–8.

——— 'Two Notes on Minor Greek Poets', ibid. 8 (1983) 143.

——— 'Five Notes on Aulus Gellius', ibid. 143–4.

——— 'More Notes on Aulus Gellius', ibid. 9 (1984) 145–51.

——— 'Aduersaria minora Gelliana et Apuleianum', ibid. 10 (1985) 111–12.

——— review of Cavazza's edn., *CR²* 37 (1987) 36–9.

Honoré, A. M., *Gaius* (Oxford, 1962).

——— 'Julian's Circle', *Tijdschr.* 32 (1964) 1–44.

——— [T.], *Ulpian* (Oxford, 1982).

Hornblower, S., *Mausolus* (Oxford, 1982).

Hornsby, H. M. (comm.), *A. Gellii Noctium Atticarum Liber I* (Dublin and London, 1936).

Hosius, C., review of Rolfe's tr.: *PhW* 48 (1928) 1155–7, 1304–5.

Housman, A. E., *The Classical Papers of A. E. Housman*, ed. J. Diggle and E. R. D. Goodyear (Cambridge, 1972).

Huetius, P. D., *De interpretatione libri duo²* (The Hague, 1683).

Huit, Ch., *La Vie et l'œuvre de Platon* (Paris, 1893).

Hultsch, F., *Griechische und römische Metrologie²* (Berlin, 1882; repr. Graz, 1971).

Inwood, B., 'Hierocles: Theory and Argument in the Second Century AD', *Oxford Studies in Ancient Philosophy* 2 (1984) 151–85.

——— *Ethics and Human Action in Early Stoicism* (Oxford, 1985).

Jackson, K. H., *Language and History in Early Britain* (Edinburgh, 1952).

Janson, T., *Latin Prose Prefaces: Studies in Literary Convention* (Stockholm, 1964).

Jocelyn, H. D., 'The Annotations of M. Valerius Probus', *CQ²* 34 (1984) 464–72 (I), 35 (1985) 149–61 (II), 466–74 (III).

Kaser, M., *Das römische Zivilprozeßrecht* (Munich, 1966).

——— *Das römische Privatrecht²* (Munich, 1971–5).

Kelly, J. M., *Roman Litigation* (Oxford, 1966).

King, Helen, 'Born to Bleed: Artemis and Greek Women', in Averil Cameron and Amélie Kuhrt (eds.), *Images of Women in Antiquity* (London, 1983) 109–27.

Kleberg, T., *Buchhandel und Verlagswesen in der Antike³*, tr. E. Zunker (Darmstadt, 1969).

Klinkers, E., 'Studie over de grammatische mededeelingen in Aulus Gellius' *Noctes Atticae*' (Diss. Leuven, 1946–7).

Knapp, C., 'Archaism in Aulus Gellius', in *Classical Studies in Honour of Henry Drisler* (New York, 1894) 126–73 [Knapp].

—— 'Notes on the Prepositions in Aulus Gellius', *TAPhA* 25 (1894) 5–33.
Knauer, G. N., *Die Aeneis und Homer* (Göttingen, 1964).
Koch, H., *Pronoia und Paideusis* (Berlin, 1932).
Krebs, J. P., *Antibarbarus der lateinischen Sprache*[8], rev. J. H. Schmalz (Basle and Stuttgart, 1962).
Kretzschmer, A. C. H. J., *De A. Gellii fontibus*, i. *De auctoribus A. Gellii grammaticis* (Posen [Poznań], 1860) [Kretzschmer].
—— 'Zu A. Gellius gegen Hrn. L. Mercklin', *JbClPh* 85 (1862) 361–8.
—— 'Entgegnung', ibid. 87 (1863) 440.
Kroll, W., *Studien zum Verständnis der römischen Literatur* (Stuttgart, 1924).
Kühner, R., rev. Stegmann, C., *Ausführliche Grammatik der lateinischen Sprache: Satzlehre*[3], rev. A. Thierfelder (Leverkusen, 1955).
Kunkel, W., *Herkunft und soziale Stellung der römischen Juristen*[2] (Graz, Vienna, and Cologne, 1967).
—— *Römische Rechtsgeschichte*[9] (Cologne and Vienna, 1980).
Kurth, W. C., 'A Commentary on Book XIII of the *Noctes Atticae* of Aulus Gellius' (Diss. Chapel Hill, NC, 1964).

Lachmann, (K.) F. (Th.), *De fontibus historiarum T. Liuii commentatio prior* (Göttingen, 1822).
Lambecius, P., *Prodromus lucubrationum criticarum in Gellii Noctes Atticas* (Paris, 1647; publ. together with id., *Dissertatio de uita et nomine A. Gellii*).
Latte, K., *Römische Religionsgeschichte* (Munich, 1960).
Lebek, W. D., *Verba prisca: Die Anfänge des Archaisierens in der lateinischen Beredsamkeit und Geschichtsschreibung* (Göttingen, 1970) [Lebek].
—— *'Pluria* und *compluria* in lateinischer Sprache und römischer Grammatik', *RhM*[2] 114 (1971) 340–8.
Lefkowitz, M. R., *The Lives of the Greek Poets* (London, 1981).
Lehrs, K., *De Aristarchi studiis Homericis*[3] (Leipzig, 1882).
Leo, Fr., *Plautinische Forschungen*[2] (Berlin, 1912).
—— *Geschichte der römischen Literatur* (Berlin, 1913).
Leopardi, G., *Scritti filologici*, ed. G. Pacella and S. Timpanaro (Florence, 1969).
Leumann, M., *Lateinische Laut- und Formenlehre*[6] (Munich, 1977).
Leuze, O., *Die römische Jahrzählung* (Tübingen, 1909).
—— 'Das synchronistische Kapitel des Gellius (Noct. Att. XVII, 21)', *RhM*[2] 66 (1911) 237–74.
Lindsay, W. M., *Nonius Marcellus' Dictionary of Republican Latin* (Oxford, 1901).
Lloyd-Jones, H., and Parsons, P. J., 'Iterum de "Catabasi Orphica"', in *Kyklos: Griechisches und Byzantinisches Rudolf Keydell zum neunzigsten Geburtstag* (Berlin (West), 1978) 88–100.
Long, A. A., *Hellenistic Philosophy: Stoics, Epicureans, Sceptics*[2] (London, 1986).
Lynch, J. P., *Aristotle's School* (Berkeley, Calif., 1972).

Maass, E., *De biographis Graecis* (Berlin, 1880).
McCall, M. H., Jr., *Ancient Rhetorical Theories of Simile and Comparison* (Cambridge, Mass., 1969).
MacMullen, R., *Enemies of the Roman Order* (Cambridge, Mass., and London, 1966).
—— *Paganism in the Roman Empire* (New Haven, Conn., and London, 1981).
Madvig, J. N., *Aduersaria critica* (Copenhagen, 1871–84).
Marache, R., *La Critique littéraire de langue latine et le développement du goût archaïsant au II*[e] *siècle de notre ère* (Rennes, 1952).
—— *Mots nouveaux et mots archaïques chez Fronton et Aulu-Gelle* (Paris, 1957).

―――― 'Le jugement d'Aulu-Gelle sur Salluste', in *Hommages à Léon Herrmann* (Brussels, 1960) 499–502.

―――― 'Fronton et A. Gellius (1938–1964)', *Lustrum* 10 (1965) 213–45.

―――― 'Aulu-Gelle et la prose métrique', in *Mélanges offerts à Léopold Sédar Senghor* (Dakar, 1977) 255–61.

―――― 'La recherche du rythme dans la *Préface* des *Nuits Attiques*', in J. Collart (ed.), *Varron, grammaire antique et stylistique latine* (Paris, 1978) 397–403.

―――― 'La préface d'Aulu-Gelle: couples et séries de synonymes ou de mots analogues', in *Letterature comparate, problemi e metodo: studi in onore d'Ettore Paratore* (Bologna, 1981) ii. 785–91.

Marchesi, C., *Storia della letteratura latina*[8] (Milan, 1955).

Marganne, M.-H., *Inventaire analytique des papyrus grecs de médecine* (Geneva, 1981).

Mariner Bigorra, S., 'Una paradoja fonemática: Váleri/Valéri', *Helmantica* 5 (1954) 141–65.

Marquardt, J., *Das Privatleben der Römer*[2], ed. A. Mau (Leipzig, 1886).

Marrou, H.-I., *Histoire de l'éducation dans l'antiquité*[6] (Paris, 1965).

Marshall, P. K., 'The Date of Birth of Aulus Gellius', *CPh* 58 (1963) 143–9.

―――― 'Aulus Gellius', in L. D. Reynolds (ed.), *Texts and Transmission: A Survey of the Latin Classics* (Oxford, 1983) 176–80.

―――― Martin, J., and Rouse, R. H., 'Clare College MS. 26 and the Circulation of Aulus Gellius 1–7 in Medieval England and France', *Mediaeval Studies* 42 (1980) 353–94 [Marshall *et al.*].

Maselli, G., *Lingua e scuola in Gellio grammatico* (Lecce, 1979).

Masselink, J. F., *De Grieks-Romeinse windroos* (Utrecht and Nijmegen, 1956).

Mayser, E., rev. Schmoll, H., *Grammatik der griechischen Papyri aus der Ptolemäerzeit*[2] i/1 (Berlin (West) 1970).

Meiggs, R., *Timber and Trees in the Ancient Mediterranean World* (Oxford, 1982).

Meisterhans, K., *Grammatik der attischen Inschriften*[3], rev. E. Schwyzer (Berlin, 1900; repr. Hildesheim, 1971).

Mercklin, L., 'Die Citiermethode und Quellenbenutzung des A. Gellius in den Noctes Atticae', *JbClPh* Supp.[2] (1857–60) 635–712 [Mercklin].

―――― 'A. Gellii Noctium Atticarum capita quaedam ad fontes reuocata', in *Indices scholarum* (Dorpat [Tartu], 1861) 3–15.

―――― review of Kretzschmer: *JbClPh* 83 (1861) 713–24.

―――― 'Zur weiteren Beglaubigung des Hrn. J. Kretzschmer', ibid. 87 (1863) 428–40.

Meuli, K., '"Das Blatt hat sich gewendet"', *Gesammelte Schriften* (Basle, 1975) i. 503–11 [repr. with different illustrations from *Schweizerisches Archiv für Volkskunde* 30 (1930) 41–50].

Meyer-Lübke, W., *Romanisches etymologisches Wörterbuch*[3] (Heidelberg 1930–5).

Mikalson, J. D., *The Sacred and Civil Calendar of the Athenian Year* (Princeton, NJ, 1975).

Millar, F., *The Emperor in the Roman World* (London, 1977).

Momigliano, A., *Alien Wisdom* (Cambridge, 1974).

Mommsen, Th., *Römisches Staatsrecht*[3] (Leipzig, 1887–8).

Mosellanus, P., *Annotationes in Auli Gellii Noctes Atticas* (Basle, 1526).

Mühmelt, M., *Griechische Grammatik in der Vergilerklärung* (Munich, 1965).

Müller, H. W., *De particularum usu Gelliano quaestiones selectae* (Königsberg, 1911).

Munk Olsen, B., *L'Étude des auteurs classiques latins au XIe et XIIe siècles* (Paris, 1982–7).

Naguevskij, D. I., *Bibliografija po istorii rimskoj literatury v Rossii s 1709 po 1889 god* (Kazan', 1889).

Nettleship, H., 'The *Noctes Atticae* of Aulus Gellius', *Lectures and Essays* (Oxford, 1885) 248–76 [repr. from *AJP* 4 (1883) 391–415].

260 *Bibliography*

Neubauer, R., *De coniunctionum causalium apud Gellium usu* (Magdeburg, 1890).
Neue, F., rev. Wagener, C., *Formenlehre der lateinischen Sprache*³ (Leipzig, 1892–1907).
Niebuhr, B. G., *Historische und philologische Vorträge* (Berlin, 1846–58).
Norden, E., *Die antike Kunstprosa*⁵ (Darmstadt, 1958).
Nörr, D., 'Iurisperitus sacerdos', in *Ξένιον: Festschrift für Pan. J. Zepos* (Athens, Freiburg i. Br., and Cologne, 1973) i. 555–72.
—— 'Rechtskritik in der römischen Antike', *ABAW* 77 (1974).
—— 'Der Jurist im Kreis der Intellektuellen: Mitspieler oder Außenseiter? (Gellius, Noctes Atticae 16, 10)', in *Festschrift für Max Kaser zum 70. Geburtstag* (Munich, 1976) 57–90.
Nutton, V. (ed.), *Galen: Problems and Prospects* (London, 1981).

Ogilvie, R. M., *Roman Literature and Society* (Brighton and Totowa, NJ, 1980).
Oliver, J. H., *The Civic Tradition in Roman Athens* (Baltimore, Md., 1983).
Otto, A., *Die Sprichwörter und sprichwörtlichen Redensarten der Römer* (Leipzig, 1890; repr. Hildesheim, 1965).
Otto, E., 'De uita, studiis, scriptis et honoribus Seruii Sulpicii, Lemonia, Rufi', in *Thesaurus iuris antiqui*² v (Utrecht, 1735), 1549–630.

Page, D. L., *Further Greek Epigrams* (Cambridge, 1981).
Pearson, J., 'Prolegomena in Hieroclem', in M. Casaubon's edn. of Hierocles (Platonicus), *De prouidentia et fato* (London, 1655).
—— *Vindiciae Epistolarum S. Ignatii* (Cambridge, 1672).
Pfeiffer, R., *History of Classical Scholarship: From the Beginnings to the End of the Hellenistic Age* (Oxford, 1968).
Pflaum, H.-G., 'Les correspondants de l'orateur M. Cornelius Fronto de Cirta', in *Hommages à Jean Bayet* (Brussels, 1964) 544–60.
Pianezzola, E., *Gli aggettivi verbali in -bundus* (Florence, 1963).
Politianus, A., *Miscellaneorum centuria prima* (Florence, 1489).
—— *Miscellaneorum centuria secunda*, ed. V. Branca and M. Pastore Stocchi (Florence, 1972) [cited by page of vol. iv].
Pomeroy, S. B., *Goddesses, Whores, Wives, and Slaves* (London, 1976).
Pontanus, J. Jov., *Giovanni Pontano: I dialoghi*, ed. C. Previtera (Florence, 1943).
Portalupi, F., *Marco Cornelio Frontone* (Turin, 1961) [Portalupi, *MCF*].
—— *Frontone, Gellio, Apuleio: Ricerca stilistica*, i (Turin, 1974).

Rabbow, P., *Seelenführung* (Munich, 1954).
Rappolt, F., *Logica Gelliana* (Leipzig, 1654).
Rawson, E., *Intellectual Life in the Late Roman Republic* (London, 1985).
Reynolds, L. D., and Wilson, N. G., *Scribes and Scholars*² (Oxford, 1974).
Riginos, A. S., *Platonica: The Anecdotes concerning the Life and Writings of Plato* (Leiden, 1976).
Ritschl, F., 'Die fabulae Varronianae des Plautus', *Parerga zu Plautus und Terenz* i (Leipzig, 1845) 71–245.
Robinson, C., *Lucian and his Influence in Europe* (London, 1979).
Roma en el siglo II: Trabajos de la Sección Latina del II Simposio de la Sociedad Española de Estudios Clásicos, Sección de Barcelona: Villanueva y Geltrú, abril 1970 (Barcelona, 1975).
Romano, B., *La critica letteraria in Aulo Gellio* (Turin, 1902).
Ronconi, A., 'Gellio e la lingua di Claudio Quadrigario', *StudUrb* 49/1 (1975) 127–40.
Ruske, L. L., *De A. Gellii Noctium Atticarum fontibus quaestiones selectae* (Glatz [Kłodzko], 1883).
Russell, D. A., *Plutarch* (London, 1972).
—— *Criticism in Antiquity* (London, 1981).

—— *Greek Declamation* (Cambridge, 1983) [Russell, *GD*].

Rutgersius, J., *Variarum lectionum libri sex* (Leiden, 1618).

Rutledge, H. C., 'Herodes Atticus, World Citizen, A.D. 101–177' (Diss. Ohio State, 1960); an illustrated summary publ. as 'Herodes the Great: Citizen of the World', *CJ* 56 (1960–1) 97–109.

Sabbadini, R., *Vita di Guarino Veronese* (Genoa, 1891; repr. Turin, 1964 in *Guariniana*, together with next).

—— *La scuola e gli studi di Guarino Guarini Veronese* (Catania, 1896).

—— *Le scoperte dei codici latini e greci ne' secoli XIV e XV*, rev. E. Garin (Florence, 1967; publ. together with next).

—— *Le scoperte dei codici latini e greci ne' secoli XIV e XV: Nuove ricerche*, rev. E. Garin (Florence, 1967).

Ste. Croix, G. E. M. de, *The Class Struggle in the Ancient Greek World* (London, 1981).

Salmasius, Cl., *Plinianae exercitationes in Caii Iulii Solini Polyhistora* (Paris, 1629).

Saxius, Chr., *Onomasticon literarium*[2] (Utrecht, 1775–1803).

Scaliger, J. C., *Poetices libri septem* ([Lyon], 1561).

—— *Problemata Gelliana* (Toulouse, 1620).

Scaliger, J. J., *Coniectanea in M. Terentium Varronem de lingua latina* (Paris, 1565).

—— *Scaligerana* (Cologne, 1695).

Schanz, M., rev. Hosius, C., *Geschichte der römischen Literatur*[4] (Munich, 1927–35, vols. i–ii only).

—— —— and Krüger, G., edn.[3], vol. iii (Munich, 1922).

Schettino, M. T., 'Questioni di biografia gelliana', *GFF* 8 (1985) 75–87.

Schibel, W., *Sprachbehandlung und Darstellungsweise in römischer Prosa: Claudius Quadrigarius, Livius, Aulus Gellius* (Amsterdam, 1971).

Schmid, W., *Der Atticismus* (Stuttgart, 1887; repr. Hildesheim, 1964).

Schmitt, A., *Das Bild als Stilmittel Frontos* (Munich, 1934).

Schoeck, R. J., 'More's Attic Nights: Sir Thomas More's Use of Aulus Gellius' *Noctes Atticae*', *Renaissance News* 13 (1960) 127–9; 'Aulus Gellius: A Post-praefatio', ibid. 232–3.

Schrader, H., *De Plutarchi Chaeronensis Ὁμηρικαῖς Μελέταις* (Gotha, 1899).

Schulz, F., *Classical Roman Law* (Oxford, 1951).

Schulze, W., *Orthographica* (Marburg, 1894; repr. Rome, 1958).

—— *Zur Geschichte lateinischer Eigennamen*, Abh. der Gött. Ges. d. Wiss., phil.-hist. Kl.[2] 5 (Berlin, 1904), no. 5.

—— *Kleine Schriften*[2] (Göttingen, 1966).

Schweiger, F. L. A., *Handbuch der classischen Bibliographie* (Leipzig, 1830–4).

Scullard, H. H., *Roman Politics 220–150 B.C.*[2] (Oxford, 1973).

Seel, O., *Die Praefatio des Pompeius Trogus* (Erlangen, 1955).

Shackleton Bailey, D. R., *Propertiana* (Cambridge, 1956).

Sherwin-White, A. N., *The Letters of Pliny: A Historical and Social Commentary* (Oxford, 1966).

Skutsch, O., *Studia Enniana* (London, 1968).

Smalley, B., *English Friars and Antiquity in the Early Fourteenth Century* (Oxford, 1960).

Smirnov, S. K., *Istorija Moskovskoj Slavjano-Greko-Latinskoj Akademii* (Moscow, 1855).

Speyer, W., *Die literärische Fälschung im heidnischen und christlichen Altertum* (Munich, 1971).

Stanford, W. B. *The Sound of Greek: Studies in the Greek Theory and Practice of Euphony* (Berkeley, Calif., 1967).

Steinmetz, P., *Untersuchungen zur römischen Literatur des zweiten Jahrhunderts nach Christi Geburt* (Wiesbaden, 1982).

Stephanus, H., letter to his son Paul, prefixed to Carrio's edn. (Paris, 1585).

—— letter to Jean de Vulcob prefixed to *Noct. Par.*

—— *Noctes Parisinae*, appended to Carrio's edn.

Straaten, M. van, *Panétius* (Amsterdam, 1946).

Stroev, P. M., *Spiski Ierarxov i nastojatelej monastyrej rossijskija cerkvi* (St Petersburg, 1877).

Suerbaum, W., *Untersuchungen zur Selbstdarstellung älterer römischer Dichter* (Hildesheim, 1968).

Syme, R., *Tacitus* (Oxford, 1958).

—— *Sallust* (Berkeley, Calif., 1964).

—— *Roman Papers* (Oxford, 1979–84).

—— *Historia Augusta Papers* (Oxford, 1983).

Sypniewska, B., 'De Claudii Quadrigarii fragmentis ab A. Gellio traditis quaestiones selectae', in *Charisteria Casimiro de Morawski septuagenario oblata* (Cracow, 1922) 149–78.

Tarrant, H., *Scepticism or Platonism? The Philosophy of the Fourth Academy* (Cambridge, 1985).

Teuffel, W. S., rev. Kroll, W., and Skutsch, F., *Geschichte der römischen Literatur*[6] (Leipzig, 1910–16).

Thompson, Stith, *Motif-index of Folk-Literature*[2] (Copenhagen, 1955–8).

Threatte, L., *The Grammar of Attic Inscriptions* i (Berlin (West), 1980).

Thuanus, J. A., *Commentariorum de uita sua libri sex*, publ. with separate pagination in vol. vii of *Historiarum sui temporis ... libri CXXXVIII*, ed. S. Buckley (London, 1733).

Till, R., *La lingua di Catone*, tr. with additional nn. by C. de Meo (Rome, 1968).

Timpanaro, S., *La filologia di Giacomo Leopardi*[2] (Bari, 1978).

—— *Contributi di filologia e di storia della lingua latina* (Rome, 1978).

—— *La genesi del metodo del Lachmann*[2] (Padua, 1981).

—— *Per la storia della filologia virgiliana antica* (Rome, 1986).

Traina, A., *Vortit barbare* (Rome, 1970).

Tränkle, H., 'Subsiciva Gelliana', *Hermes* 111 (1983) 106–14.

Triller, D. W., 'Emendationum et obseruationum in Aulum Gellium libellus' (letter to Falster, 12 June 1722), Copenhagen, Royal Library, MS E don. var. 6, fol.

Trillitzsch, W., *Seneca im literarischen Urteil der Antike* (Amsterdam, 1971).

Turnebus, A., *Aduersariorum libri triginta* (Paris, 1580).

Usener, H., *Kleine Schriften* (Leipzig, 1912–13; repr. Osnabrück, 1965).

Väänänen, V., *Introduction au latin vulgaire*[3] (Paris, 1981).

Valla, L., *Opera omnia* (Turin, 1962).

Veyne, P., *Les Grecs ont-ils cru à leurs mythes?* (Paris, 1983).

Vives, J. L., *Opera omnia*, ed. G. Mayans (Valencia, 1782–90; repr. London, 1964).

Vogel, Th. 'De A. Gellii uita, studiis, scriptis narratio et iudicium', in *Programm des Gymnasiums und der Realschule in Zittau 1860*, 1–25.

—— 'De A. Gellii sermone I. De copia uocabulorum', in *Gymnasium zu Zwickau: Jahresbericht über das Schuljahr 1861–1862*, 1–32.

—— 'De Noctium Atticarum A. Gellii compositione', in *Philologische Abhandlungen Martin Hertz zum siebzigsten Geburtstage von ehemaligen Schülern dargebracht* (Berlin, 1888) 1–13.

Wallace-Hadrill, A. F., *Suetonius* (London, 1983).

[Wasse, J.], contribution to J. Jortin (ed.), *Miscellaneous Observations upon Authors, Ancient and Modern* 2 (1732) 401–8 (signed D.); Lat. tr. in P. Burman (sen.) and

J.-P. d'Orville (eds.), *Miscellaneae obseruationes in auctores ueteres et recentiores* 4 (1734) 431–41 (signed D.D.).

Watson, A., *The Law of Property in the Later Roman Roman Republic* (Oxford, 1968).

—— *The Law of Succession in the Later Roman Republic* (Oxford, 1971).

—— *Rome of the XII Tables* (Princeton, NJ, 1975).

—— (ed.), *Daube Noster: Essays in Legal History for David Daube* (Edinburgh, 1974).

—— 'Two Notes on Manus', in J. E. Spruit (ed.), *Maior uiginti quinque annis: Essays in Commemoration of the Sixth Lustrum of the Institute for Legal History of the University of Utrecht* (Assen, 1979) 195–201.

Weil, H., *Études de littérature et de rythmique grecques* (Paris, 1902).

Whitehorne, J. E. G., '*Ad Amicos* I, 5 and 6 and the Date of Fronto's Death', in C. Deroux (ed.), *Studies in Latin Literature and Roman History* i (Brussels, 1979) 475–82.

Wilamowitz-Moellendorff, U. von, 'Ad Ernestum Maassium Epistula', in *Maass* 142–64.

—— 'Asianismus und Atticismus', *Kleine Schriften* iii (Berlin (DDR), 1969) 223–72 [repr. from *Hermes* 35 (1900) 1–52].

Wille, G., *Musica Romana* (Amsterdam, 1967).

Winckelmann, J. J., *Geschichte der Kunst des Alterthums* (Dresden, 1764).

Wind, E., *Pagan Mysteries in the Renaissance*[2] (London, 1968).

Winterbottom, M., 'Declamation, Greek and Latin', in A. Ceresa-Gastaldo (ed.), *Ars rhetorica antica e nuova* (Genoa, 1983).

Wiseman, T. P., *Cinna the Poet and Other Roman Essays* (Leicester, 1974).

—— *Clio's Cosmetics* (Leicester, 1979).

—— *Catullus and His World: A Reappraisal* (Cambridge, 1985).

Wissowa, G., review of Hosius' edn.: *GGA* 169 (1907) 727–40.

Wright, J., *Dancing in Chains: The Stylistic Unity of the Comoedia Palliata* (Rome, 1974).

Yoder, E., *The Position of Possessive and Demonstrative Adjectives in the* Noctes Atticae *of Aulus Gellius* (New York, 1928).

Zeller, E., *Vorträge und Abhandlungen* (Leipzig, 1875–7).

—— *Die Philosophie der Griechen in ihrer geschichtlichen Entwicklung*[6,5,4] (Leipzig, 1919–23; repr. Darmstadt, 1963).

Ziebarth, E., *Aus den griechischen Schulen*[2] (Bonn, 1913).

Zielinski, Th. [Zieliński, T. S.], *Das Clauselgesetz in Ciceros Reden: Grundzüge einer oratorischen Rhythmik* (Leipzig, 1904).

Zwierlein, O., *Kritischer Kommentar zu den Tragödien Senecas* (Stuttgart, 1986).

Postscript

W. S. Watt, 'Gelliana', *AC* 55 (1986) 328–32, among other interesting proposals, emends 'modestissimo' (1. 3. 10), of which an embarrassed translation is offered on p. 200, to *disertissimo*, thus granting Theophrastus his normal praise for eloquence (cf. 8. 9. lemma). For 'dedit' (19. 8. 18) he would read *uitiosum credit*, citing Rolfe's note for use of *harenae*; but of the authors named there only Vergil would count as *doctus* for Gellius, who knew the plural to be post-Republican (cf. p. 97 n. 33).

Index

Gaul, Gaulish, Gauls 26, 47, 88 n. 5, 179
n. 9, 180 n. 12, 184, 231, 232 n. 30;
Narbonese, later Transalpine 72,
74 n. 14, 116; sack of Rome 179 n.
9, 185 n. 41
Gavius, P., of Consa, crucified by Verres
143–4
—— Bassus 119
Gellius, A.: 'Agellius', *see this*; anonymous
friends 10, 17, 28–9, 82, 106, 131,
133, 218; children 13; dates 12–18,
102–3 n. 67, 104 n. 3; father and
other kin not mentioned 10; judge
10 n. 6, 13, 133 n. 42, 218–20, 223;
origin, immediate 11–12, remote 9;
social status 10

disdains *sermo plebeius* 38, 128;
errors in Greek 87, 169–71, 202,
235; false references 57, 197–8, 227
n. 4, 228; interested in athletics,
child-rearing, embassies, *see these*;
limited critical vocabulary 162; literary tastes 152–3, 162, 163; military matters 14 n. 34; moralism
29–30, 33–4, 192; *naïveté* 103, 104–
5, 198; obsolete notions of law 108
n. 28, 222, 223; puts practical
question 64; selective in archaism
36 n. 10, 132, in topics 15, 27–8,
121; teaches his teacher, 84; uses
words he disapproves 37 n. 22, 97
n. 33, 123; vilipends gluttony 203;
weak on proper names 24, 227–8
echoes in other authors:
ancient: Ammianus 16, 57; Apuleius 15 (disputed works), 16–
19; Augustine 9 n. 1, 31 n. 68;
Ausonius 107 n. 24; Deutero-
Servius 9 n. 1, 122 n. 39, 151 n.
41; Donatus 151 n. 41; Festus
119 n. 29; Gregory of Tours 9
n. 1; *Historia Augusta* 9 n. 1;
Isidore 110 n. 38; Lactantius 9
n. 1, 22 n. 17; Macrobius 22 n.
17, 87 n. 80, 121 n. 38, 189, 210
n. 86; Minucius Felix 68 n. 43;
Nonius 22 n. 17, 123 n. 48;
Priscian 9 n. 1, 22 n. 17; Servius
9 n. 1, 148 nn. 30–1, 154 n. 60;
Tertullian 15 n. 38
medieval: Boccaccio 128 n. 16;
Diceto 22 n. 17, 34 n. 76, 79 n.

37, 228 nn. 8, 10; Gerald of
Wales 34 n. 76, 87 n. 80; John
of Salisbury 33 n. 74, 34 n. 76,
57, 228; Petrarch 228 n. 10;
Petrus Cantor (false quot.) 22
n. 17; Walter Map 34 n. 76;
William of Malmesbury 22 n.
17 (false quot.), 34 n. 76, 228
modern: Bacon 24 n. 28, 204 n. 51
(false quot.); Browne 123 n. 50;
Burton 195 n. 15; Ion Luca
Caragiale 216 n. 5; Crinitus
237 n. 2; Erasmus 129 n. 18,
252; Gabriel Faernus 157; Lud-
vig Holberg 74 n. 11; Hans
Wilhelm Kirchhof 228 n. 10;
La Fontaine 103 n. 69, 157 n.
74; Lessing 27 n. 47 (from
interpolated edn.); Sir Roger
L'Estrange 182 n. 17; Mary I of
England 24 n. 28; Pedro de
Mejía 217 n. 14; Montaigne
211 n. 96, 228 n. 10; More 128
n. 16; Jacques-Louis Moreau
79 n. 37; William Painter 79 n.
37, 228 n. 10; Rabelais 57, 122
n. 39; Heinrich Steinhöwel 182
n. 17; Thomas Wilson 228 n.
10, 252
Gellius, Cn., annalist 9, 158
——, Cn., untrustworthy character
(same as above?) 9 n. 3
——, L. (*cos.* 72 BC) 9
—— Menander, L., Corinthian mag-
nate 99 n. 44
geometry 27, 213, 233 n. 45
Germania Inferior 98; Germans 229 n.
15; *see also* Hermunduri
Gibbon, Edward 1, 248, 251 n. 54
gladiators 203 n. 49
Gnostics 105 n. 12
Goethe, Johann Wolfgang von 104–5 n.
6, 238 nn. 8–9
gout 98
Gracchus, C. Sempronius 45, 65, 66, 96,
143–5, 151 n. 44, 153, 163, 176,
184, 190
——, Ti. Sempronius (*cos.* 177 BC)
213 n. 102
——, —— —— (*tr. pl.* 133 BC) 65 n.
22, 144
grammar 27, 34, 74, 88, 126–41, 192 n.